37th Annual Pacific Northwest Software Quality Conference 2019

A Culture of Quality

Portland, Oregon, USA
14 - 16 October 2019

ISBN: 978-1-5108-9360-3

Printed from e-media with permission by:

Curran Associates, Inc.
57 Morehouse Lane
Red Hook, NY 12571

Some format issues inherent in the e-media version may also appear in this print version.

Printed by Curran Associates, Inc. (2019)

For permission requests, please contact PNSQC/Pacific Agenda
at the address below.

PNSQC/Pacific Agenda
PO Box 10733
Portland, OR 97296-0733
USA

Phone: 503 223-4630

www.pnsqc.org

Additional copies of this publication are available from:

Curran Associates, Inc.
57 Morehouse Lane
Red Hook, NY 12571 USA
Phone: 845-758-0400
Fax: 845-758-2633
Email: curran@proceedings.com
Web: www.proceedings.com

37th Annual Pacific Northwest Software Quality Conference 2019

A Culture of Quality

Monday, October 14, 2019 Schedule

7:00-10:00 AM	**Registration and Wake Up with Coffee & Tea** Level 3 Skybridge Terrace			
8:00-8:15 AM	**Welcome and Highlights for the Day** Level 3 Auditorium			
8:15-9:20 AM	**Keynote** (Auditorium Level 3) **Testing the Untestable** **Angie Jones**, Developer Advocate			
	Level 3 Auditorium	**Level 1 Plaza Room**	**Level 2 Mezzanine Room**	**Level 3 Skybridge Room**
	Invited Speaker	***Quality Engineering***	***Security & Performance***	***People, Mgmt, and Leadership***
9:30-10:10 AM	**The QA/QE Role – Supporting DevOps** **the Smart Way** with **Melissa Tondi**	**Transition from monolith to microservices: a dream or a tester's nightmare?** **Natalia Pletneva** Okko	**Serverless Security: What are we up against?** **Atul Ahire** McAfee	**Timeless Skills for Modern Testers: Communication, Collaboration and Creativity** **Gerie Owen** Testing Strategist

10:20-11:00 AM		**Is This Testable? A Personal Journey to Learn How to Ask Better Questions from My Applications and Engineering Team** **Michael Larsen** Socialtext	**Staying Enlightened with Lighthouse – Tools and Techniques for Automating Website Performance Testing** **Adam Henson**	**Agile Software Quality Management – Using Quality Attributes to Communicate Product and Corporate Goals and Change Your Organization** **Ian Savage** Agile Open Northwest
11:00-11:20 AM	**Break in Exhibit Hall Level 2 Mezzanine**			
		Quality Engineering	***Automation***	***People, Mgmt, and Leadership***
11:20-12:00 PM	**Guru Jam Session with Lightning Talks** **Tariq King,** moderator	**Optimize Tests for Continuous Integration** **John Ruberto** First Data Corporation	**Using Promises with the Page Object Model** **Hal Deranek** Software Tester	**Building Automation Engineers from Scratch** **Jenny Bramble** Willowtree Apps
12:10-12:50 PM		**On-Premises to Cloud: Ephemeral Scale Testing** **Andrew Graham** Tripwire	**How to start a test automation framework and not die trying** **Juan Delgado** Universidad Panamericana Campus Aguascalientes	**Creating a Culture of Quality** **Angela Riggs**

12:50-1:50 PM	**Grab n' Go Lunch Specials Level 3 Skybridge Terrace**			
	Patio Level 3		**Level 2 Mezzanine**	**Level 3 Skybridge**
	Enterprise IT Forum		Panel Discussion moderated by **Michael Larsen & Bill Opsal** **The Release Day Crime Scene**	**Every Metric for a QA Team Has Pitfalls** **Jenny Bramble,** Willowtree Apps
	Level 3 Auditorium	**Level 1 Plaza Room**	**Level 2 Mezzanine Room**	**Level 3 Skybridge Room**
	Invited Speaker	***Quality Engineering***	***Automation***	***People, Mgmt, and Leadership***
1:50-2:30 PM	**Product Planning for Quality** with **Frank D'Andrea**	**Why We Need New Software Testing Technologies** **Carol Oliver,** Ph.D.	**Adding process to increase quality without adding tests** **Michael Millerick** Blend	**Software Based Disruptive Change Initiatives Require a Culture of Quality** **Ying Ki Kwong** Office of the State CIO
2:40-3:20 PM		**Test Scenario Design Models: What are they and why are they your key to Agile Quality success?** **Robert Gormley** SWAT Solutions	**Developing a test automation program step by step; one valuable, trusted test at a time.** **Joel Gerbino** Veterans United Home Loans	**Quality Guild: Creating a Culture** **Philip Daye** Ultimate Software

3:30-4:10 PM	**Poster Paper Jam Session** – Lobby area	**Advanced Test Case Design Methods – Going Far Beyond Boundary and Equivalence Testing** **Subei Liu** Software Tester	**Test Automation and DevOps, Where to Begin** **Robert Taylor** BlueVolt	**What It Takes to Be a Successful Scrum Master** **Anh Chi Nguyen** AKVA Group
4:10-4:30 PM	**Break in Exhibit Hall** Level 2 Mezzanine			
4:30-5:30 PM	**Keynote (Auditorium Level 3)** **Surviving the AI Testing Apocalypse,** **Dionny Santiago, Ultimate Software**			
5:30-6:30 PM	**Networking Happy Hour with Poster Paper Jam Session**			
6:30 PM	**Dine Around Portland**			

Tuesday, October 15, 2019 Schedule

7:00-10:00 AM	**Registration and Wake Up with Coffee & Tea** Level 2 Mezzanine
8:00-8:15 AM	**Welcome and Highlights for the Day** Level 3 Auditorium
8:15-9:20 AM	**Keynote** (Auditorium Level 3) **Remember This! The Science of Learning and Memory,** **Scott Crabtree, Happy Brain Science**
9:20-9:40 AM	**Break in Exhibit Hall** Level 2 Mezzanine

	Level 3 Auditorium	Level 1 Plaza Room	Level 2 Mezzanine Room	Level 3 Skybridge Room
	Invited Speaker	*Quality Engineering*	*Technologies and Tools*	*Processes, Practices, and Methods*
9:40-10:20 AM	**Agile Without Dedicated QA** with **James Shore**	**What Your UI Tests Need to Say** **Joseph Ferrara** The Climate Corporation	**Testing for cognitive Bias in AI Systems** **Peter Varhol** Telerik	**Being More Agile without Doing Agile** **Dawn Haynes** PerfTestPlus, Inc.
10:30-11:10 AM		**Standards are necessary but not sufficient for excellent software** **David Card** Experimental Software Engineering Group	**Writing Efficient Unit Tests for C++ Libraries** **Easa El Sirgany** Software Engineer	**Moving to Continuous Delivery Culture: Cutting Releases Cadence** **Andy Peterson** Costco
11:20-12:00 PM	**Poster Paper Jam Session**	**Being a modern tester for safety's sake!** **Dawid Pacia**	**Testing Mobile Software with Machine Learning: an introduction** **Jennifer Bonine** PinkLion AI	**Creating Quality with Mob Programming** **Thomas Desmond** Hunter Industries
12:00-1:00 PM	**Grab n' Go Lunch Specials Level 3 Skybridge Terrace**			
	Patio Level 3		**Level 2 Mezzanine**	**Level 3 Skybridge**

	Enterprise IT Forum		**Panel Discussion with Sion Heaney** **DevOps in Context and Practice**	**Engineering Quality Beer Jarek Szymanski,** Tektronix
	Level 3 Auditorium	**Level 1 Plaza Room**	**Level 2 Mezzanine Room**	**Level 3 Skybridge Room**
	Invited Speaker	*Security and Performance*	*Technologies and Tools*	*Processes, Practices, and Methods*
1:00-1:40 PM	**The Dark Side of Test Automation** with **Jan Jaap Cannegieter**	**Performance and Security Monitoring in the Public Cloud** **Sneha Mirajkar** Cisco Systems India	**Understanding and testing Blockchain** **John Cvetko** TFxCloud	**Agile Where Agile Fears to Tread!** **Thomas Cagley** Ultimate Software
1:50-2:30 PM		**Performance Testing with AWS X-Ray, CloudWatch, and RDS performance tools** **Daniel Kranowski** Business Algorithms, LLC	**Semi-autonomous, site-wide A11Y testing using an intelligent agent** **Keith Briggs** Ultimate Software	**Why Test Automation Initiatives Fail** **Jim Zuber** IBM

2:40-3:20 PM	**Panel on Trends in Software QA** **Testing in the Golden Age of Quality: Where are we and where are we going?** with **Jenny Bramble**	**Starting a Security Program on a Shoestring** **Brian Myers** WebMD Health Services	**Achieving a Culture of Software Quality for Android Robots** **Vivek Kumar** Total Chaos Robotics Team	**Behavior Driven Development – A Case Study in HealthTech** **Le Xiao** Alzheimer Therapeutic Research Institute
	Enterprise IT Forum, Patio Area			
3:20-3:40 PM	**Break in Exhibit Hall** Level 2 Mezzanine			
3:40-4:45 PM	**Keynote (Auditorium Level 3)** **Testing AI and Bias** **Jason Arbon, test.ai**			
4:45-5:00 PM	**Award Ceremony & Closing Remarks**			
5:00-6:00 PM	**Networking Happy Hour,** Level 3 Skybridge Terrace			

Wednesday, October 16, 2018 Schedule

7:30 – 8:30 AM	**Workshop Registration Opens**

<table>
<tr><td colspan="7">Breaks 10:00 AM and 2:45 PM, Level 2 Mezzanine Lobby</td></tr>
<tr><td colspan="7">Lunch 12:30-1:30 PM Level 3 Skybridge Terrace</td></tr>
<tr><td colspan="7">Plated service on the covered terrace, please dress for the weather.</td></tr>
<tr><td rowspan="4">8:30 AM – 5:30 PM</td><td>8:30am-12:30pm</td><td>8:30am-12:30pm</td><td>8:30am-12:30pm</td><td>8:30am-12:30pm</td><td>8:30am-12:30pm</td><td>8:30am-5:30pm</td></tr>
<tr><td>W01: Use Mind Maps to Increase Team Velocity and Communication to Customers
Jan Jaap Cannegieter
Squerist</td><td>W02: Introduction to Automated Visual Validation
Angie Jones
Developer Advocate</td><td>W03: Demystifying AI-driven Test Automation
Tariq King
Ultimate Software</td><td>W04: Efficient Testing
Melissa Tondi
Rainforest QA</td><td>W05: System Performance Estimation, Evaluation and Decision (SPEED)
Kingsum Chow
Alibaba System Software Hardware Co-Optimization</td><td>W11: Hands-on Selenium
Alan Ark
Duo Security</td></tr>
<tr><td>1:30pm-5:30pm</td><td>1:30pm-5:30pm</td><td>1:30pm-5:30pm</td><td>1:30pm-5:30pm</td><td>1:30pm-5:30pm</td><td>continued…</td></tr>
<tr><td>W06: CMD+CTRL Hackerthon
Chad Holmes
Security Innovation</td><td>W07: Test Driven Development without Mocks
James Shore
The Art of Agile</td><td>W08: Augmenting Your Test Pyramid with Layered Front-End Testing
Dionny Santiago
Ultimate Software</td><td>W09: Unit Testing: What Every Developer and Tester Should Know
Tariq King
Ultimate Software</td><td>W10: Continuous Improvement beyond Retrospectives
Adam Light
SocioTech</td><td>W11: Hands-on Selenium
Alan Ark
Duo Security</td></tr>
</table>

Table of Contents

How to Start a Test Automation Framework and Not Die Trying

Juan Delgado, Isaac Méndez

jddelgado@up.edu.mx, isaac.mendez@up.edu.mx

Abstract

Nowadays, some organizations still execute the test life cycle of their projects without test automation, which means that they also do it without the possibility of implementing the best Quality Assurance & Test Automation practices.

If you would like to start a test automation effort in your organization with a formal and mature process, this paper will help you to start and not die trying!

In the process, this paper will introduce and discuss the Android Open Source project "UP Automation Framework" a wrapper of libraries developed by the Panamerican University (Universidad Panamericana in Spanish), that will help you implement a mobile test automation framework and structure in your organization. This paper explains the fundamental principles and demonstrates how to apply them. We'll look at identifying what type of mistakes are most frequently made in your organization and choosing from a toolkit of prevention and detection practices to address these mistakes. We'll also talk about how to choose the practices that best fit your organization's software development process.

Biography

Juan de Dios Delgado has more than 15 years of experience as engineer. He has worked in all kind of IT activities including development and support, and 7 years of experience working on testing. He has a strong knowledge on the IT and business areas with a big inclination to learning and analysis of Business processes. He has experience in Functional Testing, and has also worked with Agile and Waterfall methodologies, with certification as Scrum Master and ITIL Foundations.

He has participated in several projects, in the last years. He has worked on site in the US and Europe; near shore from Mexico to the US, and offshore from Mexico and India to Europe; working strongly with Functional Testing focusing on Automated Testing and Business Analysis

He is currently working at Mobica, an award-winning software development and integration services company with a global customer base.

Also, he's a Professor at the Panamerican University in Mexico, in the faculty of Engineering. He's focused in Software Quality Assurance and involved in the development and launch of interdisciplinary programs for students.

The rest of the team were students at the Panamerican University in the last year of the major in Artificial Intelligence Engineering. This project was part of the subject named Agile and Automated Testing Engineering.

Introduction

Testing is very important for software development companies because they need to guarantee their clients that their products are multiplatform, multidevice and that they will work correctly and efficiently. It is very important to perform testing during the entire development cycle and is essential to do it starting in the first stage of the project because this will reduce cost and time when fixing the bugs.

According to Oracle, industry surveys indicate that 75% of all functional testing is still done manually.[1] That's why we decided to develop this framework in order to make automation easier and save money for companies by reducing functional testing times.

Mobica, who employs Juan de Dios Delgado, is a company that works in software development for mobile devices, so that software must work across different platforms. That means that, alongside the development, a lot of testing must be built in order to assure any user will have a good experience with the software and that the client requirements will be achieved.

The company know that the quality of the software is very important, so they put a lot of effort in their testing. That comes with the usage of many different tools to make sure this testing is done in the best possible way. Juan found, however, that having this widely set of tools can be a little messy and overwhelming.

He also noted there are a lot of common tasks that testers want to automate, and they write scripts for, like opening apps or making calls. That means that there's a lot of work that is redundant, and that resources being used on something already existing when they could be used on something else. Surely a tool that gathered all these tools and had a set of these common actions could be made.

This paper narrates how the goal of making automation easier for Android devices was approached, with a project that was developed under the Scrum methodology by Juan de Dios and his group of students in a university in Mexico. The first name of the project was UP Android Automation Framework where UP stands for Universidad Panamericana (Panamerican University). Later, we decided that the name of the project will be AMX Framework where AMX stands for Automation Mobile Experience.

Android Mobile Devices for Testing

When beginning with this project about mobile devices, we had to decide what kind of devices we would work with. When making that decision, we found out that working with iOS would be very problematic, since we worked with the equipment already owned by the students, that consisted entirely in computers working with Windows 10 and Android mobile devices, so we defined our scope with these operative systems.

It is important to acquire a wide array of devices for your mobile Quality Assurance lab. Naturally, the underlying platform plays a big role in device procurement, as it will probably need a host of smartphones and tablets from different companies.

A good cross-section of screen dimensions, processors, and manufacturers (for Android) helps to ensure your team can test apps and websites in a multi-device, multi-platform and multi OS-testing environment. Checking for overall performance on older devices is vital as well.

While working on the development of this project, we decided to incorporate a Smartphone Test Farm to assure future users can do this easily.

Android Testing Concept

In testing, every test case is formed by many steps that must be achieved in order to determine if the test was successful or if it failed. In our project, a step will correspond to a certain task that has to be executed in the android device.

We run the test cases in different devices with the goal of obtaining statistics with strong foundations. There can be exceptions where we cannot execute some steps in a specific device, in this situation we must create a different test case or add the exception in the same test case.

When some step failed, the framework will log the failure with the description and the device where it occurred. It will also log when a step was executed successfully.

In order to achieve an accurate result of the test cases, we must run them many times depending on the type of application and on the type of testing that is required.

Methodologies and Process in Class

We executed this project using an agile methodology. We have sprints with a duration of one week, but they were adjusted sometimes to suit specific requirements. We choose this duration because we have class once a week so in this way the team can work during the week and show their progress in the meeting we had at the beginning of the class.

We had two technical leads because we divided our team in two teams. This made the work easier for the technical leads and we got more features done in a sprint.

The technical leads worked along with the developers in the framework and in the reviewing of the code. The developers worked on the framework and on the creation of the database to save the information of the mobile devices. The three mobile testers worked on the test automation plan and the test cases that we used to create the demo.

The scrum master was on Bellevue, WA, and the rest of the team was on Aguascalientes, Mexico. We choose to work this way because the scrum master couldn't travel to Mexico, but we take advantage of the technology to make this work with 3 meetings per week via video call and a daily communication between the scrum master and the technical leads.

This choice is preferable when you have members of the team living in other countries and they can't travel very often, but we recommend all the team members to be collocated in the same city so they can communicate better and work smoothly.

The entire UP (Universidad Panamericana) AMX scope is described in a product backlog and is documented in Jira. We use this platform to create our Scrum dashboard where we have the historical information of all the sprints we had during the development of this project. We also have the effectivity of every sprint and we can check the sprints where we have more issues and the tasks we created in order to solve these issues.

The sprint planning prioritizes the remaining incomplete items in the product backlog and selecting the items for implementation in the subsequent sprint. At the end of each sprint, the backlog items which have been implemented in that sprint will be reviewed during the demo. Due to the duration of this project, we established that we must have a functional demo at the end of every sprint. The developers were required to do a functional testing on every task they did in order to expedite the review process. Then the demo was assembled by the technical leads which consist on a script that executed all the functions that were developed during the week and this was presented to the project manager.

Using an agile methodology helped us a lot during this project because we could adjust at any time depending on the issues or the requirements. Having a functional demo every week helped us to see our strong and weak spots in the planning and the development and we measured the scope of the project and how we could extended or remove tasks from it. The meetings helped us to review our progress, helped another members that had issues with their tasks and confirmed that we were achieving the requirements.

The members of the team that worked on this project are:

§ Juan Carlos García and Ricardo Macías – Product Owners

§ Juan de Dios Delgado – Scrum Master and Project Manager

§ Isaac Méndez – Technical Lead

§ Marco Montoya – Technical Lead

§ Rodrigo Quiroz – Python Developer

§ Ricardo Bustos – Python Developer

§ Carolina Delgadillo – Python Developer

§ Diego Camacho – Python Developer

§ Luis García – Mobile Tester

§ Jorge Ramírez – Mobile Tester

§ Miguel Salazar - Mobile Tester

1.1. The Structure of the Team

The students worked in a conventional team used in a scrum project; where members with certain skillset can take specific tasks based on their experience or in the skills that they would like to develop.

Rather than having a specific set of students assigned to specific tasks, the team had a "groupthink" approach which allowed them to have a greater diversity and flexibility that gave them a wider experience and knowledge base in order to complete a task more quickly.

The challenge was to provide additional management over the students to verify the task was completed on the time to avoid any delay in the plan. The table below depicts the roles of our team.

Roles	**Responsibilities**

Product Owner	Responsible for the overall direction of the project
Scrum master (PM)	Responsible of ensuring a good relationship between the team and product owner and progress reporting
Consultant	Responsible for design, architecture and implementation of the AMX (Automation Mobile Experience) infrastructure.
SDET (Software Development Engineer in Test)	Responsible for the development of the core of the AMX Framework
Database Engineer	Responsible for the design and maintenance of the database
UI/UX Engineer	Responsible for the overall look & feel of the AMX
Tester	Responsible for testing the various portions of the application including end-to-end deployment

Tools

We used Jira to create and track our sprints. It was very useful because we could comment on the tasks to give an update of the progress or to give feedback. Also, this helped us to have a clear view of our goals and to estimate the number of sprints that we would need to finish all the tasks.

We used GitHub to manage our source code and to have a track of every change we made to the framework. We also used pull requests to review the code, which helped us to have a functional project in the repository with excellent quality code.

We used Zephyr, a JIRA add-on, to create our test cycles, this helped us to do a test cycle for every type of device and to detect bugs on a specific device or on a specific function.

We developed our framework using Python and the following libraries: uiautomator, pytest, validators, colorama, requests, firebase-admin, pylint, invoke, git-lint, pyyaml, pycodestyle, flask and flask_cors.

The demo was developed in Angular 7 and we used Firebase as our database motor.

UP (Universidad Panamericana) Automation Framework

1.2. History

This project was originally initiated in the second semester of 2018 by professors of the Panamerican University campus Aguascalientes in Mexico in response to a request from the engineering school to implement testing in mobile devices in the Software Quality Assurance class for students of Artificial Intelligence engineering.

The students had a gap as they did not previously have classes related to the quality of software in areas such as functional testing, automation testing, performance testing, API testing, etc. Also, there were not any classes related to agile methodology to work as a team in order to accomplish a project like this in real life so with this project they have gain the experience needed in their work.

The UP Framework was proposed and designed to provide the ability to gain experience in Manual and Automated testing using tools as Jira, Confluence, Python, STF.

The UP Framework can connect devices, create automated test cases and execute the test cases in the devices with a great user experience.

This execution on mobile devices can be used for a variety of reasons including but not limited to: user experience testing on a device, market analysis, performance, compatibility, application unit testing and so forth.

1.3. Business Case

The UP Framework was a unique college opportunity for the students in the following ways: it fulfills an immediate market need and it provides Panamerican University with its first intellectual property product as an Open source project. This allows the students to develop their skills in coding, scrum, communication, and team effort.

This framework can be offered to software companies to improve their testing process and for companies that does not have a testing department and they want to implement one. It is a software framework that can adapt to the needs of the client and it is very friendly with the user.

1.4. Implementation

This project was developed with Python and the code follows the style recommended by PEP 8. PEP 8 is Python's style guide with a set of rules for how to format your Python code to maximize its readability.

We created a diagram of the workflow of the framework and based on this we created the classes and the methods that we needed in order to get a functional first version.

We choose a non-relational database hosted on Firebase because this gives us the possibility to save all the data from the device and from the logs, and we can perform fastest searches when we need to retrieve certain information.

With the help of Confluence, we can generate reports of the test cycles that can be personalized according to the requirements of the user and they can have a historical of the executions they do so they can compare the results with the previous ones.

Our framework will execute the test cases automatically so this would save work and time for the testers and the developers of the application. The executions can be configurated to determine the number of cycles, test cases, android versions, devices and the data that will be saved in the logs.

1.5. Timeline

The features outlined above, combined with the students took approximately 6 months to complete. The primary focus is the development of a testing framework in python for mobile devices using deployment procedures, methodologies and best practices in the classroom with scrum.

Bringing a project as a topic of the class was something new, never implemented before at Panamerican University, it was hard to accurately estimate the exact time required to complete the project.

We had to teach the students the test automation processes and tools, the scrum process and get help from our principal consultant in order to develop the architecture and the code reviews. With these actions and after a few sprints the project was a success.

1.6. AMX Approach

Our project is a framework for automated mobile testing in Android devices developed with Python. The goal of the framework is to help the testers by reducing the time and the effort they put in automated testing.

The testers will create the test cases by using the methods of the framework and then they will determine the number of devices and the versions of the operative system they want to test. Finally, they will run the test cycle in the mobile devices that are connected to the farm and after this the framework will show a log of all the actions that were successful and the ones that failed.

This project has a Graphic User Interface for the user to see and interact with, so they don't have to deal with the complications that can come when interacting with code.

The UP Framework is the core of this project. It has many classes with functions that are necessary to create the test cases, and with this we can do test automation in the application. We have a class for the mobile device, for the database, for android debug bridge (adb), for file management, for a logger that registers actions executed by the framework, for the basic actions you can do on a mobile app and for the mobile test farm.

The Test Suite is formed by the test cases that make specific tasks. They use the functionalities of the framework to develop a certain task. For example, they use the functionalities of starting a call, verifying it and end it for the task of making a call.

We used different Android devices like Motorola, Samsung and LG to test the application.

1.7. Structure

The following section contains an explanation of the different folders that compose the project, and the content of each one of them.

GUI Folder

An angular application that has the demo to execute the test cases of the framework.

LIB Folder

Adb Folder

Adb Controller Class has a function to run an adb command and other functions that will execute specific commands like install app, open app, close app, make phone call, download logcat, install app from PC, get the list of installed apps, toggle Bluetooth and take a screenshot.

Data Repository Folder

Data Device Class to create an object with the ID of the device and other properties like the brand, the operative system, the version of the operative system and others.

Data Repository Class that has functions to insert, update and to get all the records from the database that we have on Firebase.

File Manager Folder

File Manager Class that has functions to read and write files, to search a value on a file and to check if a directory exists on the device.

Logs Folder

Logger Class has functions that will write messages on the log file and a function to get the actual content of the logger. The type of messages are debug, info, success, warning and error.

My App Folder

My App Class to create an object with the package name of the app and it has a function to check it the app is opened.

My Device Folder

My Device Class to create an object with the ID of the device, the path of the logcat on the pc, an adb controller object, the path of the downloads on the PC and the path of the screenshots on the PC. It has functions to install an app, download an apk, install an apk from the PC, open an app, close an app, download log, open log, close log, press the back button, make phone call using the UI, clear apps, press the home button, check if an app is installed, toggle Bluetooth, toggle WIFI, end a call, pause a call, check if a call is answered in less than a minute, make a click, take a screenshot, copy files from device to PC, copy one file from device to PC and find a value on the log.

STF Device Folder

STF Device Class to create an object with the ID of the device, the URL of the mobile test farm and the token for the farm. It has functions to check if the farm is being used by a device, to add a device to the farm, to connect to a device from the farm, to disconnect a device from the farm, to get the connection address to the farm and to remove a device from the farm.

Benefits

Our framework can get testing done faster. This will help manual testers to concentrate on clever ways to find defects, instead of working on performance test inputs and verifying the output.

It also reduced the execution time by 70% in different devices and different android versions. With this result it increased test efficiency (productivity), test effectiveness and test coverage. It helps decrease the number of defects that escape to production and it helps improve test repeatability.

Our ROI projection is based on the execution of 91 cases (LTE Data) and on 10 devices.

AMX Framework Total Hours	480 hours (6 Sprints)
Effort Saved per Iteration	80
Total Manual Effort per device	8-13 hours (average)
Total Automated effort per device	5 hours (average)

References

Oracle - “When to Automate Your Testing (and When Not To)”

https://www.oracle.com/technetwork/cn/articles/when-to-automate-testing-1-130330.pdf

How the Page Object Model and Promises Work Together

Hal Deranek

Solution Architect, Slalom_build

deranek@gmail.com

Abstract

The Page Object Model is one of the bedrocks of modern website test automation. The model, based on Object Oriented Programming concepts, helps a test automation engineer break website pages down from large dynamic sets of elements into sections and patterns. Rather than having to account for 100+ elements on a webpage, we can account for the discernible sections and patterns. Place the elements within those sections and patterns. The POM is easier to implement, understand, and maintain.

This all worked well when page content wasn't terribly dynamic. With the recent rise of asynchronous platforms like React and Angular, test automation has become more difficult because of the one word that strikes fear in the hearts of most automation engineers: PROMISES! Perhaps that's hyperbolic, but I have seen enough testers struggle to work with Promises to know that it's a large problem. Fortunately, I've been able to understand Promises, when they are used, and how to resolve them within a test automation suite.

My presentation will focus on these points - describing the Page Object Model and its benefits, explaining what Promises are and how they work, and best practices around using the Page Object Model when testing against an asynchronous platform. I will provide context and examples that the attendees will be able to understand and reproduce. I will also be sure to move around, speak with energy and verve, and interact with the attendees so that everyone has a good time while learning.

Biography

Hal Deranek has worked in testing for over a decade at companies like Tableau, Slalom, and Blue Nile. He started with writing test automation suites for websites, mobile apps, and other platforms. He has grown to become an expert in test strategy and organization. Hal has led several testing teams in various projects across disparate industries. He enjoys mentoring burgeoning testers and helping them reach their potential. Finally, Hal enjoys being part of the testing community in his home city of Seattle by attending, facilitating, and presenting at various Meetup groups.

Introduction

The Page Object Model (POM) is one of the bedrocks of modern website test automation. Rather than having to account for 100+ elements on a webpage, we can account for them using discernible sections and patterns. The POM is easier to implement, understand, and maintain than code without it.

This all worked well when page content wasn't terribly dynamic. With the rise of asynchronous platforms like React and Angular, test automation has become more difficult because of the one word that strikes fear in the hearts of most automation engineers: PROMISES! Perhaps that's hyperbolic, but I have seen enough testers struggle to work with Promises to know that it's a large problem. Fortunately, I have come to understand Promises, when to use them, and how to resolve them within a test automation suite.

By the end of this paper, I will go through the following points:

- Describing the Page Object Model and its benefits
- Explaining what promises are and how they work
- Best practices for using the POM when testing an asynchronous platform

Explaining the Page Object Model

"A page object is an object-oriented class that serves as an interface to a page of your [application under test]. The tests then use the methods of this page object class whenever they need to interact with the UI of that page. The benefit is that if the UI changes for the page, the tests themselves don't need to change, only the code within the page object needs to change. Subsequently all changes to support that new UI are located in one place." — Seleniumhq.org

There are different methods of creating automated tests. The most obvious is to take a page and define everything in one file/class. As an example, take a look at this webpage:

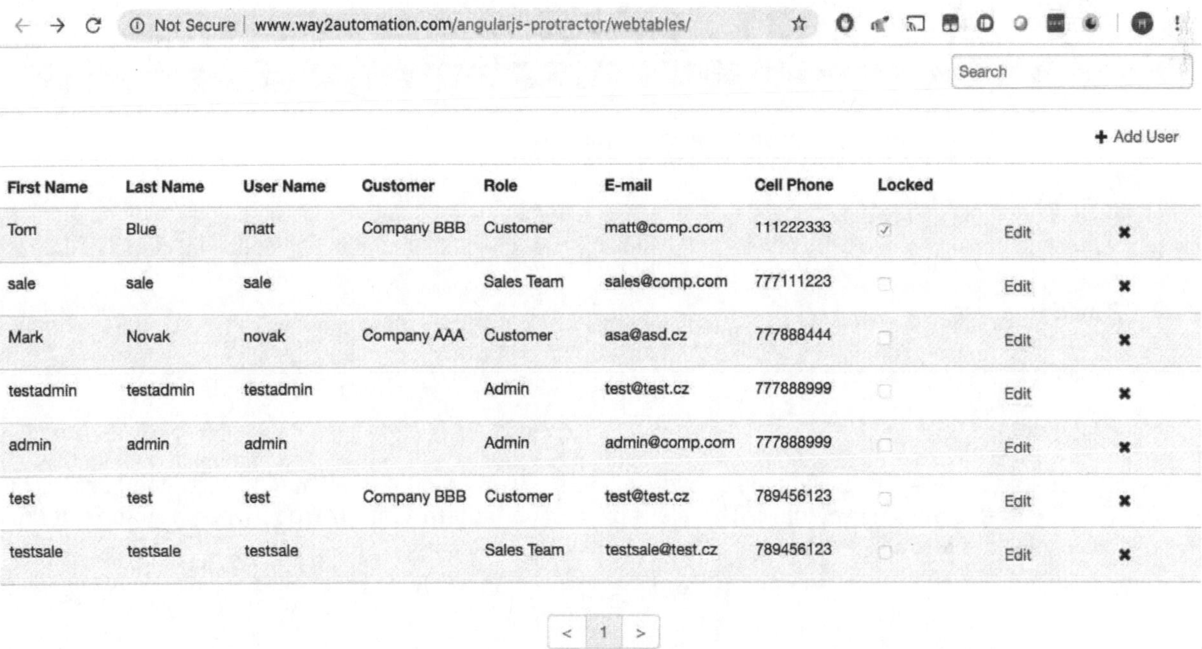

First Name	Last Name	User Name	Customer	Role	E-mail	Cell Phone	Locked		
Tom	Blue	matt	Company BBB	Customer	matt@comp.com	111222333	✓	Edit	✖
sale	sale	sale		Sales Team	sales@comp.com	777111223		Edit	✖
Mark	Novak	novak	Company AAA	Customer	asa@asd.cz	777888444		Edit	✖
testadmin	testadmin	testadmin		Admin	test@test.cz	777888999		Edit	✖
admin	admin	admin		Admin	admin@comp.com	777888999		Edit	✖
test	test	test	Company BBB	Customer	test@test.cz	789456123		Edit	✖
testsale	testsale	testsale		Sales Team	testsale@test.cz	789456123		Edit	✖

< 1 >

http://www.way2automation.com/angularjs-protractor/webtables/

How many different visible elements do you think are on this page? Counting the search input box, each user name, each Edit button, etc., there are 84 elements visible on the page. You could include them all in one large class if this page never changed, however this is a dynamic website. You can add, remove, or edit records, meaning the page will change and you can never define it in automation by declaring each object. There must be a better way!

There is! The Page Object Model is ideal for situations such as these. Rather than seeing the page as singular elements, you can look at it more as exploitable sections and patterns. The sections and patterns you define will contain the objects.

As an example, let's take a look at the website again. This time, let's break it down by sections...

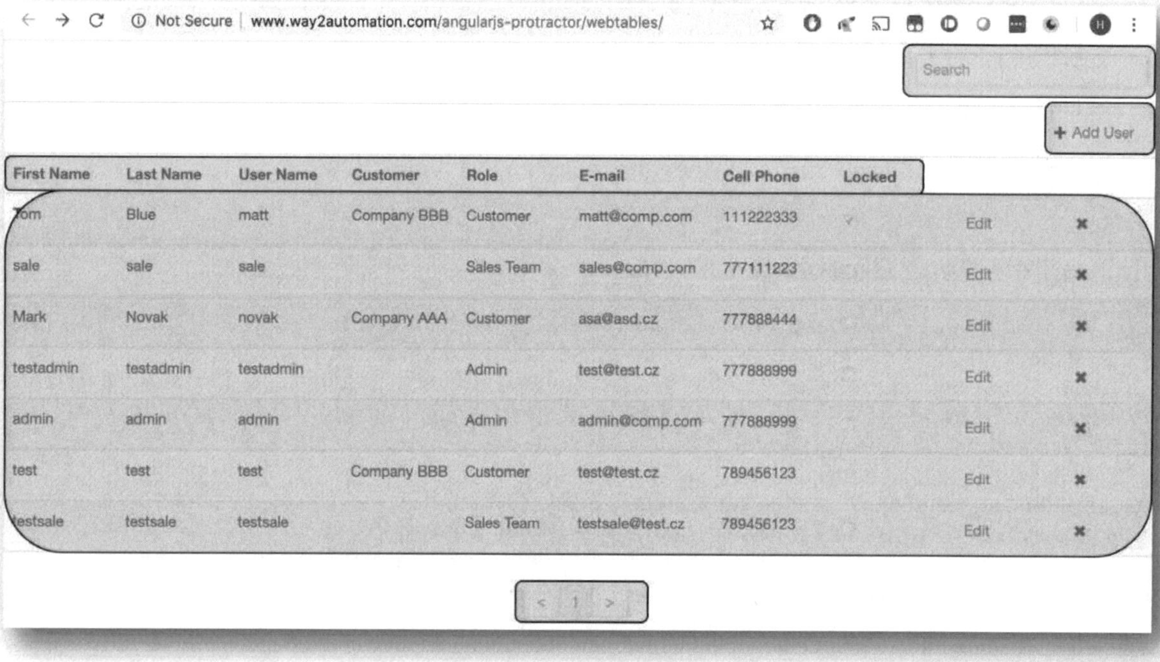

Looking at the page, there are five sections we can define:

- Search
- Add User
- Table Headers
- Table Records
- Pagination

This is a great start but the Table Records section still has a vast amount of elements. Also, the number of records is likely to fluctuate at any time. There's a distinctive pattern that emerges when you look at the records themselves: the rows.

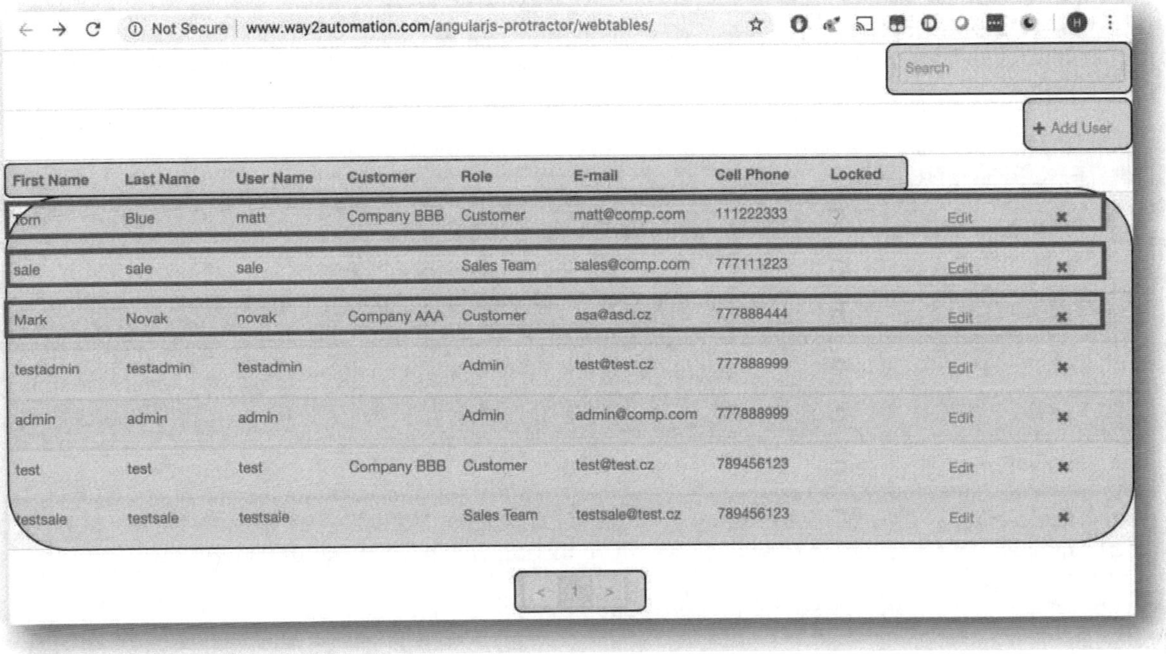

If you create a class to represent this pattern, you can grab each row's container and let the pattern handle the rest.

Code Examples

Using the section examples above, we can start coding our classes. Let's start with the Dashboard Page. We have five sections which will need their own classes. Here's what the DashboardPage class would look like:

```
export class DashboardPage {
    constructor() {}

    public get searchBar(): SearchBarSection {
        return new SearchBarSection(element(by.css('td.global-search')));
    }

    public get addUserButton(): AddUserSection {
        return new AddUserSection(element(by.css('td.actions-add-url')));
    }

    public get userTableTitles(): UserTableTitles {
        return new UserTableTitles(element(by.css('tr.table-header-row')));
    }

    public get userTableRecords(): UserTableRecords {
        return new UserTableRecords(element(by.css('tbody')));
    }

    public get userTablePagination(): Pagination {
        return new Pagination(element(by.css('.pagination')));
    }
}
```

The code above includes all five previously identified sections. One thing to note is that each returned class instance has an element passed in. This is the container. You use the container to ensure you're only looking for elements within the correct section. This is especially important for patterns like the records rows.

```
export class SearchBarSection {
    constructor(private container: ElementFinder) {}

    public get inputBox(): ElementFinder {
        return container.element(by.css('input')));
    }
}
```

Here's the class for the first section seen on the page—SearchBarSection. Since there's only one element currently in the section—an inputBox—it's not terribly complicated. Note how we search for the 'input' tag after the container. This ensures we only look for an 'input' tag within the passed-in container.

To see something more complicated, let's think about the records table. Before we work on the class of the table itself, let's think about the pattern of the record rows:

```
export class UserTableRecord {
    constructor(private container: ElementFinder) {}

    public get firstName(): ElementFinder {
        return container.element(by.css('td.firstName')));
    }

    public get lastName(): ElementFinder {
        return container.element(by.css('td.lastName')));
    }

    public get userName(): ElementFinder {
        return container.element(by.css('td.userName')));
    }

    public get customer(): ElementFinder {
        return container.element(by.css('td.customer')));
    }

    public get role(): ElementFinder {
        return container.element(by.css('td.role')));
    }
    ...
```

This class defines each element with a basic pattern, including using the container. Now that we've got the row pattern, we can start thinking about finding all the records:

```
export class UserTableRecords {
    constructor(private container: ElementFinder) {}

    public async getUserRecords(): Promise<UserRecord[]> {
        const records: UserRecord[] = [];
        for(const record of (await container.element.all(by.css('tr')))) {
            records.push(new UserRecord(record);
        }
        return records;
    }
}
```

Here we find the user rows by this code:

```
await container.element.all(by.css('tr'))
```

This will find all 'tr' tags within the scope of the container. The next line will push a new instance of a UserRecord (as defined in the previous code example) into an array. Finally, the method returns all found row elements.

...

The examples above show how you can use the POM to help with test automation – find basic patterns in the page and build them into sections. However, as previously stated, interacting with these page elements can be difficult when working with asynchronous frameworks, especially when you may have to nest these elements. Let's take a moment to look at how to work with asynchronous frameworks. Let's take a moment to discuss promises!

Explaining Promises

"A Promise is an asynchronous operation. It's called a "Promise" because we are promised a result at a future time." - https://toddmotto.com/promises-angular-q

Let's talk about promises. To translate the statement above, think of a promise as a request to perform an action. Once you've identified an element on a page, you'll want to perform an action on it – click it, get its text, determine if it's displayed, etc. These actions are promises. (Note: finding a single element itself does not return a promise. Finding multiple elements will invoke a promise.)

Why are Promises Difficult?

Asynchronous frameworks don't wait for actions to complete before proceeding to the next action. This allows for quick and dynamic websites. For example, let's say a page has 30 images to load. Traditional websites wait for the images to load in a linear fashion. An asynchronous site will ask for those images all at once and display them as they are available.

Unfortunately, automated tests almost always expect actions to occur in a linear fashion. You're going to run into problems if your test asks for an action (a promise) without accounting for the asynchronous nature of the framework. You must resolve the promises on one action before continuing on to the next.

Let's look at an example of this. In this test, I want to determine if an element is present on the webpage. I start by declaring the element in the first line and then asking to print text to the console on the second line:

```
let newElement = element(by.css('div'));
console.log(`Is the element present? ${newElement.isPresent()}`);
```

Here is the output I expect to see:

```
Is the element present? true
```

Here is the output I will actually see:

```
Is the element present? ManagedPromise::428 {[[PromiseStatus]]: "pending"}
```

What happened? Instead of "true", there's a bunch of nonsense about promises. What's going on?

Resolving Promises - the "Await" Keyword

What's going on is that I didn't resolve the promises in my code. "isPresent" is an action that I performed on the element ("newElement"). Because the framework is asynchronous, the console.log event executes before the "isPresent" promise resolves. This is why we see that the promise is "pending" – it hasn't completed the action when we asked for its output. Fortunately, there's a way to resolve the promise before moving on. Let's see how...

Here's the code I wrote before:

```
let newElement = element(by.css('div'));
console.log(`Is the element present? ${newElement.isPresent()}`);
```

To make the promise to finish executing before I proceed, I use the "await" command like so:

```
console.log(`Is the element present? ${await newElement.isPresent()}`);
```

Notice the "await" keyword before the "isPresent" action on the "newElement" element. This is telling the framework to wait for the "isPresent" action to complete before continuing on. Once "isPresent" finishes, the console.log method will execute. There's the output we now see:

```
Is the element present? true
```

Best Practices for Implementing the Page Object Model & In An Asynchronous Framework

Now that we know how to force promises to resolve on our command, let's look at how to implement this within a framework.

Using the "Get" Syntax

```
export class UserTableRecord {
    constructor(private container: ElementFinder) {}

    public get firstName(): ElementFinder {
        return container.element(by.css('td.firstName')));
    }

    public get lastName(): ElementFinder {
        return container.element(by.css('td.lastName')));
    }

    public get userName(): ElementFinder {
        return container.element(by.css('td.userName')));
    }

    public async getFullName(): Promise<string> {
        return `${await this.firstName.getText()} ${await this.lastName.getText()}`;
    }
...
```

Here is an example of using the 'get' syntax. You'll notice that the async/await keywords aren't used in these methods since they are only identifying the element they're returning. Actions are not performed so no asynchronous calls (promises) are made. Another note on using the "async" keyword on "get" methods: it's not allowed when declaring the method, though you can return a promise (see the next section).

Looking at the "getFullName" method, though, we see the keywords appear. The "async" keyword appears before the method name to declare it as asynchronous. We use "await" before the two "getText" actions to ensure they resolve before the method returns the string.

A note on constructors: by design, constructors cannot execute complex procedures. This means you cannot resolve a promise within the context of the constructor. Having the "get" methods find and return a new instance of the element each time they're called ensures you do not run into difficulties with stale elements such as when a page's data dynamically refreshes.

Returing Promises from a "Get"

There are times where a "get" statement requires either returning a promise or doing some error checking before returning. For example, you might want to validate a dynamic element is present before returning it or throw an error if it isn't present. In the code below, the method is getting all record rows. Since "element.all" returns a promise, the "get" needs to handle this:

```
export class UserTableRecords {
    constructor(private container: ElementFinder) {}

    public get userRecords(): Promise<UserRecord[]> {
        const records: UserRecord[] = [];
        return(async () => {
            for(const record of (await container.element.all(by.css('tr')))) {
                records.push(new UserRecord(record);
            }
            return records;
        })();
    }
}
```

You use the "await" keyword to ensure all the row elements have been found before you proceed to the next step.

Chaining Promises

When one line of code needs to resolve multiple promises, you'll need to chain your promises with "await". Unfortunately, "await" is not a cure all – one "await" will not resolve all promises in one line of code. As an example, let's say you wanted to get the first name from the first record in a table. The code would look like this:

```
const firstName = await (await table.userRecords)[0].firstName.getText();
```

The action breaks down like this:

1. Call and execute the "userRecords" get method on the table object, returning an array of userRecord objects. Use "await" to ensure the method finishes before moving on.
2. Select the object in that userRecord array with index "[0]"
3. Select the "firstName" object in the "userRecord" object
4. Performs the "getText" action on the "firstName" object. Use "await" to ensure the method finishes before moving on.
5. Assign the text returned by "getText" to the constant "firstName" property

Writing a Test

Now that we've gone over the Page Object Model, promises, and how to work with them in concert, we can finish up by writing a test to bring this all together. Here's the webpage again:

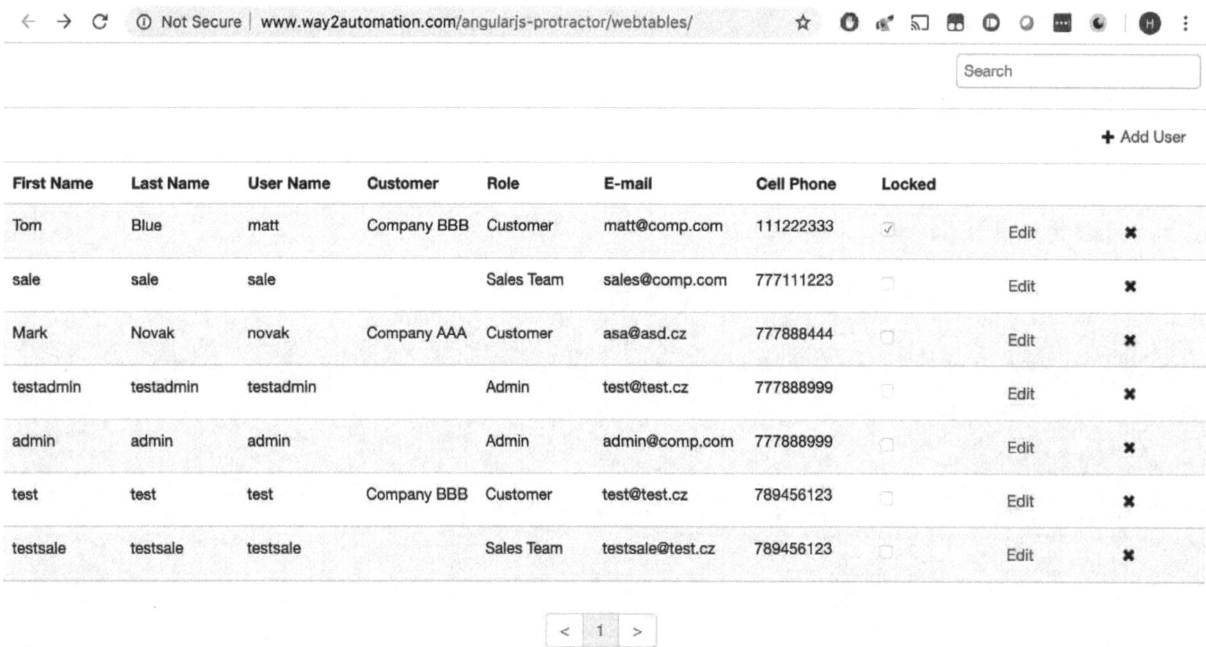

First Name	Last Name	User Name	Customer	Role	E-mail	Cell Phone	Locked		
Tom	Blue	matt	Company BBB	Customer	matt@comp.com	111222333	✓	Edit	✖
sale	sale	sale		Sales Team	sales@comp.com	777111223		Edit	✖
Mark	Novak	novak	Company AAA	Customer	asa@asd.cz	777888444		Edit	✖
testadmin	testadmin	testadmin		Admin	test@test.cz	777888999		Edit	✖
admin	admin	admin		Admin	admin@comp.com	777888999		Edit	✖
test	test	test	Company BBB	Customer	test@test.cz	789456123		Edit	✖
testsale	testsale	testsale		Sales Team	testsale@test.cz	789456123		Edit	✖

< 1 >

Let's write a basic test. I want to write a test that will validate that the first name of the third record is "Mark". To do that, I will need to:

- Find the page (dashboard)
- Find all the user records on the page
- Find the third record from the user records array
- Get the text from the First Name of that record
- Ensure that the record's First Name is "Mark"

Here's the code for that test:

```
describe('User records', () => {
    let dashboard: DashboardPage;
    let userRecords: UserTableRecord[];

    it('should use "Mark" for the third record', () => {
        dashboard = new DashboardPage();
        userRecords = await dashboard.userTableRecords.userRecords;

        const recordName= await userRecords[2].firstName.getText();
        const expectedName = 'Mark';
        expect(recordName).toEqual(expectedName,
`First name of the third record should be '${expectedName}' - is '${recordName}'`);
    }
}
```

The interesting things to note here:

- We use "await" when setting the "userRecords" property because calling the "get" method for "userTableRecords.userRecords" returns a promise
- "await" is also used within the scope of the "expect" to ensure we get the text of the "firstName" property before determining if it equals 'Mark'
- The string, `First name of the third record should be '${expectedName}' - is '${recordName}'`, is a custom error message created for this specific expectation.
    - Creating specific error messages are not required, however it is helpful from a debugging standpoint. Why? Without this, the error message seen would be something like 'Expected Frank to equal Mark' (assuming "Frank" is the name seen). Writing a specific message allows for more clear debugging. That said, it can be onerous to add a custom message to each and every assertion/expectation. You'll need to determine which option works best for your situation.
- Even though "toEqual" returns a promise, we do no put an "await" before the "expect". Why not? In this instance, the code was written in Protractor using the Jasmine testing framework. Though Protractor doesn't inherently handle promises otherwise, it does resolve promises here by default.

In Conclusion

Let's summarize what's been said above:

- Use the Page Object Model to increase code functionality, reduce repetition, and make maintenance easier
- Any action performed on an element will generate a promise
- Use the await keyword to force promises to resolve before continuing to the next action
- Use the `get` syntax to return elements in your POM class
- Chained promises need to use await within those chains

While the Page Object Model is fairly straight forward, promises are not. Using the information above, I've explained how both work on their own and when intertwined. I've also given examples to demonstrate their effectiveness. You should now be able to write automated tests for modern frameworks without issue. Good luck in all your endeavors!

Glossary

Action - an interaction with an element. Examples of an action on an element: clicking, getting its text, determining if it's displayed, sending text, etc.

Async – a keyword used in a method's declaration, requiring the method to return a Promise.

Asynchronous Call – an action that initiates a promise.

Await – a keyword placed before an Asynchronous Call to tell the framework to wait for it to resolve before continuing on.

Container – an element that contains other elements. These other elements can use the container's scope to help with location. Example of usefulness: if there is a data table, each row of data will contain elements that likely use similar identifiers. If you use the <tr> tag of each row as a container, you can access each row's columns without fear of accessing data from other rows.

Element – a singular Page Object seen on a page of your application (text, input box, button, link, etc.).

Page Object – an object-oriented class that serves as an interface to a page of your [application under test].

Page Object Model – a method for representing patterns within the architecture of your application. The patterns are collections of page objects that can be captured in a class for easy reuse.

Promise – an asynchronous operation. These are most often (but not exclusively) raised when actions are performed on Page Objects (click, sendKeys, isDisplayed, etc.).

Resolving – this term refers to a promise completing its execution.

Adding Process to Increase Quality Without Adding Tests

Michael Millerick

mmillerick@blend.com

Abstract

Blend's primary product is a customizable web application. We use a large suite of pre-merge browser-based tests to ensure its continuing functionality and quality. The tests stand up a production-like configuration of our core platform and web application and allow calls to go out to other services in our sandbox environment. We refer to these tests as end-to-end tests. As the number of engineers increased, most had little visibility into the cause of flakey tests. The flakey tests would fail builds, yet engineers had little motivation or ability to remedy the cause of the failures. This tragedy of the commons created instability and prevented code changes from merging quickly. This instability in turn made it impossible to release as often as we desired.

We set out to improve stability without removing flakey tests from the test suite. We took a multifaceted approach to process and cultural improvement. We addressed the negative feedback cycle of instability with cultural and engineering changes:

1. We defined distributed ownership and analytics for tests to create visibility and accountability.
2. We provided engineers with tools that removed the need to watch the status of tests on code changes.
3. We eliminated escape hatches that allowed engineers to bypass tests.
4. We improved the scalability of our test infrastructure.

This approach improved the pass rate of tests and reduced the tribal knowledge and barriers to merging code. The improved ease of merging, combined with the infrastructure changes, improved the rate we released new features to production to almost daily. These changes cut the time engineers waited for tests to finish by half. They also reduced the amount of infrastructure per engineer required to run end-to-end tests. Over the course of the changes described in this paper, our engineering team roughly doubled in size while we were able to hold the size of our test infrastructure constant.

This paper describes the implementation details and impact of each of the four points in the approach described above. It will also examine how the changes made for each point in the approach reinforced the need for the other points.

Biography

Michael is an Engineering Manager at Blend responsible for Quality and Automation. His automation efforts focus on engineering velocity, productivity, and quality of life. He enjoys scaling distributed systems. He enjoys accounting, finance, investing, and previously worked in the StarMine group at Thomson Reuters.

1. Introduction

Blend's primary product is a customizable web application. The large configuration space and desire to ship a product that will delight customers means that we always focus on quality. Early in the company's history, this took on the form of a large manual regression suite that QA would work through for every release candidate. This was a multi-day process and limited our ability to achieve our desired once per day release cadence.

In 2017 the engineering team began to decrease the size of the manual regression suite, primarily by transferring the majority of the manual test cases into our automated pre-merge browser-based end-to-end tests against the majority of our backend and frontend applications. This allowed us to achieve our goal of a daily release cadence of the platform, but had two consequences on the end-to-end test suite:

1. The run time for the suite, and therefore the amount of time it took to merge a Github pull request, increased.
2. Many of the newly added tests were flakey. They would fail in situations where there was no issue with the application. Running the tests did not give reliable results.

The unreliable test results eroded confidence in the suite and caused engineers to constantly battle against probability for their pull requests to pass all of the pre-merge tests. The increased run time of the suite also meant that this battle was often drawn out over the course of several hours. While we had achieved our goal of a daily release cadence, we had unintentionally decreased the velocity of the engineering team in the process.

To combat these two consequences, we built out analytics associated with our test results, built tools to help engineers merge their pull requests and regain confidence in the process, strengthened our process around merging code, and made significant improvements to our test infrastructure. Our overall goal was to increase engineers' confidence in the test suite and get to the point where flakey test results were more likely to be an indicator of bugs in the application than they were to be an indicator of a poorly written test.

2. Analytics and Distributed Ownership

We already had basic analytics on our end-to-end tests. Since early 2017, we published test result information into Datadog[1] at the end of every single test. We found the insights Datadog was able to give us inadequate because we could not view trends over a long period of time and we could not formulate complicated queries to give us insight into which tests were the most problematic. We decided to create a service, Test Center, which would store all of the data in a Postgres database and provide views into the data.

In order to decide which tests were flakiest, we first needed to decide on how to differentiate between "good" results and "bad" results. We ultimately decided that "good" results would be those where all of the tests passed within the maximum number of retries before the job finished—the ones that would result in a green status indicator on a pull request and allow the author to merge their pull request. All others would be classified as "bad". This allowed us to compare the test results for the known "good" jobs to the entire set of test results and gain information from the different trends in the two sets of data and filter out systemic, external, and infrastructure issues, from the signal in a systematic fashion.

We decided to operate under the assumption that the "bad" results that prevented engineers from merging code had one of two causes. The first are legitimate regressions in the product detected by the tests that would need to be fixed before the code was merged. The second are indicative of systemic, external, or infrastructure issues. Neither of these two situations provide signal on whether or not a given test is flakey since both are deterministic in nature. Our filtering to just test results that are indicative of flakey test behavior unfortunately also disregards results when tests are so flakey that they fail an entire run and prevent engineers from merging code. While we filter out more results than we arguably need to, we found that the information we preserved provided us with a sufficiently strong signal. We could then use that signal to investigate whether the test was flakey because of issues within the test, or because of bugs in the application that would cause the test to fail periodically (e.g. race conditions).

Test Run	Attempt	Result
1	1	Pass
2	1	*Fail*
2	2	*Fail*
2	3	*Fail*
3	1	*Fail*
3	2	Pass

To contextualize our filtering logic in an example, assume we had the information shown on the right for a test in the database. This single example test was part of three separate test runs. In the first and third test run, the test passed prior to the end of the test runs. In the second test run, the test did not pass and would have resulted in a failing status indicator on the pull request. Therefore, our filtering logic excludes the second test run from the "good" job pass rate. With the results of the second test run excluded, the "good" job pass rate for this test is 66.6% (two passes out of three total attempts). The pass rate considering all test runs is 33.3% (two passes out of six total attempts).

With these simple analytics developed, we now had a strong picture of which tests were flakier than others. The "good" job pass rate on tests ranged from about 34% to 100%. 87/373 tests had pass rates lower than 90%, which lead to substantially more failed test jobs from false positives than we wanted.

We now had a concrete picture of which tests were in the worst shape, but with so many tests in need of fixing (either by fixing the application(s) being tested or by fixing the test, the former being more preferable to fix), we needed a way to know which engineering team was responsible for fixing each test. Using the information in the git history, and with guidance from engineering leadership, we added a comment to each of the test files to denote which engineering team was responsible for each test file. The clear assignment and distribution of ownership helped us build tooling around the distributed ownership.

We had data and ownership. We followed by adding additional process. We created the notion of a technical health team to apply upward pressure on the pass rate of tests. We set a threshold "good" job pass rate, below which we categorized a test as flakey, and set how many flakey tests each engineering team was allowed to have before they would need to contribute an engineer to the technical health team for a sprint. By carefully setting these thresholds and expectations around the technical health team, we have increased our threshold for a flakey test from a 70% to 85% “good” job pass rate without any engineers added to the technical health team. If engineers were to be contributed to the technical health team, they would spend the sprint focused on improving their team’s flakey tests to reduce the likelihood that their team would need to contribute an engineer to the technical health team in a future sprint.

3. Tools

We built tools to allow the organization to push through the difficulties caused by frequently failing tests without eliminating tests from the suites. The overarching goal of the tools described below was to minimize the number of times engineers had to rerun tests on their pull requests and to reduce the likelihood that engineers would attempt to run tests on their pull requests while there was little to no chance that the tests would pass.

3.1. The Merge Bot

We built a bot that would help guide pull requests into a merged state. Pull request authors needed to get their necessary reviews, and then attach a label to the pull request in Github Enterprise. The bot would then perform the minimal amount of work necessary to merge the pull request into the appropriate branch.

The label also had the secondary benefit that it allowed us to better utilize our existing infrastructure. The label effectively formed a queue of pull requests that needed to be merged. Authors would attach the label, and then the bot would work tirelessly day and night to merge the pull requests. Before the label, we would frequently run into problems when engineers first came into the office and immediately after lunch, when engineers would attempt to run tests on their pull requests in bulk. It was a poorly kept secret that it was significantly easier to merge pull requests at midnight than it was to merge pull requests during working hours—a fact that we did not like but tolerated. The label also made it easier to recover from systemic issues in the test environment. If there were problems with tests, engineers could apply the label and have confidence that the bot would merge their pull request once the environment was stable again.

3.2. Slack Notifications

We added Slack notifications that would be sent to the pull request author when tests failed on their pull request. It contained a link to Test Center that would state which tests failed on the pull request, what the “good” job pass rate was on that test, as well as which team owned the test(s) that failed after all retries were exhausted. This provided two benefits to us:

1. It drastically reduced the difficulty for pull request authors to understand whether or not they legitimately failed tests. If the one or two tests that failed their pull request were ones with very low “good” job pass rates, then it was likely they were just unlucky.

2. It put pressure on the owners of the worst performing tests to improve the pass rate of the tests. It quickly became public knowledge which tests lead to the most frequent failures.

3.3. Issue Tracking

We use Jira to track issues and defects. We built a daily job that leveraged the Test Center data to create/close/reopen Jira issues based on the flakey tests. If a test became flakey for the first time, it would create a Jira issue in the Jira project for the team that owned the test and assign it to the lead for that team. If a test was no longer below the threshold for flakey tests, it would close the appropriate Jira issue. If a test became flakey again, it would reopen the existing Jira issue.

The automatic actions of the bot made it easier for teams to track their flakey tests. This enabled teams to be more proactive about correcting their flakey tests, since they were now visible in their backlogs rather than visible only in Test Center. The automatic actions also made it impossible for them to hide their flakey tests. If a Jira issue is closed out, and the test is still flakey a week later, the job will reopen the Jira issue and keep the team accountable for fixing their flakey tests.

3.4. Test Status Indicators

All engineers working on our core platform are in a Slack channel for developer support and notifications about the core platform. The channel topic contains indicators for the general health of the core platform in the sandbox environment. All of these indicators were manually maintained. We gave Test Center the ability to maintain the test related indicators using its own data. We use the following two heuristics to determine if it is possible for a test suite to pass:

1. Are there any tests that have failures, and zero successful results in the last hour? If so, those tests, or the portion of the application they are testing, are broken and it is not possible to pass the suite.

2. Are there any test results present in the database in the last hour? If not, it indicates an issue with the sandbox infrastructure preventing the tests from even beginning to run and it is impossible to pass tests.

The automated maintenance of the status indicators reduced our detection time for issues preventing tests from passing. Prior to this, test maintainers needed to be incredibly vigilant, or rely on engineers pointing out that tests were probably broken, to know that there were problems in the sandbox environment that needed to be resolved. These changes put a cap of one hour on our time to detection for broken tests.

4. Elimination of the Escape Hatch

When there were relatively few engineers, an "escape hatch" was created that would allow engineers to merge their code without passing any tests. This was tenable in a small engineering organization because the engineers had detailed knowledge of every area of the platform and therefore were able to make good decisions around when they could skip all of the tests without impacting any of the tests. Over time, engineers also began to use the escape hatch to bypass broken tests. This eventually turned into using the escape hatch to bypass flakey tests as the organization grew.

This was problematic. We frequently ran into this cycle:

1. There would be an issue with the infrastructure or an external service, which prevented one or more tests from passing.
2. Engineers would skip past the tests they failed in order to continue merging code during the outage.
3. The original cause of the outage would be fixed, but tests continued to fail because one or more of the pull requests merged during the outage broke one or more tests.

This would repeat in a cycle, sometimes for multiple days. Not only would engineers need to fix the original cause of the outage, but engineers would need to hunt down and fix the one or more bad pull requests that merged during the outage, an exercise that was time consuming and was only necessary because of the escape hatch. We decided that the escape hatch needed to be eliminated.

When we rolled out the merge bot discussed in the previous section, we also began tracking the number of days the organization went without skipping tests with the escape hatch. We tracked this information on a whiteboard near the Quality team and sent out a daily Slack message with a picture of the whiteboard. Initially, there was very little change in behavior. Gradually the organization became comfortable with the new workflow. As more and more engineers adopted the merge bot to merge pull requests, the organization was able to go more and more days without using the escape hatch. After about a month and a half of daily dashboard updates, we reached 10 consecutive days without using the escape hatch and disabled it entirely on 13 April 2018.

5. Scalable Infrastructure

In parallel to these other initiatives, we also migrated from Protractor[2] to WebdriverIO[3] as the framework for running our end-to-end tests. With this migration, we also built out our own test runner to run the test containers on our Kubernetes cluster rather than directly on our Jenkins servers and to parallelize the tests in a more intelligent fashion than the default behavior of the test runner. Improvements in these two areas, combined with increases to the pass rates of tests, reduced the wall-clock time of tests from 30 minutes to 10 minutes.

5.1. Test Parallelization and Sandboxes

In order to reduce the runtime of our tests, we run many tests in parallel. While we were using Protractor, we used the built in `shardTestFiles` option to parallelize the tests. We would run the tests once, see which tests failed, and rerun those tests. This led to a waterfall pattern where the retries of failed tests could only begin after all of the original tests had failed. This resulted in long periods of time where only a single test was running, and we were not effectively utilizing our infrastructure.

Our application is very configurable, which means that many of the configurations are modified over the course of our tests. Since the tests had grown from nothing under our Protractor framework, alongside a configuration space which had also grown from nothing, each individual test was not sandboxed very well. This led to flakey tests and frustrated engineers. With our switch in frameworks, we also began to leverage features from our platform to sandbox tests from each other. Our platform application supports serving multiple customers from a single instance of the platform application by completely segregating all information based on its knowledge of which customer API requests originated from. We call this feature multitenancy. We leveraged the multitenant capabilities of our platform to create N identical tenants in the platform application, which also dictated how parallelized our tests would be. We could rely on our multitenant capabilities to sandbox tests from other tests running in parallel since bugs in the implementation of our multitenant capabilities would mean that the entire test suite would fail deterministically.

We updated the setup function at the beginning of tests to reset feature flag and configuration states to a standard configuration. Our use of tenants on our platform meant that each test was isolated from each other, while our setup function guaranteed that each tenant began in the same state for each test. We updated our lint rules to require that the setup function was used properly at the beginning of every test. This forced all tests to begin with the same initial application state, which eliminated the potential for tests to fail because of state left behind by previous tests. This reduced the cognitive overhead when writing new tests since engineers no longer had to worry about the configuration changes made by other tests.

In addition to the success or failure of tests, Test Center also collects information on the run time of each test. If set to run two tests in parallel, our grouping algorithm creates two different test groups, with roughly equivalent total expected duration from looking at the historical run time information in Test Center. Assume a test suite has five total tests, four of which are expected to complete in one minute based on historical data, and one expected to complete in four minutes. Our grouping algorithm would group the four tests expected to complete in one minute each into a group and would put the single test expected to complete in four minutes into its own group. Both groups would run in parallel, and the tests would finish in about four minutes. This guarantees that all tests will finish at almost exactly the same time, which minimizes the amount of time engineers need to wait for their tests to complete.

5.2. Jenkins v. Kubernetes

We found that Jenkins did a poor job scheduling work. While the number of jobs was fairly evenly distributed across all of our Jenkins servers, the load placed on each server was rarely evenly distributed. This led to some servers being put under extremely heavy load, and they would frequently remove themselves from the cluster as the Jenkins process crashed. Our tests were already run in containers, so we started launching those containers on our Kubernetes cluster instead of on the local Jenkins server. This allowed us to specify and tune exactly how much CPU and memory was needed for the tests to run and provided a stable environment in which the tests were guaranteed to have access to the resources that they needed to run to completion.

Putting all of our test traffic on the Kubernetes cluster in our sandbox environment also helped us to stress test the cluster. The tests were the first heavy load we placed on our Kubernetes clusters, and served to stress test the infrastructure and tooling built around Kubernetes. Our most important learnings were

1. Our original cluster overlay, Weave, was insufficient for our large amount of pod churn to be handled gracefully by Kubernetes. We switched to Calico and saw a noticeable increase in network and test stability (unfortunately the increase is difficult to quantify due to there being different metrics between the two overlays).
2. How to appropriately size the nodes in our cluster for our workload and tune resource requests and limits for our application. These learnings made it significantly easier to ultimately move our core platform from Amazon Elastic Container Service to our Kubernetes cluster in May 2019.

6. Conclusion

Through all of the changes described above, we have significantly improved the pass rate of our end-to-end tests. Refer to Chart 7.1. You can see several areas where the pass rate of tests degraded, and then rebounded shortly thereafter when we fixed the bug(s) identified in the application from examining which tests had degraded the most. These downward spikes are most apparent around April 2018 and April 2019. Also visible is the large increase in pass rate (and corresponding drop in overall test time) that came with a significant performance increase in the application, the opportunity for which was identified by examining the test data in Test Center.

Improvements to test grouping and how we run the tests on our Kubernetes infrastructure have decreased the wall clock runtime of tests. Refer to Chart 7.2. When we began the improvements described above, the wall clock runtime of tests varied between 20 and 30 minutes. By improving the stability of tests, and with continuing improvements to how tests are grouped, the wall clock runtime of the tests has decreased to about 10 minutes and varies significantly less from run to run. This is notable because the CPU time used by the tests (Chart 7.3) has not decreased as much as the wall clock runtime has decreased.

Improving the pass rate of our tests has given us better signal on the health of the application from our test result analytics. When the pass rate of our tests begins to decline, we now have confidence that instability was introduced in the application and are able to quickly identify and remediate the instability. We believe this has had significant benefit on the stability, and therefore quality, of our platform and application. The majority of issues that have been corrected have been performance related, or pure race conditions in the application. The large volume of test runs has given us enough signal to identify these issues that are otherwise nearly impossible to find manually. Additionally, engineers trust the tests more which has increased their willingness to add new tests, maintain the existing tests, and address likely issues uncovered by examining the test analytics in Test Center.

7. Charts

7.1. End-to-end test pass rate

7.2. Average wall clock duration per end-to-end test suite run

7.3. Average CPU Time spent per end-to-end test suite run

References

Datadog, https://www.datadoghq.com/
Protractor, https://www.protractortest.org/#/
WebdriverIO, https://webdriver.io/

[1] A monitoring service for cloud-scale applications.
[2] An end-to-end test framework for Angular and AngularJS applications.
[3] A next-gen WebDriver test framework for Node.js.

Introduction to Test Automation and DevOps: A Case Study

Robert Taylor

rmtiv@comcast.net

Abstract

Test automation and DevOps is necessary to increase test coverage, boost efficiency, and improve the quality and quantity of a delivered product. But have you ever wondered how to begin implementing any kind of test automation or DevOps if little or none exists? Or understanding what test automation or DevOps entails?

This paper explores the challenges that beginning test automation and DevOps Engineers may face when beginning their Automation Engineer career, especially within .NET projects in an agile setting. This paper discusses a case study about test automation and DevOps separately, then the integration of test automation into DevOps, and lastly addresses common challenges beginning Automation Engineers may face. Key topics will include tools used through the case study, understanding the purpose of test automation, determining and articulating why testing needs to occur, understanding why automation is important, and learning how to integrate test automation with DevOps.

This knowledge can help beginning Automation Engineers' determine which tools may add value to their company, increase automation coverage, gather effective analytics, and increase efficiency of the Continuous Integration/Continuous Deployment (CI/CD) pipeline. The purpose is not to dictate how an Automation Engineer should do their work, but to teach or expand on what they know and understand what steps can be taken.

Finally, this paper concludes by describing how to use the information presented to quantify necessary changes and solutions to use for next iterations. That change is not static, but everything created is a living breathing thing that needs to be continuously monitored and improved upon each iteration.

Biography

Graduated from Oregon State with a B.S. in Computer Science in the summer of 2017. During my senior year and beyond, I worked on independent projects using Unity and C#, participating in Portland Indie Game Squad (PIG squad). In October 2017, I worked for Experis-Manpower Group with a focus in black-box testing on major label video games. At Experis, I learned how to use a multitude of testing methodologies and software development cycles. After a year at Experis, I joined BlueVolt in November of 2018 as a Junior test automation and DevOps Engineer. At BlueVolt I continue to build upon my knowledge of testing by adapting it with scripting to automate the testing process. Taking over the test automation I built out a Regression test suite when none-existed, implemented some performance testing, participate in all UAT testing, and managed and directed interns on where they can begin and how to begin help with test automation. I've also increased my DevOps knowledge and experience by setting up lower environments, creating a CI/CD pipeline to speed up development and testing, setting up gated check-ins, and using a wide range of tools to monitor and configure BlueVolt's production environment.

1. Introduction

Test automation and DevOps are becoming important roles through all varieties of industries. and for beginning or aspiring Automation Engineers it can be difficult on how to get involved with the tools, practices, and cultures of test automation and/or DevOps. Learning how to work with test automation and DevOps always starts with the customer, as the main objective is to server the customer effectively, efficiently, and increase the quality of the product. To achieve this, it is important to learn and understand the product's development cycle, agile processes, goals of the company, and the pain points for the different groups involved with the product (such as the product team, support, developers, QA, and customers). Coming into BlueVolt's, there were a lot of manual steps for deployments through a complex system of NAnt [18] scripts with limited DevOps implementation. There were outdated unit tests, limited code coverage, and developers were using their time to manually run regression tests at the end of each sprint. But before I could begin automating tasks it is important to get familiar with what the product is and the goals of BlueVolt.

Before creating any kind of automation, it is important to take the time and effort to understand the problem that the product is attempting to solve, what is the metrics determine the product's success , the products development cycle, and what pain points are preventing the product from being more successful. These 4 ideas can be broken up and act as signposts to help guide successful automation implementation. The first signpost is to learn about the company's product to understand what it's trying to achieve and how to serve the customer. At BlueVolt, we are a Learning Management System (LMS) that provide customer with a platform to host and create a dynamic learning system. The second signpost is to identify the goals of the product that the company's creating. At BlueVolt, the company's primary focus is the user experience, what the user can and cannot do throughout the platform and helping create a product that will satisfy different types of user's needs. Knowing this emphasize the importance of user experience for the LMS and helps focus tasks towards improving user scenario. This included expanding upon the regression suite through automation, putting tests with pipelines, create code and product quality feedback loops, create not tests to increase functionality coverage, and using performance analytics to find performance improvements.

The third signpost is about improving the CI/CD process by automating tasks so that developers only need to complete a pull request to see their code get deployed to test environments and then after testing automate processes to get the code into production. Improving these processes allow for efficient development and could decrease the downtime of the application during updates and deployments. At BlueVolt, a few improvements to the CI/CD was accomplished through automating regression tests, creating deployment pipelines, and setting up gated check-ins. These improvements have helped alleviate development pain points, improved testing, sped up the deployment process, and improved the quality of the product.

Lastly, the fourth signpost is about improving the quality of the code and product. Being able to provide effective feedback helps provides the information needed to figure out how to fix broken code, improve code coverage, and increase performance. Using automated tests to provide information as soon as a pull request is completed can help maintain the integrity of the build. Other methods to improve code and product quality can be through test pipelines, integration tests, unit tests, stress testing, setting up SonarQube, or any other tools that provides feedback about quality and performance. At BlueVolt, test automation was combined with pipelines that would check to ensure that the product could always build, database migrations always work, and code coverage of unit tests are analyzed with SonarQube. Once the product is pushed to production, Pingdom and New Relic are used to track and measure the performance.

Following the guidance of the above signposts is an excellent way to start figuring out where the problems exist. From there the problems can be broken down into investigations which will lead into actionable items for automation. Another important factor when creating automation is understanding the development stack of the product. Knowing the development stack can help provided answer into what tools to use to develop tests, test environments, and software to use so that the automation will work well with the product.

At BlueVolt, our stack is C# .NET backend with an Angular frontend where we work closely with Azure to host and deploy our product. Becoming familiar with the stack has helped direct me towards focusing on automation through Azure DevOps and Azure Portal as much as possible. Also used Jenkins and SonarQube which are used to create testing and analytic pipelines to quantify and automate code coverage, regression testing, code deployments, and other useful tasks. Automating test have been done through Protractor, JMeter, and custom scripts to test the different components, functionality, and simulate user scenarios throughout the web application. Another key component at BlueVolt is the use of a content delivery network and performance software to help deliver our product effectively. As an LMS we work with Akamai, which is a content delivery network (CDN), to improve the caching of our content to speed up our page loads and use Pingdom and New Relic to monitor performance of the production environment.

This paper will explore test automation and DevOps independently by discussing the different types of tools that have been used at BlueVolt. Each tool will be broken down into how they function and how they fit within the culture of BlueVolt. The paper will then discuss about how to use tools from test automation and tools from DevOps together to create automated testing. Lastly the paper will finish with questions that beginning Automation Engineers may face. The purpose of this paper is to show the steps taken to integrate automation at BlueVolt, introduce different combinations of test automation and DevOps together to increase efficiency, and to inspire or provide useful knowledge for others for their Engineering career.

2. Test Automation

Test automation is taking manual testing and tasks and then, "... automating the tracking and managing of all those testing needs, including how much of the system different tests cover and what other types of testing might be required to cover all the moving parts." [1] Where the goal is to use automation to create a quick, efficient, reliable way to get results. These results are valuable as it provides Quality Assurance and Developers with feedback towards improving the product. Automating tests should help find issues quickly and efficiently so that developers can resolve found issues before the next release. Another benefit of automating tests is that it allows other testers to focus on areas of the product increasing the overall test coverage.

To increase testing coverage is important to understand a wide range of testing techniques. Knowing different testing techniques will increase test coverage across the system and help find the weak points within a system. Some examples of different testing techniques are:

- **Golden Path (Happy Path) –** The default scenario of known input producing a known or expected output throughout a system.
- **Testing Edge Cases –** Testing outside of the base assumptions the expected use of the function or feature within the system.
- **Smoke Test –** Check basic functionality of a system, ensuring that the product's main feature work as expected.
- **Combinatorial Testing (All-Pair Testing) –** Testing all the difference combinations of parameters in a system to achieve 100% test coverage.

- **Performance Testing –** Testing the speed and effectiveness of the system.
- **User Testing –** A test plan to run through user simulations to ensure that functionality will work for users before a product is released.
- **Stress Testing –** Test the stability and reliability by putting a system under an extremely heavy load condition.

Knowing different testing techniques and integrating them into the development cycle will increase the product's quality. Another benefit is that knowing how to test will narrow down where to start automating and help determine which testing tool should be used.

2.1. Test Automation Tools

After knowing about the different type signposts to follow for test automation, it is time to determine which tools to start using to build out those tests. At BlueVolt our stack is a C# .NET backend, an Angular frontend, and our database lives within Azure. The focus of our product is through customer success using user interfaces, performant page response times, quick content delivery, and providing an effective learning platform that the customer can use. This information helps determined to create tests that will monitor application performance, check that UI functionality is correct, automate regression tests, and preventing breaking changes from being released into production. Knowing what test need to be created, the tools that help met these requirements were Protractor for frontend testing and a mix of JMeter and custom scripts for backend testing.

2.1.1. Selenium/Protractor

Selenium/Protractor are frontend UI testing tools to do end-to-end testing, simulation how an end-user would use the system. Selenium is a Java tool that interacts with browser page elements of a web application. This can be used to verify content is loading correctly, check that elements are interactable, simulate use navigation, combine UI commands, and to test different kinds of frontend functionality. Whereas Protractor is a test framework for Angular JS and uses Selenium to automate the browser interactions. Since BlueVolt's platform uses angular for the frontend we built out our end-to-end tests using Protractor. Along with building out a Protractor test suite, time was spent deciding where and how the Protractor test will run.

End-to-end testing should run against a clean test environment. The test environment should also be updated with completed features, that are planned to go out with a future release, so that test have a chance to catch a breaking change. For example, if a feature exists on a dev environment and introduces a broken functionality, and end-to-end tests are being ran against a different environment, those tests will never catch the breaking change until it's possibly too late. By automating test to check existing functionality, in an updated clean environment, can help expose any breaking changes quickly and efficiently so they can be fixed (or reverted) before the next release.

2.1.2. JMeter

JMeter is a "...Java test framework provides facilities for load, stress and performance testing, but it can also be used to perform regression tests and a limited set of functional tests." [2]. The tools focus is to simulate multiple users hitting an endpoint that could test the endpoint's durability, reliability, and to find its limitations (where it will break, what load it can handle, and where the stress/weak point reside within that endpoint). Another use of JMeter is the possibility to run a suite of regression tests or other tests for functionality due to the tool's ability of: having a variety of samplers that allow any kind of request simulation, assertions for verifications, and a diversity of listener to help debug the tests. [3]

At BlueVolt, JMeter is used to test our performance of our Web API endpoints, databases interactions, and perform load and stress testing. JMeter has also been used to check the configuration of our different development environments (dev, quality assurance, staging). An example of using JMeter at BlueVolt, was comparing our performance between using a SQL Server database and an Azure database. Using JMeter, a suite of tests would run to hit endpoints that reads/writes from a database tracking response time, throughput, and deviation using large amount of simulated user. Afterwards, the metrics from each were compared and analyzed to determine which database would be best for our product. JMeter was not the only determining factor for which database, but the metrics did help justify and predict how BlueVolt's product would function in the different environments.

2.1.3. Scripting

Creating custom test script through scripting language can be a powerful way to create flexible automated tests, some example of different scripting languages includes JavaScript, Python, Ruby, PowerShell, or Batch. A test script is a set of instructions that is performed on a system to quantify if the system is performing as expected.[4] Creating custom scripts allows a test to be completely customizable. A few examples used at BlueVolt are increased scalability by using any available library, determine which target(s) to test, what dataset and amount of data to use, and alter the load the test will put on the system. Custom test scripts can be dynamic for different environment, where the test is adjusted to avoid destructive testing (create, update, or delete data) if the test saw that it was running against the production environment, or can include destructive testing when ran against dev, qa, or a staging environment.

At BlueVolt, currently we do not have an abundance of custom scripts, but have made a few that check the response header, response code, and response time of our different nondestructive Web API endpoints in production. These custom scripts help check the functionality of those endpoints and can monitor the response time and other performance metrics of those endpoints. Another use of these test scripts is when we setup up other environments (through Azure Portal or on a VM) the script can be used to check Web API endpoints to ensure that the system was configured correctly.

2.2. Applying Test Automation

Test automation is finding repetitive manual testing, are of the application that can't be automated, or speeding up testing while increasing the quality of the product. Successful test automation should help improve product quality by finding bugs or broken functionality that may have been caused by a code updates and be easy to maintain/run. [5] Test automation needs to be efficient and save time it would have taken to manually test allowing other testers to focus on different areas of the product to increase overall test coverage. The goal of test automation is the serve the customer and ensure they experience a high-quality product.

One way of applying test automation at BlueVolt was that at the end of each sprint (once every two weeks) running manual regression tests were run to check the functionality of the product before being released to production. This was done to check if any breaking changes were being introduced and to fix them before the release. But by performing manual repetitive test, the tests were taking away time that the rest of the team could be using for other tasks. Also, since the tests were running once every two weeks, a breaking change may not be found until it was too late in the development cycle. But by using Protractor, an automated regression suite was built and turned something that was ran one once every two weeks manually, into something that runs on a nightly basis. This also helped relieves the manual testing from the team and finds issues the night of rather than at the end of the sprint.

Another example is when migrating from a SQL Server Database to an Azure database, tests were creates using JMeter to check product performance. Then these metrics were used to determine which type of database the company should use to improve the quality of the product. These same JMeter test were repurposed from performance and are now used to check Web API functionality of our production and test environment using non-destructive (update, add, or delete data) testing.

In this section a lot of different testing tools and techniques were explored and discussed throughout BlueVolt. The next section will go into detail about the different DevOps tools and purposes they have served at BlueVolt. Afterward the paper will discuss how DevOps and test automation can be combined to create powerful features.

3. What is DevOps

DevOps is a multitude of tools, practices, and culture shifts that expand across the agile process within a product's lifecycle. DevOps can be described as a collection of ideas and agile practices that are used between dev and ops engineers throughout a product's lifecycle. Starting from design features, through the development cycle, through test, and through production. Where DevOps "...extends the Agile principles beyond the boundaries of the code into the entire delivered service." [6] Bringing together all the different groups involved to value building quality throughout the development process.

The primary objective of DevOps, much like test automation, is to satisfy the customers wants, needs, and concerns. This can be accomplished through increased deliverability, quality, improvements to the development cycle, helping developers work efficiently and effectively, convey information about performance and metrics, promote sustainable development through agile processes, making things simple, and architecture improvements. [7] A few ways this was achieved at BlueVolt was through setting up pipelines, automating tasks, setting security policies, creating environments, working with monitoring tools, and relieving other pain points throughout the company. Improvements throughout the company means improve the deliverability of the product which then increase the service to the customer.

3.1. DevOps Tools and Applications

Like test automation, when implementing a DevOps tool, process, or cultural shift it is important to understand the issue being solved, how the implementation will solve that issue, and how can the process be iterated upon for future updates. For BlueVolt the problem DevOps is trying to solve is how to improve the deliverability of the product while improving its quality, integrity, and health. Many different tools, processes, and ideas have been implemented to help improve the product across the whole company. DevOps is used to speed up the development cycle, improve our agile practices, increase the amount of product that can be delivered, enforce a higher-quality product, and to track performance to find improvements. This can't all just be achieved with one or two tools/applications but with several different tools. Some of the tools and applications that BlueVolt uses are Azure DevOps, Azure Portal, Jenkins, SonarQube, Pingdom, New Relic, and Akami. The reason why some of these tools were chosen was due to our stack (C# .NET backend, Angular frontend, and Azure database), current issues that the company faces, and to increase future planning to prevent issue from arising.

3.1.1. Setting Up Pipelines

Azure DevOps and Azure Portal offer a wide range of DevOps opportunities to speed up the CI/CD process, provide analytics and metrics, allow the user of pipelines and agents for deployments and gated check-ins, and has a system to create, alter, and track Public Backlog Items. Azure DevOps also provides flexibility in build, deployment, and release pipeline by providing a wide range of extension from the Visual Studio Marketplace. Whereas the Azure Portal provides the capability to setup different resources that can be used for all aspect of our application. Due to the nature of the .NET project, the Azure Portal is primarily being used to setup different WebApp's providing us the ability to migrate away from Internet Information's

Services (IIS) on virtual machines (VMs) to host and run different environments. Like other monitoring tools, the Azure Portal offers analytics of the WebApps to show the performance of each on being used in the different environments. Another important pipeline application that we use is Jenkins.

Jenkins is a useful pipeline application that can be configured to run all different types of pipelines. At BlueVolt, Jenkins has been used to turn our test automation into automated testing. Where we integrate our tests with Jenkin pipelines, set specific triggers for the pipelines to automatically run, and then output the results via email after the tests are complete. This has been beneficial as the team went from running manual regression tests once every two weeks to a nightly automated test suite with emailed results. This has helped us catch and address issue well before the night we release to production.

3.1.2. Improving Delivery and Quality

Setting up Jenkins, and other pipelines, continue to help us track, find, and resolve issue well in advance, but there are other ways to help improve the quality and deliverability of the product. The product's quality and deliverability can be improved through task automation and settings up software to gather performance metrics. Some performance metrics that we gather to quantify the integrity of our product is response time, uptime, and the overall health. This is accomplished at BlueVolt through the user of Azure DevOps and SonarQube. BlueVolt uses Azure DevOps to transform our manual task into pipelines that run from triggers to improve the speed, quality, and quantity of the deliverability. Whereas SonarQube is used to help track our code coverage to find areas where we can improve our testability to improve the quality of the product.

Azure DevOps has provided us with the tools to transform our manual task into automated pipeline that will run when triggers are hit. These pipelines help us deploy to our managed test environments, release our product to production, check database migrations, and speed up the development process. To run these pipeline, Azure DevOps agents must be either installed on a self-hosted VM or there are a few that are Microsoft Hosted that can be used. The few purposes of these pipeline agents (self-hosted or Microsoft hosted) are that they can pull down a repository, build the solutions(s), run tests, run custom script, create build artifact, chain pipelines together, and then deploy the code to a VM instance or the Azure Portal. These pipelines have been effective for increasing product production and has sped up deployments to our test environment and production. Where each sprint the CI/CD automation process is continuous refined to improve the deliverability of the product.

Another way we use Azure DevOps is by setting up quality to check that no breaking changes are introduced into our managed code source. Some simple quality gate pipelines have been setup to triggers so that before a pull request is completed the changes to the different C# .NET solutions are checked to ensure they can build, that our legacy code still functions, and that a new database migration will not break the build. The purpose of these pipelines is to ensure that the quality of our product is not negatively affected, prevent bugs from being introduced into the system, keep our source control functional, and increase the deliverability of our product.

SonarQube is another product we use to help track and monitor our unit tests and code coverage. At BlueVolt, SonarQube is primarily used to analyze our code quality, find deprecated code lines, find vulnerabilities, and analyze if there is any tech debt. We combine Jenkins and SonarQube to bring automation to the process. Jenkins will start and stop a SonarQube docker container (to manager VM resources) and run the unit test through the SonarQube Scanner to gather daily reports to track the trends and health of our product.

3.1.3. Setting Up Environments

Azure Portal is used to setup our managed test environment and production. As our company grows (in clients and employees) we have been moving away from inhouse managed services and moving to the cloud. Using Azure Portal our applications have been transformed into WebApps and our static SQL Server was changed into an Azure DB with an elastic pool for dynamic scalability. As BlueVolt continues to improve our production resources, we continue to try to mimic the same types of resources to our test environments. Our test environments have moved off IIS and now use WebApps, each environment has a scaled down Azure Database, and our deployments to the managed test environment mimic production releases. Bugs and other issues can be prevented by having test environments setup similarly to production.

Setting up managed test environments are critical to test new features. A test environmental allows testers, developers, and QAs to test functionality, bug fixes, incomplete features and other agile updates without having negative effects on the production environment and database. [8] Having a test environment allows all testers to find bugs, issues, glitches that may have been introduced throughout the sprint. But there is some limitation of a test environment which prevents it from being an exact replica of production. A test environment will not have the stress of an active userbase on the system, third-party integrated systems, equivalent resources (it can be too expensive to have a test environment with exact same resources as production), or any other outside influences. Regardless, having "... a confined environment where outside influences on the code are limited, gives those involved in the production of a system confidence that their code works as expected." [9]

3.1.4. Monitoring Tools

After a product has been released to production there needs to be monitoring setup so that performance and health can be continuously tracked. The purpose of monitoring the production environment is that a healthy product:

- Protects the image of the business
- Keeps customers happy
- Prevents losing sales (if applicable)
- Obtain better search engine results ranking
- Detect hackers, ddos, and attacks
- Track performance metrics
- Provide a quick response if the site goes down [10]

BlueVolt believes that customers of the product should always have an excellent experience while developers continuously find solution to improve the product'. To accomplish this, we use a combination of Pingdom and New Relic to help track real-time performance and health metrics. These metrics help us find way to improve the performance of our product by breaking down the slow parts and making it apparent where exactly the pain point exists. Metrics are a good way to provide information about the product to the different group involved with the product to help develop the DevOps culture.

3.1.4.1. Pingdom

Pingdom is a monitoring tool that helps analyze and gather information about the uptime, transactions, page speed, and visitor insights of our product. Custom alerts can be created for uptime, transactions, and page speed tracking the response time and outages that have occurred. These alerts can be customized to monitor specific URLs or create custom scripts to monitor certain features of UI integration, specific endpoints, or third-party integrations. Then if an alert is trigged, Pingdom can be setup to send information to the team so that the performance issues can be immediately addressed.

3.1.4.2. New Relic

New Relic is a monitoring tool that uses New Relic agents to track the different performance metrics within a system. To track certain information New Relic agents can be installed on VMs, WebApp, databases, mobile devices and is compatible with C, Go, Java, .NET, Node.js, PHP, Python, and Ruby projects. At BlueVolt, we use New Relic as our primary way to track the performance throughout our VMs, WebApps, and Azure Database. It offers a wide range of customizable analytics that helps pinpoint and track down where and what transactions are cause slowdowns on the production environment. We also use this tool to create custom analytic dashboard to track the overall health and integrity of different aspects of the product. The goal of using New Relic is to find the slowdown within the .NET project and determine where performance updates could be introduced. New Relic also allow custom alerts to be created and can send alerts when a violation occurs. At BlueVolt we have created transaction speed New Relic alerts to determine if a transaction is taking longer than it should, and if a transaction is performing too slow an alert is sent to the development team to address that performance issue.

3.2. Applying DevOps

DevOps is not just tools or practices, it is applying the tool, practices, and culture changes of DevOps to every aspect of the product life cycle. It is about the different group involved with the product to become aware with the entire development cycle to improve the products quality and overall better server the customer. DevOps should be implemented from the product team figuring out what content needs to be created or adjusted to serve the customer, to the agile and scrum process of meetings, at standup, throughout planning, to the integration of different tools and application to gauge the metric of the product and help speed up the CI/CD process. "DevOps doesn't confine itself to technical implementation and execution of testing and development activities. It is a cultural shift that is needed to ensure that the strategy Is collaborative and closely monitored. Developers and operations need to work together to reduce inefficiencies and bring speed to the development activity." [15]

DevOps can be extremely overwhelming for anyone involved with the cultural shift. DevOps is about bringing together the different groups that have been separated from the software development process. [17] It is challenging to influence and provide solutions for each of the different groups, as the focus is not going to be the same between them. But different DevOps tools and practices can help build out the culture by finding solution to overlap datapoints to involve the different groups.

An idea of DevOps is to provide a feedback loop where each group involved (QA, testers, developers, product) can get key information about the product quickly and effectively. Pipelines are an excellent way to speed up the processes while proving key information about the product's lifecycle. One example is by creating and managing gated check-in, important information about the quality of the code, automated tests, and other metrics can be retrieved quickly. Pipelines can be triggered from one another to create a deployment and a release pipelines to managed test environments or to production. By creating and managing pipelines to the test environment, this allows testers to start testing new features, updates or bug fixes as soon as the developer completes the pull request. Aside from pipelines, other software tools (Azure, Pingdom New Relic) can be used to track and gather performance metrics that can be used throughout a company to quantify the healthy and integrity of the product. DevOps provides the ability to quantify the work done through the agile process and communicate throughout the organization. But DevOps cannot be just implemented, it needs to be continuously refined and build upon it's becoming more and more effective. But it all starts with taking that first step to help bring different groups together to build an effective development workplace.

4. Using DevOps to Create Automated Testing

Test automation and DevOps can be extremely powerful when combined. As DevOps can transform test automation (that runs are a push of a button) to automated testing that runs automatically. The purpose is to create a process that will help improve the agile process of the deliverability, increase scalability, and increases the quality of what is being delivered to the customers. The power of automating tests is only as good as the effort put forwards and always needs to be continuously improved upon with each iteration of new test, DevOps tools, practice, features, or anything that would work with test automation.

The purpose of testing it to increases the quality through code coverage. Some example where testing may help the produce is through exposing existing issues and help catch issues that may have been introduced with new code changes. With the application of DevOps tools and practices, the quickness, reliability, and effectiveness of test automation can be improved. The goal is to implement test automation and DevOps at different stages of the CD pipelines so that "...one or more test suites run. Each test should provide feedback. This feedback helps people understand CD pipeline status and the quality of code moving through it." [13] As a warning, this should not be confused with making every test automated as automation will not catch every issue, adhoc testing needs to be manually involved. Adhoc testing is an unstructured process that's conducted by a tester with strong knowledge of the software testing areas of the software through error guessing.[19] By having a feedback loop throughout the CD process developers can get quickly notified with faults and are able to fix the issues while the current code is still fresh within the sprint. Testers and automated testing work together to increase test coverage helping improve the overall product by finding issues before a release to help the company serve a higher quality product to the customer.

The goal of a product is the figure out how to best serve the customer. A company cannot see increase on return on investment if the customers' needs are not met, and consumers are always looking for the what works the best. If a company decides not to focus on their products deliverability, they run the risk of being passed by another competitor or will be unable to catchup to a competitor that's ahead of them. When improvements are made to the CI/CD process with automation the deliverable product becomes an improved version of itself that better serves the customers. But the deliverability of a product is not just determined by improvements to the CI/CD process, but by influencing the agile, testing, scrum processes with the DevOps culture. It is necessary to integrate DevOps ideas into the agile process to help refine the existing practices that adapts to change to better satisfy the customer through early and continuous delivery of valuable software. [14]

Automated testing should help increase the deliverability of the product by speeding up tests while maintaining or improving the test quality. Then, further improvement to product deliverability can be accomplished by adding test automation to DevOps. Doing so will help find issues effectively and quickly which can become cost effective, increase product quality, and help save the company time it would take to run test manually. [16] Creating automated testing will allow developers, product, testers, and QA to direct their focus to other agile aspects to increase the deliverability to production.

At BlueVolt we try to integrate test automation into all aspects of our DevOps tools. An example is the regression suit, where automation transformed manual test that happened once every 2 weeks into something that could be ran through a shell command. Through DevOps test automation was automated further. The DevOps tool Jenkins allowed us to remove the need of having someone starting and reporting on the test suite and turned test automation into automated testing. The ideas of adding test automation to DevOps expanded past the regression tests and endpoint tests were setup to run nightly on Jenkins to verify functionality and ensure that nothing broken throughout the day. This practice was also applied with the Azure DevOps but with different types of tests.

Azure DevOps has provided me with the resources to create validation pipelines that we use as our gated check-ins, pipelines the ensure certain tests pass before the pull request is able to be completed into a branch. This combined with branching policies has helped me and the developers ensure that no breaking changing would be entered and ensure that our branching processes are being upheld. What this means is that ensure that branches go through the correct methodologies, practices, and quality gates before making into the Release branch and ensure that our agile process is upheld. Where the gated check-ins are continuously being revised to ensure excellent code throughout the development process.

Even the monitoring tools has test within their framework that allows the developers and I track issues and send alert when certain threshold are being violated. Pingdom allows alerts to be setup for Uptime, Transactions, Page Speed, and allows custom reports to be made. Where BlueVolt determines what is an acceptable performance, and if something breaks that performance then alerts are sent out and leads into tickets to be resolved during the current or a future sprint. Just like Pingdom New Relic function similarly with the type of alerts that can be setup. For BlueVolt New Relic is used more for digging deeper into the transactions which helps single out slow performant operations and setting up alerts accordingly. Even with what BlueVolt has setup, we are continuing to expand upon each agile process either adding, creating, or refining upon what we currently have.

5. Challenges Faced by Beginning Automation Engineers

Whether working in test automation or DevOps, Automation Engineers will face a learning curve as they continue to problem solve each automation hurdle. This could be through learning about a new tool, a new process being introduced, another automation practice, or a cultural shift. To help overcome these hurdles I'm going to answer questions that I ask myself to break down most automation challenges and hurdles I have faced. These questions may not be applicable to everyone but the intent it to help show how I helped myself in learning, implementing, iterating, and maintaining the tool, processes, and tests that have been introduce throughout BlueVolt.

1. **Where to begin?**

   Get involved with the product and start learning how the product functions, who the target audience, what is the issues the product is trying to solve, what is the stack it's developed in, and where are the pain points for groups within the company. Take in information about the product and its lifecycle. It is important to take the time and focus to understand what the company is trying to deliver, what issue this automation will solve, when the automation will be used, and how does it affect the deliverable of the product. Try to fit the mentioned tool above to see how they can help introduce new ways to test, deliver code, bring out analytics, or build out the DevOps culture. Find what needs to be tested and bring automation to it, what automation can be used to increase delivery of the product, or maybe find ways to speed up workflow effectively. Sometime old implementation needs to be taken out and completely reworked because it did not fit within the agile scope of the project. Or old code, tests, tools, or process need to get revisited and upgraded to better fit future planning. Even time needs to be spent writing up documentation about different way to test, explain what certain features do, build out a roadmap, or anything else that explain in detail about the product that can be used by the different groups involved.

2. **After figuring out what needs to happen, how do I even begin working on an automated test or automated pipelines or combining the two?**

This is another hard question that a lot of beginning and aspiring Automation Engineers face and continue to face with each new project. Breaking down the task into smaller tasks can help provide steppingstones towards speeding up the creation or integration of a test or pipeline. Figuring out what the purpose of the task, where this task needs to live, what resources are needed to host the task (if it needs a VM, use a WebApp from Azure Portal, be setup in ISS, or just exist on your local desktop), and what tools may be needed to accomplish this will help guide towards a good starting point. Sometimes the first step is the hardest, but it's important to realize that nothing must be static, and it's healthy to make beginning mistakes to strengthen yourself for future tasks. Also, when applicable, go back and build upon previous tasks to improve upon them to make them better, scalable, more robust.

3. **"After finishing one task, what do I do next?"**

Figuring out what to do next can always be a tricky question. It is easy to move on and forget what was just implemented, thinking that the task is completed and never needs to be revisited but that cannot be correct. After a task is complete whether it is a new tool, process, improvement, or test it continuous needs to be iterated upon to maintain its upkeep and ensure that it is performing accurately. Looks for ways to expand upon what was just built and figure out how to use it If an automated test was created, test it in all kind of environments and start getting information out of the created test. If an automate pipeline was created, start using the pipeline and see what it's doing well and where it can be improved. Never complete one task and think it does not need to be revisited, each task should always be iterated upon into a better version of itself. Another thing to keep in mind, is that the next task could be the next step of the development cycle and how-to best build upon what's there and what needs to be created.

6. Conclusion

To reiterate, test automation is the process of taking manual ran tests and automating them though tools or applications and that they can be ran from either a button click or through a shell. Where the created test automation should run faster, accurate, maintains or improves the quality of the tests. Additionally, test automation can achieve testing that that manual testing cannot such as different types of performance testing, network testing, or testing in parallel. Whereas DevOps is a multitude of different tools, practices, and cultural shift made throughout the company. This could include building out a more robust CI/CD process, improving the agile process, and bringing the DevOps culture to all groups involved with the product. As companies move more towards automation, the test automation and DevOps practices continue to play important roles throughout product lifecycles with the goal to better serve the customer.

Test automation helps take away manual repetitive tests and turn them into s test suite that can be ran from a push of a button or easily from a Shell. Where the goal of test automation is to increase the quality of the product through increase test coverage to help create a higher quality product for the customer. Before creating and implementing test automation, it is important to look for where manual testing exists, where there's a lack of testing, carefully create a test plan, and find tools that will work well with the product's development stack. Putting the time into planning out how and what tests to automate should be just as important as the creation and implementation of those tests. Also, after automating a test it is important to continuously build upon and refine those tests.

DevOps is the implementation of tools, practices, beliefs, and ideas that evolve the culture to bring awareness for each group, involved with the product, about the product's development and lifecycle. DevOps's culture is about find the best way to covey the different parts of the product development so that it gets all the different group to be involved with most (if not each) aspects of that product. They can be accomplished through different ways such as:

- Creating automated pipelines in Azure DevOps and Jenkins to perform automated testing.
- Creating deployment and release pipelines to setup managed test environment or push new code to production
- Set up gated check-ins to ensure code quality using SonarQube
- Analyze product performance through Pingdom and New Relic

Building out a robust DevOps culture is crucial; it allows all parts of the agile sprint to be applicable to each group involved. Where developers, QA, tester, product, managers, and anyone else can be exposed to the product's roadmap. Where the roadmap can be broken down into tasks then spread across different sprints to provide continuous implementation and development to the production product.

Beginning and aspiring automation engineers face all kinds of tasks and challenges, and it can be complicated finding the answer to solve the task or overcome the challenge. I continue to face those challenges myself, which is why I broke down my problem-solving process into a few questions. The first question was figuring out how to begin. Before the creation and implementation of automation it is important to understand how the automation will better serve the customer. Get involved with the product and understand what's problem it's trying to solve, how it functions, and where pain points exist for each group involved with the products development. Find tools that will help introduce new ways to improve quality, deliverability, show more metrics, or ways to improve the DevOps culture. The second question was how to break down a task. It is easy to get lost in planning and the semantics of the problem, but it's important to understand that the solution is going to be an iterative process. Interact with the different groups involved with the product and find extra information to help figure out the problem that is trying to be solved with automation. From there break the task into its simplest form and find what needs to happen first and then build upon that until the automation is complete. The last question I discussed was determining how to build upon an existing tool, practice, or application. Find where the existing tool, practice or application is lacking by talking to the people who use it the most. This can help expose the weaknesses that will then show how it can be improved.

References

1. McMeekin, Kyle. "Test Automation vs. Automated Testing: The Difference Matters." QASymphony. https://www.qasymphony.com/blog/test-automation-automated-testing/ (accessed June 15th, 2019)
2. McKenzie, Cameron "5 Java test frameworks and tools JDK developers must know" The Server Side. https://www.theserverside.com/video/5-Java-test-frameworks-and-tools-JDK-developers-must-know (accessed June 16th, 2019)
3. JMeter. "Regression Testing With JMeter – Learn How" https://www.blazemeter.com/blog/regression-testing-with-jmeter-learn-how/ (accessed June 17th, 2019)
4. Software Testing Fundamentals. "Test Script" http://softwaretestingfundamentals.com/test-script/ (accessed June 17th, 2019)
5. Mexazros, Gerard. "xUnit Test Patterns: Goals of Test Automation" Pearson. http://www.informit.com/articles/article.aspx?p=759702&seqNum=3 (accessed June 17th, 2019)
6. Mueller, Ernest. "What Is DevOps?" The agile admin. https://theagileadmin.com/what-is-devops/ (accessed June 17th, 2019)
7. Mueller, Ernest. "A DevOps Manifesto" The agile admin. https://theagileadmin.com/2010/10/15/a-devops-manifesto/ (accessed June 17th, 2019)

8. Tetanich, Amanda. "Test Environment Benefits and Best Practices" omatic https://omaticsoftware.com/blog/benefits-of-a-test-environment (accessed June 19th. 2019)

9. Brown, Jordan. "The Importance of a Test Environment" Edge Testing. http://www.edgetesting.co.uk/news-events/blog/the-importance-of-a-test-environment (accessed June 19th, 2019)

10. 99tests "The Importance of Web Application Health Monitoring" 99tests . https://99tests.com/blog/the-importance-of-web-application-health-monitoring/ (accessed June 18th, 2019)

11. WineHQ https://www.winehq.org/ (accessed June 18th, 2019)

12. Pataki, Daniel. "How to use Pingdom to Measure (and Monitor) the Speed and Performance of a Website – Effectively!" WinningWP https://winningwp.com/pingdom/ (accessed June 19th, 2019)

13. Bailey, Joe. "Good Automated Tests are Critical to Agility" OSG IT Solutions. https://blog.osgcorp.com/automated-testing/good-automated-tests-critical-agility/ (accessed June 19th, 2019)

14. Buchanan, Ian. "Agile and DevOps: Friends or Foes?" Atlassian https://www.atlassian.com/agile/devops (accessed June 19th, 2019)

15. "4 ways to Automate Testing in a DevOps set-up" Cigniti Trvhnologies. https://www.cigniti.com/blog/4-ways-to-automate-testing-in-devops-set-up/ (accessed June 19th, 2019)

16. Moragn, Herman. "Scalability in the Age of DevOps: A Must for Success" DevOps.com https://devops.com/scalability-in-the-age-of-devops-a-must-for-success/ (accessed June 19th, 2019)

17. Wilsenach, Rouan. "DevOps Culture" MartinFowler.com https://martinfowler.com/bliki/DevOpsCulture.html (accessed June 19th, 2019)

18. https://github.com/nant/nant

19. "Adhoc Testing: A Brief Note With Examples" testbytes https://www.testbytes.net/blog/adhoc-testing/ (accessed August 13th, 2019)

Building Automation Engineers from Scratch

Jenny Bramble

Jenny.bramble@gmail.com

Abstract

Creating automation engineers from manual testers is hard. Even if testers are willing, they have a lot of hurdles to get over to feel like the same kind of subject matter experts in automation as they are in manual testing.

As a career-long manual tester making the leap to automation, Jenny Bramble has experience to explain frustrations and provide solutions. She will discuss managing the expectations of testers and their managers (what's the time frame? Why isn't this working?), techniques for teaching (such as games! Pair/mob programming! Software fundamentals!), and how to know when testers have made it (what should manual testers be aiming for when they start?).

Biography

Jenny Bramble came up through support and DevOps, cutting her teeth on that interesting role that acts as the 'translator' between customer requests from support and the development team. Her love of support and the human side of problems lets her find a sweet spot between empathy for the user and empathy for the team. She's done testing, support, or human interfacing for most of her career and is excited about the future of automation.

1. Introduction

One of my favorite bosses asked me if I wanted to consider becoming an automation engineer. This would mean moving away from my decade-long manual testing career into the realm of coding—reflecting the degree that I'd been working at off and on during that time.

I told him no.

Honestly, I was perfectly happy as a manual tester! I got to work with the applications, find the mindsets of users, and prevent major issues from reaching production. I felt valuable, engaged, and excited about my job. There was no need, I felt, to take the leap into automation so I stayed deep in the trenches of manual testing. Sure, that meant that I spent eight hours one day running login tests to make sure that every permutation on every device was covered when we made a change. And maybe there was the weekly smoke test that took 12 hours of my life. But this was what I wanted to do—I wanted to be the user and advocate for them!

Looking back, I recognize that I was blocking myself off from an entire suite of tools that I need to be the most successful tester possible. There's a lot to be gained by adding automation to our abilities--being able to take some of the more trivial things we do and clear them from our plates so that we can focus on the interesting, complex, and sometimes purely confounding edge cases or UX testing that humans are best at doing.

I'm going to address these things over the next few pages. We will follow my journey as a manual tester making this transition into an automated tester and some of the expectations I've had to adjust as well as the challenges I've had to meet.

Adding automation skills to the toolbox of a manual tester is not a trivial undertaking. There are barriers that include perception of ability, velocity, and success that can be enhanced by the concern that their previous skills are no longer needed. You can reset these expectations and meet these challenges by creating a framework for success that speaks to learning styles and support. In the end, the life of a software tester is changing rapidly and she needs to be able to continuously learn and add new tools and abilities as often as she can.

2. Assumptions

I am going to make a few assumptions about the resources and humans you have available. There are a lot of artic les and presentations that talk about some of the things I'm making assumptions about. As such, this paper is going to gloss over them and concentrate on some of the things we don't talk about as much.

2.1. Resources

To begin with, you need people: either you yourself, or a group of manual testers who are interested in moving towards automation. A passing interest, a fancy is all that it takes to start down the path of becoming an automation engineer! But the spark needs to be there.

Second, you need to have time and resources. I'll discuss more in detail what this means later, but for now, you need to be able to dedicate time to this adventure. There are several talks and papers that focus on the mechanics of finding time, so this topic is considered out of scope of this one.

Next, a support system is vital for anyone adding a new skill to their resume. This can look like a supportive boss, a dedicated mentor, a group who is also working towards the same goals, or a team that is ready to support you. Finding a mentor or a support system is somewhat outside of this paper, though I will discuss how you can support someone moving into automation.

Finally--and most importantly--you are willing to make and execute a plan. This whole endeavor hinges on your willingness to step outside of your comfort zone into a challenging new phase of your career or to help others move into a new phase of their career. It's not a trivial undertaking because it requires confronting some long-held expectations for yourself and for the people around you as well as learning how to apply a set of skills that have been honed over a long career to a new way of thinking and operating.

When I started out, I found my favorite developer and asked him to teach me Ruby. He became a huge source of support for me and nurtured my budding interest in test automation and coding in general.

2.2. Humans

There are also humans involved in every step of the plan and I will be making several assumptions about them.

Every tester is an SME in their field. No matter what you call them, anyone who has made their career in testing software is an expert in testing software. We have spent years honing and fine tuning our ability to detect places in applications that may not meet the expectations of everyone around us and that's very valuable.

Related to that, manual testing is still very important. There will always be elements of a system that cannot or should not be tested in an automation fashion. There will always be points in the process that need the eyes of a human.

The next points are also related. First: not everyone wants to be an automation engineer. Second: change is scary.

Spending your day writing code is not something that everyone wants to do. However, I feel very strongly that every tester should have automation in her arsenal--it doesn't make sense to limit ourselves when we could have these skills in addition to all our others. At the same time, change can be terrifying. You're asking yourself or a group of people to step away from something they're secure in and have known for years to something new. That needs to be recognized.

3. Adjusting Your Expectations

Everyone has expectations. They permeate every part of our careers and lives. When you're building up automation engineers from scratch, it's vital to get out in front of the expectations that people have of themselves and that others have of them.

Let's discuss some common expectations and how we can adjust our thinking.

3.1. Expectation: Perception of Ability

I'm an expert manual tester. I've been testing applications for a long time on desktops, mobile, embedded systems, and more. During this time, I've learned to stretch and grow into different types of users—super users, musicians, digital advertisers, clinical research associates, blind users, patients in hospitals, music reviewers, and more. I pride myself on my adaptability and the way that I can navigate an application with the user's mindset.

When I started out dipping my toes into automation, I hadn't coded seriously for five years. I'dd fallen behind—no one had Visual Basic or Assembly or C tests. It was all languages that hadn't been taught when I was in school or that I'd picked up in my tenure as a Linux support tech. It felt like everything I'd learned was now useless and I was looking at starting over.

If you have been an expert in manual or human testing for a while, it can be very jarring to suddenly be put in a place you no longer feel like an expert. There's a picture you have in your mind of yourself--or that you hope other people have of you--that can be hard to reconcile with being faced with an entirely new field of knowledge that you do not possess.

This perception can be a difficult force to combat because it is very subtle. Not often will people come out and directly say 'I'm stressed because I no longer feel like I am in my element.' Instead, look for signs such as timidity in moving forward or always taking on the parts of the jobs they have succeeded in before while leaving little room for the new parts that may involve coding.

3.1.1. Adjustment: Respect the Manual

To adjust for the perception of ability, start by acknowledging and respecting that manual testers have valuable skills. Be careful not to disparage the skills people have built up over years and years of work. Automation complements and does not replace the manual tester.

One of the best ways to respect a manual tester's skills is by starting conversations with 'what are we going to test' instead of moving straight into 'how are we going to test this?' That gives everyone a chance to be heard and to have their skills reinforced. It will also teach other people on the team more about testing and what they should be looking for when they are passing a feature along.

I've found it incredibly valuable to sit with my developers and walk through PRs together—especially ones that involve unit tests. Not only does this give me a chance to look more deeply into the application code, but I can often find places that aren't covered in a way that I would cover when I apply my manual tester's skills.

3.1.2. Adjusting: Reset Your Mindset

Speaking of mindsets, you need to reset your thinking and reset your tester's mindsets. We have a natural tendency to assume we will be just as good at one thing as we are at something tangentially related.

Don't expect someone to be just as good at writing code as they have been at manual testing.

Do expect them to apply their stellar manual skills to the business of writing code. They won't churn out feature tests as quickly but no one knows the system from a user's perspective like someone in the trenches who's seen all the bug reports and handled all the defects. Even if you don't know the code, you know the paths users take in the app.

3.2. Expectation: Perception of Velocity

Let's talk more in depth about velocity.

Velocity is one of the metrics that is widely used—everyone wants to know how fast something will appear in the Done column. We talk about points, sizing, and commitments weekly if not more often. We press each other in stand up to make sure that things are moving.

When you're first learning something entirely new, it's hard to estimate how long it will take you. In fact, you don't know enough to even guess at what your velocity might look like. Using other people's velocity can undermine you as they have a much deeper toolbox to use than your new automation engineers.

3.2.1. Adjustment: Velocity is Not Objective

We can see here that an objective view of velocity is not beneficial to your automation engineers. Holding people to expectations they cannot meet is a toxic situation.

Work with your team members to determine what they think they can complete in a sprint and give them the ability to make adjustments as they learn and become better at estimating.

Above all, don't fall into the trap of comparison. It's often easy to think that a group will have the same velocity, but as people ramp up, their velocity will need to change.

3.3. Expectation: Perception of Success

Success is a funny thing—there's a lot of expectations around what success looks like. Everyone in the process has an idea of what the end goal is and often these ideas are not aligned.

One of my favorite conversations always starts with 'are you done?'

Done with what? What does it manes to be done with a whatever thing I'm being asked about? Often times, the person asking isn't even sure what I'm doing, much lesswhat done would look like when I reach it. This puts me in a mush deeper conversation than anyone had expected starting out.

3.3.1. Adjustment: Define Your Success Metrics

Success or 'done' looks like something different every sprint and every week. If we don't sit down and define some success metrics for our adventures, we're going to have a hard time reaching success.

These metrics can be anything that makes sense for your team. Each team is different and in a different place, but there's a few constants.

As you're pulling together metrics to use, remember that they should be reevaluated often. There is also a chance for people to game the metrics or to use them as weapons against other people. You can help prevent this by checking in often with the team and making sure that your metrics still fit your needs.

Here's some metrics I've seen used.

- Everyone on the team interacted with a pull request
  - Putting one in
  - Commenting on a PR
  - Being part of an in person review
  - Merging something
- Golden Path or happy path is automated
- A person in particular has learned how to do something of note
  - Scrolling and tapping on iPhone
  - Using intents in Espresso
  - Creating a new page
- There are 15+ tests
- We got tests running in CI
- No one cried this week

The important thing is to define success. This will sometimes be driven by business, but really should be done by the test engineers and team at large. Start out the project with everyone's individual goals as well as team wide goals. This will let people feel like they are succeeding on both levels.

4. Set Up a Framework for Success: How Can You Actually Make This Work?

4.1. What Do You Know Now?

I've said before that I'm an expert manual tester. This will never change. As long as I'm testing, I'll be improving that expertise and sharpening my skills.

While it can feel that way, automation is not an entirely new skillset. It is an augmentation to the skillset I already have. It's a tool in my toolbox that lets me apply the skills I've already gained and honed in a different way.

This is a skill set built on top of my existing skills. I know I say 'scratch' in the title, but no one really starts from absolute zero. You don't wholesale drop your other skills to pick up automation. Everything you've done in your career and in your life is a stepping stone to make your automation better.

On top of knowing how to test, you also know how to use tools and language. Think about the last time you picked up a new test case management system—how long did it take you to start really utlizing it? I've switched between three or four test case management systems in the past year. It's difficult, but we're used to ramping up quickly and becoming useful.

We also know how to use language. I often say that test engineers are the morale center of teams in large part because we do a significant amount of the communication on teams. We discuss defects with developers, product, and sometimes end users. We spend most of our days doing some sort of communication within our teams. This is an incredible skill when it comes to automation—coding is, after all, communicating what tasks you'd like a computer to perform for you. Once you get the hang of where to start, using your natural communication skills will help you far more than you can imagine.

Another of the top things a test engineer has is her logic skills. We puzzle through defects and convoluted systems. We spend our days asking questions and digesting the answers. This ability to work through an issue is often hard won by many years of work and is invaluable when you sit down to learn to code. Not only do you have to tell the computer how to step through a task, but you often have to find creative and interesting work arounds. Using your deduction and logic skills will let you have a much easier time with these tasks.

The final thing we'll discuss is your ability to learn.

No successful test engineer shies away from learning. Every new feature, use case, situation, or application that we run up against is an opportunity for us to learn. We have to learn in order to proceed through the situation — if we completely stopped learning, we'd be unable to test once we had a new feature. We have to learn what ig does, how it can be used, and who would be using it in order to do our jobs.

Adding automation to our skillset is not much different — it feels different, but in the end, we're learning a new way to communicate and to do our jobs better.

4.2. What Do You Need to Know?

When you're setting out to become an automation engineer, the first thing you think about doing is learning to automate. Don't fall into this trap.

Instead, learn to *code*.

When we talk about writing code as a test engineer, we often start by talking about automation frameworks and how to get our tests working. Instead, we should start by talking about how we can create quality code on the same levels as our developers. This isn't to say that we should expect ourselves to code at the same level as our coworkers who have been exclusively coding for their entire careers; more to say that we should aspire to have clean, efficient code that follows the standards of your platform and company.

In that same vein, the software development lifecycle at your company is another vital component. As test engineers, we often feel like we've got a really good grasp on the SDLC—but when you look at it from a developer-centric perspective, it can look really different. Talk to your developers about how they move from tickets to code reviews and do your best to follow those procedures.

One group that I work with creates UI automation subtasks for each story. These subtasks are groomed, pointed, and slotted into sprints just like any other work. We move them through in progress to code review to testing. When they hit testing, they're usually been running on our build server for a few builds, so we're not looking at the code as it's written so much as we're double checking the manual testing that isn't covered by our automation. If we determine that there is more automation to do, we'll send the ticket back to the start of the workflow. This means that if a developer picks up a UI automation ticket, they're using a process that they are familiar with. It makes it much easier to share tasks.

And remember—automation code is production code. It tests production and is a vital part of the pipline for getting features to users. You have a responsibility to yourself and your users to write clean, maintainable code that is treated just as seriously as application code. If you wouldn't do it in prod, don't do it in your test suite.

5. What If You Don't Want to Step Away From What You've Always Done?

That's okay! Sometimes, the job we want is exactly the job we have.

However, the world of software is changing rapidly around us. Software testing is wildly different than it was years ago and will be wildly different in several years' time. If we expect to still be working in this field and making meaningful contributions to our teams, then we need to take advantage of every opportunity and advancement. This is why we go to conferences, read blog posts, and network. Humans want to advance, and we want to be better than we were. This is not a profession in which you can let yourself grow stagnant and still succeed. This is a profession of growth.

Automation is one way we grow. It is an incredibly valuable tool to add to your toolbox of skills and we are shorting ourselves and our commitment to quality if we refuse to investigate this tool. When we prepare ourselves for the challenges that we're going to see in the next 5-10 years, then we also prepare our software for those challenges.

Software development is not going to slow down and it's certainly never going to stop changing around us.

Building automation engineers is one of the ways we rise to meet those challenges.

Quality Guild: Creating a Culture

Philip Daye, Jr.

philip_daye@ultimatesoftware.com

Abstract

Organizations adopt Agile methods to reap the benefits of shortened feedback loops and a quicker release cadence. Agile teams are made up of cross-functional people formed around a product or feature. This often leads to teams that focus almost exclusively on their individual product areas, which easily become siloed. This is a hidden cost to adopting Agile practices.

Isolated teams will seek solutions for similar challenges, unaware of what others have already done. Fragmented solutions make collaboration difficult and put the health of the product at risk. This becomes increasingly troublesome as the organization grows and tries to scale development. In a culture of silos, how does an organization provide guidance and standards to its teams?

Many organizations attempt to solve this problem by creating a centralized team focused on quality processes, but it too often becomes siloed as well. This new, centralized team often has difficulty penetrating the isolation of Agile teams, and thus, their proposed solutions do not reflect the needs of those they serve. As quality is decentralized, and quality and test engineers are federated out to teams, community leadership becomes an increasingly important mechanism for preserving enterprise level coordination and cooperation.

This paper describes the process one organization, Ultimate Software, undertook, to build a company-wide quality guild, which promotes the shared interests, challenges, and goals of the quality professionals within the individual Agile teams. The guild collaborates to build and evaluate new tools, propose improvements to testing practices, and share findings with the rest of the organization. By breaking down the barriers, the quality guild promotes a sustainable and consistent culture around quality, with less duplication of effort, expanded opportunities for individual engineers, and improved operations.

Biography

Philip Daye is a Software Test Lead for Ultimate Software, a developer of HCM software and a perennial on Fortune's Best Companies to Work For list. Philip has more than two decades of experience in software development, testing, and delivery for companies of all sizes. From his earliest days as a software tester to today, Philip has pursued a passion for quality, which has led him to hone his craft by studying and researching the latest advances in the field, applying it to his current work, and then sharing it with others.

In his current role, Philip helps document quality practices, consults with teams on how to apply those practices, and develops and delivers training on testing and test techniques. As an active participant in the broader testing community, he has taken on co-organizing the South Florida Test Automation meetups.

1. Introduction

The Merriam-Webster Dictionary defines culture as "the set of shared attitudes, values, goals, and practices that characterizes an institution or organization" (Merriam-Webster Dictionary, n.d.). This culture is "the integrated pattern of human knowledge, belief, and behavior that depends upon the capacity for learning and transmitting knowledge to succeeding generations" (Merriam-Webster Dictionary, n.d.). For a company, its "internal culture may be articulated in its mission statement or vision statement" (WhatIs.com, n.d.).

72% of CEOs that participated in an Inc. survey said that "Maintaining company culture" was "the hardest part about managing a growing workforce" (Inc., n.d.). As a company grows, subcultures will emerge around shared work areas, common job types, or mutual project boundaries (such as a feature-based development team) (Leading Agile, 2015). This paper presents an approach for maintaining cross-team, functional collaboration within a projectized organization. The supporting case study specifically examines how a common quality subculture was intentionally maintained in an otherwise decentralized Agile environment with fully distributed quality assurance personnel and responsibilities. How can the shared values of a subculture around roles be aligned with those of the teams and the overarching goals of the company?

2. Ultimate Software

Ultimate Software is a Human Capital Management (HCM) solution provider. The company's "People First" principle permeates all aspects of the business, including our approach to our employees and customers: "At Ultimate Software, we take care of our employees, and we know it will show in the way they take care of you" (Ultimate Software, n.d.). Our corporate mission statement continues the theme of improving "the personal work experience for you and your people - the power behind the business" (Ultimate Software, n.d.). To be People First, we recognize that our organizational structure must be responsive to our customers and to our employees. As such, there must be a balance between the needs for product development and people development. Career development is often built upon improving skills within a functional domain such as software development or quality engineering. Being People First requires that the organization provides clear paths for employees to improve and expand their functional skills and responsibilities.

The development organization has adopted Agile, with Kanban as the work-in-progress management tool. Accordingly, teams include personnel to specify, architect, produce, and validate product features. These teams "produce a working, tested increment of product" (Leading Agile, 2015). As HCM encompasses a complex domain, several functional teams are often grouped together to work on a common product sub-domain (e.g., Pay, Tax, or Talent).

At one point, all development teams were located at Ultimate Software's corporate headquarters in Weston, FL. Maintaining a quality culture was a simple process as quality engineers would see each other in the hallways and open areas. Inter-team coordination along functional lines was as easy as gathering in a single conference room. Quality issues were addressed quickly.

As the company began to grow rapidly, the development teams could no longer be located in the same building. Where culture initially grew organically from daily interaction, a more deliberate approach was needed to promote and share that original quality culture. This was addressed through the use of a centralized command structure where a few managers and architects dictated monolithic solutions. While this maintained a relatively common solution set for a short period of time, as the company continued to scale, such a structure quickly became intractable as product lines diverged. Addressing these new product needs, teams adopted new technologies and architectures, which required greater team autonomy.

Through growth and acquisition, development has spread to both coasts of the United States as well as into Canada and Europe. Each new office location adds greater physical separation between teams. Where it once was possible to bring all of the testers in the organization together in one conference room to share information and hold discussions, the logistics of space and time no longer make this possible. As teams grow, it becomes increasingly difficult to have conversations together and ensure that every voice is heard. Where the quality organization once had a unified culture, it has split into subcultures, overshadowed by the individual teams' cultures.

As Ultimate Software's offerings have grown to meet the increasing demands of the HCM market, the need for inter-team coordination has also grown. It's no longer possible for any single person to be capable of comprehending all of the sub-domains and architecture used across the company's products. The company is no longer able to rely on architects or centers of excellence to satisfy all coordination requirements.

The core values that define a culture depend on them being taught and shared. As test engineers were assigned to feature teams, and as new people joined, the sharing became fragmented. With less cross-team interaction, teams began to pursue solutions for similar problems without understanding what other approaches were available, or that their current pursuit had been tried. As an example, a commercial test tool for a legacy product was no longer available or supported. It would not be usable on newer operating systems. Either a replacement would be needed, or regression testing would become a manual effort - adding a number of days to a release. Several teams worked independently towards a solution. In itself, this is not bad, but some of the approaches would not have worked for all teams. Also, teams ended up repeating work. This is the impact of siloed teams - no sharing of information, duplication of effort, and solutions that don't meet all teams' requirements.

What if the same fragmentation was occurring in quality practices and principles? What if quality was being defined outside of the community of testers, and without consulting the test architects that had crafted a set of standard practices best suited for the needs of the organization?

A solution was needed that would allow test engineers to share information, tools, and practices and through which organizational standards could be communicated out to the teams.

3. The Quality Guild

3.1. Community of Practice

Agile teams are cross-functional to facilitate the delivery of increments of the product, but there's value in test engineers communicating with their peers, sharing their multiple experiences and knowledge. The Community of Practice is one way to support function-centric discussions and collaboration (Scaled Agile, Inc., 2018).

Communities of Practice are "organized groups of people who have a common interest in a specific technical or business domain. They collaborate regularly to share information, improve their skills, and actively work on advancing the general knowledge of the domain" (Scaled Agile, Inc., 2018).

3.2. Scaling Agile: Spotify

One example of Communities of Practice is found in the organizational model used by Spotify and laid out in "Scaling Agile @ Spotify with Tribes, Squads, Chapters & Guilds" (Crisp's Blog, 2012).

Spotify organizes feature teams into Squads. Squads working in related areas are organized into Tribes (Crisp's Blog, 2012). These Squads and Tribes are analogous to Ultimate Software's Teams and Domains. The difference is that Spotify then has Chapters that organize along a function within a Tribe. The Chapter, combined with the Squad and Tribe, form a management matrix with the individual contributor reporting to their Chapter lead (Crisp's Blog, 2012). Ultimate Software does not have this matrix structure.

Finally, the concept of the Guild is to bring together those with a common interest from across Squads and Tribes - from across the organization. Spotify defines the Guild as "a group of people that want to share knowledge, tools, code, and practices" (Crisp's Blog, 2012). This is the Community of Practice. The Squads and Tribes maintain their autonomy, while the Guild allows for sharing and learning that cuts across both. A culture is built on the sharing and teaching of common values and goals.

3.3. Ultimate Software: The Quality Guild

Figure 1, below, is a diagram of the Guild structure at Ultimate Software. Test engineers from feature teams, across Domains, are able to gather and discuss issues related to quality practices and tooling.

As noted earlier, centralized control doesn't scale and often becomes siloed. Guilds are decentralized and self-organizing. In the book *The Starfish and the Spider*, the authors describe two persons critical to launching decentralized groups: the catalyst and the champion. The catalyst is the person who gets a decentralized organization launched and then cedes control. The champion pursues the idea and takes it to the next level (Brafman and Beckstrom 2006).

The Quality Guild's catalyst was Tariq King, Distinguished Architect and Sr. Director of Quality Engineering. He provided the vision and the critical management support needed to launch the guild. The Quality Guild also required a champion, someone who could act as "guild coordinator" and who would organize and facilitate regular meetings. The author was selected for this role.

Initially it was decided to invite only one test engineer from each feature team, preferably a test lead or a test engineer acting in that capacity. This was done to keep the size of the group manageable as it got started.

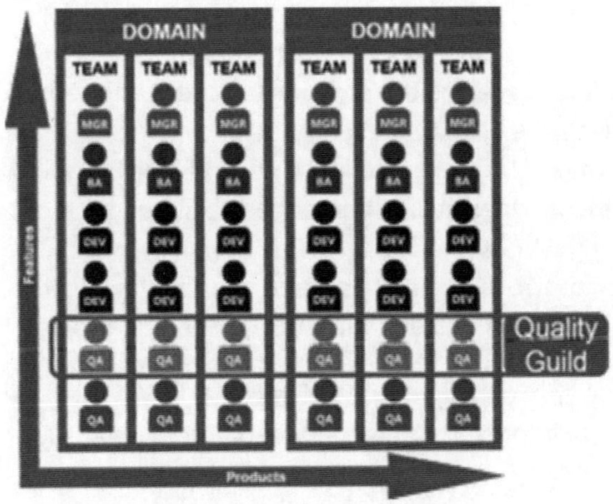

Figure 1: Teams, Domains, and the Quality Guild

The initial meetings were run similar to a "meetup," with a fixed agenda based around a presentation. While this was successful at first, it quickly became difficult to arrange presentations and the topics for discussion began to stagnate. There was also a sense that too many of the discussions focused around one tech stack and some members felt they weren't getting any true value from the meetings. This led to a fall in attendance.

In addition to the meetings, a channel was setup in Slack to create a more immediate way to share information. This was a place to not only ask questions and share ideas, but to share links to interesting posts and tools. With Slack being a primary communication tool at Ultimate Software, it became the natural choice for the guild.

Three approaches were taken to address the problems with the meetings:

First, membership was opened more broadly. While it still isn't open to every test engineer, those who express an interest are extended an invitation.

Second, instead of soliciting presentations and using a static agenda prepared by the facilitator, we adopted Lean Coffee to generate our agenda. Lean Coffee is referred to as an "agenda-less meeting" (Lean Coffee, n.d.) because the agenda is not fixed in advance. Typically, participants would write topics on cards and then the cards would be voted on and discussions would start with the topic that got the most votes. We chose to use an electronic board that stays up between meetings, allowing members to add topics whenever they want, and also to vote on what interests them. Some variations of Lean Coffee will timebox discussions, allowing for votes for more time. We decided not to restrict the discussions that way. Since we use an electronic board, we also carry topics over from meeting to meeting - along with their collected votes.

Third, the Quality Guild has started forming Working Groups, chartering them to address particular issues. They are expected to complete the work and disband. The length of time a Working Group will exist is based on the work to be done. Participation is voluntary, so those involved are generally more passionate about the topic. Each Working Group chooses its own chairperson to organize and facilitate the work. At the time of this paper, there are four active Working Groups:

- **Test Case Management:** Gathers requirements for tooling to support test case creation and maintenance, reviews available options, and proposes solutions.
- **Root-Cause Analysis:** Develops standards and processes for collecting root-cause analysis data on escaped defects and develops tools and reporting to use in process improvement.
- **Test Coverage Metrics:** Develops the process to collect and report data regarding teams' efforts around testing of features.
- **Accessibility Testing:** Develops architecture and quality guidance addressing accessibility testing, architecting for accessibility, and accessibility conformance reporting.

Working Groups are expected to give regular updates to the Quality Guild on their progress, which also gives an opportunity for the broader community to ask questions and provide feedback on the work.

"Typical guilds live and die by the participation and motivation of their members" (AZ Central, n.d.). Fortunately, these initiatives have improved participation and the Quality Guild is growing.

4. Results

The Quality Guild, on its own or working in conjunction with Architecture, has provided key insights, assistance, and work on documentation, test case management, root-cause analysis, test coverage metrics, accessibility testing, and training.

4.1. Documentation

Ultimate Software is developing an internal site for documentation related to our architecture, development, and quality standards.

The Quality Guild provided source material on each team's internal processes for reviewing automated GUI-level system tests. This formed the basis for a document on standards for these tests. Where there was consensus, the standard was added to the document. Those where there might be disagreement, and areas where there was no guidance, were reviewed by a quality architect for input. The final document was reviewed by the Quality Guild. The document is now live and is considered the standard for Ultimate Software.

In addition to this direct contribution, guild members have also participated in other quality standard documentation being written by the quality architecture team. Their assistance has included identifying the priority of documents to be created and reviewing the documents before internal publication. The documents developed and reviewed have included guidance on test case authoring, the test pyramid, exploratory testing, risk-based testing, test planning, performance testing, and on production readiness from a quality perspective.

Some of the documentation codifies existing practices and will serve as training material for new testers (and a reference source for everyone). Others, such as risk-based testing, are practiced by some teams, but adoption will increase with published guidance. Since teams use different technologies and architectures, many of the documents have to be written for a broad audience. For instance, the test pyramid material does not define a single pyramid for all teams, but instead discusses the rationale behind the pyramid and provides guidance on how to use it as a heuristic for developing an effective test portfolio.

The documentation site is still relatively new, so the Quality Guild members reviewing documentation are helping to drive adoption of the site. Likewise, quality architecture is actively encouraged continued involvement, including contributing documents and assisting with future maintenance.

4.2. Working Groups

4.2.1. Test Case Management

A prior informal investigation of this topic, held before the working group existed, had generated a set of requirements that must be met by any new tool acquired or built for the authoring, maintenance, execution, and reporting of manual test cases. These requirements were reviewed and refined by the working group and included the following:

- Integration with tools, such as our issue tracking system (Jira) or an API to provide the integration
- ability to version test cases
- a configurable interface
- report generation
- ability to execute and collect results for manual tests

Based on the requirements, a select number of vendors were contacted about trials of their tools. These tools were deployed, and the working group reviewed and scored them against the requirements. The tools showed some level of integration with Jira, but little else in the way of APIs for extensibility. Most had interfaces that were not intuitive and often cumbersome to navigate and use.

We also surveyed open source test management tools, without finding a single tool that met a sufficient number of our requirements to justify selecting it for further evaluation.

Due to the somewhat lackluster response to all of the commercial tools reviewed, and the lack of open source alternatives, the chairperson, working with another engineer, developed a prototype of an internal tool, as an additional option. This prototype is currently being reviewed by working group members. The members of the full Quality Guild will be invited to comment on the prototype as well.

The working group is on track to recommend either funding the acquisition of a commercial tool, or the development of an internal tool within the next month. A problem that had been discussed for a few years will have been moved forward by the working group within a matter of months.

4.2.2. Root-Cause Analysis

The purpose of root-cause analysis of defects is to determine what happened, why it happened, and how to reduce the likelihood of another defect like it happening again in the future. Defects that escape the development process and are discovered in a production environment are the costliest to fix in terms of time taken from new features and damage to the company's reputation with its customers.

This working group quickly developed guidance based on IBM's Orthogonal Defect Classification (Chillarege, et.al. 1992) for collecting relevant information about escaped defects. The guidance used questions like: What happened? Why did the defect occur? When should it have been found? and How can it best be avoided in the future? Using this guidance and model, a pilot program was created, engaging seven development teams. The pilot data was collected in Google Forms.

With the pilot completed, a retrospective was held and some of the data collected was reviewed. One key point was that the collection of the data caused the teams to have discussions around their defects and how they might prevent similar ones in the future. Since this is a key goal of root-cause analysis, everyone agreed this was a positive result. The teams did note that collecting the data in a Google Form instead of in the defect did not fit their workflow. None of the teams showed a desire to continue to collect this data after the pilot ended, unless the data could be collected in the centralized issue tracking system used by Ultimate Software (Jira).

The working group now has two primary tasks to complete:

- First, it must work with the Jira administrator to add fields to the defect form so that root-cause data is collected along with the defect itself, as the teams clearly desire.
- Second, they must develop guidance on how teams must collect and analyze the data and develop experiments on improving the team's development processes to prevent particular classes of bugs in the future.

4.2.3. Test Coverage Metrics

This working group is developing a model for collecting data indicating how well a feature has been tested. The first task they had to accomplish was to define, for the sake of knowing what to measure, what a feature is: a business facing capability, or an internal process. Building on this, they have created a draft proposal for guidance on collecting data to build a coverage metric. It was decided that feature coverage would be somewhat aligned with the concept of the test pyramid.

Metrics to collect include:

- Unit level test coverage
- Integration level test coverage
- System level test coverage
- Compliance test coverage

- Performance test coverage

Note: Compliance testing includes non-functional concerns other than performance, such as security, data privacy, accessibility, and regulatory.

For unit level test coverage, teams will use code coverage reporting from SonarQube to provide the coverage percentage.

Code coverage is a quantitative metric. There has been no consensus on similar quantitative metrics for the other levels of testing to be reported, so teams will be asked to provide a qualitative metric for each of those. The data is to be provided in the form of a percentage of coverage they believe their team has achieved for a given feature.

Given the complexity of determining this metric, the working group is currently focusing on two intermediate steps: ensuring all teams are reporting unit test code coverage via SonarQube and developing tooling that will assist in the collection of qualitative metrics. Part of that tooling is a Taxonomy Manager that allows teams to build a tree-like structure of their product, grouping related features together in branches and leaves. There is also consideration of adding risk analysis data to this taxonomy so that test coverage of individual features are weighted by risk to provide further insight into the overall health, based on test coverage of a product.

4.2.4. Accessibility Testing

The World Wide Web Consortium (W3C) has developed the Web Content Accessibility Guidelines (WCAG) "with a goal of providing a shared standard for Web content accessibility" (W3C, n.d.). Most countries that have adopted accessibility standards base them on adherence to WCAG.

The company cannot meet either its People First commitment, or its legal obligations, if our solutions are not broadly accessible. This working group is focused on developing architecture and quality guidance addressing accessibility testing, architecting for accessibility, and accessibility conformance reporting.

Members of this working group have delivered an introductory class on accessibility to a team designing interface controls for future projects. The goal is to have these controls support accessibility "out of the box." This introductory material will be used as the foundation to develop more in-depth training for developers and testers throughout the organization.

The working group is currently preparing a proposal for an approach that will aid teams in determining their current level of conformance, planning and executing any remediation required, and then remaining in conformance.

Work was completed to integrate an open source accessibility test library, aXe (https://github.com/dequelabs/axe-core), into Aeon (https://github.com/UltimateSoftware/aeon), a test framework developed in-house, so that teams could begin to include automated accessibility checks into their system tests that run against the web interface of UltiPro, Ultimate Software's core product.

Another project that is currently being pursued is Agent A11y. Agent is an open source AI-driven testing agent that explores web pages (https://github.com/UltimateSoftware/AGENT). Leveraging the Agent platform to run a static analysis tool such as aXe will allow us to autonomously collect information on accessibility issues. Additionally, Agent A11y is able to perform certain dynamic accessibility tests such as tab order and element focus checks.

4.3. Training Classes

One of the ways the Quality Guild perpetuates the quality culture at Ultimate Software is to share knowledge. That includes how we train our own people on testing.

Internal training is an integral part of the career experience of employees of Ultimate Software in general, and quality engineers in particular. Every tester joining the company is invited to attend a black box testing techniques class. Additionally, a class on white box testing techniques is available. Members of the Quality Guild have been instrumental in reviewing and piloting a new class on Session-Based Test Management. The feedback was extremely valuable and is being used to complete the final draft before rolling it out to all of our test engineers.

Originally, all test-related training was done by test architects, but over time it became clear that more trainers would be needed. Test leads have been selected to be prepared to deliver the training themselves. This is an important part of their career growth, opening new opportunities as their impact on the organization increases. This is similar to how the Marine Corps "tap outstanding performers to fill instructor slots, regarded as one of the high-profile tours of duty" (Freedman 2000). Because they will be responsible for teaching newer testers these techniques, leads are challenged to deepen their own knowledge of testing and quality engineering.

5. Future Work

The Quality Guild is like exploratory testing in that we try an experiment and see what happens. Based on the results of that experiment, we may keep doing something, or we may move on and try something else. Looking ahead, areas that we will be experimenting in are Attendance and Engagement, Diversity, and Working Groups.

5.1. Attendance and Engagement

Participation in the Quality Guild is strictly voluntary and in addition to a test lead's usual work, therefore we cannot penalize someone when they don't attend meetings. That said, we have tracked attendance for almost a full year now. The purpose is not to be concerned with individuals, but to see which teams and domains aren't being represented. Those teams will miss critical information that's shared and have no input into decisions that are made if they don't have a presence at the meeting.

We also want to continually review attendance to determine if there are people on the invite who have been promoted or moved to a different functional role and are no longer interested in participating. Replacing them allows us to focus on improving representation from the teams.

5.2. Diversity

As of August 2016, Ultimate Software reported that 49% of the total workforce were women (Ultimate Software, n.d.). Unfortunately, our initial invite list did not reflect this diversity. We noted it at the time but were unable to identify additional qualified individuals already in the company. Since then, opening the membership to include those expressing an interest has improved the situation, but there's a long way to go. Opening it further, as planned, may also improve the diversity of the guild.

Beyond passive approaches, one of the purposes of the Quality Guild is to provide mentoring to engineers who want to grow and could eventually become leaders. Greater outreach needs to be fostered and diversity needs to be an issue kept before us.

5.3. Working Groups

Working Groups would benefit from a greater emphasis upfront on their charter, including stipulating completion criteria. The current working groups had to take a vague requirement and refine it into a mission with a clear goal, which delayed their addressing the problem they had gathered to solve. Also, an early, clear charter might attract other members to participate.

Additionally, all of the current chairpersons come from central teams, such as Architecture and the Quality Center of Excellence. There is a goal to make sure that as often as possible, the chairperson, or a co-chairperson, come from a feature team, since they are the most impacted by the guidance and tools produced. This is also an ideal place to mentor more junior members.

6. Conclusion

This paper has examined Ultimate Software's Quality Guild as a way to promote a shared culture among quality professionals from across the feature teams that build and deliver software. That software improves "the personal work experience" for our customers and their employees - "the power behind the business" (Ultimate Software, n.d.).

We looked at Spotify's model for communities of practice, which they named guilds, as a way to create a decentralized team that could sustain their culture while addressing the issues that impact the feature teams. In this way, teams would learn from each other.

Working together, the Quality Guild has helped with the development of documentation to provide guidance on test approaches that work across Ultimate Software. Working groups have been created to address specific issues that teams are facing (the need for test case management tooling and root-cause analysis to drive process improvement) to organizational issues (such as the need for measures of product health and assessing the accessibility of our products, a moral and legal requirement). The guild is also concerned with the development of the individual quality engineer and so it is actively involved in the development of classes and preparing test leads to teach, as well as to mentor others.

As a result of discussions within the guild, new tools have been created, or are in the process of being created, that will solve problems teams are currently facing. This includes tooling around test case management, metrics collection, test planning, and accessibility testing.

Culture is about shared values and goals. Ultimate Software has a strong culture built around the principle of "People First." The Quality Guild is an outgrowth of that culture, through which we have instilled and grown a sub-culture of quality that also strive to achieve this principle.

References

Agile Coffee. n.d. "What is Lean Coffee?" Accessed June 8, 2019. http://agilecoffee.com/leancoffee/.

Agile Transformation. 2015. "What is an Agile Team and How Do You Form Them?" Accessed June 8, 2019. https://www.leadingagile.com/2015/02/what-is-an-agile-team-and-how-do-you-form-them/.

AZ Central. n.d. "Culture and Subculture in Business." Accessed June 15, 2019. https://yourbusiness.azcentral.com/culture-subculture-business-3801.html.

Brafman, Ori and Rod Beckstrom. 2006. *The Starfish and the Spider: The Unstoppable Power of Leaderless Organizations.* New York, NY: Penguin Group.

Chillarege, Ram, I.S.Bhandari, Jarir Chaar, M.J.Halliday, D.S.Moebus, Bonnie Ray, M.-Y.Wong. 1992. "Orthogonal Defect Classification - A Concept for In-Process Measurements." *IEEE Transactions on Software Engineering* 18: 943 - 956.

Crisp's Blog. 2012. "Scaling Agile @ Spotify with Tribes, Squads, Chapters & Guilds." Accessed June 8, 2019. https://blog.crisp.se/2012/11/14/henrikkniberg/scaling-agile-at-spotify.

Freedman, David H. 2000. *Corps Business: The 30 Management Principles of the U.S. Marines.* New York, NY: HarperBusiness.

Hootsuite. 2014. "Guilds: Get Stuff Done Together." Accessed June 8, 2019. https://medium.com/hootsuite-engineering/guilds-get-stuff-done-together-3d0826209390.

Inc. n.d. "Preserve Your Company's Culture As You Grow: 5 Steps." Accessed June 15, 2019. https://www.inc.com/paul-spiegelman/company-culture-manage-growing-workforce.html.

Lean Coffee. n.d. "Lean Coffee Lives Here." Accessed June 8, 2019. http://leancoffee.org/.

LinkedIn Pulse. 2015. "Guilds, Tribes, Chapters & Squads... and SCRUM. What?!," Accessed June 8, 2019. https://www.linkedin.com/pulse/guilds-tribes-chapters-squads-scrum-what-arjan-bos/.

Merriam-Webster Dictionary. n.d. "Culture." Accessed June 14, 2019. https://www.merriam-webster.com/dictionary/culture.

Pink, Daniel H. 2009. *Drive: The Surprising Truth About What Motivates Us.* New York, NY: Riverhead Books.

Poppendieck, Mary and Tom Poppendieck. 2003. *Lean Software Development: An Agile Toolkit.* Boston, MA: Addison-Wesley Professional.

Prowareness. 2016. "How to get Great Scrum Guilds." Accessed June 8, 2019. https://www.scrum.nl/blog/get-great-scrum-guilds/.

Scaled Agile, Inc. 2018. "Communities of Practice." Last modified September 21, 2018. https://www.scaledagileframework.com/communities-of-practice/.

Ultimate Software. n.d. "Our Culture." Accessed June 14, 2019. https://www.ultimatesoftware.com/Ultimate-Company-Culture.

Web.com. 2017. "A New Agile Guild Model." Accessed June 8, 2019. https://medium.com/webcom-engineering-and-product/agile-guilds-the-yodle-way-47dc00f6cd3a

WhatIs.com. n.d. "corporate culture." Accessed June 14, 2019. https://whatis.techtarget.com/definition/corporate-culture.

World Wide Web Consortium. n.d. "Web Content Accessibility Guidelines (WCAG) 2.1." Accessed July 20, 2019. https://www.w3.org/TR/WCAG21/.

Software Based Disruptive Change Initiatives Require a Culture of Quality

Ying Ki Kwong, PhD, PMP
Office of the State CIO
State of Oregon
ying.k.kwong@oregon.gov

Philip Lew, PhD, PMP
XBOSoft
philip.lew@xbosoft.com

Jack McDowell
Office of the State CIO
State of Oregon
jack.mcdowell@oregon.gov

Abstract

The meaning of quality – whether in the software product we develop or the organization that develops it – needs to evolve over time to adapt to changes in business requirements and environmental factors. The authors observe that not all software-based Change Initiatives are created equal. Some occur within an enterprise with stable enterprise architecture, while others require a significant paradigm shift to transform an enterprise and disruptively shift business or operating models. We believe managing complexity, promoting active organizational learning, and treating change as a common Enterprise Language are key understandings that project leaders and participants must acquire in order to successfully lead transformative change initiatives. These understandings are important to transformative Change Initiatives and are the foundation of a quality culture necessary for a modern enterprise to continually learn, sustain, and renew itself. This paper will outline key success factors in "crossing the chasm" to implement disruptive Change Initiatives in large enterprises.

Biography

Ying Ki Kwong is the Statewide Quality Assurance Program Manager in the Office of the State CIO in Oregon state government. Prior to this role, he was IT Investment Oversight Coordinator in the same office and was Project Office Manager of the Medicaid Management Information System Project in the Oregon Department of Human Services. In the private sector, Dr. Kwong was CEO of a Hong Kong-based internet B2B portal for trading commodities futures and metals. He was a program manager in the Video & Networking Division of Tektronix, responsible for worldwide applications & channels marketing for a line of video servers in broadcast television applications. In these roles, he has managed software based systems/applications, products, and business process improvements. He received the doctorate from the School of Applied & Engineering Physics at Cornell University and was adjunct faculty in the School of Business Administration at Portland State University. He holds the PMP certification since 2003.

Philip Lew, CEO of XBOSoft, oversees strategy, operations and business development since founding the Company in 2006. In a span of 25 years he has worked as a developer, product manager, and held roles at the executive level both in USA and Europe. He also serves as an Adjunct Professor at Alaska Pacific University. He has spoken at conferences such as STPCon, PNSQC and Better Software East-West, StarEast-West while his papers have been published in ACM, IEEE, Project Management Technology, Network World, Telecommunications Magazine, Call Center Magazine, TeleProfessional, and DataPro Research Reports. Philip Lew is a certified PMP and holds a BS and a Masters Degree in Operations Research and Engineering from Cornell University and a Ph.D. in Computer Science and Engineering from Beihang University. He loves bicycling and has traveled the world visiting more than 60 countries to quell his passion for exploration and learning.

Jack McDowell is an Operations & Policy Analyst for the State of Oregon's Statewide QA and E-Government Program. Before this, he was a web developer and the chief editor of a community newspaper in Arlington, Virginia. He holds a Master's degree in political science from the University of Oregon and a certification in ITIL.

1. Introduction

Changes in the modern enterprise are increasingly managed as projects that are enabled or supported by enterprise software or IT systems (henceforth "Change Initiatives"). Some Change Initiatives deliver relatively simple improvements to existing business practices, such as digitizing paper workflows. In contrast, some Change Initiatives are transformative in nature and impact major business processes or basic operating models or paradigms, such as mergers of previously independent or autonomous organizations.

Transformative Change Initiatives are prone to failure. Although failure is often associated with failed software implementation, technology and software development are seldom the root cause. A common root cause may be a lack of collaboration among business units or disconnect between IT and business management. Closer collaboration between IT and business staff can be achieved through the use of certain software development life cycle (SDLC) methods – e.g. Agile, the Unified Process, and Joint Application Development (JAD). If used correctly, these SDLC methods can contribute positively to overall quality, typically by avoiding defects in requirement gathering or by enabling early detection and correction of defects [Jones 2012].

We believe iterative SDLCs, including Agile that implement changes incrementally with frequent course corrections, are important to manage quality in Change Initiatives. However, we also believe that SDLC is one aspect of overall quality; with other considerations being an organization's ability to articulate the desired change accurately, to work with contractors effectively, and to manage change in the context of complex organizational dynamics [Kwong 2018]. In this context, Enterprise Architecture methods are often used by large enterprises to align business goals and objectives with IT systems design [Ross 2006]. There appears to be no shortage of management methods, techniques, and philosophies, but Change Initiatives remain highly risky.

We observe that some transformative Change Initiatives are doomed to fail when leaders and participants are not aware of the magnitude of the change needed and the dynamics at play during enterprise change. This may be so even when IT and business management are willing and able to work closely. In this paper, we will characterize different types of Change Initiatives in the modern enterprise. A descriptive model of organizational change and relevant dynamics will be presented. Leveraging this understanding, we present possible approaches for assuring quality and mitigating risk in transformative Change Initiatives. This paper expands on Section 7 Organizational Dynamics in our PNSQC 2018 paper [Kwong 2018].

2. Change Initiatives and Enterprise Architecture

Projects in an enterprise's portfolio can be categorized into projects required to run or grow an enterprise and projects required to transform an enterprise [Maizlish 2005], as depicted in Figure 1.

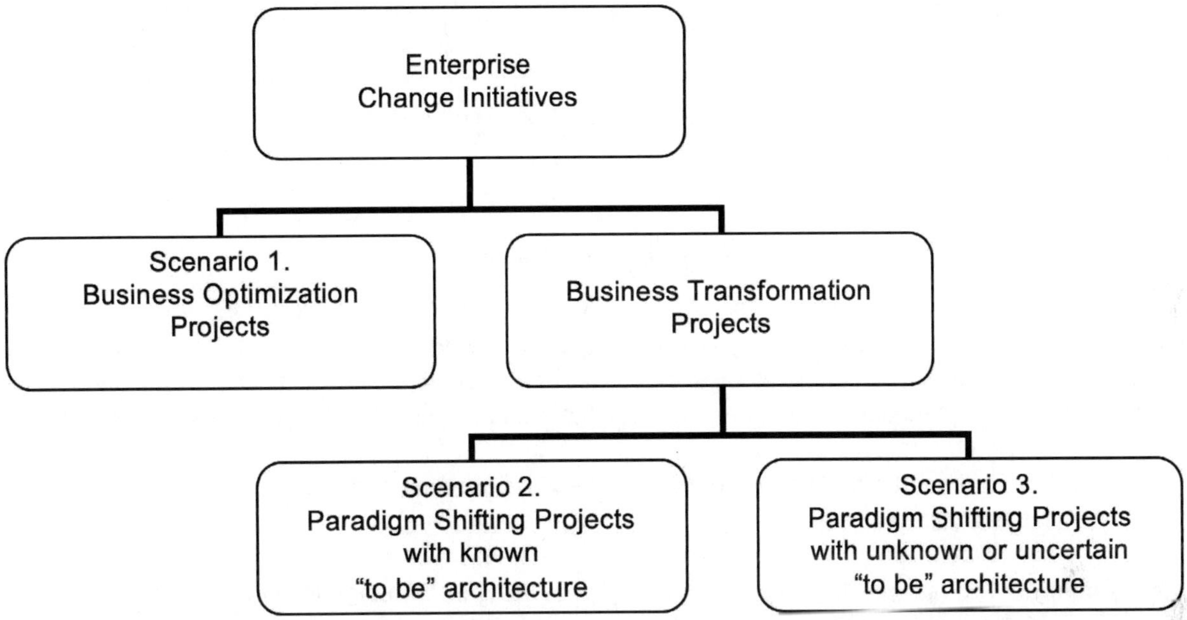

Figure 1. Enterprise Change Initiatives can be broadly classified into two categories: projects that optimize business operations or support growth based on the current operating paradigm (Scenario 1) and projects that transform an enterprise. Among these projects, there are projects with known "to be" architecture (Scenario 2) and those that have unknown or uncertain "to be" architecture (Scenario 3).

Projects required to run or to grow an enterprise may not require significant changes to business models or business processes and may focus on optimizing existing workflows or user experience. Typical goals for this category of projects may include: improve process efficiency, improve customer satisfaction, and reduce operational costs [Jones 2012]. These types of projects likely do not require significant changes to the organization's Enterprise Architecture (EA), whether formal EA is in use or not.

Projects required to transform a business usually involve major business process or technological changes. Historically, IT executives may associate projects required to transform an enterprise with the following: implementing an ERP system, building a data warehouse to support cross-functional needs, or implementing middleware to integrate heterogeneous systems [Ross 2002]. These types of initiatives are likely major undertakings of an enterprise, which require large IT investments whose outcome can significantly affect the future performance of an enterprise.

Transformative Change Initiatives of qualitatively greater scope and complexity are increasingly common in large enterprises. According to the Federation of Enterprise Architecture Professional Organizations (FEAPO), transformative changes typically include large mergers or acquisitions, rapid adoption of new business models, the shift from one overarching operating model to another. These kinds of Change Initiatives require "transformational enterprise architecture" in order to realize the desired business benefits [Architecture & Governance 2013]. Furthermore, new solution approaches that drive or enable new business models must be delivered in increasingly compressed time frames. According to Adrian Cockcroft, former Chief Architect of Netflix, "enterprises have hit a turning point" with respect to cloud technologies, software-as-a-service (SaaS), and DevOps [Bloomberg 2014].

In summary, the magnitude, complexity, and velocity of cross-functional change needed often conspire to create great challenges to stakeholders of Change Initiatives. These initiatives may not be "normal" enhancements or optimization of existing paradigms; they may be "paradigm shifting" [Kuhn 1970] in the sense that the enterprise's Enterprise Architecture is to be disruptively transformed, as categorized in Figure 1.

3. Enterprise Change as Complex System Dynamics

A modern enterprise can be modeled as a complex value network of many functions and participants. Therefore, enterprise change over time can be viewed and analyzed as complex systems dynamics. The business literature contains many examples of the application of complexity theory to the analysis of business ecosystems, emphasizing the importance of the interdependence between participating parts.

Kwong & Harmon analyzed the dynamics of value networks based on non-equilibrium dynamics [Kwong 2007]. When this analytical approach is applied to complex enterprises, there are three distinct scenarios:

- **Scenario 1:** Business Optimization Projects[1] – This type of Change Initiative occurs within a stable operating environment with stable operating paradigms. In this scenario, the magnitude of change at the enterprise level is small, and the basic operating paradigm of the enterprise and EA are not changed appreciably. Change initiatives here are business optimization in nature, and normal project management methodologies work well.

- **Scenario 2:** Paradigm Shifting Projects with known "to be" architecture[2] – This type of Change Initiative transforms an enterprise from its current operating paradigm to a stable new one. Here, the magnitude of enterprise change is large and entails significant changes to operating models and EA. This type of Change Initiative can usually be guided by industry or domain-specific designs ("dominant designs" [Utterback 1996]) or an accepted maturity model.[3] As a result, strategies and roadmaps toward the "to be" state of the enterprise can be developed, at least in principle. However, a poorly understood or executed Change Initiative may deliver a "to be" state of the enterprise that is less optimal than planned or, even worse, less optimal than before the Change Initiative. Houchin and MacLean observe that in many organizations, especially in the public sector, enterprise change gravitates toward a new stable equilibrium [Houchin 2005]. They argue that complex organizations strive to maintain stability through the establishment of organizational structure and culture; much like living species, social groups, and nations. As an example, a Change Initiative usually requires personnel roles & responsibilities to be adjusted. In a large enterprise, it may be impractical to change the position descriptions of all staff and their reporting relationships in a short timeframe. As a result, certain practices may be retained and may well "live on" through a Change Initiative, constraining the pace of change. One challenge of a Change Initiative in a mature organization is to balance beneficial change with necessary stability.

- **Scenario 3:** Paradigm Shifting Projects with unknown or uncertain "to be" architecture[4] – This type of Change Initiative also transforms the enterprise from its current operating paradigm to a new one. Unlike Scenario 2, the "to be" state of the enterprise for Scenario 3 cannot (or cannot yet) be fully elaborated or understood, owing to the rapid changes in business requirements or overall business environment. This type of Change Initiative does not have the benefit of dominant designs or accepted maturity models.[5] In this Scenario, clear strategies and roadmaps are not possible, or roadmaps are valid only for a limited time and must be updated frequently. Anderson observes that enterprise changes do not necessarily result in a long-term equilibrium [Anderson 1999]. When changes in business environment are more significant and rapid than an organization's ability to bring about beneficial change, a previously successful enterprise may fail [Christensen 2003].

Change Initiative	**Nature of Change**	**Magnitude of Enterprise Change**	**Gap between "as is" and "to be" states**	**Strategies and plans age or become obsolete quickly?**
Scenario 1	Business Optimization Projects	Small	Small	No
Scenario 2	Paradigm Shifting Projects, with known "to be" architecture	Large	Large and with guidance of applicable dominant design or maturity model	No
Scenario 3	Paradigm Shifting Projects, with unknown or uncertain "to be" architecture	Large	Large and without guidance of applicable dominant design or maturity model	Yes

Figure 2. Change Initiatives as analyzed using the analytical approach of Kwong and Harmon [Kwong 2007].

4. Navigating the Process of Transformative Change

Transformative change is, by nature, a cross functional undertaking. In our experience, the following aspects are especially important in navigating the process of transformative change: managing complexity, organizational learning, adopting an enterprise language for change, and working toward a culture of quality for change.

A. Managing Complexity

Transformative Change Initiatives are inherently complex undertakings because stakeholders in large enterprises have certain collective characteristics that do not lend themselves to simplification [Page 2009]:

- diversity – the great number of participants and their differences in background, training, and values;
- connection – the participants' perspectives are affected by each other's perspectives;
- interdependence – the participants' actions are affected by each other's actions;
- adaptation – participants can change or adapt their perspectives and actions.

Curlee & Gordon observe that traditional project management methodologies have weaknesses with respect to managing complexity. There are aspects of the work of project managers[6] that "are either not fully explained or are treated as solely linear concepts" in the PMBOK [Curlee 2011]. Indeed, recent editions of the PMBOK provide substantially more guidance on stakeholders' management and on the use of iterative / Agile methods to help manage real-world complexity.

In the authors' experience, the following considerations are important in managing complexity in Transformative Change Initiatives:

- Review goals and objectives in a business case frequently to assure that they are up to date.
- Review the project plan frequently to assure that it aligns with the current business case. This includes scope (inclusive of functional, non-functional, security and other requirements), schedule, budget, resources, and other aspect of the project plan that may need to be adjusted when the business case is updated.
- Incorporate slacks in project schedule and budget. Project schedules and budgets should not be so "lean" as to eliminate the possibility of flexible response to unanticipated issues or problems. Slack may be locally non-optimal but enables overall project robustness, especially in enabling response to the unexpected that inevitably arises.
- Encourage diverse perspectives among stakeholders; especially ideas that may not initially appear to align with an organization's "dominant logic" which often leads to "group think." However, this must be balanced with decision-making processes that are timely, enable greater weight be given to the perspectives of stakeholders with the deepest topical expertise, and avoid analysis-paralysis.
- Encourage synergistic links between stakeholders that exploit the diverse knowledge, experiences, and background of the stakeholders. Leverage positive interdependences between stakeholders' thinking that lead to cooperation, organizational learning, synergy, and win-win scenarios.
- Attend to small issues and conflicts between stakeholders early on, in order to avoid the sort of "self organized criticality" associated with irreversible loss of mutual confidence, trust, and the ability to work together effectively. Consensus is helpful, but there needs to be a way for the team to move forward when complete consensus is not possible or cannot be achieved quickly.

B. Organizational Learning

While "out-of-the-box" thinking may be welcomed by some, it is well known that social and cultural considerations may impede the diffusion of innovation [Rogers 1995] and the widespread adoption of new technology [Moore 1991]. Transformative Change Initiative requires the adoption of new enterprise paradigm, business processes, and technology by an enterprise. This entails the mass adoption of a new "worldview" within the enterprise, with requisite change in mindset made possible by organizational learning.

To support organizational learning, a variety of tools and methods have been found useful. Many mature organizations have adopted Enterprise Architecture (EA), which is the "fundamental organization of a system embodied in its components, their relationship to each other and to the environment and the principles guiding its design and evolution" [Zachman 1997]. Zachman considers EA to be an ontology for a modern enterprise or an Enterprise Language to support change. The Enterprise Language of EA enables formal description of the "as is" state and possible "to be" states of an enterprise. So, different enterprise designs can be framed conceptually, detailed, reviewed, and approved -- typically in cross-functional work groups or review boards.

In highly disruptive contexts, in which transformative change is expected to be relentless, traditional EA methods may be viewed as overly burdened by process and documentation and ineffective for just-in-time organizational learning. In reference to traditional EA methods, Cockcroft noted that "monolithic apps that need rigid architecture with rigid architecture review boards that maintain central control" may not work [Bloomberg 2014]. In order for new technologies to act as enablers of innovation and transformative change, "the goal of architecture was to create the right emergent behaviors." Managers need to "set up feedback loops and change the management style" in order to foster continuous enterprise learning.

C. Enterprise Language for Change

EA typically starts with natural language descriptions of knowledge in an enterprise. Zachman speculates that EA, as the Enterprise Language for organizational change, can be informed by the process of natural language change [Zachman 2014].

Important characteristics of natural language change include [Sole 2010]:

- different languages developed due to spatial (geographic) or cultural separations (e.g. power distance) – necessitating translation between groups that do not speak the same language or dialect;
- languages are subject to the forces of competition and "foreign invasion";
- languages may require expansion in order to address new things or new concepts;
- languages must evolve over time or risk decay (diminished use) or death [Zuckermann 2012].

By analogy with the four bullets above on natural language change, we infer the following characteristics of EA in the context of enterprise change:

- historical functional separations in an enterprise created different "languages" among professionals and managers – necessitating translation between groups by "multi-lingual" cross-functional specialists, architects, or managers;
- the different "languages" in use in an enterprise can beneficially "invade each other" – ideally converging on a single dominant language for the enterprise (a sort of "Enterprise Language" whether formal EA is used or not);
- different "languages" in use and the emergent Enterprise Language must incorporate new concepts from other paradigms, within but also outside the enterprise;
- the Enterprise Language must evolve over time to enable innovation and change or risk decay or extinction due to enterprise level decay or death.

Wittgenstein said, "If a lion could talk, we could not understand him." The idea is that without common experiences and understanding, there cannot be communication with shared meaning. At the start of a transformative Change Initiative, different functions within an enterprise would likely understand the meaning of a proposed paradigm shift and associated changes differently. The organizational learning that follows, if done well, imparts common experience and shared meaning on the desired enterprise change among stakeholders. To accelerate this process of organizational learning, an effective Enterprise Language for organizational change can be helpful. From Section 2 and Section 3 of this paper, we believe our classification of the three types of Change Initiatives (Scenario 1, 2 or 3) and their associated dynamics provide a viable taxonomy -- an Enterprise Language -- for communicating the nature of enterprise change during Change Initiatives.

D. Toward a Culture of Quality for Change

There is no simple list for what constitutes a culture of quality for change. In addition to the focus areas covered above (managing complexity, organizational learning, and common enterprise language for change), we believe stakeholder training that emphasizes the following would be important in transformative Change Initiatives:

- Address enterprise-wide paradigm change early; especially with respect to major operating model change, business process change, staffing change, and other changes that are significantly different from prevailing organizational practices or culture.
- Adjust scope / quality requirements based on evolving changes in the business and external environment that take into account necessary or beneficial changes; not ignoring or resisting them on the ground of scope creep or change control.
- Develop project roadmaps that integrate relevant business functions and IT.
- Put in place project governance that integrates work teams and relevant business functions.
- Coordinate cross-team / cross-function dependencies methodically and carefully.
- Assure end-to-end functionality of work products across all business functions.

5. Agile in Transformative Change

Agile methods call for incremental delivery of change and frequent course corrections. As discussed in Section 4, these are good practices where transformative Change Initiatives are concerned. So, it is not surprising that Agile is gaining momentum in delivering Change Initiatives and, more generally, in enterprises seeking more "agile ways of working" [Aghina 2018].

Agile is used to handle uncertainty in requirements as new features are requested and their priorities shift in real time. Agile sprints produce frequent software releases based on direct input from the business. This tight coupling with the business supports early detection of defects in requirements and designs; as high level user stories / scenarios are elaborated to produce detail requirements that support design, development, and implementation.

In chasing agility, projects often ignore or can only poorly understand the uncertainties and associated risks introduced by the Backlog. With relentless sprints, it is easy to view completed sprints as a proxy for progress. The "risk trap" is poor understanding of the probability and impact of the actual project risks associated with implementing certain user stories incorrectly (scope / quality risks) and actual velocity falling short of the expected (schedule / budget risks) [Nuottila 2016].

In traditional project management (waterfall SDLC), overall risk of remaining work in a project decreases as the project progresses (Figure 4.2). However, an unmanaged Backlog can result in increasing uncertainty with time and a higher likelihood of project failure (Figure 4.3). We have observed failed projects as a result of this type of poorly executed Agile or iterative SDLCs. The lesson learned is: over emphasis on sprint statistics without attendant efforts to manage the Backlog can compromise the health of a transformative Change Initiative.

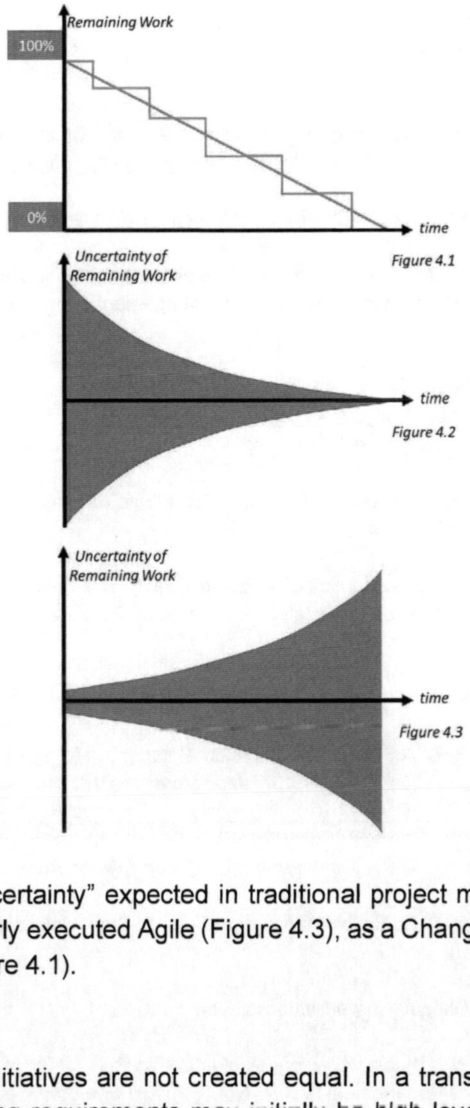

Figure 4. The “cone of uncertainty” expected in traditional project management (Figure 4.2) vs. the unmanaged Backlog in poorly executed Agile (Figure 4.3), as a Change Initiative proceeds by “burning down” work over time (Figure 4.1).

6. Conclusion

We have shown that Change Initiatives are not created equal. In a transformative Change Initiative, the business case and corresponding requirements may initially be high level and non-specific. This type of Change Initiative often has requirements that are ambiguous and need to be carefully elaborated. This elaboration requires cross-functional work teams that engage in managing organizational complexity, achieve organizational learning, and converge on a common Enterprise Language of change. Throughout the life of a transformative Change Initiative, complex organizational dynamics is always at play. For this process to be successful and repeatable, a culture of quality for change needs to emerge. These considerations are important even if an enterprise uses Agile or iterative SDLCs.

References

[Aghina 2018] Aghina, W., Ahlback, K., De Smet, A., Lackey, G., Lurie, M., Muraka, M., and Handscomb, C., "The Five Trademarks of Agile Organizations," McKinsey & Company, January 2018. Available at https://www.mckinsey.com/business-functions/organization/our-insights/the-five-trademarks-of-agile-organizations

[Anderson 1999] Anderson, P. "Complexity Theory and Organization Science," Organization Science, Vol. 10, No. 3, May-June 1999, pp. 216-232. Available at https://pdfs.semanticscholar.org/fb23/409e0ed1257af816c96cb5b555838287a50a.pdf

[Architecture & Governance 2013] "A Common Perspective on Enterprise Architecture," Architecture & Governance, vol. 9, Issue 4, 2013, pg. 14. Available at https://feapo.org/wp-content/uploads/2018/10/Common-Perspectives-on-Enterprise-Architecture-Final-1-copy.pdf

[Bloomberg 2014] Bloomberg, J. "Agile Enterprise Architecture Finally Crosses the Chasm," Forbes, 7/23/2014. Available at http://www.forbes.com/sites/jasonbloomberg/2014/07/23/agile-enterprise-architecture-finally-crosses-the-chasm/print/

[Christensen 2003] Christensen, C.M. The Innovator's Delemma, HarperBusiness, New York, 2003.

[Curlee 2011] Curlee, W. and Gordon, R.L. Complexity Theory and Project Management, John Wiley & Sons, Hoboken, NJ, 2011. See especially the section entitled "What is lacking in current project management knowledge regarding complexity," in Chapter 2 (Going Beyond the PMBOK Guide).

[Hong Kong Monetary Authority 2016] "Whitepaper on Distributed Ledger Technology," Hong Kong Monetary Authority, 11/11/2016. Available at https://www.hkma.gov.hk/media/eng/doc/key-functions/finanical-infrastructure/Whitepaper_On_Distributed_Ledger_Technology.pdf

[Houchin 2005] Houchin, K. and MacLean, D. "Complexity Theory and Strategic Change: an Empirically Informed Critique," British Journal of Management, Vol. 16, pp. 149-166 (2005).

[Jones 2012] C. Jones and O. Bonsignour, *The Economics of Software Quality*, Boston: Addison-Wesley, 2012, ISBN: 978-0-13-258220-9. See page 246 for relevant paragraphs on Waterfall SDLC and page 281-282 for relevant paragraphs on defect severity levels.

[Kuhn 1970] Kuhn, T. The Structure of Scientific Revolutions, Second Edition, The University of Chicago Press, Chicago, 1970.

[Kwong 2007] Kwong, Y.K. and Harmon, R.R. "A Structural Complexity Perspective for Understanding Value Networks," Proceedings of PICMET 2007 in Portland, Oregon, August 2007; and references therein. Available at: http://www.researchgate.net/publication/4281537_A_Structural_Complexity_Perspective_for_Understanding_Value_Networks

[Kwong 2018] Kwong, Y.K. & Lew, P. "Quality & Risk Management Challenges When Acquiring Enterprise Systems," PNSQC 2018.

[Maizlish 2005] Maizlish, B. and Handler, R. IT Portfolio Management Step-by-Step: Unlocking the Business Value of Technology, Wiley, Hoboken, NJ, 2005; near Exhibit 4.12.

[Moore 1991] Moore, G.A. Crossing the Chasm, HarperBusiness, New York, 1991.

[Nuottila 2016] J. Nuottila, K. Aaltonen, and J. Kujala, "Challenges of adopting agile methods in a public organization," International Journal of Information Systems and Project Management, Vol. 4, No. 3, 2016, page 65-85; and references cited therein. Available: http://www.sciencesphere.org/ijispm/archive/ijispm-040304.pdf.

[Page 2009] Page, S. E. Understanding Complexity, Chantilly, VA: The Teaching Company, 2009. Lecture 1 (Complexity – What is it? Why does it matter?). This is part of a collection of 12 lectures recorded on DVD. Professor Page is Professor of Complex Systems, Political Science, and Economics at the University of Michigan Ann Arbor and a member of the External Faculty at the Santa Fe Institute.

[Rogers 1995] Rogers, E.M. Diffusion of Innovations, Fourth Edition, The Free Press, New York, 1995.

[Ross 2002] Ross, J.W. and Beath C.M., "Beyond the Business Case: New Approaches to IT Investment," MIT Sloan Management Review, 43 (2), Winter 2002, pp. 51-59. See table on p. 51 (Characterizing IT Investments).

[Ross 2006] Ross, J.W., Weill, P., and Robertson, D.C. Enterprise Architecture as Strategy, Harvard Business Review Press, Boston, August 1, 2006.

[Sole 2010] Sole, R.V., Corominas-Murtra, B., and Fortuny, J. "Diversity, competition, extinction: the ecophysics of language change," Journal of the Royal Society Interface, 2010. (doi:10.1098/rsif.2010.0110)

[Utterback 1996] Utterback, James M. Mastering the Dynamics of Innovation 2nd Edition, Harvard Business Review Press; 2nd edition (October 1, 1996)

[Zachman 1997] Zachman, J.A. "Enterprise architecture: The issue of the century," Database Programming and Design, 10 (3), 1997, pp. 44-53.

[Zachman 2014] Zachman, John A. Private communication, Salem, Oregon, October 21, 2014. The conversation was partly stimulated by international travels and multi-lingual situations experienced by Mr. Zachman and the authors.

[Zuckermann 2012] Zuckermann, G. "Stop, revive and survive," The Australian Higher Education, June 6, 2012. "Death of a language" is called linguicide. It occurs when its last native speaker dies. "Language eating" is called glottophagy. Among natural languages or dialects spoken by smaller ethnic groups, the driving force for glottophagy is globalization and homogenization. Available at http://www.theaustralian.com.au/higher-education/opinion/stop-revive-and-survive/story-e6frgcko-1226385194433

Acknowledgements

The authors acknowledge helpful discussions with (in alphabetical order of last names): Bob Cummings, Capers Jones, Robert Harmon, Paul Hempel, Alex Pettit, and John Zachman.

---

[1] The game theoretical parallel of Scenario 1 is single-person games; e.g. individual small firms seeking to optimize performance in the presence of overall market forces that it cannot affect appreciably.

[2] The game theoretical parallel of Scenario 2 is multi-person games; e.g. non-cooperative games in which players make decisions independently and cooperation is self-enforcing. Given perfect information flow, non-cooperative games have global optimal strategies called the Nash equilibrium.

[3] For example: the Capability Maturity Model Integration (CMMI), Medicaid Information Technology Architecture (MITA), or the Environmental Protection Agency's Cross-Media Electronic Reporting Rule (CROMERR).

[4] There is no game theoretical parallel of this scenario, because the "rules of the game" change too rapidly to enable stable strategies.

[5] For example, the current state of distributed ledger / blockchain technology used for smart contracts in finance and trading applications [Hong Kong Monetary Authority 2016].

[6] These aspects include harnessing complexity, stakeholder communications, virtual teams, and leadership.

What It Takes to Be a Successful Scrum Master

Anh Chi Nguyen

anguyen@akvagroup.com

Abstract

This paper focuses on the lessons learned along the way as I transitioned from Developer to Scrum Master. I'll share my own personal story in why I decided to take on this transition. My main desire was to help people. I wanted to help my fellow developers and product owners to solve daily Scrum communication problems and adopt an Agile mindset. However, with my lofty aspirations, it was a tough mission. As a developer at my organization, you mostly work alone at your desk. But I quickly realized that I could not do things on my own terms anymore. Rather, I needed to collaborate with people and look for solutions which could work for all. Rather than "ME", it is now a "WE". As a Scrum Master, my tasks have become more abstract and personnel related.

In sharing my story, I'll discuss what I have experienced working in a Scrum Master role for more than 4 years. This includes my successes, challenges, and yes... failures. I hope that this can provide valuable insight (including tips and lessons learned) to other developers & testers who may be considering transitioning to a Scrum Master role. Some particular points I'll cover include:

1. Understand human psychology to decode team behaviors. Why is it that some team individuals behave in 'odd ways' that you can't understand on the surface? What's going on here?!

2. Select communication methods that could help your team to solve collaboration problems. Keep in mind, what works for you does not mean it will work for your team. Test it and adjust!

3. How to measure and interpret work progress in your team and look for team improvements.

4. Do Agile vs. Be Agile learned lessons

Biography

Anh Chi Nguyen holds a MSc degree in Information Systems at Norwegian University of Science and Technology (NTNU). She has worked in Nordic IT industry for 12 years where of 4 years as a Scrum Master. Her current job is Agile Coach for AKVA group where she coaches multiple development teams to adopt an Agile mindset through a practical set of Scrum practices.

1. Introduction

Scrum is no longer a new topic in IT industry. Yet, challenges of doing Scrum effectively persist. Back in 2007, I was a software developer when my past Norwegian company started to adopt Scrum in my team. Norwegian software companies are known for their flat culture, which is an advantage to adopt Scrum. However, there are certain real-life challenges when working with Scrum that you hardly find explanation in Scrum training and books. My paper will cover some of these challenges reflected from my own experience.

2. Psychology Approach to Understand Human Behaviours

Most communication conflicts are caused by misreading others' behaviors. In Scrum, communication conflicts may happen frequently. This is because teams are empowered to make important decisions together without hierarchical authority. To solve communication conflicts effectively, I chose to look at human psychology.

2.1. Background of DISC Model

DISC stands for Dominance, Influence, Stability and Compliance. This model is invented by an American psychologist named William Moulton Marston. The author proposes a technique to categorize people's behavioral traits into these types of DISC in order to understand their emotional reactions. For each type, there are certain communication challenges. Below is an illustration of main traits in each DISC type.

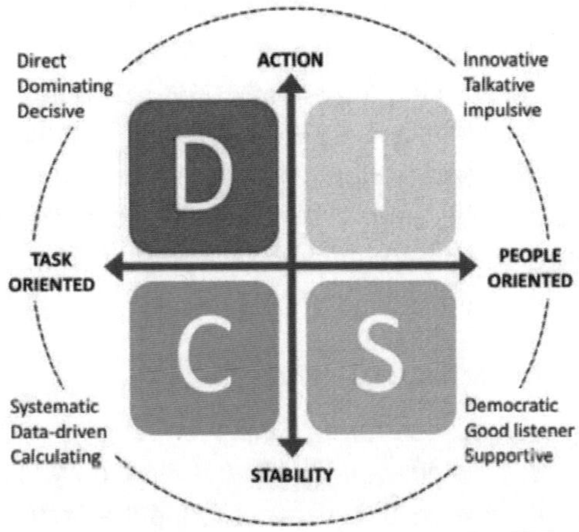

DISC model [1]

In my experience, everyone is a combination of these four types. However, their dominant type can highly influence their overall reactions. By knowing about their dominant type, I could adjust my communication approach to obtain a more effective result and improve collaboration.

2.2. My Stories

I was Scrum Master before I learned about the DISC model. There were certain situations that I could have handled better if I had been equipped with a proper understanding of how different others were from me. DISC helped me to gain a fundamental understanding of human behaviors, and I made better decisions in this field with my tasks.

2.2.1. The Agreeable Person

Agreeable people can initially be perceived as polite and peaceful, yet they can be a frustrating factor in teamwork where we require individual opinions and consensus. I had such an experience with Dave, a developer who is the agreeable type. One time, Dave came to me and complained that his Sprint work got disturbed by our elite colleagues Alf and product owner Bob. In the team, we all knew there was some tension going on between Alf and Bob on product decisions and we had not found an effective resolution.

Bob felt developers need to comply with the design he wanted for his product, while Alf argued how the product interacted should be a developer's decision. They both went for their own ways, and Dave felt stuck, uncertain and disturbed as a team member.

To prevent unnecessary tension, I brought Alf to talk with Dave first and discuss how to help him remove work disturbance. Alf suggested a few collaborative things and Dave agreed with them all. Surprisingly, the same outcome happened when I brought Bob to help Dave remove work disturbance. I knew suggestions from Alf and Bob were different and impossible to implement both, but Dave just accepted them. I must emphasize that Dave accepted both Alf and Bob's suggestions when he was in the room *with each of them*. When he left the room, he came to me and complained that Alf and Bob's suggestions made him stress out. That made me feel frustrated. What did not work here? I had brought them to communicate and agree on a solution. I could not understand Dave. If he thought Alf and Bob's suggestions were difficult for him to try, he could have told them when he was in the room with them. Why had he accepted it and now complained? At last, I had to gather them all again to clarify product goals and role scopes; we formed a new mutual agreement.

Had I known about the DISC model, I would have helped all of them more effectively sooner. Later, when learning about the DISC types, I reflected on this story and realized that Dave's behavior traits were considered as those of the Stability type, so he always tended to avoid conflict. On the other hand, Alf presented a Compliance type which tended to judge every detail in a logical aspect and fought for what he felt to be correct. Bob was a typical Dominance type who chose to see his plan implemented with a strong will and might overlook important details. When a Dominance type communicates his goal with a Compliance type, he could get into conflict due to their different focus. Unfortunately, Dave was brought in between them, and with his Stability nature of good collaboration and conflict avoidance, it made sense he felt totally helpless.

2.2.2. Anxiety Spreading Due to Differences in Perception

One time I worked to kick start Agile processes for an R&D team in an accounting software company. They had strong domain knowledge, but their old-fashioned software development slowed them down in a competitive market. Management planned to hire external consultants to speed up development for new short-term projects which they hoped to roll out for an early win. The team had a history of "anti-outsider" which hindered management to hire external experts.

Management gathered us to confirm about external hiring. I sensed there was an underneath tension from developers towards management's decision. Henry, my boss who was a Dominance type, briefly announced about the hiring and requested the team to prepare an onboarding plan for newcomers. Ted, a backend developer who was a Stability type, expressed concern about why Henry needed to hire outsiders this time. He felt that the team with several years of experience should have been considered to take charge of new projects. He also reasoned that bringing new people to the team now would affect their productivity due to time spending on training the new ones. Henry explained to them that it would have taken too much time if the team had handled new projects, due to their lack of modern technical competence. Henry emphasized a wish to roll out new products as soon as possible. Therefore, he suggested the team to transfer domain knowledge to the new ones and let them handle new projects alone. As a Dominance type, he was very direct and to the point in conversation. Arvid and Luke, Compliance type developers, said no word but they wrote something in their notebooks. Three other Stability type developers Larry, Jane and Laura exchanged comments but preferred not to say it out loud. As a Scrum Master, I had to observe my team well to detect hidden reactions. My job was to facilitate discussion but not actively attend the discussion. I asked if the team had more concerns to bring up with Henry. Luke raised questions about how long those people would stay with the team. Henry showed the gesture of being unsure but confirmed that he would soon find out when the new guys started their first project. Arvid wrote something more while Ted looked puzzled at Henry but said nothing. The meeting was dismissed in agreement that the team would prepare an onboarding plan as soon as possible.

The next day, Larry and Jane came to talk to me. They were worried about management's hiring decision. I asked them why they didn't say a word in the meeting yesterday. They explained that they needed to discuss with their team first. I realized there was a border in communication which separated "my side" and "your side". They worried about their future when management focused on hiring outsiders. They could be replaced one day if the management kept on bringing in outsiders. I was struck with their thought. Although I knew Stability type was not comfortable with change and I was aware of the team historic issue, it seemed Larry and Jane perceived the situation too pessimistic. Worse, their anxiety spread to the rest of the team. Ted, then Luke came to me the day after and expressed the same anxiety. The team could not work productively, so I had to step in. I called in everyone and confirmed that I would help them find out more details about the hiring plan from management. I showed them my booked meeting with management in the upcoming week. I also assured them that the outsiders would not involve any potential replacement to the team. I had confidence to say this because I was in a discussion with management where this issue was brought up as a team mental challenge, and we all agreed a hiring plan would not involve replacement to current employees. Had Henry and I have remembered to mention about this agreement with the team, they would have not built up anxiety and spread it to others. Henry and I simply thought the team should not have been concerned as management had already checked for them. This story taught me a lesson about being aware of differences in perception. What I perceive and make sense of can be different from others. I need to put myself in their shoes to feel how my message is perceived. In addition, I ask assertive questions to ensure that my audience understand correctly about what I intend to communicate.

3. Communication Approach Based on Development Stages

3.1. Background of Tuckerman's Group Development Stage

Bruce Tuckman has provided a clear path of how a team develops its maturity from Forming stage to Adjourning stage. At each stage, the team exposes certain traits. Although the path seems to be linear, real-life teams have their own tempo with a few back and forth shifts. If we are aware of the team's current stage based on Tuckman's predefined traits, we can find effective ways to improve the team's communication and productivity.

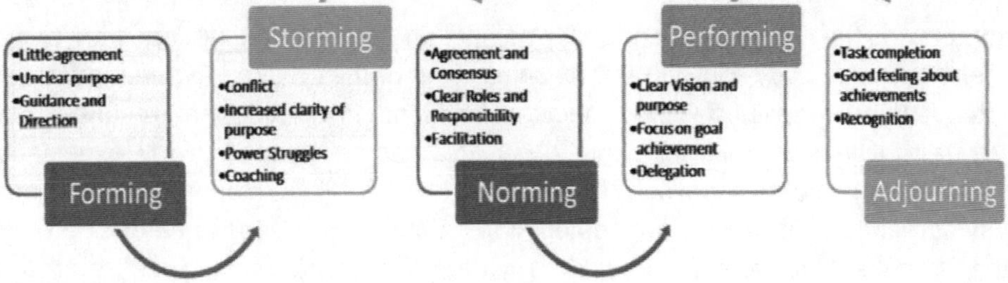

Tuckman's stage of team development (2)

3.2. My Stories

For some reason, I have been mostly working with teams belonged to Storming, Norming and Performing stage. My stories present some memorable challenges I have collected through my Scrum Master journey.

3.2.1. Team Struggles to Move Forward

I had been assigned to a team which had several skilled developers but struggled with moving forward. Team productivity was low, and everyone felt unhappy about their progress. They missed delivery deadlines and no one from outside the team managed to step in and take charge. Management told me that they had talked to the team several times, but they could not reach a solution. The team said their productivity was struggling due to a work distraction of helping newcomers onboard and offboard quite often, while management believed newcomers would never affect team productivity since they were skilled people. I suggested the team to hold a Retrospective session. We connected the events which happened along recent Sprints with respective velocities. We found out that the team got productivity issues at each new onboarding and offboarding period due to unpredicted time spent on helping newcomers. In addition, team development stage seemed to shift back and stay long in Storming since there was not enough time for the team to stabilize team spirit before a new onboarding and offboarding event. We shared our findings with management. Management now understood the problem and agreed with the team to decide a new scope of work and resources, so that the team could get stabilized soon and improve productivity.

3.2.2. Team Struggles to Implement a Change

One time I had been assigned to a software team which had a history of change avoidance. The team contained people who worked together for many years and was at Norming stage. Everyone understood their peers' working style and kept a decent collaboration. But, new change suggestion is an unfavorable topic in the team. I was aware of that and tried to figure out how to help them overcome this hindering.

At one meeting, I introduced a new routine on technical documentation to the team. Being aware of the team change avoidance tendency, I was careful to present my idea which contained only a few simple steps to try. Three developers showed positive signs towards the idea and three others looked reserved. I asked how the team thought about this idea. Jane, one of those positive developers, said she would like to try it and she thought the idea should be also applied for release notes to customers. She is an Influence type person and full of new ideas and positive spirit. I complimented Jane on her opinion with a smile and waited for others to give inputs to the idea so that we could agree to start applying it tomorrow. I looked for inputs from the reserved ones. They looked at each other. Fred, one of them, finally said they would not hinder the team if the team chose to apply this change. I was not experienced enough to understand his intention correctly. At that moment, I just thought he was agreed about applying the change in his team. Two days later, I came to the team to check out how the change was going. Fred and one of the reserved developers told me that they didn't do anything yet about it. I was surprised. I asked for a reason. They told me the team didn't start applying the new routine and that was not their fault. More than that, they emphasized that they didn't hinder the team about applying this change. To me, they looked like frustrated victims in this case. I came to Jane, the developer who showed most positive engagement towards the change discussion. I wanted to hear what she thought about this case. Opposite to my expectation, she just confirmed that the team should decide what to do with my idea. A big BUT appeared in my head, "... BUT you guys already agreed to try it with my suggested steps. What more needs to be decided?" I didn't know what to say other than thank you and went back to my desk. For the first time, I realized the real problem with this team. Team accountability was lacking. Empowerment was lacking. It seemed that individuals waited for someone else to make decision. That's exactly what hindered them to grow to a Performing team. They needed an action plan and someone to hold them accountable for their delegated tasks in the plan. The next day, I gathered the team to set out a minimum workable plan which could be delegated to all team members and we agreed on a weekly follow up session. One week later, the change seemed to start showing signs in their documentation routine. The team also showed better engagement and enthusiasm towards this change as they could finally see the progress. I came to learn that sometimes a team struggled to implement a change because they had no one to give guidance and follow up. Scrum Master should guide them to create a workable plan and make them accountable for implementation.

4. Team Progress Measurement

Scrum Master does not only help team to achieve excellent communication, but also knows how to measure and interpret team progress.

There are several courses and training materials giving you guidance on what and how to track work progress in a Sprint as well as what you should do when you detect a problem. To prevent repeating these topics, I will only provide you some personal insights that goes beyond pure theory.

4.1. Velocity is Not Everything

Velocity can be tracked by number of tasks or story points in a Sprint. This indicator is essential to help team forecast Sprint capacity, but Scrum Master needs to understand it properly in order to benefit from it. Factors such as team atmosphere and product focus may affect velocity numbers so it's important to be aware of them and evaluate team performance in the big picture.

4.1.1. High Velocity but Delivery Delay

I had been assigned to work with a Scrum team that looked very productive from outside. I was surprised to hear management complain about their delivery delays, because I saw each Sprint velocity based on the data looked very strong and stable on the chart. However, I soon found out the hidden cause to delivery delays. Something was going on with the product focus. The product owner was too busy with two teams, so he could not always manage the product backlog priority on time. The team also had a problem with having him available to clarify the tasks. He at times could not attend some of the Sprint planning meetings. In order to protect their Sprint velocity, the team had to pick up whatever tasks in the backlog that they could proceed with. In addition, there was no available burndown chart to reflect where the Sprint scope started to creep i.e. new tasks were added into the Sprint after Sprint planning. I brought the team together with management to present my findings and asked for suggestions. Management took charge of getting the product owner a solution for his more availability in the team. I helped the team to refine our measurement approach which emphasized on product focus, scope and time. We still used velocity as an indicator but we would not depend solely on it like before. After all, we had learned that numbers could hide us from seeing real issues. When there is a lack of communication like in this case, product development will get in trouble regardless of how good the velocity numbers look.

4.1.2. Struggle to Get a Stable Velocity

One of my past teams was upset because after six Sprints, they still could not get a stable velocity. The team was coming into the Performing stage and they all wished to stabilize the velocity for a better capacity prediction. Yet, they seemed to struggle to achieve it. I also shared that frustration as I didn't know the root cause of our struggle. Looking back at earlier Sprints, the team observed stable results in some Sprints, and unstable results at some other Sprints. Velocity seemed stable for a while, and then unstable again. There might be some pattern there, I thought at last. I then gathered the team and suggested we put all the previous Sprints' velocities together with a timeline, then we saw a pattern. We found out the Sprints before a release as well as the Sprints during a release, there appeared to be an unstable velocity. We explored deeper in our reflection and found that those Sprints usually connected with a lot of testing and fixing. The team had to deal with emergency work like customer support, stakeholders meeting and bug fixing. These efforts were not counted as user story points for velocity. Worse than that, these efforts normally happened unexpectedly and therefore came in the Sprint after the team finalized a forecasted Sprint work. We all now understood why we had that pattern. Learning about this insightful analysis, we came to modify our measurement by setting a velocity-free reservation for each Sprint. This means we reserved a time buffer up to 20% of a Sprint for handling emergency incidents in that Sprint. With the new measurement, my team felt more confident in velocity prediction as well as sufficient time handling should emergency tasks have happened.

A lesson here was do not plan a 2-week Sprint with an expected 2-week velocity work. There is always an unknown factor somewhere which may show up right after we settle the plan, for example, sick leave, critical bug found, unplanned downtime or meetings etc. These emergency cases certainly affect the Sprint velocity. Therefore, reserving a velocity-free time buffer in a Sprint will help secure planned velocity better.

4.2. Spring Work Means Work Forecast, Not Work Commitment

Many factors contribute to planned Sprint tasks unachievable at the end of a Sprint. It is therefore insufficient to judge team commitment using Sprint work as the only indicator. Scrum Guide 2011 [(3)] also made the change from "commit" to "forecast" to reflect this reality. Here is a list of the most troublesome factors to a Sprint in my experience.

- **Communication problems**

  Communication problems cause team individuals to have frustration, confusion and lack of motivation towards Sprint work. Sometimes it happens because of different perceptions on the message communicated between sender and receiver. Sometimes it happens because of human behavior misunderstandings between sender and receiver. Looking back at the DISC model and my shared stories in section 2, you can obtain insights on how to better understand your peer colleagues in a working context. My advice to you as a Scrum Master is, always pay attention at daily team communication and Sprint workflow to detect early communication issues.

- **Unplanned meetings, external emergency requests and similar issues**

  One of the biggest disturbances which developers call as "a mental drain", comes from outside the team. Ironically speaking, external disturbances share team's Sprint time but not its Sprint work. Team members can always be exposed to external disturbances. Scrum Master should help team to protect themselves by setting "unavailability" rules which inform external side about when the team becomes unavailable. External sides can still reach the team by a written message like email or message via chat program, but they must expect there will be delay in receiving an answer.

  I have set a 10 AM rule for all my teams which means they are not available for external requests before 10 AM every morning. With this rule, my teams can optimize a quiet morning to concentrate on their work. In addition, I set the no-meeting Wednesdays in their calendar so they can expect all Wednesdays are only reserved for internal team discussions or no gatherings at all except daily stand up. My teams think the rules help them focus more on Sprint work and able to plan out the day for both internal and external matters.

- **Technical problems affect development progress such as server downtime, expired licenses, and unforeseen forbidden access**

  These problems are popular and it's difficult to predict them all at Sprint planning. Therefore, it would be wise to always reserve a time buffer in a Sprint. This time buffer can be then used for critical bug fixing, extra meetings, technical problems etc, which helps the team protect planned capacity for the Sprint work (mentioned in section 4.1.2).

5. Do Agile vs Be Agile

Scrum methodology is a double-edged sword. The approach that Scrum Master chooses to lead Scrum process in team can either yield benefits or cause burdens for them. Following Scrum practices by the book is good with caution. By that, I mean Scrum Master needs to understand team maturity level and their specific needs for Scrum in order to help them build a workable process.

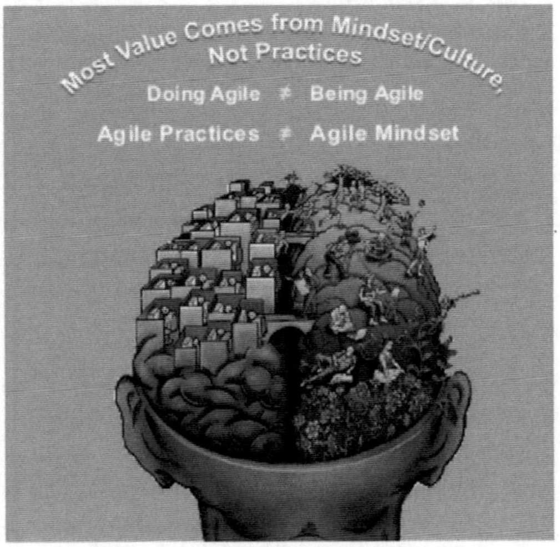

Doing Agile vs. Being Agile (4)

5.1. Adding resource does not increase team capacity (velocity) immediately

One common problem of management, especially from sales and finance department, is that they believe adding resource to a process yields an instant benefit. In real-life development scenarios, this belief can face challenges. I have shared a story illustrated a similar case in section 3.2.1.

While there is an expectation that velocity will increase soon after adding new resource, reality may show a different result. Indeed, velocity can drop since team members must share their Sprint time with newcomers in an onboarding process. Internal disturbance is expected to the fullest when onboarding newcomers. Instead of setting a high velocity goal in early Sprints, management and team should allow velocity adjustment to accommodate the change and look for insights into new potential capacity of the team.

5.2. Agile does not welcome all kinds of change in product development

I've worked with management who wanted to adopt Agile because they believed it would welcome all changes. In theory, this belief can be valid. However, adopting Agile in theory and reality still present a big gap. My experience shows that unnecessary changes of scope, political influences, individual motivation conflicts, etc should not be considered as productive changes which Agile supports. Indeed, these kinds of change only cause negative effect to team process. People, who allow these changes to happen and expect that Agile will fix them, are misusing Agile's "embrace change" principle.

Once I came to work with a corporate team which was directed by two managers. Jake was product manager and Luke was technical manager; both were assigned to collaborate on a new product development. Trouble happened when they had different interests for the product and manipulated product roadmap in their favor. Jake was passionate to build more product features, while Luke aimed for delivering a technical masterpiece. They influenced team members to gain their support. Somehow, the team was split in three groups: Jake's group, Luke's group and a neutral group. Communication in team was frustrating when priority kept changing in product roadmap. The team lost both motivation for the product and trust for the managers. At that time, I was very new to the team and Scrum Master role. I didn't expect to face this complex situation. The Scrum books I had read didn't mention any similar case. I felt stuck to see two passed Sprints which were unproductive. Worse than that, Jake and Luke expected Agile process would embrace these changes in product development; they requested me to find a solution. I decided to ask for help in my company's internal Scrum Master group. Luckily, one of senior Scrum Masters, Mark, agreed to step in to help my struggling team. He had much Scrum Master experience in corporate teams and earned high respect from management.

Mark called in a meeting with Jake, Luke and me. He explained to all of us that what was going on now in my team was a result of a political conflict between the two managers. I had eye-opening moment when Mark went on explaining why this conflict likely introduced unnecessary change in scope and affected team collaboration. He referred to the unproductive Sprints which the team had just experienced. Jake and Luke reasoned that their interests were aligned with a purpose of making the product better. Mark listened to them carefully and then replied in a neutral way "Yes, political conflicts may start from a good will of making a better product. However, when two parties choose not to be open minded to consider each other's opinions in a mutual concern for the product, collaboration goes broken. The conflict then only creates frustration and bad team spirit." The room was silent as Mark let his message sink in for the managers. Then Mark offered to help them solve this conflict by building an agreement on product goal and responsible scope. He set the agreement's code of conduct: trust and accountability. Mark said to Jake and Luke that they needed to build collaboration on trust and accountability. He advised the managers to optimize product development by using each other's strength and keep each other accountable. Mark suggested that the managers should collaborate on the product backlog priority before coming to Sprint planning with the team. Keeping one mutual priority for Sprint work will help team focus on the right thing and move forward. The meeting gave me deep insight about how Agile process could help solve anti-Agile issues. I realized that true power of Agile stayed in building a mindset around it, and this mindset will be used to navigate direction through real-life challenges in Scrum teams.

5.3. Exceptions in Sprint Can Be Positive

5.3.1. Sprint Length

Scrum process encourages teams to keep a stable Sprint length to benefit velocity measurement and capacity prediction. However, it's not always simple to keep desired length because of team availability. How productive is it to have two-week Sprints in summer time in Norway when developers take overlapped four-week vacation? Or in Christmas holiday when people combine holiday and family vacation? Or the team simply attends a one-week conference? Keeping two-week length in these cases is frustrated and ineffective. My teams usually extend Sprint length to four weeks or even six weeks to cover frequent lack of resource in these occasions. We have a good long Sprint planning before anyone starts vacation, then the team organizes internal sync (update round) every time a member gets back to work from vacation.

5.3.2. Sprint Review

Scrum books make an impression that team must demonstrate something that they have achieved at Sprint review session. At least, that's the reason to invite stakeholders and all who are interested in the product to come at the Sprint review. But what if that Sprint contains most of back-end work and impossible to have a visualized demonstration? It's not good to cancel the Sprint review as the team did achieve something, but how to show it then? My experience showed that a presentation from the team can be a good solution in this case. With visualized illustrations and user-oriented explanation, the team can inform stakeholders about their achievement in an effective way.

Working with Agile / Scrum, you must be prepared to face unknown challenges. Don't be caught up in rigid process from limited teamwork scenarios in Scrum books. You should be open-minded and question purposes behind a suggested process. Scrum framework is meant for adopting and adjusting to suit your team's specific needs. Scrum practices should be there to serve your team, not vice versa.

6. Conclusion

I hope my shared stories will provide insight about challenges you may encounter in your Scrum Master journey. Although the stories come from my own experiences with a limitation on specific teams, working environment and culture, they reflect common challenges in real-life Scrum teams. The key to success is to keep an open-minded attitude and continuous learn and improve your soft skills. Good luck!

References

1. Right people group. The four different communication types. "Cheatsheet to customer communication." https://rpg-cify0074508w.netdna-ssl.com/wp-content/uploads/2018/09/DISC-profile-cheat-sheet-to-customer-communication.pdf (accessed June 10, 2019).

2. Wageningen University & Research. Tuckman (forming, norming, storming, performing). http://www.mspguide.org/tool/tuckman-forming-norming-storming-performing (accessed June 10, 2019)

3. Scrum Guides. Scrum Guide Revisions. https://www.scrumguides.org/revisions.html (accessed August 3, 2019)

4. Agile Exchange. Doing Agile ≠ Being Agile. https://agilityexchange.com/doing-agile-is-not-being-agile/ (accessed June 15, 2019)

Timeless Skills for Modern Testers: Communication, Collaboration and Creativity

Gerie Owen and Peter Varhol

gerie.owen@gerieowen.com; peter@petervarhol.com

Abstract

As testers in today's world of agile and DevOps, we are challenged to champion quality in new and unique ways and to develop innovative test approaches that focus on customer value. It is in using not only our technical expertise but more importantly, our creativity in bringing innovative techniques such as test optimization, Behavior Driven Development (BDD) and others to our test practices that we can make our most valuable contribution.

We determine both what to test and how to test and we test jointly with developers. We assess risk and communicate this to our teams and stakeholders through our stories. Our ability to innovate comes from not only our technical skills, but also from our skills in communication, collaboration and creativity.

In this paper, Gerie and Peter will discuss the key skills that the modern testers need to be innovative: communication, collaboration and creativity. Using real-life examples, Gerie and Peter show how we can create intersections of creativity both individually and as a team. You will learn how to look at issues in multiple, unexpected ways to eliminate your own associative barriers. Finally, you will learn how create true innovation by connecting seemingly unrelated ideas generated by teams of multiple disciplines.

Biography

Gerie Owen is a Testing Strategist and Evangelist. She is a Certified Scrum Master, Conference Presenter and Author on technology and testing topics. She enjoys mentoring new QA Leads and brings a cohesive team approach to testing. Gerie is the author of many articles on technology including Agile and DevOps topics. Gerie chooses her presentation topics based on her experiences in technology, what she has learned from them and what she would like to do to improve them.

Peter Varhol is a well-known writer and speaker on software and technology topics, having authored dozens of articles and spoken at a number of industry conferences and webcasts. He has advanced degrees in computer science, applied mathematics, and psychology, and is Managing Director at Technology Strategy Research, consulting with companies on software development, testing, and machine learning. His past roles include technology journalist, software product manager, software developer, and university professor.

1. Introduction

Of the many roles that testers take on in Agile and DevOps teams, probably one of the most important is that of champions of the quality assurance process. This role is critical to achieving the ongoing success of the organization, especially during digital and business transformations. As testers we enable transformations by transforming testing.

In the 2016-17 World Quality Report (Buenen and Muthukrishnan, 2017), Buenen and Muthukrishnan report that digital transformation is the top IT strategy that presents both opportunities and challenges to quality assurance and testing groups [1]. The report noted a fundamental shift in the role of QA and testing from getting products released with as few defects as possible to improving business performance through transformed customer experience and updated business operations leading to revenue growth.

To transform our test practices, testers must innovate; the usual quality assurance and testing approaches in today's business environment will not meet the needs of Agile and DevOps as well as business transformations.

Our technical skills are important; however, it is in using our expertise in testing strategy and design and risk analysis that we can make our most valuable contributions. We determine both what to test and how to test and we test jointly with developers. We assess risk and communicate this to our teams and stakeholders through our stories. We implement new techniques including test optimization, continuous testing, Acceptance Test Driven Development (ATDD), Behavior Driven Development (BDD), Test Driven Development (TDD) and shift left. So then, our expertise comes not only from our technical experience; but more importantly, from our skills in communication and collaboration.

Although we do not always know the right answer, we can find the most innovative solutions through conversation, collaboration and creativity. True innovation doesn't happen in a vacuum; it almost always requires the intersection of seemingly disparate fields. True innovation is hard and it begins with communication and collaboration.

2. Communication

Communication is simply an exchange of information; however, communicating effectively is an art. Communication is the foundation for collaboration and creativity; it is virtually impossible to collaborate and innovate without engaging in effective communication.

Effective communication begins with talking to people directly, face-to-face, if possible. When our teams are distributed, it is extremely important to use high-quality audio and video tools that can simulate face-to-face conversations.

As we focus on how to how to best use JIRA, HipChat, Slack, project management products, incident and defect tracking solutions, and a myriad of other software tools as a part of our development and delivery environment, we often lose sight of the most fundamental and powerful tool available – talking to people, to our team members, management, customers, and other stakeholders.

Rather than burying ourselves in tools and devices, software and search engines, we can do more for our overall application quality and delivery processes by simply talking to the people around us. While a focus on software may produce more data, knowing and understanding the thought processes, expectations, pain points and ideas of the stakeholders will result in more innovative ideas as well as provide a filter for developing optimal solutions.

In Reclaiming Conversation: The Power of Talk in a Digital Age (Turkle, 2016), Sherry Turkle points out that when we communicate through texts and emails, we lose the spontaneity and exchange of ideas that come with direct conversation [2]. These direct conversations lead to a flow of ideas that may lead to unexpected solutions to issues. It is exactly this spontaneous exchange of ideas that enables collaboration, creativity and innovation.

Communication is the enabler of collaboration and communication coupled with collaboration provide the underpinning for innovation. Communication is the key component of the systems development lifecycle, no matter what methodology is espoused. Whether an organization has embraced agile and iterative methodologies or DevOps or uses a waterfall approach, teams must communicate effectively among themselves and with their stakeholders. Testers and test managers must use their communications skills to tell the story of the quality of the release and explain the business risk of releasing in the current state.

For any initiative, especially transformational innovative initiatives, to be accepted and implemented, they must be clearly and effectively communicated to multiple stakeholders at various levels throughout the organization.

3. Collaboration

Collaboration is one of the most critical skills for testing professionals today. As information systems technologies become increasingly more complex and development methodologies focus on increased velocity, individual testers and test teams cannot possibly provide effective testing alone. Testing must become a team effort. Transforming testing requires implementing shift-left techniques such as TDD, BDD and ATDD. Implementing these techniques require testers to collaborate across roles and functions; working more closely with developers, operations professionals and the business than ever before.

Collaboration is about people working together to achieve goals. It is a process through which people work as a group to achieve a common purpose. Through collaboration, teams learn about themselves both as individuals and as members of teams. Energy is created through disagreement and through the intersection of ideas, new possibilities emerge.

Although it may seem like a simple process, effective collaboration can be difficult to achieve. In CIO View: Ten Principles for Effective Collaboration (Graham, 2011), Dr Graham Hill offers ten principles that organizations can use to develop a framework for their collaboration process.
They are:

1. Focus on achieving business results
2. Develop collaboration as a capability
3. Define a decision-making structure that includes information sharing and authority
4. Champion personal accountability
5. Instil cooperative standards for information-sharing, dialog and discussion
6. Expect, encourage and make use of the natural divergences and convergences
7. Manage trade offs
8. Define and enforce high standards of personal behaviour
9. Develop a flexible organizational structure that enables collaboration
10. Employ collaboration tools and systems to support ownership[3].

Due to nature and functional goal of QA teams, there are several aspects of the collaborative process that are of particular importance. These include clear communications, traceability and visibility. A QA team must collaborate not only within the team, but as part of a cross functional team. The team may be distributed across various time zones, making collaboration via the usual social collaboration tools such as Skype or video conferencing, useful as only part of the solution.

Collaboration is the process that enables creativity and therein lies its true power. In Group Genius: The Creative Power of Collaboration (Sawyer, 2017), Keith Sawyer shows how collaboration is the only way to achieve breakthrough creativity and true innovation. Sawyer offers seven characteristics of innovative teams:

1. Innovation happens over time when the right ideas are combined in the right structure.
2. Collaborative team members practice deep listening; each member listens attentively rather than planning what they will say next.
3. Collaborative team members build upon each other's ideas.
4. Initial ideas are accepted without having meaning at the time; meaning can be built upon later.
5. Questions emerge that spawn new problems, issues, ideas and solutions.
6. Innovation comes from lots and lots of failed ideas; it is not an efficient process
7. Innovation emerges from the bottom up; often in self-organized and self-managed teams[4].

Group flow is the peak of collaboration. In Flow: The Psychology of Optimal Experience (Csikszentmihaly, 2008), Mihaly Csikszentmihalyi defines flow as a state in which an individual or a group is completely absorbed in a task, almost in a higher state of consciousness. When flow happens in a group, they are performing at their highest level of ability and are finding personal fulfilment in the process. In his study of flow, Csikszentmihalyi found that environment is critical to achieving flow. In the environment that promotes flow, the challenge must match the skillset, the goal must be clear, immediate feedback is required and the team must be free to concentrate on the task at hand. To achieve the highest levels of collaboration that lead to innovation it is important to facilitate and enable this environment[5].

For teams to collaborate, it is important that all team members feel empowered to make suggestions and build off of each other's ideas. This requires emotional intelligence as well as the ability to resolve conflicts using empathy. Testers can foster collaboration by using their requirements review skills by looking at ideas in different ways and asking probing questions that enable the team to think outside the box.

4. Creativity

Creativity is the basis of innovation. So why is innovation so hard? Our natural tendency in approaching a challenge is to analyze the issue from a framework of our current knowledge and expertise. In this way, our innovation becomes incremental, building upon what we have done in the past. Then, by collaborating with colleagues from within our own field, we "innovate" new versions of the same old ideas, furthering our incremental innovation. We may improve on our processes in this way; but we don't create anything truly new in direction. This is sometimes known as directional innovation.

Therefore, to create something totally new, actually the only way to create a completely new innovation, is to combine ideas from different, usually disparate fields. A field is not necessarily our line of work, it can be any area of study in which we are interested and have become well-versed. Our fields can come not only from our educational experiences and previous jobs, but also from our hobbies, travels and other interests. Ground breaking innovation begins when individuals or groups combine their expertise in various fields to solve a problem.

In the Medici Effect: What Elephants and Epidemics Can Teach Us About Innovation (Johansson, 2006), Frans Johansson suggests that the process of combining ideas requires "stepping into the intersection". He describes the intersection as the place where "different cultures, domains and disciplines connect and established concepts clash and combine through which ground breaking new ideas are generated". To describe the process of stepping into the intersection, he coined the term, the "Medici Effect" [6]. This is because it was through the Medici family's patronage of many disciplines in Florence in fifteenth century Italy that experts where brought together producing an era of many innovations.

In today's world of Agile, DevOps and distributed teams, we have the opportunity to collaborate with colleagues from many different, often disparate areas of expertise. Since we and our colleagues also have additional fields of study, the opportunities for intersection expand exponentially. Although collaborating with our diverse colleagues yields many opportunities for stepping into the intersection, ground-breaking innovation will not happen unless our teams are able to associate their disparate fields of study. In other words, it is not just about putting together seemingly unrelated fields; It is finding the relationships between them.

This is usually difficult because it is the opposite of our typical problem-solving process. Our minds analyze problems by association. We solve problems based on past successful actions which is useful in most situations: however, association doesn't encourage different perspectives or exploring unrelated concepts. This becomes an issue when we are addressing a problem that we cannot solve using this approach.

So then, when we are trying to solve a difficult problem that seems to beg for an innovative solution, we need to form not only a team of people from disparate fields, but more importantly, those people need to be open-minded and able to find these associative relationships easily. Frans Johansson describes these people as having low associative barriers. How do we recognize these people among our colleagues and teams?

Although they are often people who have been exposed to different cultures are curious and are self-taught in many disciplines, there are some personality characteristics that make them predisposed to having low associative barriers. Specifically, they have a growth mindset, they are able to look at problems intuitively with limited bias and the ability to use their adaptive unconscious to the appreciate the important of initial impressions and gut reactions. Let's take a more in-depth look at each of these characteristics.

In Mindset: The New Psychology of Success (Dweck, 2007), Carol Dweck describes a mindset as the way in which we mentally approach life and its challenges. Understanding mindsets explains why brains and talent don't bring success, how they can stand in the way of it and why praising brains and talent doesn't foster self-esteem and accomplishment, but can jeopardize them. Dweck described two types of mindsets, 'fixed' and 'growth'[7]. People of a fixed mindset believe that intelligence is based on what a person is born with whereas people of a growth mindset believe that intelligence can be developed.

As a result, people of a fixed mindset continually try to prove their intelligence and they see failure as a personal reflection of their intelligence. On the other hand, people of a growth mindset look at failures as opportunities to learn; they believe what they have now is a starting point and work to improve their intelligence and abilities. It follows that people of a growth mindset are better innovators as they are willing to risk failure as they explore new ideas.

The ability to think intuitively plays an important role in innovation. In Thinking Fast and Slow (Kahneman, 2011), Daniel Kahneman describes two distinctly different decision-making processes which he terms System 1 and System 2 thinking. System 1 thinking is fast and deliberate whereas System 2 thinking is more intuitive. Cognitive biases or errors in judgement based on beliefs that we are predisposed to have are the result of dichotomies between System 1 and System 2 thinking[8].

There are several biases that may limit our ability to relate seemingly unrelated concepts. These include representativeness, the confirmation bias, congruence and framing. Representativeness and the confirmation bias describe our usual approach to decision-making. Representativeness is at play when people tend to make judgements about situations based on how similar the situation under consideration is to others with which they are familiar. The confirmation bias is displayed when people consider only the information which supports what they have decided is true. It is easy to see how these biases impact true innovative thinking.

Congruence and framing impact our ability to generate atypical or unusual solutions. Congruence, or the tendency of experimenters to plan and execute tests on just their own hypotheses without considering alternative hypotheses limits the ability to try seemingly unworkable solutions to problems. Framing impacts our approach to risk. It is due to framing that people make different, sometimes opposite, choices depending upon how the information was presented. We are less likely to try a solution that has a 50 percent change of failure than one that has a 50 percent chance of success, even though both solutions literally have the same likelihood of both failure and success.

People who are able to use their adaptive unconscious are better able to innovate. In Blink: The Power of Thinking without Thinking (Gladwell, 2007). Malcom Gladwell defines adaptive unconscious as "our mental processes that work quickly with little information" [9]. Of course, as with System 1 and System 2 thinking, it is important not to rely exclusively on one or the other; however, by allowing ourselves to make quick assessments about ideas without association to other ideas, we can limit the effect of cognitive bias. Malcolm Gladwell terms the recognition and use of adaptive unconscious, "Thin Slicing". It is usually an unconscious feeling, but following those intuitions can lead to intersectional innovation.

As testers, we must challenge ourselves and our colleagues to work together to solve our challenging technological problems and improve our methodologies using intersectional innovation. And how do we do this? We must understand that true innovation comes from the Intersections of seemingly unrelated fields of study and that intersectional innovators have low associative barriers and work as individuals and teams to lower those barriers. We can become innovators by: reversing assumptions and examining different perspectives being aware of our biases, having a growth mindset and using our adaptive unconscious to think without thinking.

5. Conclusion

Communication, collaboration and creativity are the key skills that testers need to champion quality and enable innovation among their cross-functional teams. As testers, we must embrace failure and use it as a learning experience individually, as a team and as an organization. In The Element: How Finding Your Passion Changes Everything (Robinson and Aronica, 2007), Sir Ken Robinson and Lou Aronica suggest that if we are not prepared to be wrong, we will never come up with anything original[10]. Truly innovative teams will generate many ideas and initiative that fail in their quest for true intersectional innovation; we must foster an organizational culture that not only accepts this but embraces and encourages failure.

References

1.Buenen, Mark and Govind Muthukrishnan, 2017. *"World Quality Report 2016-1".*, 8th Edition. https://www.sogeti.com/globalassets/global/downloads/testing/wqr-2017-2018/wqr_2017_v9_secure.pdf (accessed June 16, 2019)

2.Turkle, Sherry, 2016. *Reclaiming Conversation: The Power of Talk in the*

Digital Age. New York: Penguin Books.

3. Hill, Graham, 2011. *"CIO View: Ten Principles for Effective Collaboration".* https://www.zdnet.com/article/cio-view-ten-principles-for-effective-collaboration/ (last accessed June 1, 2019)

4. Sawyer, Keith, 2017. *Group Genius: The Creative Power of Collaboration.* New York: Basic Books.

5. Csikszentmihalyi, Mihaly. 2008. *Flow: The Psychology of Optimal Experience.* New York: HarperCollins Publishers.

6. Johansson, Frans, 2006. *The Medici Effect: What Elephants and Epidemics Can Teach Us About Innovation.* Massachusetts: Harvard Business School Publishing.

7. Dweck, Carol. 2007. *Mindset: The New Psychology of Success.* New York: Ballantine Books.

8. Kahneman, Daniel, 2011. *Thinking, Fast and Slow.* New York: Farrar, Straus and Grioux.

9. Gladwell, Malcolm, 2007. *Blink: The Power of Thinking without Thinking.* New York: Little, Brown and Company.

10. Robinson, Ken and Lou Aronica, 2007. *The Element: How Finding Your Passion Changes Everything.* New York: Penguin Books.

Creating a Culture of Quality

Angela Riggs
riggs.ang@gmail.com

Abstract

The idea of quality in software is often synonymous with the role of Quality Assurance engineer, or assumed to only happen at a specific point in the software development lifecycle. Instead of siloing quality this way, you can help create practices that support quality throughout the whole company! By replacing the silo with a widespread culture of quality, you allow more visibility into the benefits of quality, and how those practices can support the business and the people.

Over a two-year period, I helped lead the creation of this quality culture at a software agency, and I want my experiences and lessons learned to help you do the same! My talk will break down into three general areas:

- How to effectively advocate for a culture change, including techniques for change management and introducing new processes
- How people across departments can participate in a culture of quality (it's not limited to testers and developers!)
- Why a company-wide culture of quality is important, and how the company can benefit from it

I want you to feel inspired and prepared to advocate for positive change at your own company! Everyone will have their own unique set of challenges along the way, but this talk will help set you up for success when you begin implementing the kind of change that leads to a culture of quality.

Biography

Angela believes that empathy and curiosity are driving forces of quality, and enjoys solving a variety of challenges from this perspective. Her work in quality has ranged from feature testing to leading department-wide process changes. She works to understand and create quality experiences for users, engineering teams, and the organization as a whole.

1. Understanding Quality

The concept of *quality* isn't always well-defined. It's often assumed to be equivalent to *testing*, or synonymous with the role of Quality Assurance Engineer. Neither of those definitions accurately capture the entire breadth of work and effort that *quality* entails, although they are part of the whole. While working at my first job as a QA Engineer, I came to realize that quality is something everyone contributes to at all levels, from sales to engineers to leadership.

However, having this understanding didn't automatically mean that everyone shared my perspective, or that they were immediately ready to implement this vision of quality. Over a two year period, I worked with leadership and my colleagues across departments to understand and create our own culture of quality. I learned how to lead and advocate for change; how to communicate a shared understanding of process; and how to collaborate so that everyone feels heard and involved in the changes being made.

2. Creating a Culture of Quality

Change is hard, and it's emotional. We have a tendency to react negatively to change of any kind, especially large changes that we don't have control over - such as creating an awareness and culture of quality throughout your tech or software company. This type of cultural change is where the intersection of change management and core needs is important, combined with thoughtful onboarding processes for your employees and colleagues.

Change management is a phrase that you might have heard from leadership at your company, but it can be difficult to do well. Change Management is the approach and set of processes used to prepare and support people and companies when organizational change is happening. There are some standardized approaches to how change management can be handled, but my experience has shown that any approach needs to be planned around the people being affected by the changes that are coming. One of the best ways to do that is to understand people's core needs, and take them into consideration when planning, implementing, and iterating organizational change.

2.1 Core Needs

When people are faced with change, especially unexpected change or change that someone else is creating, they often experience what's called an "amygdala hijack" - more informally known as the "fight or flight" response. An amygdala hijack can happen when people's core needs feel threatened, and change is often perceived as a threat to those needs.

In order to help mitigate the "fight or flight" response, effective change management needs to take core needs into account. It's important to understand what these core needs are, and how people react when they feel (remember, change is *emotional*) that their core needs are at risk. I like using Paloma Medina's BICEPS model to define and describe core needs: Belonging, Improvement, Choice, Equality, Predictability, and Significance.

2.1.1 Belonging

The first core need is Belonging. People like to have a sense of community and kinship - to feel that we're a part of something and we're being cared for. At work, this might look like having a good relationship with our engineering team, or feeling purposefully included in work activities. Organizational change makes us worry that our needs won't be understood or taken into account, and we're afraid that change will cause us to lose out or be left out of something.

2.1.2 Improvement

Generally speaking, people don't really like to feel stagnant. We like to know that we're able to set goals for personal and professional improvement, and that we'll be supported by our company to meet those goals. Change has the potential to introduce setbacks. Sometimes we're afraid that changes will require us to set goals we don't agree with, or that the change will distract us from the work we're doing to meet those goals.

2.1.3. Choice

This is a big one. People want choices - we like options and flexibility. We want to know that we have ownership over our environment and working conditions. We like being empowered with some level of autonomy, where we have ownership to be a decision-maker. Change can remove that autonomy and ownership, and make us feel like we have less control. It makes us afraid that we won't have a voice in the decisions being made, or that the decisions someone makes will be bad for us.

2.1.4. Equality

At work, we want to know that we have access to resources as our colleagues, whether that's time or money or opportunity. We want transparency, and the same access to information that the people around us get to have. We want management to make decisions that are fair and affect everyone equally. When change comes along, people worry that the balance of equity will shift and they'll be worse off than they were before. Some people worry that the burden of change will be unfair, and they'll have to support other people without being supported in turn.

2.1.5. Predictability

People like predictability, and the comfort of knowing our routines. We like being able to prepare in advance. For instance, it's good to know that your company's work is stable, so you can focus on doing your job without wondering if you'll still have one tomorrow. Predictability allows us to get ready for upcoming challenges, so we can be successful. Change, even positive change, is uncomfortable and disruptive to our daily work. It also makes us worry that we won't be prepared for things introduced by change, like new goals or expectations from leadership.

2.1.6. Significance

People like to feel valued. We like to know that our work contributes to the company or the people around us in some way, and we take pride in being recognized for the work we do. We also think about the title or role that we're in currently, and how we want to continue gaining status by the work that we do. When change happens, we worry about a loss in current status or recognition, or that our work won't be valued in the same way anymore.

2.2. Change Management that Considers Core Needs

Creating a culture shift was introducing a lot of change - new workflows, new tools, and a new way of looking at our work. In order to effectively manage all of these changes, we had to take those core needs into account. We needed to make sure our changes weren't a threat to people's needs, and we also needed to make sure we proved it to everyone through our actions in change management.

Thinking of people's need for Predictability, make sure your changes include transition periods so your teams have time to adjust. Most of our process and tool changes started on a small scale, usually a single product or team. This allowed us to find and solve blockers quickly in early stages with shorter feedback loops.

Feedback is an important part of change management. It helps ensure that the changes you're making will meet the needs of the people you're expecting to change. Proactively asking for feedback also lets your team know that collaborating with them while change is being implemented, and their voices matter while it's happening. This all comes back to the core needs of Significance and Choice. People need to know that their expertise and their opinions are valued, and important to the process of creating this new culture. Ask for their input when you're still in the planning stage, get their feedback while changes are being rolled out, and make time to listen to their suggestions or pain points after.

When you're having these conversations with your teams, it's also helpful to include the reasoning and context behind the decisions being made. Be transparent about the problems you're trying to solve, and include that context: *Why are we doing it this way? Why is this a pain point? Why should we change it? Why haven't we changed it before? Why will this iteration make it better?* The factors that you considered when you decided to implement a change are the same questions that everyone else will ask when that change comes along. This calls back to Belonging and Equality - making sure people feel understood, that their needs are being considered during these changes, and that they all have access to the same information as you do.

Proactively giving people access to information and communication is also important. People like being kept in the loop, and well-informed people can make better decisions. This relates to our need for Equality - making sure people know they're not being left out, and offering them transparency around process and the decision-making that goes into creating a culture of quality. When your teams are involved in the conversations, they're also more invested in the decisions that are being made. That means they'll be an active part of the culture shift, which increases your likelihood of success.

2.3. Onboarding

During all of these changes, we also had to consider onboarding, which was closely tied with our change management. Onboarding can be really difficult to execute well - something many people experience when they've started a new job. And although onboarding usually refers to ramping up new employees to the company, I'm using "onboarding" to talk about ramping up existing teams to new tools and workflows. It's a different context, but offers a lot of the same challenges.

But what does onboarding mean in this context? Onboarding includes making sure people know what they need to know, when they need to know it. It's knowing who to ask when they have a question, and knowing where information is stored. When you're onboarding your team to new workflows and tools, you also have to balance the time and effort of that against their existing responsibilities. As much as you can, try to simplify the process of onboarding for your team. If you can reduce the churn and uncertainty that goes along with messy onboarding, it's much easier for them to focus on the actual work, and successfully address and be a part of the changes that are happening.

2.3.1. Simplify the Process of Onboarding

In creating a culture of quality, some of the engineering teams incorporated more testing automation to their projects. In an effort to reduce the overhead of learning, I practiced "I do / we do / you do" during our testing sessions. With this practice, you can start by doing a demo for your team - run through the testing setup, and write and execute a test. Then let one of the developers on your team guide you through writing another test, or let them guide while someone else drives. This practice helps you make sure your team can understand and use their tools effectively before you hand it over for them to continue on their own. However, keep in mind that "handing it over" doesn't mean you never come back to it. Part of reducing the complexity of onboarding means checking in with the teams, and being available for feedback or troubleshooting. People can be hesitant to speak up when there's an issue, so it's up to you to work with your team to make sure things are going smoothly. If things aren't going well, take the time to understand what the blocker is, and find out what they need in order for it to work.

Because we were able to improve the process of onboarding for our teams, they had much less resistance to trying out new things. When you can lower the barrier of use with efficient onboarding, your team will be much quicker to adopt new tools and processes into their workflow.

3. Practicing a Culture of Quality

So let's say you've tackled your change management - everyone's needs are still being met, everyone agrees that the changes are useful and working for them. What does this culture of quality end up looking like? How are people actually doing this in their day to day work? The important thing to remember is that no single tool, test, or person can guarantee quality. In order to be truly effective, everyone needs to support and contribute to it. We had management, sales, product managers, architects, developers, and testers all involved in focusing on quality and helping change our company culture. Quality is the responsibility of everyone who interacts with or makes decisions about the product.

3.1. Management

To start with, a culture of quality needs buy-in from management. This culture won't be created top-down, but management does have to support the work going into it. Management can influence the conversations around change, and their support gives you certain authority and credibility to the rest of the company. They're also in charge of the money! If you're trying out new tools or trainings as you're creating this culture of quality, they can give you budget approval, which is pretty nice to have.

3.2. Sales

Your sales team is also a part of this culture! They're in a perfect position to seed the ground early for conversations about quality. At my company, I partnered with our sales team to develop collateral on the process and benefits of quality. The sales team used that information when they responded to proposals, when they reached out to prospective customers, and even included it in contracts. Including the topic of quality in their process meant that our clients at least had a basic introduction to the idea of quality, and it's involvement in our development process.

3.3. Architects

If your company does discoveries or architecture phases, this is another chance to enhance your culture of quality. Architects take a long view of the work - they're trying to match up current state with future needs, and make sure the work can safely scale. During discoveries, architects can start thinking about high-level testing needs, and make recommendations for project architecture that will allow for easier testing down the road. The architect role can also act as a communication bridge, and make sure the product managers, developers, and testers all understand the general outline of work being planned out.

3.4. Project Managers

Your project managers also play a part in this culture of quality. Because of their relationship with your stakeholders, Product Managers can advocate for the benefits of including quality practices throughout a project. If stakeholders don't hear about the importance of quality until the project has already started, they'll feel like paying for quality means sacrificing their MVP. Product Managers can tell the stakeholder why quality is worth the team's time, and why it's worth paying for.

3.5. Software Engineers

Software engineers also contribute to creating a quality of culture. When it comes to building the product, I know that test-driven development is not always possible - timelines may be short, or maybe there's a lot of legacy code. However, TDD can always be supported by engineering teams, and setting goals to increase coverage with each pull request is great way to encourage it.

Software engineers can also contribute through code reviews. When engineers review each other's work, it means more people are familiar with what's being built. This helps decrease the chance of silos happening, where a single software engineer is responsible for part of the product, and can never hand it off for help or collaborating. Ideally, code reviews offer a way for engineers to communicate with each other - to ask questions and learn from someone else's work; or to share ideas around other solutions. It prompts a conversation around quality, and how the work someone is doing contributes to those standards.

3.6. Testers

When we were creating a culture of quality, it was really helpful for teams to have a dedicated, embedded tester. When software engineers are immersed in their work, it's easy for them take on a ground-level view of the project. Having a tester on the team offers the chance for a higher-level view - seeing the whole forest instead of just a few trees. A dedicated tester also means there is someone to focus on other opportunities for quality - integration or regression testing, increasing automation, and creating best practices for release management.

3.7. Everyone is Responsible

These roles and responsibilities are some of the ways we practiced our culture of quality, but it's not the only way for that culture to exist. If you have a Site Reliability or DevOps team, a design team, a security team - they all share in the responsibility of contributing to the culture of quality. Ultimately, a great culture of quality is flexible, with the ability to meet changing requirements.

4. Benefitting from a Culture of Quality

So - we've talked about what your culture of quality might look like in practice, and now you're familiar with some of the challenges that come along with making these changes. But why have a culture of quality at all? As you're thinking about what quality means for your teams and your company, make sure you're including the benefits of this culture in your conversations.

When you create a culture of quality, you're creating a better way for people to work together. You're building a stronger foundation of communication, and a shared understanding about the process and benefits of quality. With a culture of quality in place, you also get an increase in the actual quality of work being produced, because quality is not only encouraged, it's supported by the entire process. That increase in quality leads to increased confidence in the work you're doing, whether you're selling the project or writing the code.

4.1. Cultures Improvements from a Culture of Quality

Beyond that, a culture of quality leads to a culture of empowerment and trust. A culture of quality means your design team is empowered to build in accessibility, even if it changes the stakeholder's initial vision. It means that management trusts their engineers' expertise. It means that people and teams across verticals are empowered to say "Let's do this right", and those decisions are trusted by everyone else.

A culture of quality also leads to a culture of pride. Working within a culture of quality enables you to take pride in your work, because you're confident that it was the best work you knew how to do at the time. Having a company culture where people are empowered and trusted to do their best work, also leads to a culture of morale.

4.2. Morale as a Quality Indicator

Morale is a vital aspect of any company! Good morale within a company gives teams a sense of purpose, working together toward common goals. Morale speaks to the level of psychological safety, which is also really important. Psychological safety means that people feel safe trying new things because mistakes aren't punished. It means people feel comfortable saying "I don't know", because they know they'll be offered opportunities to learn. And morale generally means that people are happy and confident coming to work.

Morale is important to quality because morale is quality indicator. Improved morale is a result of creating this culture; but once it exists, morale becomes a strong part of what allows that culture of quality to thrive. When people and teams have high morale, they feel good about the work they're doing, and they're more engaged in the work. They're willing to take chances and innovate, and they have better relationships with their teammates. In other words, the benefits of morale reinforce the benefits we get from creating a culture of quality in the first place: people working together with a shared goal of improving quality; teams that enjoy coming to work and solving problems together; and a company that is able to have confidence in the work it produces for stakeholders and clients.

5. Creating Your Culture of Quality

How can you use my experiences here to begin creating a culture of quality within your own organization? First and foremost, I hope you take away the idea that you are empowered to begin establishing this culture!

Successfully creating a culture of quality requires effective change management, clear communication, and purposeful collaboration with your colleagues and leadership. Focus on small, incremental changes with feedback loops - make sure the people adjusting to change have their voices heard, and their needs taken into account. Create open lines of communication to build trust and transparency. It helps to give people advance notice before a change goes into effect, so they have time to ask questions and adjust to the new process or workflow. And finally, make sure you're working *with* the people you work with! Involving other people allows them to have a stake in the decisions and changes being made, which increases the likelihood of successfully implementing this culture of quality!

And of course, reap the benefits! A culture of quality enhances your ability to build and launch high-quality products that meet your stakeholders' needs - and that's a culture that benefits everyone.

Agile Software Quality Management

Ian E. Savage

IESavage0000@gmail.com

Abstract

This paper introduces a discipline -- Agile Software Quality Management (ASQM) – to reach consensus on what we will build next to provide the most value to the most people – internal and external.

This discipline, ASQM, is a framework that helps us resolve conflicting product priorities, and to enumerate risks, and to budget for and manage those risks.[1] ASQM uses a new structure for these communications: ***quality priorities tables***.

A cornerstone for ASQM is a usable operational definition of agile quality: Quality for a cycle is some function of the salient product attribute(s) in context for that cycle:

$$\mathbf{Q}_{\text{cycle}} = \mathbf{f}\ (\mathbf{q1}, \ldots, \mathbf{qN})_{\text{cycle}}$$

This definition says that quality varies from place to place and time to time. What is important one day may not be important the next day – you may have solved all of yesterday's problems. Likewise, what is unimportant one day may be pivotal the next. The priority tables may change from day to day and certainly from cycle to cycle.

ASQM relies upon normalizing the Iron Triangle "**project** constraints" of cost, schedule, and scope as **product** qualities. Once these constraints are normalized, they can be prioritized and specified along with any other important quality attributes.

These **quality priorities tables** use existing technology: Vic Basili's Goal-Question-Metric, Robert Grady's (et. al.) FURPS, and Wirfs-Brock's Landing Zones with some small additions by the author.

This paper will be most useful for Agile teams who want more effective cycle/sprint planning and cleaner communications between major players in their eco-systems.

Biography

I've had the pleasure to be associated with some fine communities: Agile Open Northwest, PNSQC, AgilePDX, SAO/TAO, Tech Alliance of Central Oregon, SAO QASIG (TAO Quality Forum) and working in interesting Pacific Northwest firms including Tek, ASG, Bidtek, CFI, Tiger Systems, McAfee, and Intel,

Introduction

Q: What should we test?
A: Whatever keeps you awake.

This paper presents a straightforward way to plan and document your testing objectives in a way that empowers everyone on an Agile team. When we applied part of this at McAfee with good success, the entire company started thinking in terms of quality goals, questions, and metrics.

Teams sometimes "lose their testers" when their company adopts agile methods. That is an antipattern. Another antipattern is to maintain a separate testing organization. The alternative, the one presented in this paper, incorporates solid testing methods from giants in the testing community: Juran, Basili, Grady, Wirfs-Brock, and others. I call it Agile Software Quality Management or ASQM.

The material is presented in five sections:

1. Normalizing the "Iron Triangle" – thereby integrating management people into the "whole team"
2. Quality priorities tables – setting cycle-specific goals and handling the resultant risks
3. An operational definition of quality – a function of "the vital few" qualities (ala Juran)
4. Scaling ASQM – from limited WIP/flow to very large systems (smaller is better)
5. Conversations – examples of priority/quality tradeoff discussions

My proposal: ***Quality priorities***[2] are the elementary drivers of acceptance tests in Agile shops. These quality priorities can be engineered before each implementation cycle - allowing your team to focus on, say, ***performance*** in one cycle, ***security*** in the next, and ***reliability*** in the next. This gives you a logistical framework to promote/demote work within your backlog. At scale, an organization can drive its entire engineering operation using ASQM.

With ASQM all team members are expected to ask questions, suggest improvements, and implement those improvements. It blends quality management techniques with agile software methods to guide and document your path through the management of a software solution.

The paper covers a lot of ground, hopefully in a way that builds usable stuff as it goes. Setting the stage, it begins with a review of the traditional "project constraints" of the Iron Triangle and then smites those constraints. It presents how ASQM varies as WIP limits vary, discusses the efficacy of small cycles, then finishes up with examples of short examples of quality trade-off discussions.

To implement ASQM, organizations adopt a flexible operational definition of quality wherein 1) any quality can become the top priority for a cycle; 2) any team member can promote and champion any quality attribute; and 3) your team extends and adapts ASQM to your projects and your contexts.

Major potential learnings:

- Aligning business goals with engineering goals
- Using metrics to articulate context-specific engineering goals
- Using risk management to select salient quality attributes
- Appreciation for the simplicity of short cycles
- Quality priorities tables that drive design decisions

1. Normalizing the "Iron Triangle"

Q: You really expect senior management to attend iteration planning meetings?
A: If they care, yes. But it's your shop.

1.1. Integrating management into the team

In the current world, circa 2019: schedule, scope, and cost are typically viewed as sacrosanct project constraints that control the course of a development project.[3] And "quality" is "just supposed to emerge" as shown here. Seems like that isn't going per plan in some shops. Let's look at a managed approach:

ASQM asks managers and engineers to jointly decide cycle priorities, goals, and measurements (metrics). Unlike the traditional Iron Triangle and its constraints, the agile team is flat and all team members are expected to contribute. Here's my contribution: I believe Iron Triangle constraints can be recast as ***product qualities*** and managed as other qualities are managed. More on that later.

Perhaps you release every few minutes. Will you hold a meeting for each release? Yes. Members who cannot be present can delegate their vote(s). But it is your shop. Meet how you meet. Do meetings mean clanking chairs, sidebars, loss of focus? No. You can use technology.

Figure 1: Ye Olde Iron Triangle... the ball-and-chain view of projects.

If you think of quality as some amorphous, squishy blob, then dive deeper. Quality is defined in Section 3. It says that the quality of any cycle is some function of the cycle's attainment of its salient attributes.

Data normalization is a stepwise process that creates data structures (tables) that need no special pre-processing to read, write, and operate upon seamlessly. This same normalization technique can be applied to the Iron Triangle – an arbitrary structure that most software companies seem to have adopted that has Schedule, Scope, and Cost as the ***project constraints*** – those things that project management typically handles. But these ***project constraints*** can be normalized such that they can be treated as ***product qualities***. Once normalized, they can be prioritized along with the rest of the product qualities. Specifically, once these transformations are understood, the Iron Triangle fades away because...

Schedule > ***Availability***	*Availability* has an internal and external component (see below)
Scope > ***Capability***	*Capability* is another name for feature / functionality
Cost > ***Affordability***	*Affordability* also has an internal and external component

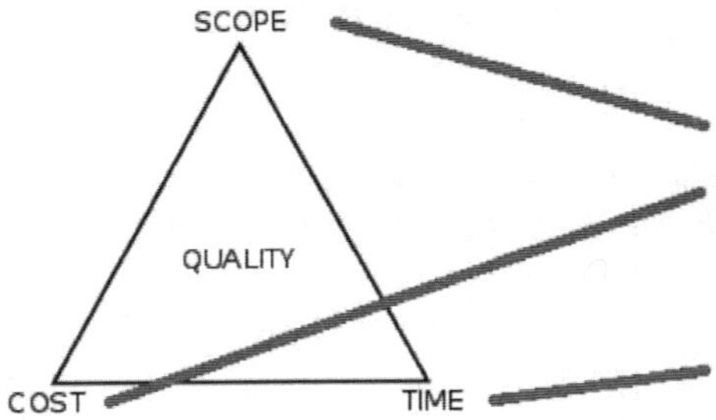

Priority	Questions	Metrics	Method	Lower Limit	Upper Limit
Capability					
Affordability		1. Sprint budget 2. Cost to buyer			
Availability					

Figure 2: Recasting the constraints as qualities

Why recast the project constraints as product qualities? Two reasons:

1. doing so makes them easy to define, measure and track.
2. it elevates project management and general management to the same level as the "Whole Team" and puts them at the same table, facing the same direction.

Once accepted as the norm, the prioritization process becomes more direct and effective, the team works better because all the members understand 1) the business and 2) the technology that will be used. See also Jeremy Lightsmith's Lean Coffee.

Once the project constraints are normalized, they become product qualities that can be prioritized along with all the familiar quality attributes - the "ilities" and others – as shown in Figure 2.

1.2. Implications

Once the "project constraints" are recognized as manageable product qualities, they can be evaluated, ranked, and prioritized along with all the other quality attributes. The next section shows how that might look in three different environments: a limited WIP shop, a more traditional software shop, and a big shop.

For now, let's look at the high-level implications:

1. Project management, program management, and people management will rethink their roles. They may all want to be involved in deciding the cycle goals, and some will want to help manage the backlog queue in a hands-on way. That is, some will be more involved than others in cycle planning and micro decisions making.

2. Software engineers will rethink their role as code adders and realize they need a clear understanding and appreciation for quality attributes in general and for the business-related stuff: product direction, market opportunities, value chain planning and mapping, etc. so they make better detailed design and coding decisions.

3. To facilitate those two things, both groups will need to actively listen to one another's issues and concerns. This non-trivial change changes their lives and the organization for the better. This is the big payday. The demise of the Iron Triangle removes barriers between organizational units: There is no longer a need for a separate PM/PO and for disconnected general management. Everyone gets on the bus and speaks in the same language. In any

given context, our oral and written communications are less error-prone when we use the same words and definitions. Every team needs people who listen for ambiguity (topical, lexical, and deeper) and point it out.

4. In general, this expands the set of Agile practitioners to include general management (who are mostly concerned with ***profitability*** and ***affordability***) and product management (who are mostly concerned with ***availability*** and ***capability***). Expanding the set of Agile practitioners to include these managers in quality planning brings the true whole team to the table and gives them a framework to discuss salient attributes in context. In ASQM, the whole team can decide which qualities are important, what questions the testing must answer, the things to be measured to answer those questions, and the lower-limit and upper-limit (the "landing zones") for each quality.

Summary: Normalizing the Iron Triangle's project constraints into measurable quality attributes:

- equalizes decision making
- opens dialogs
- allows direct comparison of qualities based on their merits and the business conditions

The next section demonstrates how to create and manage a **Quality Priorities table** based on quality attributes, and discusses the differences between:

qualities-to-assure,
risks-to-manage, and
risks-to-accept.

2. Quality Priorities Tables

Q: Suppose we adopt this "everyone is equal" mentality. How does that help?
A: It enables simpler prioritizing.

2.1. (New) Quality Priorities Tables

Since schedule, scope, and cost become ***availability***, ***capability***, and ***affordability***, that "terrible triad of tyranny," the Iron Triangle, is no longer operant. We need it no longer. Indeed, the death of that Iron Triangle frees us to compare qualities directly – on a level playing field.

Focusing on one quality attribute affects design decisions made during that cycle/iteration. If ***security*** is your primary focus, your software will have fewer attack surfaces. If ***performance*** is your primary focus, you may have more attack surfaces – and you will make those design decisions mindfully.

Quality priorities tables allow us to responsibly answer the difficult question: "How will we know the product is ready for prime time?" **Answer: When all the landing zones are green, we ship it.**

But ASQM holds potential for more than rigorous quality assurance. It also can change your daily life. Normalizing the Iron Triangle constraints into simple product quality attributes is a sea change for organizations that have siloed functional groups like Product Management, Sales and Marketing, Development, Maintenance, Testing/QA. These departments will not instantly disappear, they will fade away once the organization coalesces around short release cycles with consensus on small, well-defined increments.

Note: ***Affordability*** and ***availability*** may always be in your Quality Priorities tables. Don't be overly concerned... that's a reasonable business decision. With the constant involvement of managers on the team, engineers will gain more appreciation for those business realities.

Your team will eventually reach its equilibrium as your team goes through the forming, norming, storming team maturation stages. Norms develop and practices synchronize. As co-equal qualities, ***affordability*** and ***availability*** take shape through several cycles, and your team eventually finds its proper and fitting risk aversion/acceptance level. Juran, in his watershed book on quality control (*sic*), taught us that quality assurance is simply a matter of assisting management to make good decisions.

The other face of the test/risk coin is risk. We test because we want knowledge about our software. But because we cannot test everything, we must live with some risk. Quality priority tables give us the tool we need to juxtapose our testing against our risk analysis – to present the complete test plan for any cycle.

So, here is the new playing field. The Quality Priorities table with three sections represent descending magnitude of risk:

Qualities to Assure						
Priority	**Questions**	**Metric**	**Method**	**Lower Limit**	**Upper Limit**	**Result(s) [Red | Green]**
Most important property						
Next MIP (optional)						
...						
Last MIP (optional)						

Risks to Monitor						
Risk	**What is the risk?**	**Probability**	**Potential Impact $**	**Risk Budget $**	**Trigger**	**Mitigation**
Highest risk						
Next highest risk						
...						
Last high risk						
Risks to Accept						
Ignorable risks 1...	**What is the risk?**	**Probability**	**Potential Impact $**	**Avoidance measures**	**Reasons**	**References**

Figure 3: The Quality Priorities table layout

2.1.1. Qualities to Assure

These are the properties that are critical to the success of the current release. If any of the qualities in this section are not met (i.e. they do not fall between the Lower Limit and Upper Limit), the software is not ready for release. Fewer entries in this section means the less overall testing is needed. Ideally, N = [0|1] (lowest possible WIP).

Priority ~ which property is critical and must be measured/tracked? Example: ***Reliability***

Question ~ question(s) we have about this priority. Example: "What is the uptime?"

Metric ~ the specific thing we will measure. Example: (uptime) / (uptime + downtime)

Method ~ how we will gain that information? Example: automated monitoring

Lower Limit ~ four nines (99.99%)

Upper Limit ~ five nines (99.999%)

Result(s) [Red | Green] ~ [red | green | yellow | {}]

2.1.2. Risks to Monitor

These second-tier properties indicate some quantifiable risk to the organization. To qualify for this section, a property must be something that would cause an interruption in the flow of software to end users, operations/production, or whatever is appropriate for your shop. Actively managing this second section indicates a healthy team.

Risk ~ which property presents a risk? Example: ***Usability***

What is the risk? ~ A short description such as "New UX will be rejected by some customers."

Probability ~ A number between zero and one. (Risks with a probability of zero can be accepted.)

Potential Impact $ ~ What's the most money the organization could lose if the risk occurs?

Risk Budget $ ~ Probability * Potential Impact $. Budget this much to prepare for risk occurrences.

Trigger ~ The thing(s) that tell us that the risk has occurred.

Mitigation ~ The thing(s) we will do to control the effects of the risk using the Risk Budget.

2.1.3. Risks to Accept

These are the dicey areas that every company accepts every day without documenting it. Put your very best people in charge of these **risks to accept** because there's no money allocated to deal with these problems. Your best people can smell problems and they can navigate organizational chutes and ladders to prepare the organization for potential failures in these low-probability areas.

These people must have the organizational horsepower to elevate a risk into Section 2 or even Section 1. Mid-level managers can be effective risk analysts.

This third section lets you enumerate qualities you are expressly NOT testing. This is an important list. You will make mistakes of omission and of commission. Learn from each mistake. Don't take these low-running risks lightly. These risks are not negligible.

Just like Lean Coffee topics, attributes are reprioritized continually or after each delivery using something super simple like index cards or PostIt® notes. As Ward Cunningham and Kent Beck say: "What's the simplest thing that could possibly work?" If you choose to reprioritize continually, make sure all team members are advised quickly – the goals of the next cycle can affect their design decisions in the current cycle.

2.2. Example Quality Priorities/Risks

Below are a few examples quality priorities tables. Your issues are different so your mileage will vary.

2.2.1. Safety first

"***Safety*** is our highest priority" says the aircraft supplier, "but we need to get our planes back into operation ASAP." Okay, the first two lines of our Quality Priorities table – our top two priorities – would be ***Safety*** and ***Availability***:

Qualities to Assure						
Priority	**Questions**	**Metric**	**Method**	**Lower Limit**	**Upper Limit**	**Result(s)**
Safety	Do our planes have fatal software flaws? How many lesser flaws do we have?	Unhandled faults Weighted MTBF	Static analysis Evaluating failures found in “final test” (simulations, exploratory testing, etc.)	zero zero hours	zero[4] 10 hours[5]	Green[6] Red
Availability	When can our planes fly again?	Calendar	Track remediation progress vs plan	January	June	Yellow

Risks to Monitor						
Risk	**What is the risk?**	**Probability**	**Potential Impact $**	**Risk Budget $**	**Trigger**	**Mitigation**
Marketability – short term	Reduced customer acceptance	25%	$500m	$125m	Largest customers place orders with competitors	Deep discounts for early adopters

Certifiability	FAA reluctance	50%	$100m	$50m	Planes grounded beyond EOY	Constant contact with FAA
Risks to Accept						
Risk	**What is the risk?**	**Probability**	**Potential Impact $**	**Avoidanc e measures**	**Reasons**	**References**
Marketability – long term	Substantial loss of market share	low	All of it	Constant market analysis	Senior mgmt approval	Internal restricted access docs.
Others		high	$100m	TBD	No data	N/A

Figure 4: Hypothetical Quality Priorities table – safety as primary driver

2.2.2. Cash is king

"We are in business to make money. *Profitability* is our highest priority" says the CFO and the GMs agree.[7]

Qualities to Assure						
Priority	**Questions**	**Metric**	**Method**	**Lower Limit**	**Upper Limit**	**Result(s)**
Profitability	Are we competitive?	Net return from operations	GAAP	20%	N/A	Green[8]
	Are we improving?	Total CoQ and YoY financial results.	CoQ tracking	-10% / year	-20% / year	Red

Risks to Monitor						
Risk	**What is the risk?**	**Probability**	**Potential Impact $**	**Risk Budget $**	**Trigger**	**Mitigation**
Marketability – short term	Reduced customer acceptance	25%	$500m	$125m	Largest customers place orders with competitors	Deep discounts for early adopters
Certifiability	FAA reluctance	50%	$100m	$50m	Planes grounded beyond EOY	Constant contact with FAA
Risks to Accept						
Risk	**What is the risk?**	**Probability**	**Potential Impact $**	**Avoidanc e measures**	**Reasons**	**References**
Marketability – long term	Substantial loss of market share	low	All of it	Competitiv e analyses	Senior mgmt approval	Internal restricted access docs.
Others		high	$100m	Unknown	N/A	N/A

Figure 5: Hypothetical Quality Priorities table – profitability as primary driver

2.2.3 Maslow's favorite

"***Security*** is our highest priority" say the security providers and many companies.[9]

Qualities to Assure						
Priority	**Questions**	**Metric**	**Method**	**Lower Limit**	**Upper Limit**	**Result(s)**
Security	Is it penetrable? Does it fail safely?	Successful breaches Privilege elevations	Penetration testing Be-bugging	Zero zero privilege escalations	Zero zero privilege escalations	two zero
Risks to Monitor						
Risk	**What is the risk?**	**Probability**	**Potential Impact $**	**Risk Budget $**	**Trigger**	**Mitigation**
Availability	Memory leakage	20%	$100k	$20k	Leakage observed in sys tools	Memory tracing
Performance		10%	$100k	$10k	Throughput degradation	Performance monitoring
Risks to Accept						
Risk	**What is the risk?**	**Probability**	**Potential Impact $**	**Avoidance measures**	**Reasons**	**References**
Testability	UI changes break our GUI tests	20%	$20k	UX team involvement	Status quo	See John Doe

Figure 6: Another hypothetical Quality Priorities table – security

2.3. Other continuing agile testing of course

Using these quality priority tables to test the salient qualities is insufficient by itself. Several other testing practices (such as those listed below) are employed by responsible agile teams. These are part of the team's rhythm and do not need to be repeated in each cycle's quality priorities table.

- TDD / BDD
- T2B (top two boxes on customer feedback)
- Automated, randomized capability testing (background processing) to simulate production
- Analytics and telemetry
- Exploratory testing

Repetitive manual regression testing (which has an impossibly low ROI) is expressly excluded from this list of high ROI testing methods. It is replaced by1) automated, randomized capability (feature/functionality) testing and 2) frequent unit test executions with no tolerance for broken tests.

3. Background: Operational Definition of "Quality"

Q: Where do we put QA?
A: She leads the meetings.

So finally, we get to the question "What is quality?" This question comes around every time we have a significant change in software paradigms. Obviously, we have experienced such a change with the advent of lightweight / agile methods around the turn of the century.[10]

Agile software engineering can be scary: What do we do without testers? How do we engineers test software? How do we know it's good enough? Relax, breathe, all will be fine. ASQM gives us a simple way to plan and execute software testing and to reach consensus on 1) what will be built and 2) when it is truly ready for use in production ("done done").

As seen above, ASQM provides a framework to communicate about important software goals. It helps us to resolve conflicting product objectives, set priorities, and to enumerate and manage risks. ASQM uses these new quality priorities tables work through these difficult and important communications. But these priorities tables require an operational definition of quality – one that promotes action and limits risk. Here is that definition:

For any cycle, quality is a function of the salient quality attributes for that cycle in context:

$$\mathbf{Q_{cycle} = f\,(q1, \ldots, qN)_{cycle}}$$

That is... the quality of any deliverable is some function of its salient attributes.

This definition asserts that quality is context sensitive, it varies from cycle to cycle as the needs of the team change with each cycle. As you have seen above, each of the important qualities – q1 through qN – have their own metrics and targets / acceptable limits. The fewer, the better.

This context-sensitive, cycle-specific operational definition of quality lets us create better software by using quality priorities tables focused on important quality attributes.[11]

So why do we need this new tool (quality priority tables) and this new definition of quality (function of salient attributes)? Because software quality is definable, it is discussable, it is manageable. And it helps everyone in your development stack by identifying where you will focus your testing efforts, what you consider as success, what risks you are assuming and what risks you are tracking.

The following sections discuss how these quality priority tables help management, product owners, and engineering.

3.1. Helping management

An operational definition of quality suggests a strategy to resolve conflicting requirements and, significantly, to include general management and product management on the "whole team" and thusly eliminate appeals to higher authorities and opaque office politics. This reduces the "hidden factory"[12] that saps an organization's energy and profits. As you saw in Section 1, engaging these management types in quality goal setting is as simple as recasting schedule, scope, and cost as product attributes and inviting them to join your decision-making.

3.2. Helping project management / owners

Product owners are caught between two worlds: management and engineering. Successful POs have great organizational skills and technical skills. ASQM gives them a tablet they can use to defining "quality" for the next iteration. And it gives them a template that provides a limited lexicon to bound those quality discussions.

3.3. Helping engineering

Effective use of ASQM gives engineers specific quality targets and provides them and management with visibility and alignment. Quality priorities tables also make engineers wade into the management world of risk analysis and mitigation. Risk management is the other side of the testing coin. Product qualities that present a significant risk are tested. Qualities that fall below the must-be-tested threshold are then treated as risks – some that require monitoring (e.g. with triggers and mitigations) and some that do not require rigorous monitoring but need the attention of your best players. Agreeing on the cut-lines between these sets is non-trivial and it is the gist and grist of ASQM.

3.4. Silo-busting

To implement ASQM, an organization starts by understanding the normalization described above, articulating any serious blocking issues, and filling out a quality priorities table. Once your team has defined cycle quality a few times, then you can extend the model as appropriate for your context.[13] And the PO/PMs among you can talk with your fellow PMBOKs, the managers to other managers, and engineers to other engineers.

But don't stay in those silos. If you find ASQM useful, gather your comrades and share. Every product group deserves a couple evangelists.

The rest of this paper presents how ASQM varies as WIP limits – speaking to the efficacy of small cycles and finishes up with a few examples of quality trade-offs:

- ***affordability*** vs ***X***
- ***affordability*** *vs* ***availability*** vs ***reliability***
- ***affordability*** vs ***availability*** vs ***capability***

- ***affordability*** vs ***availability*** vs ***performance***
- ***affordability*** vs ***availability*** vs ***security***

4. Scaling ASQM

Q: Is ASQM for everyone?
A: Some orgs might be too big.

Will it scale… this Agile Software Quality Management?

Since we are talking about a new field, let's consider how those four words may relate to one another. Then we'll talk about scaling.

On its surface, the term ASQM has several possible meanings. Deciding as a team your definition of ASQM will set the course for your team. Agile can succeed at any level of the organization – it's basically adopting a pattern of inspection and adaptation. Results will vary depending on several factors such as the proportion of skilled Agile Level 2 team members (see Cockburn) and management commitment to active participation.

But are we talking about the agile management of software quality or the quality of agile software management? You decide. It is your organization. You are responsible for your responses to your organization's needs. As your team matures, you can make structural and organizational changes to deliver even better results on a team-by-team basis.

Will your successes be repeatable? Probably. ASQM grows by word of mouth. Success breeds success. If you will feel comfortable with goal-driven engineering, you will feel comfortable improving your capabilities and you will get good value from quality priorities tables. However, if you have scaled agile by simply relabeling your legacy processes, then you will get some value from using quality priorities tables but not the organizational transformation that ASQM can provide.

If you try to expand one super-huge instance of ASQM, your challenges will be many. Big projects will always have big project problems. Sorry. The idea of small goals and quick feedback is antithetical to big projects.

There is hope. Large organizations with extremely well-defined interfaces, low coupling, high cohesion, excellent customer involvement, a quality improvement ethos, learning organizations with compassionate management, etc. those organizations can make ASQM work. Let the author know how that goes. The main problem is that huge projects always have too much communication because there are too many communication channels. That is a subject for a different paper but see "Old and Big" in the table below.

There is no hypothetical size limit for ASQM: the quality priorities tables are resizable. You can test as many qualities as your context indicates, likewise with risks. Of course, your teammates may pull you back from the brink during planning – hey, pay attention – you want fewer items, not more. The more qualities in the mix, the more interdependencies you have between qualities, and the more task switching (lost time, technical debt, and frustration) you will experience.

If you are looking to consolidate reporting, to aggregate data for corporate reasons, you may struggle. The leading "A" of ASQM[14] means Agile approaches work best in small groups. Some authors, notably Jorgen Hesselberg, have written persuasively about enterprise transformation. It is non-trivial. Communication becomes less reliable as team size increases. If you find yourselves in a "***thar be dragons***" mode of writing big one-size-fits-all programs and policies and procedures, stop and rethink your commitment to your customers. Agile doesn't fit some organizations. See also Larsen and Shore's Agile Fluency work.

But scaling goes both ways: bigger and smaller. What would happen if you put energy into making cycles as short as possible? What would happen if you assure just one quality per cycle? My contention is that as the cycle time goes to zero, the risk associated with secondary quality attributes goes to zero. If so, then driving down the cycle time to its absolute minimum would drive down the number of defects inserted into the software. This remains an open question and worthy of more study. See also #NoProjects and #NoEstimates on Twitter.

For now, let's focus on the more typical projects: large, medium, and small. The table below divides software engineering shops into those three sizes – you can supply your own magnitudes.

Project Size	Team Size	Zeitgeist
Old and Big	Characteristics: Many people, perspectives, alliances, motives, styles, plans, desires. Many misunderstandings, corners cut, late projects, stress.	"the software problem" 1950s-present
Middling	Characteristics: Fewer side effects than with big projects. Team size limited by cognitive capacity - the rule of seven plus or minus two. Well-defined modules, data, and interfaces	Structured Systems RUP 1980-present
Small	Characteristics: Tests as guardrails for more continuous testing. Limited WIP. many:1 sets of eyes (pairing, mobbing). Large automated test-base that keeps the rubber on the road. Extremely few bugs. Excellent customer relationships. Better predictability.	ZD for software DevOps 2000-present

4.1. Implications for large, medium, small WIP shops

Most organizations aim for growth at any cost… at their peril. As Larsen and Shore (cited above) have taught us with their Agile Fluency work, different organizations should be at different levels of agile fluency because their business doesn't require full dials-to-11 agile software engineering capabilities.

4.1.1. Implications for large WIP shops (aka "Big Projects")

Large organizations with large projects must track more qualities than smaller orgs with smaller projects. Large projects affect more things. So, your quality priorities tables may have many qualities in the "Test" section and many concerns listed in the "Risk" sections. It could have five, 10, 15 qualities and even more risks to manage.[15]

Some qualities are interdependent, so some effects are complex. My advice is to simplify as much as possible and when interdependencies remain, include all the related qualities, set targets for each, then simplify by aggregating into a placeholder quality attribute such as "***Maintainability****-related goals.*"[16] Whatever works in your environment/context... inspect and adapt.

Management/Engineering cost is exponential with size, not linear. Many small, well-defined projects with well-defined interfaces, are easier and less expensive to manage.

Expected results of ASQM in large shops

Lots of meetings, lots of closed-door meetings, some alignment meetings

Levels of approval and synchronization

Big roll-out after several "dogfooding" trials

Early adopters, early majority, late majority, but not the stalwarts. Offer them a severance.

4.1.2. Implications for medium WIP shops

Somewhat smaller companies are better prepared than the behemoths to make quick moves. Smaller companies can adopt ASQM easier than large companies. They have demonstrated to themselves the efficacy and sufficient quality of their products. But now the world changes. Disruptive stuff happens. Adapt.

Expected results of ASQM in medium shops

Some buy-in trouble. Structured systems are very attractive. Listen acutely to the nay-sayers – they may be right – radical engineering isn't for everyone. Listening is the only way to find consensus.

4.1.3. Implications for small WIP shops

Already in the habit of working closely with customers and delivering value frequently, small shops can take more risks. Small companies can pivot. The most they stand to lose is the WIP – a week or two (or less) of work. A well-run small company is eager for finding and filling market spaces. You don't bet the company on any one project. You don't need to because over the months and years, you have reinvested all those well-earned Tugmans into evolving your organization's quality culture.

Small companies can grok the idea of having only one item in WIP [see also mob programming]. As a steppingstone to straight-through-processing [see Product Flow], the team can have multiple small feature teams: two to four people if those people can represent the various departments in your organization. Feature teams can work in parallel and must keep current with design changes from adjacent feature teams. No big problem. The team can work out their resolution norms with working agreements / terms of engagement.

Expected results of ASQM in small shops

Extremely nimble business moves

Ability to disrupt major markets

Very high ROI with very small losses

4.2. Cycle duration

Like organizational size, cycle size greatly influences your ability to implement Agile and ASQM.

4.2.1. Huge cycles

N/A. Huge cycles cannot exist in Agile environment unless we use artificial meanings for "huge" and "Agile." Big, old projects had far too many people, creating far too many associations and queues to be effective. That's why so many projects from the last century ended in failure.

In these agile times, using huge cycles require suppression of disbelief, or magical thinking.

4.2.2. Middling cycles

The middling-size cycle is most common in this second decade of the twenty-first century. This is the "chaordic edge" that Jim Highsmith recommends we agilists skate along. If we are too comfortable, we're not engage enough, not pushing ourselves hard enough. If we are too uncomfortable, we might crash.

As a purist, I feel that these one-week or two-week iterations are a mistake. They mask inefficiencies and ineffectiveness. They allow engineers to move undone work to next cycles without analyzing their failures.

4.2.3. Tiny cycles – Limiting risk by limiting scope

Using tiny cycles requires diligence. In Agile we want frequent releases and quick feedback. Inspect and adapt is even more important than delivering working software because adaptations allow more effective delivery for all of time.

Also, the smaller the changes, the fewer side effects generally, so lower risk.

It may be possible to focus on one quality for some cycles because the cycle is tiny, the testing drives the change(s), and the change is well-understood (e.g. easily explainable to a teammate on a white board).

4.3. Quality planning with ASQM

Now here's the big payoff: These quality priority tables can be used to engineer your software solutions.

4.3.1. Run/Drive Engineering

"The spec is the test." Therefore, the test is the spec by the identity principle. When we practice test-driven development (TDD), we are intentionally equating the specification (typically an early/left activity) with test planning (typically a late/right activity).

Since quality priorities tables specify each goal – including the acceptance criteria – these quality planning tables can also be used to implement the desired change(s). They can specify ***capability*** changes (formerly feature/functionality) as easily as any other quality. Indeed, once implemented, they can be deployed and sent along with the modified software to the IV&V[17] group or to the customer.

4.3.2. Qualities normalize the Iron Triangle constraints

As we saw in Section 2, ***availability***, ***affordability***, and ***capability*** are the Agile quality equivalents of schedule, cost, and scope. And they always need to be considered. A product team must have a very good reason to put them low in the priorities queue. These are very important qualities as evidenced by their traditional assignment to very important people in organizations: product managers, general managers, and such. Once these people are convinced that they can take a seat at the table, they become members of the "Whole Team" that Agilists speak about. They are no longer just welcome to attend planning meetings;

they are expected to do so. That supercharges Agile teams as they get into their define-develop-deliver rhythm.

The presence of these manager types on your "whole team" gives your team the horsepower needed to refine and decompose product direction into epics and from epics into stories. The three "project constraints" over time will wither away as more teams in your organization adopt the quality priorities approach.

As your customers and management team become more involved, your discussions about the next MVP[18] become more meaningful, your communications improve, and you know that you deliver usable stuff on Friday (for instance). Your sales and marketing people will know it, too. You may hear the aircraft supplier say "***Safety*** is our highest priority, yes. But we also must have it by Friday. Yes, you can increase the sprint budget by up to 15%." The quality priorities tables support these multi-dimensional product needs.

5. Conversations re: Competing Qualities

Q: Which quality is more important?
A: Let's talk here and now.

Salient qualities drive design decisions. For instance, a focus on ***performance*** would have completely different effects than a focus on ***security***. One result of a focus on ***performance*** would be to have fewer page swaps whereas a focus on ***security*** would tend to have fewer attack surfaces. So, the practice of partitioning **capability** (nee ***functionality***) into modules may differ from cycle to cycle.

Because the focus will change from time to time, we must not paint ourselves into corners – unless we like spending time rewriting systems. And if we rewrite systems, we still must decide which are our most important aspects/properties/qualities from time to time as context varies.

Below are some imaginary conversations about which quality should be superordinate and which subordinate.

5.1. Affordability vs X

Affordability is the biggie, so the biggies get to call this dance. Your company's president may well want to see how this works. When she does, she will be an active participant in the detailed planning. She will always be interested in ***affordability***. That's how important ***affordability*** is – those people with P/L responsibility are ultimately responsible for significant costs, losses, and profits. And garden variety quality is important: A colleague of mine once used this example: "Volkswagens and Mercedes both have brakes. The latter are better."

There are two parts to ***affordability***: 1) what does it cost the company to produce it 2) what are the customers costs (initial and ongoing).

Affordability 1: Producer's cost

Initial cost to develop (planning and execution)

market (requirements, rollout)

support costs

Affordability 2: Customer costs:

Initial cost layout

Purchasing decision, hardware, software, internal support

Installation costs

Support costs

Will it take some money? Will it pay for itself? When? Like many other quality improvement efforts – and ASQM certainly will improve quality – there are initial startup costs. Yes. But the costs avoided by having common understandings about the cycles content will pay for themselves almost immediately. The guardrails provided by the automated tests will pay for themselves many times over.

5.2. Affordability, Availability, Reliability

Availability: For the purposes of this example ***availability*** means when the software will be ready for the customer or, for large shops, general ***availability***.

Let's suppose ***affordability***, ***availability***, and ***reliability*** are selected as the three salient qualities. How would the discussion go?

> ***Affordability*** champion: "This must cost the customers less than $8k and it cannot cost us any more than 20 person-weeks."
>
> ***Availability*** champion: "Person-weeks? Oh, okay I get it. Well I need the first three epics done by Thanksgiving for the big blast-off."
>
> ***Reliability*** champion: "Do all three of those epics need everything we've specified? I fear that we are over-committed. Can any of those epics be beta quality?"
>
> ***Affordability*** champ: "What do you mean by 'beta quality'?"
>
> ***Reliability*** champ: "Is 99% uptime good enough?"
>
> ***Affordability*** champ: "What's that mean '99%'?"
>
> ***Reliability*** champ: "The software will be up 99% of the time users need it."
>
> ***Affordability*** champ: "That'll work for the Thanksgiving demo."

5.3. Affordability, Availability, Capability

About ***capability***: Software shops using some form of test-driven development (TDD) will be able to appreciate this advice: Don't wait until some arbitrarily late point in your development cycle to verify that the expected functionality is present and performs as expected. In these times, feature functionality / ***capability*** really must be demonstrated before quality attributes testing begins. Goals for ***affordability*** and ***availability*** are more attainable when basic ***functionality*** is treated as an entry criterion to acceptance testing. [See EITVOX]

Therefore, an ***affordability***, ***availability***, ***capability*** quality priorities table may not be necessary. This radical advice will be adopted slowly. It is an outright rejection of the beat-it-to-fit/paint-it-to-match mentality.

5.4. Affordability, Availability, Performance

Performance is always a concern – ever since the manned moon missions in the late 1960s. The USA was challenged to send a man to the moon and return him safely to Earth by the end of that decade. We didn't have the abilities and certainly didn't have the technology – we had to dream it up – starting from scratch...

> ***Performance*** champion: "We need to minimize the weight of everything. How much does the software weigh?"
>
> ***Affordability*** champion: "I don't care about that. We will spend whatever it takes to win the race."
>
> ***Performance*** champion: "I must know the weight of everything on the vehicle."
>
> ***Availability*** champion: "Wait. Software has no weight."
>
> ***Performance*** champion: "What?! Everything has a weight. Don't risk the mission!"
>
> ***Availability*** champion: "Okay. You see this punch card?"
>
> ***Performance*** champion: "Yes (thinking 'now we're getting somewhere.')"
>
> ***Availability*** champion: "You see these holes?"
>
> ***Performance*** champion: "Yes, yes of course (thinking "now we're getting somewhere)."
>
> ***Availability*** champion: "Add up the weight of all these holes and that's the weight of the software."
>
> [Decision: Software does not present a weight risk.]

5.5. Affordability, Availability, and Security

> ***Security*** champ: "***Security*** is everything. We could lose the business with another vulnerability like that last one. Let's get it right or call it quits."
>
> ***Affordability*** champ: "Well, we only have so many resources for that task."
>
> ***Availability*** champ:" We can outsource most of that verification, right?"
>
> ***Security*** champ: "If we want our enemies to know our vulnerabilities."
>
> ***Affordability*** champ: "Oh – good point. Let's double the budget. I'll talk with the CFO."

6. Conclusion, Summary, Further Research

The idea that we can fully specify an iteration using quality priorities does not appear elsewhere in the literature. <u>Some</u> in the software world still believe that manually rerunning test cases – mind-dulling, soul-stealing ***functionality*** testing – is a good way to qualify products for distribution. That is way too primitive. Those days were never here – we never needed brute force functionality testing. It is wasteful and – NOW – it has been superseded by quality priorities tables and continually reworking the backlog.

Applications of ASQM outside of software seem easy to find. After all, what is a thing other than some function of its attributes? Perhaps there are some non-attributes that help describe things. The author would like to know.

It is entirely possible that an organization with multiple related teams can employ synchronized/parallel small cycles. That is outside the scope of the present paper. The author would also like to know your experiences with that: How are the teams related? How do they interact? Please share the near term and long-term results.

References

Traditional Iron Triangle defined: https://en.wikipedia.org/wiki/Project_management_triangle (accessed August 16, 2019).

Dr. Victor Basili's (University of Maryland): Goal, Question, Metric: https://en.wikipedia.org/wiki/GQM (accessed August 16, 2019).

Grady, Robert; Caswell, Deborah (1987). *Software Metrics: Establishing a Company-wide Program*. Prentice Hall. p. 159. ISBN 0-13-821844-7.

Juran, Joseph: https://www.juran.com/blog/a-guide-to-the-pareto-principle-80-20-rule-pareto-analysis/ (accessed August 16, 2019).

---

[1] Testing after all is an exercise in risk management.

[2] In this paper these terms are basically equivalent: qualities, attributes, goals, properties, priorities.

[3] Indeed, this author previously held that prudent project managers should assign Fixed, Firm, Flexible, or Fluid to project constraints.

[4] Typically, the UL will differ from the LL. But releasing critical flight systems software with known fatal flaws is indefensible so the UL is zero – you cannot ship known-defective mission-critical software.

[5] See "defect density" calculations."

[6] The Results column enables Quality Priorities tables to be used as BODs (big overhead displays).

[7] This makes sense only for software that is NOT safety-critical, e.g. games.

[8] These Quality Priorities tables can be used as BODs (big overhead displays) via this Results column.

[9] Software security people say there are two categories of companies: those that have been hacked and those that don't know they have been hacked.

[10] While the agile movement is typically associated with the Agile Manifesto, several lightweight methods were gaining popularity in the late 1990s.

[11] Other than this footnote, you will not see "non-functional requirements" anywhere in this paper. The term non-functional already has a meaning in natural language: broken. It serves no purpose in the software industry. Quality attributes are not broken.

[12] http://knowledgehills.com/six-sigma/cost-quality-defects-hidden-factory.htm

[13] The author would love to hear your experiences implementing ASQM. Use the email atop this paper.

[14] Resources abound about software quality management – Weinberg's Systems Thinking is an excellent starting point.

[15] A student asked whether all the IEEE quality attributes would appear in one of these Quality Priorities tables. I believe the answer is "Yes, and in the real world of practicalities, not very often."

[16] Maintainability-related qualities include serviceability, extensibility, portability, and others.

[17] IV&V = Independent Validation and Verification. In the software world it is incorrectly called "QA."

[18] MVP = Minimum Viable Product

Agile Where Agile Fears To Tread!

Thomas M Cagley Jr.
Tom Cagley & Associates LLC
tcagley@tomcagley.com

Abstract
Over the years managers have told many stories about why Agile cannot work and software development using Agile can't be tested. These are excuses to avoid change. They were not valid then and they are not valid now. Taking a less prescriptive definition has allowed teams to create hybrids of lean and Agile techniques to address real-world testing work that spans the entirety of an organization's priorities. Join Tom Cagley as he shares five key scenarios that are cited in which Agile "don't" work. Tom will explore each fallacy and provide insights into practical solutions. He will also explain why testing of all types is often the key to making Agile work, providing a palette of techniques to enable rather than avoid adaptive techniques. You do not want to miss this opportunity to hear how Tom's years of experience in Agile has led to very decisive solutions to address your challenges.

Biography
Tom Cagley is president of Tom Cagley & Associates. He actively seeks out process problems across the development environment and facilitates problem-solving. Mr. Cagley has over 20 years of experience in the software industry. He has held technical and managerial positions in different industries as a leader in software methods and metrics, quality assurance and systems analysis. Mr. Cagley is a frequent speaker at metrics, quality and project management conferences. His areas of expertise encompass management experience in methods and metrics, quality integration, quality assurance and the application of the SEI's CMMI® to achieve process improvements. Mr. Cagley is the past president of the International Function Point Users Group. He also is an active podcaster, hosting and editing the Software Process and Measurement Cast (www.spamcast.net) and blogger (www.tcagley.wordpress.com).

1. Agile Where Agile Fears to Tread
In 1516, a few weeks before the modern project management and new team-based program management approaches, a Bavarian nobleman enacted the Reinheitsgebot[i] (German Beer Purity Law). The law defined the ingredients in beer. Water, hops, and barley was the one true set of ingredients. There are those that want to set and enforce similar purity laws for modern methods and frameworks. For some, Agile is Scrum, Extreme Programming, SAFe, or Kanban. The argument is that you need to pick one but never combine approaches to address your specific culture or scenario. Combining frameworks is a bridge too far. Requiring framework or technique purity is a false requirement, and is often used to eschew less command and control concepts and techniques in certain situations.

These are five scenarios which are often used as examples where Agile is difficult or daren't go:

1. Mainframe Development and Enhancements

2. Maintenance
3. Commercial Off The Shelf Packages (COTS)
4. Software as a Service (SaaS)
5. Outsourced (Contract) Work

Mainframe: The reasons generally quoted for why Agile can't be used revolve around three macro issues. The first is that large mainframe projects are hard to break up into a component that is deliverable in a short iteration. The second is that much of what goes on in this environment happens behind the scenes. Lots of work occurs in batch processes or in file transfers that have no user interfaces, so its difficult to involve users or the business. Third, when not doing large projects, most teams complete many small enhancements and fixes.

Maintenance: The rationale quoted for why maintenance doesn't fit Agile is typically two-fold. The first is a problem with the difficulty in planning many projects of varied sizes that are typically put into the maintenance bucket. The second and potentially more problematic issue is the emergence of significant production issues that require priority.

COTS: The major issue of fitting Agile into a COTS project is transparency. The firm that builds (or owns the software) has its own process and will deliver what they deliver when they deliver it. A related problem is that most testing is a black box (hard to know what is happening with the code) negating the power of test-driven development.

SaaS: This type of software has concerns similar to COTS with the complication of the software running in the cloud. Why does it matter 'where' the software lives?

Outsourced Work: Issues in this scenario include lack of transparency, contract structure, delivery cadence and potentially testing/acceptance processes.

In each of the five scenarios, the reasons quoted for why Agile can't work have been used over the years to avoid change. They lacked validity then, and they are not valid now. Rather than asking why adaptive approaches won't work, a better question is how can we address the 12 principles in the Manifesto[ii] using a mixture of frameworks and techniques to deliver value. Agile is currently the buzzword *du jour* in IT departments across the world. As the frenzy has grown, the definition of the word has become - fuzzier. The looser definition has allowed teams to create hybrids techniques to address real-world work that spans the entirety of an organization's priorities.

2. Mainframe Projects

Change is never easy when there is fear, the end state is unclear, or when there is a threat to what made you successful in the first place. Doing something different is hard (Karten, 2009), even now when we are well into the Agile age with any number of second and third generation transformations going on. However, many people don't use modern approaches because of the mistaken assumption that frameworks are all or nothing. The first of the five major categories viewed as no-go zones for adaptive and small-scale iterative approaches are mainframe projects.

Tom Henricksen, MyITCareerCoach.com, stated in correspondence[iii], "I have seen resistance to using Agile around mainframe projects. The main issue that comes up is the coordination and communication." In large project scenarios, another issue is that it is hard to break the project up into components that are deliverable in short iterations. There are several solutions to that are useful get started injecting agility into these type of large projects:

1. Adopt Scrum techniques even if you are doing waterfall. Daily standup meetings and retrospectives are examples of techniques that help communication, coordination and process improvement.

2. Focus on flow (Tendon & Muller, 2015), develop a Kanban board that mirrors how work progresses and then track your work. When you SEE bottlenecks hold a retrospective and solve the problem. This step will set up an iterative inspect and adapt loop. Life will start to improve.

3. Where multiple teams participate in group planning events (for example SAFe's PI) provide powerful platforms for coordination. Synchronizing planning also gets everyone on the same schedule.

4. Pair or mini-mob using coders and testers to interpret the requirements and to define tests before coding (test first).

5. Consider borrowing the concept of an architectural runway[iv] from SAFe that provides the architectural, network and technical direction, and components for the development teams. The runway should stay just ahead of the team's(or teams') needs so that they can quickly react. What does quickly mean here? Might be good to define that with data.

6. Use the classic three amigos technique to break the work down into smaller pieces. The piece of work should be small enough to meet a solid definition of done in the iteration (cadence) you are using. The work needs to be potentially implementable. In terms of iteration cadence, I am a big fan of shorter iterations but there is no law that an iteration has to be two weeks or 2 days. Having spent a considerable part of my early career working with folks that wrote macro assembler, COBOL, IMS, DB2 and more I have never seen a piece of work that wasn't refinable into smaller chunks, coded, tested, and put under configuration control before working on the next story. Empathize the importance of adopting 1-week sprints or 2-week sprints. Too short and too long end up hindering teams.

There is no reason why Agile practices can't apply to large mainframe projects. Adopting some techniques might require changing organizational structures to remove boundaries or might require building new infrastructure, but the use of techniques is still possible.

3. Maintenance

The second category that tends to draw consternation from those resistant to Agile is maintenance. There are two issues raised to explain why this type of work doesn't fit well. The first is the difficulty in planning the many projects of varied sizes put into a single bucket. Note – most organizations aggregate small enhancements and maintenance into the same budget. The second and potentially more problematic issue occurs by expediting emergency production issues. These two primary issues boil down to predictability which, if pushed, could be further reduced into a discussion of coordination.

One of the first team transformations I participated in involved two teams supporting the implementation of the PeopleSoft HR modules. The two teams had slightly different focuses, but could and did help each other out. The backlog was a mixture of enhancements, upgrades, support tickets and software defects on external customizations and reports. The flow was somewhat chaotic. The organization was not interested in directing work that was more stable and predictable to one team and the more erratic flow to the other (no one wanted to have defects and support tickets as the only component of their daily to-do list). Each story followed the same pattern of work: definition, prototyping, coding and configuration, testing, release notes, and implementation. The ultimate solution the team adopted based on two months of experiments was a Kanban heavy form of Scrumban (Reddy, 2015). As part of the transformation, Product Owners began working closely with the team and were able to review and perform user acceptance testing while the work was progressing rather than waiting until the end of the sprint. The solution included the following "ingredients":

1. Adoption of Kanban: The teams defined their process and developed work in progress (WIP) limits for each step. (Burrows, 2014) This allowed both teams to visually identify bottlenecks and the impact of "unplanned" work entering the workflow. The agreement to only pull work when there was room for it to move was one of the hardest concepts to implement. However, after the teams had implemented it, the ability to visualize the flow of work provided a critical tool to identify and try out process improvements.

2. Coordinated Planning: Both teams planned together. Many pieces of work required software code and/or configuration changes that were highly related. When the teams discovered these items, they combined them to minimize contention between teams.

3. Adoption of multi-level planning. The whole team developed a quarterly product roadmap (as a form of release planning) for enhancements. The roadmap left the team with enough capacity to meet their service level agreement for support tickets and most defects. The second level of very tactical planning occurred formally every two days with the whole team rearranging the ready queue in light of the current brush fires (high priority defects).

4. Bi-weekly retrospectives and daily stand-ups. The teams retained two classic Scrum ceremonies out of the basic Scrum playbook. The teams used formal introspection to review process changes and to define the next tweak. They used daily stand-ups to identify bottlenecks and adjust the flow of work.

5. Slack. The team began its journey with a plan for 100% capacity utilization. Any unanticipated impact caused them to miss commitments (a story for a different time). The two teams freed one FTE as slack to catch emergencies or to swarm to a problem if someone else got in trouble the team rotated the "reliever" (they were in a baseball town) to get everyone exposure and training.

6. Runways. We will return to this topic when we address commercial off-the-shelf (COTS) directly. However, the vendor's release plans act as guidance on what is in the package, what the team will need to add, and what the team will need to configure. Knowing what is coming reduces rework and is useful for prioritizing the backlog. This runway or guidance approach is useful for any COTS package that provides a heads up on what is coming.

7. Breaking work down into smaller pieces[1] (Steve Tendon and Daniel Dorian, 2018). They adopted the user story concept of disaggregation into stories that are demonstrable and potentially implementable. As the team got into the habit of focusing on flow, there was a natural tendency to make stories smaller. One of their "learnings" from the first retrospective was that large stories tended to get stuck when complications arose.

The team, with a little coaching, was able to make their process more Agile by combining lean, SAFe and other ideas. This was not possible until they began to shift their mindset. Doing the work and the organization had to decide to change how they performed and managed the work. Sergio Brigido[v] said it best in his response on LinkedIn about why maintenance and other scenarios are difficult; "Not that I believe that it´s not possible to have a system maintenance (at least in respect to functional changes, on mainframe or different) operating under an adaptive mindset, but what I see is that we are very far to really have the necessary organizational mindset change to achieve that desired state." The process of adopting Agile (in a broad sense) begins by establishing a goal then adopting the proper mindset. Process changes combined with feedback bolster and reinforce the new mindset.

4. Commercial Off the Shelf Packages

Buying a package to perform a major function in an organization is rarely as easy as buying and implementing an app on your smartphone. Package implementations often include:

5. Integration with other applications
6. Configuration
7. External customizations
8. Conversion of current data
9. Training users
10. Communication and change management activities
11. Business process re-engineering
12. Buying and installing the package
13. Hardware and network changes

Purchasing Microsoft Word and installing it on your computer might not be as complicated as this list suggests; however, installing packages like PeopleSoft, SAP or Workday will require most, if not more, than this list of activities. Implementing Commercial Off-The-Shelf (COTS) software for anything substantial is a complicated endeavor (albeit less complicated than building the whole thing yourself). The most common reasons given for why an Agile approach to these efforts won't work are three-fold:

1. Coordination amongst all of the teams and organizations
2. Transparency between the organization and software vendor(s)
3. Implementations for packages are typically are either comprised of a big bang or a few biggish banglets.

Coordination:

COTS implementations for major packages are large projects and involve many different teams. Many of the same solutions that we noted for mainframe projects are germane to this scenario.

1. Adopt a Scrum of Scrums (SoS). SoS's foster focused cross-team coordination by getting a small set of representatives together on periodic basis for micro-planning and coordinating the work between Agile teams. (Dalton, 2019)

2. Implement visual management using a Kanban board and other information radiators. Make sure everyone can see the progress toward the goal. This will help involvement and will support self-

organization.

3. Follow a common cadence of joint planning at a strategic and tactical level. Consider the 90-day product increment adopted by SAFe combined with everyone participating in team level planning at the same time (every 1 to 3 weeks based on a common sprint/iteration cadence).

4. Leverage the package to seed the project's architectural runway.

The COTS package will have a required footprint including code structure, components, and infrastructure; use the package to seed the organization's architectural runway. The subtitle of the movie Dr. Strangelove put it best, "How I Learned to Stop Worrying and Love The Bomb." When you buy a major package you often have just bought the structure for a big piece of your business.

Transparency:

Transparency might be the hardest problem to solve. Each organization will have its own methodology for implementation. The level of transparency spelled out in the contract defines how the organizations will interact. If you are going to use Agile to coordinate and communicate it must be in the contract. Building many coordination steps into the contract before signing will solve much of the transparency problem. Another recommendation is to review the timing for when the COTS vendor releases draft release notes. The earlier and more in-depth the draft release notes, the easier it will be for teams to integrate the flow of work into standard iteration planning and execution.

Implementation:

It is difficult to implement a package in production a little bit at a time. Most organizations put packages into production all at once or in large chunks. An Agile approach often cannot impact that trajectory. However, much of the activity (integrations, conversions, configurations, coding and more) can use best practices identified earlier, such as small pieces of work completed in short iterations that deliver production-ready code.

Coordination, transparency, and implementation make implementing and maintaining major COTS packages complicated. No methodology will make these efforts easy, but the structure and techniques that improve communication and generate faster feedback will improve coordination, transparency and reduce the risk of the typical big bang implementation.

5. SaaS

Software as a service (SaaS) is one of the most significant trends of the early 21st Century. SaaS is a scenario in which a person or organization access a piece of software hosted outside of the company via the internet. You use the software as long as you want, you don't need the infrastructure to host the software and you don't have to worry about dealing with the code. The organization using these types of solutions needs to configure the software, manage the data, code and integrate organization-specific solutions outside of the package and manage internal uses. Significant distributed cloud solutions rarely are "plug and play". Even straightforward applications, such as Slack, often need administration and support inside the organization. Large packages, such as Workday, need teams to support, configure and administer the implementation. Some organizations using distributed cloud solutions to meet their information technology needs find it difficult to leverage approaches like Scrum; however, with the correct mindset and a flexible approach, Agile is useful in this environment.

Teams and organizations cite several problematic scenarios for why Agile is not a good fit for SaaS. We will focus on on-going release scenarios after the initial implementation of the package.

1. The package is a black box, which obscures the activity until the users receive a release. Most SaaS providers do their best to provide release notes to organizations to help them know both what is coming and what has arrived (note the definition of 'best' varies). The issue is that the release is not always available in test environments before they are releases nor do organizations always have the option of whether or not to accept the change.

   Suggestions for addressing this issue: Ensure that your vendor provides good release notes and a solid test environment that is available before release dates. Use the release notes to drive user stories and the acceptance tests for the user stories. Planning for this type of release needs to incorporate the internal changes needed. Write and prioritize user stories for the internal work. Use automated testing tools that incorporate both the package and integrated functionality if possible, to incorporate continuous testing.

2. Configuration is not coding. Functionality is often controlled by setting which change the behavior of screens or whether specific functions are visible or available. Occasionally teams make the argument that because they are not coding they can just wing changes (that's not Agile). Rather they can make changes on the fly without a user story, prioritization by Product Owners or even testing. I call this the big boom approach. There are several flaws in the logic. First, doing work that isn't prioritized by the Product Owner takes time away from delivering value. At best adding extra work into an iteration of any size requires stretching the boundary, or at worst abandoning committed functionality. Daniel Vacanti's Actionable Agile Metrics for Predictability (Vacanti, 2015) lays out the negative impact of adding expedited work to a process.

   Suggestions for addressing this issue: Treat configuration like any other type of change you would make in an Agile project. The means generating user stories, prioritizing with the Product Owner(s), testing the change (this means you need a test region with test data that mirrors production). Develop tests before you make the change. This is a form of test-first development that will allow you to understand whether you have completed their task. Using test first thinking will also help to ensure that the user story is well-formed and thought out.

3. SaaS vendors and internal cadences don't match (Rothman, 2016). I recently spent time with a team supporting the package solution delivered on a weekly basis and two major releases during the year. Deliveries of software happened like clockwork. The internal team used a Scrum-y version of Scrumban with a two-week cadence. At first, the team had difficulty determining how the solution providers schedule could integrate with their schedule.

   Suggestions for addressing this issue: Forget for a moment the techniques and ceremonies from the frameworks or methods you are using and consider the principles of Agile. The techniques you are using should deliver value by making how you work more adaptable. Review the approaches you are using and tailor them to meet your environment. Use the principles from the Manifesto to test the approach. For example, in this case, a sub-team reviewed the changes that the vendor anticipated in each major release (a variant of the Three Amigos approach). The sub-team crafted user stories and incorporated those stories into the larger backlog. For the weekly release, a team member playing a Business Analyst (BA) role swept the weekly release notes and crafted user stories of any changes that required testing or where optional changes in the portion of the solution they used. The team reviewed the new user stories for incorporation into the backlog at the standup meeting every Monday.

Many of the solutions to address using Agile in a SaaS environment are similar to those teams using a commercial off-the-shelf package (COTS) environment. Most of the suggestions require a mindset that approaches adaptable approaches by asking how the principles in the Manifesto can address those issues, rather than immediately jumping to why these approaches don't fit. Using any approach in this type of environment feels different than for systems of engagement developed and maintained within the organization. Different does not mean impossible but does require both conscious decisions about how a team or organization will work and an adaptable mindset.

6. Contracts and Outsourcing

The final category of reputed places Agile fears to tread is the land of contractual relationships. Outsourced work is the primary denizen of the land of contracts. In all but the simplest scenarios, asking another firm to do work for you generates a formal relationship. In most cases, the legal document is a proxy for intimacy and trust that occurs inside a single organization. Fences make good neighbors to keep relationships orderly; in the business world, formal agreements take the place of fences to establish boundaries. Boundaries constrain the free flow of information and ideas, which is antithetical to Agile principles. There are four core reasons organizations and practitioners see issues of high-trust approaches in low trust environments. None of these issues is insurmountable (Atkinson & Benefield, The Curse of the change control mechanism, 2011) if negotiated and written down upfront. Some of the issues are:

1. **Transparency** – Agreements establish boundaries and obligations between the parties. Obligations are often tied to payments and in some cases performance incentives and penalties. All of the parties in the contractual arrangement have a variety of goals that include delivery of an output (generally software), maximization of profit by the outsourcer and minimization of expense by the outsourcee. All goals in a contract, taken together, generate a behavioral equilibrium so that everyone gets what they need. Unfortunately, not all behaviors are useful which makes sharing information less likely. A classic example is a scenario where someone is over budget or behind schedule but thinks they can fix the problem. In this case, they feel incented to avoid the pain of exposure until they know they can't fix the problem. Highly structured agreements exacerbate this issue.

   Solution: Before signing the contract build in the participation required by Agile for all parties. The Product Owner must be from the outsourcer, the outsourcer needs to take part in all planning activities, involve the Product Owner (or proxy) in the daily stand-ups, and they should have access to the backlog management tool. After signing: involve the outsourcer in the demonstration and the team is adhering to their definition of done.

2. **Access** – Interactions between team members and the business are often constrained. Often point people assigned for each role. These people act as a funnel for all conversations and decisions. This is often done as a configuration management technique. Only the identified point people can accept inputs or changes to the scope of work or tweaks to the requirements. Access is a specialized form of transparency. Agile principles and techniques explicitly assume that the team(s)

have access and interact with the business daily (sometimes stated as continuously). Also, there is an expectation for the Product Owner (from the business) to manage and prioritize the backlog.

Solution: Before signing, explicitly build Agile roles into the document. For example, build the Product Owner role (part of the business) as part of the team. Identify the need for intimate, daily (or close) communication with the team. In the contract make it OK for team members to talk with the business without a chaperone. If at all possible, embed the Product Owner and/or subject matter experts with the team (full time if at all possible). After signing, this issue is more difficult to solve post. One possible solution to generate the conversation between the team and the business is to embed the Product Owner and/or point persons with the team at least on a part-time basis. This fix generates conversation by forcing access. In the longer-term embedding helps to foster trust.

3. **Delivery Cadence –** Agile techniques expect that the team will deliver "potentially" implementable functionality on a periodic basis. The periodic delivery gets value to the client sooner and provides a feedback mechanism. Many agreements only recognize value by the final outcome. The contact views anything else as a distraction that might take the focus away from the real payout.

   Solution: Before signing, build in delivery on cadence. After signing, deliver each iteration and map the stories (or work units) delivered to the ultimate goal. By linking each delivery to the ultimate goal in the contract everyone involved will stay focused on the agreed-upon obligations.

4. **Trust –** Signed agreements are tools to explicitly define the obligations of all parties in lieu of trust or a handshake. The goal is to enforce trust because the penalties are painful. Agile assumes that the parties have a common goal. The common goal creates an environment in which everyone involved has a clear understanding of how the team and business will behave.

   Solution: Before and after signing, establish a common goal. Recognize that each party might have other goals that conflict. State the conflicts and made them subservient to the common outcome. If team members believe that there are ulterior motives, trust will be elusive. Use embedding, joint planning, and retrospectives to make a contractual relationship more Agile.

Contracts are tools to create fences (Atkinson & Benefield, 2013). Most Agile principles and techniques get rid of fences between the business and the team or between the outsourcee and the outsourcer. Legal agreements can explicitly prohibit interaction or they can create scenarios where participants are afraid to interact. Once signed negotiation to embed any techniques is painful. Adopt techniques such as joint planning, attending demonstrations and stand-up and sitting with the team (even if it is just occasionally) to help build trust and inculcate principles.

7. Conclusion

Agile is a mindset first and a set of techniques second. Saying that adaptive approaches won't work is less about technique but about a fear of a mindset or being satisfied with the status quo. Rather than saying what can't work it is better to question how can we address the 12 principles using a mixture of frameworks and techniques to deliver value. The Manifesto establishes goals that provide a solution path. In the end, the reason Agile has become important not only in software but most business domains is that it helps people deliver value. Who wouldn't want a value-based mindset?

References

Atkinson, S., & Benefield, G. (2011). The Curse of the change control mechanism, *Society for Computers & Law Publication*.

Atkinson, S., & Benefield, G. (2013). Software Development: Why the Traditional Contract Model Is Not Fit for Purpose. *Hawaii International Conference On System Science.* IEEE.

Burrows, M. (2014). *Kanban from the Inside.* Sequim: Blue Hole Press.

Dalton, J. (2019). *Great Big Agile.* New York: Apress.

Karten, N. (2009). *Changing How You Manage and Communicate Change, Focusing on the human side of change.* Cambridgeshire: IT Governance Publishing.

Reddy, A. (2015). *The Scrumban [R]Evolution: Getting the Most Out of Agile, Scrum, and Lean Kanban.* Hoboken: Addison-Wesley Professional.

Rothman, J. (2016). *Agile and Lean Program Management.* Practical Ink.

Steve Tendon and Daniel Dorian, T. Y. (2018). *Tame Your Work Flow.* Amsterdam: LeanPub.

Tendon, S., & Muller, W. (2015). *Hyper-Productive Knowledge Work Performance.* Plantation: J. Ross Publishing.

Vacanti, D. S. (2015). *Actionable Agile Metrics for Predictability.* Amsterdam: LeanPub.

---

[1] Consider Steve Tendon and Daniel Dorians MOVE concept where the smallest outcome is pursued iteratively.

---

[i] Reinheitsgebot, Wikipedia, accessed April 3, 2018, https://en.wikipedia.org/wiki/Reinheitsgebot

[ii] Agile Manifesto, Manifesto for Agile Software Development, accessed April 3, 2018, https://agilemanifesto.org/

[iii] T Henricksen (personal communication and LinkedIn, February 14, 2018).

[iv] Architectural Runway, accessed August 16, 2019, https://www.scaledagileframework.com/architectural-runway/
[v] S. Brigido (personal communication, LinkedIn, February 17, 2018)

Creating Quality with Mob Programming

Thomas Desmond

Thomas.Desmond@HunterIndustries.com

Abstract

Mob programming is a software development approach where the whole team works on the same thing, at the same time, in the same space, at the same computer (Zuill 2016). Mob programming is all about collaboration, teamwork, helping others, and developing great software. With it, we get improved communication, consistent exchange of knowledge, enhanced idea generation, and more learning.

In my organization, we mob program on every aspect of our production code. Every line of code, every test, every release is developed using mob programming. Because of the high quality of our software developed with mob programming, we went a year and a half without any bugs reported in our production software. The software we release is developed drastically different because of mob programming.

In this paper, we will explore how the mob programming software development approach produces quality software in my organization.

Biography

Thomas Desmond has been developing software utilizing mob programming for over three years. He is passionate about learning, teaching, and helping others perform their best. Mob programming has become his preferred method for developing software. Thomas has also incorporated mob programming concepts when teaching university courses.

1. Mob Programming Fundamentals

1.1. What is Mob Programming?

"All the brilliant minds working on the same thing, at the same time, in the same space, on the same computer." (Zuill 2016) In my organization, we mob program on every aspect of our production code. Currently, we have nine separate mobs working full time.

So, what does mob programming look like in my organization? We have up to five developers all working together at the same time on the same thing driving the software forward. We do all software development practices together: architecture design, code development, testing, deployment, kanban, prioritization, EVERYTHING. It may help to think of mobbing as a more extreme version of pair programming. Instead of two people working together, we generally have up to five members all working together.

We may be at a single computer, but we are not huddled closely together around one small screen. We have one desktop computer attached to 80-inch monitors with multiple desks surrounding the monitors. We have plenty of space to sit, work, and move around. The image below is an actual mob set-up.

1.2. How did Mob Programming Begin?

"Having an environment where awesome things can happen, pretty much guarantees that awesome things WILL happen." (Zuill 2016)

Mob programming did not start overnight. Mobbing has continually improved over the past seven years, starting slowly and expanding into what it is today.

It began with a teammate that needed help with a feature they were tasked to complete. They did not feel like they would meet the deadline, so they called upon their peers for help. They all got together in a conference room. They collaborated and worked together to come to a solution and did end up meeting their deadline. The team enjoyed working together and continued it. They held a retrospective every day to discuss their progress.

The collaboration, working on the same task and daily retrospectives continued. With each retrospective, they found ways to improve their processes and work better together. Eventually, they were given a permanent space to mob program.

This was the very beginning of mob programming. It has now, seven years later, expanded to nine mobs in my organization. We want to always find ways to turn up the good and mob programming worked well for the team. Mob programming is still evolving today but began because a group of people saw it as a beneficial way to develop software.

1.3. Driver-Navigator Model

When people first think of mob programming, they often think of it as one person at the keyboard writing the code while the others watch. It is not like that at all. We take a much stricter paradigm coined "Driver-Navigator". The person at the keyboard is the driver while everyone else is a navigator. The driver is not allowed to implement their ideas. They are taking the input of the navigators and translating that into code.

Llewellyn Falco expressed the statement that "For an idea to go from your head into the computer, it MUST go through someone else's hands". The navigators describe their ideas in English to the driver, who then translates that into code. If an idea cannot be explained in plain English and understood by the driver, then it would not go into the code.

For the driver-navigator model to work, it is crucial to ensure the driver is never talking through their ideas and coding at the same time. It is the responsibility of everyone on the mob to ensure that this does not happen.

We have found that the driver-navigator model forces people to have to explain and discuss ideas with others. At a minimum, one other person, the driver, has to understand the idea enough to put it into code. The shared understanding of the code and being forced to explain code in English brings out quality code.

The driver-navigator roles are also not static. They change often. Using a timer, we rotate roles between driver and navigator, so everyone gets a chance to present ideas and navigate through the solution. Depending on the team, rotations are done each five to fifteen minutes. The forced rotation gives everyone the chance to navigate and prevents one person from navigating the code endlessly.

While the driver and navigator are essential roles in mob programming, there are many other roles that can be present. For more information on the driver-navigator roles and the other roles that can be seen in a mob, take a look at Mob Programming: The role-playing game (Larsen 2016) or the IBM experience report on mob programming patterns (Keeling 2019).

1.4. Zero Bugs

In my organization, we have a set of lofty goals. The lofty goals are meant to be statements that we would want to be true if we were in the perfect software development environment. One of the lofty goals is to have zero bugs in production.

Zero bugs may seem like an unattainable goal for most teams, but the first mob team at my organization was able to improve the quality of the software being released to the point of having zero reported bugs in production for a year and a half. Having zero bugs was made possible because they were mob programming.

To this day, we still have very few bugs. When a bug is reported, it becomes the top priority for the team. We only return to feature development once the bug has been resolved. We have so few bugs that we do not use a software bug tracking tool. Each project has a physical whiteboard to be used as a kanban board to keep track of tasks. The board is broken into three sections: To Do, Doing, and Done. When a bug is reported it goes immediately into the Doing column. The kanban boards gives us and interested stakeholders visibility into what we are currently doing, what has been completed, and what still needs to be done.

2. Ways Mob Programming Creates Quality

2.1. Communication

The number one benefit of mob programming is communication. We are face to face with our teammates for the entire day. We are always talking to one another. The driver-navigator model forces us to be continually collaborating, working together, debating ideas, etc. The immense amount of communication that occurs in a mobbing environment breeds quality software.

Fewer formal meetings need to occur when mobbing. If we need to discuss something as a team, we are already together. If a product owner wants to see our progress, we are all together ready to give a demo. Mob programming as defined by the Agile Alliance, "Ironically through the use of ongoing, "working meetings" Mob Programming ensures that work, knowledge creation and decision making are joined together thus leading to much better alignment and more effective action." (Mob Programming)

Questions get answered immediately. If we do not understand why we are doing something in the code, we can stop and get our questions answered. We do not need to struggle through confusing code on our own. We do not have to queue up questions to ask a coworker once they are available. Mobbing allows us to ask for help and clarification from those around us immediately.

2.2. Knowledge Sharing

When you have a group of three or more people all working on the same feature at the same time, knowledge is shared amongst the individuals. We code through the solution together, sharing how and why we made our decisions.

Jason Kerney describes how mob programming benefits from systems like transactive memory. If multiple people share the same experience, they are then able to remember different aspects of that experience. They can recall the information better and put all the pieces together (Kerney 2015).

It is not possible to remember every piece of a solution. However, with mob programming, the shared experience of coding through a solution means we can, as a team, better remember how and why something was done.

We have a shared redundant knowledge of the software among the team. Quality is increased because of the transactive memory and shared experiences in a mob.

2.3. Idea Generation & Development

With mob programming, we are no longer working alone to come up with solutions to our architecture, implementation, and testing problems. We have multiple team members to discuss ideas with face to face immediately. One study came to the following conclusion that mob programming led to a more creative problem-solving environment. They came up with higher quality solutions because of the mobbing environment that they were in (Aune 2018).

Having a group of people to work together with through a problem together also helps to reduce stress. I never feel as if the entire responsibility of finding the right solution lies solely on me. I can leave at the end of the day not worried about how I would take on the next day's tasks. I know I have my teammates to help tackle the hard problems together.

Quality is heightened when we generate our ideas together as a team. We come up with more creative solutions to our problems and experience less stress around having to solve every problem alone.

2.4. Elevated Learning

When programming in any setting, we are always learning. Learning how to use a new tool, framework, language, or technique. In a mob, we are always sharing what we learn with each other. Knowledge is quickly disseminated among the team.

Karel Boekhout studied a mob programming team and found that the team had grown much faster in development skills and development processes while mob programming, compared to traditional individual development (Boekhout 2016). The group setting of the mob is conducive to learning. We gain the knowledge of the others on the team.

I joined a new project team that used a mobile development technology that I had never used before. Nine months after joining that team, I accepted a position as a lecturer to teach that very same technology at a local university. Going from zero knowledge to teaching a university-level course on the subject would not have been possible for me had I not been mobbing.

We are encouraged to share and encouraged to bring everyone around us up to the same level. The interactions and navigation in mobbing lead to amplified learning. Quality is increased when everyone is learning more and at a fast pace.

3. Mob Programming Things to Consider

3.1. The Work Environment

The mobs in my organization are all collocated together in a single building. We do all of our work on-site and do little to no work remotely. Having the teams together, face to face is an important aspect that has made mob programming successful for us.

It has been studied that there is a correlation between the proximity of teams and the amount of collaboration on the teams. By having our mobs close all the time, we can achieve the highest level of collaboration (Kiesler 2002). Mob programming is all about collaboration and is a big part of how we create quality software.

Some teams perform mob programming remotely; INNOQ is one example. They have put together an excellent resource for how they successfully mob program remotely (Harrer). Remote mobbing may work for some teams, but at my organization, we do almost all our work onsite.

A time-lapse video published to YouTube titled "A Day of Mob Programming 2016" gives an overview of our work environment and what we do every day. (https://www.youtube.com/watch?v=dVqUcNKVbYg&t=1s).

3.2. Mob Team Size

Having an infinite number of team members could bring quality to a whole new level. However, we know this is impossible, and there must be a maximum number of people on a mob team to prevent benefits from declining or stagnating.

As of writing this paper, few formal scientific studies have been conducted revolving around mob programming, especially team size. Yet, there has been a large number of studies surrounding pair programming. Woody Zuill breaks down mob programming, using data from pair programming studies, to provide estimates of the correlation between team sizes, costs, and the quality of work produced.

It is hard to provide an exact number that makes up the perfect mob. However, based on the work completed by Zuill and my empirical evidence, mobs should be made of four or five members. Zuill's extrapolations found diminishing returns with team sizes any larger than six. For a full breakdown of Zuill's calculations, see section 3.10 titled A Simple Cost Analysis of Mob Programming in his book "Mob Programming A Whole Team Approach" (Zuill 2016). Zuill goes into details of costs effectiveness, expected quality metrics, and effects of the mob team size.

3.3. Developer Fatigue

Mob programming requires a lot of focus. Working with a group of people and trying to focus on development tasks all day can be very draining. One study found that mob programming, "strengthens the team, but can also be draining on energy and mood because of the intense focus required". (June 2018)

In an experience report by Aaron Griffith, he talks about how mob programming can be draining and over stimulating especially for introverts. Being among a group of people, and having little to no alone time can be demanding (Griffith 2016).

Having dedicated breaks and time to complete personal tasks can help alleviate fatigue. In my organization, we mob for up to 7 hours a day. We then have one hour of learning time a day that can be done individually or in a group. This learning time can be the perfect opportunity to be alone, learning something and recharging.

Mob programming is still something that takes some getting used to. In order to keep the quality high and consistent, we need to ensure we do not overwork ourselves.

3.4. Team Psychological Safety

For mob programming to be successful, teams need to be psychologically safe. Team members must feel comfortable to challenge one another, be able to share constructive feedback, and trust each other. Just being kind to one another is not enough. Feeling comfortable enough to give candid feedback and have a healthy debate is vital to creating quality software.

In a study completed by Google, they found that psychological safety was the number one factor in how successful their teams were. They described psychological safety as "Team members feel safe to take risks and be vulnerable in front of each other" (Rozovsky 2015). Psychological safety is not about just being polite, but instead being able to be vulnerable with one another. Google has proved it is what leads to truly outstanding teams.

Psychological safety can be built up over time by framing work as a learning problem, being able to acknowledge fallibility, and modeling curiosity (Edmonson 2014). In order to create quality software, we need to feel safe with one another.

4. Conclusion

In my organization, we have found mob programming to be a successful methodology for developing quality software. The nine mobs work full time every day on production code because of the results we have experienced.

The quality that comes with increased communication, spreading of knowledge, creative idea generation, and heightened learning has led us to mob on all aspects of our production software. Mob programming is very different from traditional programming and has its obstacles like the work environment, developer fatigue, and requiring psychological safety. However, when mob programming is done well, it can be very conducive to creating high-quality software.

If you are interested in learning more about mob programming or getting started with mobbing yourself, Woody Zuill's book, Mob Programming A Whole Team Approach available on LeanPub is a great first resource. It goes deeper into what mobbing is, how to start mobbing on your teams, and the problems mobbing tries to alleviate.

References

Aune, Ole Kristian & Echtermeyer, Christian & Sørensen, Elias. (2018). Mob Programming: A Qualitative Study from the Perspective of a Development Team. https://www.researchgate.net/publication/328150167_Mob_Programming_A_Qualitative_Study_from_the_Perspective_of_a_Development_Team.

Boekhout K. (2016) Mob Programming: Find Fun Faster. In: Sharp H., Hall T. (eds) Agile Processes, in Software Engineering, and Extreme Programming. XP 2016. Lecture Notes in Business Information Processing, vol 251. Springer, Cham

Edmondson, Amy. Building a Psychologically Safe Workplace. May 4, 2014. https://www.youtube.com/watch?v=LhoLuui9gX8.

Falco, Llewellyn. "Llewellyn's Strong-style Pairing." June 30, 2014. https://llewellynfalco.blogspot.com/2014/06/llewellyns-strong-style-pairing.html.

Griffith, Aaron. "Mob Programming for the Introverted." Agile2016 Conference, August 2016. https://www.agilealliance.org/resources/experience-reports/mob-programming-for-the-introverted/.

Harrer, S., Christ, J., & Huber, M. (n.d.). Remote Mob Programming. https://www.remotemobprogramming.org/

Keeling, Michael, and Joe Runde. "Harvesting Mob Programming Patterns: Observing How We Work." Agile2019 Conference, August 2019. https://www.agilealliance.org/resources/experience-reports/harvesting-mob-programming-patterns-observing-how-we-work/.

Kerney, Jason. 2015. "Mob Programming - My First Team." Agile2015 Conference, August 2015. https://www.agilealliance.org/resources/experience-reports/mob-programming-my-first-team/

Kiesler, Sara. Distributed Work. MIT Press, 2002. https://mitpress.mit.edu/books/distributed-work

Larsen, Willem. "Mob Programming: The Role Playing Game." https://github.com/willemlarsen/mobprogrammingrpg.

"Mob Programming." https://www.agilealliance.org/glossary/mob-programming.

Rozovsky, Julia. "The Five Keys to a Successful Google Team", November 17, 2015. https://rework.withgoogle.com/blog/five-keys-to-a-successful-google-team/.

Zuill, Woody. "Answering a Few Questions." Mob Programming. November 2012. https://mobprogramming.org/answering-a-few-questions/.

Zuill, Woody, and Kevin Meadows. Mob Programming A Whole Team Approach, October 29, 2016. https://leanpub.com/mobprogramming.

Moving to a Continuous Delivery Culture: Cutting Releases Cadence

Andrew Peterson

andrew.peterson@costcotravel.com

Abstract

You will learn how a growing organization transforms from a release cycle including three sprints lasting five weeks to a single two-week sprint release cycle. You will be guided in the challenges that the testing organization has had to overcome in order to test things faster, earlier and more often as they change their culture to a more continuous delivery model. This was done not only with traditional functional testing, but also the larger non-functional testing such as security and performance. These teams were able to raise the confidence of build candidates as they moved from 10 releases a year to 26 and the other benefits associated with a more frequent release cadence.

Biography

Andy Peterson has spent more than 20 years in IT roles with the last dozen in a QA specific role including Software Development Engineer in Test (SDET), QA Lead, and QA Manager. He is currently the QA Manager for Costco Travel's Products and Markets group. Before that, he was the QA Lead for initiatives such as their platform and international efforts. Originally from Michigan, he moved out to the Pacific Northwest in 2006. Since then he has been through a lot of the regional hobbies like mountain climbing and wine making. Currently, he is busy trying to keep up with two daughters.

1. Introduction

Like so many other organizations, our organization within Costco Travel has been on a path to deliver value to our members and users more continuously with the same or better quality. We have been on a long journey that has had many challenges. Our organization has iterated through changes to develop and release at a faster cadence. There was initially little automation. Longer sprints and stabilization sprints were required to meet the quality bars early on. These stabilization sprints were the biggest challenge for the QA teams. Teams were forced to stop focusing on delivering new features or architecture and instead shift our time and energy on system stabilization, integration testing, performance testing, security testing and preparation of the system for release.

2. Reducing Deployment Timelines

The need for the reduced deployment timelines was due to the need to get feedback from the business faster. If we were going to do something incorrect, we would rather know after two weeks rather than five weeks. There were also many interruptions within the deployment in the form of an overabundance of hotfixes and stabilization sprints. Finally, estimation is easier for a shorter time than it is for a longer time frame, so IT is able to give the business a more confident idea of what it can deliver.

2.1. The Agile Beginnings

Before Costco Travel turned to agile, we used a traditional waterfall software development methodology in which we would deliver one or two releases a year. In 2012, we began the agile transformation. Initially we started with a five-week release consisting of a three-week functional sprint followed by a two-week stabilization sprint. There was no successful QA automation until 2014.

2.2. The First Disruption

In 2015, we moved to two two-week feature sprints followed by a one-week stabilization sprint. In this phase, we were able to make the work done during stabilization smaller, yet we were still not able to deliver more frequently than ten times a year. The deployments required the site to have scheduled downtime during the deployment. Therefore, we continued to keep with a five-week release cycle by changing one stabilization sprint into a feature week and dividing those four feature weeks into two sprints. This also gave us the opportunity to practice between the functional sprints in the release to see if we could get the stabilization work done.

During this phase there were two key steps that occurred that made the following phases much easier to attain for both the business operations and product development: no downtime deployments and feature flags.

2.2.1. No Downtime Deployments

The most important advance needed for this was moving to a model where Costco Travel stayed up during deployments. Our eCommerce site was going dark ten times a year and as we grew, we lost hundreds of thousands of dollars each time. This had to be stopped before we could get out of the five-week cycle cadence and move to the four. The biggest problem was with the database and the content management systems and making sure that we were backwards compatible so that we could continuously deploy throughout the day. Schema changes in the database would need to be phased in through several releases as backwards compatibility would require the database to be read by either the current version of the code or the next version of the code that is being deployed. On the eCommerce site, no new sessions would be allowed on a percentage of servers until it the current sessions were severed. At this point, the new code would be deployed to the application servers and they would be turned on and monitored. The remaining application servers would be updated in the same way.

2.2.2. Feature Flag

A feature flag is a variable that can control whether a feature is available to the system. This will allow features to be tested in a lower environment with the feature flag turned on. It can then be turned off for regression testing and in production because it isn't fully complete or the business is not ready for it. In order to reduce the cadence of the deployments though, these needed to be used in most projects and at a lower level. Feature flags allowed for a feature to be turned on at any time which decoupled the idea of a release of a feature from a deployment of code. Another benefit is that if a severe enough defect was discovered, there was an option to just switch the feature flag off again.

2.3. Un-Stabilization

In 2018, the third phase finally removed the stabilization sprint as the QA and DevOps teams were able to get all of the work we needed to do. Automation and the ability to get work in during the feature sprint made this possible. This change was the biggest and most important move for QA. Because it was still expensive in DevOps and QA effort to deploy more frequently to production, only one production deployment was done every 2 sprints. The two feature sprints would go into production every four weeks. This allowed us three additional deployments into production and it aligned the deployments with the business periods.

2.4. Sprint is a Release

In May of 2019 after eight months without a stabilization sprint, Costco Travel was able to deliver the sprints to production independently. This doubled the frequency that value is delivered to our members and users. These 26 releases allow for faster iteration if there is a needed course correction.

3. QA Implications

3.1. Functional Testing

3.1.1. Adding Automation

There is no surprise that the key to the QA portion of the reduced cadence was the introduction of automation. At Costco Travel, there was none in the beginning, so it was a big effort.

3.1.1.1. Pre-2013 – Automation investigated

The first Quality Assurance team members at Costco Travel were travel agents that were selected based on willingness and aptitude for the application. A QA Manager was brought over from Costco's home office to help develop the effort with QA processes in mind. A few outside QA hires were also brought in from outside. There was still little experience with automation. There were a few trials of automation products but none took off with the team.

3.1.1.2. 2013 – Initial volunteer effort

In 2013, two new quality assurance engineers joined and began an effort in their free time to put together a framework using Microsoft Test Manager and Rational Functional Tester. A volunteer group of interested QA came together weekly and made some progress in getting together a suite of 19 end-to-end tests that were scheduled and run a few times a week. These tests tested the base happy path scenarios for login and purchase of our basic travel product offerings. The tests were fragile and took a lot of maintenance and troubleshooting but they were the beginning.

3.1.1.3. 2014 – Getting full time SDET support

After realizing how long it was going to take to go from the initial 19 tests, especially with the troubleshooting, management was convinced to hire two six month contractors. 162 tests were initially identified for these two to automate. In addition to doing those tests, they converted to Selenium from Rational Functional Tester and also rewrote the initial 19 tests that were running.

3.1.1.4. 2015 – First Full Time SDETs

Following the contractor trial we were able to create three full time and permanent SDET openings, one of which was filled with an original contractor. These three became the start of the Engineering Productivity Team. This team took on the framework, creation of tools for automation, reporting of automated runs, and integration of the automation into the build pipelines. For the first few years, they were the main coders of the automation as well.

3.1.1.5. 2017 – Hired performance and security experts

The hiring of performance and QA security engineers to the Engineering Productivity Team was also a key step in the process. Before this time, we had one QA engineer running all of these types of tests and reporting them. The two new experts were joined and were able to take on the traditional testing done during the stabilization sprint as well as spread it throughout the sprints.

3.1.1.6. 2018 – SDET on every scrum team

It wasn't until 2018, that the Engineering Productivity was fully staffed and there was an SDET on every scrum team. This was over four years from the time Costco Travel had our first dedicated SDETs. It was a slow process. At this point, the automation of features is being kept up by the Scrum team SDETs and the Engineering Productivity team can concentrate on framework and tools.

3.1.2. Creation of a Dedicated Automation Environment

As the automation suites grew, the time needed for the QA environment grew. The scrum teams needed to get updated features for testing regularly. They would often have to either wait for an automated test pass to finish or start a deployment causing the remaining tests to run in the suite to fail. The opposite would also occur when a functional tester would be in the middle of a test scenario or using specific test data and an automated test would come through and blow away a cache or some other needed test object. A dedicated automation test environment was developed to prevent this from occurring. This also allowed the automation or deployments to run nearly around the clock without fear of interrupting the other teams. This was key in allowing the growth of automation regression to run concurrently with the functional testing going on in the scrum teams. It also created a healthy competition to see whether the scrum team tester or the regression automation would catch bugs first.

3.1.3. Gatekeeping Environments

The development of a dedicated automation environment allowed us to use it as a smoke test environment for a build. This became a key feature to be added into the Costco Travel Jenkins deployment pipelines, which prevents a bad build from blocking testing our standard QA environment. After a successful development build is deployed into the automation environment it is smoke tested. If these basic tests would not pass, the pipeline would stop until a more stable build would pass. This gatekeeping has saved us countless hours of time from broken builds, severity 0 bugs and other problems from sneaking into the normal QA environment.

3.1.4. Getting Automation into Scrum Level Work

Once Costco Travel was able to staff the scrum teams with SDETs and move the majority of the regression test automation from the centralized automation framework team to the scrum teams with the direct feature knowledge. This accelerated the automation development and improved the quality of the automation greatly. Now the Engineering Productivity Team could concentrate on the framework and tools.

3.1.4.1. Reduce Test Debt

There was a reduction in test debt when the regression automation shifted to the scrum teams. This occurred because the scrum teams were able to add the "regression test complete" to the definition of done of the feature. This was not a possibility when it was being done by an external team that was accumulating work from over a dozen teams and those teams were growing at a rate faster than the centralized team could handle, especially while also maintaining test framework and tools.

3.1.4.2. Ownership and Accountability

The other benefit to pushing the automation work to the scrum team was heightened sense of ownership of the tests. Regression tests are being automated by the team that initially tested the feature, the teams would be also analyzing automated results and is ultimately responsible for the quality of that feature. This makes that most knowledgeable team the one that is accountable to those tests.

3.1.5. Manual Testing

Manual Testing has not been completely removed, but it has been drastically scaled back. We have goals to reduce the manual test suite to under three hours. All of the existing Priority 1 manual regression tests have been revisited and triaged. The QA leadership worked with our Engineering Productivity Team and marked about a third of them as able to automate or already automated. There was about another third that were marked as lower priority and we didn't have to run manually for every release. That final third of the tests that remained ended up being manual fit into a few different categories. These included tests that (1) were too complex to automate, (2) were too risky to automate, or (3) need eyes, emotions or evaluations of humans. In addition, we decided not to run these for every version in the release. This greatly reduced the workload needed for running these tests.

3.2. Non-Functional Testing

3.2.1. Security

Costco Travel's security tests were initially built to do the basics of keeping Payment Card Information (PCI) and Personally Identifiably Information (PII) compliance. This meant that one tester was creating the scripts in IBM AppScan, running the scan with set default policies, and validating the report. These scans would take the better part of a day to run if nothing went wrong and they were performed in a shared environment. If there were identified vulnerabilities, engineers did not have much time to analyze and potentially fix if needed.

In planning for getting to a more continuous model, the organization realized that it needed to do more frequent scans earlier. Our engineers complemented the regular release runs with daily smaller runs that looked for higher priority vulnerabilities using IBM's policy called "The Vital Few". This allowed us to match up new issues with a specific check-in so the new vulnerability bug was easier to assign to the respective team. Also, we were deploying major versions weekly to pre-production. These full versions were still all being fully scanned making more full policy scans run. All of these scans were built into Jenkins, so we did not have to run them manually. We also were able to integrate other tools, like Sonar, a static analysis tool, while checking in code.

3.2.2. Performance

As with the security testing, almost all of the performance testing was performed in the stabilization sprints. This testing was all done in the same pre-production environment as both the functional testing and the security testing. This meant we had to make sure that only performance testing was done in order to have a similar baseline.

The obvious problem was the need for a dedicated environment. A dedicated performance environment was spun up so they did not have to fight with other process resources in the pre-production environment. The new performance environment was also built on non-virtual servers as production was to provide similar performance results. This environment also allowed for the ability to deploy a new build daily instead of the weekly or sprint build which went into the pre-production environment allowing for a daily performance run. This made it much easier to track down performance issues with fewer check-ins or changes to the infrastructure. The dedicated environment also gave the opportunity to have control and administration of analytical tools; such as Splunk and Dynatrace. Access for the QA team was not possible to the pre-production environment. The performance engineers were able to run full tests after each sprint version, which we were doing more frequently. In addition, they were running smaller scenarios daily. Self-service scripts are also now being developed for scrum teams that have specific needs for performance verification so that the teams actually doing the code can see results specific to them. The resources needs of setting up and maintaining the new environment, tools and test runs were made available when we brought on the new performance engineers along with some resource help from devOps from time to time.

4. Demonstrated Benefits

4.1. More Frequent Value Delivered

During Costco Travel's initial agile roll out there were only 10 releases a year in five-week releases. This was the case for the first several years. We were able to deliver value more frequently when we moved to the four-week releases. This four-week release model also aligned with the 13 business periods which synchronized the business and IT organizations. We are currently deploying 26 releases a year. In addition with providing business value faster, it also allows the business to pivot as needed, as it gains more information with the analytics and sales that we are actually generating. See Figure 1.

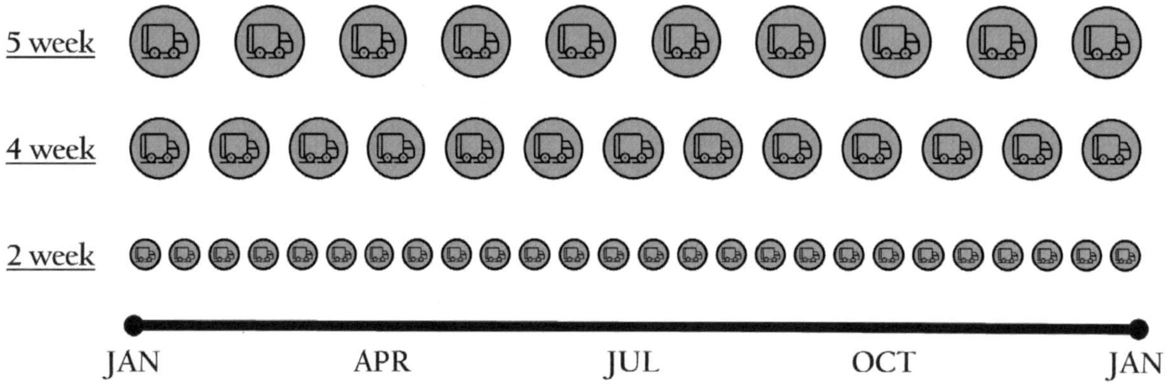

Figure 1: Timeline comparison showing the number of deployments that deliver value to the customer as Costco Travel deployed more frequently.

4.2. Lower Production Defect Fixes Needed

The analysis of the number of escaped defects shows another interesting piece of information that was unexpected. During the timeframe that Costco Travel was releasing under the 2:2:1 week release cadence, there were an average of 15 escaped production defects fixed per week. In the 2:2 week release cadence, immediately after, there was only an average of only 12. If you remember the 1 week in the 2:2:1 week was a stabilization sprint. You would think that if you dedicated an entire week to stabilization that you would have fewer escaped production bugs to fix, but this was not the case. Instead we are now successfully doing a better job of stabilizing the feature work within work sprints.

4.3. Fewer Hot Fixes

One of the most striking improvements has been the reduction of hot fixes. This has been an amazing overhead time savings as many features have had to be pushed out when critical defects have taken precedence over scheduled scrum work. This also causes entire build cycles which takes the time for additional regression testing and devOps deployment activities. These would not normally take place. Finally, any out of ordinary process gets less oversight, testing and monitoring which increases risk compared to having these defect fixes go out with a regularly scheduled release. As seen in Figure 2, there has been a distinct trend downward in the in the past two years. Even the spikes which represent major feature releases trend downwards. There are two general reasons for this trend. The organization is maturing and becoming more stable as automation is developed faster, by testers that are closer to the features and it is run more frequently. Another factor is the amount of time in between releases. A user doesn't have to wait five weeks for a defect to get fixed anymore. That defect could go out with limited impact in the two-week regular cycle.

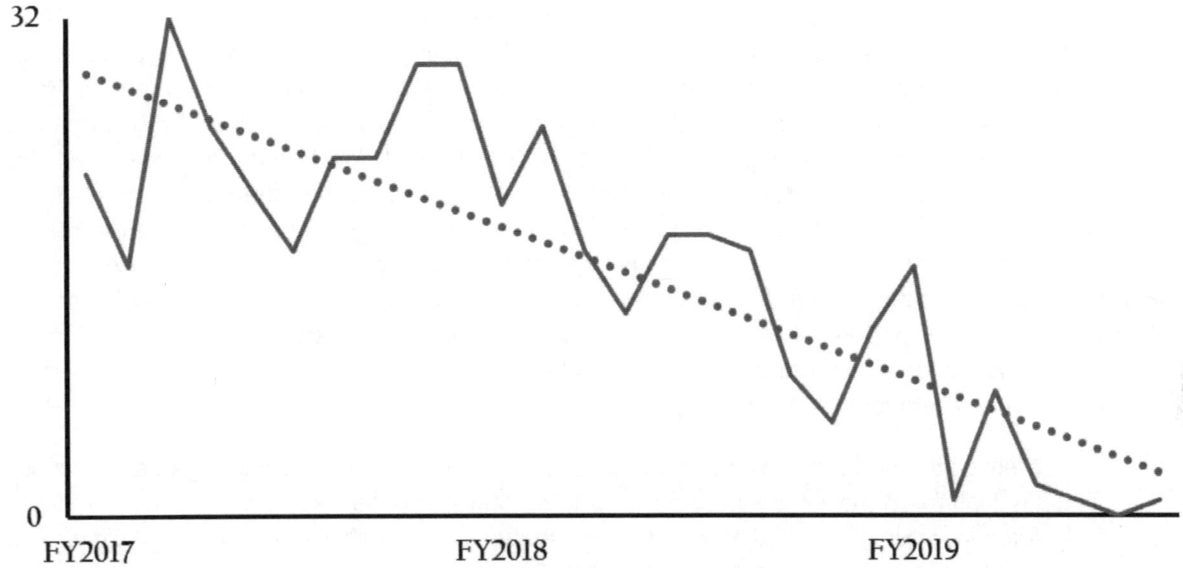

Figure 2: Actual hotfix items (solid) and trend line (dotted) of hotfix items in releases between fiscal year 2017 and fiscal year 2019.

5. Missteps

As with any process change or set of changes, there is bound to be failures. Costco Travel has had its share of missteps as well. There are a few highlighted here to give an idea of what can happen. Remember that one of the core concepts of Lean thinking and Agile is to iterate and continually improve. It is important to keep making small steps that will either produce small failures to learn from or small wins to build off of. This paper will only highlight three of the QA specific missteps while working toward a faster release cadence.

5.1. Use Experience to Start an Automation Effort

The first and most important misstep for QA was to start an automation effort without testers who have automated tests at a large scale. There are several tools on the market that make it seem so easy to automate your application testing. Writing a test may be easy, but developing the infrastructure, reporting, processes, etc. around it and then maintaining them is not really thought about. There were several attempts with different products to get off the ground with varying degrees of success at Costco Travel. Nothing was useful until we hired dedicated SDETs that would focus on the framework and initial tests. Even these were not the end product, but they were the first serviceable automation.

5.2. Tread Lightly Adding BDD to a Mature System

Costco Travel did make an attempt to go to a behavior driven development model (BDD) using Cucumber. This proved difficult because of how mature the systems and documentation was. A couple of proof of concepts were attempted including one that was going to go back and rewrite all of the previous user stories into Gherkin format. This proved to be just too large of a rewrite just for the tests. It also showed how standard writing styles are needed to make the coding clean and easy to maintain. We also tried to do a proof of concept of a small project independently. The idea was to use BDD on projects going forward. This did not move forward because there would have to be more than one process and we still wouldn't have had all of the user stories in one location.

5.3. Don't Let Your Test Run Time Get Away

The final misstep highlighted in this paper is the need to manage test run time. This is one that we still run into here and there. Costco Travel's focus was on the run time of testing. We would regularly get test suites bogged down because tests were continually added and not looked at for efficiency or even need at times. The main problem was the need to focus on the UI testing which by nature are slower. To build on that testers would create an entirely new end to end test using a similar workflow to one that already existed. There were also situations where certain tests did not have the importance to run every day or build. We had test run goals of five minutes for a simple smoke test of an environment. A few months later, a tester would ask why the pipelines were taking so long and part of the reason was because this smoke test was running for 25 minutes – nearly five times longer than it should. We would see this at all levels of our tests. Our Continuous Acceptance Tests (CAT), which was the basic build level certification, would get to the point where it would run for 45 minutes and the team would know we would have to do something to reduce it. Here are a couple of remedies that were employed:

- Actively go through similar workflows and develop permutations that could regression test as many features as possible with as few end-to-end trips as possible.
- Enforce the coding standard of adding a new feature to an existing end-to-end test if it is available over creating another end-to-end test.
- Creating a prioritization in which we could group regression tests by tests that would highly impact the end-user and those that would not impact the end user and we could run the later less frequently and in off-peak lab hours.
- On the hardware side, make sure that we were running as many tests concurrently as possible. There was a significant effort that went into determining how many Selenium nodes could fit onto the virtual machines that were allotted and at a lower level, how many instances of each browser could run on each of those nodes.

6. Next Steps

6.1. Mindset Shift

Costco Travel has gotten to the stage where we cannot simply continue to shrink our sprints or deployments. We need to start thinking about how to get the value out more dynamically. We need to start peeling away from our monolithic core so that we can deploy independent services (Fowler 2019). These independent services must be backwards compatible so that we don't have to depend on one specific release cycle. Costco Travel is already developing proof of concept services that should plug and play into our current architecture including automated test frameworks that will allow for the continuous testing to complement the continuous integration and continuous deployment of these specific services.

6.2. Testing at a Lower Level

Costco Travel has developed an amazing UI testing platform. Even though we are good with UI testing, this type of testing is big, bulky, and time-consuming to run. Code changes causing failures early on in an end to end test may prevent many other tests from getting run until those tests are fixed. These tests also rely heavily on outside influence such as Selenium, individual drivers, browsers, and device hardware. There was no UI test automation strategy early on at Costco Travel and incoming automation testers had to deal with a mature product with little test hooks into lower layers. This left us with more of a goblet looking test model (See figure 3) instead of a traditional pyramid model (Cohn 2009, 311). The future move to a service oriented architecture such as a microservices architecture will allow us for us to work with the architects and developers to get test hooks in place and an accessible service layer to test on.

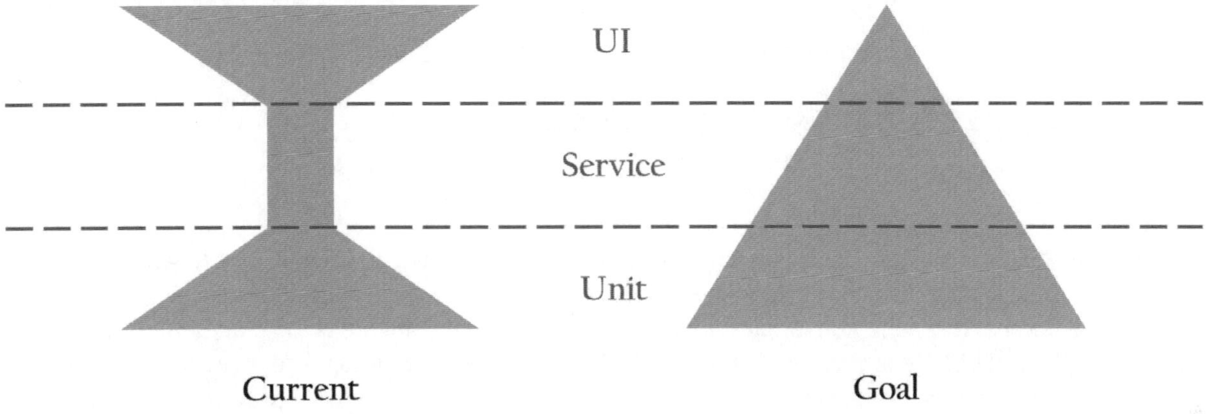

Figure 3: Current model of test distribution with more unit and UI tests and the ideal distribution (right) where there are more service layer tests than Costco Travel has now relative to UI tests.

7. Conclusion

Costco Travel has shown progress in its journey from a manual five-week release with only three weeks of value added work to a much more automated two-week deployment cycle with almost full value capacity. It is easy for existing mature systems to feel that it is too difficult to make progress, but this is not true. A continuous improvement approach must always be in place. In Costco Travel's situation, we focused on getting to closer to a continuous deployment and continuous integration model. They were a large successful monolith with a realization that additional value could be delivered faster. Starting from scratch was out of the question because we did have success. We took small strides. This can be seen in ratcheting up the QA department slowly over the years. The release cycles did not cut to two weeks all at once. It was a slow, continuous improvement. Mistakes were made, identified and reworked before moving on. Victories were celebrated. The roadmap is still in place and the journey is still continuing as Costco Travel is attempting to change the architecture so that it can have more individual independent services. These services will be testable on a lower service level, which will also be independent of the rest of the existing monolith and other services.

References

Cohn, Mike. 2009. *Succeeding with Agile: Software Development Using Scrum*. Addison-Wesley Professional.

Fowler, Martin. 2019. "Microservices Resource Guide" martinFowler.com, https://martinfowler.com/microservices/ (accessed August 15, 2019).

IBM Knowledge Center. 2019. "Security test Policies", https://www.ibm.com/support/knowledgecenter/en/SSW2NF_9.0.2/com.ibm.ase.help.doc/topics/c_security_test_policies.html (accessed August 15, 2019).

Behaviour Driven Development (BDD)

A Case Study in Healthtech

Stefania Bruschi, Le Xiao, Mihir Kavatkar, Gustavo Jimenez-Maggiora

bruschi@usc.edu, xiaole@usc.edu, kavatkar@usc.edu, gustavoj@usc.edu

Abstract

Behavior Driven Development (BDD) is a software development practice that leverages a simple domain-specific language to enhance the effectiveness of testing within the Software Development Life Cycle (SDLC). The biomedical research applications developed at the University of Southern California - Alzheimer's Therapeutic Research Institute (USC ATRI) are subject to multiple regulatory requirements. Compliance with these requirements must be tested formally following current software quality assurance best practices and methods. As part of a comprehensive test battery, BDD plays a critical role to ensure each software release meets internal quality standards and complies with applicable regulatory requirements.

The BDD infrastructure developed at USC ATRI provides an extensive set of functionalities: from testing data integrity and replicating user interactions to efficiently communicating test results, analytics, and dysfunctional operations. This scalable infrastructure can accelerate development, speed up the execution of cross-platform testing across multiple browser-device-operating system combinations, standardize validation, facilitate the redesign of existing User Interfaces (UIs) and enhance the readability of test documentation.

This case study demonstrates our journey of building and incorporating BDD in our day-to-day development workflows using a real-world use case. Also, we describe the infrastructure set-up, the test execution, automation and get a real-world perspective on the strengths and limitations of BDD.

In our view, a key advantage of the BDD methodology is that it seeks to build a robust communication channel between software quality engineers (SQEs) and business analysts (BAs) in which the expected behaviors of the system are described in a business readable and domain-specific language. By breaking down siloed communications between stakeholders, BDD allows SQEs to apply tests based on semantically valid business requirements without the need for translation to a distinct technical schema. BAs, for their part, can focus on ensuring that the cases being tested are meaningful, representative, and can easily be traced back to their requirements, leading to increased engagement in the testing process.

Biography

Stefania Bruschi, MS, MBA, is a Senior Programmer Analyst at USC ATRI with a broad range of computer programming experience and proven track record in team leadership and development.

Le Xiao (MS, MBA) is Programmer Analyst at USC ATRI focusing on full stack development and automation testing.

Mihir Kavatkar, MS is Programmer Analyst at USC ATRI. He is a Full Stack Software Engineer and deep learning enthusiast with experience in delivering modern web applications.

Gustavo Jimenez-Maggiora, MBA, is the Director of Informatics for USC ATRI. He is a recognized expert in the field of clinical research informatics in Alzheimer's Disease and Related Dementias.

1. Introduction

Software testing is a broad term collectively applied to a variety of activities along the software development life cycle and beyond, aimed at different goals (Tuteja and Dubey 2012). Historically, challenges in software development and real-time usage have served as motivation for the advancement of new software testing techniques and the technologies which underpin those techniques with the ultimate goal being able to detect flaws in an application before releasing it to consumers. As its benefits have become better understood, software testing has become a widely adopted and important practice, especially in industries that are highly regulated. Health Technology, or Healthtech, defined as "the application of organized knowledge and skills in the form of devices, medicines, vaccines, procedures, and systems developed to solve a health problem and improve quality of lives" (World Health Organization n.d.) is one such industry.

The Alzheimer's Therapeutic Research Institute (ATRI) at the University of Southern California (USC) is an academic organization leading a consortium of academic institutions dedicated to the acceleration of therapeutic interventions for Alzheimer's disease (AD). It is collectively committed to developing new models of AD to test, characterize biomarkers and develop and minimize variability through enhanced quality control of outcome measures by applying novel analytic methods and enact highly innovative regulatory pathways. USC ATRI is currently conducting 18 clinical trials via a network of clinical trial sites in multiple countries to accelerate the development of effective therapies for AD (Keck School of Medicine of USC n.d.). There are multiple sections and functional areas at USC ATRI that participate in different stages of a clinical trial's life cycle (Figure 1: Organizational Structure of USC ATRI). Among these, the Informatics section takes the lead in building the computing and data infrastructure that supports the scientific and operational aspects of the clinical trials conducted by USC ATRI.

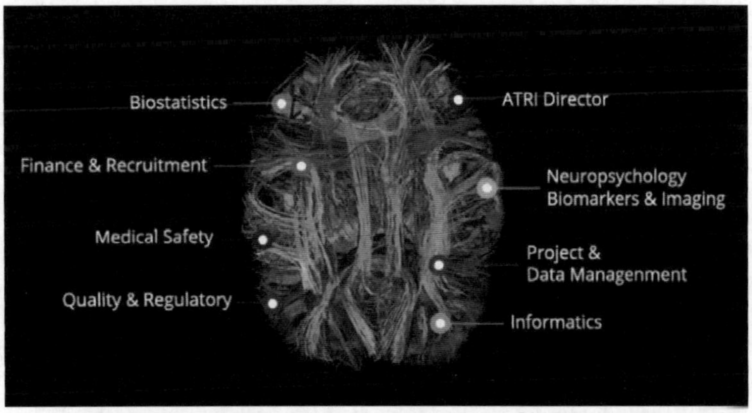

Figure 1: Organizational Structure of USC ATRI

A key system within USC ATRI's computing and data infrastructure developed by the Informatics section is the ATRI Electronic Data Capture (ATRI EDC) system. This web-based system provides clinical research teams with multiple applications to manage their daily scientific and operational workflows and data management activities. This system is an example of a Healthtech application that is subject to regulatory requirements regarding its development and operation, with a strong emphasis on software quality. To address these requirements more efficiently and maintain a feature development roadmap which is responsive to our project goals and user feedback, the Informatics section restructured its development workflow to incorporate the Behavior Driven Development (BDD) methodology. We describe our BDD implementation and discuss the impact this approach has had on our ongoing development of this system in the sections that follow.

2. Objectives

This case study describes the integration of Behavior-Driven Development (BDD) into our Healthtech software development lifecycle. Specifically, we (1) develop a cloud-based platform that supports the process of requirements gathering, testing and reporting; (2) develop CI/CD automation workflows; (3) describe the tools and services that are required to build our BDD platform.

3. Overview

3.1. Electronic Data Capture (EDC) System at USC ATRI

The ATRI EDC system is a software solution designed to support data management activities for a clinical trial, from study start-up through study completion and publication of results. The driving principle behind such a system is to provide research teams with a set of reusable tools for collecting, storing, and sharing clinical research data. The following are the key features of our system; (1) user authentication and role-based security; (2) electronic case report forms (eCRFs); (3) real-time data validation, integrity checks, and other advanced techniques to ensure data quality; (4) Audit capabilities; (5) Document storage and sharing; (6) Data Export functionality for use in statistical analysis workflows; (7) Reporting on the different operational data collected by the system; (8) Secure data storage and backup capabilities. Importantly, as an example of a Healthtech application used to establish new medical treatments, the development and use of this system for research purposes are subject to regulatory requirements.

3.2. Data Quality, Integrity and Regulatory Compliance

The development of new drugs and biologics is a capital-intensive, time-consuming, and highly regulated process. The clinical success rate for a new compound is estimated to be 12%, development costs per new approved drug or biologic are estimated to be $2.6 billion (2013 dollars), and development timelines are estimated to be 96.8 months (DiMasi, Grabowski and Hansen 2016). Regulatory authorities supervise the marketing of new compounds based on evidence generated in clinical trials. Regulators define quality standards for evidence presented in support of new drug applications. Quality standards for the construction and operation of the computer software and systems used to collect and manage clinical trial data are also regulated.

The ATRI EDC system is used to collect data in support of new drug and device marketing applications to the U.S. Food & Drug Administration and international regulatory agencies. When used for this purpose, a computer system is subject to multiple regulations including Title 21 of the Code of Federal Regulations Part 11 (U.S. Food & Drug Administration 2003) and The General Principles of Software Validation - Guidance for Industry and FDA Staff (U.S. Food & Drug Administration 2002) guidelines. The consequences of non-compliance with these standards are high; data collected in a computer system which is not compliant may be rejected by the regulatory agency, potentially putting the approval of the entire new drug application at risk.

Title 21 of the Code of Federal Regulations Part 11, or Part 11, describes the record-keeping requirements that a computer system must meet to assure its electronic data and signatures will be eligible for submission to the FDA. These procedural and technical requirements ensure the authenticity, reliability, and integrity of system data and specify the use of written operating procedures, access controls, and immutable audit trails.

The General Principles of Software Validation guideline promotes the use of good software engineering practices and risk management when developing software used in clinical and research applications. The guideline recommends the Software Development Life Cycle (SDLC) approach, which consists of discrete phases such as planning, testing, traceability, and configuration. In this approach, testing, verification, and validation are considered distinct activities. Software verification "provides objective evidence that the design outputs of a particular phase of the software development life cycle meet all of the specified requirements for that phase". Software validation, on the other hand, provides "evidence that all software requirements have been implemented correctly and completely and are traceable to system requirements". Based on the software's risk profile, this evidence allows us to develop an "acceptable level of confidence" that the software satisfies all requirements and user expectations before release.

We rely heavily on the concepts and methods defined in the aforementioned guidelines and the expert guidance of quality assurance consultants to support the conclusion that the ATRI EDC system is validated and compliant with Part 11. Historically, however, the implementation of these methods was reliant on a costly, error-prone, manual approach which limited the number of times we could realistically revalidate the system. This approach also suffered from poor reproducibility and scalability. Given the rapidly evolving needs of science and clinical research which drive our system requirements, we decided to find a new approach to validation.

4. BDD Methodology and Strategy

Behavior-Driven Development (BDD) (Lazar, Montogna and Parv 2010) is an agile software development methodology that encourages collaboration between developers, software quality engineers (SQEs), business analysts (BAs) and non-technical stakeholders in a software project. It encourages teams to use conversation and concrete examples to formalize a shared understanding of how the application should behave. BDD combines the techniques and principles of Test-Driven Development (TDD) with ideas from domain-driven design and object-oriented analysis and design to provide software development and management teams with shared tools and a shared process to collaborate on software development.

Despite these potential benefits, adopting the BBD methodology can be a daunting task for development teams. Incorporating additional effort into use case discovery and testing as well as integrating specialized tools and infrastructure required to support BBD carry risks and costs that may dissuade some teams. Automation, however, can play an important role in recovering these upfront costs and mitigating risks. These considerations are especially important to small organizations such as ours which have limited resources.

To de-risk our team's adoption of BDD, we made several strategic choices: 1) we chose to focus on a specific software project, the ATRI EDC, 2) we chose to focus on a specific goal - validation and regulatory compliance - which BDD was capable of solving effectively, 3) we scoped the project to ensure that automation was a requirement, thus allowing us to recoup our upfront costs rapidly, and 4) we chose to build our BDD infrastructure by using a modular architecture that integrates various cloud-based component services.

As a next step, we enlisted the help of a medical device quality assurance consultant to provide an objective review of our plans to introduce BDD into our existing validation model, which is based on the V-model (Mathur and Shaily 2012), an approach which envisages the SDLC as a series of design, development, and testing stages (Figure 2: V-model (Mathur and Shaily 2012)). Each design and development stage (e.g. planning, requirements, specifications) is associated with a corresponding testing stage (e.g. testing, verification, validation). Importantly, this model promotes a high degree of traceability between related stages.

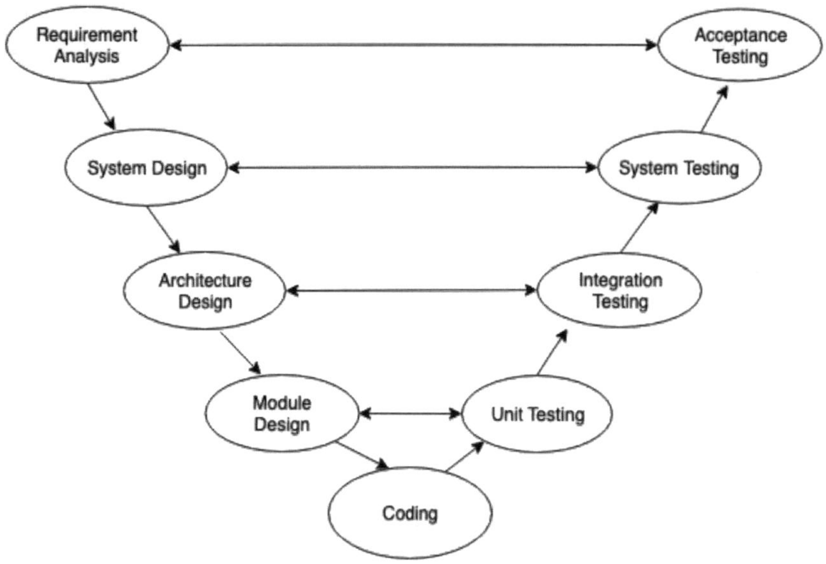

Figure 2: V-model (Mathur and Shaily 2012)

Our BDD-enabled validation exercise was rooted in the fundamental principle of BDD, which posits that user behavior should drive application functionality. User-oriented use cases and test scenarios were developed using Gherkin syntax (cucumber.io n.d.), a highly accepted standard in the software testing community used to describe user behavior utilizing business readable, domain-specific language. These artifacts serve as inputs to our BDD infrastructure, which automates test generation, execution, reporting, and documentation.

Once the initial validation of the ATRI EDC system was completed we continued to work to further incorporate BDD into our development workflow. Ultimately, we established a process where new development starts with a requirements discovery process which seeks to be inclusive of multiple stakeholder perspectives. Requirements are broken down into use cases and test scenarios using Gherkin syntax to ensure the full project team can participate in the review process. The final Gherkin documents are used by our BDD infrastructure to support automated testing, documentation, verification, and validation. As new user requirements emerge, this cycle can be repeated efficiently.

5. Infrastructure Overview

The Behavior Driven Development (BDD) infrastructure enhances the testing framework of a software application and must be integrated into the culture and software development life cycle of an organization. We implemented the BDD infrastructure as a plugin that can be used across multiple projects with minimal training. When developing a BDD infrastructure, it is crucial to consider each of the following aspects: transparency in the organization, scalability of the overall system and processing pipelines, automation in the integration with a software implementation, version control, maintainability, simplicity, compatibility, and cross-browser support. Finally, the BDD infrastructure must automate the creation and distribution of reports and traceability matrices.

Figure 3 provides an overview of BDD infrastructure we developed.

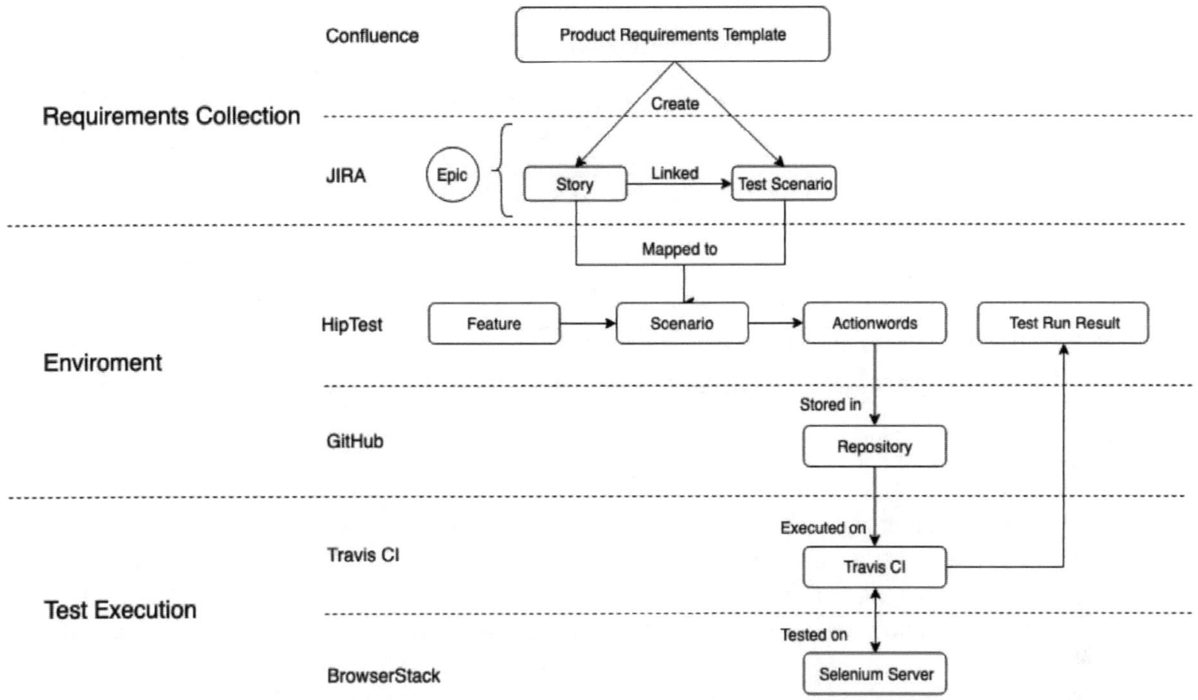

Figure 3: BDD Infrastructure

6. Requirements Collection

The integration of the BDD methodology within the early stages of the SDLC process is critical. Following the V-Model shown in Figure 2, planning BDD tests during the requirement analysis stage is an effective strategy to increase collaboration between stakeholders and to define linkages between requirements and acceptance tests.

To increase transparency and facilitate communication between different cross-functional teams, we use an integrated project workspace made up of Atlassian Confluence, a knowledge base tool, Atlassian Jira, an agile project management tool. Atlassian tools allow teams to initialize linkages between requirements and BDD test scenarios and maintain the association between tasks generated at any stage in the SDLC and requirements and BDD test scenarios. This process minimizes disruption to the coding and testing phases but helps software quality engineers (SQEs) and business analysts (BAs) automatically generate reports that can be distributed to project stakeholders.

6.1. Requirements Hierarchy

Defining a requirements hierarchy is one approach to break down the requirements into understandable and readable parts.

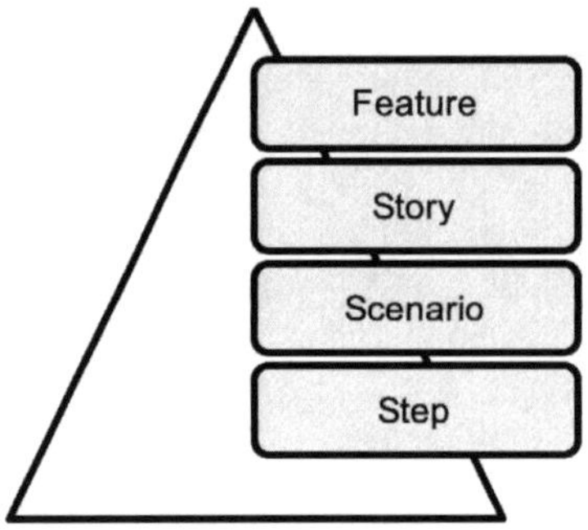

Figure 4: Feature Structure

In Figure 4, we define the following hierarchy:

- **Feature** is a summary of new functionality to be developed and tested.
- **Story** is the end-user use case that needs to be addressed and the expected outcome is interpreted from the software or system requirements.
- **Scenario** is the basic unit of functionality which scopes out the user behaviors. A story could have many scenarios to test different outcomes.
- **Step** in a scenario is a simulation of user behavior which is verified against the expected behavior. There can be many steps to satisfy a test scenario.

A similar convention is followed by HipTest (SmartBear Software n.d.), a collaborative testing platform in the cloud from SmartBear Software that allows the software delivery team to co-design acceptance tests.

7. Environment

7.1. Following standards

Writing test scenarios must follow standards that ensure readability and maintainability. We used Gherkin language, a highly accepted standard in the testing community, to describe the test cases. "Gherkin is designed to be non-technical and human-readable, and collectively describes use cases relating to a software system. The purpose behind Gherkin's syntax is to promote behavior-driven development practices across an entire development team, including business analysts and managers. It seeks to enforce firms, unambiguous requirements starting in the initial phases of requirements definition by business management and in other stages of the development lifecycle". (cucumber.io n.d.)

7.2. Collaborative Testing Platform

The BDD infrastructure requires a collaborative testing platform allowing the design of the test scenarios, test execution, and test refactoring.

Our selection was based on the following criteria:

- **Improve trackability** – the testing platform is integrated into our agile project manager tools, Jira, via plugins.
- **Automate report (i.e. traceability matrix)** – the testing platform provides standard reports and APIs.
- **Minimize disruption of SDLC process** – the testing platform generates executable code and feature files that can be translated into many programming languages including all the scenarios and action words.

- **Automate maintainability across multiple releases –** the testing platform supports test refactoring and automated report generation synchronizing test scenarios and keeping feature files up to date.
- **Visibility and One stop shop –** the testing platform provides a rich reporting framework that aggregates test results and Gherkin-based descriptions.
- **Keep the overall system lean –** the testing system provides reusable action word across features.
- **Security –** the testing platform requires encrypted communications between component services.
- **Cost-effectiveness and Total Cost of Ownership –** the testing platform requires modest subscription costs and minimal or no licensing fees.

Based on the listed selection criteria, HipTest (SmartBear Software n.d.) was selected as the best match for our requirements.

7.3. BDD Plugin

The BDD plugin is the core of the BDD Infrastructure where all the preliminary work of creating stories and scenarios comes together. Our BDD plugin uses the Python-based Django framework. The BDD plugin includes several modules as shown in Table 1. The code structure of the plugin is crucial for its future reusability.

Feature Files	The HipTest command line interface (CLI) helps to build a set of feature files which describe the scenarios and the steps that are required to accomplish them. These feature files are the entry point to the tests (SmartBear Software n.d.).
Step	A step is a user behavior description. In the plugin, it builds a mapping between a step described in a feature file and implementations which are referred to as action words.
Action Word	An action word is a set of actions taken to implement user behaviors. Developers use an action word to define the logic of the test (SmartBear Software n.d.).
Page Object	The page object pattern is used in the context of web testing for abstracting the application's web pages to reduce the coupling between test cases and application under test (Spadaro, et al. 2013).
Fixtures	A fixture is a collection of pre-defined sample data that can be used to support development and testing (Django n.d.).

Table 1 - BDD Plugin module

8. Test Execution

Figure 5 illustrates the environment utilized by our BDD infrastructure to support cross-platform, high performance test execution.

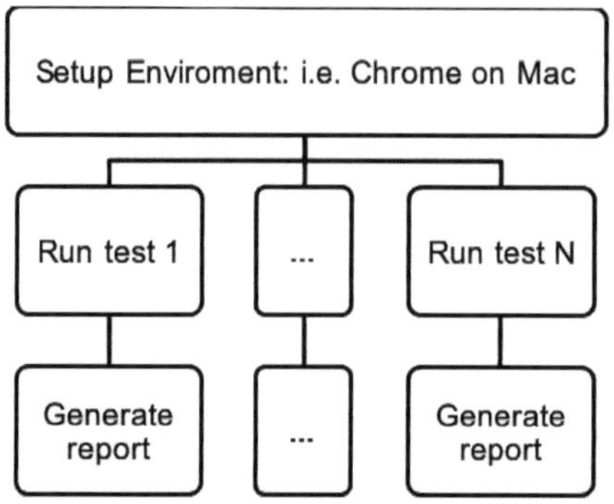

Figure 5: Test Execution

8.1. Parallel Test Running

Monitoring multiple test runs is time-consuming and involves manual work. Automating the parallel execution of tests is a crucial requirement for an effective BDD infrastructure. Travis CI (Travis CI n.d.) is a continuous integration (CI) tool that can be integrated with source code version control systems such as GitHub to streamline test execution at different stages enabling parallel testing runs. Each concurrent job has a makefile which defines the BDD test environment's build directives and dependencies.

8.2. Test Running on a Cross-Browser Platform

For web development, the BDD Infrastructure must enable developers to execute their tests across multiple combinations of operating systems, devices, and browsers. This need has become increasingly important as the smartphone market continues to grow and diversify (Prasad and Mesbah 2011).

To support this requirement, we chose BrowserStack, a cloud-based cross-browser testing solution, that allowed us to manage our costs, provide our developers with reasonable test execution times, and collect video-based troubleshooting and execution reports (Gowthaman and Kaalra 2014).

Furthermore, BrowserStack supports integration with Travis CI and enables automation testing to run through Selenium. After each test execution is complete, the test results are sent to HipTest through integration with Travis CI.

9. Reporting Requirements Traceability Matrix and Test Results

A critical component of a software or system validation project is the creation of a requirements traceability matrix (RTM) (Wikipedia, the free encyclopedia 2019). In this context, the purpose of the RTM is to ensure that all requirements are covered by the test protocol.

Our BDD infrastructure generates a new RTM report for each software release which supports backward- and forward-traceability between requirements and related tests. Links to detailed cross-browser platform test results are also provided to facilitate quality reviews.

9.1. Current process

The current reporting process relies on Jira, HipTest, and Confluence APIs and the BDD plugin's environment file and test-specific makefiles to build and upload a detailed report of use cases, tests, and test results to Confluence. This information is subsequently used to generate the RTM. These reports are reviewed by the QA team and project stakeholders to confirm requirements and review discrepancies.

9.2. Potential Improvements

The current reporting process displays the RTM as a set of reports that can be viewed in Confluence or exported as a PDF document. This static, table-based approach limits our ability to analyze historical data using statistical or visualization tools. Platforms such as Amazon Web Services (AWS) or Google Cloud Platform (GCP) provide reliable, scalable, and cost-effective cloud computing services that could be used to optimize our reporting process. The use of these services would allow us to store, analyze, and draw inferences from the rich testing data we are collecting. Efforts to implement these improvements are already underway.

10. Discussion/Lessons Learned

The integration of the BDD methodology into our software development life cycle began with a comprehensive review of our processes, practices, and tools. Once complete, this review revealed several gaps which we addressed over 3 months, from September to December 2017. In the following 3 months to March 2018, we collaborated with a medical device quality assurance consultant to retrospectively apply the BDD approach to validate the ATRI EDC system and ensure compliance with 21 CFR Part 11 guidelines. After this, all subsequent development of the ATRI EDC system has been conducted using the BDD approach. This experience has provided us with a better understanding of the advantages and shortcomings of the BDD approach, which we discuss below.

In our experience, a key advantage is that BDD increases communication which results in better collaboration. It helps multiple teams agree on a standard for formalizing the test requirements which are used to automate testing and document generation, elements which are important for system validation. Every step, from requirements gathering to test execution, is traceable and transparent to all stakeholders. Time-consuming tasks, such as documentation and testing, are largely automated by BDD allowing teams the flexibility to focus on other priorities. To ensure continuous compliance before every release, comprehensive testing reports are generated which allow all project stakeholders to review and confirm that defined test scenarios are meaningful and cover product requirements. The automation available using BDD saves time and cost, critical to small organizations such as ours. Finally, significant changes can be deployed with thorough validation and test requirement coverage so that the development process is accelerated.

Despite the above advantages, BDD also has a few shortcomings. First, the Gherkin syntax attempts to make tests human-readable and therefore constrains human language. Because of this, It may not able to capture nuance and intention. Second, test execution follows a top-down approach within a feature file and hence ignores conditional situations. In other words, "if-else" conditions cannot be used to cover alternate use cases. A solution to this limitation is to replicate the test scenario for each conditional use case. Finally, different browsers have their respective web drivers and test scenarios rely on these to perform user behaviors. Some web driver versions may not be compatible with the latest browser and the tests may fail for these browsers. A solution to this problem is to restrict the version of the browser where the automated tests are executed. A limitation to this solution is that the tests are not executed on the latest browser which can result in unexpected results.

11. Conclusions

In the fast-paced environment of medical research and information technology, our development teams historically struggled to keep up with rapidly changing user scenarios and requirements. This served as the initial motivation for moving our software development model from waterfall to agile. The agile development approach has provided our teams with numerous advantages such as short iterations, focus on consumer requirements, and increased developer engagement. Despite these gains, challenges still exist; being able to rapidly add a new feature to a project doesn't necessarily mean that the new feature will meet user requirements or stakeholder expectations. More often than not, this mismatch is due to gaps in communication between end-users, stakeholders, and developers. This is one of the areas where the process of Behavior Driven Development, a methodology that extends traditional agile approaches, truly shines. By design, BDD strives to keep the whole project team in sync, maintaining one standard language (Gherkin), to describe use cases and test requirements. Just as importantly, BDD facilitates the inclusion of both the end-user defined requirements and the technical perspectives required to achieve them.

Interestingly, traditional BDD implementations consider automation an optional requirement. This case study demonstrates different strategies and services we used to automate BDD. By automating the execution of our BDD test battery, we attained several benefits including tighter collaboration and communication, faster feedback, and continuous compliance with 21 CFR Part 11 guidelines. Adding automation allowed us to create a sustainable BDD-based validation model which is a critical requirement for Healthtech projects.

Finally, the key advantage of including BDD in our software development approach has been the creation of a more inclusive environment where all project stakeholders are engaged in a more frequent and meaningful manner. This ongoing engagement has ultimately reduced the number of misunderstandings and inconsistencies that can occur at the end of the project. BDD has strengthened the interaction between the entire project team leading to significant efficiencies.

12. References

cucumber.io. n.d. *Gherkin Reference.* Accessed 08 23, 2019. https://cucumber.io/docs/gherkin/reference/.

DiMasi, Joseph A, Henry G Grabowski, and Ronald W Hansen. 2016. "Innovation in the pharmaceutical industry: New estimates of R&D costs." *Journal of Health Economics* 20-33.

Django. n.d. *Providing initial data for models.* Accessed 08 23, 2019. https://docs.djangoproject.com/en/2.2/howto/initial-data/.

Gowthaman, Dr. K, and Bhavnesh Kaalra. 2014. "Cross Browser Testing Using Automated Test Tools." *International Journal of Advanced Studies in Computer Science and Engineering* (IAASSE).

Keck School of Medicine of USC. n.d. *About the Alzheimer's Therapeutic Research Institute.* https://keck.usc.edu/atri/about-atri/.

Lazar, Ioan, Simona Montogna, and Bazil Parv. 2010. "Behaviour-Driven Development of Foundational UML Components." *Electronic Notes in Theoretical Computer Science (IEEE).*

Mathur, Sonali, and Malik Shaily. 2012. "Advancements in the V-Model." *International Journal of Computer Applications.*

Prasad, Mukul, and Ali Mesbah. 2011. "Automated Cross-Browser Compatibility Testing." *International Conference on Software Engineering.* ICSE. 561-570.

SmartBear Software. n.d. *Execute the tests and create feature files.* Accessed 08 23, 2019. https://hiptest.com/docs/create-feature-files-for-automated-execution/.

—. n.d. *Hiptest.* https://hiptest.com/.

—. n.d. *HipTest at a glance.* Accessed 07 17, 2019. https://hiptest.com/docs/about-2/.

—. n.d. *HipTest: Use action words.* Accessed 08 23, 2019. https://hiptest.com/docs/use-action-words/.

Spadaro, Cristiano, Filippo Ricca, Diego Clerissi, and Maurizio Leotta. 2013. "Improving Test Suites Maintainability with the Page Object Pattern: An Industrial Case Study." *Proceedings of the 2013 IEEE Sixth International Conference on Software Testing, Verification and Validation.* IEEE.

Travis CI. n.d. *Travis CI.* Accessed 08 23, 2019. https://travis-ci.com/.

Tuteja, Maneela, and Gaurav Dubey. 2012. "A Research Study on importance of Testing and Quality Assurance in Software Development Life Cycle (SDLC) Models." *International Journal of Soft Computing and Engineering (IJSCE).*

U.S. Food & Drug Administration. 2002. "General Principles of Software Validation." *www.fda.gov.* January. https://www.fda.gov/regulatory-information/search-fda-guidance-documents/general-principles-software-validation.

—. 2003. "Part 11, Electronic Records; Electronic Signatures - Scope and Application." *www.fda.gov.* 08. Accessed 08 14, 2019. https://www.fda.gov/regulatory-information/search-fda-guidance-documents/part-11-electronic-records-electronic-signatures-scope-and-application.

World Health Organization. n.d. "Health technology assessment: What is a health technology?" *World Health Organization.* Accessed 08 13, 2019. https://www.who.int/health-technology-assessment/about/healthtechnology/en/.

Standards are Necessary but Not Sufficient for Excellent Software

David N. Card
card@computer.org

Abstract

Software is becoming increasingly pervasive in business systems and everyday life. Software is the glue that holds together complex systems. It is impossible to talk about the quality of a software dependent system without discussing software quality. A software dependent system is a system that can't perform its intended function if the software doesn't work correctly. However, since software is invisible, systems developers often do not give it sufficient attention. Nevertheless, inadequate quality can put businesses and lives at risk.

This paper provides a systematic overview of software quality in the context of a system. This includes static, dynamic, and customer/user perspectives. Quality standards have been widely adopted in recent years. However, these standards only address static aspects of quality, e.g., conformance to requirements. Moreover, the author's experience shows that these standards are often incompletely implemented. This is facilitated by a lack of appropriate feedback on the quality status of software products. As described here, objective measurements and independent in-process audits can be part of the solution.

Biography

David N. Card is an independent consultant working in the areas of software quality assurance for aerospace, automotive, and marine systems. He is also a research associate of the Experimental Software Engineering Group of the Universidade Federal do Rio de Janeiro, Brazil. Previous employers include Computer Sciences Corporation, Det Norske Veritas, and Lockheed Martin. Mr. Card is the author of many articles and two books on the topics of software quality, reliability, estimation, and performance management. He has worked with scores of software engineering organizations seeking to improve their performance. He does not promote any single methodology. He has also participated in many project reviews and accident investigations.

1. Introduction

The term "software quality" has been redefined so many times that its meaning has become unclear. In this paper we introduce the term "software excellence" to encompass most interpretations of software quality. Excellent software meets requirements and is defect-free, safe, reliable and secure from cyberattack. Figure 1 identifies these properties. Note that they are not orthogonal dimensions. They are overlapping and dependent. For example, research (Woody, 2014) shows that 50% of security exploits are linked to defects introduced during development and maintenance. Consequently, establishing an engineering process that minimizes defects is critical to achieving software excellence. The practices of an effective engineering process are defined in process models and standards (e.g., International Standards Organization, 2017)

2. How Do Standards and Models Fail?

The Capability Maturity Model – Integration (CMMI) (Chrissis, et al.) is popular in the aerospace and automotive industries. The CMMI is used to assign a maturity rating or score to an organization's software engineering process. However, organizations that are assessed as high maturity often do not operate with high performance, especially with regard to quality. There have been several significant examples in recent years, although these are not discussed publicly.

How does this happen? Software and systems development are human intensive activities, typically conducted in complex organizations. Established past performance may predict future performance, but good behaviors (maturity) may not be maintained in situations of stress. The CMMI assumes that the QA role will maintain quality performance, but project management usually has greater power while focusing on cost and schedule. Integrated Software Dependent Systems (ISDS) (Det Norske Veritas, 2012) is similar to the CMMI but is intended to be used to monitor ongoing software development processes. It does not assume that because an organization can correctly answer a questionnaire or has demonstrated good performance in the past that it will deliver good performance on the current project.

Another problem is that process models may be incomplete and/or poorly implemented. This may be due to a misunderstanding of process requirements. For example, the concept of "peer reviews" is well define in software engineering literature, but I have seen examples of implementations ranging from peer reviews that find no defects to peer reviews of the same artifact repeated multiple times.

Software development is a human activity subject to human weaknesses such as misunderstanding and overconfidence, Experienced developers often believe that their skill enables them to take shortcuts without suffering consequences. ISDS addresses this by requiring in-process audits.

A current issue is the myth that Agile eliminates the need for processes. The Agile manifesto (Beck, et al., 2001) specifically de-emphasizes processes (Individuals and interactions over processes and tools), but that does not mean that processes are unnecessary. In fact, rigorous processes (especially Configuration Management) are essential to an effective Agile project, where different parts of the product are being developed and tested at different times, with the expectation that they will all integrate easily at the end. The most effective Agile organization I have encountered developed software for cable TV set top boxes. They followed a disciplined process that incorporated Agile practices such as Scrums and Sprints. The Quality Assurance organization provided intensive coaching on the methods to be employed and Project Management enforced the process regardless of cost and schedule challenges.

3. Nature of Quality

Quality may be viewed from many perspectives. Figure 1 illustrates some of them. This discussion focuses on software, but applies to software dependent systems, in general. A similar approach (de Rocha and Travassos, 2017) also includes the factor of service quality, which may be important for some products. Figure 1 shows that achieving software excellence requires taking static, dynamic, and operational perspectives to ensure high performance.

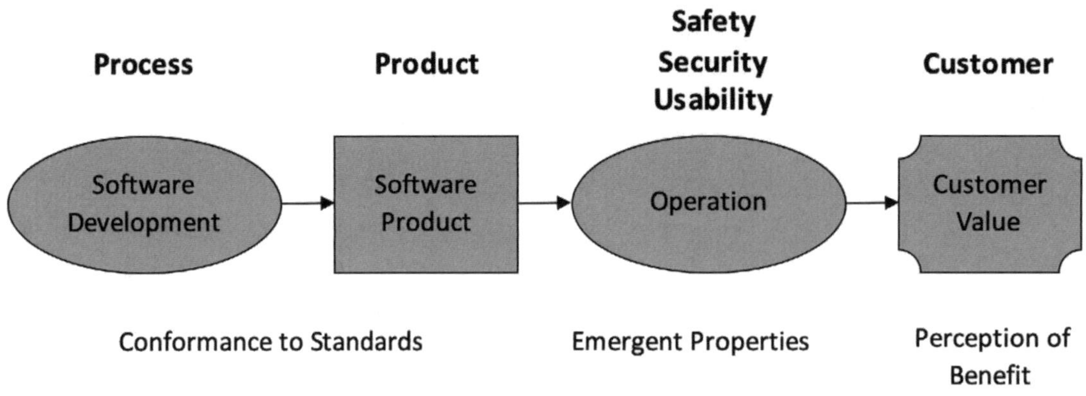

Figure 1 - Model of Contributors to Software Excellence

The software engineering process may be more or less capable of producing a good product. Process quality may be defined in terms of process standards or process reference models based on "best" (or at least "good") practices. Of course, in order to provide benefit, these practices must be implemented by the developers.

The software product, itself, may be evaluated in terms of conformance to appropriate product standards. The process perspective has proven to be more important for software quality than for typical manufacturing industries, because software product standards have proven harder to agree upon, and logically, different standards are needed for different products. Software product standards typically define characteristics that are associated with successful operational use and maintenance of the software. Software product standards commonly focus on user interface and networking issues. Data may also be considered a software product that can be standardized for specific applications such as maps

The operating software may be evaluated in terms of the quality of service provided, such as security, safety and usability. As emergent properties, these qualities are not amenable to standards. They must be evaluated in the overall system context. For example, the safety of a software component depends on how the user interacts with it as well as the mechanical equipment attached to it. Conformance to product standards (such as "no single point of failure") cannot ensure safety, but can make it easier to achieve. While Safety is a special concern for offshore vessels, most safety analyses assume that software is 100% reliable, but reliability also depends on the context of use. Security has largely been ignored in this industry. For example, many suppliers deliver software with a hard-coded password. Nevertheless, quality (as freedom from defects and nonconformance to requirements), is a pre-requisite for both safety and security. Research shows that 50% of all security vulnerabilities are due to software defects (Woody, 2014). Clearly, software quality has an immense effect on the operator's and customer's perception of the product, even if it is not the only factor.

The customer's satisfaction is based on his experience with the product as compared to his expectations of it. Satisfaction is a state of mind, not a physical state. Managing customer expectations is as important in achieving customer satisfaction as managing operational quality. Establishing standards for customer satisfaction is very difficult.

As indicated in Figure 1, the software process and software product are the views of software quality that are most amenable to standards. How do standards fit into software quality assurance? Standards provide expectations of activities to be performed or outcomes to be achieved. Satisfaction of these expectations can be confirmed by direct observation (verification), i.e., in-process audits.

4. Recommended Solution

In addition to in-process audits, appropriate measurements should be to monitor whether or not real quality performance meets expectations. Simple data from peer reviews (defects, effort) tell us about the performance of design and code activities. The author observed two illustrative cases where the number of reported defects from peer reviews was low. Audit and observation of the peer review activities in these projects showed that in one case (Case1) the peer reviews were pro forma – peer reviews lasted five minutes and few defects were recorded. In the other case (Case 2), the team conducted two rounds of peer reviews – in the first round defects were found and recorded; the second peer review occurred after defects had been fixed. Both teams were trying to do a good job, but in Case 1 the objective of peer reviews was not achieved, while in Case 2, the cost of peer reviews was doubled and important defect data was lost. A program of regular in-process audits would have led to earlier detection and correction of these situations.

The message is that simple data helped to identify that something unusual was going on, but that it was necessary to directly observe the behaviors in order to diagnose and correct the problem. Thus, our focus on measurement and in-process audits to ensure effective implementation of processes. Requirements Traceability is another activity where there are many technical approaches, but where developers may lose sight of the objectives.

In order to maintain a focus on quality, defects should be monitored throughout development. The author has had success with a Weibull modelling approach for agile and highly iterative processes. The Weibull model is suited for processes where defects are continually being introduced and removed from the system, but at different rates (Card, 2002). Figure 2 shows an example of a Weibull analysis of data from implementation and testing of a control system for marine navigation based on a standard design. The Weibull curve represents the theoretical optimum (i.e., frontier) performance of this verification process. However, in any given testing interval there are likely to be inefficiencies, e.g., holidays, delays, poor planning – so the actual performance tends to fall below the optimal performance leading to a "frontier" behavior (Zu, et al., 2001). In this case regression on the actual data, e.g. (Dola, et al. 2014) will not give us the correct (frontier) Weibull model. Instead we *impute* the Weibull parameters using the criteria that the observed peak of the distribution should coincide with the peak of the theoretical model, and the slope of the observed data should match the slope of the theoretical model. (The Delta Delta line in Figure 2 compares the slopes.) As both curves pass through the origin we can identify Weibull parameters to estimate the tail of the frontier model. The result shown in Figure 2 indicates that additional testing and fixing is needed to reduce the defect level and increase reliability.

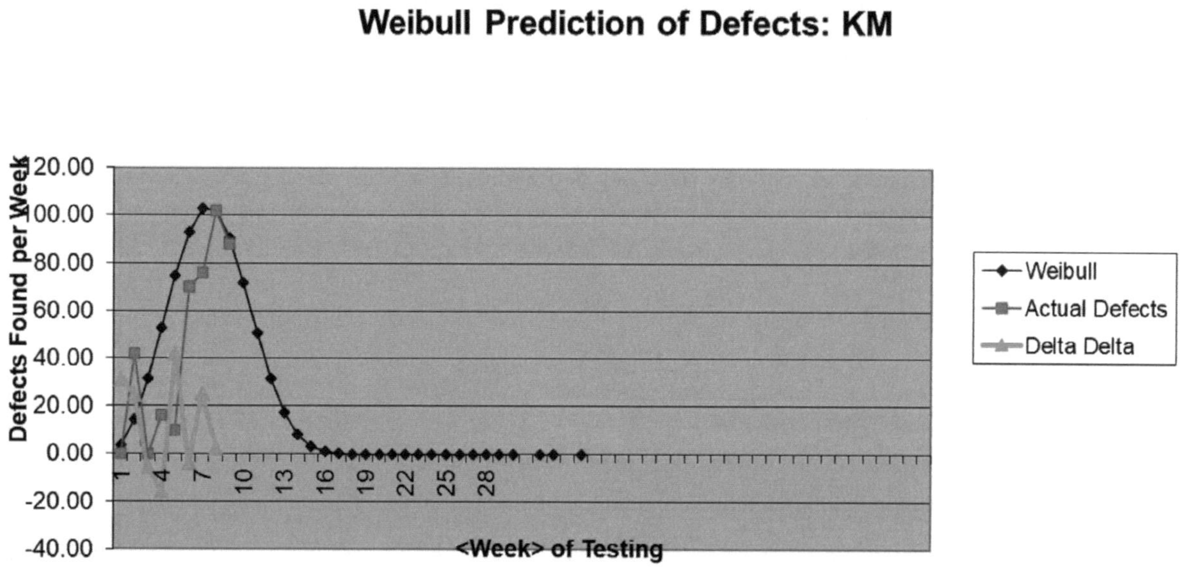

Figure 2 - Weibull Analysis of Defects [SM1]

5. Summary

Achieving software excellence in a complex system requires many different activities, not just implementation of standards and process models. Moreover, implementation of process models must be re-enforced through timely feedback. Agile processes require re-enforcement, too. Organizations that make major investments in methods and tools often fail to invest in feedback mechanisms to make sure that they are effectively implemented.

Process models and standards are necessary, but not sufficient, for excellent software. FAA standards require rigorous development and testing activities similar to those of the CMMI. However, failure to update a safety analysis after a late design change can result in disaster.

Similarly, rigorous development and testing of an offshore safety system that ignores how the operators can/will react to anomalous situations can result in failure to avoid disaster.

Nevertheless, good implementation of standards and process models creates an environment where safety, security, and operations studies can be successful. These processes ensure that artifacts (e.g., designs) necessary for FMECAs and usability studies are available.

6. References

D. Card and L.G. Chua, Ensuring Software Reliability, Safety, and Security, *Proceedings: RINA international Conference on Computers in Shipbuilding*, 2017

A.R. de Rocha and G.H. Travassos, QPS – Modelo de Referencia para Avaliacao de Produtos de Software, *Universidade Federal do Rio de Janeiro*, 2018

WOODY, C., *Predicting Software Assurance Using Quality and Reliability Measures*, Software Engineering Institute, 2014
Stamatis, D H., *Failure Mode and Effects Analysis*, ASQ Press, 2003

Ogale P., M. Shin and S. Abeysinghe, Identifying Security Spots for Data Integrity, *Proceedings: IEE Computer Software and Applications Conference*, 2018

Det Norske Veritas (DNV), OS D-203, *Integrated Software Dependent Systems (ISDS)*, December 2012

CARD, D., A Software Integration and Process Model for Offshore Vessels, *Proceedings: Asia-Pacific Software Engineering Conference*, 2013

CHRISSIS, M., M. PAULK, and S. SHRUM, *Capability Maturity Model - Integrated*, Addison Wesley, 2003

Dola D.R., M.D. Jaybhaye, and S.D. Deshmukh, Estimation of System Reliability using Weibull Distribution, *International Proceedings of Economic Development and Research*, 2014

Zu T., M. Wen, and R. Kang, An optimal evaluating method for uncertainty metric in reliability based on uncertain data envelopment analysis, *Microelectronics Reliability*, August 2017

Beck, Kent, et al., https://agilemanifesto.org/, 2001

International Standards Organization, ISO/IEC 12207, *Systems and Software Engineering: Software life Cycle Processes*, 2017

Card, D., Managing Software Quality with Defects, *IEEE Computer Software and Applications Conference*, 2002

[SM1] Chart axis titles are overlapping the chart impacting readability

What Your UI Tests Need to Say

Joe Ferrara
joe.ferrara@climate.com

Abstract

UI tests that only execute steps and return a Pass or a Fail are not very useful. While this kind of automation gets you much further along in your automation, it requires close examination of the test code and its logs to figure out what went wrong. One of the best practices you will learn is that the test should communicate what it is doing plus provide a precise statement of what went wrong. Other best practices having to do with test results communication are reporting results to a test case management system and communicating to stakeholders on the status of test runs. Aspects of test reporting such as the different audiences that care about test report data will be covered. Audiences range from the individual engineer to senior management.

In this talk, I will use Swift code for iOS to illustrate fine grained ways that tests communicate progress and status, such as ways to use assertions, screenshots and other test artifacts to your advantage. I will also describe a component written in Swift that our team developed that writes test results to a test case management system, TestRail®. The best practices and experiences shared are applicable to software platforms besides iOS.

Biography

I am a Staff Engineer with over 20 years of experience ranging from development, test and test development for numerous companies. I spent over 10 years at Microsoft developing consumer software and testing the software. I spent some time at startups in Seattle plus consulting with several companies including White Pages and Starbucks. My focus for the past several years has been mobile application testing, mainly on the iOS platform. I currently work as a front-end Test Architect at The Climate Corporation. I have led the development of a UI test automation project and now consult with other front-end projects regarding test engineering.

1. Introduction

Effective communication from your automated tests to members of your team is important for any team process and for continuous integration and continuous deployment (CI/CD) pipelines. With effective communication, issues can be investigated quickly and understood efficiently. Whether you are part of a large test engineering team or just one or two people, your time is valuable. Being able to zero in on an issue quickly frees up your time for testing and development.

In this paper, I illustrate the best practices that I have worked through in my work with UI test automation development. My most recent experience is with testing iOS apps using the Swift language. My examples are based on this platform, though the material is applicable to other toolchains. I first lay out the reasons why communication is important and then get into specifics applicable to authoring the test function in code and communication to individual engineers, the test case database and to any member of your team.

At The Climate Corporation, we decided to choose a UI test framework that allows us to write tests in the same language that our development team codes with. This decision has allowed us to fully engage the development team in reading, writing and maintaining UI tests. The test framework we use, XCUITest, is included in Apple's Xcode along with the unit test framework, XCTest. The benefit for the team is that we could leverage each other's work. We have worked as a team to write regression tests that bring us to a more complete automated CI/CD pipeline. Developers also can use UI tests to automate bugs and use that automated test script to verify the bugs got fixed.

2. Preparing for Writing Tests

2.1. When to Write UI tests

There are at least three phases of a project where UI tests can be written. One is before the feature is written. This is difficult with a test that manipulates a UI, but it is not impossible. At least outline in high level code what is supposed to happen and failing by default.

A second phase is while the features are being implemented. Working with the app developers can ensure that the automation is buildable and gives early feedback to stakeholders.

A third phase is to automate an existing set of tests for features that have already shipped. A motivation for doing so is to cut down on the time required for manual testing and to enable the continuous integration pipeline to run faster and with fewer manual resources.

2.2. What to Communicate When a Test Fails

When writing a test, it is tempting to do whatever it takes to write code that passes the given test case or specification you have for the test. This is ultimately what you want, but it is also important to keep in mind what happens when the test fails. A future "you" or anyone else on your team may need to deal with this.

In addition to cases when the application under test fails, your test can fail due to the runtime environment, an error in the test code, a change in the underlying test framework or change in the operating system.

When planning for implementing tests you have to specify for yourself how your tests will communicate. This includes assertion messaging, logging, screen shots and text attachments. You can build some of the enabling functionality into your test framework. For example, in our most recent iOS project, we implemented code in the common **tearDown()** logic so that a snapshot of the UI element tree is saved to a text file attachment that is always available as a test artifact. For logging, we wrapped the most basic "print" function with one which can direct where text is sent so as to accommodate a cloud testing framework.

3. Aspects of Assertion Messages

3.1. Assertions

Assertions constitute the core of your communication. Other than simply seeing that a test failed, the assertion message will often zero in on what the failure is. To the extent possible, providing enough information to get to a root cause is ideal. The assertion logic and messaging work in concert with additional test artifacts like screen shots, attachments and logging.

The assertion functions provided in XCTest are **XCTAssertTrue()**, **XCTAssertFalse()**, **XCTAssertNil()**, **XCTAssertNotNil()**, **XCTAssertEqual()**, **XCTAssertNotEqual()**, **XCTAssertThrowsError()**, **XCTAssertNoThrow()**, **XCTAssertGreaterThan()**, **XCTAssertGreaterThanOrEqual()**, **XCTAssertLessThat()**, **XCTAssertLessThanOrEqual()** AND **XCTFail()**. Each assertion function takes an optional parameter for a message.

XCTAssertTrue() could be used for most types of assertions, however in that case the intent is more difficult to understand from reading the code and you lose any default messaging the test framework gives you. Of the assertions shown here for XCTest, only the ones having to do with NSExceptions need some specific assertion function. Although the other specialized assertions can be replaced with **XCTAssertTrue()**, this is not recommended.

I often see code that does something like 'XCTAssertTrue(!someFlag, "something went wrong")'. Here, the thing that might get lost in a quick scan of the code is the exclamation operator just to left of `someFlag`. It is better to just use **XCTAssertFalse()** instead, so that the intent is very clear just from reading the function name.

XCTAssertEqual() and **XCTAssertNotEqual()** are examples where the assertion function provides for a default message before whatever message is specified in the parameter. It is much better to be explicit that you are testing for a comparison so that when it fails the XCTest framework it will include the compared values in the message.

3.2. Messages for Assertions

3.2.1. Do Include a Message

I have seen engineers write assertions in UI tests that lack any message. I have found that when I get a failed test case with no error that I am, at first, at a loss as to what is going on. I am forced to go into the code and tease out what is being checked and what happens before the assertion is fired. Going into the extra steps is certainly not impossible and might only add a few minutes to writing a bug report or determining that one is not needed. However, why waste time when a clearer communication is easier to do?

3.2.2. Include Context

No matter what type of assertion is used, it is good to include additional data in the message that include the names of the elements being compared -- additional information on what precedes the assertion. I have sometimes had the opportunity to add a hint on what could be going wrong. For example, if some setup is required in a test and lack of doing that setup fires off an assertion, then why not inform the reader about the setup requirement?

In addition to being aware of coding guidelines while writing code, code reviews are a great opportunity to catch cases where context is not being provided. Some teams create short guidelines for code reviews. From a test engineering point of view, it is valuable to advocate for these sorts of guidelines and participate in writing them.

3.2.3. Consider Custom Assertions

XCTest and many other frameworks will allow for some method to write custom assertions. This allows the developer to write very specific verifications particular to their application. Doing so can often eliminate duplicate code and make it easier to both comprehend and maintain.

When you see many assertions that look similar and do something special before each call, you have a candidate for a custom assertion. For example, I want to assert that a substring shows up within a string.

Below is an example for code that will benefit from a custom assertion.

```
let myList = ["apple", "orange"]
var searchFor = "apple"

XCTAssertTrue(myList.contains(searchFor),
    "Mylist: \(myList) does not contain \(searchFor)")
searchFor = "orange"

XCTAssertTrue(myList.contains(searchFor),
    "Mylist: \(myList) does not contain \(searchFor)")
searchFor = "banana"

XCTAssertTrue(myList.contains(searchFor),
    "Mylist: \(myList) does not contain \(searchFor)")
```

Below is the custom assertion that can be used instead of **XCAssertTrue()**. The function usage is shown first.

```
CXCTAssertListContains(myList, searchFor)

extension XCTest {
    func CXTCAssertListContains(list: [String], searchFor: String,
        message: String = "", file: StaticString =            #file,
            line: UInt = #line) {
    let errorMessage = (message == "") ?
            "List `\(list)` does not contain `\(searchFor)`" : message
    XCTAssertTrue(list.contains(searchFor), errorMessage,
```

```
                        file: file, line: line)
        }
    }
```

When naming your custom assertion, it is clearest to not use the same prefix as the test framework. So, in the example, instead of using `XCT` use `CXCT` where `C` stands for Custom.

4. Communicating to the Engineer

4.1. Organizing Test Case into Steps

In XCTest there is a function, **runActivity()**, which is used with a named closure to show test code in a distinct step. That name shows up in the report's hierarchy making the report easier to comprehend.

Sample Code

```
XCTContext.runActivity(named: "Verify starting state") { _ in
  XCTAssertTrue(demoScreen.labelStaticText.exists,
         "Demo Label element is missing")
  XCTAssertTrue(demoScreen.labelStaticText.label == "",
         "Demo Label is not empty")
}
```

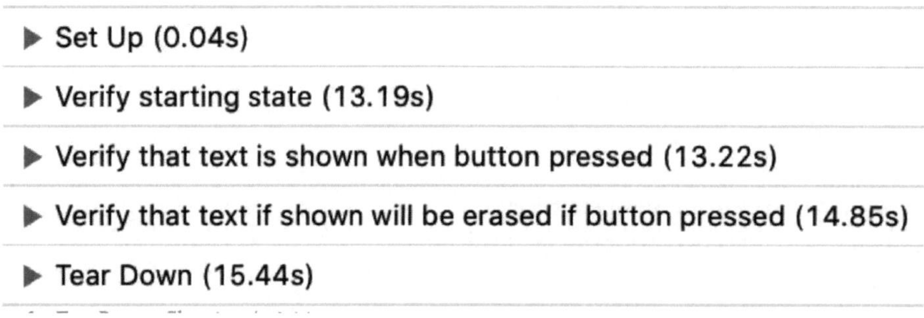

Figure 1 - Test Report Showing Activities

4.2. Screen Shots

4.2.1. Screenshots Created Automatically

In XCUITest, the system framework automatically takes screenshots whenever there is some change in the state of the app. I find these useful, though sometimes it is a bit time consuming to match up which automatic screen shots to pay attention to. It is also sometimes the case that when the test fails, the most relevant screen shot is not the last one.

4.2.2. Screenshots Created in Code

Adding code to a test case that saves a screen shot as an attachment allows for the test author to specify a name or to even do something like take an image of some subset of the screen. A reason for doing this rather than only relying on automatic screen shots is that if some UI state more than one step before an error is related to the screen where the error occurs. For example, in an app that has a form for entering data the test could modify data and then navigate through a few other screens before landing on one where it needs to assert that the data is displayed correctly. By keeping a named, manually attached screen shot, it is easier to make a comparison between what the test actually entered in the new value and the later screen where it displays the new value.

An example for adding an attachment in code is shown below.

```
let screenshot = app.windows.firstMatch.screenshot()

let attachment = XCTAttachment(screenshot: screenshot)

attachment.lifetime = .keepAlways

attachment.name = "Enter new value in `Name` field"

add(attachment)
```

4.2.3. Screenshots Retention

Screenshots can be useful even when the test passes. These can be configured to persist for all test runs. I find these useful when a test is inconsistently failing or when I am trying to compare an earlier integration's passing result to the current integration's passing result. It is typically possible for a CI/CD pipeline to have the capability of deleting these artifacts after some amount of time has passed.

4.3. Keeping Key Screenshots

Some tests will fail with some data verification from screen to screen. It would be useful to not only have detailed data on the final screen that is up when the assertion fires but to also have the first screen with the data that was compared against. By naming these screen shots and having them readily available for failures, it helps when investigating the issue.

4.4. Code Clarity

4.4.1. Accessibility Identifiers

Accessibility identifiers are more of a coding detail, though the clarity of your code makes it easier to have coherent assertion messages and diagnosis support. In iOS apps, the developer can associate an accessibility identifier with any element on the screen. There are a few ways to do this though demonstrating these is out of the scope for this paper.

Having a naming convention is important. One convention is to start with a name for the screen, then the name of the element and then the name for the type of element. For example, a name for the user name text field on a Sign In screen is **SignIn_Username_TextField** is useful.

How you deal with system elements such as those in iOS itself is important. For these you could be forced to use labels or position in the element tree. One work-around is to copy the localization string into a place accessible by the test framework and then use a utility function to get labels using an internal identifier.

5. Communicating to the Test Case Management System

5.1. Design

The Test Case Management system used on my projects is Gurock Software's TestRail® tool. It is a server-based service that stores our team's test cases, test plans and test results. It is a useful place to store documentation for test cases. It supports creating detailed reports based on past test runs. Our team needed a way to write results from UI tests automation runs to TestRail®. We used one of the REST endpoints, "api/v2/add_result_for_case", provided by our TestRail® instance.

An executed test result in our TestRail® instance can be set to Pass, Fail, Untested, Retest, or Blocked. Custom attributes are also defined in our system to store build label, comment, device and operating system. The build label and comment are passed into the reporter component. The device and operating system data can be determined in code at runtime. When passing data to the TestRail®, we include an API key and test Run ID. The API key is used instead of account and password in code to improve security. The Run ID is needed by TestRail® so it knows where to write results.

Our use case for using the TestRail® API was simply to record basic results from UI tests. Our UI automation writes Pass or Fail results to TestRail® for each test case using a REST endpoint. A test case where a result is not written remains Untested by default. Retry and most Blocked test case results are not supported with automation but used manually. If a test result is set to Nil then the test result is set to Blocked. Each result also includes the meta data supplied by the TestRail® client and system derived data. Each test result is made for the correct test case since that ID is also passed in.

In each test case we assign an ID string to an instance variable representing the test case ID. If we supply a comma delimited list of IDs then the results get written to multiple test cases. It is my recommendation that a class instance method is the preferred way to store a test ID so as to hide variables from the test case and make it easier to make changes. The sample function signatures below support setting a single ID or an array. You could consider validating the string form in the function body and returning a Boolean result or throwing an error. See below.

```
func setTestCaseId(id: String)
func setTestCaseId(id: String[])
```

5.2. Implementation

5.2.1. Determine Test Result

In the test's teardown function, one of the steps is to set the test case result based on the XCUITest **TestResult** variable. XCTest has a class variable named **testRun** which is an instance if the **XCTestRun** class. A variable in the **XCTestRun** class is **failureCount**. In the case of running one test case, this will get set to 1 if the test fails. This information can be used to set the **testResult** variable that gets pass into **reportToTestRail**().

5.2.2. Configure Test Result Data

The code for setting up the test data in **reportToTestRail()** is too long to document here, so below are the steps used for this function. The high-level description is that data about the test run and the test case is collected from environment variables and by calling system functions.

Step 1: Convert the test case ID string into an array of test case IDs even if there is one test case ID.

Step 2: Loop over the elements of the test case IDs array and set variable passed in as environment variables. Data that is set is for App version, Bot name, Bot integration ID, Host name, Comment, Assertion message, TestRail® account name, and TestRail® API key.

Step 3: Loop over elements of the test case IDs and call a function in the TestRailClient class, **reportResult()**, so that the results are written to TestRail®.

5.2.3. Convert Test Result Data to JSON

The test case result, build label, comment and assertion message are converted into a JSON string using a function named **buildJson()**. The JSON string is passed into **postResult()** with parameters for the TestRail® account credentials, test case run ID and test case ID.

The function, **buildJson()** determines the device and OS version. The return value is a **Data** object that is passed on to the REST endpoint in a later function.

5.2.4. Call TestRail® REST Endpoint

The request parameters are set and TestRail® credentials encoded so that the REST end point can be called.

Below is the code for setting the endpoint's URL.

```
let urlToPost = "https://mycompany.testrail.com/index.php?/api/v2/add_result_for_case/" +
testRunId + "/" + testCaseId
```

5.2.5. Log Errors

Any errors are determined and logged. Data from errors should at least include an HTTP status code but can also include full details from the call's response. If an error occurs the TestRail® result is left as its default value of Untested. Further investigation should proceed using logged data.

6. Communicating to the Team

Two routes that come up at this level of communication are summaries of test status as well as input to an issue tracking system where test execution data is communicated to all team members.

Test results flow through a CI/CD pipeline.

A summary of details about the executed tests help to keep management apprised of the health of the software and its readiness for shipping. Information that should be included for high level reporting include which tests fail, pass, and not tested. A couple of additional characteristics are revealing which test cases require another run or those that are blocked. These additional characteristics are most commonly associated with manual test results.

Tools such as TestRail® provide for reporting capabilities that can be used for visualizations such as a pie chart. Another component of TestRail® is more advanced reporting which can combine test status with other properties defined for each test case such as its type, priority and severity.

For test results dashboards and reports, assertions messages and other lower level details are not commonly found as it is possible to drill down into details through the TestRail® result and then the integration results.

6.1. Reports

Reports should include the following information. Percentages by test status in conjunction with a pie chart visually makes clear how many failures occurred as well as how many test cases passed. Something that can fit on one page is useful for sending to the team daily to provide a bird's eye view of the application's health. A high-level report can also be incorporated into a dashboard that some team members will use to get some more detail. This dashboard can dig deeper into the data and show the history for test status from build to build as well as a history of the specific test cases that fail and issues created as a result of test failures. Exploring this view gives the reader a sense of the application's stability over time.

6.2. Issue Tickets

Information communicated by UI tests in conjunction with artifacts from the build process and pipeline steps is needed for the creation of issue tracking tickets. Tickets are created either manually or through automation found in the CI/CD pipeline. A detailed look at aspects of issue tracking is beyond the scope of this paper, but several key things are worth noting.

A tool for tracking application issues is useful for storing bug reports as well as stories and tasks for software development. Reporting features can reveal the number of issues found over time, each issue's persistence over a number of builds, and a measure of test flakiness. The data associated with a test failure is useful for the contents of a ticket. Artifacts such as assertion messages, logs, attachments, and a reference to the test case management system are also important.

Deciding what data to communicate and how to do so is crucial for forming actionable issue tickets and facilitating ease of analysis by the engineer. Issue tickets are typically triaged manually by a group of team members that includes test engineering, development, and product. The information that your test communicates into the ticket should be clearly stated so that a diverse group of team members can understand the issue quickly and then make appropriate decisions about next steps. Another team member who benefits from effective communication is either yourself or someone else who needs to manually reproduce an error reported from tests. This helps with testing around the issue and determining if it can be reproduced. It is also at this point that test flakiness can be revealed.

7. Conclusion

Improving what your UI tests say supports faster issue diagnosis and better decisions from team members. Team members other than the test case coder benefit from high quality communication so that a clear picture is formed that is not missing details. Other team members who may not have been involved or remember details of a test or its feature under test need that information to make good decisions. Appropriate assertions and a precise message to indicate what has gone wrong is essential.

When communicating to the Engineer, you have the responsibility to include precise details, context and intent. Precise details come into play when constructing assertion messages that include state and relevant data. Context is adding any information about what leads up to the assertion. Intent is found in the code when choosing an appropriate assertion function to use and how the test code is organized with an eye towards how the test results will be displayed when test execution is done.

When communicating to the test case management system, you have the responsibility to forward test status, application metadata such as build label, device, and OS. Assertion messages are also useful.

When communicating to the team, you have the responsibility to provide clear information concisely using data derived from lower level communication. The sum of all the levels of communications provides enough detail to write actionable issue tickets.

8. Resources

TestRail® – https://www.gurock.com/TestRail

TestsRail® API - http://docs.gurock.com/TestRail-api2/start

XCTest documentation - https://developer.apple.com/documentation/xctest

XCUITest User Interface Tests - https://developer.apple.com/documentation/xctest/user_interface_tests

Test Scenario Design Models

What are they and why are they your key to Agile Quality success?

Andrea Gormley, Robert Gormley
anniegormley99@gmail.com, hotspur99@hotmail.com

Abstract

Customer satisfaction is considered the most important criterion for successful product delivery by a majority of Agile teams (52%). Yet as Digital Disruption continues to fuel the need for hyper speed IT delivery, many Quality teams are being left behind as they continue to leverage an old-world testing paradigm focused on Functional & Regression Testing built on traditional, linear test case design that is not customer centric. What's more, traditional test case design has become an antipattern for most product teams as it neither serves to validate the many different emerging layers of software architecture nor does it establish a core understanding of what should be built into automated tests.

What if, instead of traditional test case design, Quality teams could focus on building scenario-based outlines of user behaviors in a consistent, ubiquitous narrative to not only connect product functionality to users but also to establish a tight boundary for automated testing of acceptance criteria? Welcome to the world of the Test Scenario Design Model, where user behavior is king and test cases are short, concise, and business language-driven. In this paper, we explore what the Test Scenario Design Model is, how it can help Agile Quality teams accelerate their testing and show how Test Scenario Design Models tie to traceability and Quality metrics to truly measure your product team's Agile health.

Biography

In her role as a Principal Quality Consultant, Andrea works with organizations to master the art of Agile Quality. Her strengths in Lean Agile processes and business transformation allow her to develop practical and pragmatic Quality solutions for product teams to implement and refine. Andrea excels at helping organizations align on Quality goals, implement meaningful behavior-driven Quality processes, and mentoring less experienced resources on Agile Quality.

In his role as Chief Essentialist of Continuous Quality, Robert provides executive level total quality management strategy through efficient and effective testing, leveraging test automation and global service capabilities. Industry experiences include finance, healthcare, retail, security, wearables, IoT, Big Data, AI, and MBL. Robert helps organizations create lean agile processes that allow product teams to deliver business value with built-in quality. Robert uses his Master's in Education to help train and mentor all levels and types of resources in the ways of Total Quality.

1. Introduction

In its most recent survey on the State of Agile, VersionOne states that 52% of their respondents believe that success within an Agile initiative is measured by customer/user satisfaction and that success for an Agile project is measured equally by customer/user satisfaction at 46% (VersionOne 2019, 11). These percentages represent a jump for the customer/user satisfaction measurement as previously only 44% and 28% (respectively) of respondents believed this in 2016. Given the raise in the importance of customer/user satisfaction, most savvy IT folks would expect that Quality strategies within Agile organizations would naturally gravitate toward validating customer/user experience to ensure their satisfaction. Surprisingly, in multiple Quality reports at the end of 2018, 75% of respondents suggested their Quality strategies were focused on Functional and Regression Testing. These Quality strategies typically focus almost entirely on testing at the UI level to ensure proper navigation, functionality, and completion of simple rote tasks but do little to address customer/user satisfaction concerns. What's more, in many of these same organizations focused on Functional and Regression Testing, the key driver for testing is the over reliance on linear, repetitive test cases that don't place the customer/user at the center of the testing effort.

How then does an Agile Quality team ensure both built in quality and meet customer needs and satisfaction? What if, instead of traditional test case design, Quality teams could focus on building scenario-based outlines of user behaviors in a narrative that not only connects product functionality to users but also establishes a tight boundary for automated testing of acceptance criteria? We have been employing the use of Test Scenario Design Models, an approach to test case design based on the work of Cem Kaner's Scenario-based Exploratory Testing, Hans Buwalda's Soap Opera Testing, and ISO 25010's Product Quality and Quality in Use Models, to solve the challenge of placing the customer/user at the center of the Agile testing paradigm. In doing so, we have been able to help Quality teams be more successful in achieving both efficiency and effectiveness in Agile testing while ensuring that products being built deliver on the promise of customer/user satisfaction. The use of Test Scenario Design Models has allowed our teams to create clear traceability to user stories and acceptance criteria, the cornerstones of business value delivery for Agile teams.

2. What Are Test Scenario Design Models?

How do you define Test Scenario Design Models? They are scenario-based outlines of user behaviors in a consistent, ubiquitous narrative that allow you to focus on testing at every layer, not just the UI. In this section, we'll go through the details of what Test Scenario Design Models are and the history behind them.

2.1. Scenario-based Testing

Cem Kaner once defined a scenario as "a hypothetical story used to help a person think through a complex problem or system" (Kaner 2003, 1). Hans Buwalda expanded the scenario definition by saying that when used in the context of Soap Opera testing, the scenario is "based on real life, exaggerated, and condensed" (Buwalda 2004, 31). When we put the two definitions together, we have a new definition (a workflow) that places the user at the center of the testing effort while emphasizing the end-to-end nature of the testing approach. However, if you read carefully into both definitions, the biggest short-coming in both approaches is highlighted: the system under test must be mostly complete, a criterion that most Agile product teams could not meet until the end of a project. Additionally, the problem with most in-flight Agile Quality efforts is that the original testing strategy typically focuses entirely on Functional and Regression testing, an approach that does not look at scenario-based test design and execution.

2.2. ISO 25010's Product and Quality in Use Models

In order to circumvent the shortcomings of the end-to-end testing needing a nearly complete system in order to test, we've brought in ISO 25010's Product Quality and Quality in Use models. The Product Quality model of ISO 25010 emphasizes testing at a feature and functional level to assure the static properties of software and dynamic properties of the computer system (ISO 25010, 2011). By focusing on features and functions, the Product Quality model allows testers to focus on continuously developed increments of software during in-flight Sprints. The Quality in Use model of ISO 25010 emphasizes both the context of software use and satisfaction of users to measure the level of quality maturity in the system under test. In

Figure 1, you can see how scenario-based tests run horizontally from one transaction to the next to test a complete workflow. Whereas in Figure 2, you can see that scenario-based tests tied into ISO 25010 run both horizontally and vertically to carve out transactions as discreet modules because you are testing at both feature and functional levels while considering how the modules come together as a whole workflow. Note how, in most cases, user stories and their accompanying acceptance criteria are typically written in stand-alone fashion like the transactions in Figures 1 and 2. The main point of combining scenario-based test design with ISO 25010 is to enable a product team to always be working toward a releasable product that delivers end-to-end functionality by always testing for it. A product team that delivers code in isolation will always deliver poor quality (lack of integration) and a product team that delivers code in end-to-end workflows will likely never deliver code with any sort of speed.

2.3. Test Scenario Design Model Details

As you can see in Figures 1 and 2, a Test Scenario Design Model focuses on creating discreet transactions that can stand-alone but are part of a larger workflow. Note that each transaction is broken down into 4 specific parts: the UI/UX, Data Management, Integration, and Risk. The UI/UX component of a transaction should reflect the behavior of the user against the system and the response of the system to that behavior. Note, we aren't talking about the UI exclusively as focusing only on the UI simply validates that the system meets requirements but ignores fit for use. Data Management is a key component of a Test Scenario Design Model as most modern systems simply store, manager, or distribute data. As such, making sure that you are validating both system and inherent data characteristics as well as semantic and syntactical attributes of data is becoming increasingly important. Properly analyzing data requirements allows you to develop the best test data management strategy while also identifying the complete data set required to test both your transaction and workflow. Integration points are important to understand as the basis of a Test Scenario Design Model is an end-to-end workflow. Ensuring that integrations/hand-offs from one transaction (and in some cases one system to another) to the next are tested successfully is vital to testing workflows. The areas where defects tend to cluster most in modern systems are at points of integration. Emphasizing this testing is important for improving your teams defect detection efficiency. The final component of a Test Scenario Design Model is Risk. Because testing exhaustively is impossible (ISQTB, 2011), understanding where risk lies at a transactional level is important for not only understanding where to test but also how much to test. Working in Sprints predicates that QA teams have to be able to follow a more risk-based testing approach in order to meet testing goals but also to ensure team velocity.

3. Why Use Test Scenario Design Models?

Back in the day (you know you're old when you say that!), we used to proudly talk about the number of test cases we had written; the larger the number, the better we felt we were doing our jobs. That all changed when we became part of an Agile product team because Agile favors "working software over comprehensive documentation (Agile Manifesto, 2001)" and everyone knows having thousands of manually written test cases has little value for an Agile product team. There are those who would argue (Robert used to be one of them) that writing detailed test cases helps in automating the test cases. However, we now argue that the increased technical skillset of Quality Engineers means they require less mundane details (read UI); rather they value a complete story that helps them test the different layers of software systems. In addition to testing the different layers, automation that leverages Test Scenario Design Models focuses on creating modular, stand-alone tests at a transaction level, thus making it easier to script and much more reusable. The stand-alone, transactional nature of the automated tests allow you to exponentially expand test coverage by simply juxaposing variations of transactions one after the other in order to create better coverage of all scenarios. Traditional, linear tests have a limitation in that they have a singular intent (not parameterized, modular, or mutable) which limits reusability.

Test Scenario Design Models are built on fundamental testing principles. We've already noted that exhaustive testing is impossible (Testing Principle 2 according to ISQTB) so explicitly writing out every permutation of test case is a wasted effort. We also note that testing early (Testing Principle 3 according to ISQTB) or shifting left improves testing efficiency and effectiveness while reducing overall cost. Analyzing and planning test strategies for individual user stories while maintaining the focus on the whole picture allows you to build more comprehensive tests during pre-testing. Capers Jones, in his book *The Economics of Software Quality*, notes that pre-test activities are 25% more likely to find defects compared to the act of testing itself (Jones 2012, 5). What's more, we know that testing is context sensitive (Testing Principle 6 according to ISQTB), that is to say, the more we know about what we are testing, the better we are at finding flaws in the system. Test Scenario Design Models allow you to focus testing at the Product Quality level but also emphasizes that end-to-end testing should always be the goal to ensure customer satisfaction is delivered. Understanding the end-to-end behavior of the customer is truly aligning your testing to the context of why the system is being built.

One final point on why using Test Scenario Design Models is key to Agile Quality success is that they are easy to create. We like to use the Gherkin language to help us provide a consistent business language that is easy to write, read, and maintain. Leveraging Gherkin allows you to both connect your models back to the user story and develop fairly detailed traceability to the acceptance criteria. Those teams practicing Behavior Driven Development can leverage the Gherkin syntax to feed into their Feature Files of creating automated tests through tools like Cucumber, SpecFlow, and JBehave. We've seen how creating Test Scenario Design Models has reduced test case creation by over 25% or more depending on how long you've used them. In addition to taking less time, we've seen a reduction in the number of tests written by as much as 8 to 1. As more and more organizations embark on the journey to DevOps, Quality teams are going to be put under considerable pressure to reduce test execution time and parallelizing the test execution will only save so much time. It's going to be up to the Quality teams to achieve a dramatic reduction in the number of test cases in order to support quick deployment times key to DevOps.

4. How to Build Test Scenario Design Models?

When building Test Scenario Design Models, start by doing the following:

- List possible users, analyze their interests and objectives
- List "system events" and understand how the system handles them
- List "special events" and what accommodations the system should make for them
- Work beginning to end and break scenarios down into "transactions" tied to UI/UX, data, integrations, and risk

It's important to note, per Cem Kaner, that your scenario is credible. Kaner writes "it not only could happen in the real world; stakeholders would believe something like it probably will happen (Kaner 2003, 2)". Buwalda similarly notes that his Soap Opera tests were written to come up with "stories based on the most extreme examples that had happened, or that could happen in practice (Buwalda 2004, 32)". Avoiding the "what if" game (when testers sit and think about all the "what ifs") of test case design is the key of building the right level detail into the Test Scenario Design Models.

4.1. Getting Started with a Narrative

When we teach people to create Test Scenario Design Models, we start by getting them to write a short story about an experience most people have had before; buying something online at Amazon. We give them a few simple instructions:

- Avoid focusing on details like buttons, instead focus on user behavior
- Identify what event is the starting point and what event is the end point of your story
- Call out key data points

Here's an example of what we see:

Merrick received an e-mail from Amazon about the latest iPhone accessory. He was hooked, he had to have it. He clicked on the link provided and landed on the page for the accessory. He chose his color (red) and initiated the checkout process. Unfortunately, Merrick couldn't remember his password to log-in so he had to initiate the reset password process. He did that and received an e-mail which gave him his temporary password. He reset it, logged-in, and went to buy his accessory. Before he could check out, Merrick had to add credit card information since he hadn't saved it the time before. He entered his credit card info and clicked buy to confirm his order. Apparently, everyone who received the bulk e-mail rushed to buy the accessory and since Merrick had to reset his password, the red-colored accessory was out of stock!

4.2. Breaking It Down to Transactions

Once we have stories created, we ask our students to break down the stories into discreet transactions. For the example above, here's how it looks broken down by transaction:

- Merrick received an e-mail from Amazon about the latest iPhone accessory
- He clicked on the link provided and landed on the page for the accessory
- He chose his color (red) and initiated the checkout process
- Unfortunately, Merrick couldn't remember his password to log-in so he had to initiate the reset password process
- He did that and received an e-mail which gave him his temporary password
- He reset his password
- Logged in
- Navigated to his accessory
- He entered his credit card info and clicked buy to confirm his order
- The accessory was out of stock

4.3. Using Gherkin

Once we've broken down the story in to discreet transactions, we ask our students to focus on flushing out the details for each transaction using the Gherkin syntax of Given, When, Then. For the example we are using, the Gherkin would look like this for the first discreet transaction:

- **Given** Merrick has received an email from Amazon with a link to an iPhone accessory
- **And** he has clicked on the link provided in the email
- **And** he has been taken to the Amazon page for the iPhone accessory
- **When** he adds the Red accessory to his cart
- **And** clicks on the <Complete Order> button
- **Then** Amazon will initiate the checkout process

4.4. Layering on UI/UX

With the Gherkin created, we have our students focus on layering the UI/UX underneath it to guide testers on test execution. Note: the guidance shouldn't be detailed steps, they should be more focused on providing identifiers or behaviors to be used to imitate the user. For the example above, here's what the UI/UX guidance looks like:

- UI/UX: Email
- UI/UX: Amazon iPhone accessory page
- UI/UX: <Add to Cart> button
- UI/UX: <Complete Order> button
- UI/UX: Login or Proceed as Guest page

4.5. Adding the Data Layer

The next step to creating a Test Scenario Design Model is to identify, at a high level, the data required to complete a transaction. When you work through the data, it's important to make sure you consider the inherent (what the data looks like when it is in its raw, newly created form) and systematic (what the data looks like after it has been handled by a system) nature of the data. It's also important to include considerations for data syntax (structure) and data semantics (form) as you add the data layer to your Test Scenario Design Model. If we continue with our previous examples, you would add the data layer in the following way:

- Data: Temporary password (syntax & semantics)
- Data: Username (syntax & semantics)
- Data: Valid, corresponding password (syntax & semantics)
- Data: Credit card information (syntax & semantics)

When you are identifying the data needed for your Test Scenario Design Model, avoid falling into the "find every possible combination" trap. The modified condition/decision coverage (MC/DC) testing approach shows that even with testing each entry and exit point, the number of test cases needed for complete code coverage is finite. Here's an example we use to illustrate this point with our students. We ask our students the following question: if you are testing login functionality with just username and password, how many test cases do you need to test the login functionality completely? Before you (our readers) answer the question, let us give you some of the answers we've seen in practice at a number of different clients. We've seen up to 100+ test cases used to test login functionality. When we ask why these clients have so many test cases for validating login functionality, we always hear the same answer; "we make sure we test every combination possible". When we tell them the correct number of test cases is 4, they do not believe us and ask us to prove it. Here's the mathematical proof for why there are only 4 test cases:

- Test case 1: Username = T, Password = T, Result = Pass
- Test case 2: Username = T, Password = F, Result = Fail
- Test case 3: Username = F, Password = T, Result = Fail
- Test case 4: Username = F, Password = F, Result = Fail

Note that every combination of "business rule" applied to this proof is simply repeating one of the above 4 test criteria. For instance, one case we get all the time is "what if the username has a special character in it?" If your username field accepts special characters, it invokes test case criterion #1 and if the username field does not accept special characters, it invokes test case criteria #3 or #4.

4.5 Integrations, Integrations, Integrations

Once the data layer has been added to the Test Scenario Design Model, add integration areas for your transaction. As modern systems have become increasingly complex, the number of integrations within software systems has dramatically spiked, as has the importance of testing these integrations. When you add integrations, be sure to focus on sources of data, data locations, services, and security attributes or protocols. For the example above, the integrations would look like this:

- Integration: Bulk email
- Integration: Content manager
- Integration: Authentication service
- Integration: Add product to cart service
- Integration: Credit card validation service
- Integration: Checkout service fulfillment

If you find yourself identifying upstream and downstream dependencies, you are on the right track!

4.6 Don't Forget Risk

The final piece of a Test Scenario Design Model is risk. Risk, used here, is focused on prioritizing transactions based on business value. This definition of risk is sometimes difficult for tester to understand because they equate risk to severity or likelihood of failure. When we ask our students what level of Risk they would attribute to the login transaction, the most common (and by far the most immediate) response is high. When we ask "why" they gave that response, our students say login functionality is critical for a website. When we say that in the Amazon example the Login transaction is low risk, we get a lot of incredulous looks. We remind our students that Amazon's core business is to sell something to its customers. Whether or not those customers are signed on or not does not make any difference to Amazon because they can complete a purchase as a guest. Therefore, the login transaction does not represent a significant risk to Amazon's business if it does not work. At this point, we remind our students about the importance of context to testing especially as it applies to user-centric design.

As you look to assign risk to your transactions, do not lose sight of the fact that integrations should play an important part in determining your risk designation. Transactions that feature in many of your Test Scenario Design Models should always have a higher risk designation. If we refer back to the example of Amazon, the payment transaction would be high not only because the business value is high but also because every business critical scenario for Amazon would leverage that transaction.

4.7 Putting It All Together

If we put everything together from our previous sections, our Test Scenario Design Model would look something like this:

Note that this Test Scenario Design Model is not complete, we've only included three of the transactions as a sample. The full Test Scenario Design Model is actually 7 transaction. We've boxed up the transactions like a card which can be helpful if you are running Kanban (each box could be a Kanban card) or if you like using a physical Agile board (treat each box as a testing task to move along the board until it is done) but it's not necessary to do this.

Before we end this section, we want to highlight a few keys points from the Test Scenario Design Model we've included here as our example. The first point to highlight is how the **Given** statement for Transaction 2 and Transaction 3 are the **Then** statements from Transaction 1 and Transaction 2 respectively. Note that a link is created between the transactions but that the link is not creating a dependency as each transaction could be run independent of the linked transaction. For instance, Transaction 3 can be run at any point in time as long as the user has something in their cart and they proceed to checkout. You can see that there are also links in other areas of the transaction like in the UI/UX and Integration details but that these links are also independent of each other when it comes to test execution. This point is important because one of the features of Test Scenario Design Models is that they are built in a modular way so that you can easily juxtaposition individual transactions in order to create more scenarios and expand system coverage quickly.

The second point to highlight is the language and syntax used to create each transaction. The Gherkin language gives each transaction description a consistent and easy to follow narrative. That narrative provides a tester with a clear test objective and a concise criterion by which they can determine if the Test Scenario passes or fails. The syntax is succinct but comprehensive, it gives the tester enough information to guide their exploration of the system but also provides enough flexibility for the tester to use their analytical skills and experience to identify defects.

The third point to highlight in this example is that fact that not every transaction has to have details at every layer. In this example, Transaction 1 and Transaction 3 have no data details because no data is necessary as an input for the transaction to be completed. Avoid the compulsion to add details to every layer for the sake of "completing" the transaction details because Test Scenario Design Models emphasize the minimal viable product principle.

Final, the hardest part of teaching people how to create Test Scenario Design Models is getting them to break from the old paradigm of testing that emphasizes quantity over quality. You do not need endless numbers of test steps to figure out how to test a system, you simply need high quality guard rails that keep you on the right path. We often get pushback here from people who ask "how can you completely test the system if you don't explicitly call out what to test in detailed test cases?" It's a fair question especially for organizations that rely heavily on a traditional testing approach where much of the testing is conducted manually. However, according to recent studies like the one done by Dimensional Research, over 87% of QA teams say they have both executive and financial support to implement and use test automation (Dimensional Research 2018, 2). Test automation is an important factor here because the right strategy around test automation eliminates the need to worry about "completely" testing a system. Take for example a team that is leveraging data models and iteration factories in the test automation they write. By virtue of leveraging a data model and iterating data through it, an automated test can literally execute hundreds of permutations of data inputs in a single test run. Making use of Test Scenario Design Models does not mean you move away from good fundamental testing strategies that combine the right balance of people, process, and tools. Test Scenario Design Models enable QA teams to focus less time on meaningless tasks like writing thousands of manual test cases so that they can focus more time on high value, user-centric test execution and test automation.

5. Test Scenario Design Model Metrics

As we worked to help organizations implement Test Scenario Design Models, one thing has become clear to us: traditional "testing" metrics are not going to work as a reporting mechanism. This fact was made clear to us when our clients asked us to provide statistics like how many test cases had we created and how many test cases were being run every day. Since the emphasis of Test Scenario Design Models was to reduce the number of test cases being written while increasing the coverage of critical business scenarios, we could not report on simple test case counts. We started to move the reporting conversation away from numbers of test cases and toward operational readiness by business function. By directing the conversation to readiness, we were able to talk more directly about quality measurements instead of testing statistics. When we tied in test automation numbers, the product owners became excited about the fact that not only were business critical scenarios being tested in an end-to-end manner but that a small but powerful set of business-value driven test cases were being run on at least a daily basis. We continuously pushed organizations to emphasize customer satisfaction as the most important measure of success and since POs were satisfied, traditional testing metrics became a thing of the past.

5.1 Defect Removal Efficiency

As the need to focus on traditional testing metrics faded, we were able to start focusing on quality metrics like defect detection efficiency, defect removal efficiency, volatility index, and quality throughput. One of the most important metrics you can report on while leverage Test Scenario Design Models is defect removal efficiency (DRE). "The DRE metric measures the percentage of bugs or defects found and removed prior to delivery of the software (Jones 2011, 1)." Why we find this metric important is because it is focused on removal of defects, not just the detection of them. The one variation on this metric that we always add for Agile teams is to measure not on production escapes but by escapes into User Acceptance Testing. By measuring against UAT, we are able to see how well our quality strategy is performing in removing defects before our customer uses the software in two-week increments. The timing of the data allows us to pivot our quality strategy to focus on the activities that help remove the most defects on a frequent basis.

5.2 Defect Detection Efficiency

Understanding how well your quality strategy is performing at defect detection is important for measuring the success of Test Scenario Design Models. That is why we typically like to combine our DRE metric with defect detection efficiency (DDE). The DDE is "the number of defects detected during a phase/stage that are injected during that same phase divided by the total number of defects injected during that phase (http://softwaretestingfundamentals.com/defect-detection-efficiency/)." That is to say "the ultimate target value for Defect Detection Efficiency is 100% which means that all defects injected during a phase are detected during that same phase and none are transmitted to subsequent phases (IBID)." Providing metrics that show defects injected, detected, and removed by phase depicts the level of quality maturity that you are operating with especially as you transition into leveraging Test Scenario Design Models. One additional metric that we use is a pareto analysis of defect detection activities such as static code analysis, unit testing, functional testing, regression testing, user story grooming, etc. The Pareto diagram of the top defect detection activities allows product teams to rapidly pivot to activities that are helping the team identify defects as quickly as possible.

6. Conclusion

As we have guided our clients in their transition to Agile, we have most prevalently seen the challenge breaking from the old testing paradigm that favors quantity of test cases over the quality of test cases. We have sought to bring forth a way where QA teams can focus on building scenario-based outlines of user behaviors in a global narrative to connect product functionality to user-centric designs in order to test We believe that Test Scenario Design Models is that way forward. Test Scenario Design Models allow you to build succinct but comprehensive end-to-end scenarios that test systems and software based on business value priority.

References:

Adaptavist. *Future of Automation Report*, https://www.adaptavist.com/atlassian-apps/future-of-automation-report/, 2018.

Black, Rex. *Managing the Testing Process: Practical Tools and Techniques for Managing Hardware and Software Testing*, Wiley, 2009.

Beck, Kent. *Test-Driven Development*, Addison-Wesley, Boston, MA 2002.

Buwalda, Hans. *Better Software*, www.stickyminds.com, February 2004.

Capgemini. *World Quality Report*, www.worldqualityreport.com, 2018.

Dimensional Research. *Testing Trends for 2018: A Survey of Development and Testing Professionals, Feb. 2018.*

International Organization for Standards. ISO 16085, https://www.iso.org/standard/40723.html.

International Organization for Standards. ISO 25010, https://www.iso.org/standard/35733.html.

International Organization for Standards. ISO 25012, https://www.iso.org/standard/35736.html.

International Organization for Standards. ISO 25030, https://www.iso.org/standard/35755.html.

International Organization for Standards. ISO 25040, https://www.iso.org/standard/35765.html.

International Software Testing Qualifications Board. https://www.istqb.org/, 2018

Jones, Capers, Bonsignour, Olivier. *The Economics of Software Quality*, Addison-Wesley, Upper Saddle River, NJ 2012.

Jones, Capers. *Software Defect Origins and Removal Methods*, www.namcook.com, 2013.

Jones, Capers. *Software Defect Removal Efficiency*, https://pdfs.semanticscholar.org/4e1b/c72a0324664e46e1404c6dc5ce3ed266020d.pdf, 2011.

Kan, Stephen H. *Metrics and Models in Software Quality Engineering*, Addison-Wesley, Upper Saddle River, NJ 2005.

Kaner, Cem. *An Introduction to Scenario Testing*, http://www.testingeducation.org/BBST/testdesign/Kaner_ScenarioIntroVer5.pdf, April 2013.

PractiTest. *State of Testing Report 2018*, http://qablog.practitest.com/wp-content/uploads, 2018.

SmartBear. *The State of Testing 2018*, https://smartbear.com/resources/ebooks/state-of-testing-report-2018, 2018.

VersionOne. *The 12th Annual State of Agile Report*, https://explore.versionone.com/state-of-agile, 2018.

VersionOne. *The 13th Annual State of Agile Report*, https://explore.versionone.com/state-of-agile, 2019.

On-Premises to Cloud: Ephemeral Scale Testing

What are they and why are they your key to Agile Quality success?

Sam Gomena, Andrew Graham, Anthony Spurgeon, Tripwire
sgomena@tripwire.com, agraham@tripwire.com, aspurgeon@tripwire.com

Abstract

The proliferation of cloud technologies has caused software development, testing, tools, and applications to face a new set of challenges. One such challenge, is determining if a non-native cloud application can be converted to work within and take advantage of a cloud. Such a migration brings about the potential for high reward. It also increases scalability demands for development and testing in this new domain.

The viability of applications developed before the rapid expansion of cloud computing must be evaluated before migrating them into the cloud. Cloud environments offer pathways for increased product reach. This expanded reach comes with the expectation that non-native cloud applications will scale according to the potential for greater demand.

This paper demonstrates an approach for testing non-native cloud applications at cloud scale. Specifically, we will cover test design considerations, tooling, lessons learned, and key takeaways from working to overcome these challenges.

Biography

Sam Gomena is a Software Engineer at Tripwire on the performance testing team. He is a senior in Portland State University's Computer Science program.

Andrew Graham is a Software Development Engineer in Test for Tripwire. He is the technical lead for the performance testing team and is actively working on enabling Software as a Service efforts. Andrew graduated from Portland State University in 2014 with a Bachelor of Science in Computer Science.

Anthony Spurgeon is a Software Engineer at Tripwire on the performance testing team. He is a senior in Arizona State University's Software Engineering program.

1. Introduction

Proliferation of cloud technologies has quickly changed expectations and opportunities for software applications. Applications deploy to the cloud while serving users on demand, all at scale. Non-native cloud applications were designed either before the advent of the cloud or without initial consideration for deployment. This rapidly evolving space is providing a second wind for non-native cloud applications.
Non-native cloud applications are at a design disadvantage, as they were not engineered to be served at the scale that a cloud has the potential to provide. To add to the complexity, users can connect and disconnect from cloud applications rapidly. Applications must be prepared for the following circumstances:

1. High load
2. High connection flux

"High load" is a subjective term depending on the application and the conditions around its use. In the scope of this paper, the definition of high load will be arrived at in two parts. First, it is the peak quantity of connections to the application under test over some period. Second, that peak quantity will be applied to the application under test for an extended period. In combination, these two parts create the conditions that we will accept as high load.

High connection flux, in the scope of this paper, describes the rate at which new connections are established and existing ones expire. It is important to note that we consider both connections and disconnects. Each operation comes with some computational cost for the application under test. These operations will be referred to as onboarding and offboarding, respectively.

These requirements, high load and high connection flux, lead to the development of the ephemeral scale testing outlined in this paper. Ephemeral scale testing intends to create the conditions necessary to simulate both criteria in an efficient, controlled, and reproducible manner. The goal of the ephemeral scale test is to provide a development team with confidence of an application's ability to perform at scale in a cloud environment.

Ephemeral scale testing will be described in three sections: Test design, test tooling, and a case study.

1.1. Problem Statement

How do we design a test that allow us to determine, with confidence, that an application can perform in a cloud-based environment? How do we design and implement a tool capable of simulating high load and high connection flux?

2. Test Design

Ephemeral scale testing, put simply, is a scale test that adds an element of onboarding and offboarding to the application under test. These two capabilities meet the criteria of high load and high connection flux.

2.1. Application Under Test

The application under test, for the purposes of this paper, is comprised of two basic components:

1. Agents installed on assets
2. Console

2.1.1. Components

Agents are responsible for reporting information to the console and they are installed on assets. Assets are systems, physical or virtual, that a user wants to monitor. The number of agents can range from dozens to thousands at any given point in time. Agents can connect and disconnect at will.

For the sake of simplifying the test we will say the following about agents:

1. An agent is installed on some asset
2. An asset needs to:
    a. Be provisioned
    b. Do some work
    c. Destroy itself when its work completes
3. An agent on such an asset will:
    a. Attempt to connect to the console
    b. Do its own work
    c. Attempt to disconnect once its work completes and is reported

The console, which is a component of the application under test, is responsible for aggregating the results of all the agents. There is only a single console for the purpose of our test. Users consume the reports from the console.

The console must:

1. Perform some onboarding procedures when a new agent wants to connect
2. Waits for the agent to do its work
3. Receives the agent's report
4. Perform off-boarding procedures once the agent disconnects

2.1.2. Behavior

If the console is over-saturated, then it will begin to queue onboarding agents. As mentioned earlier, the assets hosting agents have their own work to accomplish. If they finish work before the agent connects to the console and does its own work, then the opportunity is lost. The asset will destroy itself and the agent will never have reported.

To simplify the relationship between an asset and the agent that is installed on it we will simply refer to this pair as the agent. The agents cannot exist without an underlying asset, so we consolidate them into a single entity from here forward. The agents are a component of the console. The application under test in this setup is the console itself.

2.2. Test Tool Requirements

To reiterate, the ephemeral scale test must meet two requirements:

1. **High load**: quantified by the peak maximum number of agents that exist at one time
2. **High connection flux**: quantified by the rate at which new agents are instantiated and existing agents expire.

2.3. Test Tool Design Considerations

For the ephemeral scale test to achieve the above requirements it must be able to:

- Provision a large quantity of test agents (mock or real)
- Control or simulate the lifetime of the agents

Generating a large quantity of agents at a given point in time is only part of the problem for the ephemeral scale test. It must be able to provision many agents at a varied or constant rate over some period. The test can specify the desired peak agents in order to satisfy the high load requirement.

During the test the current quantity of agents will not be constant; however, it may reach a peak quantity multiple times over the course of the test.

High connection flux is met by defining batches of agents with lifetimes. A batch is a term used to define some positive, non-zero quantity of agents. Batches are defined in a list before the execution of the test. The agents in a batch share a common configuration and lifetime. Lifetime is defined as the duration, in minutes, that an agent exists.

To reiterate, an agent on an asset will:

1. Be provisioned

2. Connect to a console
3. Do work
4. Disconnect
5. Destroy itself.

That cycle represents the lifetime of an agent. For simplicity, the agent's lifetime and the asset's lifetime are treated as synonymous.

When the test begins, it starts a clock that ticks at a user defined interval. The test will attempt to acquire a random unused batch from the list of batches. The batch will perform their lifetime tasks, and then the batch is freed back into the list.

The test checks for an unused batch to deploy every tick. If no batches are available, it simply waits for another tick to check again. Since each batch has its own individual lifetime there will be a varying number of agents transitioning through the various stages of their lifetime cycle.

2.4. Value Proposition

The test will determine at what rate and scale the application under test can handle onboarding and offboarding of agents.

During a successful test run, an application under test will continue to handle onboarding and offboarding procedures. Ideally it would not develop an onboarding queue. No agent connections will be missed. This behavior proves that the application under test can continue to work optimally under conditions that a cloud environment would provide.

A failure will result in the application under test being unable to properly handle new connections for onboarding procedures. The application under test will begin to grow a queue of connection requests. If a queue of connection requests from agents begins to grow, then the risk of those requests becoming invalid increases.

The agents are only meant to live if they have work to do. If the console does not onboard the agents and receive their work, then it is a missed opportunity. Depending on the scenario, it can be considered poor performance or outright failure on the part of the console.

2.5. Limitations and Considerations

The number of peak agents that can be generated across all batches is strictly limited by the hardware on which the test is executing. As a concrete example, we typical use the following physical attributes for asset virtual machines running the agents:

- 1 virtual CPU
- 2 gigabytes memory
- 40 gigabytes disk; thin provisioned

We typically run this test in a vSphere cluster with the following attributes:

- 1 THz compute / 6 TB memory
- 1 PB datastore
- 10 Gb network link

Using the above physical hardware, we have run this experiment with a peak of 10,000 agents.

3. Test Tooling

The ephemeral scale test tool is a Go application. It was designed to satisfy the previously stated requirements of high load and high connection flux. It deploys predefined batches of assets at various rates. Those assets are subsequently provisioned with agents, do work, and are destroyed after a given lifetime.

3.1. Language Consideration

We decided to create the ephemeral scale test in Go. There were several reasons that influenced this decision, as follows:

- **Goroutines:** Goroutines are lightweight alternatives to traditional threads. Goroutines allow the ephemeral scale test to deploy and provision many assets concurrently.
- **Portability:** Our teams operate in a variety of development environments. We require that our ephemeral scale test be able to do so as well.
- **Familiarity:** Our team already had experience working with Go.
- **Existing Tooling:** The ephemeral scale test leverages pre-existing tools and libraries that were already written in Go.

We considered Python and Ruby as alternatives for the ephemeral scale test. Both languages are represented in much of our current tooling. As a team, we are trying to move away from Ruby, and have decided not to develop any new tools in the language. We continue to use Python elsewhere, but we determined that it did not allow for the same level of efficient concurrency as Go.

3.2. Design Implementation

The ephemeral function is the backbone of the test. A ticker is instantiated here. The ticker is a clock that provides a time interval and allows the test to check for and interact with free resources at regular periods.

Each batch is a collection of assets to be deployed, configured, and destroyed. A batch also encompasses some relevant metadata, as shown:

The lifetime of each asset is represented below. During its lifetime, the asset is provisioned, an agent is installed and configured, and finally the asset is destroyed when its time is up. Status for the batch's lifetime is returned through a channel to the parent thread. Channels, in Go, allow for bi-directional communication between threads.

The ephemeral scale test itself is simple. Every tick, the test checks for any available resources to be deployed. If this check finds any available resources, a new lifetime function is started for the resource.

Within this goroutine, the available batch generates its assets which exist for the duration of their lifetime. Assets are provisioned and agents are configured on those assets. The assets and agents do their work. Once an asset's lifetime expires, the asset is destroyed. Once all assets in a given batch are destroyed, then the batch is freed up. This process continues for the duration of the ephemeral scale test.

Much of the heavy lifting itself (the deployment and configuration of the assets and agents) is handled by existing internal tooling and libraries. These tools were also written in Go. Interaction between the ephemeral scale test and these tools is through an interface that the ephemeral scale test provides.

The result is that, given a proper configuration, once the ephemeral scale test is begun, it will operate for its given duration without further input. During the test, it will deploy batches of assets running various operating systems for given lifetimes, destroy them, and repeat indefinitely.

4. Practical Application

A Tripwire customer who was in the process of transitioning from on-premise to cloud operations tasked Tripwire with demonstrating the viability of monitoring assets in a cloud environment. The customer was transitioning from on-premises operations to cloud operations. They wanted to ensure that their assets could continue to be monitored in the new environment. An extra challenge was added in that assets would no longer be static and there was no guaranteed lifetime – meaning they could come and go so long as they had utility.

Our team had a hypothesis that our application would function appropriately in a cloud environment. We needed to quantify performance and behavior in order to assure the customer that our hypothesis was correct. Enter ephemeral scale testing: We needed to understand if the application under test could onboard and offboard assets fast enough and at scale, and to know if the application could keep up with the flux of connections.

4.1. Application Under Test

The application under test is a combination of two applications that work jointly to monitor assets. As aforementioned, assets are systems, physical or virtual, that a user intends to monitor. For the sake of focusing on the ephemeral scale test itself we'll use the term monitor in the most general sense. Agents are installed on assets and have the responsibility of monitoring their behavior and files based on rules received from the console. The console aggregates data from the agents and presents a consolidated report to the user.

The application under test, while not the primary focus of this paper, will be generally described as follows:

4.2. Test Setup

Test setup initially consisted of installing a console on a Linux machine running in Amazon Web Services. The console was static for the duration of the test. The ephemeral scale test was setup on a remote machine and configured to deploy agents according to the specifications of the customer. An overview of the specifications we were provided is as follows:

- Asset peak volume: 5,000
- Asset lifetime range: 10 minutes to 60 minutes

We then defined limits for the test:

- Test duration of 72 hours
- Asset peak volume of 10,000
- Mixture of Windows and Linux virtual machines
- Batch ranges of 25 to 250 agents
- Batch lifetime ranges between 10 minutes to 60 minutes

4.3. Considerations and Limitations

Once started, the test requires no interaction. We relied on logging built into the product itself.

Initial runs were hindered by high resource consumption on the machine running the ephemeral scale test. This was easily overcome by quadrupling the test machine's memory.

The agents were deployed exclusively in an on-premises vSphere cluster. The console was deployed in an Amazon Web Services datacenter on the West coast. There was a latency overhead communicating between on-premises assets and the public cloud-based console. That latency did not have remarkable effect on our test. The customer's stated use case was to begin with a hybrid on-premises and public cloud solution. Their mature state would have both the console and agents running in a public cloud. It was not specified whether they would use separate datacenters available in the public cloud.

The agents used for the test did not do any substantial work. That is, once created, the only program running on the virtual machine was the agent software and any native programs used by the operating system. This likely allowed an agent to provision quickly. In comparison, an agent running alongside a process intensive application may have a harder time allocating resources for monitoring, or sending data to the console.

We used both Windows and Linux virtual machines for agents. The Linux based virtual machines were headless and thus lighter weight than their Windows counterparts.

An important factor in using an on-premises cloud for the assets was the cost prohibitive nature of a public cloud. For instance, a t2.micro instance in Amazon Web Services costs $0.0116/hr at the time of our test. At 72 hours with a peak of 10,000 agents, we predicted that the average number of assets existing at any point in time during the test would be approximately 5,000. Our testing would have conservatively cost $4,000 ($0.0116/hr * 72 hrs * 5,000 mean assets = $4,176) per test run.

Physical attributes of assets were not necessarily specific to the customer use case. It was not considered an important attribute; we cared more about asset lifetime. A machine may have done work 'faster' or 'slower' depending on its physical attributes. Lifetime of the asset was the sole requirement provided by the customer.

4.4. Results

We picked a peak agent volume twice as large as the customer's requirements. We wanted to ensure that we exceeded the customer's expectations. We did not empirically find an upper limit, nor did we calculate a theoretical upper limit. The tests results supported our hypothesis that the application under test could handle the high load and high connection flux of a cloud environment.

The console did not experience any meaningful onboarding queue and all assets were able to communicate with the console within their designated lifetimes.

As a pass-fail test for this particular test scenario, the application under test passed and the tool performed as designed.

5. Closing Remarks

Testing non-native cloud applications at scale is a daunting endeavor. As with any testing, before beginning it is important to have a well-defined understanding of:

- Why you are testing
- A baseline of quantifiable results that will determine success
- Whether the test itself will measure something meaningful

With respect to the ephemeral scale test, we needed to provide a customer with confidence that the application under test could help them transition into a cloud environment.

The baseline of results that determined that success was that no assets would miss connection with the console. The test run that we performed had double the assets that the customer expected, and the console behaved beyond expectations. During testing it witnessed 100% onboarding and offboarding success with no assets missing a connection during their lifetime.

5.1. Additional Use Cases

The ephemeral scale test provided high confidence that the application under test, a non-native cloud application, could operate in a cloud environment. The test has since been used for other applications as outlined here:

- **Stress testing:** We found that the tool works quite well for fine-tuning stress tests to pinpoint areas of fragility. For instance, we ran an auxiliary test that required a constant influx of data.
- **Functional scale testing:** While somewhat obvious, we were easily able to extend the tool to run an arbitrary test suite against the application under test. This allowed us to provide additional benefit and metrics to a functional test cycle.

There is additional utility to be found in software and environment testing. For example, situations that require the generation of a high volume of ephemeral assets.

References

"Documentation." Documentation - The Go Programming Language. Accessed June 12, 2019. https://golang.org/doc/.

"Documentation." Documentation - AWS Elastic Compute Documentation. Accessed June 14, 2019. https://docs.aws.amazon.com/ec2/?id=docs_gateway

"Documentation." Documentation - Go by Example: Goroutines. Accessed June 15, 2019. https://gobyexample.com/goroutines

Is This Testable? A Personal Journey to Learn How to Ask Better Questions from My Applications and Engineering Team

Michael Larsen
mkltesthead@gmail.com

Abstract

Have you ever felt like you were working at cross purposes with an application you were developing and testing? Have you wished that there were easier ways to interact with your application? Do you struggle with the fact that efforts to automate your application under development yield less than satisfactory results? Perhaps you discover that for every answer or solution what results is more and more questions. I decided to undergo a process of better understanding of what made the applications I work with testable in the first place. Through that process, I've learned a few things that may be helpful to anyone looking to make their product more responsive to both human and external program interactions.

Biography

Michael Larsen is a Senior Quality Assurance Engineer with Socialtext/PeopleFluent. Over the past two decades, he has been involved in software testing for a range of products and industries, including network routers & switches, virtual machines, capacitance touch devices, video games, and client/server, distributed database & web applications.

Michael is a Black Belt in the Miagi-Do School of Software Testing, helped start and facilitate the Americas chapter of Weekend Testing, is a former Chair of the Education Special Interest Group with the Association for Software Testing (AST), a lead instructor of the Black Box Software Testing courses through AST, and former Board Member and President of AST. Michael writes the TESTHEAD blog (http://mkltesthead.com) and can be found on Twitter at @mkltesthead. A list of books, articles, papers, and presentations can be seen at http://www.linkedin.com/in/mkltesthead.

1. Introduction

Testability is a topic that can take many pages and many experiences to cover. My experiences with Testability came into focus by working through the "Thirty Days of Testability" challenge that the Ministry of Testing put together. By going through this process, I learned a great deal about what makes applications and services testable. Testability is not some unimaginable outcome. It requires communication, involvement, and a willingness to look at a product objectively and determine what would help make it more testable and, potentially, more usable by everyone.

2. Making Testability a Primary Focus

Testability can be described as:

> "The logical property that is variously described as contingency, defeasibility, or falsifiability, which means that counterexamples to the hypothesis are logically possible. The practical feasibility of observing a reproducible series of such counterexamples if they do exist."

> "In short, a hypothesis is testable if there is some real possibility of deciding whether it is true or false based on real experience. Upon this property of its constituent hypotheses rests the ability to decide whether a theory can be supported or falsified by the data of actual experience. If hypotheses are tested, initial results may also be labeled inconclusive."

That may seem like overkill when it comes to testing software. In truth, I consider it a great place to start. What is the goal of any test that we want to perform? We want to determine if something can be proven correct or refuted. Thus, we need to create conditions where a hypothesis can be either proven or refuted.

How we do that will vary from project to project. Simple programs may be considered with a few examples and paths through the visible interface. More complex applications may require interacting with a variety of interfaces, including but not limited to:

- operating systems
- desktop and mobile platforms
- desktop and mobile applications
- web browsers
- web servers
- database servers
- load balancers
- third-party applications and libraries
- cloud devices

Regardless of the level of complexity of application, the goal is the same. We either confirm our hypothesis is correct or we prove our hypothesis is wrong. If we cannot verify our hypothesis, then we must call into question the very methods which we will examine why it isn't going to work for us. What do we do if we determine we can't? For me, the question of "testability" falls into this area, addressing why we cannot effectively confirm or refute a hypothesis. In short, if there is an aspect that acts as a barrier or lessens our effectiveness to be able to perform actual experiments and make decisions based on the data provided, we have testability issues we need to examine.

3. Getting Specific with Hypotheses Using Data [AP1] [AP2]

One of the aspects that I think is important is to look at ways that we can determine if something can be performed or verified. At times that may simply be our interactions and our observations. Let's take something like the color contrast on a page. I can subjectively say that a light gray text over dark gray background doesn't provide a significant amount of color contrast. Is that hypothesis reasonable? Sure. I can look at it and say, "it doesn't have a high enough contrast."

That is a subjective declaration based on observation and opinion. Is it testable? As I've stated it, no, not really. What I have done is made a personal observation and declared an opinion. It may sway other opinions but it's not really a test in the classic sense.

What's missing? Data. What kind of data? A way to determine the actual contrast level of the background versus the text. Can we do that? Yes, we can, if we are using a web page example and we have a way to reference the values of the specific colors.

Since colors can be represented by hexadecimal values or RGB numerical values, we can make an objective observation as to the differences in various colors. By comparing the values of the dark gray background and the light gray text, we can determine what level of contrast exists between the two colors. Whether we are using a program that can create a comparison or an application that can print out a color contrast comparison, what we have is an objective value that we can share and compare with others.

"These two colors look to be too close together"... this is not a testable hypothesis.

"These two colors have a contrast ratio of 2.5:1 and we are looking for a contrast ratio of 4.5:1 at the minimum" ... this is a testable hypothesis and it also contains data points to support it[AP3] .

4. What Do Your Logs Say?

Some of the most effective and often overlooked sources of data for how an application performs are the application log files. One of the reasons that log files are often overlooked is the sheer amount of information present. Log files are great places to see the history of events and actions that have taken place in a system. The downside is that the sheer volume of information can be overwhelming.

Additionally, it is important to have a clear understanding of what I mean by "the application" when I discuss log files. Do I mean the actual application I work with? How about the extended suite of applications that plug into ours? I mention this because, for each of the components that make up our application, there is a log file or, in some instances, several log files to examine.

To use one of the products I have worked on, we have a large log file that is meant to cover most of our interactions. Even then, there are so many things that fly past that it can be a challenge to figure out exactly what is being represented. Additionally, there are logs for a number of aspects of our application and they are kept in separate files, such as:

- installation and upgrades
- authentication
- component operations
- third-party plug-ins
- mail daemons
- web server logs
- search engine logs

and so on.

There are a variety of ways to parse this information and examine it with scripts after the fact but that requires that we understand what we are looking for in the first place. As for me, looking in log files is a voyage of discovery.

I have found that using simple screen multiplexers such as "screen", "tmux" or "byobu" and splitting one of my windows into multiple fragments allows me a clear look at a variety of log files at the same time. This way, I can see what is actually happening at any given time from a variety of perspective. Additionally, I get used to seeing which log files post updates after system interactions.

Some logs fly by so fast that I have to look at individual timestamps to see dozens of entries corresponding to a single second, while other logs get updated very infrequently, usually only when an error has occurred.

Putting together an aggregator function so that I can query all of the files at the same time and look for what is happening can be a plus but only if they use a similar format. Unfortunately, this is a common problem. If we have multiple log files, it would be helpful to have all of the resulting log files be formatted in a similar way, such as the following example:

log_name: timestamp: alert_level: module: message

repeated for each log file.

Let's use the example of a user updating a database field. It's possible that this action might be reflected in multiple places. It might show up in a log for the web server, for the database server, for the backup server and perhaps other locations where the log will be recorded (search results, access logs, error logs, etc.).

Having an option to gather all log files into an archive and have them archived each day (or whatever time option makes the most sense) also provides considerable benefits. If at all possible, try to make the messages put into the log files human-readable.

5. Identify a "Partner in Crime"

If I had to find out what the three biggest customer impacting issues related to my product are, how would I get that information? Working with support engineers and sales engineers should be a first line of contact for every software tester or person involved with software quality.

I am fortunate in that I have a terrific point of contact in the guise of a great customer engagement engineer. I can count on one hand the number of times when I have announced an update on our staging server and not heard a reply from this person of, "hey, what's new on staging?" They make it their responsibility to be clear and up to date with every single feature and every option available in the product and when it is deployed. They also make a lot of sample accounts and customizations to our product to push the edges of what the product can actually do.

One of the examples we use frequently is a site that is cloned from one of our most active customers. We set up our test environment to match theirs in every aspect. These include the number of front-end servers, load balancing devices, back end servers, database replication schemes, customer accounts, and views to data and applications that we display through widgets in the application dashboard.

By putting together these environments and creating examples that reflect what our customers actually see, we can more effectively look at the methods and means to interact with those systems the way our customers do, not necessarily in the ways we think or would like them to.

6. Are We Using Feature Analytics?

In my company, we have two applications we use and monitor for Analytics. One is for overall HTTP traffic and demographics:

- what pages get hit the most?
- what browsers are used the most?
- what time of days do people most use the application?
- how many parallel connections are we maintaining at any given time?[AP4]

This helps me define what I should prioritize in my testing[AP5] , as well as to the load our application might be subjected to. By addressing or considering these areas, we can ask specific questions or develop experiments that will help to provide answers. How many concurrent users will be accessing the system? How will we know? What processes will be running during those interactions? Do we have enough physical or virtual memory to interact with those processes?

The second tool we use is based on feature analytics, as in "what features in our product are our customers actually using?" As an example, there have [AP6] been situations where customers have asked for specific features to be included in our application. These requests range from "this would be nice to have" all the way to "if this feature is not included, we cannot purchase the product." What is a development team to do? Depending on the level of feedback and urgency, it is possible that a great deal of effort will be put into developing the features that have been requested. There are times where this makes a lot of sense, such as when a feature (take Responsive Design as an example) may be the make or break feature for a large organization. The want to have a site that will allow for display on multiple devices and not have to rely on separate apps for desktop and mobile. With tens of thousands of users, making a feature development priority is easy to in this case.

At other times, we have had requests that have been labeled as very important to make a sale for a large organization, only to later see that the adoption of that feature was low to non-existent. Additionally, applications or pieces of functionality that may think might be the most significant may be to a small but vocal subset. How do we actually determine if these features are actually being used? By having feature level analytics that can be examined and monitored, it is possible to both determine what features are actually being used at a variety of customer sites as well as see trends of what are not being used. This can help us determine the priority of testing efforts and areas that both need to be tested as well as make decisions about future development efforts or even support for these components.

Looking back to the original definition of proving a hypothesis, sometimes the most important hypothesis to prove is "does it make sense to keep a piece of functionality working the way that it is?" We can make guesses but implementing feature analytics can give us data that we can them make actionable decisions about. If features are actively being used, we know that efforts for continued feature enhancement is desired and necessary. IF features are not, we can objectively evaluate how and when they are being used, or how little, and make a determination as to whether or not they should be gracefully deprecated or removed from the product completely.

7. Automatable Does Not Necessarily Mean Testable

Alan Richardson has written an effective blog post around the differences between "Automateable and Testable." (Richardson, 2019). Just because you can automate something doesn't necessarily means it's testable. Automat-ability means that something else (a program, a shell script, or an API) can interact with it. However, while that is capable to be done, it doesn't necessarily mean that it's going to be a good experience for a user. It also does not mean that the hypothesis related to the test will necessarily be proven or refuted.

"Testability is for humans. Automatability (Automatizability) is for applications." (Richardson, 2019)

An example can be seen with an applications menu bar. It is possible to click on the various elements and open other pages within the application. Those interactions can be automated. However, those interactions give us no indication if that path makes the most sense or if the design of that interaction could be improved. Can we select each of the elements in the navigation bar and then move to another page? The answer is yes if we click with a mouse or call out the elements and click them with an automated script. Can we navigate between the pages using nothing but a keyboard? Based on traditional automation techniques, we may or may not know if that is true.

Testability can add a number of options to a program and can help to make a system more enjoyable for a user. It may help with making an application more automateable but it doesn't guarantee that it will.

8. Ask the Following Question: "How Am I Going to Test This?"

In my organization, stories get defined and features are determined during our story kickoff or design workshop. As a quality advocates, it is my duty to ask, "how am I going to test this?" every time I am part of these meetings. What might be the results of some of these questions? It's possible that I might determine it would be helpful to:

- add calls to the API so that I can query and set values without having to fire up a browser and look at a bunch of things on the screen.
- create actual configuration enhancements of an application so that I can tweak various things while I'm setting up a test environment.
- make sure that elements are named well (whenever possible) and that duplication is minimal.
- ensure that the error output is understandable and helps me understand what has happened and what I can do about the error.

Testability hooks are often put in at points where testing might prove difficult, but we won't be able to determine where those difficult areas are if we don't have these conversations. Also, there may be friction between the development team and the testing team if these conversations are not held early in the development process. It is much easier to add a testing hook early in the process rather than later or as an afterthought. To paraphrase a Chinese proverb, "the best time to plant a shade tree was twenty years ago. The second-best time to do it is now."

When I have had discussions about testability issues, I have found the greatest successes come from examining areas that have led to bugs. While it is not productive to say, "why didn't you find that bug?", it is often helpful to examine where we might have prevented it or how we might prevent it going forward. Without laying blame, I have found that these are opportunities to look at ways of introducing testability hooks, since rework is already underway for that particular issue.

9. Get a Handle on Your Test Data

Depending on the product under test, the data we need to effectively test that application may be simple or complex. In my day-to-day testing work I deal with a lot of users and data that would be generated by those users.

At the basic level, everything is associated with an account, so often the most effective method to load test data (as well as to protect it and to use it from a known starting point) is to import an account that is already set up with the information I want to use. I actually have several of these and each is set up to help me deal with a variety of issues. I have accounts created for Localization, Responsive Design, Accessibility & Inclusive Design, and Large Customer simulation.

Additionally, I have data that deals with the components of our system so that I don't have to constantly reconfigure those elements (that includes text examples, HTML and Markup formatting, videos, user details, language preferences, etc.). The key here is that I try to limit the use of test data that tries to be all things to all circumstances. While it can be helpful to include a lot of details in one place, it can also complicate the situation in that there is "too much of a good thing" as well as too many variables to chase.

Another way that I try to keep test data useful and fresh is that I determine the methods that can best generate the data that I use and help me to keep track of everything in a noticeable way. One of those methods is that I have general and specific scenarios. When I do tests with large numbers of users I generate that data with a tool called "Fake Name Generator". This has been my go-to tool for more than a decade and it provides individual details I can call up one at a time to use, or I can get bulk downloads with tens, hundreds, or thousands of users. The system limits you to 100,000 users for any given request, but over time, it is possible to generate several hundred thousand or even millions of users.

10. Conduct Regular "Show and Tell" Sessions

As the release manager and build manager for each of our releases, one of my responsibilities has been to gather a cross-section of the broader engineering, sales, and support teams so that we can show them the new stuff going out with our next release.

Additionally, we have as part of our "definition of done" to demo any feature we are working on to our product owner and/or our chief sales engineer. This is a great time to walk through the feature, show as many parameters as we can and to listen to their questions. Much of the time it's a fairly straightforward "show and tell" but every once in a while, we have some deeper discussions. These longer conversations often serve to point out that the new feature we are demonstrating may have some follow-on stories to consider. Often, it's a chance to see and determine how well we have answered the product owner's/representative's expectations so that we can adjust accordingly in the future[AP7] [LM8] [LM9] . It is also a good opportunity to make sure that the programming and testing efforts are focused on the same goal or are at least in the same ballpark.

These sessions frequently help us to ask the earlier considered question of "How am I going to test this?"

11. Pair with Your Developers and Test Together

I'm[AP10] fortunate in that I have developers that are willing to pair and look [11] at stuff with me. As we have G-Suite as our main communication platform among the team, it's easy to demo stuff and talk out what is being tested. We are a small team and technically speaking, with management out of the equation, our engineering team is equally balanced between programmers and testers. Thus, it's not an imposition or overly burdensome to get together and pair with developers. Another opportunity that is available is to look at the code and examine unit tests that have been created or need to be created. By doing so, we can have a starting point to see what the programmers have determined is important to be tested at this level and to help initiate conversations about what else could or should be covered or to identify areas where there may be gaps.

Lisa Crispin has written a handy guide on "Pairing with Developers: A Guide for Testers" (Ministry [AP12] of Testing, 2019). Lisa's article is a great resource and while I have little to add to it specifically, I can share a few things that I have found help considerably with pairing with developers.

1. Have a specific goal for the session: By developing a very specific charter around an area that is either difficult to test or that may require more knowledge that the developer has, being super specific really helps with this process. Often when I approach and have a question that has very clear parameters (or as clear as I can make them) I'm much more likely to be able to block out time with them. More times than not, we range farther than that specific area because we're into it and we're both able to get more done together than separately.

2. Block out a specific time interval: set an appointment, set the desired time (about an hour is my usual suggestion, no more than two). We frequently blow past the single hour time set aside but we're usually good about heeding the two-hour limit. Beyond two hours we tend to lose focus but up to that point is usually very effective.

3. Do your homework in advance: This goes with number 1, but if I'm going to try to understand something that's going on in the code, it helps for me to have reviewed it first (if possible). Greenfield development efforts don't always allow for that but since our current efforts are mostly focused on revamping existing functionality, there's plenty of opportunities for me to read up and understand the parameters the developers are working with. I may not understand all of it but at least I am ready to start sessions with a list of questions.

12. Identify Your Dependencies

Most modern applications are not self-contained. They rely on a variety of third-party or open source components to allow them to run, as well as external libraries and other dependencies that may not be clearly outlined. If an application uses a micro-services architecture, it adds to the complexity of testing when there are external groups that control what is being displayed and how it looks or if it's even available. This is the case with my company currently and we are actively trying to deal with it.

To this end, one of the more helpful approaches I have found is to create a specific test environment with users that have permissions to access multiple connecting applications. This allows for the micro services applications to interact with each other in a meaningful way and to allow me to examine more of the interactions between systems. This way I can determine how many issues are specifically associated with our product and which issues are associated with other applications my product is interacting with.

13. Check Your Source Control History and "Feel the Heat"

A term I discuss [AP13] with my team frequently is to "look for the heat" in the source code. That is to say, where are we making frequent changes? What other components do those changes interact with? The closer the level of interaction, the greater the level of "heat". The farther away, the less heat there is, or likelihood that those components will be involved in the most recent changes. In short, where there is heat is where we need to focus our testing efforts. By doing that, by examining existing unit tests, integration tests and end to end tests (if they exist) we can see if we are effectively covering these areas or if more specific testing is needed. Again, going back to the original definition, do we have enough information? Do we have enough of a handle on the capabilities and inner workings on these areas to determine if the changes made are working as we want them to?

By using our source control history, it is possible to find out which parts of our system change most often.

As a recent example, we have been involved in an update to a more responsive design. To that end, it means that there is a lot of change to our front end and how it is displayed with regard to the device or user agent making the calls. By contrast, our legacy interface changes very little and the workflows, IDs and respective interactions are well defined and rarely change. However, there are certainly instances where new code does interact with components that effect that older code and thus have an effect on how that legacy interface responds. By looking at the source code changes and getting a feel for what has been modified, I can also determine which areas in our legacy interface might need to be looked at once again.

14. Conclusion

There are a variety of methods and tools that we as quality engineers and quality advocates can leverage to help make our products more testable. It all starts with us being able to identify areas that are potential issues, as well as being able to talk about them in a meaningful way with our development teams. Additionally, we need to be willing and able to look at our systems objectively and identify the areas we can test effectively first, so that we can better define and describe the areas that have deficiencies. There is no easy fix to testability. The process is ongoing. It requires focus and consistent communication. It requires a willingness and an ability to encourage the development team to likewise consider testing the product actively and looking at it from a variety of perspectives.

While the process may be slow and challenging, with consistent effort and a willingness to keep asking questions, it will be possible to narrow down the areas where we have to as "is this testable?" It may not be possible to make every area perfectly testable, but we can certainly make our applications more testable over time and that is an outcome I think everyone would welcome.

References

Ministry of Testing. "Thirty Days of Testability". Ministry of Testing, https://www.ministryoftesting.com/dojo/lessons/30-days-of-testability (accessed July 20, 2019).

Wikipedia. "Software Testability." https://en.wikipedia.org/wiki/Software_testability (accessed July 20, 2019).

Alan Richardson. "Testability vs Automatability - in theory". Evil Tester, https://www.eviltester.com/2018/01/testability-vs-automatability-in-theory.html (accessed July 20, 2019).

Fake Name Generator. https://www.fakenamegenerator.com/ (accessed July 20, 2019).

Crispin, Lisa. "Pairing With Developers: A Guide For Testers". Ministry of Testing. https://www.ministryoftesting.com/dojo/lessons/pairing-with-developers-a-guide-for-testers (accessed July 20, 2019).

Advanced Test Case Design Methods – Going Far and Beyond Boundary and Equivalence Testing

Subei Liu
liu.subei@xbosoft.com

Abstract
Complete and effective test case design will make the test more effective. There are various types of designing techniques, each of which is suitable for identifying a particular type of errors. Additionally, we need to select the right set of relevant test design techniques for the particular application and particular types of functions within an application. In this paper, I'll discuss some advanced design techniques for test cases. This will enable you to develop deeper test cases, get better test coverage and expand your toolbox for test case design and thinking. Along with examples, you can get better understanding of not only on the techniques themselves, but also when to use each one depending on the situation.

Keywords: Black-box test design techniques, Equivalence partitioning, Boundary value analysis, Cause–effect graph, Decision table testing, Functional structure diagram, Orthogonal array testing, Error guessing, Scene graph

Biography
Subei Liu, graduated from agricultural university of Hebei, China with a major in computer science and technology. She has more than 6 years' experience on software testing, testing all kinds of platforms and also trains for new recruits for XBOSoft. She has a deep understanding of software testing, and specializes in test design.

1. Introduction
In our modern society, change is no longer constant. Rather, it's accelerating. And this acceleration is caused by technology. Software has become the nervous system of technology as these technology-based systems are increasingly dependent on software. The software quality of these systems is particularly important because software failures can lead to very serious consequences. Software today is written by humans (notice we said today) and humans make mistakes. So, how do we ensure that the final software delivered to users meets their needs with high quality? Software testing.

However, with agile development methods, software testing often falls to the wayside. Back in the days of waterfall, discussions on software testing naturally included test cases. However, test cases have gotten lost with the agile tendency towards minimal documentation. New software testers may think that they can test software as soon as they get it. They are eager to find all the flaws in the software immediately, just as developers may rush to write code without thinking of design and architecture. However, software testing requires an engineering perspective. Before specific test implementation, we need to understand what to test and how to test. Even if we have no formal test cases per say, we need to formulate our test design to guide the implementation of testing. Otherwise, not only will your testing be ad-hoc, but you'll also miss testing critical areas where defects can often hide. This paper sets out to describe and show examples of various test design methods that we've successfully used in many projects.

2. What Are Test Cases?

A test case is an output of test design, which directly reflects the idea of test design. A software program should function and perform as designed. If the program does not work properly or behave as designed, it means that the software programmer has created a defect in the software. Of course the design could be defective as well, but that is outside the scope of this paper. A beautiful test case is not only an excellent embodiment of the design idea, but also easy to execute and understand its flow, with readability and traceability is generally a set of test inputs, execution conditions and expected results, prepared for a particular goal to verify whether the program meets a specific requirement and does not complete redundant operations, namely, to ensure the following two points:

a. The program did what it was supposed to do
b. The program isn't doing anything it shouldn't be doing

Therefore, as the basis for test implementation, test cases should be carefully designed to cover the design of the program under test.

3. Black-Box Test Case Design Techniques

The design of test cases is an important link in the process of software testing, and it is the only way to achieve the test goal. The success of a software test depends on the success of its test case design.

The common test case design methods of black box test include: equivalence class partition, boundary value analysis, error guessing, cause-effect graph, decision table, Orthogonal array, functional graph method, etc.

3.1. Equivalence partitioning

This is a very common and important test case design method. We divide the input domain into several regions, and choose a few representative data for each region to test, so that we can avoid using a lot of testing data and avoid blindness. Thereby reducing the total number of test cases that must be developed. When use this method, we find the input conditions first, and divide the equivalence, then design test cases.

There are two different cases of equivalence partitioning, valid class and invalid class. A valid equivalence class is a collection of input data that is reasonable and meaningful for a program's specification. A valid equivalence class verifies that a program has achieved the functionality and performance specified in the specification. While an invalid equivalence class is a collection of input data that is unreasonable or meaningless to the program specification.

In general, when designing test cases, one test case should cover as many valid classes as possible, while invalid equivalence classes require one-to-one coverage. For instance, if an input for email address can be saved with valid values letters and numbers together as expected in one test case, for sure it works with only letters or numbers in two different test cases. While for invalid values, email address cannot be saved with invalid values Chinese characters and asterisk together, you have to test for each one separately to see whether each invalid value is not supported as expected.

3.1.1 Example

The input value is student achievement, ranging from 0 to 100.

3.1.2 Strengths and Weaknesses

Strengths

Test with less representative data instead of full test with all data.

Weaknesses

1. Not consider detailed relationship between inputs and outputs, this may cause some logic errors.

2. Needs to understand the detailed requirements, and it is easy to omit equivalence classes when the requirements are not clear.

3.2 Boundary-value analysis

Boundary-value is another classical black box test method and often used together with equivalence partitioning as a supplement. In programming, a number of errors tend to occur at the boundaries of input or output data, so the method of using boundary values can often detect errors. Boundary value analysis considers not only the input conditions but also the test conditions generated by the output space.

Values of the boundary can be taken as min, min+, Max -, Max and norm, rather than typical or arbitrary values in equivalence classes. When define the boundary values, data domain in requirements is very important for choosing which one as boundary. For instance, if the level of precision is two decimal places for numbers/amounts, the one less than 1 is 0.99, while if the level of precision is three decimal places, the one less than 1 will be 0.999.

Common boundary values:

1) For integers of 16 bits, 32767 and 32768 are boundaries.
2) The first and last lines of the report.
3) The first and last element of an array.
4) The 0th, 1st and penultimate times of the cycle.
5) The cursor is at the top left and bottom right of the screen.

3.2.1. Example 1

We can use the example in 3.1.1 to analysis boundary values for inputs:

Boundary value of valid equivalence class	Boundary value of invalid equivalence class
0	-1
100	101

3.2.2 Example2

Here is another example to analysis boundary values for outputs:

Rules for park admission tickets:

1). Children under 1.2m in height are free.
2). Children between 1.2m (including 1.2m) and 1.4m in height can get half price.
3). People over 70 years old (including 70 years old) can get free tickets.
4). Half fare for students in school (excluding on-the-job students).
5). No charge for families of revolutionary martyrs and soldiers on active duty.

We can divide the equivalence into full, half and free tickets, see table:

3.2.3 Strengths and Weaknesses

Strengths

1. Test cases are easy to automate.
2. Small design workload

Weaknesses

1. Based on the domain of data, the logical relationship of data is not recognized.
2. A large number of test cases can be generated which will need long execution time of test cases.

3.3. Error guessing

Error guessing is a method of designing test cases based on experience and intuition that surmises all possible errors in the program.

When use this, we list all possible errors and error prone special scenarios in the program, and select test cases based on them.

3.3.1 Example

For input:

1). Single Spaces, multiple Spaces
2). Special characters (<script>)
3). Date format in different browser languages.
4). Time limitation for submit
5). Two people modify the same form.
6). etc.

There are no definite steps and they are carried out largely by rule of thumb.

3.3.2 Strengths and Weaknesses

Strengths

1. Give full play to people's intuition and experience.
2. Brainstorm

3. Easy to use
4. Fast and easy to carry out

Weaknesses

1. It is difficult to know the coverage of the test
2. A lot of unknown areas may be lost
3. It is subjective and hard to replicate

3.4. Cause–effect graph

The cause-effect graph is a method of designing test cases by analyzing various combinations of input conditions graphically. It is suitable for checking various combinations of input conditions of programs.

Both the equivalence method and the boundary value analysis method focus on the input conditions, but do not consider the various combinations of the input conditions and the mutual constraints among the input conditions.

If the various combinations of input conditions must be considered during testing, the number of possible combinations would be astronomical, so the design of test cases must be considered in a form suitable for describing combinations of multiple conditions and corresponding multiple actions, which requires the use of causal diagrams (logical models).

3.4.1 Example

Product description: there's a vending machine software that handles boxed drinks for $1.50 each. If you put in $1.50 coins, press the "coke" or "Sprite" button, and the corresponding drink will be delivered. If you put in $2 coins, return $0.5 coin with the beverage.

Test cases design steps

1). Determine the cause and effect in the requirements.

#	Cause / Input	#	Effect / Output
C1	Put in $1.50 coins	E1	Refund $0.50 coin
C2	Put in $2 coins	E2	Dispense Coke
C3	Press the "Coke" button	E3	Dispense Sprite
C4	Press the "Sprite" button		

2). Determine the constraints between inputs.

#	Cause / Input	Constraints
C1	Put in $1.50 coins	Exclusive: Either C1 or C2
C2	Put in $2 coins	
C3	Press the "Coke" button	Exclusive: Either C3 or C4
C4	Press the "Sprite" button	

3). Determine the causality between input and output.

#	Cause / Input	#	Middle status	#	Effect / Output
C1	Put in $1.50 coins	Cm1	Coin-in	E1	Refund $0.50 coin
C2	Put in $2 coins			E2	Dispense Coke
C3	Press the "Coke" button	Cm2	Pressed	E3	Dispense Sprite
C4	Press the "Sprite" button				

4). Draw the cause-effect graph.
To distinguish, black lines are used for inputs and green lines for outputs.

5). Convert graph to a decision table. (see 3.5)
6). Design test cases from decision table. (see 3.5)

3.4.2 Strengths and Weaknesses

Strengths

1. The causal-effect graph method can help us select test cases efficiently and design multiple input condition combination test cases according to certain steps.

2. Causal-effect diagram analysis can also point us to problems in software specification descriptions.

Weakness

1. The causal relationship between input conditions and output results is sometimes difficult to get from the software requirements specification.

2. Even if these causal relationships are obtained, the complex causal relationships lead to a very large causal diagram and a huge number of test cases.

3.5. Decision table testing

Decision tables are tools for analyzing and expressing situations where different operations are performed under multiple logical conditions.

In some data processing problems, the implementation of certain operations depends on the combination of multiple logical conditions, that is, different operations are performed for the combined values of different logical conditions. Decision tables are suitable for such problems.

3.5.1. Example

Go on with the example for vending machine software.

Test cases design steps:

5). Convert graph to a decision table.
a. Take the values of C1, C2, C3 and C4 from small to large in binary system.

	Cause / Input			
#	**C1**	**C2**	**C3**	**C4**
1	0	0	0	0
2	0	0	0	1
3	0	0	1	0
4	0	0	1	1
5	0	1	0	0
6	0	1	0	1
7	0	1	1	0

8	0	1	1	1
9	1	0	0	0
10	1	0	0	1
11	1	0	1	0
12	1	0	1	1
13	1	1	0	0
14	1	1	0	1
15	1	1	1	0
16	1	1	1	1

b. Analyze whether the intermediate results are valid or not.

The green highlighting rows are the valid input configurations.

	Cause / Input				**Middle**	
#	**C1**	**C2**	**C3**	**C4**	**Cm1**	**Cm2**
1	0	0	0	0	N	N
2	0	0	0	1	N	N
3	0	0	1	0	N	N
4	0	0	1	1	N	N
5	0	1	0	0	N	N

6	0	1	0	1	Y	Y
7	0	1	1	0	Y	Y
8	0	1	1	1	Y	N
9	1	0	0	0	Y	N
10	1	0	0	1	Y	Y
11	1	0	1	0	Y	Y
12	1	0	1	1	Y	N
13	1	1	0	0	N	N
14	1	1	0	1	N	N
15	1	1	1	0	N	N
16	1	1	1	1	N	N

c. Obtain the following simplified version (that is, when intermediate results Cm1 and Cm2 are true).

	Cause / Input				**Effect / Output**		
#	**C1**	**C2**	**C3**	**C4**	**E1**	**E2**	**E3**
1	0	1	0	1	T	F	T
2	0	1	1	0	T	T	F
3	1	0	0	1	F	F	T
4	1	0	1	0	F	T	F

6). Design test cases from decision table.

#	Input	Expected Result
1	Put in $2 coins, Press the "Sprite" button.	Refund $0.50 coin, Dispense Sprite
2	Put in $2 coins, Press the "Coke" button.	Refund $0.50 coin, Dispense Coke
3	Put in $1.5 coins, Press the "Sprite" button.	Dispense Sprite
4	Put in $1.5 coins, Press the "Coke" button.	Dispense Coke

3.5.2 Strengths and Weaknesses

Strengths

The decision table fully consider the combination of input fields, and each rule covers multiple input conditions and consider the constraint relationship of input, the risk of missing measurement is reduced.

Weakness

When too many input items, the number of rules goes up by 2 to the n, the decision table will be very large, using the decision table to merge will cause logic loss, business confusion and error.

3.6. Orthogonal array testing

Orthogonal array testing is a scientific method of designing experiments by selecting a suitable number of representative points from a large number of data.

For example, when test for an account sign up, there are three fields (Username, Password, Confirm password for input. Each field has 2 options (fill in or not fill in). In traditional design, we need to test 2*2*2=8 times. However, use orthogonal table L4(2^3), 4 times can cover the testing.

Composition of orthogonal tables

An orthogonal table is a special form, usually expressed as Ln(m^k). The representation of L is “this is an orthogonal table”, n represents the number of trials or rows of orthogonal tables, k represents the number of factors that can be arranged or the number of columns in the orthogonal table, m represents the maximum number of values that can be obtained by any single factor, and n = k * (m - 1) + 1.

3.6.1 Example

Create an account by provide: Username, Password, Confirm Password.

Test cases design steps:

1). Analyze the factors (variables): Username, Password, Confirm Password.

2). Value of variable: Yes (fill in), No (not fill in).

3). Choose an appropriate orthogonal table: here we use L4(2^3).

0	0	0
0	1	1
1	0	1
1	1	0

Reference

Orthogonal table online: https://www.york.ac.uk/depts/maths/tables/orthogonal.htm

Available Tools: http://www.pairwise.org/tools.asp

4). Map the value of the variable to the table.

#	Username	Password	Confirm Password
1	No	No	No
2	No	Yes	Yes
3	Yes	No	Yes
4	Yes	Yes	No

5). Take the combination of the various factor levels of each row as a test case.

6). Add a combination of test cases that you think are needed but do not appear in the table.

3.6.2 Strengths and Weaknesses

Strengths:

Test cases are reduced reasonably by using orthogonal test method, so test rime and cost is reduced too.

Weaknesses:

This method treats each state point equally, the key is not prominent. It is easy to spend a lot of time on test design and execution in functions or scenarios that are not commonly used by users, while there is no extra focus on testing in the use of important paths.

Although the orthogonal test design has the above shortcomings, it can find the optimal level combination through all tests, so it is very popular among practical workers.

3.7. Functional structure diagram

Function structure diagram is used to show the dependency of functions, it is also a feature breakdown structure diagram. Each box in the diagram is a function module or function point. It is recommended to use the form "verb + name" when describing function points

3.7.1 Example

Test for an instant messenger Wchat which has the common functionalities, such as login, add friends, chat with friends, post information, etc.

3.7.2 Strengths and Weaknesses

Strengths

Functional structure can show global structure of production.

Weakness

Only feature breakdown structure, not single points of functionality.

3.8. Scene graph

Almost all software today uses event triggers to control the flow. When an event is triggered, the situation will form a scene, while different triggering orders and processing results of the same event will form an event flow. This idea in software design can also be introduced into software testing, which can more vividly depict the scenario when the event is triggered, which is beneficial for test designers to design test cases and make test cases easier to understand and execute.

The scene approach generally consists of basic and alternate flows, starting with one process and iterating through all the basic and alternative flows to complete all the scenarios.

Basic flow: represented by a straight black line, is the most basic and simple path through the use case (the program starts and ends without any errors).

Alternative flows: in different colors, an alternative flow can start with a base flow, or it can start with an alternative flow, execute under certain conditions, and then rejoin the base flow or terminate the scenario.

Start with the base flow and combine the base flow with the alternative flow to determine the test case scenario:

1	Basic Flow			
2	Basic Flow	Alternate Flow 1		
3	Basic Flow	Alternate Flow 1	Alternate Flow 2	
4	Basic Flow	Alternate Flow 3		
5	Basic Flow	Alternate Flow 3	Alternate Flow 1	
6	Basic Flow	Alternate Flow 3	Alternate Flow 1	Alternate Flow 2
7	Basic Flow	Alternate Flow 4		
8	Basic Flow	Alternate Flow 3	Alternate Flow 4	

3.8.1 Example

The production is an application of online shopping for books.

Test cases design steps:

1). Draw flow chart according to requirement document.

2). Determine the basic flow and alternative flow according to the flow chart.

Basic Flow	Access to website, Select books, Put books in cart, Login, Pay, Generate order
Alternate Flow 1	Login user doesn't exist
Alternate Flow 2	Username or Password error
Alternate Flow 3	Insufficient account balance

3). Determine the scenario based on the basic and alternative flows.

1	Successful shopping	Basic Flow	
2	User doesn't exist	Basic Flow	Alternate Flow 1
3	Incorrect username or password	Basic Flow	Alternate Flow 2
4	Insufficient account balance	Basic Flow	Alternate Flow 3

4). Generate test cases for each scenario.

5). Review all test cases generated, remove the redundant, and determine test data values for each test case.

3.8.2 Strengths and Weaknesses

Strengths

Business processes can be overridden.

Weaknesses

Only validate business processes, not single points of functionality.

In general, the methods of equivalence class, boundary value, error guessing, decision table and orthogonal array are adopted to verify the single point of function, then the scene method is adopted to verify the business process.

4. General Principles

Here are some general principles for when to use which test design techniques.

1. If the variables are independent, you can divide the domain and use equivalence partitioning. Turn an infinite number of tests into a finite number of tests.

2. Boundary value analysis is a method that used in any software test.

3. Error guessing helps us to supplement the original test cases with additional ones.

4. If the combination of input conditions needs to be considered, the causal graph method and the decision table method can be used

5. If the relationships between inputs and outputs are large, orthogonal array method can be used to reduce test cases.

6. If the functionalities of a system are complicated, functional structure can be used to breakdown functionalities.

7. The system with clear business process can choose scene method to design test cases.

8. Check the designed test case logic coverage against the program logic, and add enough test cases if the required coverage standards are not met.

References

Books: Glenford J. Myers, Tom Badgett, Corey Sandler. The Art of Software Testing (Third Edition)

GuXiang. 2017, Software testing technology in action, China post and telecommunications press

Cem Kaner, Jack Falk and Hung Quoc Nguyen. 2006 Testing Computer Software (Second Edition)

Why We Need New Software Testing Technologies

Carol Oliver, Ph.D.
carol@carolcodes.com

Abstract
Mobile and IoT software must perform in a dramatically greater variety of environments than traditional software. Yet the core testing technologies in widespread use today do not directly address this vast environmental variability. Cloud-based device testing is bridging the gap for now, but it is an incomplete solution. This paper presents a Release-Readiness Levels Framework that provides vocabulary and a structure for discussing the gaps between what software testers would like to be able to test and what the existing tools and technologies enable them to test. This paper then identifies the existing software testing technologies that might be extended to better meet practitioner needs, describes the requirements for entirely new software testing technologies to target the needs of mobile and IoT software testing into the future, and offers a glimpse into how the emergence of new testing technology is likely to proceed.

Biography
Dr. Carol Oliver earned a B.S. in Computer Science from Stanford University and a Ph.D. in Computer Science from Florida Institute of Technology. In between, she worked for about 15 years for campus infrastructure IT services at Stanford University, where she did some web app and a lot of middleware software testing.

1. Introduction
My academic research argues that practitioners need a new generation of tools to support mobile and IoT (Internet of Things) software testing. In this paper, I will present a brief history showing how mobile and IoT software differs significantly from traditional software. Then I will present the Release-Readiness Levels Framework, a tool for discussing the possible extents of software testing on a project – and for features and smaller details within any project. Next, I will survey the Seven Core Software Testing Technologies available today, highlighting their strengths and limitations and how those different technologies can fulfill (or not) the needs of the Release-Readiness Levels. Finally, I will present the requirements for the next generation of software testing technology and tools, and set context for how the emergence of the new technology is likely to proceed.

This paper is drawn from my Ph.D. dissertation (Oliver 2018) and many details and specific citations have been omitted from this paper in the interests of time and space; they are available in my dissertation, which is the primary reference for this paper.

1.1. Scope Note
Many types of testing concerns need addressing when preparing software for production release. Application usability and accessibility, installation and update accuracy, security and performance, etc. All these are very important concerns, but this work limits its attention to Functionality Testing.

1.2. Vocabulary Note

This work discusses code moving from Development Focus to Testing Focus. These phrases are used to emphasize that no adherence to any particular software development methodology is implied (e.g. Waterfall, Agile, etc.). In a company with separate departments for development and testing, this change in focus corresponds to sending the code from one department to another. In a one-person shop, this change of focus corresponds to removing the Developer Hat and donning the Tester Hat. Who does the work and when that work is done are not in scope in this paper. The scope of this paper is what work it is possible to do and why that work may be worthwhile.

Development Focus work is about trying to find a way to make something work. Testing Focus work is about challenging what has been created to see if it will hold up no matter what adverse circumstances occur. These are two creative efforts with a shared purpose (the production of successful software) but different – and contradictory – goals.

2. Major Phases of Computing and Software Testing

History tells how software testing came to be what it is today. A look at the arc of computing history reveals how software testing is inevitably entwined with the state of computing technology.

The earliest computers created a 100% known software execution environment: Programs were written in each computer's particular language to take advantage of each computer's unique capabilities and restrictions. Unless a moth flew into the hardware[1], the full context of the computer while running the program was predictable. Mainframes diversified, computing languages abstracted, and programs came to be written for multiple hardware platforms. The software execution environment could no longer be fully predicted, but the variations between computing execution environments remained relatively constrained.

The emergence of desktop computing created an explosion of change. Many new hardware manufacturers emerged, making both new computers and various accessories to extend their capabilities. Peripherals all spoke different hardware languages and operating systems relied on the hardware manufacturers to create functioning drivers to enable their devices to work on consumers' systems. For some years, computing saw rampant device driver incompatibilities. When a consumer purchased desktop printing software, the consumer needed to check if their printer was on the list of compatible printers for that program. It was hard to predict the execution environment for software, and strange errors occurred (e.g. a program might not run if a peripheral not even used by that program was attached to the system).

Then standards emerged and the operating systems with consumer-market dominance took over the bulk of interfacing to hardware (C. Kaner, pers. comm.). Most hardware manufacturers implemented exactly that interface, most software manufacturers programmed for only that interface, and the operating system passed information across the border. Execution environments for programs became largely predictable again, and problems related to environmental conditions became a relatively small aspect of software testing.

The emergence of mobile computing created another explosion of change, several magnitudes larger. There is now a very rapid change cycle for hardware, operating systems, and applications. Rather than years, merely months pass between major changes in each category. A few consumers change quickly to the most recent everything; many lag a few revisions behind state of the art (Android Open Source Project 2018); and a few still run systems others have consigned to museums (Google Tech Talks 2013). Just that aspect of environmental conditions is wildly variable for mobile apps.

The mere aspect of mobility adds to the unpredictability of environmental conditions while a program runs. As they move about the world, mobile devices change their network connectivity methods and parameters, and they are impacted by changes in the geography and weather conditions around them. Anecdotally, network connectivity around skyscrapers and device stability in extreme temperatures are both problems. Exacerbating the unpredictability problem, mobile devices consume input from a wide variety of sensors that previously were specialty equipment but now are commonplace, like magnetometers and accelerometers. Applications are expected to respond to a great deal of that data, and sometimes the mobile operating system imposes the new conditions on the programs whether the programs handle them gracefully or not (e.g. screen orientation changes, dimming the screen in response to changes in ambient light, replacing the active network connection details at any moment, etc.). These types of environmental unpredictability cannot be solved by standardization of interfaces; they are inherent aspects of mobile computing.

IoT software shares many of the environmental characteristics of mobile computing, especially the deep reliance on embedded sensors.

This history shows that mobile and IoT apps operate within a fundamentally different scale and scope of environmental unpredictability than programs in any prior computing era. To be effective, automated software testing tools need to address this unpredictability directly.

3. Release-Readiness Levels Framework

When I worked as a practitioner, specific tacit goals underpinned my software testing activities. As I met other senior testers and discussed experiences with them, I found resonance in how we approached our software testing efforts. We all wrestled with the question of judging when software was performing well enough that we could recommend its release. Our project managers made the release decisions, but they expected us to render professional judgments and supporting evidence to inform those decisions.

We lacked a good framework for discussing the options. Historically, the ISO/IEC/IEEE 29119[2] standards and their predecessors have not been entirely helpful. Guidance on managing the testing process or doing requirements traceability does not directly answer the core problem: How to judge if the software will perform adequately in the field. There is tension between how much testing is feasible to do and how much productive information about the range of field conditions is needed to enable sound decision-making.

My Release-Readiness Levels Framework (Figure 1) captures one perspective on how to assess that tension and how to discuss what additional testing might be desirable at any point in the project. Underlying this model is the concept of exposing the software to increasingly difficult challenges, thereby increasing knowledge about the variety of conditions in which the software will perform acceptably.

Each level in the Release-Readiness Levels Framework applies to individual features, communicating feature sets, and to the program as an integrated whole. The further testing goes through the levels, the further confidence develops that the software will behave desirably in a wider variety of circumstances.

Note that this is a map of the testing *possibilities* – not a statement of required steps. The appropriate point at which to release the software in question is a Project Management decision and varies for each program and often for each release.

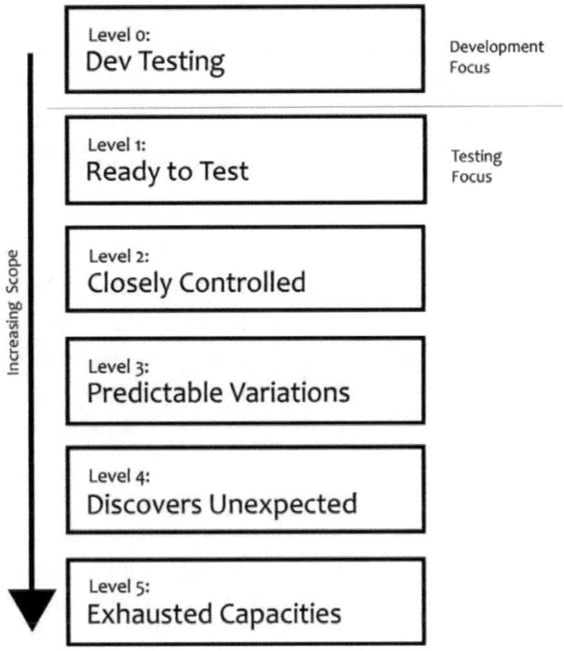

Figure 1. Release-Readiness Levels Framework

3.1. Level 0: Dev Testing

Level 0 testing occurs during Development Focus, and its goal is to assess whether the intended functionality has been implemented. Characteristically, very small aspects of program behavior are analyzed separately from all other behaviors of the program. In modern software development, Dev Testing consists mostly of unit tests, but this is also where style checkers and other static code analyzers are usually applied.

Software released at Level 0 (Dev Testing) may contain missing, partly-functional, and incomplete features. It may not install cleanly into any environment other than the Development Environment, and it may not work as a cohesive whole even if it installs cleanly. Professional software development shops usually test further than this before production release.

3.2. Level 1: Ready to Test

The goal at Level 1 is to assess whether the installed software is ready to be challenged by Testing Focus work. Characteristically, functionality is tested only surficially, just enough to show whether the program crashes with trivial case or permits access to all features of current interest; it is common in the early stages of a project for features to be missing or known to be not ready for Testing Focus yet.

Specific behaviors checked at Ready to Test tend to focus upon whether the install process worked correctly and upon the basic stability of features to be tested. Happy-path scenarios in which the software is used exactly as intended are checked, along with the most common or most predictable error-path scenarios.

Software released at Level 1 (Ready to Test) should install properly into expected operating environments but may break if used even slightly differently than anticipated, whether by user action, data state, or an operating environment that was not tested.

3.3. Level 2: Closely Controlled

The goal at Level 2 is to assess whether features work when challenged by tests with carefully controlled parameters. Characteristically, test data is hardcoded but may occasionally be drawn from small lists. Testing activities consist of challenging the program's assumptions in various ways, subjecting it to atypical usage patterns, data that is potentially hard to process, easily-triggered system and environmental interruptions, etc.

Software released at Level 2 (Closely Controlled) is likely to suffer many field failures on systems that differ from Development and Testing Environments; it may also break if used in unanticipated ways or if used on a continuous basis for some block of time, as characteristically tests at this level consist of very brief runs of the app to test a specific behavior, followed by resetting the app to a clean state before testing the next specific behavior. Such run intervals provide clear boundaries between tests, making it easy to identify which test failed, but these runs are markedly shorter than most scenarios in which users will actually use the app.

3.4. Level 3: Predictable Variations

The goal at Level 3 is to assess whether features of the program continue to work when test conditions are significantly loosened and many predictable variations in those parameters are exercised. Test cases at this level take different values at each execution, drawing specifics from large sets rather than fixed details or small lists of possibilities. Characteristically, Predictable Variations tests intensely vary one or a few variables while holding others constant, as the knowledge sought is about how those specific variations alter the program's response.

Software released at Level 3 (Predictable Variations) is markedly more stable in a diverse variety of conditions than software released at Level 2 (Closely Controlled), but it may still experience a moderate number of field failures. These stem largely from unexpected patterns of use and from untested environmental and data conditions. The more aspects of environmental unpredictability not tested, the higher the likelihood of finding many problems after release.

3.5. Level 4: Discovers Unexpected

The goal at Level 4 is for testing to uncover problems that no one on the project could predict, sometimes that no one on the project could imagine. Experienced practitioners regularly exchange tales of finding bugs like this, often accidentally, because modern programs are complex and contain many tacit dependencies within themselves, with their operating environment, and with their data.

In various ways, a program and its operating environment tested at this level are placed under stress. Many of the test techniques for finding these unpredictable bugs consist of HiVAT (High Volume Automated Testing) techniques, such as long-sequence tests, long-duration tests, and random variations of structured input (i.e. fuzzing). Characteristically, the scale of tests increases dramatically at this level. HiVAT techniques are intended to efficiently run hundreds of thousands, millions, or scrillions of specific tests.

Senior technical testers in the practitioner community have created HiVAT testing efforts for decades, but the approach typically requires programming expertise and these techniques are not widespread in general practice.

Software released at Level 4 (Discovers Unexpected) tends to experience some field failures as combinations of conditions are discovered in the field that were not reached by intensive testing, but these failures are rarer than at earlier levels.

3.6. Level 5: Exhausted Capacities

The goal at Level 5 is for testing efforts to exhaust their capacities, given the capabilities of the suite of tools and techniques and the time available. Stresses upon the software are dramatically increased, sampling scope approaches closer to exhaustive, and system testing increases the variations in exercising interleaved, cooperating, and coexisting features.

This level of testing intensity is typically done when the risk of failure is extremely high (e.g. data-processing logic that could corrupt the database if done wrong, life-support systems, high-impact infrastructure systems, etc.). Possibly the best-known example of Level 5 (Exhausted Capacities) testing is the preparations made for Y2K as computing approached the year 2000.

Computing professionals not involved in the Y2K transition often lack understanding of the details. The problem was caused by a vast quantity of legacy code that assumed all years fit the format 19xx, and so stored only the last two digits to distinguish the year; the imminent arrival of the year 2000 meant all that code was going to break and comparisons for which data was older or newer would be incorrect unless four digits were compared. Surficially, the answer appears to be as simple as just replacing two-digit storage with four-digit storage.

However, the reality was a great deal more complex than that. Many companies attempted to patch their legacy software only to find that every patch spawned multiple new problems; the harder they tried to fix their code, the less functional their software became. In the United States, many banks sold themselves to the few banks with Y2K-compliant software, and antitrust regulators approved the sales because the financial infrastructure of the country had to continue to work reliably (C. Kaner, pers. comm.).

Problems riddled software at all levels, and companies in a vast array of disciplines created entire duplicate computing systems and networks so they could advance the date in this test environment and see what would break and what fixes actually worked. That degree of duplicate computing hardware alone cost an exorbitant amount (easily millions or billions or more, worldwide), and very significant human time was invested in testing and retesting critical systems. Y2K was a worldwide test effort that covered years. Popular understanding is that Y2K was a lot of noise made about nothing, because when the clock turned over, only very minor things broke; the reality is that Y2K was an incredibly successful, Level 5 testing effort that exhausted the capacities of the people, technology, and time invested in it.

Software released at Level 5 (Exhausted Capacities) experiences the fewest possible field failures, but some failures remain possible.

3.7. Release-Readiness Levels Recap

To properly assess whether mobile and IoT software will perform adequately in their field conditions of massive environmental unpredictability, software testing efforts need to include tests at Level 3 (Predictable Variations) and Level 4 (Discovers Unexpected). Some critical behaviors within many apps likely deserve tests at Level 5 (Exhausted Capacities); in some cases, whole software systems may merit that level of testing (e.g. autonomous vehicles). So, what levels of testing are enabled by our current software testing technologies and tools?

4. Core Software Testing Technologies

The process of software testing involves creating tests, executing them, and evaluating what happened as a result. Whether manual or automated, executing a test relies on specific technology to make it function.

These software testing technologies are mechanisms for exercising a program in directed ways or for obtaining information about the software's behavior. They are the keys which enable different test methods, the gateways which define the character of what kinds of tests are possible.

I identified seven core testing technologies present in today's readily available tools and the academic research literature:

1. Physical devices
2. Virtual devices (emulators and simulators)
3. Simulation environments
4. Mechanisms for interacting with the Visual GUI Tree
5. Image-comparison
6. Code manipulation (e.g. xUnit, code instrumentation, etc.)
7. System monitoring

Each technology enables certain kinds of tests and is better-suited to some types of investigations than others. Existing tools and testing approaches fulfill a technology's potential to differing degrees, and each implementation of a technology may be evaluated in terms of how well it handles the environmental unpredictability characteristic of mobile and IoT software.

4.1. Physical Devices

Testing on physical devices is the baseline testing technology. When programs were written for just one computer, testing the program meant running it to see if it worked, at least well enough for the intended purpose at that time. Beginning programming students do the same thing today.

As computers diversified, software testing on physical devices expanded to include compatibility assessments between the program and different execution environments. In the desktop computing era, software development companies typically had test labs containing a variety of supported equipment. Companies could buy representative hardware for all their major supported systems and expect to use those machines for years; significantly new systems came out every few years when chipsets changed, and the operating systems updated every few years as well.

In the mobile era, the comprehensive in-house test lab has ceased to be feasible. Instead of dozens of distinct hardware platforms, there are thousands in use worldwide (OpenSignal 2015). New device models appear at least once a year from most device manufacturers, and sometimes more frequently than that; operating systems receive frequent major updates (sometimes several times per year) and nearly continuous minor updates. The scale and pace of mobile environment changes make maintaining traditional in-house test labs of physical devices for all in-scope systems prohibitively expensive.

Thus, the environmental unpredictability problem mobile software testing faces for this technology is simply access to a diverse-enough collection of physical devices.

4.1.1. Accessing Sufficient Diversity

One strategy is to test only on the top 10-15 devices in use by a mobile app's target users, broken into strata of high-end devices, mid-range devices, and low-end devices; which devices belong in which grouping changes very quickly, as new devices are released. This is an example of Level 2 (Closely Controlled) testing because the test data varied here is a small list (10-15 devices). Despite its limitations, this strategy should work adequately for reasonably homogeneous target populations; as the diversity of target users increases, more of their systems will not be represented in this sampling strategy.

Arguably, the most common option in modern app development is cloud-based testing. Fundamentally, these cloud services leverage existing software testing technologies to provide networked manual or automated access to physical devices hosted and maintained by the cloud service provider; various providers exist and exactly who is in business changes over time. Because so little can be inferred about the stability of software on other devices based upon its behavior on one device, mere replication of tests across many different mobile devices is not very informative. Tens or even a few hundreds of devices tested is still a small fraction of the possible thousands of devices that a mobile app could be deployed to, so it is difficult for mere replication across devices to lift testing beyond Level 2 (Closely Controlled). Further restricting the power of cloud-based device testing, the kinds of tests that can be performed on such devices are bounded by the testing interfaces provided by the service, and that limits their power.

4.1.2. Technology Strengths and Limitations

The greatest strength of testing on physical devices is trustworthy realism about how apps will behave on that device. Although that observation seems obvious, fidelity to reality is a great enough issue in mobile app testing that the point is emphasized by academics and practitioners alike (Delamaro, Vincenzi, and Maldonado 2006; Ridene and Barbier 2011; Muccini, Di Francesco, and Esposito 2012; Nagowah and Sowamber 2012; Gao et al. 2014; Vilkomir and Amstutz 2014; Knott 2015).

One of the motivators for the emphasis on realism is the mobile fragmentation problem. Mobile hardware varies greatly in chipsets; screen size, display resolution and pixel density; number and types of network interfaces, sensors, and embedded devices (e.g. camera, speakers); quantity of working memory and local storage space; and battery performance. The current state-of-the-art solution to this vast variety is to test on a sufficient number of real devices, where "sufficient" is interpreted individually by every software publisher.

Some limitations apply to using physical devices as a testing technology. Mobile devices are consumer devices, and (Google Tech Talks 2013) points out that consumer devices are not designed to run 24x7, so hardware used for extensive testing will fail after a few months and need replacing.

4.1.3. Implementation Limitations

Another pragmatic limitation on the number and type of tests executed remains the financial cost of testing. Even though cloud-based testing services have dramatically lowered the costs to software producers of provisioning and maintaining physical devices, these services still cost money. Budget and service constraints limit the testing minutes purchased for a project, forcing tradeoffs in what is tested and how extensively.

Cloud-based pools of physical devices vastly improved access to a variety of devices, but there is little variety in the physical or network environments of server rooms, providing little opportunity to exercise the embedded sensors and other equipment in cloud-based mobile devices. Examining these aspects of mobile devices in any detail still requires physical access to the appropriate device, and the common solution is for individuals to move around the world, interacting with each device one at a time. The obvious problems in scaling this approach explain the appeal of crowdsourcing[3] testing, but that approach lends itself to haphazard data collection and great challenges in repeatability.

Again, cloud-based testing is limited in its possibilities by the testing interfaces that the service providers support. Generally, it is not possible to extend or replace a provider's testing framework, so tests are constrained to the types and design styles the provided frameworks support.

4.1.4. Physical Devices Technology Summary

Testing on physical devices yields highly trustworthy results but also incurs test-management overhead costs that can be significant, somewhat limiting scale. Cloud-based providers close the gap in trying to examine the effects of all the combinations of hardware and operating system versions, but they do so in a server room environment that provides little scope for exercising the embedded sensors and other equipment in mobile devices. A robust solution to scaling testing that exercises embedded sensors and equipment is either not yet invented or not yet widely available. The types and design styles of tests run on cloud-based devices are limited to what the provider's frameworks support; support for custom testing needs is quite rare.

4.2. Virtual Devices

Virtual devices leverage readily-available and affordable hardware to mimic the specific hardware and operating environment of less easily obtained systems. The manual analog is the collection of techniques involved in desk-checking, where a human reads through the code, pretending to be the computer, analyzing how the program is going to run.

Computer-based virtual environments appear to have their roots in the first time-sharing operating systems of the 1960s (Creasy 1981; Pettus 1999). Over the next several decades, computing professionals developed a decided preference for emulators over simulators. Simulators ran faster, but they characteristically used the full resources of the host computer to perform the computing tasks. Emulators created representations of the foreign hardware within the host computer, using just the resources the real device would have available and using a virtual chipset to execute the foreign program at the binary or system-call level. Testing on simulators gave an approximation of how the program would behave on its target computer, but the exact fidelity in representing the emulated device created great trust in the results obtained while using the emulator.

At the beginning of the mobile era, devices were especially resource-constrained, making it difficult to run testing software on the physical devices. Vendors addressed this problem by providing virtual devices to enable testing (Satoh 2003). Although traditional programs tend to be developed on their target platforms, mobile apps are developed on desktop computers and deployed to mobile devices later. Consequently, virtual devices are everyday tools during mobile app development today.

4.2.1. Technology Strengths and Limitations

The primary strengths of virtual devices for mobile apps today are enabling development tasks on non-mobile systems and the ease of switching between devices. The practical matter of cost savings is another strength inherent in the technology, as the actual physical devices are not a factor.

The history of simulators and emulators from the desktop era has shaped expectations about them in the mobile era. When the term "emulator" is applied (e.g. the Android Emulator), the implication is that it will provide the exact fidelity trustworthiness of the prior era.

Unfortunately, there are significant limitations to the virtual devices representing mobile devices. Although the mobile CPU, OS version, RAM, and screen size, resolution, and pixel density are virtually represented, it is well-understood that sensors and other embedded hardware commonly are not. Functionality involving the camera, GPS, accelerometer, microphone, speakers, gyroscope, or compass; sensors for ambient light, pressure, temperature, humidity, or proximity; and network connections like Bluetooth, Wi-Fi, NFC (Near Field Communication), and cellular communication for 3G, 4G, etc. – all these are difficult or impossible to test on virtual devices, especially those provided by the platform vendors (Muccini, Di Francesco, and

Esposito 2012; Griebe and Gruhn 2014; Knott 2015, 115). It is not clear that including all these embedded components in a virtual device would even be useful; most of these are pure input mechanisms, not manipulated by either the user or the program. Merely representing them as pieces of hardware in a virtual device is not enough to make them usable; a different technology is required.

4.2.2. Implementation Limitations

The Android ecosystem faces another set of serious limitations, stemming from its open-source nature. Microsoft controls their operating system, and Apple controls both their hardware and software, so these ecosystems may not have the same problem.

However, the Android OS is commonly customized by both hardware manufacturers and cell service providers. Some of this customization is required to make Android work on the equipment; other aspects are customized for user experience, and sometimes these changes are very significant functionality differences. Complicating matters, most of these customizations are proprietary and therefore not publicly documented.

This means the best the Android Emulator can do after setting up the partial-hardware representation of a device is layer on a stock version[4] of Android OS. Seen in that light, it is not just that features to send context data to the virtual device are awkward to use or unavailable, it is that testing on a virtual device *lies* about how well things will work in the field. The virtual devices are idealized deployment environments that incompletely and inaccurately represent the real devices. This limits the power of testing on Virtual Devices to Level 1 (Ready to Test) because the information obtained is only a ghost of reality.

This explains why experienced practitioners strongly advise testing primarily on physical devices in real environments (Knott 2015, 3–4), limiting the use – if any – of virtual devices to only the most basic, simplistic tests (Kohl 2012, 278–79; Knott 2015, 52).

4.2.3. Virtual Devices Technology Summary

Testing on virtual devices enables effective development of mobile apps, since development is done on different systems than where the software is deployed. However, all mobile virtual devices lack completeness; significant hardware components are routinely omitted, and Virtual Device technology alone is insufficient to exercise the sensors and other embedded equipment even if they were included. The Android Emulator diverges even further from exact fidelity in representing a physical device because it can only apply a stock version of the Android operating system, absent all proprietary customizations made by hardware manufacturers or cell service providers.

4.3. Simulation Environments

Simulation environments take simulation beyond the device level, instead creating virtual representations of various aspects of the world surrounding the mobile device. Academic work has mostly studied networked communication scenarios and a few richer environmental context simulations.

There is little discussion in the practitioner literature about simulation environments being used for mobile software testing. This suggests that good tools for useful mobile simulation environments are not generally accessible to practitioners.

4.3.1. Technology Strengths and Limitations

Simulation environments bring realistic deployment scenarios into a controlled lab environment, allowing intensive variation of specific aspects of interest without the expense of travelling to the correct conditions or waiting long enough for the correct conditions to occur. Theoretically, this should enable testing at Level 3 (Predictable Variations), Level 4 (Discovers Unexpected), and Level 5 (Exhausted Capacities).

Most applications of simulation environments also involve sophisticated modeling of the conditions of interest, to ensure the simulation meaningfully represents real conditions. For example, performance testing of websites typically involves estimates mixing percentages of different representative types of users so that realistic traffic and session loads can be generated. This complexity tends to isolate use of simulation tools (like those for performance testing websites) to only a few, highly-specialized testers brought in as consultants when a company has a specific need. Simulation environments are rarely used – if at all – by most practitioner software testers.

4.3.2. Implementation Limitations

The primary limitation of simulation environments applied to mobile testing today is that there are so few instances exploring it. A secondary limitation is that existing tools focus on testing user-generated events in short bursts but do not enable testing extended usage scenarios (an hour or more) (Meads, Naderi, and Warren 2015); this means that the simulation environments are not representative of reality in terms of how users will use the apps, the devices, the network resources, etc. Furthermore, the focus on user-generated events means little testing is being triggered by sensor readings or background services, despite those being extremely common vectors of input to modern mobile and IoT devices.

4.3.3. Simulation Environments Summary

Simulation environments contain rich potential to assist in testing mobile and IoT devices, but their potential is not well-addressed at this time. Academic work investigates networked communication scenarios and some environmental context simulation, but the scope of the tests is limited overall. Practitioners seem to have no useful access to tools for applying simulation environments to testing mobile apps.

4.4. Visual GUI Tree

Mechanisms for interacting with the Visual GUI Tree form arguably the most commonly used GUI application testing technology in use today. The Visual GUI Tree is the hierarchical arrangement of objects forming the rendered display of a modern GUI. All the currently-visible objects on the screen (e.g. buttons, images, etc.) are part of it, but so are many invisible objects that control how objects on the screen are placed (e.g. layout managers which arrange contained objects in a row horizontally, vertically, or in a grid). Assistive technologies like screen readers for blind users leverage the Visual GUI Tree, so it has wide availability on desktop systems, in web browsers, and on mobile devices.

To encode a test accessing the Visual GUI Tree, some absolute identification of the object in question is required. The earliest interaction mechanisms identified objects based on their coordinates on the screen, and that remains a common fallback mechanism today. Some interaction mechanisms scrape the screen to locate specific text, which is then used to identify the object of interest; this allows the text to appear at different coordinates and not break the encoded test. The most reliable means of accessing a specific object is to use a distinctive attribute of that object, commonly some kind of identifier or xname value. If such a unique identifier is not available, then the object's XPath location in the Visual Tree (i.e. the path of elements that must be traversed to reach the desired element) may be used to navigate precisely to the desired object. Once a desired GUI object is located, testing frameworks interact with it as an object, entering text or sending click commands; more mobile-centric frameworks provide gesture commands, such as swiping the screen in a particular direction.

Tools using the Visual GUI Tree are prolific and widely used today, as this is an excellent technology for replicating user interactions with a GUI. The vendor-provided automation tools for each mobile platform use this technology, as do GUI Record and Replay tools. All the cloud-based device services primarily leverage the Visual GUI Tree to replicate user interactions.

Most of the tests implemented in Visual GUI Tree tools are Level 2 (Closely Controlled) tests, restricted to specific data hardcoded into each test, repeated verbatim with every test run. This level of detail is the baseline scenario for automated testing. Unfortunately, it is rare for these tools to offer features to parameterize test case data, much less to determine it programmatically at runtime, features that are required to enable tests at Level 3 (Predictable Variations).

Whether customizations to extend the power of tests is possible in Visual GUI Tree tools usually depends on how flexible a programming language the tool uses as its test scripting language. The need to program scripts in a more sophisticated manner is at odds with the marketing of these tools, much of which focuses on enabling testing by non-programmers, so features enabling coding flexibility are not a high-priority for many tool-makers.

In recent years, an increasing number of testing services have advertised pre-packaged test suites designed to test any app without human effort. These typically install the software and apply Random Monkey testing to the GUI, looking for crashes. Anecdotally, these generic test suites are finding bugs in many mobile apps, but they necessarily cannot be checking substantial functionality of any of them because no generic test suite can know anything about the functionality of any program. Consequently, these tests operate at Level 1 (Ready to Test).

4.4.1. Technology Strengths and Limitations

Ever since GUIs became widely-implemented using objects, interacting with those objects by accessing the Visual GUI Tree has become widespread across desktop, web, and mobile applications. It is an excellent way to automate interaction with a GUI in a manner that replicates how humans interact with it, through exactly the same objects accessed in almost the same ways.

When the Visual GUI Tree works, it works very well, but it cannot work when it cannot uniquely identify an object. (Chang, Yeh, and Robert C. Miller 2010) note that sometimes GUI objects are not given unique identifier attributes. This happens rather frequently in practice, because developers often have no need of such identifiers to uniquely access the object; consequently, the identifiers required by Visual GUI Tree testing tools may only be added by special request to accommodate testers. As a matter of human process, this is not a reliable system; it is tedious work for the developers and adds clutter to their code.

When unique identifier attributes are unavailable, Visual GUI Tree tools fall back to XPath navigational routes to objects or to specific coordinates on the screen. Neither of these works with variable GUI elements – items that may change position in a list as more data is added to the application, or items that are programmatically populated into a display template based on runtime selection filters.

Consider a kitchen pantry app that is asked to display only the perishable items expiring in the next week. Each of those items is selected for display at runtime based on the state of the database and the value of the timestamp when the query is issued; in mobile apps, these are typically displayed as individual GUI objects, but there is no reliable identifying attribute that can be assigned to them and expected to persist across repeated queries. Sometimes identifiers are dynamically created for such elements while the program runs, but new values are dynamically created the next time the program runs, rendering scripting a repeatable test impossible. There is also no guarantee that each type of item will be unique (how would one distinguish between five different bananas?), and elements may not be populated into the display in the same order every time. The identification information simply is not naturally present to set up repeatable tests that will succeed across runs of the application. Automating tests in these situations quickly becomes more a matter of coordinating and maintaining test data (self-verifying records or known-state of the whole database) than about testing the behavior of the app.

The Visual GUI Tree also does not handle any case where one GUI element combines several different behaviors within it, determined by position of interaction on the element rather than by its object identity. Image maps on web pages are good examples, as clicking on different parts of the image triggers different actions. Many mobile games have visual control screens that surficially resemble image maps, where things the user can choose to do are carefully integrated into an overall image.

The Visual GUI Tree is excellent technology for testing behaviors triggered by user actions, but not sufficient for testing behaviors not triggered by user actions. Context-dependent inputs from various sensors and most error scenarios need another testing technology applied before they manifest, because they result from something else happening while the user is using the app.

4.4.2. Implementation Limitations

On the one hand, using the Visual GUI Tree for testing is a mature technology that has been well-developed across several generations of computing platforms, with well-understood recurrent difficulties and well-known solutions to those difficulties. On the other hand, certain usage limitations have never been robustly supported.

Examples from desktop applications (Chisholm 1997; Nyman 1999; Borjesson and Feldt 2012; Bauersfeld and Vos 2014) and web applications (Stocco et al. 2014) note that custom objects are not handled well in Visual GUI Tree tools. Custom objects derive from established objects but behave differently, often using the technology in non-standard ways (e.g. a list element that contains different background colors for each list item but no text, making a color-picker). The testing tools that rely on the Visual GUI Tree only know about the standard GUI widgets; they cannot know about the custom-created ones, and few tools enable programming extensions to the tool to allow accurate processing of custom GUI widgets.

In a similar vein, (Nyman 1999) and (Nguyen et al. 2014) document difficulties in handling GUI components with context-dependent text strings, such as windows titled after documents or error messages with non-constant details. Sometimes the record-and-replay usage scenario for Visual GUI Tree tools is blamed for the lack of features to handle this need, as the naïve understanding of record-and-replay expects exact repetition of all details and does not imagine tuning the recorded script to be more powerful and to handle variations fitting specific patterns.

(Chang, Yeh, and Rob Miller 2011) point out that some textual data that is read programmatically from object attributes may not be formatted the same way as the text string is displayed on screen. Date and time stamps are particularly likely to diverge. Where the discrepancy matters, this ought to be easily addressed with a little code during Testing Focus work. However, this faces the same difficulty as handling custom GUI widgets and handling parameterized scripts: Much of the marketing around these tools focuses on enabling testing by non-programmers, so features enabling coding flexibility are not high-priority for the tool-makers.

(Gronli and Ghinea 2016) note that mobile apps reliant on animations and clock-based display changes can exhibit erratic failures when tests are replayed, due to timing issues that render some GUI widgets inaccessible or not present when the test script expects to find them. This is something of a surprise, as the need for a "wait for element" feature is well-established in the history of using these tools prior to the mobile era; however, (Google Tech Talks 2013) suggests that new instantiations of using this technology may be independently rediscovering this need rather than considering it essential from the beginning.

4.4.3. Visual GUI Tree Technology Summary

The Visual GUI Tree is both an excellent and dominant technology for testing mobile apps, but the technology suffers from a persistent lack of capacity to handle custom objects and display patterns that vary in specific details, such as error messages. These limitations are exacerbated by variable GUI elements, which are becoming more common in mobile apps because it saves memory to not instantiate elements not visible on the screen; typically populated as list elements at runtime, these elements commonly lack unique identifiers, reliable paths to their location in the GUI Tree, and unique text contents. Another testing technology is required to test behaviors that result from context-data input or most error conditions, as these situations are not triggered by user actions.

4.5. Image Comparison

Image comparison tools take a snapshot of the rendered display of a running program then compare that snapshot to a reference image previously captured. Either whole-image or part-image comparison may be done. The manual version requires humans to visually compare images to a reference standard.

Testing tools at least as far back as the 1980s used whole-image comparison techniques (C. Kaner, pers. comm.), doing pixel-by-pixel comparisons of whole windows. These tools were fragile (every tiny change invalidated the reference image, even if an element just shifted left by one pixel) and fell out of general use, but there has been a resurgence in their use for testing mobile apps, where they are used to compare an entire screen's content to a baseline image (Knott 2015, 109).

The second generation of this technology is part-image comparison, which analyzes the snapshot of a running program to see if it contains the reference image somewhere within the whole picture. This is much more resilient to changes in the GUI layout. (Potter 1993)'s demo tool Triggers is commonly cited as the first work of this kind, although (Horowitz and Singhera 1993) used bitmap part-images in their fully-implemented GUI testing tool XTester, which went far beyond a demo implementation of the idea.

However, comparison of part-images did not occur widely until the introduction of Sikuli in 2009; the technology required advances in computer vision algorithms and in hardware capacities to become practical (Yeh, Chang, and Robert C. Miller 2009). Sikuli emerged from work seeking to help users confused by a GUI icon find help documentation without needing to guess the icon's text name. (Chang, Yeh, and Robert C. Miller 2010) applied Sikuli specifically to automated testing, focusing primarily on the benefits of unit tests established to check the implementation of Visual-Meaning behaviors, such as the Play button on a video player changing images from the Play triangle to the Pause bars[5] after the Play button was clicked; their scope limited itself to checking the GUI layer only, without any underlying connections to application functionality, so in this example nothing would be known about whether or not the video player could successfully show recorded video.

4.5.1. Technology Strengths and Limitations

Part-image comparisons are significantly better-suited for testing Visual-Meaning situations than tests that try to use the Visual GUI Tree for this purpose. (Groder 10/26/2016) contains an enlightening example test case in which the image searched for on-screen is that of Lake Superior rather than of a traditional GUI element object. The picture of Lake Superior is a more accurate indicator of the intended content than any other; if the image claims to be of Lake Superior but actually depicts an elephant, tools using the Visual

GUI Tree data will not notice the problem, but image-comparison technology should. However, searching the whole screen for part-image matches is a computationally expensive operation. This means these tests run slowly, which limits how many are worth running.

Another problem with using image-comparison for tests is that the technology can only deal with what is currently visible on the screen – if the target is scrolled off the visible portion of the screen or occluded by something else, image comparison cannot find it (Chang, Yeh, and Rob Miller 2011; Groder 10/26/2016). Scrolling may alleviate this problem, but anything that cannot currently be seen cannot be tested.

4.5.2. Implementation Limitations

The current set of image-comparison tools is hampered in effectiveness by several technology problems that may be addressable with improved code and algorithms. One impact of these is that the tools do not cope gracefully with differences in image size, color, or style (St. Amant et al. 2000; Chang, Yeh, and Rob Miller 2011; Borjesson and Feldt 2012; Groder 10/26/2016; Gronli and Ghinea 2016; Garousi et al. 2017); Sikuli was designed to address these variations (Yeh, Chang, and Robert C. Miller 2009), but in practice it is not functioning well enough. Practitioners relying on image comparison tests also have to rely on workarounds they need to implement themselves to get around tools that can only recognize one baseline image per screen; this implies that every device tested requires its own library of baseline images (Austin Test Automation Bazaar, pers. comm.). This means tests relying on this data are at best Level 2 (Closely Controlled).

Some commercial testing tools, like Eggplant, are encouraging companies to replace their Visual GUI Tree test suites with Image Comparison test suites, selling this next-generation of tools as based on how users interact with applications rather than on "outdated" code-centric testing approaches[6]. What that pitch does not make clear is that the resulting test scripts require collecting and maintaining a mammoth library of GUI element images, because images need to be collected for each individual element in all its states (selected, enabled, disabled), in every language, in every platform look-and-feel, in various sizes, etc. Collecting and maintaining all that test data is a significant and continuing operational cost, consuming time and energy testers could otherwise spend on testing the app instead of maintaining test data.

Image Comparison is also a poor technique for text recognition. (Chang, Yeh, and Rob Miller 2011) points out that existing OCR[7] techniques are designed for printed pages; thus, they expect white backgrounds, high-resolution text, and rectilinear layouts. Yet screen images may be significantly lower resolution than paper, contain colorful backgrounds, and be laid out much less predictably – all details which challenge the success of text-recognition via images. (Borjesson and Feldt 2012) observed a 50% failure rate in Sikuli's ability to distinguish between the single characters '6' and 'C'.

Lastly, the existing tools poorly handle moving image data, whether in GUI animations or in extracting data from video clips (Borjesson and Feldt 2012; Chang, Yeh, and Robert C. Miller 2010). It is not clear how much this is a limit of the technology, how much a limit of the computer vision algorithms, and how much a limit of the hardware processing resources in use at this time. However, mobile platforms seem to be standardizing on applying more animation to GUI elements for interface usability reasons (Tissoires and Conversy 2011), so this limitation to the tools is a significant challenge.

4.5.3. Image Comparison Technology Summary

Computer vision technology has enabled the ability to test for Visual Meaning problems, which is a great advance, but even part-image comparison is not suited for all purposes. The approach fundamentally cannot address functionality not visible on the screen; as such, it cannot trigger tests for incoming context data nor for most error conditions. Large libraries of images are currently required to apply the tools across platforms and different display characteristics, and searching for images on the screen slows the tests compared to looking for an identifying attribute via the Visual GUI Tree. Image-comparison of text is error-prone because OCR algorithms are designed for a much higher resolution and sharper contrast scenario. Image Comparison Technology is an excellent complement to Visual GUI Tree Technology, but it is not suited to be a complete replacement of it.

4.6. Code Manipulation

This large category encompasses many types of code analysis and modification. All the techniques utilize some insight into the code's details to enable testing, and all require programming.

In modern software development, arguably the most commonly used of these techniques is the xUnit framework. Primary use of xUnit tests is by developers during code creation and code maintenance activities; tiny, specific, very quick execution unit tests are the backbone of most Continuous Integration systems, serving as quick-feedback flags if code changes break the build (Beck 1999, 59–60). These kinds of unit tests form a very important foundation for stabilizing code before it passes from Development Focus to Testing Focus.

Other applications of Code Manipulation Technology include code coverage tools, which report the percentage of the lines of source code executed during a test suite run; code style-checkers and other static code-inspection checkers; and a variety of approaches that directly modify that app code to create mock responses from external resources, primarily network accesses. At the extreme end of Code Manipulation approaches are cases of modifying the Android distribution itself to enable functionality required for testing purposes; it is unlikely that practitioners are going to these lengths.

4.6.1. Technology Strengths and Limitations

The scope and variety of Code Manipulation testing approaches is vast. Essentially, anything can be implemented, so long as it can be coded. Human capacity to address the problem is the limiting factor, not the testing technology. The cost, though, is that some of the knowledge required is deeply technical, and people with that knowledge are often in very senior development positions instead of in testing positions.

4.6.2. Implementation Limitations

More significant limitations on Code Manipulation testing approaches come from the mobile security policies on the devices, which significantly restrict inter-application communications relative to desktop behaviors. (Amalfitano et al. 2015) notes that every Android app (e.g. an app under test and a test tool app) runs under its own user identity rather than sharing the same identity with other applications launched by the user of the computer, as is common in traditional desktops. This leads to a need to set up the test tool to run in the same process as the app under test, rather than independently of it, which demands a tight integration between the tool and the app's source code (Takala, Katara, and Harty 2011; Amalfitano et al. 2012). Different apps can communicate only through the features provided in Android's Binder inter-process communication system (H. van der Merwe, B. van der Merwe, and Visser 2012). Binder calls in turn require global JNI[8] references (Yan, Yang, and Rountev 2013), and JNI is Android's integration mechanism with C/C++ libraries and code. As a further difficulty, Android's test automation frameworks limit tests to interacting with one Activity[9] (Kropp and Morales 2010), meaning that these built-in test mechanisms cannot be used to automate tests that flow between Activities – roughly equivalent to the different visible pages a user sees while navigating through an app.

4.6.3. Code Manipulation Technology Summary

Code Manipulation is an extremely versatile testing technology, capable of testing at all Release-Readiness Levels, with the caveat that it can grow extremely complicated. xUnit frameworks are in widespread use in industry, as are code coverage tools and static analysis style checkers. These are all used primarily while code is in Development Focus. In academia (and perhaps in some highly technical development shops), code is being modified to provide mock responders for external resource requests, primarily network accesses; this is a step towards Simulation Environments. The extreme complexity end of Code Manipulation involves researchers creating customized versions of the Android distribution just to enable their testing activities; this is technically out of reach of most practitioner shops.

4.7. System Monitoring

System monitoring represents all mechanisms for observing and noting device-level system behavior while an app is running.

4.7.1. Technology Strengths and Limitations

System monitoring of the core computing system is a mature and well-developed technology. CPU usage, memory usage (RAM), and disk usage are fundamental diagnostics on most computing systems. Because computers have been networked together for so long, monitoring of network communication interfaces is fairly robust, including wireless signal strength. But monitoring and diagnostic queries of other embedded equipment and sensors is less clear; sometimes these hardware components cannot be queried via software and require external monitoring devices (e.g. power meters to measure battery demand).

4.7.2. Implementation Limitations

Very few testing approaches or tools are manipulating device system-state, even though that can have a dramatic effect on software behavior. Resource-starved computers can behave oddly and fail in unexpected ways. The impacts of misbehaving sensors and other embedded equipment are acknowledged but poorly mapped; computing professionals know systems can be affected by these things, but the types of impacts are not well-understood.

4.7.3. Built-in Program Diagnostics

Similar to how system monitoring inspects and makes visible device-level system behavior, diagnostics built into a program inspect and make visible internal program state while software is running. Such diagnostics are more like features of the program than they are like Code Manipulations made for testing purposes after the features pass out of Development Focus. These built-in diagnostics may take the form of logging messages to log files as code execution passes through certain points; assertions and exception checking within the code's logic may be used. In some cases, comprehensive diagnostic languages and controls may be built into the software to allow inspection of hundreds of different details about the execution of the software as it runs; this was common in testing devices like switchboard telephones and laser printers (C. Kaner, pers. comm.) and seems likely to be vital in the testing of IoT software.

4.7.4. System Monitoring Technology Summary

System Monitoring is primarily applied to core computing elements and network communications, but other sensors and embedded equipment are rarely monitored. Built-in software diagnostics features are powerful testing tools, but they require extensive Development Focus work to design and implement; they provide an entire alternate interface to interacting with the software than the routes used by the ordinary traffic handled by the software.

Because System Monitoring gathers data from a running system, it works in concert with other software testing technologies, widening the view of environmental and program state gathered from tests executed via other technologies. Monitoring the system with generic monitoring functions (e.g. CPU usage, network usage, etc.) increases the Level 2 (Closely Controlled) information available about test execution conditions. Programs with extensive built-in diagnostic features can be flexible enough to uncover Level 4 (Discovers Unexpected) test execution conditions.

4.8. Mobile Software Testing Technologies Recap

As a software testing technology, Physical Devices yield highly trustworthy results. Cloud-based providers greatly expand access to the thousands of active mobile device types but do so in a server room environment that provides little scope for exercising embedded sensors and other equipment in mobile devices. No robust system for testing embedded components at scale is apparent. Cloud-based testing options are limited to what the frameworks supported by that service support, and customized testing options are quite rare.

Virtual Devices effectively support Development Focus activities, but all mobile virtual devices lack completeness because significant hardware components are routinely omitted; Virtual Device technology alone is not capable of exercising sensors and other embedded equipment. Although pre-mobile expectations lead computing professionals to expect high-fidelity behavior from virtual devices labeled as "emulators", the Android Emulator only represents an idealized runtime environment because it cannot know about the proprietary customizations of the Android OS made by hardware manufacturers and cell service providers.

Simulation Environments contain rich potential to exercise all the embedded equipment in mobile devices, but they are complex and do not seem to be available to practitioners.

The Visual GUI Tree offers direct access to the GUI objects users use, but historically fails to handle custom objects or objects which match a general pattern but vary in details (like error messages). It also does not handle variable GUI elements that are conditionally present based on runtime details, may appear in different places within a data set (like a list), and do not naturally contain uniquely identifying attributes. Visual GUI Tree technology alone is not capable of exercising sensors and other embedded equipment.

Image Comparison technology – especially part-image comparisons powered by computer vision technology – filled a significant gap in automated GUI testing, enabling the testing of Visual Meaning problems. It runs more slowly than tests via the Visual GUI Tree, cannot address GUI elements not fully visible at the expected time, and currently does not handle basic display variations well. Changes in size, color, or style confuse the current tools, which also struggle with moving image content and with accurately reading text on-screen. Image Comparison technology alone is not capable of exercising sensors and other embedded equipment.

Code Manipulation approaches can do anything software can do, but they rapidly grow quite complicated to create. Tools that propagate to industry typically encapsulate a small set of behaviors. The widespread use of xUnit frameworks, code coverage tools, and style checkers shows that well-packaged behaviors will be extensively used by practitioners. Some mobile mocking tools exist for testing requests of external resources, but these are primarily limited to network access.

System Monitoring is robust for watching core computing elements and network communications but is not commonly used for checking sensors, other embedded equipment, or internal program state. Although this technology may be applied during Development Focus to isolate issues, very few Testing Focus tools or automation approaches incorporate system-state conditions to test mobile apps.

Overall, the great variety of environmental unpredictability faced by mobile and IoT apps is poorly addressed because five of these seven technologies do not handle testing input from embedded sensors and equipment at scale. Most of the existing testing tools and research efforts function at Level 1 (Ready to Test) or Level 2 (Closely Controlled). Yet the remaining levels are where the capacity to truly address widespread environmental unpredictability – the hallmark condition of mobile and IoT computing – becomes viable. Simulation Environments and Code Manipulation technologies can do this, but at the cost of high complexity.

In practice, cloud-based access to physical devices is somewhat mitigating the paucity of tools that can be used at Level 3 (Predictable Variations), Level 4 (Discovers Unexpected), and Level 5 (Exhausted Capacities), but these cloud services exercise only the device environment variable, not the embedded sensors and equipment of mobile devices.

5. Vision of a New Generation of Software Testing Tools

The high-level review of computing history in Section 2 established that mobile and IoT computing are operating within a fundamentally different scale and scope of environmental unpredictability than programs in any prior computing era.

The Release-Readiness Levels discussion in Section 3 clarified that mobile and IoT software need to be tested at Levels 3 (Predictable Variations) and Level 4 (Discovers Unexpected) to adequately assess likely field behavior within this vast environmental unpredictability. Some specific behaviors and some whole software systems need to be tested at Level 5 (Exhausted Capacities) because of their inherent life and safety impact or their core data integrity impact.

Touring the seven core testing technologies in Section 4 showed that most existing tools and research efforts function at Level 1 (Ready to Test) or Level 2 (Closely Controlled), with a very few stretching partly into Level 3 (Predictable Variations). Only two software technologies provide means for exercising the functionality related to embedded sensors and equipment – Simulation Environments and Code Manipulation. Unfortunately, these two technologies quickly become very complex to apply, so their reach into the general practitioner testing population is limited.

What most practitioners need to perform more effective mobile and IoT software testing are new tools that directly address the gaps not covered by the existing array of tools.

5.1. Requirements for Next Generation Testing Tools

Therefore, to improve automated testing of mobile and IoT software, new approaches are required that meet the following requirements:

- **Requirement 1:** Directly target functionality dealing with embedded sensors and equipment.
- **Requirement 2:** Scale easily to vast variations in data readings, data fidelity, data delivery methods, etc.
- **Requirement 3:** Constrain technological complexity to be within reach of non-specialists.

Because Simulation Environments and Code Manipulation technologies satisfy Requirements 1 and 2, initial steps to produce new software testing tools are likely to be technically complex and to require programming skills to apply them.

However, even these tools need to be within reach of non-specialists. In my dissertation work, attempting to build a tiny tool of this new generation, I encountered the need to be proficient in hardware device driver implementation, Linux kernel programming, cross-language programming and compilation, graphics subsystem implementation at the OS level, analyzing and fixing complex build dependencies, and navigating and deciphering very large codebases. That is a broad and deep set of technical skills, rare among senior developers and rarer amongst software testers. That skill set is more likely to be satisfied by a team of senior developers and build mavens than by one individual.

Therefore, when I use "non-specialists" in Requirement 3, I mean: Experienced software testers with competent, generalist programming skills but without special technical expertise in any of the subsystems comprising mobile or IoT computing environments and without special technical expertise in the mathematical modelling commonly associated with simulation efforts.

Once several new tools and software testing technologies have been developed to sufficient maturity, it will become possible to package some of those features into much more generally-accessible tools, as has already happened with code coverage tools and style checkers.

5.2. One Vision of New Types of Tools

Extremely briefly, my vision for a new testing technology addressing these requirements combines integration testing and compiler knowledge. Integration testing combines multiple individual units of functionality into features of varying sizes and scopes without involving the application as a whole. Inside the program, data flow for these features begins in specific places and ends in other specific places. Interfaces written for mobile and IoT software communicate with these beginning and ending points, and the compiler knows how to connect these interfaces to the objects in the program's code that do the work – it has to know this information to successfully build a deployable application.

I envision testing environments that help testers interact with arbitrary paths through the source code by exposing these data-flow beginning and ending points and allowing testers to specify the data details inserted at the data-flow beginning points, as well as any other critical program state. Tests would then conclude after the actual source code processes the data, and the results of that processing would be read at the data-flow ending points. Such compiler-assisted testing tools would allow testers to perform rich Simulation Environment testing on custom slices of functionality, without requiring fully-featured reality-based environments and without requiring testers to understand all the underlying code – just the intent of the feature and how to manipulate data at the endpoints.

6. Conclusion

Mobile and IoT computing operate within a fundamentally different scale and scope of environmental unpredictability than programs in prior computing eras. Accurately assessing the field performance of software for such devices requires testing at Level 3 (Predictable Variations), Level 4 (Discovers Unexpected), and Level 5 (Exhausted Capacities) – yet most existing tools and research function at Level 1 (Ready to Test) or Level 2 (Closely Controlled), with very few stretching partly into Level 3 (Predictable Variations). This is not good enough.

Mobile and IoT computing need better software testing tools, ones that directly handle vast environmental unpredictability and operate easily at great scale. I have one vision for a possible new direction for tool development, but this is a large and complex problem. It needs the skills and experience of many minds brought to bear upon it. What types of tools can you imagine that would be useful to the field?

7. References

Amalfitano, Domenico, Anna Rita Fasolino, Porfirio Tramontana, Salvatore de Carmine, and Gennaro Imparato. 2012. "A toolset for GUI testing of Android applications." In *Software Maintenance (ICSM), 2012 28th IEEE International Conference on*, 650–53.

Amalfitano, Domenico, Anna Rita Fasolino, Porfirio Tramontana, Bryan Dzung Ta, and Atif M. Memon. 2015. "MobiGUITAR: Automated Model-Based Testing of Mobile Apps." *IEEE Softw.* 32 (5): 53–59. https://doi.org/10.1109/MS.2014.55.

Android Open Source Project. 2018. "Distribution Dashboard." (Updates every 7 days.). https://developer.android.com/about/dashboards/.

Austin Test Automation Bazaar. 2016. Various conversations, January 15.

Bauersfeld, Sebastian, and Tanja E. J. Vos. 2014. "User interface level testing with TESTAR; what about more sophisticated action specification and selection?" In *SATToSE*, 60–78.

Beck, Kent. 1999. *eXtreme programming eXplained: Embrace change / Kent Beck.* Reading, MA: Addison-Wesley.

Borjesson, Emil, and Robert Feldt. 2012. "Automated system testing using visual gui testing tools: A comparative study in industry." In *Software Testing, Verification and Validation (ICST), 2012 IEEE Fifth International Conference on*, 350–59.

Chang, Tsung-Hsiang, Tom Yeh, and Rob Miller. 2011. "Associating the visual representation of user interfaces with their internal structures and metadata." In *Proceedings of the 24th annual ACM symposium on User interface software and technology*, 245–56.

Chang, Tsung-Hsiang, Tom Yeh, and Robert C. Miller. 2010. "GUI testing using computer vision." In *Proceedings of the SIGCHI Conference on Human Factors in Computing Systems*, 1535–44.

Chisholm, Brad L. 1997. "Automated Testing of SAS System GUI Applications." In *Proceedings of the Twenty-Second Annual SAS®Users Group International Conference*. http://www2.sas.com/proceedings/sugi22/APPDEVEL/PAPER10.PDF.

Creasy, Robert J. 1981. "The origin of the VM/370 time-sharing system." *IBM Journal of Research and Development* 25 (5): 483–90. ftp://ftp.cis.upenn.edu/pub/cis700-6/public_html/04f/papers/creasy-vm-370.pdf. Accessed May 08, 2018.

Delamaro, M. E., A. M. R. Vincenzi, and J. C. Maldonado. 2006. "A Strategy to Perform Coverage Testing of Mobile Applications." In *Proceedings of the 2006 International Workshop on Automation of Software Test*, 118–24. AST '06. New York, NY, USA: ACM. http://doi.acm.org.portal.lib.fit.edu/10.1145/1138929.1138952.

Gao, Jerry, Wei-Tek Tsai, Ray Paul, Xiaoying Bai, and Tadahiro Uehara. 2014. "Mobile Testing-as-a-Service (MTaaS) -- Infrastructures, Issues, Solutions and Needs." In *High-Assurance Systems Engineering (HASE), 2014 IEEE 15th International Symposium on*, 158–67.

Garousi, Vahid, Wasif Afzal, Adem Çağlar, \.Ihsan Berk Işık, Berker Baydan, Seçkin Çaylak, Ahmet Zeki Boyraz, Burak Yolaçan, and Kadir Herkiloğlu. 2017. "Comparing automated visual GUI testing tools: An industrial case study." In *Proceedings of the 8th ACM SIGSOFT International Workshop on Automated Software Testing*, 21–28.

Google Tech Talks. *Breaking the Matrix - Android Testing at Scale.* GTAC 2013, 2013. https://www.youtube.com/watch?v=uHoB0KzQGRg.

Griebe, Tobias, and Volker Gruhn. 2014. "A model-based approach to test automation for context-aware mobile applications." In *Proceedings of the 29th Annual ACM Symposium on Applied Computing*, 420–27.

Groder, Chip. 2016. "Objects vs. Images: Choosing the Right GUI Test Tool Architecture." Unpublished manuscript, last modified March 25, 2018. https://www.stickyminds.com/presentation/objects-vs-images-choosing-right-gui-test-tool-architecture.

Gronli, Tor-Morten, and Gheorghita Ghinea. 2016. "Meeting Quality Standards for Mobile Application Development in Businesses: A Framework for Cross-Platform Testing." In *System Sciences (HICSS), 2016 49th Hawaii International Conference on*, 5711–20.

Horowitz, Ellis, and Zafar Singhera. 1993. "Graphical user interface testing." In *Proceedings of the Eleventh Annual Pacific Northwest Software Quality Conference*. Vol. 4, 391–410. http://www.uploads.pnsqc.org/proceedings/pnsqc1993.pdf. Accessed April 18, 2018.

Kaner, Cem. 2017a. Conversation, June 2017.

———. 2018b, October 11.

Knott, Daniel. 2015. *Hands-on mobile app testing: A guide for mobile testers and anyone involved in the mobile app business.* New York: Addison-Wesley.

Kohl, Jonathan. 2012. *Tap Into Mobile Application Testing:* Leanpub. http://leanpub.com/testmobileapps.

Kropp, Martin, and Pamela Morales. 2010. "Automated GUI testing on the Android platform." *Testing Software and Systems*, 67.

Meads, Andrew, Habib Naderi, and Ian Warren. 2015. "A Test Harness for Networked Mobile Applications and Middleware." In *Software Engineering Conference (ASWEC), 2015 24th Australasian*, 1–10.

Muccini, Henry, Antonio Di Francesco, and Patrizio Esposito. 2012. "Software testing of mobile applications: Challenges and future research directions." In *Proceedings of the 7th International Workshop on Automation of Software Test*, 29–35.

Nagowah, Leckraj, and Gayeree Sowamber. 2012. "A novel approach of automation testing on mobile devices." In *Computer & Information Science (ICCIS), 2012 International Conference on*. Vol. 2, 924–30.

Nguyen, Bao N., Bryan Robbins, Ishan Banerjee, and Atif Memon. 2014. "GUITAR: An innovative tool for automated testing of GUI-driven software." *Automated Software Engineering* 21 (1): 65–105.

Nyman, Noel. 1999. "A look at QARun, a GUI test automation tool." *Software Testing & Quality Engineering* (Jan/Feb): 54–56. https://www.stickyminds.com/better-software-magazine/look-qarun-gui-test-automation-tool. Accessed March 25, 2018.

Oliver, Carol. 2018. "First Steps in Retrofitting a Versatile Software Testing Infrastructure to Android." Ph.D., Florida Institute of Technology.

OpenSignal. 2015. "Android Fragmentation (August 2015)." Accessed March 25, 2018. http://opensignal.com/reports/2015/08/android-fragmentation/.

Pettus, Sam. 1999. "The History of Emulation and its relationship to computer and videogame history." https://www.zophar.net/articles/art_14-2.html.

Potter, Richard. 1993. "Guiding Automation with Pixels (Abstract): A Technique for Programming in the User Interface." In *Proceedings of the INTERACT '93 and CHI '93 Conference on Human Factors in Computing Systems*, 530. CHI '93. New York, NY, USA: ACM. http://doi.acm.org.portal.lib.fit.edu/10.1145/169059.169526.

Ridene, Youssef, and Franck Barbier. 2011. "A model-driven approach for automating mobile applications testing." In *Proceedings of the 5th European Conference on Software Architecture: Companion Volume*, 9.

Satoh, Ichiro. 2003. "A testing framework for mobile computing software." *IEEE transactions on software engineering* 29 (12): 1112–21.

St. Amant, Robert, Henry Lieberman, Richard Potter, and Luke Zettlemoyer. 2000. "Programming by Example: Visual Generalization in Programming by Example." *Commun. ACM* 43 (3): 107–14. https://doi.org/10.1145/330534.330549.

Stocco, Andrea, Maurizio Leotta, Filippo Ricca, and Paolo Tonella. 2014. "PESTO: A tool for migrating DOM-based to visual web tests." In *Source Code Analysis and Manipulation (SCAM), 2014 IEEE 14th International Working Conference on*, 65–70.

Takala, Tommi, Mika Katara, and Julian Harty. 2011. "Experiences of System-Level Model-Based GUI Testing of an Android Application." In *Proceedings of the 2011 Fourth IEEE International Conference on Software Testing, Verification and Validation*, 377–86. ICST '11. Washington, DC, USA: IEEE Computer Society. http://dx.doi.org.portal.lib.fit.edu/10.1109/ICST.2011.11.

Tissoires, Benjamin, and Stéphane Conversy. 2011. "Hayaku: designing and optimizing finely tuned and portable interactive graphics with a graphical compiler." In *EICS '11 Proceedings of the 3rd ACM SIGCHI symposium on Engineering interactive computing systems*, edited by Fabio Paternò, Kris Luyten, and Frank Maurer, 117–26.

van der Merwe, Heila, Brink van der Merwe, and Willem Visser. 2012. "Verifying android applications using Java PathFinder." *ACM SIGSOFT Software Engineering Notes* 37 (6): 1–5.

Vilkomir, Sergiy, and Brandi Amstutz. 2014. "Using combinatorial approaches for testing mobile applications." In *Software Testing, Verification and Validation Workshops (ICSTW), 2014 IEEE Seventh International Conference on*, 78–83.

Yan, Dacong, Shengqian Yang, and Atanas Rountev. 2013. "Systematic testing for resource leaks in Android applications." In *Software Reliability Engineering (ISSRE), 2013 IEEE 24th International Symposium on*, 411–20.

Yeh, Tom, Tsung-Hsiang Chang, and Robert C. Miller. 2009. "Sikuli: Using GUI screenshots for search and automation." In *Proceedings of the 22nd annual ACM symposium on User interface software and technology*, 183–92.

[1] The historical first bug, found in 1947. See http://www.computerhistory.org/tdih/September/9/.
[2] http://softwaretestingstandard.org/
[3] The practice of outsourcing testing to a crowd of people, mostly without any technical training, in an attempt to obtain useful feedback about how the software will perform for real users (Knott 2015, 141–45).
[4] (Google Tech Talks 2013) explains that all Android Emulator images are rooted (i.e. the user account has been given root access, meaning full control of the OS), although consumer devices generally are not; and that the Android OS applied in the Emulator has been modified to be more test-friendly and to do more logging. For testing purposes, these are practical, probably desirable things, but they further distance the results from exact fidelity.
[5] Notice how you had to pause and translate those word-descriptions into the pictures and ? That's the essence of a Visual-Meaning situation: The picture conveys the meaning directly and anything else just points to the intended meaning through a stand-in representation.
[6] This sales tactic is afflicting web-based tests also. (Stocco et al. 2014) is about a tool to automatically transform DOM-based tests to image-comparison ones. DOM (Document Object Model) is the object-based representation of a webpage.
[7] Optical Character Recognition
[8] Java Native Interface
[9] An Android Activity is approximately the same as one screen view of an app, similar in concept to the scope of a webpage.

Transition from Monolith to Microservices: A Dream of a Tester's Nightmare?

Natalja Pletneva
nspletneva@gmail.com

Abstract
The changing and developing business needs of the IT industry require that technologies adopt and adjust themselves to meet their demands and, at the same time, allow advancement of new techniques and fundamental methods of architecture in software design. The result of such activity is a transition from monolith to microservices and building a definitely new architecture.

Today microservice architecture is widely implemented in various areas of software development. However, the changes in the testing process often lack the attention they deserve.

Microservice Testing is a new idea which changed the testing approaches and prioritization of testing levels. Moreover, it changed the working culture and the way teams work together.

The paper illustrates effective methods that can be applied to overcome challenges while testing applications designed with microservices architecture, as well as the main opportunities that arise when testing microservices.

Biography
I am a QA Engineer at Okko, a premium VOD service in Russia. I have been testing the service on different platforms such as Smart TV, Android, iOS, and PlayStation. Lately, I have been focusing mainly on the backend testing, functional automated testing and web applications. Along with that, I have got a Master's degree and wrote a thesis on Operation Support System/Business Support System in IoT.

1. Introduction

Every more or less successful product comes to a state where adding new features to an existing code base becomes so complicated that the cost of new functionality exceeds all possible benefits from its use. The most popular approach to solving this problem at the moment involves splitting one large piece of code into many small projects, each of which is responsible for its specific functions. When creating such a system, it is necessary to think ahead and develop a type of interaction between these separately working pieces so that future changes would require minimal development and testing costs.

There are a lot of expert articles on the web that show us the importance of such an approach and talk about which architecture can be called good and which not so good. Of course, every article or method like those is logical and consistent, and especially if the described method is proved out in practice. Nevertheless, the issue of testing when switching to microservices and the changes in the test process often do not receive the attention they deserve.

2. Monolith Architecture. Challenges in Testing Monolith

2.1. Monolithic applications and their problems

In the classic approach to software development, monolithic application architecture is used as a single unit. When developing applications, as a rule, a three-tier client-server architecture is implemented. In this case, the application consists of three main parts (Fig. 1): the client part (User Interface), a database (Database) and the server part (Business Logic Layer and Data Access Layer). The server part of the application processes HTTP requests, performs business logic, receives and modifies data in the database, and also selects the necessary HTML pages and data for display and sends them as an HTTP response to the client (browser). This server-side application is a monolithic structure, and any changes in it require deployment of a new version of this application.

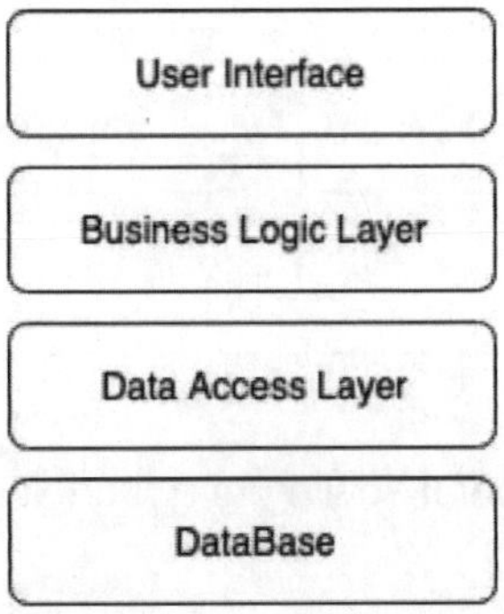

Figure 1. Monolithic application architecture.

We all know that, by making changes in one place of the monolithic program, you can cause damage in other parts of it.

Monolithic architecture means that your application is a large module where all components are designed to work together with each other, shared memory and resources.

The fact is that the components in the monolith can have very complex and non-obvious relationships. Classes calling methods, receiving other classes as inputs, generating new classes that need to be packaged into functions.

This architecture works fine for small and simple applications. But let us imagine you want to improve the application by adding new services and logic to it. Perhaps you even have another application that works with the same data (for example, a mobile client). But monolithic application can only be changed by scaling out horizontally (Fig. 2) by running several instances of it using load balancers.

The application architecture will change a bit:

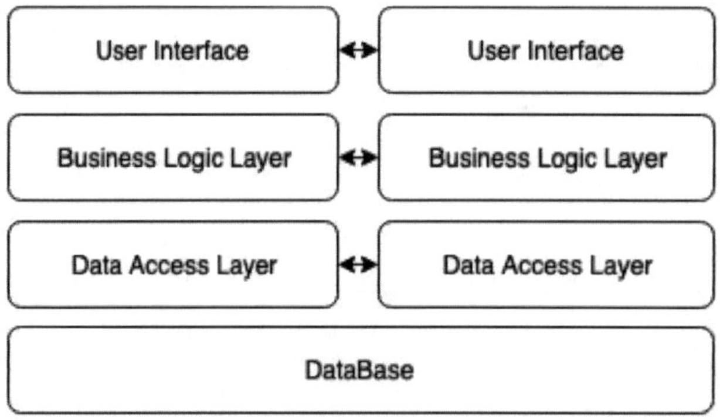

Figure 2. Horizontal scaling of a monolithic application.

In any case, as the application grows and develops, you encounter problems with monolithic architectures:

- Support is more and more difficult.
- In such an architecture, it is always tempting to reuse a class from another module, rather than take data from the database. Thus, an extra connection arises, which should not be the case in the original architecture.
- It is difficult to understand monolith, especially if the system passed from generation to generation, the logic was forgotten, people left and came, but there were no comments and tests.
- If any of the components stops working for any reason, then the entire application will collapse as well.

- Monolithic systems just require more complex environment (when the whole system has to be compiled, built and ran).
- It is expensive to make any changes.
- Since you have to mount everything in one place, this leads to the fact that switching to another programming language or switching to other technologies is problematic.
- And one of major problems in monolithic architectures is that they are hard to scale. Normally you have an option to increase the computer power, but not scale horizontally. For instance, you cannot scale just a particular module. This is one of the reasons why microservices became so useful with highly scalable applications.

Sooner or later you realize that you can no longer do anything with your monolithic system. The customer, of course, is disappointed: he does not understand why adding the simplest function requires several weeks of development, and then stabilization, testing, etc. Surely, many faced these problems.

2.1.1 Example of monolith testing problems

Imagine that our monolithic application is an IVoD (Interactive Video on Demand - a video content delivery system that allows viewers to select content (video) and view it at a convenient time (upon request) on any device designed to play video (web, tablets, smartphones, game consoles, etc.). It is an application in which the user is offered a huge catalogue of movies for watching in different qualities for different rights: EST (Electronic Sell Through), SVoD (Subscription Video on Demand) and TVoD (Transactional Video on Demand).

This project is characterized by a huge number of overlapping business scenarios, movies can be watched on different platforms (TV, mob), and gifts can also be offered to users (movies for free, trial periods).

In this case, we meet the following obstacles:

- **Data.** Obtaining test data is a separate scenario due to a large number of combinations of input parameters. To create a crystal-clear user for a script, you first have to run it through the entire system, which requires more time and more expertise. Of course, there are workarounds (changes through the database), but from a testing point of view, this is not legitimate.
- **Performance Testing.** Maintaining a separate environment for stress tests is quite expensive, and the load of the test environment can negatively affect the work of colleagues.
- **Bug Analysis.** Analysis of the bugs is difficult because we have one monolith, one end point, and it is quite difficult to understand which module the failure occurred in. Thus, the life cycle of the bug is increased.
- **Test Automation.** The monolith cannot be dismantled and not tested, therefore the first question that arises at the beginning of the autotest path on the monolith is: where to start? Due to the strong interconnection in the monolith, writing "clean" unit tests will not work since you still have to use additional data from other blocks, make stubs and resort to other tricks. Thus, the cost of tests grows and the time to maintain them increases. And what if a new specialist comes to the project? Not only will he have to figure out the monolith, but he will also not be able to understand the whole value of the autotest code. It seems to be very expensive.

These inconveniences led to the development of architectural style of microservices: building applications as a set of services. In addition to the ability to independently deploy and scale, each service also receives a clear physical boundary that allows different services to be written in different programming languages and tested independently. They can also be developed by different teams.

3. Microservice Madness

It is not surprising that the video service application presented above also encountered the main difficulties of the monolith. Business ideas coming up constantly and introduction of new features resulted in grow of monolith, and adding a new feature started to seem not worth the potential benefits of the feature itself (Fig 3).

In view of all these difficulties, it was decided to create a set of new services grouped in several servers, in which there will be separate APIs for working with all business functions - the so-called transition to microservices, which solves the main problems of the monolith:

- Less code for one service.
- Implementation independence.
- No single point of failure.
- Independent deployment.
- Independent testing.

3.1. Architecture "before"

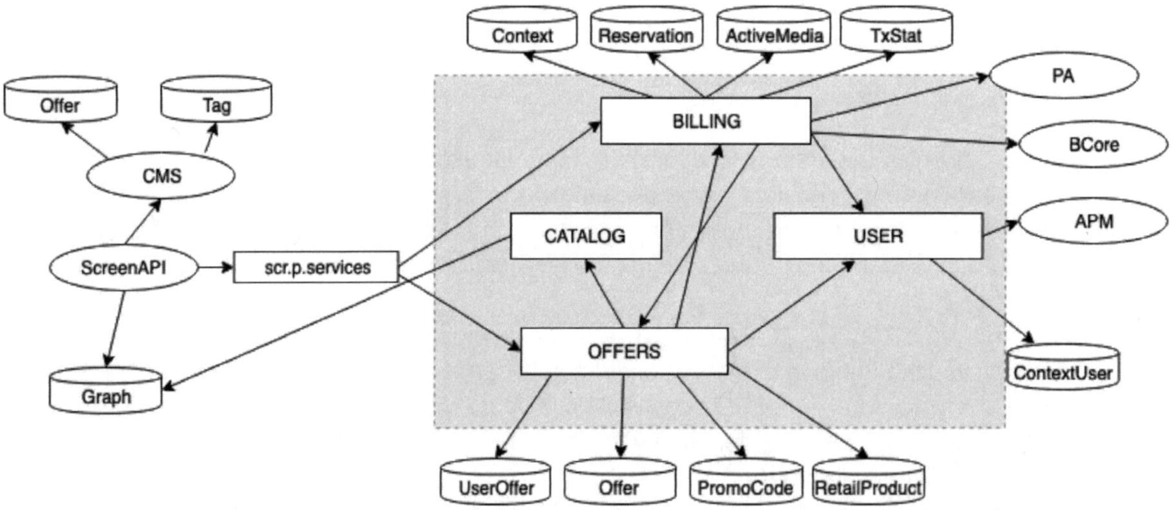

Figure 3. Architecture "before".

There are obvious problems with the monolithic architecture scheme presented above (Fig. 3):

- Strong interconnection between services.
- If the services are just divided into separate applications, the number of network operations is too high, and transactions fall apart.

- Often different services get the same information - this is inefficient and, moreover, makes services "all-knowing".
- A lot of unnecessary checks, performance may suffer.
- The life cycle of bugs is increased because it is difficult to analyze any problems.

3.2. Architecture "after"

Microservice architecture is an approach to creating applications, meaning the rejection of a single, monolithic structure (Fig. 4). That is, instead of executing all the limited contexts, several small applications can be used, each of which corresponds to some limited context.

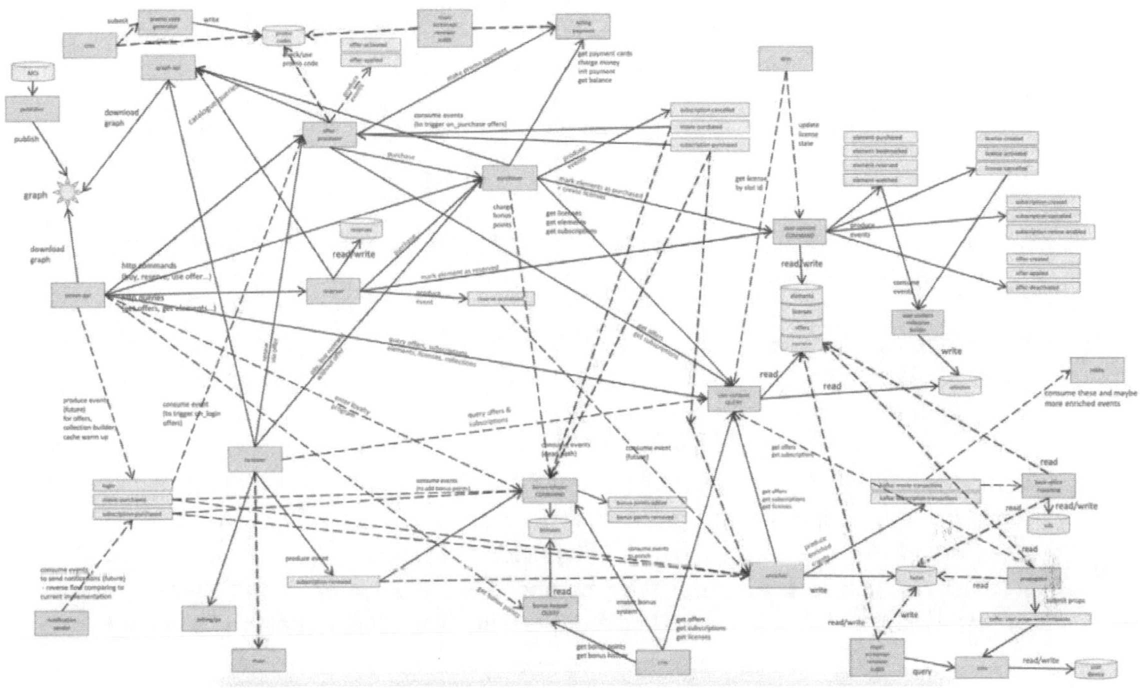

Figure 4. Architecture "after".

Another view on the microservices system is where every component is connected to a message bus (kafka/rabbit/etc) and sends and receives messages from it (Fig 5). It is a less scary image of the diagram above.

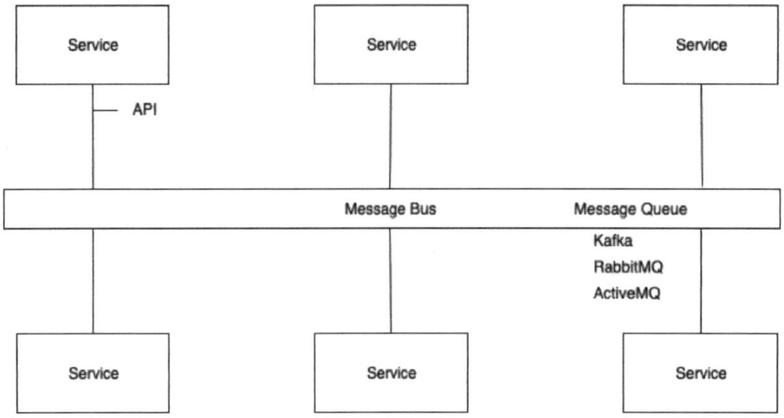

Figure 5. The diagram of a messaging system between microservices.

Microservices were gradually separated and new functionality was written independently from the main application. The new components provide:

- Independence of change.
- Testing independence.
- Independence from any technologies.
- Isolation of business logic and work with the database from other components (since one component now communicates with the database separately), which in future will allow moving to any other database particularly.
- Ability to optimize the execution time of complex scenarios.
- It is also possible to scale in/out every component of the system individually.
- Microservices allow for separate (isolated) testing, when the rest of environment is fake.

In the case of a monolith, in order to replace any piece in this system, we cannot roll it out separately. You need to rebuild and completely update the backend. This is not always rational and convenient. What happens when switching to microservice architecture? We take the backend and divide it into its component components, dividing them by functionality. We determine the interactions between them, and we get a new system with the same front-end and the same databases. Microservices interact with each other and provide the same business processes. For the user and system testing, everything remained as before, the internal organization has changed.

What would be the point? You can make a change in the microservice X, which implements some of its functionality, and immediately roll it out to work. It all sounds very good. But, as always, there is one catch: you need to check how microservices interact with each other.

As a result, for testing, we get a number of services, each of which can pull the rest, and which exchange the data randomly:

- A set of functionally complete services.
- Interaction between them occurs either synchronously via http/https or asynchronously through the manager, if a mixed type of architecture was selected, when services interact either

directly; or via a messenger, when a component subscribes to a message queue and listens to it.

- Standard messaging interface for all services.

4. How to Test It?

Expectation:

Today, there are several ways to structure tests on microservices: for example, a honeycomb test that focuses on integration tests. This is the theory of moving to a higher level in the test pyramid, which also contains the priority of integration tests. A lot was mentioned about the test-division approach on levels - modular, contract, integration, functional and end-to-end - a huge number of ideas and proposals. It sounds excellent, but in practice, not everything turned out to be so easy.

Reality: «situation of absolute mess is normal: all tests pass, but nothing works».

Based on the definition of microservices, it may seem that microservices for testing is a great idea, but things need to be clarified a bit.

Further I will discuss some basic misconceptions and pitfalls of the transition to microservices so that you could take them into account when you decide whether microservice architecture is right for you or not.

4.1. The Illusion «It is Easier»: distributed transactions are never easier

Every time a new technology appears, there is a feeling that now we have to study everything from the very beginning. But this is usually not the case. For example, when mobile applications appeared, almost all the technologies that we knew before remained unchanged. We had to deal only with the new client part, in connection with the advent of new operating systems and programming languages. And when the Internet of Things appeared, in addition to hardware and embedded code, the server part also changed a little - new protocols and new ways of processing large amounts of data in real-time appeared. But when it came to be building a microservice architecture, really serious changes appeared at once on many levels, and not only with regard to technology.

Starting the transition to microservices, the first basic thing that will have to face is the separation of the old monolithic code into small services and placing them into an architecture already familiar to us (for example, SOA). Dividing code is not too difficult. Difficulties begin when setting up load balancing, restoring, and automatically scaling these services, but the greatest difficulties can arise when testing such new applications. Here, new approaches and testing tools are required, as well as a lot of expertise and knowledge in the field of microservices.

On the surface, everything may seem simple: you have clearly defined inputs and outputs for the API that the service should provide - what could be the difficulty?

When several remote services are involved in a single request, the complexity greatly increases. Can I refer to them in parallel or do I need to apply sequentially? Are you aware of all possible errors in advance (at the application level and at the network level) that can occur at any time, at any part of the chain, and what will these errors mean for the request itself? Each of the distributed transactions often requires its own approach to error handling. And to understand all the mistakes and how to solve them is a very, very big job.

Before you start testing microservices, you need to determine approaches and the number of tests, based on the existing architecture and application features. Based on the experience of testing the video delivery application discussed above, I would like to highlight the main points in testing microservices:

4.1.1 Unit testing

For the most part, the developers are responsible for the unit tests. They make sure that the individual unit of the code base (test subject) is working properly. You can also use imitations (mocks) or stubs, which, instead of implementation, give out believable data, simply hard-coded. In our case, the tester acts more as a reviewer. And the unit tests are not enough here since errors are maybe at the junction of services.

4.1.2 Integration testing

The basis of our test suite consisted of integration testing. During integration testing, the correctness of interaction of various microservices with each other is verified. This is one of the most crucial tests of the whole architecture. With a positive test outcome, we can be sure that the whole architecture is designed correctly and all independent microservices function as a whole in accordance with expectations.

4.1.3 You have a lot of services - you have a lot of APIs. What is the problem with the API?

An API is not just code that is accessible to an external customer, it is a large number of supporting tasks that need to be addressed, and the code that stands behind the API is not the biggest problem. You will need:

- Documentation with examples of how to use your API, including a comprehensive description of all possible errors.
- Means of validating requests (declarative schemes, at least for oneself, at most - publicly available).
- Tools for testing and experimenting with APIs - isolated environments, sandboxes for debugging.

If you have one application, then the API publishing point is about the same. If you have a service architecture, each service requires all this infrastructure support. If each service is created using different technologies, your problems have just tripled.

4.1.4 A hybrid testing approach was chosen, and testing was added in production.

It is necessary to monitor the entire service, collect as much data as possible - both for analyzing the current situation and for analyzing incidents. The tester is responsible for monitoring using the modern Jaeger (distributed query tracking system), there are more research testing and user interaction.

In addition to these 4 points, you also need new tools and approaches, like system observability techniques and tools (assigning every message in a scenario a traceable id across all components)
Thus, there are no fewer tests, it has not become easier: since microservices work simultaneously alone and in conjunction with other loosely coupled services, it is necessary to test each component both separately and as a part of a whole.

4.2. The Illusion «It is faster»

Each service is a separate, functionally complete unit and it has its own set of tests. Although now we do not have to emulate user actions, it is enough just to build the REST request correctly, but we live under the conditions of monolith and microservices that work together. All of this must be managed simultaneously, which gives us rise to an even greater number of points of failure, the number of tests requires more expertise.

Suppose you decide to do everything conscientiously and provide your services with tests.

With unit tests, everything is good and even better than with ordinary applications - you have clearly described inputs and outputs.

But now you need to emulate external services with which you interact - you do not want to re-raise the entire ecosystem of services after each change (moreover, if you have resorted to using separate development teams for each service, you personally may not require infrastructure / knowledge in order to raise the services of another team).

The problem is that your stubs and mocks, which successfully emulate your immediate environment, actually protect you far from as much as you think, even if you update them neatly and they always exactly match the interfaces of the services you use directly.

Imagine this situation:

Your service A goes to service B, which in turn relies on service C, which you do not directly interact with.

Service B was written by smart guys, and it knows how to handle different variants of data from service C, without noticeable damage to himself, and even give you something similar to the result. Your tests pass; on test environments with real services, services A, B, and C have no problems with each other.

But here your distant colleagues from service C roll out new formats that are successfully processed by the current version of service B, and are returned to you after being processed by service B. No one has any idea of how it can respond – but it still works.

And you (service A) - fail. All your tests pass, all tests of services B and C pass. Even pairwise integration pass. But all together it does not work - this is why system observability tools are necessary, to understand first which component exactly did not work in this scenario, to avoid browsing logs of every component individually.

At the same time, the versions of services A and B, at the moment of the interaction of which the problem occurs, have not changed.

Even if all the data formats that you exchange are covered with schemas and validators, they cannot protect from everything, and you will encounter the described problem.

Some kind of more or less noticeable confidence that everything will work gives us the deployment of a full set of services in a test environment and run of typical scenarios on a fully working system.

Even if we forget about the fact that such checks are slow, every service can be developed with different technologies, it can take a considerable amount of time to initialize or require specially configured databases. And with such data sets that will allow you to get rid of your end-to-end scenarios (these sets will need to be maintained by various teams up to date, by the way), all you know is that a specific set of service configurations seems to be working. And if you want to be constantly confident in the performance of the entire complex, you need to roll it all out together.

Thus, we spend a lot of time on interaction between teams, on finding errors, new requirements, but the worst thing is that when we divide microservices between test engineers (each tester is in charge for and understands his own field), we get an uncertain area of responsibility:

In this case, when testing microservices there can be one big global difficulty - the interaction between teams.

It requires constant synchronization with the teams. Errors can live simultaneously in several services and require changes at the level of several teams - synchronization and coordination of efforts are necessary. In addition, people may lose their sense of responsibility and try to push as many problems as possible to another team.

4.3 . The illusion «This is better for testing»

We encounter some key issues when testing the microservice architecture:

4.3.1 Team Coordination

As many independent teams manage their own microservices, it becomes very difficult to coordinate the entire software development and testing process.

4.3.2 The Complexity

There are many microservices that communicate with each other (Fig. 6). We must make sure that each of them works properly and is resistant to slow reactions or failures from other microservices. You definitely need to test full system threads to see if the services understand each other, in particular when one of the services responds with error messages.

4.3.3 Performance

Since there are many independent services, it is important to test the entire architecture under traffic conditions that are close to production. If you work with queues, many of them may have asynchronous events and timeouts that may come into work. You can try to model each of such scenarios individually, but performance tests, when many parallel threads load one of the queues with an unexpected number of messages, can reveal many errors.

4.3.4 The problem of collecting logs in one place

To test a problem, you need to download all the involved microservices. Debugging becomes a non-trivial task, and all the logs need to be collected somewhere in one place. At the same time, you need as many logs as possible to figure out what happened. To track the problem down, you need to understand the whole path that the message went. Unit tests are not enough here since errors are likely to be at the junction of services.

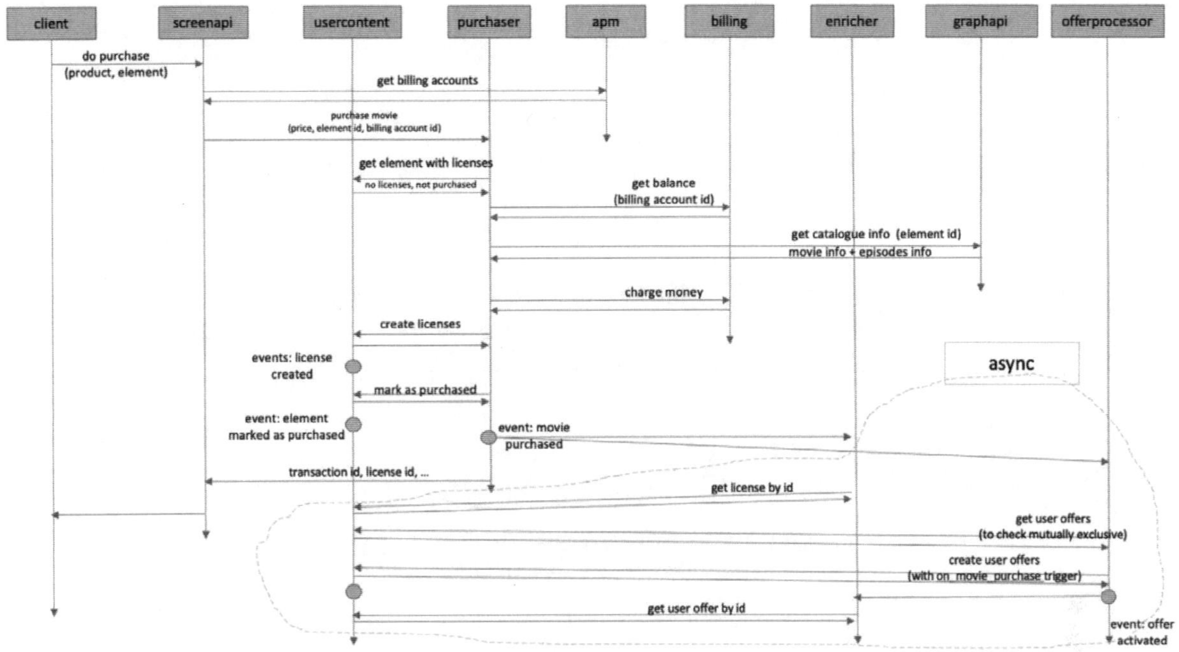

Figure 6. Sample scenario: movie purchase.

Automated testing plays a very important role in the modern software development process. It allows you to always maintain the working of the product, make changes and refactor. The microservice approach adds its difficulties to the testing issue since it is necessary to verify the correct interaction of microservices under various working conditions. For full testing of microservices, it is necessary to deploy a complex testing environment on special servers, which requires large human and material costs.

Many scenarios are easier to automate at unit testing level, where you do not need to start an HTTP server to host a service or service mock. This is particularly the case for negative scenarios. Usually, we can work closely with developers of such services, and every time QA finds that automating a scenario is too expensive at the system level, we can ask developers to add a test to their unit testing suite.

5. Conclusion

All considered illusions do not detract from the obvious advantages of microservice architecture. Consider an example.

When we came up with the idea of switch to microservices, It was decided to first separate the billing and the offers granting service - the so-called free periods of using the service.

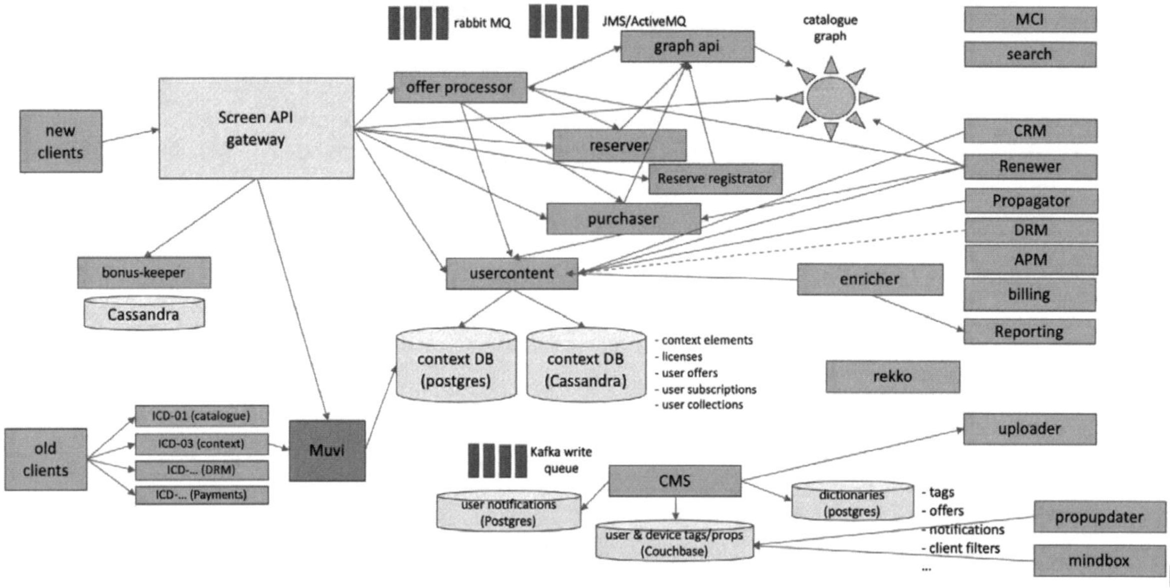

Figure 7. Switch to microservices: first iteration.

To output the component data from the monolith, it was necessary to isolate a couple of services, and in the end, we got this (Fig.7):

Graph API:

- provides GraphQL API for catalogue graph
- listens to publication event from publisher
- downloads catalogue graph and keeps it in memory
- if your app cannot load graph in memory, use this service

User-content:

- proxies read and write access to user entities (context):
  - user offers
  - user subscriptions
  - licenses & context elements (purchases, bookmarks, etc.)
  - user collections
- dumb service, CQRS (command-query) pattern
- supports Postgres and Cassandra implementations
- produces events, but nobody consumes them yet but itself
- does not interact with other services

Purchaser:

- wraps movie/subscription purchase logic
- handles purchase/pay requests of main API(ScreenAPI) and offer-processor

- works with Graph API (to get info about prices, etc.)
- works with User-content (checks/creates licenses, subscriptions)
- works with billing/APM (checks balance, linked cards)

Offer-processor

- wraps offer activation and offer usage logic
- also handles promo code activation requests
- works with user content
- listens to purchaser pay events to activate specific offers
- listens to the main API (ScreenAPI) events (login/register) to activate offers
- creates user notifications when offer is activated

Business logic was isolated from the monolith, but, of course, not removed. Everything seemed to be tested. Both the monolith and the microservices included the A / B split (using the CMS internal split service) and worked on the test environment.

Initially, the path of individual component testing was chosen: each microservice was covered with unit tests, plus a contract test of the interaction of microservices inspired by trends was conducted. Of course, no one forgot about integration, but more attention was still paid to the integration between monolith and microservices, and not between different microservices. The main task was to bring microservices to the monolith without harm.

On the appointed day X, everything was implemented in the production environment. And it lasted only five minutes. Because such promising microservices did not go off the first try, and not at the second, and even not at the third.

It was a great fiasco experience, from which we drew certain conclusions:

- Contract testing is a lot of sizzle and no steak, because in practice, we have not found a long-lasting good solution here. Although in some cases it certainly works.
- Sometimes the test environment does not coincide with the production environment for various reasons: from the configuration of hardware to the load. Therefore, it is necessary to carefully consider the model of the load on services (and not to repeat our mistake).
- To test microservices, a higher-level approach is needed, more system testing, as well as end-to-end tests.
- Each service should fall as painlessly as possible for the system as a whole and scale separately: what really worked. The fallen part of microservices did not destroy the entire service. Chaos Monkey testing was successful.

Microservices provide flexibility in choosing the type and level of testing that can be used since microservices can implement some central business functions or something small, when the level of testing may be lower. But before moving on to microservices, you need to think about all the possible details and issues in order not to face any problems in the future. In testing, there are pros and cons of this approach, so you need to take into account the current situation in the team and be prepared for huge amounts of work. Although we still live under conditions of monolith and microservices, now I can say that the transition experience may be very positive.

In our case, microservices are a dream and salvation: it is an opportunity to organize and structure testing processes, strengthen automation and, eventually, conduct testing faster and better.

Experience says: you cannot fight trends, but you can fight fluctuations. Let your choice of architecture be the personal trend, based on the requirements of the system, and not the point's position on the technology's hype-cycle.

Optimize Your Tests for Continuous Integration

John Ruberto
JohnRuberto@gmail.com

Abstract

"Test early, test often." If you've worked with me, you are probably sick of hearing me say that. But it's common sense that if your tests find a problem shortly after that problem was created, it will be easier to fix. This is one of the principles that make continuous integration a very powerful strategy.

But, too often our existing tests don't work well running continuously. They may have false positives that need to be triaged by a person or the tests may take a long time to run.

Come to this presentation to see how I evaluate test suites by two criteria: value added and time to execute. Then, I'll provide five strategies to improve the value of your tests so they are worth executing more often or speed up your tests so they can be run more frequently.

These methods combined have helped teams gain the maximum value from their automated test suites.

Biography

John Ruberto takes an engineering approach to building quality into software. He is currently helping clients with testing and quality strategies at Testlio. He has previously held positions up to VP of Quality Engineering at First Data, Concur, Intuit, Alcatel, PhoenixBIOS, and Boeing. He holds a BSEE, MSCS, and MBA.

1. Introduction

"Test early, test often." If you've worked with me, you are probably sick of hearing me say that. But it's common sense that if your tests find a problem shortly after that problem was created, it will be easier to fix. This is one of the principles that makes continuous integration a very powerful strategy. To illustrate this, consider for example, a continuous integration system that finds a bug in the code, while running tests that run along with the build. There may have been only 1 person making a change since the previous successful execution. That person will know that the code they just checked-in caused the failure. Now, consider a different bug that was found a week later. The entire team may have made updates that caused the bug. Just finding the offending code change may take a lot of time and effort.

Many times I've seen teams that have many automated tests but are not using those tests as part of a continuous integration program. Two common reasons stated by the team are the tests take too long to execute, or they are not reliable enough to give accurate results themselves and it will take humans to interpret the results. These issues can be overcome.

2. Rate Test Suites by Value & Time

When assessing these suites, I start with a simple exercise. First, I draw two axes on a white board. The vertical axis shows the value of the tests and the horizontal axis shows the time it takes the suite to execute.

The team and I then write down the name of each test suite on a sticky note and place them on the appropriate place on the board. The chart below shows an example of a grid, showing how each test suite measures.

2.1. Rank By Value

When we talk about the value of the tests, it's based on the team's subjective opinion, so we keep the choices pretty simple: No Value, Moderate Value, High Value, and Very High Value. We base this opinion on the reliability of the tests, or the tests' ability to give accurate results each time they are executed, and the level of confidence the tests give the team for the quality of the system.

For example, some test suites are a must-have when it comes to making a decision, but the results are a little flaky, and when they fail sometimes for no apparent reason, a person has to re-execute those failing tests manually. We might still call this test suite High Value, but if it ran accurately every time, we would call it Very High Value.

On the other side of the coin, sometimes there is a test suite that gets executed because it's part of a checklist, but no one really knows what the results mean. Maybe the original author has left the team and no one picked up the ownership of that suite. We would put that suite in the No Value category.

2.2. Rank By Time

The horizontal axis is easier to determine: It's simply the number of minutes that it takes to execute that suite.

Now that you have an assessment of each suite, it's time to think about improving your suites by making them more valuable (moving up in the diagram) or by helping them execute faster (moving to the left).

3. Categories of Tests

For continuous integration, I like to target the tests into four categories:

- Tests with Very High Value that execute in ten minutes or less

These tests can run with every build. These are used to accept the build for further testing; the team should consider the build failed until these tests pass. Your developers will not want to wait more than ten minutes to get the build results.

- Tests with High Value or better that execute in an hour or less

These tests can run continuously. For example, you might configure these tests to execute every hour and start again as soon as they are complete. If there isn't a new build ready yet, you can wait until the next build completes.

- Tests with High Value or better that take longer than an hour to execute

These tests can run daily—or, usually, nightly, so that the results are available when the working day begins for your team.

- Tests with Moderate Value

These tests can run once per week or once per release cycle.

Notice that I did not include tests with No Value. These should be improved to add value, or just dropped from your execution. It doesn't make sense to keep test suites that don't add value.

I chose the time boundaries of ten minutes and one hour based on input from the development teams. They want to get quick feedback. You can imagine a developer waiting for the build results to complete successfully before going to lunch. Your timelines may vary based on your realities; this is just a framework to show the thought process behind selecting the tests that run with the build versus hourly.

A huge benefit for executing the tests this frequently is that you are likely to have very few code changes between a successful test run and a failed test run, making it easier to isolate the change that caused the test to fail and for a responsible dev to consider a fix.

4. Strategies for Making Improvements

There are several strategies that have been useful for optimizing existing tests for the continuous integration suites. Here are five proven practices.

4.1. Create tiny but valuable test suites

Choose the most important tests and pull them into a smaller suite that runs faster. These are usually very gross-level tests, but they're necessary to qualify your system or app for further testing. If these tests don't pass, it doesn't make sense to proceed.

A good starting point would be to create a new entity and perform the most important operation on that entity. For example, if it's a note-taking app, the test would be to create a note, add text, close the app, then reopen and verify that the text was saved. If your note-taking app can't save a note, there isn't much use in proceeding to other tests.

We often call these build acceptance tests or build verification tests. If you already have these suites, great; just make sure they execute quickly.

Taking this concept a step further, you might consider trying to make each test as independent as possible. If each test case can run completely independently, then the most important tests can be run first. The "Atomic Check" pattern is described in a book called MetaAutomation (Griscom 2018). According to Griscom, "… the automation code needs explicit preliminary verifications to do two things: 1. Fail the check faster by detecting a failure case earlier 2. Fail the check with detailed and specific root cause information. ." Having more atomic tests also facilities parallel execution.

4.2. Refactor the test setup

Tests generally have a setup, then perform verification. For the note-taking example, to verify that the app opens with the previous text present, you first have to set up the test with the text. Examine how your tests are doing the test setup and see if there is a better way.

For example, one team had a suite of UI-driven tests that took a long time to execute and had many false failures due to timing issues and minor UI tweaks. We refactored that suite to perform the test setup via API commands and do the verification through the UI. This updated suite had the same functional coverage, but it executed 70 percent faster and had about half the false failures caused by UI changes.

4.3. Be smart with your wait times

We have all done it: A flaky test keeps failing because the back end didn't respond in time or some resource is still loading, so we put a sleep statement in. We intended that to be a temporary workaround, but that was a year ago now. This situation is compounded when you run the same tests on multiple environments.

The team builds the delays to match the slowest environment, so even the tests running in a more capable platform has to wait as long as the slowest platform.

Look for those dreaded sleep statements and see if you can replace them with a smarter wait statement that completes when the event happens, instead of a set period of time. The wait statement in most test frameworks will watch for an event, perhaps for a locator to appear, then proceed. The wait statement usually includes a timeout, which can be set for your original sleep duration.

4.4. Trigger tests automatically

You may have several test suites that are normally initiated by a person during the test phase of a project. Often, it only takes a little shell scripting to be able to include these tests in the continuous integration suite.

Security and performance tests are two examples of types of tests that might be performed by a specialist who is not part of the standard test team, so those tests might not be configured for automatic execution. The other benefit of running these tests frequently is that the problems that are found are frequently difficult to fix, so if the problem is identified sooner, the team has more time to fix it. These tests are often classified as Very Valuable, but they take more than an hour to execute, so they are typically executed daily.

4.5. Run tests in parallel

Virtual machines and cloud computing services coupled with tools that help automatically set up environments and deploy your code make it much more affordable to run tests in parallel. Examine the test suites that take some time to execute and look for opportunities to run those tests in parallel.

On one team, we had a very vital test suite that contained five hundred test cases. This suite took several hours to run, so we didn't execute it very often. It was a very broad-based test, touching many different features. We were able to break that suite up into about a dozen different suites that could run in parallel, so we could run the tests more frequently (nightly instead of weekly), and we could tell more quickly where any problems lay because the new suites were organized by feature.

4.6. Incorporate manual tests into your continuous integration program

Often, it's difficult to find all of the problems through automated tests. "Inevitably, when users try an application in real life, they discover that there is room for improvement." (Humble 2011)

Striking the balance between a comprehensive automation suite, and a stable (non-flaky) set of test cases is difficult. Some tests are naturally left to real humans to execute, including exploratory, usability, and even one-off tests (Crispin 2009).

It may sound strange to incorporate manual tests into a Continuous Integration system, but with today's technology and marketplace, it can be done with similar effort and infrastructure as an overnight performance test.

Many companies have test teams that reside overseas, working in a different time zone and there are crowd-sourced testing companies that have testers across the world.

I've worked with a project where we incorporated a manual test suite that executed overnight. The Continuous Integration (CI) system would push the build to the test provider's platform and notify the test manager to proceed. The test team executed their tests and published the results a few hours later, overnight from the development team.

5. Conclusion

Improving the value of your test suites and the time it takes to execute them can help you optimize your existing test suites to fit into a continuous integration program.

References

Crispin, Lisa and Gregory, Janet, 2009, Agile Testing, A Practical Guide for Testers and Agile Teams, Addison-Wesley

Griscom, Matt. 2018. MetaAutomation, ISBN 978-0-9862704-2-0

Humble, Jez and Farley, David, Continuous Delivery, Reliable Software Release Through Build, Test, and Deployment Automation, 2011, Addison-Wesley

Severless Security: What Are We Up Against?

Atul Ahire, Harvijay Kapoor, Shanu Mandot
Atul_Ahire@McAfee.com, Harvijay_Kapoor@McAfee.com, Shanu.Mandot@Gmail.com

Abstract

Developing applications using serverless architecture helps one get relieved from the daunting task of constantly applying security patches for the underlying operating system and application servers. These tasks are now the responsibility of the serverless architecture provider. From a software development perspective, organizations adopting serverless architectures can now focus on core product functionality, and completely disregard the underlying operating system, application server or software runtime environment.

Due to these benefits, there is a lot of demand for going serverless right now. There is a community forming around these designs and major cloud service providers such as Amazon Web Services (AWS), Microsoft and Google are all pushing the concept. Large enterprises are even jumping on board.

Serverless is real, and it's here now. And yet, serverless is no silver bullet from a security perspective. Analysis of over 1,000 open-source serverless applications revealed that 21% of them have critical vulnerabilities or were misconfigured, according to security researchers (PureSec 2018). They also cited that six percent had their sensitive data, such as application program interface (API) keys and credentials, stored in publicly accessible repositories. Serverless architectures introduce a new set of issues that must be considered when securing such applications.

This paper explains some of the most prevalent security issues in serverless applications, their impact and how we can mitigate them. This papers also covers some of the tools and solutions which can be helpful to detect the security issues introduced with serverless architecture.

Biography

Atul Ahire is Software Development Engineer in Test at McAfee, with more than 7 years of experience in Software Development, Test Automation, Build Release and Deployment. His areas of interest include Cloud solution design, deployment, and DevOps.

Harvijay Kapoor is Partner integrations lead at McAfee, with 10 years of experience in Software Development. He is skilled in Project Management and handling Implementation Activities for Cloud SaaS Product Integrations. Solutioning, Client Engagement, Demos, Trainings and Post-sales Support are his main areas of strength.

Shanu Mandot is QA Lead at TechChefs, with 7 years of experience in Software QA. Her areas of interest are Security Testing and Agile methodologies.

1. Introduction

Traditionally, we have built and deployed web applications where we have some degree of control over the HTTP requests that are made to our server. Our application runs on that server and we are responsible for provisioning and managing the resources for it. There are a few issues with this approach:

a. We are charged for keeping the server up even when we are not serving out any requests.
b. We are responsible for uptime and maintenance of the server and all its resources.
c. We are also responsible for applying the appropriate security updates to the server.
d. As our usage scales we need to manage scaling up our server as well. And as a result, manage scaling it down when we don't have as much usage.

For smaller companies and individual developers this can be a lot to handle. This ends up distracting from the more important job that we have; building and maintaining the actual application. At larger organizations this is handled by the infrastructure team and usually it is not the responsibility of the individual developer. However, the processes necessary to support this can end up slowing down development times as we cannot just go ahead and build our application without working with the infrastructure team to help us get up and running. As developers we've been looking for a solution to these problems and this is where serverless computing comes in.

Serverless computing (or serverless for short), is an execution model where the serverless platform provider (like AWS, Azure, or Google Cloud) is responsible for executing a piece of code by dynamically allocating the resources. They only charge for resources used to run the code. The code is typically run inside stateless containers that can be triggered by a variety of events including http requests, database events, queuing services, monitoring alerts, file uploads, scheduled events (cron jobs), etc. The code that is sent to the cloud provider for execution is usually in the form of a function. While serverless abstracts the underlying infrastructure away from the developer, servers are still involved in executing our functions.

By its very nature, Serverless addresses some of today's biggest security concerns. By eliminating infrastructure management, it pushes its security concerns to the platform provider. Unfortunately, attackers won't simply give up, and will instead adapt to this new world. More specifically, serverless will move attacker's focus from the servers to the application and defenders should adapt priorities accordingly.

2. Serverless Overview

Let us understand the basics of serverless architecture and its importance.

2.1 What is Serverless Computing?

Serverless computing, does not mean that we no longer use servers to host and run code; nor does it mean that operations engineers are no longer required. But consumers of serverless computing no longer need to spend time and resources on server provisioning, maintenance, updates, scaling, and capacity planning. Instead, all these tasks and capabilities are handled by a serverless platform and are completely abstracted away from the developers and IT/operations teams. As a result, developers focus on writing their applications business logic. Operations engineers can elevate their focus to more business-critical tasks.

In practice, this approach can work in two different ways:

1. Functions-as-a-Service (FaaS) typically provides event-driven computing. Developers run and manage application code with functions that are triggered by events or HTTP requests. Developers deploy small units of code to the FaaS, which are executed as needed as discrete actions, scaling without the need to manage servers or any other underlying infrastructure.

2. Backend-as-a-Service (BaaS) are third-party API-based services that replace core subsets of functionality in an application. Because those APIs are provided as a service that auto-scales and operates transparently, this appears to the developer to be serverless.

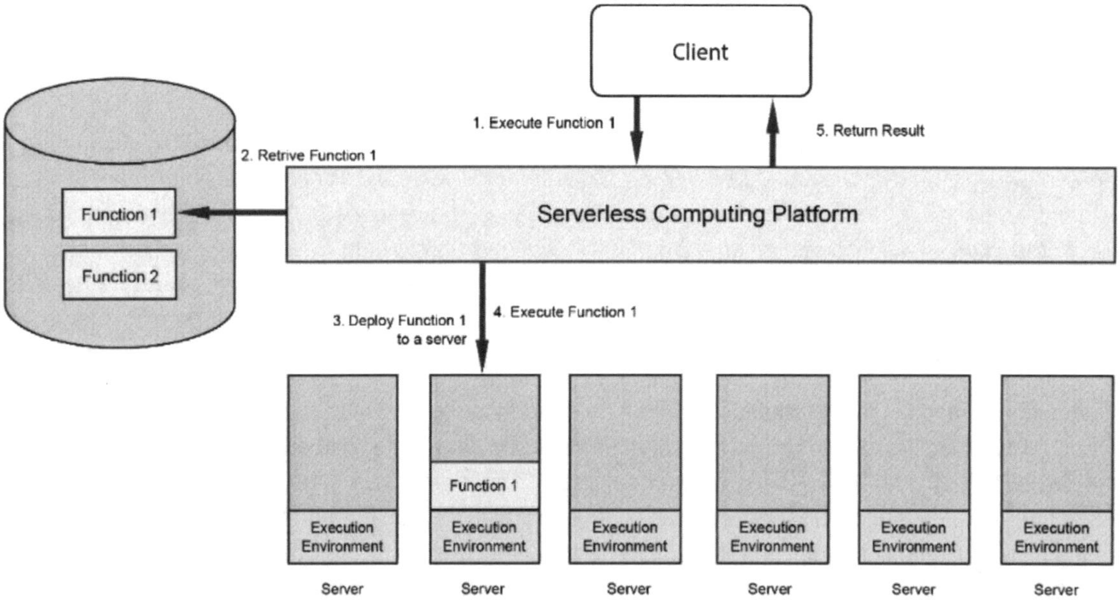

2.2. Why is Serverless Important?

Adoption of serverless delivers the following benefits:

1. **Zero Server Ops**: Serverless dramatically changes the cost model of running software applications through eliminating the overhead involved in the maintenance of server resources. Without provisioning, updating, or managing server infrastructure, a company can save significant overhead costs. In addition, since a serverless FaaS or BaaS can instantly and precisely scale to handle each individual incoming request, the serverless approach automatically scales down the compute resources so that there is never idle capacity.

2. **No Compute Cost When Idle**: One of the greatest benefits of the serverless approach from a consumer perspective is that there are no costs resulting from idle capacity. For example, serverless compute services do not charge for idle VM or containers. When there's no work being done, there are no charges being racked up.

3. **Time to production**: The serverless development model aims to radically reduce the number of steps involved in conceiving, testing, and deploying code, with the aim of moving functionality from the idea stage to the production stage in days rather than months.

3. Security in Serverless Architecture

When you host the application in public cloud, the security responsibilities get distributed between the application owner and the public cloud service provider. Who is responsible for what depends on the cloud service model you use and is referred as shared security responsibilities model.

In serverless architectures, the serverless provider is responsible for securing the data center, network, servers, operating systems, and their configurations. However, application logic, code, data, and application-layer configurations still need to be robust and resilient to attacks. These are the responsibility of application owners.

Companies adopting serverless should ensure that they provide trainings and create awareness among their employees and help them understand the new shared responsibilities model.

The following image demonstrates the shared security responsibilities model, adapted to serverless architectures:

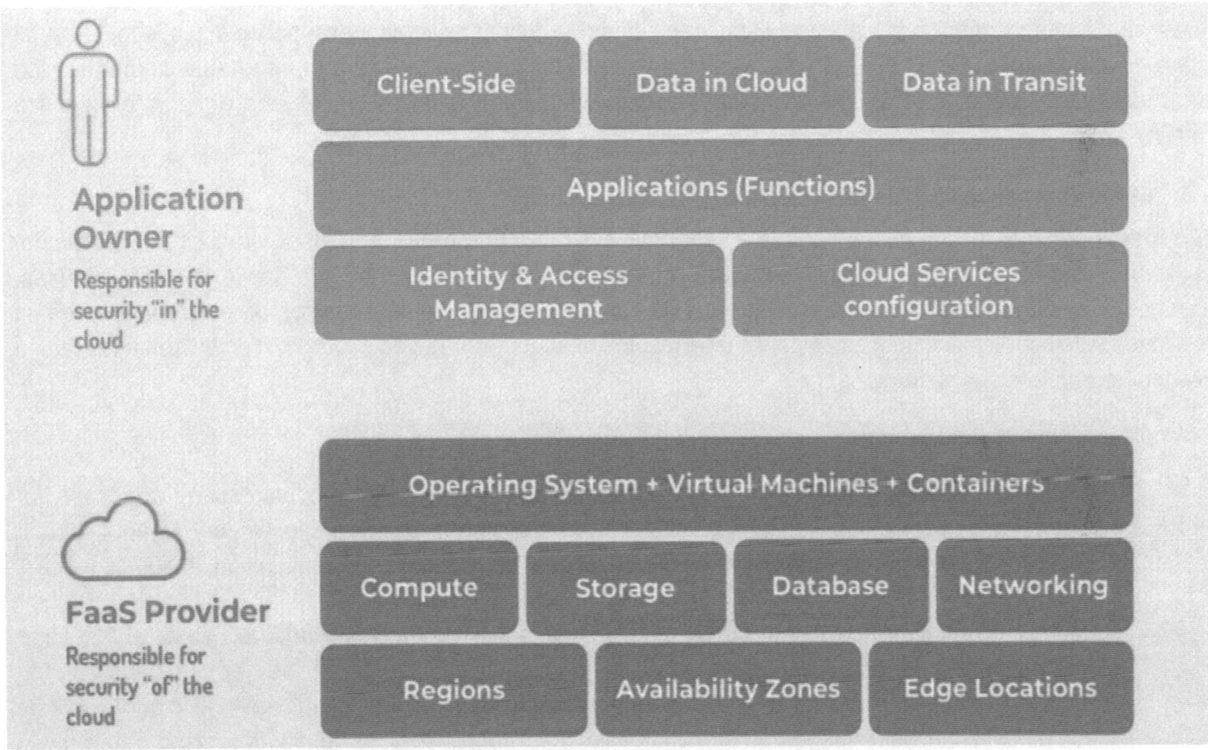

4. Serverless Security Challenges

Serverless architectures introduce a new set of issues that must be considered when securing such applications. These include:

4.1. Increased attack surface

Serverless functions consume data from a wide range of event sources, such as Hypertext Transfer Protocol (HTTP) application program interfaces (APIs), message queues, cloud storage, internet of things (IoT) device communications, and so forth. This diversity increases the potential surface dramatically. Many of these messages cannot be inspected by standard application layer protections, such as web application firewalls (WAFs). Example, web application firewalls (WAFs) are only capable of inspecting HTTP(s) traffic to the serverless application, but will not provide protection on any other event trigger types like cloud storage events, stream processing events, message queue events etc.

4.2. Attack surface and system complexity

Serverless design patterns call for web applications to be broken into constituent functions that are then reassembled in a serverless context. The attack surface in serverless architectures can be difficult for some to understand given that such architectures are still somewhat new. Many software developers and architects have yet to gain enough experience with the security risks and appropriate security protections required to secure such applications. Visualizing and monitoring serverless architectures is still more complicated than standard software environments as developers must make many decisions about which functions within their applications to expose to end users and then securely and accurately do so.

As an example, when we think of authentication in traditional applications, it can be applied using single authentication provider for entire domain/app and execution of proper authentication becomes simple. However, in Serverless applications, each serverless function acts as nano-service requiring unique authentication. Moreover, cloud services used by serverless application also require unique authentication and therefore, application of proper authentication grows tremendously complex and difficult to visualize upfront.

4.3. Inadequate security testing

Performing security testing for serverless architectures is more complex than testing standard applications, especially when such applications interact with remote third-party services or with backend cloud services, such as Non-Structured Query Language (NoSQL) databases, cloud storage, or stream processing services. Additionally, existing commonly used automated scanning tools are currently not adapted to examining serverless applications.

Example of some of the commonly used scanning tools are:

- **DAST (dynamic application security testing)** tools will only provide testing coverage for HTTP interfaces. This limited capability poses a problem when testing serverless applications that consume input from non-HTTP sources or interact with backend cloud services.
- **SAST (static application security testing)** tools rely on data flow analysis, control flow, and semantic analysis to detect vulnerabilities in software. Since serverless applications contain multiple distinct functions that are stitched together using event triggers and cloud services (e.g., message queues, cloud storage or NoSQL databases), statically analyzing data flow in such scenarios is highly prone to false positives. These rule sets used in these tools will need to evolve to provide proper support for serverless applications.

5. Critical Risks with Serverless Applications

While Serverless isn't inherently bad for security, its sheer scale emphasizes some very critical security risks. Maintaining control and security requires a paradigm shift in our thinking. Below are some of the most prominent security risks categories for serverless architecture and few best practices one can follow to mitigate them:

5.1. Function Event Data Injection

At a high level, injection flaws occur when untrusted input is passed directly to an interpreter before being executed or evaluated. Injection flaws in applications are one of the most common risks to date and have been thoroughly covered in many secure coding best practice guides.

In the context of serverless architectures, however, function event-data injections are not strictly limited to direct user input (such as input from a web API call). Most serverless architectures provide a multitude of event sources, which can trigger the execution of a serverless function. Examples include:

- Cloud storage events (e.g., Amazon Web Services Simple Storage Service (AWS S3), Azure Blob Storage, Google Cloud Storage)
- NoSQL database events (e.g., AWS DynamoDB, Azure Cosmos DB)
- SQL database events
- Stream processing events (e.g., AWS Kinesis)
- HTTP API calls
- IoT device telemetry signals
- Message queue events
- Short message service (SMS) notifications, push notifications, emails, etc.

This rich set of event sources increases the potential attack surface and introduces complexities when attempting to protect serverless functions against event-data injections. This is especially true because serverless architectures are not nearly as well-understood as web environments where developers know which message parts shouldn't be trusted (e.g., GET/POST parameters, HTTP headers, etc.).

The most common types of injection flaws in serverless architectures are presented below:

- Function runtime code injection (e.g., Node.js/JavaScript, Python, Java, C#, Golang) (OWSAP Code Injection 2013)
- SQL injection (OWSAP SQL Injection 2016)
- NoSQL injection (OWSAP NoSQL Injection 2016)
- Publish/Subscribe (Pub/Sub) Message Data Tampering (Security Compass Blog 2016)
- Server-Side Request Forgery (SSRF) (OWSAP SSRF 2016)

Example:

Consider a job candidate curriculum vitae (CV) filtering system, which receives emails with candidate CVs attached as Portable Document Format (PDF) files. The system transforms the PDF file into text to perform text analytics. The transformation of the PDF file into text is done using a command line utility (pdf to text). The developer of this serverless function assumes users will provide legitimate PDF file names and does not perform any sanity check on incoming file names (except for rudimentary examinations to ensure file extensions are indeed ".pdf"). The file name gets embedded directly into the shell command, and this weakness allows a malicious user to inject shell commands as part of the PDF file name.

Mitigation Steps:

- Never trust input or make any assumptions about its validity.
- Never pass user input directly to any interpreter without first validating and sanitizing it.
- Make sure code always runs with minimum privileges required to perform its task.

- If you apply threat modeling in the development lifecycle, ensure consideration of all possible event types and entry points into the system; do not assume input can only arrive from the expected event trigger.
- Inspect event data using a Serverless Security Platform (where applicable, organizations may use a web application firewall instead, to inspect incoming HTTP/HTTPS traffic to the serverless applications; note: application layer firewalls are only capable of inspecting HTTP(s) traffic and will not provide protection on any other event trigger types).

5.2. Broken Authentication

Since serverless architectures promote a microservices-oriented system design, applications built for such architectures may contain dozens (or even hundreds) of distinct serverless functions, each with a specific purpose.

These functions are weaved together and orchestrated to form the overall system logic. Some serverless functions may expose public web APIs, while others may serve as an "internal glue" between processes or other functions. Additionally, some functions may consume events of different source types, such as cloud storage events, NoSQL database events, IoT device telemetry signals or even SMS notifications.

Applying robust authentication schemes—which provide access control and protection to all relevant functions, event types, and triggers—is a complex undertaking, and can easily go awry if not executed carefully.

Example:

Imagine a serverless application which exposes a set of public APIs, all of which enforce proper authentication. At the other end of the system, the application reads files from a cloud storage service where file contents are consumed as input to specific serverless functions. If proper authentication is not applied to the cloud storage service, the system is exposing an unauthenticated rogue entry point—an element not considered during system design.

Mitigation Steps:

- Organizations should use continuous security health check facilities provided by their serverless cloud providers to monitor correct permissions and assess them against existing corporate security policies.

- As an example, Organizations using AWS infrastructure should implement AWS Config rules to continuously monitor and assess their environment. Examples of AWS Config rules include:

    - Discover newly deployed AWS Lambda functions
    - Receive notifications on changes made to existing AWS Lambda functions
    - Assess permissions and roles (Identity and Access Management (IAM)) assigned to AWS
Lambda functions
    - Discover newly deployed AWS S3 buckets or changes in security policies made to existing Buckets
    - Receive notifications on unencrypted storage
    - Receive notifications on changes made to existing AWS Lambda functions

- It is recommended that we should use authentication facilities provided via the serverless environment or by the relevant runtime. For example:
    - AWS Cognito or single sign-on (SSO)
    - AWS API Gateway authorization facilities
    - Azure App Service Authentication / Authorization
    - Google Firebase Authentication
    - IBM Bluemix App ID or SSO

5.3. Over-Privileged Function Permissions and Roles

Since serverless functions usually follow microservices concepts, many serverless applications contain dozens, hundreds or even thousands of functions. Resultantly, managing function permissions and roles quickly becomes a tedious task. In such scenarios, organizations may be forced to use a single permission model or security role for all functions—essentially granting each function full access to all other system components.

When all functions share the same set of over-privileged permissions, a vulnerability in a single function can eventually escalate into a system-wide security catastrophe. Thus, a serverless function should have only the privileges essential to performing its intended logic—a principle known as "least privilege."

Example:

Consider a function which receives data and stores it in DynamoDB table using "DynamoDB put_item()" method. While the function sole logic is to store data into database, the developer made a mistake and assigned full permissions to that function as shown below:

```
Effect: Allow
Action:
-'dynamodb:*'
Resource:
-'arn:dynamodb:us-east-1:*******:table/TABLE_NAME'
```

The appropriate, least-privileged role should have read:

```
Effect: Allow
Action:
-'dynamodb:PutItem'
Resource:
-'arn:dynamodb:us-east-1:******:table/TABLE_NAME'
```

Mitigation Steps:

- The "blast radius" from a potential attack can be contained by applying Identity and Access Management (IAM) capabilities relevant to your platform, and ensuring each function has a unique user-role (run with the least amount of privileges required to perform its task properly).
- Organizations should adopt an automated solution (such as a serverless security platform) for statically scanning serverless function code and configurations, flag over-privileged IAM roles and automatically generate least-privileged roles.

5.4. Inadequate Function Monitoring and Logging

One of the key aspects of serverless architectures is the fact that they reside in a cloud environment, outside of the organizational data center perimeter. As such, "on premise" or host-based security controls become irrelevant as a viable protection solution. This in turn, means that any processes, tools and procedures developed for security event monitoring and logging, becomes obsolete.

While many serverless architecture vendors provide extremely capable logging facilities, these logs in their basic/out-of-the-box configuration, are not always suitable for the purpose of providing a full security event audit trail. In order to achieve adequate real-time security event monitoring with the proper audit trail, serverless developers and their DevOps teams are required to stitch together logging logic that will fit their organizational needs. Many successful attacks could have been prevented if victim organizations had efficient and adequate real-time security event monitoring and logging.

There are many ways in which an attacker can exploit the fact that serverless applications lack proper application-layer logging, as an example:

- Attempts to inject malicious SQL payloads (SQL Injection) in event-data fields, which will not appear in standard cloud-provider logs.
- Attempts to send brute-force authentication requests
- Attempts to invoke functions with additional event-data fields containing malicious data

Mitigation Steps:

- Organizations adopting serverless architectures should augment log reports with serverless-specific information, such as:
    - Logging API access keys related to successful/failed logins (authentication).
    - Logging attempts to invoke serverless functions with inadequate permissions (authorizations).
    - Logging all successful/failed deployment of new serverless functions or configurations (change).
    - Logging any change to function permissions or execution roles (change).
    - Logging any change in function trigger definitions (change).
    - Logging the outbound connections initiated by serverless functions (network).
    - Logging all serverless function execution timeouts (failure reports).
    - Logging concurrent serverless function execution limits once reached (failure reports).

5.5. Insecure Application Secrets Storage

As applications grow in size and complexity, there is a need to store and maintain "application secrets." Examples include:

- API keys

- Database credentials
- Encryption keys
- Sensitive configuration settings

One of the mistakes related to application secrets storage, is to simply store these secrets in a plain text configuration file that is a part of the software project. In such cases, any user with "read" permissions on the project can get access to these secrets. The situation gets much worse if the project is stored on a public repository.

Also, in serverless applications, each function is packaged separately. A single centralized configuration file cannot be used which leads developers to use "creative" approaches such as using environment variables. While environment variables are a useful way to persist data across serverless function executions, in some cases, such environment variables can leak and reach the wrong hands.

Mitigation Steps:

- It is critical to store application secrets in a secure, encrypted storage environment and maintain encryption keys in a centralized encryption key management infrastructure or service. Most serverless architecture and cloud vendors offer such services, and also provide developers with secure APIs that can easily and seamlessly integrate into serverless environments.
- Organizations that decide to persist secrets in environment variables should always encrypt data. Decryption should only occur during function execution and by using proper encryption key management

5.6. Denial of Service and Financial Resource Exhaustion

In the past decade, denial-of- service (DoS) attacks have increased dramatically in frequency and volume. Such attacks became one of the primary risks facing nearly every company with an online presence.

While serverless architectures bring promises of automated scalability and high availability, they also come with limitations and issues which require attention.

Most serverless architecture vendors define default limits on the execution of serverless functions, such as:

- Per-execution memory allocation
- Per-execution ephemeral disk capacity
- Maximum execution duration per function
- Maximum payload size
- Per-account concurrent execution limit
- Per-function concurrent execution limit

Depending on limit and activity types, poorly designed or configured applications may result in unacceptable levels of latency, or even render applications unusable.

As an example, an attacker may send numerous concurrent malicious requests to a serverless function which uses the package until the concurrent executions limit is reached. As a result, this will deny other users access to the application. An attacker may also push the serverless function to "over-execute" for long periods, essentially inflating the monthly bill and inflicting a financial loss on the target organization.

Mitigation Steps:

- Write efficient serverless functions that perform discrete, targeted tasks.
- Set appropriate timeout limits for serverless function execution

- Set appropriate disk usage limits for serverless functions
- Apply request throttling on API calls
- Enforce proper access controls to serverless functions

5.7. Flow Manipulation in Serverless Function execution

Business logic manipulation is a common problem in many types of software and serverless architectures. However, serverless applications are unique, as they often follow the microservices design paradigm and contain many discrete functions. These functions are chained together in a specific order, which implements the overall application logic.

In a system where, multiple functions exist - and each function may invoke another function - the order of invocation may be critical for achieving the desired logic. Moreover, the design might assume that certain functions are only invoked under specific scenarios and only by authorized invokers.

Business logic manipulation in serverless applications may also occur within a single function, where an attacker might exploit bad design or inject malicious code during the execution of a function, for example, by exploiting functions which load data from untrusted sources or compromised cloud resources.

Example:

Consider application logic for a serverless application which calculates cryptographic hash for files uploaded into a cloud storage bucket. The sequence in application logic is as follows:

- **Step No. 1:** A user authenticates into the system.
- **Step No. 2:** The user calls a dedicated file-upload API and uploads a file to a cloud storage Bucket.
- **Step No. 3:** The file upload API event triggers a file size sanity check on the uploaded file, expecting files with an 8 KB maximum size.
- **Step No. 4:** If the sanity check succeeds, a "file uploaded" notification message is published to a relevant topic in a Pub/Sub cloud messaging system.
- **Step No. 5:** As a result of the notification message in the Pub/Sub messaging system, a second serverless function—which performs the cryptographic hash—is executed on the relevant file.

This system design assumes functions and events are invoked in the desired order. However, a malicious user may manipulate the system in two ways:

1. If the cloud storage bucket does not enforce proper access controls, any user may be able to upload files directly into the bucket, bypassing the size sanity check (which is only applied in Step No. 3). Malicious users may upload numerous large files, essentially consuming all available system resources as defined by the system's quota.
2. If the Pub/Sub messaging system does not enforce proper access controls on the relevant topic, any user may be able to publish numerous "file uploaded" messages—forcing the system to continuously execute the cryptographic file hashing function until all system resources are consumed.

In both cases, an attacker may consume system resources until the defined quota is met, and then deny service from other system users. Another possible outcome is an inflated monthly bill from the serverless architecture cloud vendor (also known as "Financial Resource Exhaustion").

Mitigation Steps:

- Protecting serverless applications against business logic manipulation can be done by leveraging serverless security platform capable of enforcing normal application flow and verifying that functions behave as designed.
- In addition, organizations should design the system without making any assumptions about legitimate invocation flow. Developers should set proper access controls and permissions for each function.

5.8. Obsolete Functions, Cloud Resources and Event Triggers

Like other types of modern software applications, over time some serverless functions and related cloud resources might become obsolete and should be decommissioned. Obsolete serverless application components may include:

- Deprecated serverless functions versions
- Serverless functions that are not relevant anymore
- Unused cloud resources (e.g. storage buckets, databases, message queues, etc.)
- Unnecessary serverless event source triggers
- Unused users, roles or identities
- Unused software dependencies

During a preliminary attack reconnaissance phase, malicious users will usually begin by mapping the serverless application, looking for the path of least resistance. Obsolete functions / cloud resources, unnecessary event source triggers or IAM roles are the most likely targets for abuse.

As an example, developers might leave event source triggers, which are unaccounted for and are probably not monitored properly. Such event triggers may enable an attacker to bypass authentication mechanisms or abuse business logic.

Mitigation Steps:

- Organizations should continuously perform discovery and pruning of obsolete serverless assets, cloud resources, IAM roles and any unknown serverless code that might have been deployed outside of the normal development process.
- Such discovery can be automated by using a cloud security posture management (CSPM) solution, or a serverless security platform (SSP).

6. Serverless Security Tools/Solutions

Following are some of the commercially available tools and solutions which can be used to secure the serverless applications:

6.1. Serverless Security Platform (SSP) by PureSec

PureSec's SSP is designed exclusively for serverless applications, and provides an end-to-end application security solution for serverless, which is tightly integrated into the CI/CD process.

The PureSec serverless security platform provides protection for applications using AWS Lambda, Azure Functions, Google Cloud Functions and IBM Cloud Functions so you can ensure that your functions are free from risk and safe from threats at every stage of the application lifecycle.

6.2. Protego

Protego is an application security platform that targets full-lifecycle security, from deployment to runtime. The web-based UI application surfaces security-focused visualizations, including the security posture explorer, third-party vulnerability reports, and policy manager.

The platform combines cloud account scanning to detect and address problems with roles and permissions; an analytics engine using machine-learning and deep-learning algorithms to detect threats, anomalies, and malicious attacks; and runtime protection that inspects and filters function-input data.

The Protego platform supports AWS, Google Cloud Platform, and Azure, and functions using Node.js, Python, and Java runtimes.

6.3. Synk

Snyk is one of the popular solutions to monitor, find and fix the vulnerabilities found in the application's dependencies. Recently, they have introduced the integration with AWS Lambda and Azure Functions which allow you to connect and check if a deployed application is vulnerable or not.

6.4. DivvyCloud

DivvyCloud, which Gartner identifies as a CSPM (Cloud Security Posture Management) solution, touches the following Cloud Management Platform categories:

- Identity, Security, and Compliance
- Monitoring and Analytics
- Inventory and Classification
- Cost Management & Resource Organization (at a peripheral level)

DivvyCloud is designed to effectively manage the perpetual shift of cloud infrastructure. By combining continuous real-time monitoring and a range of automation, along with the right cultural approach and processes, can enable an organization to solve cloud security issues around governance of multi-cloud, compliance based on a range of standards (CIS, NIST, HIPPA, etc), and security concerns tied to common misconfigurations issues.

7. Conclusion

Serverless is an exciting evolution in the world of infrastructure. It isn't inherently better or worse for security, compared to other infrastructure models, but it does change how we operate our software, and requires we adapt how we secure it. The Serverless ecosystem, including best practices and tools, is being shaped now. Serverless designs are becoming mainstream. The business advantages are undeniable. The top security challenge remains tackling the myth that "security's taken care of by our providers." Once that's shattered, there is real work to be done to secure these designs.

As adoption of the cloud continues and matures, securing serverless applications is an inevitable requirement, as many enterprises are adopting this approach to their cloud applications. The goal of security is to ensure that our data is being handled in the manner we expect. In a serverless world that means map out our data, write high quality code, trust (but verify!) what our provider is doing and monitor our application extensively. In our paper we have tried to list some of the important risks what top industry practitioners and security researchers with vast experience in application security, cloud and serverless architectures believe and some of the best practices industries adopting serverless can use to mitigate them.

References

2018. Martin fowler's blog. "Serverless Architectures". https://martinfowler.com/articles/serverless.html (Accessed June 20, 2019).

2018. PureSec Blog BY Ory Segal. https://www.puresec.io/blog/puresec-reveals-that-21-of-open-source-serverless-applications-have-critical-vulnerabilities.

2017. Open Web Application Security Project(OWASP). "Top 10-2017 Application Security Risks". https://www.owasp.org/images/7/72/OWASP_Top_10-2017_%28en%29.pdf.pdf

2016. Security Compass Blog, "Publish-Subscribe Threat Modeling". https://blog.securitycompass.com/publish-subscribe-threat-modeling-11add54f1d07

2018. Steven J. Vaughan-Nichols. "Servers? We don't need no stinkin' servers!". Linux and Open Source Journal.

2016. Open Web Application Security Project(OWASP)."SQL Injection". https://www.owasp.org/index.php/SQL_Injection

2016. Open Web Application Security Project(OWASP)."No SQL Injection". https://www.owasp.org/index.php/Testing_for_NoSQL_injection

2016. Open Web Application Security Project(OWASP). "Server-Side Request Forgery (SSRF)". https://www.owasp.org/index.php/Server_Side_Request_Forgery

2013. Open Web Application Security Project(OWASP)."Code Injection". https://www.owasp.org/index.php/Code_Injection

2019. Cloud Security Alliance. "The 12 Most Critical Risks for Serverless Applications". https://blog.cloudsecurityalliance.org/2019/02/11/critical-risks-serverless-applications (Accessed July 14, 2019).

Amazon Web Services. "Shared Responsibility Model". https://aws.amazon.com/compliance/shared-responsibility-model (Accessed June 20, 2019).

Amazon Web Services. AWS Lambda - https://aws.amazon.com/lambda (Accessed June 15, 2019).

Google Cloud. Google Cloud Functions - https://cloud.google.com/functions (Accessed June 15, 2019).

Microsoft Azure. Azure Functions - https://azure.microsoft.com/en-in/services/functions (Accessed June 16, 2019).

Serverless Security Platform by PureSec. https://www.puresec.io/serverless-security-platform (Accessed July 20, 2019).

Protego Platform. https://www.protego.io/platform (Accessed July 20, 2019).

Open Source Security Platform by Snyk. https://snyk.io/product (Accessed July 24, 2019).

DivvyCloud:"Unified Visibility and Monitoring". https://divvycloud.com/unified-visibility-and-monitoring (Accessed August 16, 2019).

Performance Testing with AWS X-Ray, CloudWatch, and RDS Performance Tools

Daniel Kranowski
kranowski.pnsqc.2019@bizalgo.com

Abstract
With a distributed, asynchronous system built on AWS, we have a variety of AWS performance measurement tools to use - which one makes the most sense? Our system under test starts with an Elastic Container Service (ECS) Docker app driving high-frequency messages into Kinesis, then to Lambda and a Relational Database Service (RDS) database. We want to measure propagation delay of messages through the system and analyze other parameters that explain or improve the existing performance. We'll look at multiple techniques for measuring performance: AWS X-Ray; AWS CloudWatch Metrics and Logs; and RDS Enhanced Monitoring & Performance Insights. We'll see how to obtain performance data in the AWS console or via command-line, and we'll characterize the pros and cons of each approach.

Biography
Daniel Kranowski is Lead Software Engineer and Principal at Business Algorithms, LLC, a business software services company based in the Portland, Oregon metro area. With over 20 years of software experience, his job roles have included software development, test, devops, and project management, at companies of all sizes and various industries. After working in multiple programming languages, today his preferred "full stack" starts with AWS and statically typed JavaScript. His personal code repositories are at https://github.com/daniel-kranowski. He can be contacted for consulting opportunities at www.bizalgo.com.

1. Introduction
The conversation starts with a question: "What is the propagation delay for a message traversing this distributed, asynchronous system?"

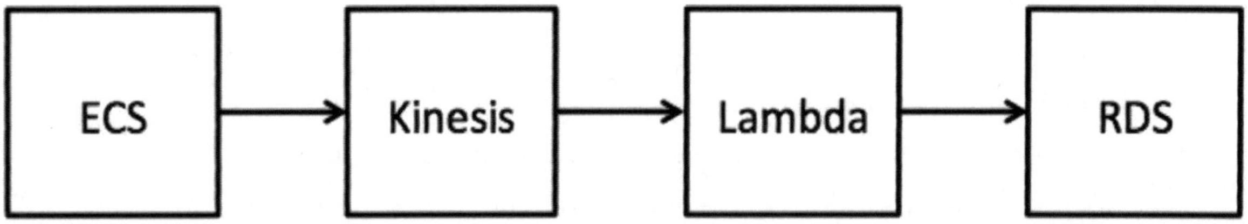

All those system blocks are in Amazon Web Services (AWS):

- AWS Elastic Container Service (ECS), for running Docker containers.
- AWS Kinesis, a messaging service.
- AWS Lambda, a service for running serverless applications.
- AWS Relational Database Service (RDS).

We have a Docker container driving high-frequency messages onto Kinesis. Lambda is listening, it picks up the messages, parses them, and persists the results into the database. We're not showing the larger system, where a thousand users are clicking some button in a website to trigger those messages, and they are sitting patiently in front of their screens waiting for the impact when their specific app can tell it has landed in the database. But that's why we care: users expect quick results, and if the app is slow we lose their business. So we need to do some high-quality performance analysis on this system. We want to know the propagation delay, and if it is not fast enough, we need to dig deeper and identify the specific bottlenecks in the system where performance could be explained and improved.

There are many tools for performance analysis on a distributed system. This is a 100% AWS system, and I can't think of any vendor more qualified to offer performance data on AWS services than AWS itself. So let's consider these:

- AWS X-Ray
- AWS CloudWatch Logs & Metrics
- AWS RDS Enhanced Monitoring & Performance Insights

The code for this system lives here: https://github.com/daniel-kranowski/aws-perfmon-01. The programming languages it uses are TypeScript for the ECS app and Lambda function (NodeJS runtime), and Terraform to automate the AWS infrastructure.

In this paper, the important items for discussion are the lessons learned about how to measure performance, not the exact performance of this system.

2. Synchronous Clocks in the Performance Analysis of an Asynchronous System

Before we get to the AWS performance tools, let's think a moment on the topic of **clocks**. Imagine someone on our team has done a performance test on this system, and reported to us "It takes 500 milliseconds for a message to get from ECS to RDS." We should have a few specific questions about that number: How exactly did we obtain the start and end timestamps? What clock did we use - was it the local clock on a workstation here in the office, a system timestamp from the VMs we are actually measuring, or time from the clock of a completely separate system? There are other questions to ask, such as whether the test payload fairly represented production data, or whether the tested system omits relevant network hops or other components of the real production system. But here we will focus on the question of the clock.

When calculating propagation delay through a distributed system, *the ideal performance analysis must be made using a single clock*, or clocks that we have reason to believe are completely in sync with each other. Propagation delay is equal to end time minus start time. If we capture the start time on our local machine when the test request is sent out, and we capture the end time on a deployed machine when it detects the arrival of the test message, can we calculate an accurate propagation delay by subtracting these two timestamps? There will be skew between the local clock and the deployed machine clock. Ignoring timezone differences, the two clocks could easily be seconds or minutes apart, which means our calculated result will be too fast or too slow by seconds or minutes. In a measurement where milliseconds count, can we feel confident in the propagation delay calculated using timestamps with an unknown amount of clock skew?

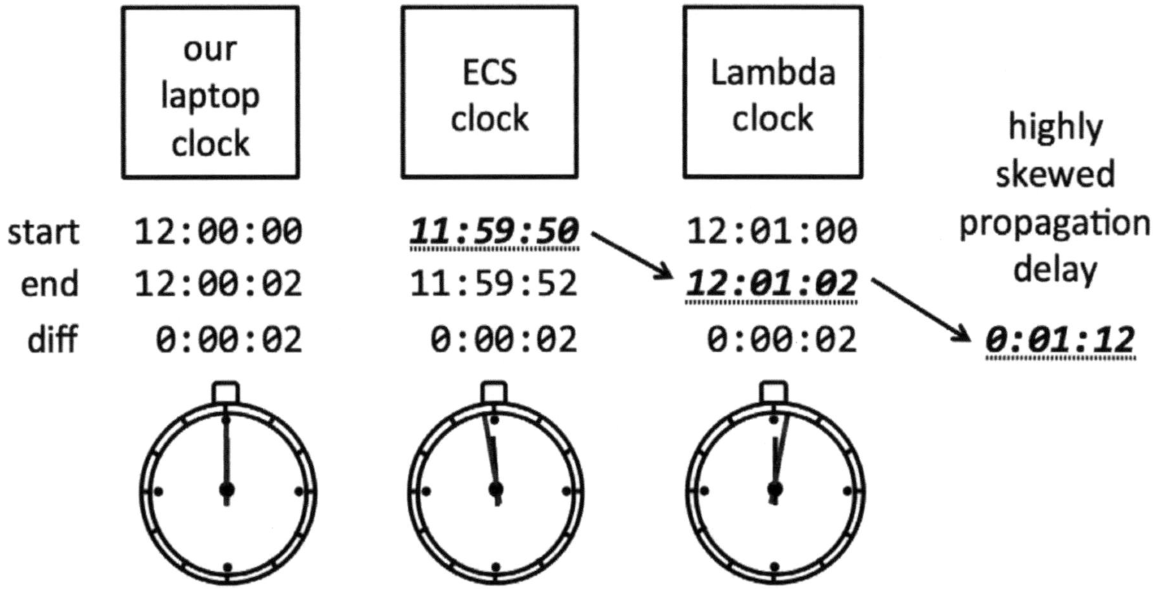

In a round-trip system test, like a synchronous request/response, there is only one clock for measurement purposes, and it lives on the client side. We throw the boomerang, and it comes back to us. No clock problem there. But the system under test described in this paper is a one-way trip, because it involves asynchronous messaging: the Kinesis component. Now we're throwing an envelope in the mailbox, and the clock on the wall where we dropped it off is not the same clock our recipient is looking when it gets received on the other end. The asynchronous aspect of the system is what makes it much harder to measure an accurate propagation delay.

With that concern in mind, now let's consider the AWS-based approaches to performance analysis.

3. AWS X-Ray

AWS X-Ray is a service for analyzing timing in distributed systems. It is focused on **timing**, and does not venture into other metrics of system performance. Because it is designed for systems with high throughput, it uses a **sampling** approach, which means it records data on a fraction of all the messages passing by, not all of them.

We can understand AWS X-Ray using three basic concepts: **services**, **traces**, and **segment uploader clients**. Below we have the Lambda service making two SQL queries to the RDS service, sending a custom metric to the CloudWatch service, then uploading data segments to the X-Ray service, with the X-Ray daemon as its intermediary:

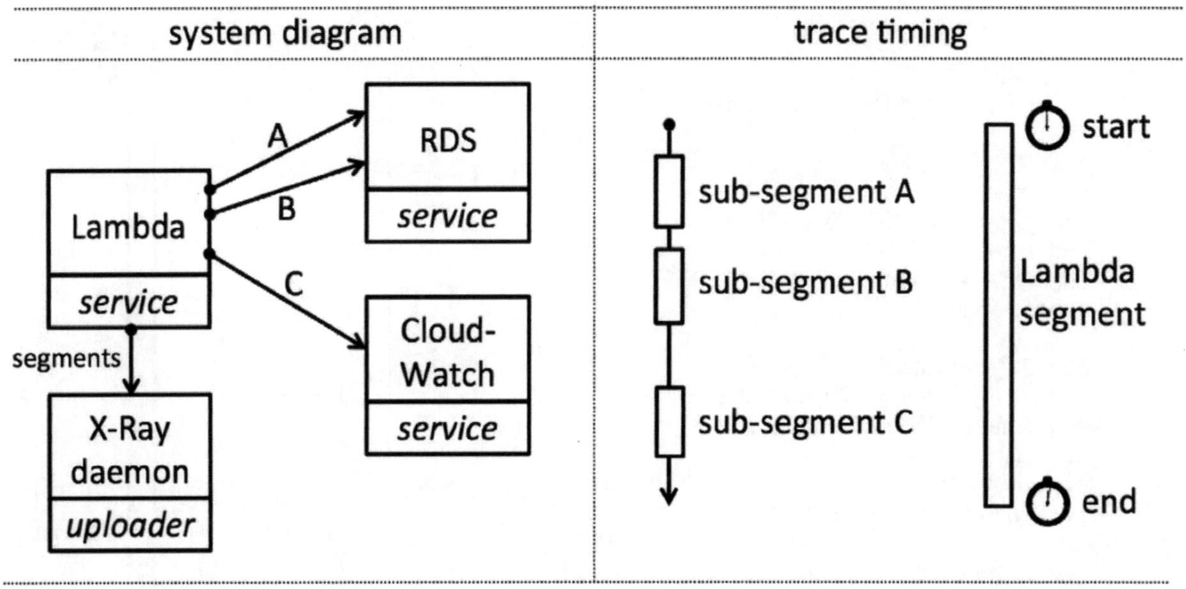

Except for X-Ray itself, the services are AWS services like Lambda or RDS whose performance we want to measure. Traces are the lines that connect them, and the propagation delay question we're trying to solve here is represented by the duration of an average trace, in milliseconds. A trace is composed of **segments**, such as the main Lambda segment, and sub-segments, such as a single SQL query to RDS. Below is an example X-Ray trace in JSON format for the above system. Many details have been removed from the JSON to make the code snippet shorter:

```
{
 "Duration": 0.202,
 "Id": "1-5d54524b-d8a31d6c6bc1e31072c986d2",
 "Segments": [
	{
	"Document": {
	"start_time": 1565807179.6620595,
	"end_time": 1565807179.851746,
	"origin": "AWS::Lambda::Function",
	"subsegments": [
	{
	"name": "Invocation",
	"start_time": 1565807179.6621196,
	"end_time": 1565807179.8506436,
	"aws": {
	"function_arn":                    "arn:aws:lambda:us-west-
2:123456789012:function:aws-perfmon-01-msg-consumer"
	},
	"subsegments": [
	{
	"name":              "msgdb@aws-perfmon-01-rdscluster.cluster-
asdfasdfasdf.us-west-2.rds.amazonaws.com",
	"start_time": 1565807179.69,
	"end_time": 1565807179.71
	},
	{
	"name":              "msgdb@aws-perfmon-01-rdscluster.cluster-
asdfasdfasdf.us-west-2.rds.amazonaws.com",
	"start_time": 1565807179.691,
	"end_time": 1565807179.72
	},
	{
	"name": "CloudWatch",
	"start_time": 1565807179.771,
	"end_time": 1565807179.831,
		"aws": {
		  "operation": "PutMetricData"
	}
	}
	]
	}
	]
	}
	}
 ]
}
```


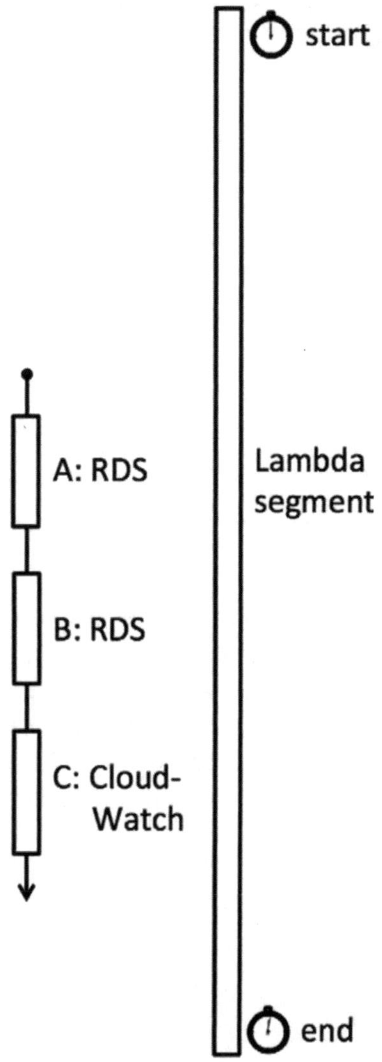

X-Ray trace

X-Ray doesn't record traces unless we configure the services to upload segments using the X-Ray API. There are many ways to do it:

- ***AWS CLI*:** Call aws xray put-trace-segments on the command-line, with the segment as a JSON string argument.
- ***X-Ray Daemon*:** Run a central daemon process, as an intermediary between our clients and the X-Ray service.Clients send the segment JSON to the daemon, which forwards them to X-Ray.
- ***AWS JavaScript SDK*:** The JavaScript SDK has an X-Ray wrapper that instruments the core AWS client object, so that the client sends a segment for every AWS service our code connects to.
- ***AWS Java SDK*:** The Java SDK has several options, including a servlet filter for webapps that starts a trace on receiving a request (the round-trip measurement model); and a general purpose X-Ray recorder that sends a segment for every AWS service call, when added as an interceptor on the Java client object for that service.

Instantiating our own Daemon is the most labor-intensive solution. Using the CLI eliminates the need to set up a Daemon, but we will still need to manage X-Ray segment formatting, and integrate the CLI calls into the application under test. The SDKs are easiest, because they take care of the low-level details for us.

Here is an example of instrumenting a NodeJS Lambda function, using the AWS JS SDK in TypeScript:

```
import * as AWS from 'aws-sdk';
import * as AWSXRayCore from 'aws-xray-sdk-core';

AWSXRayCore.captureAWS(AWS);    // AWS object is now instrumented for X-
Ray.

export async function handler(event, content) { ..... }
```

Simply by having called captureAWS(), this Lambda function handler will now automatically send a segment to X-Ray to record the start and end of the Lambda function's invocation. Additionally, if the handler uses the AWS client object in an expression to communicate with another AWS service, that will automatically send a sub-segment. Behind the scenes, the Lambda service runs an X-Ray daemon as intermediary to receive these segments and forward them to the X-Ray service.

SQL queries to an RDS database are performed over a database connection. The AWS client object is not involved in the connection or the query, so our Lambda function needs additional instrumentation in order to record time spent in the database. In our example, we use the mysql JavaScript client library to make connections and perform queries to an RDS Aurora MySQL database. The X-Ray SDK has a wrapper for that library, which can capture it just like it captured the AWS object:

```
import * as mysql from 'mysql';
import captureMySQL = require('aws-xray-sdk-mysql');
const capturedMySQL = captureMySQL(mysql);
const { createPool } = capturedMySQL;
const pool: Pool = createPool({
```

```
        host:      'aws-perfmon-01-rdscluster.cluster-asdfasdfasdf.us-west-
    2.rds.amazonaws.com',
        port: 3306,
        user: 'username',
        password: 'password',
        database: 'msgdb'
    });
```

By creating a database connection through the capturedMySQL object, the subsequent query will automatically send a segment to X-Ray to record the start and end time inside RDS.

If we run our performance test, we can log into the AWS console and see the X-Ray Service Graph:

And here is an example trace, where the Lambda function made six calls to the database and then called CloudWatch:

If we want a copy of our traces for offline analysis, we can download them with the AWS CLI:

```
aws xray get-trace-summaries \
      --start-time "2019-08-14T11:25:00.000-07:00" \
      --end-time   "2019-08-14T11:30:00.000-07:00" \
      --filter-expression 'service(id(name: "aws-perfmon-01-msg-
consumer",
                                     type: "AWS::Lambda::Function"))'

aws xray batch-get-traces \
      --trace-ids 1-5d54524b-d8a31d6c6bc1e31072c986d2 \
                1-5d34910e-71883e81bd6506cefb7768af
```

This all sounds great so far, but there is a fly in the ointment. Notice we have no X-Ray coverage for the Kinesis system block that feeds messages into our Lambda. There's a reason for this: X-Ray works great for the round-trip request/response model, but not so great for a one-way asynchronous model. X-Ray could capture the time to put a message on the Kinesis stream, but measuring the time *across* the stream is another matter. Kinesis does not have its own X-Ray daemon like Lambda, and we cannot spin up our own daemon behind the AWS curtain where Kinesis receives PUT messages and delivers GET messages. To build up a trace that covers our system path from start to finish, the best we can do is to leverage the compute nodes on either end of the Kinesis stream, which in our case are the ECS Docker container and the Lambda.

To make that work, the ECS and Lambda compute nodes would need to manage the trace id, so that segments are uploaded and attached to the right trace. The trace starts in the ECS app, which must produce an id and put it somewhere on the message. Upon pushing that message into Kinesis, the ECS app must send a segment to X-Ray saying "For trace id 123, the ECS service started work at time1, and at time2 it finished." When the Lambda function receives the message, it must parse out the trace id, do its work, and send its own segment to X-Ray saying "For trace id 123, Lambda received the message at time3, and finished processing it at time4." There is no way to make note of Kinesis in these trace segments.

It might be worth going down that road, but for one other issue: the compute nodes would need to individually fill in the start time and end time of the segment. That's right, two clocks used in distributed performance analysis! We've identified that as a risk, but there's a chance this still could work out. ECS and Lambda are both inside the AWS ecosystem, and the VMs hosting them are all probably using the same Network Time Protocol (NTP) servers, and if we stick with a single AWS region then the network latency between them is minimized. So it's possible the two clocks are "reasonably" in sync, as reasonable as it gets when we are measuring delays on the order of milliseconds. But ECS and Lambda are unreliable candidates for this because their internal supporting VMs are constantly popping in and out of existence, which is a basic part of the design and sales pitch for these AWS services. Docker containers and especially Lambda functions are short-lived, and their capacity to scale in or out is strong evidence that the AWS internal VMs which host them will also be short-lived. In a word, they are *ephemeral*. This matters because NTP sync is not instantaneous when a VM spins up, and I can tell you I see Lambdas that do not know what time it is right after a Lambda cold start. We will see evidence of this in the next section, using a CloudWatch Custom Metric for system propagation delay.

When a compute node's supporting VM has been running for a minute, then we can be sure NTP sync has occurred, however good that may be. But we have no direct visibility into the VMs underpinning ECS and Lambda, and evidence shows that the new instances start out with unsynchronized clocks.

4. AWS CloudWatch

AWS CloudWatch encompasses a handful of features, and for performance analysis I'll consider Logs, Dashboards, and Metrics. I think it's fair to say more people have used CloudWatch than, say, X-Ray, so there is perhaps nothing new and shiny on the surface here. But humor me for a moment.

4.1 AWS CloudWatch Logs

AWS CloudWatch Logs are an available route for troubleshooting other AWS services. For example, ECS and Lambda put their standard output into CloudWatch Logs by default. Logs are organized in a three-level hierarchy of Log Groups, each of which contains Log Streams, each of which contains Log Events (the actual log texts). Looking at logs is an indispensable tool for understanding *why* a compute service is slow: we can find stacktraces or other clues in the output that explain what is happening.

More pertinent to our propagation delay question is the fact that CloudWatch Log events have a timestamp. In fact, they have two of them. The reference API for GetLogEvents shows:

- timestamp: The time the event occurred.
- ingestionTime: The time the event was ingested.

The first one, timestamp, is the same one on the PutLogEvents operation, which means it is set by the compute node or service that uploads the log event. This is the same clock sync situation we were in with X-Ray, where we were trying to decide whether ECS and Lambda were a reliable source of clock data. However the ingestionTime *is set by the CloudWatch service itself*, and even though it is behind the AWS curtain, we can be sure its supporting VMs are long-lived and not ephemeral like ECS and Lambda VMs. CloudWatch is under constant request load from all accounts in the entire AWS ecosystem, unlike our little ECS container or our particular Lambda function, where traffic varies. Moreover, CloudWatch is a single service, which means one clock, not many clocks. Within a given AWS region there may be some network latency missed between ECS and CloudWatch, or between Lambda and CloudWatch, but weigh that against the more robust premise of using ingestionTime as a central clock to measure a distributed, asynchronous system path. This advantage is not to be ignored. We could conceivably design our distributed system to write log events for "start" and "end," then use the API to parse out the start/end ingestion times and calculate the propagation delay.

On the other hand, there is a significant disadvantage with basing our performance analysis on CloudWatch Logs, which can be summarized neatly by saying the API is a royal pain in the neck. Searching for text in CloudWatch Logs is very hard, because it is not an indexed system like Elasticsearch, or other SaaS indexed logging systems like Splunk and Loggly. The CloudWatch Logs API does have an operation for global searching, FilterLogEvents, but let's be careful using it or we could be sitting for hours while it scans every log event in the filtered log streams. To deal efficiently with log events from the CloudWatch API, we need to be prepared to process every log event in a log stream.

4.2. AWS CloudWatch Metrics

AWS CloudWatch Metrics are the starting point for performance diagnostics on an individual block in the system. AWS is the infrastructure provider, and they are the only ones who can truly supply us with accurate information about infrastructure metrics. We don't have to take any action for CloudWatch to record these metrics on all our resources; it is always recording them, which is handy for morning-after troubleshooting.

A **metric** is simply a time-series dataset that gives the numerical value of some system indicator over time. We can download the numbers using the API, or we can use the AWS console to plot metrics as a graph in the browser. CloudWatch Dashboards are a feature for remembering the metric graphs we like to see most often. These console graphs work very well, and we can even export their configuration in JSON to automatically recreate our desired Dashboards in an infrastructure automation language like AWS CloudFormation or Terraform.

Every AWS service has a developer documentation page with a list of metrics specifically recorded for that service. Here is a brief selection:

- ECS CloudWatch Metrics
  - `CPUUtilization, MemoryUtilization`
- Kinesis CloudWatch Metrics
  - `GetRecords.IteratorAgeMilliseconds, IncomingBytes`
- Lambda CloudWatch Metrics
  - `Duration, IteratorAge, Invocations, Errors`
- RDS CloudWatch Metrics
  - `CPUUtilization, DatabaseConnections, ReadIOPS`

That's where we go when we are digging into specific performance of a particular service or resource. X-Ray can't give us that information, only CloudWatch. But what about the total propagation delay in our distributed, asynchronous system? Drumroll please: we present CloudWatch Custom Metrics, by which anyone can create an arbitrary metric, even across a distributed system.

To create a Custom Metric, use the `PutMetricData` operation in the CloudWatch API. It is up to our creativity how to apply this, but one approach for our system under test is for the first compute node in the chain (the ECS Docker container) to take note of its start time, and make that an attribute of the message sent over Kinesis; then the last compute node in the chain (for us that is Lambda) calculates propagation time by subtracting the start time from the current time, and the Lambda then calls `PutMetricData` to store that propagation delay number in CloudWatch. Here is how it could be written in TypeScript for a NodeJS Lambda:

```
import {AWSError} from 'aws-sdk';
import * as CloudWatch from 'aws-sdk/clients/cloudwatch';
const cloudwatch = new CloudWatch();
const now: Date = new Date();
const propDelay: number = now.getTime() - ecsStartTime;
cloudwatch.putMetricData(
      {
      MetricData: [
            {
                  MetricName: "SystemPropagationDelay",
                  Timestamp: now,
                  Unit: 'Milliseconds',
                  Value: propDelay,
            }
      ],
      Namespace: "my-namespace",
      })
      .promise()
      .catch((err:      AWSError)      =>      console.log('Error',
JSON.stringify(err)));
```

We can download metrics later for offline analysis using GetMetricData from the CloudWatch API:

```
aws cloudwatch get-metric-data --metric-data-queries '[
  {
      "Id": "m1",
      "MetricStat": {
      "Metric": {
        "Namespace": "my-namespace",
        "MetricName": "SystemPropagationDelay"
      },
      "Period": 60,
      "Stat": "Average",
      "Unit": "Milliseconds"
      }
  }
]' --start-time "2019-08-14T18:25:00Z" --end-time "2019-08-14T18:30:00Z"
```

And of course we will be able to view the Custom Metric using the CloudWatch Metrics console GUI, which works very well:

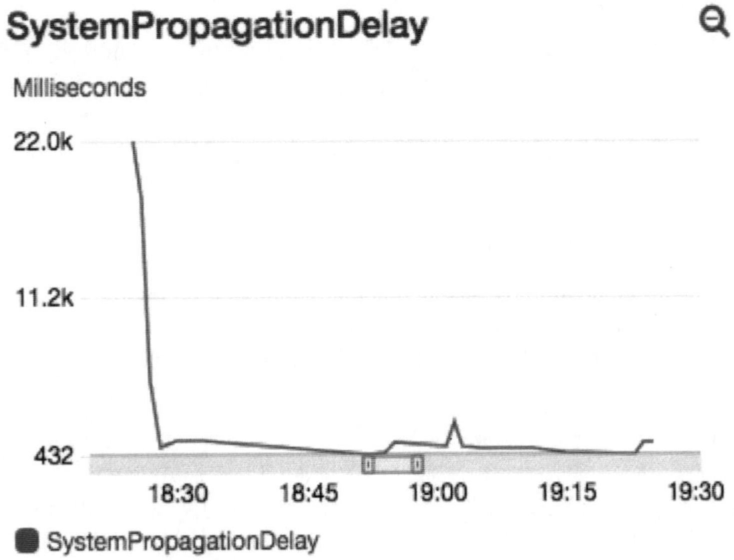

As noted strenuously above, there is some concern with the robustness of an approach that uses both the ECS clock and the Lambda clock. It is a weakness of the Custom Metrics approach. In fact, notice how the above SystemPropagationDelay metric is initially 22 sec, which seems unreasonably large, then normalizes to a more reasonable delay around 432 msec, presumably because the Lambda has finally synchronized its system clock to NTP.

Now is a good moment to switch gears. We have obtained the overall propagation delay number we were looking for. But we are still wearing our performance engineering hat, and we should ask a new question: How do we make the propagation delay quicker? Is there an obvious bottleneck in the system that we could optimize? Our system has a relational database, and AWS offers additional performance tools that are specific to RDS which can give us actionable information about the database that we cannot obtain from X-Ray or CloudWatch.

5. AWS RDS Enhanced Monitoring & Performance Insights

Let me start by saying the names are just too long. AWS does not do us the honor of abbreviating them, so I'll make the acronyms myself:

- RDS Enhanced Monitoring (RDS-EM)
- RDS Performance Insights (RDS-PI)

These are optional, added-cost features we can enable on a new or existing RDS database instance to get more advanced diagnostics. They won't tell us the propagation delay of our entire system under test, but they will help us diagnose more deeply when we have indications that the relational database is a source of slowness. The time to enable these features is *before* the performance problem happens, because, unlike CloudWatch, with RDS-EM and RDS-PI they only record performance data after we explicitly tell them to do so.

These features operate at the database instance level, not an entire database cluster. To enable RDS-EM requires an instance restart, as does RDS-PI for MySQL databases.

5.1 AWS RDS Enhanced Monitoring

RDS-EM extracts data from the operating system (OS) of the internal supporting VM on which the RDS instance runs. With RDS-EM, we get two new datasets: OS-level numeric metrics, and an OS process list. The process list is like what we would see with Linux "top" or "ps", where each process is shown with its memory and CPU usage. I have not yet encountered a "smoking gun" situation where I used RDS-EM and saw a specific database process hogging all the memory or CPU, but this is the only place where such an event could be discovered.

As for the OS-level numeric metrics, we get about sixty of them, and we can either graph them in the RDS console, or download them as JSON. There are some CloudWatch Metrics that appear redundant with RDS-EM metrics, but the latter offer much more detail. For example, CloudWatch Metrics for RDS offers `CPUUtilization`, while RDS-EM offers `cpuUtilization.{guest, idle, irq, nice, user, wait, ....}`, and `loadAverageMinute.{one, five, fifteen}`. CloudWatch Metrics for RDS offers `FreeableMemory` and `SwapUsage`, while RDS-EM Metrics offers `memory.{free, active, cached, hugePagesFree, mapped, ....}`. RDS-EM gives more granular metrics.

Notice I said we graph them in the RDS console, not the CloudWatch console. That is unfortunate, because the RDS-EM graphs are not as configurable or as easy to use as CloudWatch graphs. CloudWatch graphs let us customize the axes, specify a precise historical time window, plot arbitrary metrics on the same graph, perform functions on the data, and in my humble opinion they look better too. Also we can set CloudWatch Alarms on a CloudWatch Metric, to be notified whenever the metric exceeds a threshold, and that isn't supported with RDS-EM metrics. Finally, it would just be simpler UX to have just one data graphing functionality in AWS rather than multiple.

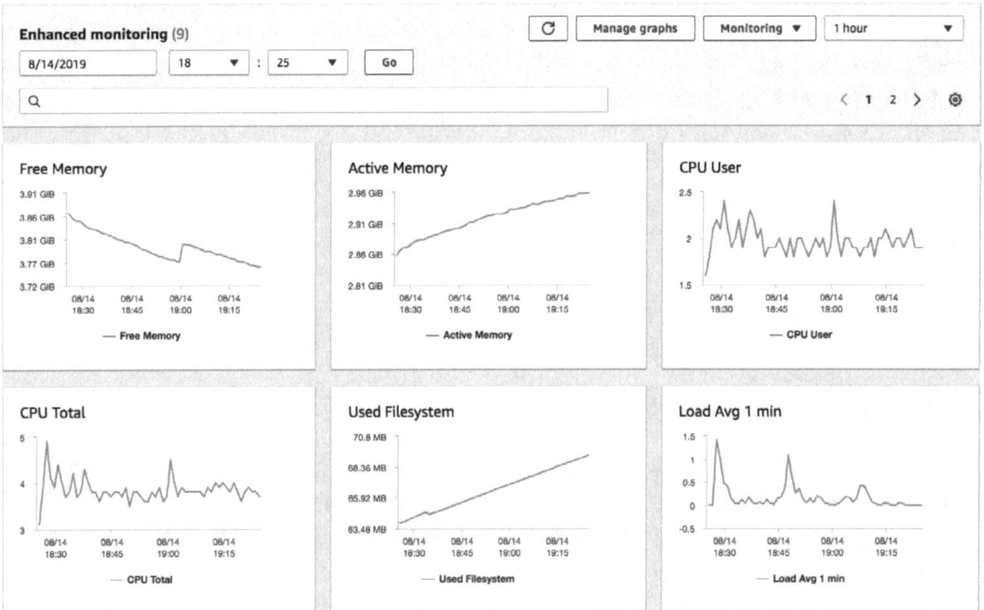

I see several reasons why RDS-EM graphs don't integrate with CloudWatch Metrics graphs. First, the time units don't always align: RDS-EM numeric metrics can be recorded on a granularity of 1, 5, 10, 15, 30, or 60 seconds, while CloudWatch Metrics are graphed on periods of 1, 5, 10, 30, or multiples of 60 seconds. The RDS-EM metrics are recorded on just one granularity, while CloudWatch Metrics are available on all periods for 15 days, 5 minute periods for 63 days, and 1 hour periods for 15 months. Also, the RDS-EM data is stored separately in CloudWatch Logs, rather than behind the AWS curtain, wherever CloudWatch

Metrics stores its data. RDS-EM writes a JSON datafile to a CloudWatch Log Group called `RDSOSMetrics`, once per granularity interval. I am not privy to AWS internals, but conceptually those reasons do not appear to be utter blockers from AWS someday offering the ability to graph RDS-EM data using the CloudWatch Metrics and Dashboards widgets, which are superior for graphing. AWS, if you are listening, think about integrating RDS-EM graphs with CloudWatch Metrics graphs!

To amplify one last point: RDS-EM data is stored in CloudWatch Logs, and our cost for using RDS-EM is simply the cost of using CloudWatch Logs.

5.2 AWS RDS Performance Insights

RDS-PI is a grab bag of additional metrics and the colorful PI Dashboard. RDS-PI metrics overlap a lot with the RDS-EM metrics, but the color charts are unique to RDS-PI.

The key concept in the RDS-PI Dashboard charts is the new **DBLoad** metric, which is the count of active sessions on the database instance. An active session is "a connection that has submitted work to the DB engine and is waiting for a response from it," which I interpret to mean any session that has transmitted manipulation SQL like INSERT, UPDATE, SELECT; or definition SQL like CREATE, ALTER. If `DBLoad` is 5, then the database instance is actively processing SQL statements for 5 concurrent clients during the entire 60 second measurement interval. RDS-PI integrates with CloudWatch Metrics here by offering three new metrics, which we can graph alongside any other CloudWatch metric or Dashboard: `DBLoad`, `DBLoadCPU`, `DBLoadNonCPU`. By itself, that's not major news, because there is already a CloudWatch Metric for RDS called `DatabaseConnections`, which appears to have the same meaning.

Where RDS-PI brings its unique value is the PI Dashboard, which is shown on the RDS console, not the CloudWatch console. This is the diagnostics tool where we can slice up the contributors to `DBLoad` in two dimensions, obtaining the "performance insights" that might just pinpoint the culprit of a database slowness problem. This is the colorful chart I was talking about, and it looks simply fabulous in a screenshot, unless we happen to use dull grayscale like I did here:

But hang on a minute, we won't get any value from the PI Dashboard until we learn its operating model. The Average Active Sessions (AAS) chart plots Sessions (aka `DBLoad`) versus time, and the area under the waveform is stratified into color-coded layers, according to the active **dimension**: Waits, SQL, Hosts, or Users. When we change the *Slice-by dimension* in the chart legend, the top line of the waveform stays the same but the color-coded layers change. If we slice-by SQL, the chart shows how many database sessions are occupied with the various types of SQL statement, and we could think about trying to optimize how those statements are used in the client application. If we slice-by Waits, we will see the session allocation to the engine-specific types of database wait states, which for Aurora MySQL might include `io/aurora_redo_log_flush` (waiting on a write to disk storage) or `synch/mutex/innodb/aurora_lock_thread_slot_futex` (waiting on a MySQL record lock). If we move the mouse left or right along the X-axis of time, the legend shows the exact number of sessions allocated to each value of the current slice-by dimension. In the above screenshot, at the selected point in time, the `io/aurora_redo_log_flush` Wait type has the largest contribution to DBLoad, compared to other Wait types, and it contributes 0.28 of the 0.32 total number of sessions. Since data granularity is fixed at 60 seconds, it means the database is in that wait state for 0.28 x 60 = 16.8 sec, from a total of 0.32 x 60 = 19.2 sec processing time, during this one-minute measurement interval.

RDS-PI gives us a second dimension of insight on the same displayed time window. In the *Load-by table* below the chart, choose a second dimension (again: Waits, SQL, Hosts, or Users) and we are rewarded with a table of color-coded bar graphs. In our screenshot, the COMMIT SQL command has the largest contribution to `DBLoad`, compared to other SQL queries, and it contributes 0.03 sessions, or 0.03 x 60 = 1.8 sec of processing time, on average, during all the 60 second intervals currently displayed in the AAS chart. The X axis spans one hour from 11:25 AM to 12:25 AM, so there are 60 measurement intervals of one minute each. The total sessions at the selected time point is 0.32, but the average sessions over the entire hour is a smaller number, 0.03.

When we put those two dimensions together, this tells us the `io/aurora_redo_log_flush` Wait type has the most database load, and the COMMIT SQL query is most responsible for that Wait type. We can get similar information directly from the database system tables, such as Aurora MySQL's table `performance_schema.events_waits_current`, but the RDS-PI color charts make it visually easier to identify.

There's no way the RDS-PI slice-by/load-by model could reasonably integrate its two-dimensional time series data with CloudWatch Metrics and Dashboards. It will always be a separate data graphing tool. So we won't be able to set CloudWatch Alarms on RDS-PI dimensionally-sliced datapoints, like the AAS chart and the Load-by bar charts. Also, just like with RDS-EM, the graphing features of RDS-PI are not as configurable or as easy to use as in CloudWatch.

In addition to the dimensional AAS chart and bar charts, enabling RDS-PI gives us access to dozens of "Performance Insight Counters." The **PI Counters** are plain old time-series data, and cannot be sliced like `DBLoad`. About half of these counters are engine-specific datapoints, like `Innodb_rows_read` and `Table_locks_waited` for MySQL, and the rest are the same OS-level numeric metrics provided by RDS-EM. Unlike RDS-EM, with RDS-PI we cannot download PI Counters over the AWS API, and the datapoint granularity is limited to just one point per 60 seconds, so for access to OS-level metrics we see that RDS-EM does a better job. The engine-specific data are helpful, because although we could obtain them separately by a select statement into the appropriate system table, like the `events_waits_current` table, RDS-PI offers the convenience of selecting them iteratively and storing the time-series. Again, none of these PI Counters can be graphed in CloudWatch, only in the less desirable graphing UX on the RDS console.

RDS-PI is unique for the way it provides dimensionally-sliced insight into the `DBLoad` metric, but it does not provide that capability for any other indicator. If the `DBLoad` metric is a large number, that is clearly a problem and we would want to delve into the dimensional analysis to see why so many database sessions have accumulated, but I could imagine a situation of database slowness caused by a small number of very bad user sessions, causing a small `DBLoad`, and the AAS chart would not draw our attention to that. Don't get me wrong, the slicing of DBLoad is very helpful, but I think it would add huge additional value and "actionable intelligence" if we could use the RDS-PI dimensions to slice other existing RDS CloudWatch Metrics, like CPU and memory usage, network throughput, IOPs, and operation latency. Maybe that's very hard to do, behind the AWS curtain, but I can still dream.

6. Conclusions

The use of AWS Kinesis messaging made our system asynchronous. Calculating the propagation delay through an asynchronous, distributed system is much more difficult than timing a synchronous, round-trip request, because it is hard to find a single clock to measure an asynchronous activity from start to finish. If the start/end clocks are separate, their skew becomes our timing error, and when we are measuring time on the order of milliseconds, even small error is significant. Ignorance of the precise skew casts doubt on the validity of the result. Our system under test also included AWS ECS and AWS Lambda, which are designed for ephemeral infrastructure, and since their supporting VMs are likely also ephemeral, those services are more susceptible to clock error when a fresh VM has not yet synced with NTP.

AWS X-Ray is for measuring the timing of a distributed trace through the nodes of an AWS service graph. It collects trace segments from specific integrated AWS services, and from compute nodes that use the X-Ray API. Because X-Ray relies on the client to supply start/end times, the trace result in our asynchronous system is subject to clock error. Additionally, X-Ray cannot directly represent the propagation delay across the Kinesis service, although the delay can be implied by the start/end times of X-Ray segments transmitted by the services on either end of the Kinesis stream. If the task is to measure system propagation delay, X-Ray is best used with a system based on synchronous requests. X-Ray is also helpful to get a general sense of the timing health of an isolated service node, or to drill into sub-segment timing of an isolated node. X-Ray is for timing measurements and not other kinds of metrics.

AWS CloudWatch Logs is a plausible answer to the clock error problem on an asynchronous system, because it records log event ingestion time using its own clock. CloudWatch VMs should be long-lived, not ephemeral, therefore presenting a stable clock. If the compute nodes at both ends of the system under test write to CloudWatch Logs, we can calculate propagation delay as time2 minus time1 because the ingestion times are based on a central source of timing truth. The pitfall of using CloudWatch Logs for performance measurement is its lack of search indexing, and the subsequent difficulty in locating the necessary log events.

After the initial collection of propagation delays through the entire system, we will still need to drill down and ask where the bottlenecks are, and how they can be explained and improved. X-Ray measures the typical delay in isolated nodes. To explain the delay, we need AWS CloudWatch Metrics. Its graphing capability in the console is very mature, and we do not need to take any action to enable data recording of predefined service metrics. Using Custom Metrics, we have another solution for measuring propagation delay through an asynchronous system, although like X-Ray it is subject to clock error.

Because the system under test uses an AWS RDS relational database, we considered RDS Enhanced Monitoring and RDS Performance Insights. They add greater detail on OS-level numbers and engine-specific datapoints that are not available in CloudWatch Metrics. However, RDS-EM, RDS-PI, and CloudWatch Metrics are mutually incompatible systems. Except for three `DBLoad` metrics, we cannot graph RDS-EM and RDS-PI metrics in CloudWatch Metrics (nor use them to trigger CloudWatch Alarms), and instead must use separate graphing widgets on the RDS console that are not as good. The strength of RDS-PI is not its counter metrics, but rather its two-dimensional approach to slicing up the contributing factors in database load.

To sum it all up, we have multiple tools at our disposal in AWS for measuring performance and drilling down for more details. Our strategy for using one or more of these tools will be guided by the types of AWS services in our system, like Kinesis or RDS, which have different levels of support for performance analysis. Finally, when reporting propagation delay, we will always remember to be very clear about how start/end times are measured, including an honest acknowledgement where timing error is unknown.

References

AWS Developer Guides:

- CloudWatch

https://docs.aws.amazon.com/AmazonCloudWatch/latest/monitoring/WhatIsCloudWatch.html

- RDS Enhanced Monitoring

https://docs.aws.amazon.com/AmazonRDS/latest/UserGuide/USER_Monitoring.OS.html

- RDS Performance Insights

https://docs.aws.amazon.com/AmazonRDS/latest/UserGuide/USER_PerfInsights.html

- AWS X-Ray

https://docs.aws.amazon.com/xray/latest/devguide/aws-xray.html

X-Ray Daemon on GitHub:

- https://github.com/aws/aws-xray-daemon

JavaScript 'mysql' client library:

- https://www.npmjs.com/package/mysql

The code to stand up this AWS system and run the performance test:

- https://github.com/daniel-kranowski/aws-perfmon-01

Performance and Security Monitoring in the Public Cloud

Sneha Mirajkar, Vittalkumar Mirajkar, Narayan Naik
SMirajka@cisco.com, Vittalkumar_Mirajkar@mcafee.com, Narayan_Naik@mcafee.com

Abstract

As business workloads move to public cloud, organizations must continue to maintain data and application security, optimize performance, and resolve issues as quickly as possible. However, getting access to large incoming traffic data in the public cloud can be a challenge and so is building strategies to access or tap traffic that is moving between cloud instances and then decide on a strategy for data filtering and grooming to help the security and performance monitoring layer to work efficiently and cost-effectively.

This paper, in addition to exploring the pros and cons of different approaches to security and performance monitoring in the public cloud, also provides an insight into how a filter-scanner sitting in the cloud instance and a security layer between cloud instances can provide the required security not only to the incoming traffic but also to the resting data, without compromising on the performance, mimicking the private cloud capabilities.

In a public cloud, traffic moving between different application and databases, referred to as east-west traffic is more difficult to intercept. When an organization uses a public cloud, the underlying infrastructure is completely transparent and seeing data is even more challenging. By embedding a network filter-scanner inside each cloud instance that is spun up, the filter-scanner can access all the data generated, eliminate all unnecessary info like duplications, erroneous data and more, in that instance and deliver it to security and performance layer, which then analyzes data packets/payload for anomalies and patterns in the data to enforces the business logic, i.e. ACLs to allow the request further or deny the same, creating incidents and reports to postmortem later, achieving security and performance at full strength in public cloud, preserving the benefits of cloud computing. Along with on-demand scalability, reduced time to resolution and easy operation on public cloud, which till now was limited to private cloud.

Biography

Sneha Mirajkar is a Senior Software Engineer at Cisco, with 12+ years of experience in software testing and extensive hands-on in test automation using Python, AWS, web-services. She has expertise in AWS applications.

Vittalkumar Mirajkar is a Software Architect at McAfee, with 12+ years of testing experience ranging from device driver testing, application testing and server testing. He specializes in testing security products. His area of interest is performance testing, soak testing, data analysis and exploratory testing

Narayan Naik is a Software Engineer at McAfee, with 11+ years of experience in exploratory testing and performance testing. He holds an expertise in providing consultation to enterprise customers for features and compatibility of various security products and security solutions deployed. His areas of interest are inter-compatibility test areas, performance testing and encryption product lines.

1. Introduction

As workloads move to the cloud, organizations must adjust their strategies for accessing and monitoring traffic. They first need to tap traffic that is moving between cloud instances and then decide on a strategy for data filtering to help their monitoring tools work efficiently and cost-effectively. The solution proposed here, enables data processing to be done in the cloud and then delivered directly to cloud-based security tools. The best overall monitoring strategy for many organizations will be a hybrid approach that supports continued use of powerful customized tools, combined with newer cloud-native tools available. With this approach, security is maintained at full strength, while the organization continue their transitions to cloud computing without having to compromise on performance, thus having the benefits of a private cloud while working on public cloud infrastructure (Ixia 2019).

2. Increase in Cloud Adoption and Its Challenges

Public cloud, as indicated by the workloads and compute instances growth, is growing faster than the private cloud. Public cloud adoption is fueled by greater need for agility, cost consideration and increase strengthening of public cloud security. Enterprises might adopt a hybrid approach where some of the cloud computing resources are managed in-house and some are provided by an external provider. Cloud bursting is an example of hybrid cloud where many mission critical workloads and daily computing requirements are handled by a private cloud, but for sudden spurts of demand the additional traffic demand (bursting) is handled by a public cloud.

Services like Amazon Web Services (AWS), Google Cloud, Microsoft Azure, and others offer much less expensive multi-tenant services on shared infrastructure with elastic compute and storage capabilities. Public cloud adoption continues to expand rapidly with AWS S3 growing over by over 650% between 2006 and 2013.1 Predictions for public cloud workloads show it growing at least 400% from 2015 to 2020.2

While the overall cloud workloads and compute instances are growing at a Compound Annual Growth Rate (CAGR) of 26 percent from 2016 to 2021, for the same period Public Cloud is expected to grow by 28 percent where as Private cloud at 11 percent. By 2021, there will continue to be more workloads and compute instances (73 percent) in the public cloud as compared to private cloud (27 percent) (Cisco 2018).

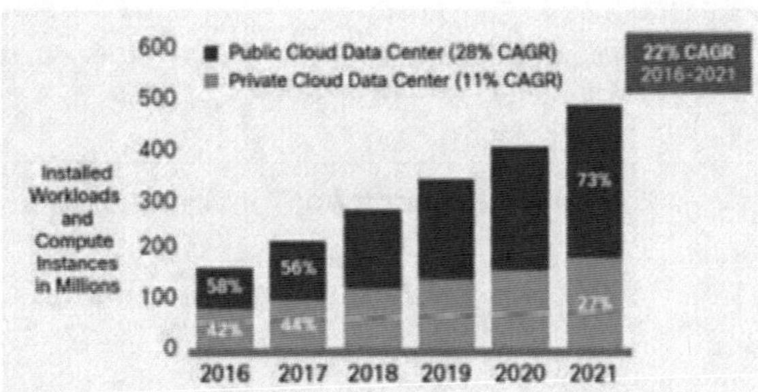

Average Workload and Compute Instance Density = (Total Physical Servers * Virtualization Rate (% of Physical servers are virtualized) * VM density (Average VMs per virtualized physical server)) + Non-virtualized Physical Servers) / Total Physical Servers.

Figure 2.1: Public vs. Private cloud growth between 2016 to 2021

2.1 The most serious attacks include:

Data breaches: If your cloud provider suffers a data breach, you may suffer exposure of sensitive customer information that could lead to serious financial or legal consequences, as well as damage to your brand.

Denial of service: These attacks take advantage of vulnerabilities in Web servers, databases, or other resources to disrupt a cloud service, sometimes as a distraction while another attack is taking place.

Insecure interfaces: The connectors of digital services are the most exposed part of any system and are frequently targeted. If the mechanisms used to manage systems, move data, and conduct admin tasks are compromised, an attacker can get access to almost anything.

System vulnerabilities: In multitenant computing, vulnerabilities in one environment can lead to an attack on an adjacent tenant with shared resources. The source is often poorly implemented or unpatched software.

2.2 Public Cloud Vs Private Cloud, a quick look

Below table gives a quick comparison at a broad level between Public Cloud vs Private Cloud. (Sungardas 2019)

	Private Cloud	**Public Cloud**
Infrastructure	Single-Tenant: Dedicated hardware and network for your business managed by an in-house technical team.	Multi-Tenant: Shared network hosted off site and managed by your service provider.
Business requirement	High performance, security, and customization and control options.	Affordable solutions that provide room for growth.
Best use	Protect your most sensitive data and applications	Disaster recovery and application testing for smaller, public facing companies.
Scalability	Can be managed in house. Extreme performance – fine-grained control for both storage and compute.	Depends on the Service Level Agreement but usually easy via a self-managed tool the customer will use.

Support and maintenance	Your technical administrators.	Cloud Service Provider's technical team.
Cost	Large upfront cost to implement the hardware, software and staff resources. Maintenance and growth must also be built into ongoing costs. CapEx.	Affordable option offering a pay as you go service fee. OpEx – Pay as you go, scale up, scale down as needed, charged by the minute.
Security	Isolated network environment. Enhanced security to meet data protection legislation.	Basic security compliance. Some may offer bolt-on security options.
Performance	High performance from dedicated server.	Competing users can reduce performance levels.

2.3 Security considerations for Public cloud

As enterprises adopt public cloud, the potential attack surface expands to include attacks on the cloud provider, as well as the provider's other clients. Most providers employ strong security measures, but they still face the same threats as traditional networks, the only difference is that, as a customer, you do not have as much control over what is done to safeguard against these threats.

In the current scenario, the public cloud is shared with multiple tenants. Thus, creating a larger need for securing moving traffic between the instances in public cloud (Johnson 2017).

Security is a shared responsibility by the user and provider, that requires constant attention and investment by both providers and organizations.

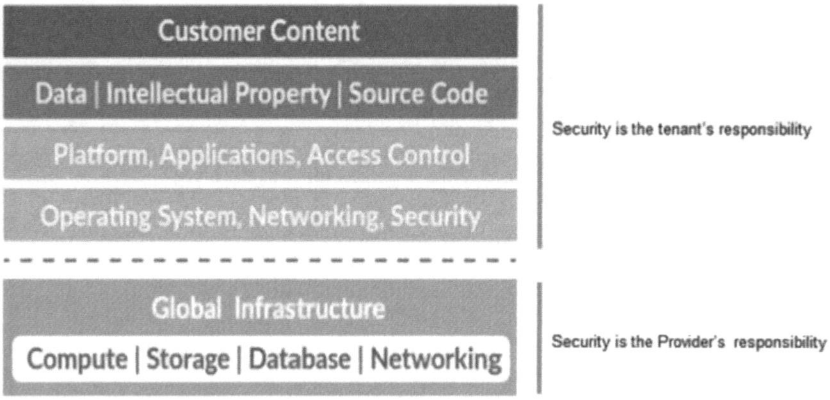

Figure 2.2: Public cloud shared responsibility model

3. Data Security Approach in Public Cloud

The approach we are presenting here to handle the authorized upload of files which may/may-not be malicious, is by getting complete transparency to cloud data. In order to achieve this, a simple customized **network scanner** is deployed as a component in each of the cloud instances spun up. How does this work? The **cloud filter platform** gets access to data in public cloud through the **network scanner**. The **network scanner** makes copies of all the data passing through the cloud instance. The captured data is filtered and sent to a **cloud filter platform,** that aggregates data from multiple sources, processes as necessary to remove duplicates and unnecessary info, isolates data of interest and delivers it to security solutions located in the cloud. A centralized, web-based interface is used to manage the **cloud filter platform** across the entire enterprise that is using the public cloud. Customized filtering policies are configured for policy enforcement.

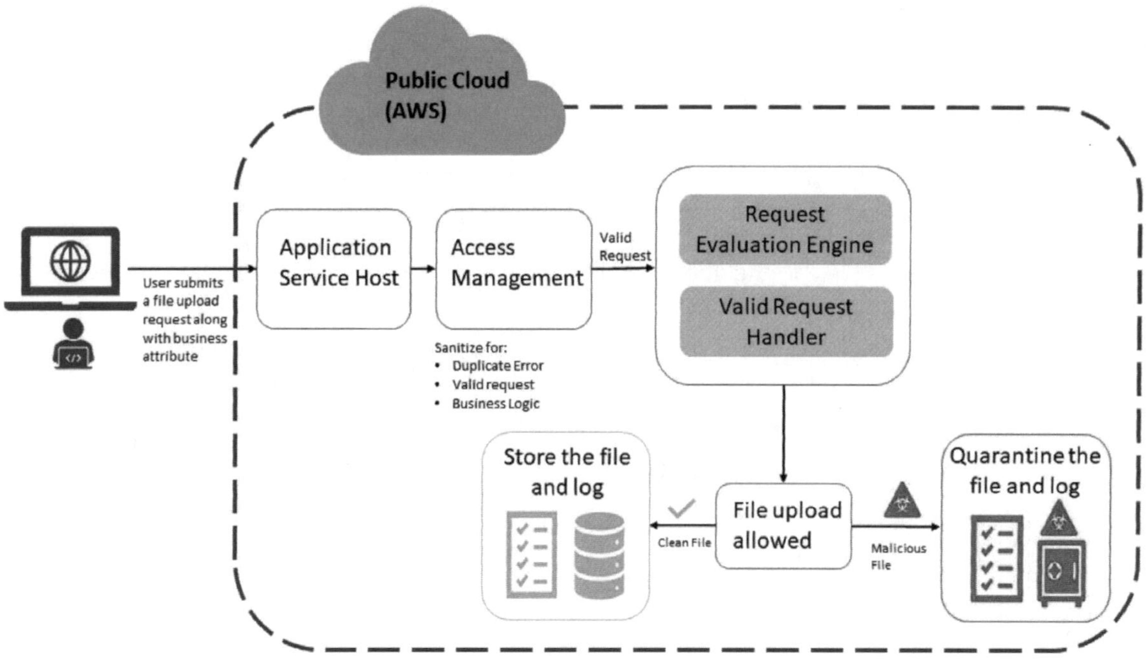

Figure 3.1 Data security approach in public cloud

4. Implementation of the Suggested Approach in Public Cloud

The test environment chosen here is with AWS public cloud. The user end point is mobile device (A laptop connected to public network), the vendor storage is Dropbox and an AWS hosted cloud filter platform.

The proposed solution consists of establishing a 3-way handshake between the end point, cloud vendor and cloud filter platform. The 3 main entities being the public end point, the vendor storage and lastly the cloud filter platform.

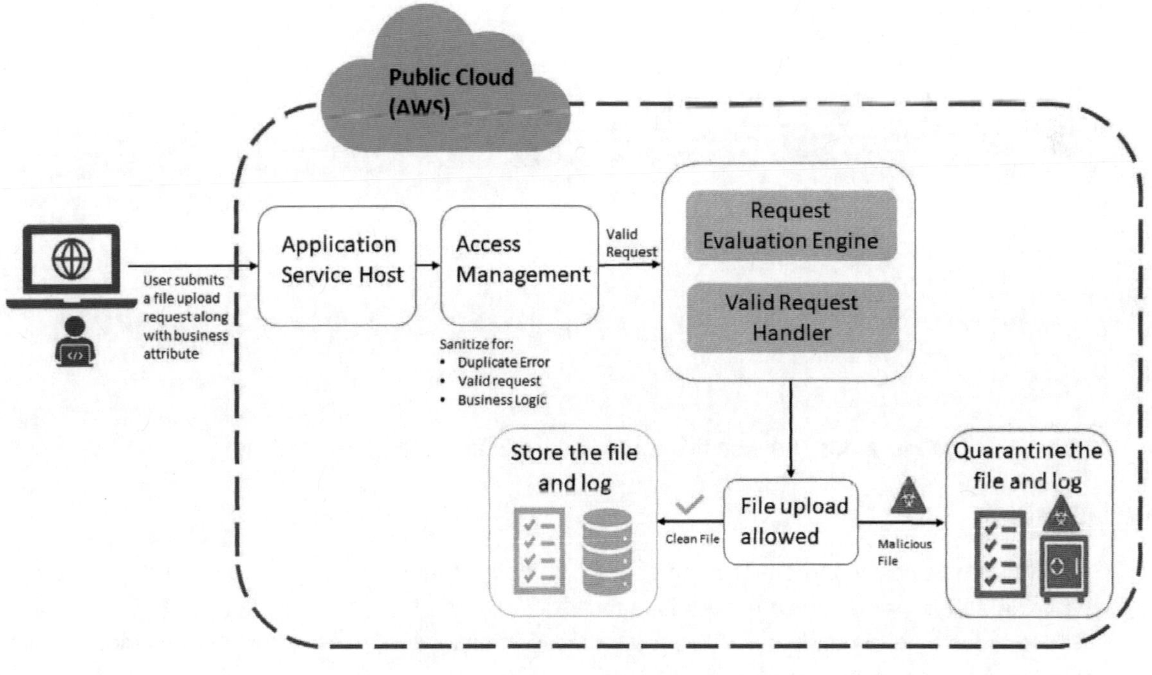

Figure 4.1 Three-way handshake.

Once the data is uploaded to the cloud vendor by the authorized end point, the polling agent (part of message queue) updates the queue with the delta of the changed values in the cloud vendor storage at the end of the scheduled polling time, this contains the metadata json of newly added files.

The metadata will be consumed by the scanner/filter for analysis, identifying potential malware (VirusTotal 2019), invoking the corresponding quarantine action. The non-malware metadata is then consumed by the downloader for the files to be downloaded and scanned for violations against given set of rules (Google 2019), (StackArmor 2019), calling for corrective actions such as updating the administrative contacts of the violations and access restrictions.

In the above approach, the performance is not compromised as the malware detection scan is executed on the file metadata, thus not waiting for the file to be downloaded. Secondly, for the policy violations, scans are triggered on the downloaded files and not the actual files, this leads to no variations in the performance of the cloud eco-system. Furthermore, with increase in the frequency of the API calls made to the cloud vendor to fetch more data, performance can be improved, since the data can be processed much faster to have more substantial results in given time.

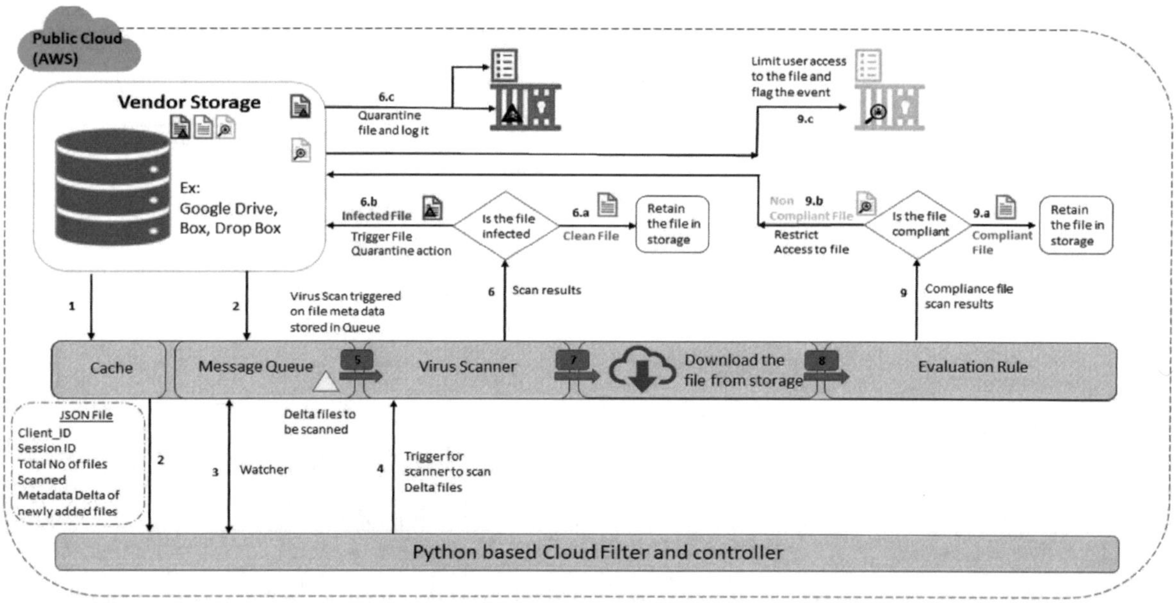

Figure 4.2 The workflow of file analysis and corrective actions

Advantages:

- With the flexibility and on-demand scalability, data collection and filtering can be automatically initiated each time a new vendor is launched.
- Reduced time to resolution – threat identification and issue resolution is in real time.
- Increased security in public cloud.
- Performance can be hiked since container technology is used for filtering and processing in the cloud instance.
- Custom policies to decide on the course of corrective measures.

Disadvantages:

- Restricting access to the uploaded files until the scan is completed may come with additional cost of implementing access restrictions.
- Increased cloud expense – Cloud capacity must also support traffic collection and filtering.
- Tool costs – containerization using the latest version of Docker will need constant upgrade.

5. Results

The graphs represent how the security is enhanced with the above approach. This shows increased security With (Red) vs Without (Blue) the above approach on increasing number of files, over a period of time.

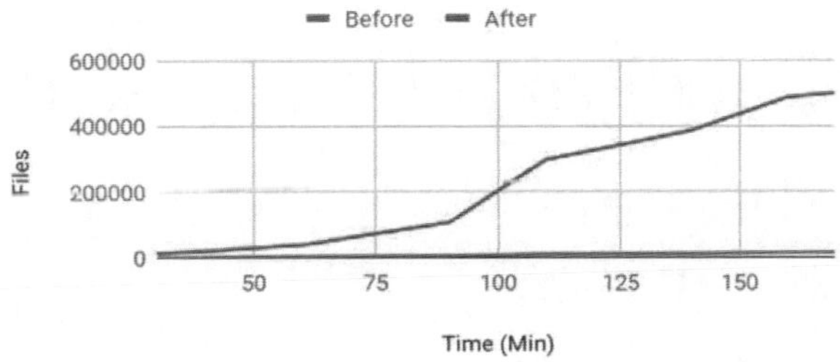

Figure 5.1 Result graph With and Without potential security risks.

6. Conclusion

Security and performance management in the public cloud has been a major concern. Of the multitude of security concerns in public cloud, one of the most prominent being malware detection and policy violations. These can be achieved by deploying the approach discussed in this paper. The complete solution is built using open source tools and readily available virus information database ex: virustotal.com

The possible trade-offs here could be handling the additional logging and spike in CPU usage based on the data handled.

7. References

Cisco. 2018. "Cisco Global Cloud Index: Forecast and Methodology, 2016–2021 White Paper." Nov 19. Accessed May 2, 2019. https://www.cisco.com/c/en/us/solutions/collateral/service-provider/global-cloud-index-gci/white-paper-c11-738085.pdf/index.html.

Google. 2019. *Cloud Data Loss Prevention.* Accessed April 5, 2019. https://cloud.google.com/dlp/.

Ixia. 2019. *Security and Performance Monitoring in Public Cloud.* Accessed May 2, 2019. https://www.ixiacom.com/resources/security-and-performance-monitoring-public-cloud.

Johnson, Stephanie. 2017. *Only YOU Can Secure Your Data in the Public Cloud (In My Best Smokey the Bear Voice).* Oct 23. Accessed May 4, 2019. https://blog.paloaltonetworks.com/2017/10/can-secure-data-public-cloud-best-smokey-bear-voice/.

StackArmor. 2019. *Data Loss Prevention (DLP) on AWS S3.* Accessed May 15, 2019. https://stackarmor.com/data-loss-prevention-with-stackarmor-threatalert/.

VirusTotal. 2019. *https://www.virustotal.com.* Accessed 2019. https://www.virustotal.com.

www.sungardas.com. 2019. *The Difference Between Public and Private Cloud.* Accessed May 10, 2019. https://www.sungardas.com/en/about/resources/articles/difference-public-private-cloud/.

Starting a Security Program on a Shoestring

Brian G. Myers
brian@safetylight.dev

Abstract

You are part of a small development team building a web application, and now someone tells you your product must be secure. Maybe the requirement comes from an auditor, or maybe from a prospective client. No one on your team was hired for security expertise. What should you do? How can you make meaningful progress with minimal knowledge? Where should you start?

You could hire experts, get training, identify risks and threats, prioritize your findings, design solutions, and implement them. That is the right way to go, but it makes for a slow start with a lot of heavy lifting up front. For people who do not have that option I propose a much easier way to get quick results and long-term improvements with minimal initial investment: just incorporate a vulnerability scanner—I will suggest a free one—into your software development process.

This paper explains how setting up a simple vulnerability management program will give immediate results, make your application more secure, improve your secure development lifecycle, help your team develop security expertise immediately relevant to their project, and meet some likely compliance requirements.

Along the way I will provide tips for choosing a vulnerability scanner. I'll show how to understand what the scanner finds, explain simple steps to turn use of a scanner into a vulnerability management program, and point out resources to help with questions that may arise.

Biography

Brian Myers (Ph.D, CISSP) has been working in security for five years and in software development for—well, long enough for his resume to include time at Borland and Netscape. He has written three books on Windows programming and taught introductory computer courses at the University of California, Berkeley. In his current job as Director of Information Security at WebMD Health Services Brian guides the work of multiple teams building a web platform in a HIPAA-regulated environment. He also serves on the CS/IS Industry Advisory Board at Western Oregon University.

1. Introduction

This paper suggests an approach to starting a security program in a company that does not yet have one. It focuses specifically on how QA can take a leading role in initiating a key part of any security program: vulnerability management. It assumes you belong to a smallish company with no security program, no budget for security, little experience in security, and minimal access to experts or formal training.

The impulse to improve your company's security posture might arise for a number of reasons. Maybe a potential customer is asking for details about how you protect their data. Maybe a security audit is headed your way. Or maybe you want to learn about security because it's fun and security experience is in demand.

Setting up a complete security program is a considerable effort. A complete program would include, for example, physical facility security, hiring practices, vendor management, training, risk management, and other areas for which you'd normally hire an information security professional. But even without all that expertise you can still make a reasonable start at driving security awareness and knowledge into your teams by starting small. The other parts can come later when the business discovers it needs them.

The problem of course is where to start without having to study up on large and unfamiliar areas. One of the main advantages of the approach I suggest is that it points you very quickly to particular bits of knowledge that are immediately relevant to your particular project. You do have to be willing to learn, but you can take it one small piece at a time.

Furthermore, not much technical knowledge is needed to follow the process this paper describes. All it takes is the ability to read HTML and HTTP traffic. For the purposes of this paper, I will assume my readers can make some sense out of this:

```
POST http://10.133.1.4/mutillidae/index.php?page=login.php HTTP/1.1
User-Agent: Mozilla/5.0 (X11; Linux x86_64; rv:60.0) Gecko/20100101 Firefox/60.0
Accept: text/html,application/xhtml+xml,application/xml;q=0.9,*/*;q=0.8
Accept-Language: en-US,en;q=0.5
Referer: https://10.133.1.4/mutillidae/index.php?page=login.php
Content-Type: application/x-www-form-urlencoded
Content-Length: 88
```

```
Connection: keep-alive
Upgrade-Insecure-Requests: 1
Cookie:    uid=24;    showhints=1;    PHPSESSID=rpiq3oo77e7rssp2gbjv6gfus2;
username=brian
Host: 10.133.1.4

username=brian&password=qwerty%27+AND+%271%27%3D%271%27+--+&login-php-
submit-button=Login
```

In particular, it will help if you can see that in the last line someone is posting to the server a very odd value for a password. (The odd value is underlined.) That is a scanner-generated value probing for a possible vulnerability, and understanding that will help you reproduce the problem. That is all the technical expertise needed to get started with a web vulnerability scanner.

2. What are Vulnerabilities?

First, what is a vulnerability? What are we trying to find?

A vulnerability is weakness in a system that can be exploited by a malicious actor to perform unauthorized actions. Scanners look for actions that might leak data, destroy data, or make the data inaccessible. For a standard introduction to common types of vulnerabilities, consult the OWASP Top Ten Project (see Resources section.) OWASP is an international non-profit whose purpose is to help companies create secure software, and one of their projects is a periodically updated list of the most common vulnerabilities that software development teams are likely to encounter.

Common vulnerability types include SQL injection, cross-site scripting, cross-site request forgery, and information disclosure. If you don't know what those are yet that's fine. Using a scanner is a good way to start learning about them.

3. Tools for Finding Vulnerabilities

A Google search for *vulnerability scanners* turns up scores of them. *Scanners* is a very broad category, however. Knowing what kind of vulnerabilities you want to find will narrow down the choices considerably.

3.1 Types of scanners

Scanners fall into at least four categories that differ in where they look and what they find.

Scanner Type	Scanner Target Area	Findings	Popular Examples
Network	Server and network infrastructure	Infrastructure configuration and patching problems	OpenVAS Qualys Nessus

Static Application Security Testing (SAST)	Application source code	Suspect program logic (missing input validation; buffer overflow risks...)	Coverity AttackFlow SonarQube
Composition Analysis	Third-party libraries	Third-party libraries with known vulnerabilities	OWASP Dependency Check WhiteSource BlackDuck Sonatype
Dynamic Application Security Testing (DAST)	Running application	Weaknesses in web pages (XSS, injection...)	WhiteHat AppSpider Netsparker

Table 1 - Types of vulnerability scanners

All four types matter, and software development companies generally need all of them. But you have to start somewhere, and for the scenario I have imagined—a small company with a web application—the best starting point is likely dynamic testing (DAST.) A DAST scanner doesn't look at source code or at build artifacts. It visits the web pages in a running application and interacts with each one to see if it can find vulnerabilities a malicious actor might exploit.

3.2 What Exactly Does a DAST Scanner Do?

Operating a DAST scanner generally involves four basic steps.

1. Configure the target.
First you tell the scanner what website to scan. This usually involves providing a URL and instructions for logging in to the site. Some scanners allow configuring secondary settings such as what vulnerabilities to look for in the scan, how much bandwidth the scanner is allowed to use, and whether to include AJAX calls in the scan.

2. Attack the site.
Next the scanner starts sending HTTP requests to the site in order to find problems. This involves three different operations. Some scanners execute all three steps at once while others ask you to initiate each as a distinct operation.

a. Find the pages (crawl the site)
The scanner starts with the target URL, look for links, and follows them recursively to discover as many pages as it can in the web site.

b. Passive scan (discover pages and read them)

The scanner examines the contents of each GET request and flags certain potential problems such as missing HTTP headers, insecure cookies, or exposed system information.

c. Active scan (feed pages unexpected input)
The scanner passes malicious values to the web server on query strings and forms. It sends the server values that are designed to turn up problems. It may fill in forms with extremely long input values, unexpected characters, semi-random "fuzzed" values, SQL commands, or any other hostile input that might produce unwanted behavior.

3. Create a report.
When the scan is done the scanner makes the results available in reports. Most scanners produce executive summary reports for managers as well as details report for development teams. The scanner reports are your source of information for reporting defects.

The first two steps of a scanner attack, crawling and passive scanning, are read-only interactions and do not change anything in the site. An active attack, however, is likely to add, modify, and delete database records. An aggressive scan could also conceivably make the server so busy that other concurrent users suffer. In general, do not run a vulnerability scanner against a production environment.

3.3. How to Choose a Scanner

NIST and InfoSec have both issued papers on selecting scanners (see the *Resources* section below.) Table 2 presents a consolidated list of desirable features compiled from multiple sources.

Scanning Functions	
Transmission Protocol Support	HTTP/S, HTTP compression, XML...
Breadth	Types of vulnerabilities it can detect
Accuracy	False positive rate
Authentication Mechanisms	Form-based, NTLM, Kerberos, SSO...
Session Management	Detect login, logout, session expiration...
Configurable Aggressiveness	Rate throttling, vulnerability type selection...
CI/CD Integration	Automation support

Reporting	
Executive Summary	Overview of results with breakdowns and subtotals
Information Per Finding	Name and description Location, inputs, context Severity CVE or CWE Remediation guidance
Changes and Trends	What has changed since the last run Are we getting better over time
Machine-Readable Output	XML (for example)
Support	
Documentation	Manual, reference, guide, wiki...
Training	Tutorials, videos, consulting...
Community	Active forums
Vendor Track Record	Reliability, expertise, release history
Commercial Considerations	
Price	Licensing + professional services
Location	SaaS or On Premise
Consulting	Training, integration...

Table 2 - Criteria for evaluating vulnerability scanners

Given the scenario we are imagining—a team with little expertise and no budget—I limited my selection of candidates to scanners that:

- Are free to use

- Have been recently maintained
- Detect a good range of vulnerabilities
- Provide informative reports of findings
- Can be integrated with a build process

In practice the first two criteria eliminated most of the contenders. A large number of the commonly mentioned free scanners are not actively maintained. Of those that are, some are special-purpose and so fail the third criteria (range of vulnerabilities.)

Product	**Free**	**Last Release**	**Active**	**General Purpose**
Arachni	Yes	2017	No	Yes
Brakeman	Yes	2019	Yes	No
Grabber	Yes	2013	No	Yes
Grendel-Scan	Yes	2012	No	Yes
IronWasp	Yes	2015	No	Yes
OWASP ZAP	Yes	2019	Yes	Yes
RatProxy	Yes	2009	No	Yes
Scan My Server	Freemium	2019	Yes	Yes
Skipfish	Yes	2012	No	Yes
SQLMap	Yes	2019	Yes	No
Vega	Yes	2016	No	Yes
W3af	Yes	2019	Yes	Yes
Wapiti	Yes	2019	Yes	Yes

Watcher	Yes	2017	No	Yes
WATOBO	Yes	2017	No	Yes
WebScarab	Yes	2011	No	No
Wfuzz	Yes	2019	Yes	No

Table 3 - Application vulnerability scanners I found mentioned in reviews

Eliminating those that have not been recently maintained immediately produces a much more manageable list. I allowed one inactive product—Arachni—into the list of finalists because know-ledge-able reviewers praised it highly.

Product	Last Release	Notes
Arachni	2017	Out of date library dependencies
OWASP ZAP	2019	Thriving community
Scan My Server	2019	Limited to scanning one domain once a week
W3af	2019	Out of date library dependencies
Wapiti	2019	Limited set of vulnerabilities

Table 4 - Application vulnerability scanners that met my initial criteria

3.4 Recommendation

I tested most of these by attempting to install them and running them against two well-known test websites with known vulnerabilities (*Mutillidae* and *Juice Shop*; see Resources.) Two of the scanners quickly dropped from consideration. W3af has dependencies on long-out-of-date libraries that prevented me from installing it even on Ubuntu, the system where the creator says W3af is tested. (Someone more persistent than I might be able to make it work.) Wapiti installed and ran, but it missed some findings that other tools reported. It works, but there are better options. That left three contenders: Scan My Server, Arachni, and OWASP Zed Attack Proxy (ZAP.)

Scan My Server is the easiest of the three to use, but the free license allows scanning only one domain once a week. Also, since the product is SaaS, the test site must be accessible on the public internet. The free version of Scan My Server could work for monitoring an existing site but is clearly not meant to support ongoing software development.

Arachni was in many ways the scanner I wanted: a command-line tool you can point at a site, leave running, and then get a clear report with all the right info. Unfortunately, like W3af, Arachni depends on long out-of-date libraries. Installing it required finding a workaround, and even then a broken dependency interfered with plugins needed for automating authentication. The scanner can't log in to a site. That's a deal-breaker. The creator has acknowledged the problem on the support forum but the code base has been inactive for two years and the problem remains.

OWASP ZAP wins my recommendation here because it is actively maintained, easy to install, detects a good range of vulnerabilities, and is supported by a community of developers producing plugins, documentation, video tutorials, code updates, and regular releases. It is not, however, as easy to use as some, and the reporting function is weak.

The OWASP ZAP scanner is designed in part as a tool for penetration tests. Much of its design is intended to support interactive exploratory testing. It produces reports, but overall the scanner is built to support analyzing results directly from the user interface. ZAP does include automatic attacks designed to uncover a range of possible vulnerabilities. As you learn more about vulnerabilities some of the interactive features may interest you as well. It's a tool you can grow into.

4. Understanding the Results

Each potential problem that the scanner reports come with two sorts of details. Some of the details explain generally what kind of vulnerability was found and what the standard defenses for such a vulnerability are. Other details explain exactly what the scanner saw on your web page that aroused suspicion.

4.1 Information About the Vulnerability

Table 5 lists generic details the ZAP scanner provides about each vulnerability. The scanner will show the same values for these fields every time it finds the same kind of vulnerability.

Item	Description
Alert Name	The name of a potential risk that may exist in the application.

Description	Generic information about the vulnerability to explain what the scanner thinks it found.
Risk Level	The degree of risk the vulnerability may create.
Confidence	How likely the alert is to represent a genuine vulnerability.
Solution	Generic advice for mitigating vulnerabilities of this type.
CWE ID	A Common Weakness Enumeration identifier from the catalog of flaws maintained at cwe.mitre.org. The CWE ID is useful for researching details about the specific vulnerability.
Reference	URL(s) pointing to more detailed information about the vulnerability. ZAP may point to a Microsoft blog, an OWASP reference page, or some other reputable source.

Table 5 - Details to explain the type of vulnerability found

4.2. Information About the Attack

The next table lists details the ZAP scanner provides to explain why it thinks your specific page might have a problem. These details tell what the scanner sent to the web server and what it saw in the response.

Item	Description
URL	The page where the risk was found.
Method	The HTTP verb that produced the suspect result (typically GET or POST.)

Parameter	A specific place in the HTTP message that ZAP manipulated to produce the vulnerability. It is the name part of a name/value pair in the query string or in a form. To understand what happened you'll want to find the parameter with this name and look at the value that ZAP assigned to it.
Attack	An excerpt from the HTTP message that the scanner sent to the application. It is the piece of the message that the scanner crafted as an attack attempting to uncover a vulnerability.
Evidence	An excerpt from the HTTP message that ZAP received from the server. The excerpt is the part of the message where ZAP sees a problem.
Request Header & Body Response Header & Body	The complete HTTP traffic from which the scanner concluded you may have a vulnerability. Often the Parameter, Attack, and Evidence values are enough, but sometimes you need to see the entire interaction for context.

Table 6 - Details to help you reproduce the problem in your application

Understanding what the attack did is critical. You must understand the attack in order to reproduce the problem. People new to vulnerabilities may find this step difficult at first, but it is a valuable learning opportunity.

The next step is key: how easy is it to understand what the scanner tells you? Can you reproduce the problem? Would you be able to describe it to a developer? Making sense of the findings is not as hard as it may initially seem. I will demonstrate with three examples of problems ZAP found in the Mutillidae site.

4.3 First Example: Path Traversal

Table 7 lists the most useful details from a ZAP report of a path traversal problem. *Path traversal* occurs when a malicious person invents URLs to request files that should not be accessible. An improperly configured server may return files that are not meant to be part of the web site's content.

Item	**Description**
Alert Name	Path Traversal

URL	http://10.133.1.4/mutillidae/index.php?page=%2Fetc%2Fpasswd
Risk	High
Parameter	Page
Attack	/etc/passwd
Evidence	root:x:0:0

Table 7 - Details ZAP provided about a path traversal vulnerability

In this particular case the scanner says it manipulated a parameter called *Page*, crafted an attack value of */etc/passwd*, and found in the response evidence that the attack had succeeded. The evidence is the string *root:x:0:0*. Readers familiar with Linux may find that report perfectly clear. In case you do not, here is what happened.

The browser encountered a URL with a query string value named *page*. This was the original URL:

https://10.133.1.4/mutillidae/index.php?page=login.php

The scanner tried replacing *login.php* with the name of a different file. It requested a well-known Linux operating system file that has nothing to do with any web server:

http://10.133.1.4/mutillidae/index.php?page=/etc/passwd

And of course in HTTP special characters such as slashes must be HTML-encoded, so the actual attack the scanner sent to the server looked like this:

http://10.133.1.4/mutillidae/index.php?page=%2Fetc%2Fpasswd

To reproduce the problem, paste the attack URL into the browser. Instead of rendering the login page, the browser renders the contents of the /etc/passwd file where Linux stores information about system users (see Figure 1.) Obviously the scanner has indeed found a real vulnerability in the Mutillidae site. It also provided enough information to reproduce the problem and create a defect report.

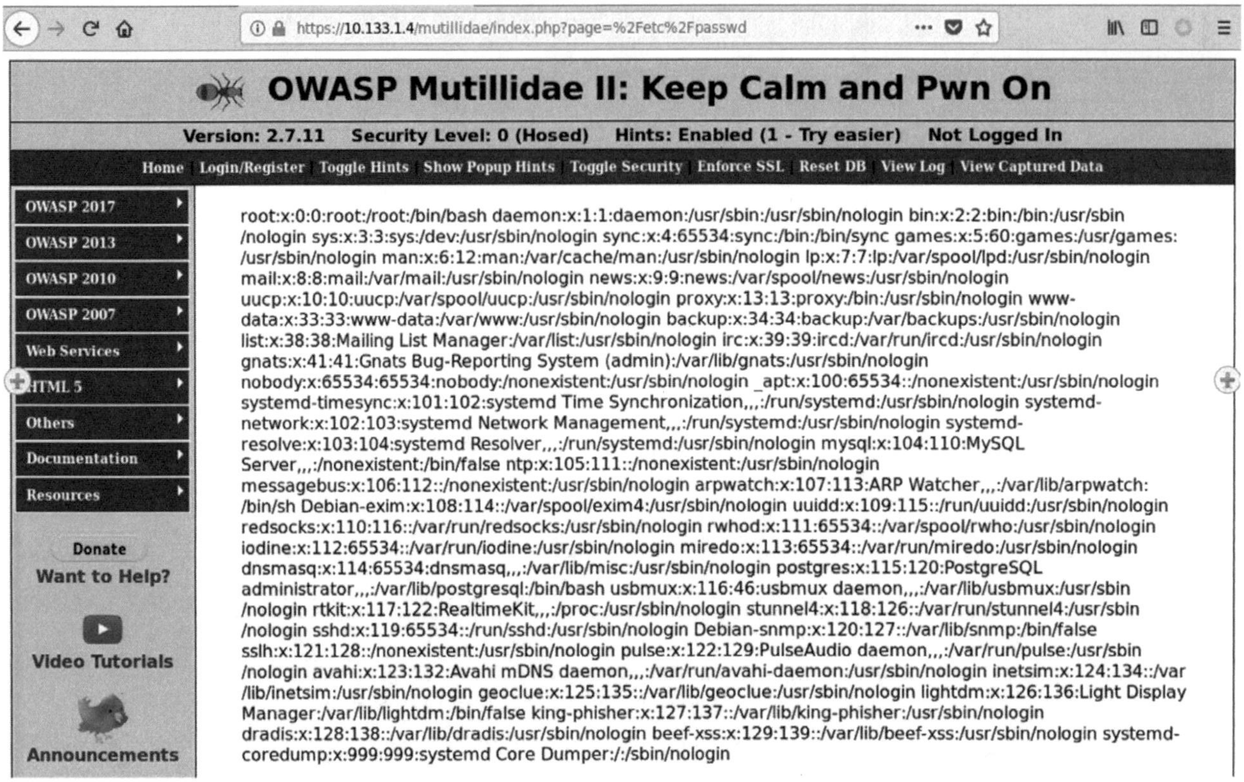

Figure 1 - The result of a path traversal attack in a vulnerable website

4.4 Example Two: A False Positive

Most scanners are not 100% accurate. They sometimes draw your attention to things that are not really problems.

Item	Description
Alert Name	Session ID Cookie Accessible to JavaScript
URL	http://10.133.1.4/mutillidae/index.php?page=register.php
Risk	Medium
Parameter	showhints
Attack	cookie field: [showhints]
Other Info	session identifier cookie field [showhints], value [1] may be accessed using JavaScript in the web browser The url on which the issue was discovered was flagged as a logon page.

Table 8 - Details ZAP provided about an allegedly insecure cookie

The scanner noticed in the HTTP REQUEST a cookie value that lacked an httponly attribute:

Cookie: showhints=1; PHPSESSID=rpiq3oo77e7rssp2gbjv6gfus2

There are in fact two cookies on this line—showhints and PHPSESSID—and neither one has the httponly attribute. The alert for the showhints cookie is wrong: showhints is not a session identifier. It is a flag governing a minor behavior in the user interface. It is true that the showhints cookie could be accessible to malicious JavaScript, but the cookie setting does nothing sensitive: it just turns on or off the display of hints in the user interface. You can safely ignore this alert.

(The ZAP scanner also generated the same warning for the other cookie, PHPSESSID. *That* alert is valid. PHPSESSID is indeed a session identifier and should have the httponly attribute.)

4.5 Third Example: SQL Injection

In this last example ZAP is reporting something more complicated: a SQL injection vulnerability. (If you are not already familiar with SQL Injection you can easily find documentation on the web[1].)

Item	Description
Alert Name	SQL Injection
URL	http://10.133.1.4/mutillidae/index.php?page=login.php
Risk	High
Parameter	username
Attack	brian' AND '1'='1' --
Other Info	The page results were successfully manipulated using the boolean conditions [brian' AND '1'='1' --] and [brian' AND '1'='2' --]

Table 9 - Details ZAP provided about a SQL injection vulnerability

The URL is the site's login page, and the attack involves a parameter called *username*. ZAP has attacked by submitting unusual values for the user name when logging in. The *Other Info* section says that the attack actually involved *two* attempts to log in, not just one:

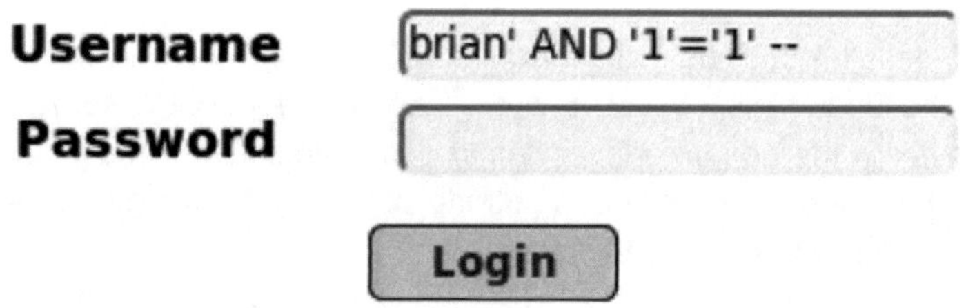

Figure 2 - The first part of ZAP's attempt to find a SQL injection vulnerability

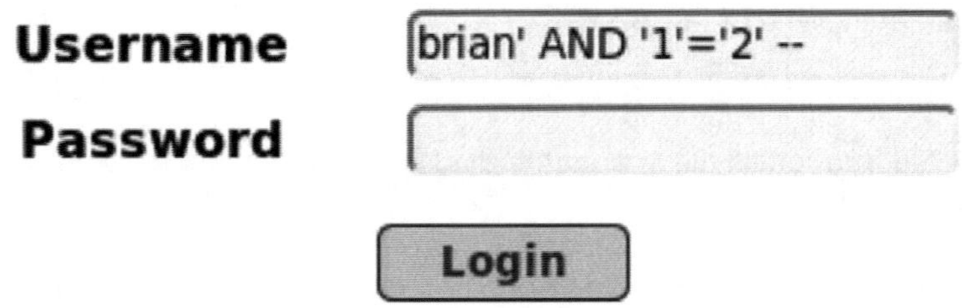

Figure 3 - The second part of ZAP's attempt to find a SQL injection vulnerability

Of course the site has no users with names like *brian' AND '1'='2' --* . Both logins should fail for the same reason: no such user exists. The scanner tries both logins, compares them, and notices that in fact they do *not* produce the same result. The fact that the results differ strongly suggests one of those inputs altered the semantics of some SQL statement on the back end. No user should be able to do that!

Attempting to reproduce the scanner's SQL injection attack in the Mutillidae site reveals that the first post actually succeeded in logging in with no error message at all! (If you try this, be sure to include the final space after the two hyphens for each input. The presence of the space is not obvious in the screen shots, but you can see it clearly in the *Other Info* field where the space appears between the last hyphen and the right square bracket: "--]".)

4.6 Risk Ratings

The scanner did not understand that the first POST produced a successful login. The scanner reached its conclusion solely from noticing that the results of the two POSTs differed. It does not try to determine how a hacker might exploit a flaw, only that a flaw exists. Understanding how much damage a hacker might do with that flaw in your particular site would be very useful, but it is beyond the capacity of a scanner to determine. ZAP rated the SQL Injection risk High because SQL injection often results in serious problems such as exposed data, not because on this particular page the attack achieved an unauthorized login.

Knowing the actual danger in your site would help in assessing risk and prioritizing work, but accurate assessments generally require knowledge of how hackers work. Experienced development teams may well be able to determine that the actual risk in their own site is lower (or higher, but more often lower) than the scanner's rating. Without that kind of experience, though, the best indicator is the risk level assigned by the scanner.

In this case the scanner is certainly right: this SQL injection is a high-risk defect.

4.7 Gaining Expertise

People new to application vulnerabilities may find their first scanner report daunting. It's full of phrases like *Path Traversal*, *SQL Injection*, *Information Disclosure*, and *Cross Site Scripting*. But as with many things in software development, hard tasks become much easier when you take small steps and iterate. The scanner helps immensely: it produces a prioritized list of security topics that would be worthwhile to learn because they are relevant to *your* web application. This is a great way to begin learning more about application security. Pick the scanner findings up one at a time in order. Take whatever time you need to learn the first one, and then go on to the next. Maybe each item takes a day, or maybe a week. Research each new vulnerability until you can make sense of the scanner's attack report and reproduce the problem for developers. Any speed, even a slow one, counts as progress. Your expertise increases item by item.

Lots of resources are available to explain vulnerabilities: web sites, forums, videos, meetups—I'll list some in the Resources section at the end of this paper.

4.8 Am I Invulnerable Now?

Suppose you have worked through all the scanner findings and fixed every reported issue. Does that mean your site has no vulnerabilities?

Unfortunately, no. It means only that the site has none of the vulnerabilities the scanner knows how to find. Not all vulnerabilities are easily discovered by a script. Some are too complex for easy scripting. Some involve non-deterministic behavior. Some are newly discovered or not well known. And some are in the infrastructure—the network and servers—not the application.

But addressing scanner findings certainly makes an application harder to hack. It means you have at least avoided a set of common, well-known problems. That is a worthwhile accomplishment. And along the way you may derive other benefits as well, as I'll suggest next.

5. Managing Vulnerabilities

I hope at this point you are convinced that with a manageable amount of effort you can download a scanner, get results for your application, and turn the results into actionable work items. If you continue to scan periodically, to understand the findings, and to work with your teams to fix them, you will be doing more than fixing vulnerabilities. You will also be:

- making yourself more knowledgeable about security—which was, I imagined at the start, one of the motivations that might draw you into an effort like this.

- spreading knowledge by drawing your team into conversations leading to fixes. A more informed team should produce fewer vulnerabilities to start with.

And with that effort you are beginning influence your team's approach to quality. But you can go further. With just a little more effort you can turn what you have already started into a *vulnerability management program*. The goals of a management program include:

- ensuring the vulnerabilities are found and fixed systematically
- monitoring progress to see how you are doing and where you can improve
- creating an audit trail so you can prove to customers and auditors that you are doing the right things

The center of a vulnerability management program is a document—perhaps a working agreement on a wiki—in listing actions a team will take in order to accomplish those goals. Be sure to say who is responsible for performing each action and when they will do it.

Here's an example:

> **Working Agreement for Vulnerability Management**
>
> **Purpose**
>
> This procedure ensures that the software development team systematically eradicates risky vulnerabilities from their code.
>
> **Process**
>
> 1. QA must run a vulnerability scan at least monthly and save scan reports in a shared folder.
> 2. QA must create stories for any items that in their judgement merit a High or Critical severity rating.
> 3. Developers must triage Critical items within one business day and High items within one week.
> 4. Teams will prioritize triaged vulnerabilities appropriately for the risk each represents.
> 5. QA will call a quarterly meeting to review vulnerability activity with management.
>   - The meeting will evaluate progress and consider improvements.
>   - The report and notes for each quarterly meeting will be saved in the shared folder.

Figure 4 - An example of a vulnerability management procedure

Adjust the frequency of activity and the severity thresholds to suit your situation. This agreement allows teams to override the scanner's decision about severity if their investigation determines that in their website the vulnerability introduces more or less risk that the scanner's generic estimate. And importantly, the agreement results in *artifacts of compliance*—evidence to show auditors. Artifacts include:

- the working agreement (auditors like written procedures)
- saved scan reports to show the scans were run with the expected frequency
- defect reports to prove that risky findings were processed and resolved
- quarterly reports to prove the team is monitoring progress and adjusting as necessary to get the best results

If your efforts haven't received attention from management yet, maybe they will when you start reporting on the quantity and severity of vulnerabilities found over time. You can look for patterns in the results. Are we more secure this month than we were last month? Are certain code areas more prone to vulnerabilities than others? Why? Do certain types of vulnerabilities occur more often? If so, perhaps it's time for a brown-bag presentation on how teams can avoid falling repeatedly into a particular trap.

6. Awareness and Training

As a team gains experience finding and fixing vulnerabilities they generally make choices about how to solve certain common problems within their own codebase. They may choose particular defenses for session fixation or cross-site request forgery. They may build a library of regular expressions for validating user input. They may make decisions about what error messages should or should not say. Start recording these decisions on your wiki, and you have a *Secure Coding Guidelines* document for the team to follow.

Share the *Secure Coding Guidelines* with new team members. And now that we are talking about onboarding, maybe new team members should also view YouTube videos about common vulnerabilities to ensure that everyone starts with at least a basic understanding of what vulnerabilities are and why they matter. Training and guidelines become part of your vulnerability management strategy.

By now we have gone much farther than you might have imagined when I first talked about running a scanner: you have a team of people trained to find vulnerabilities; practices agreed and documented for producing secure code; a vulnerability management program that produces quantifiable reports to identify trends and improve processes; and training to ensure that new team members are capable of participating in your security process.

7. Next Steps

We have accomplished much, but vulnerability management is only one piece of a complete security program. Security has a place in every phase of the product development lifecycle, as Table 10 suggests.

Lifecycle Phase	**Security Activities**
Initiation and Requirements	· Identify security requirements along with functional requirements.
Design	· Identify security risks and consider possible ways to reduce risk. (Look up *threat modeling* for help here.) · Identify use cases and abuse cases to drive requirements. · Evaluate third-party libraries for security and reliability.
Implementation	· Follow *Secure Coding Guidelines.* · Do code reviews. · Write test plans that include security requirements. · Write unit tests that include security requirements. · Run scanners (static, dynamic, third-party, and network) · Integrate automated tests with the CI/CD pipeline. · Ensure only approved changes are deployed to Production.
Operations/Maintenance	· Manage vulnerabilities. · Monitor site activity for potentially malicious behavior. · Patch out-of-date software.

Disposition	· Remove code that is no longer needed. Reduce the attack surface. · Periodically purge data that is no longer need. Hackers can't steal what isn't there.

Table 10 - Security activities appropriate to each phase of a software development lifecycle

8. Summary

At the beginning I promised to show how QA can take a leading role in initiating a key part of any security program: vulnerability management. Even with no budget and little security experience you can run a free vulnerability scanner to get a prioritized list of things to learn and fix. This is a great way to start improving both your product's security and your own professional expertise.

To review, these are the basic steps:

1. Talk to team members informally about exploring what a scanner uncovers. Be sure they're willing to participate.
2. Choose a scanner such as ZAP. Run it on your web application.
3. Pick the most important vulnerability in the report and learn about it. When you understand it well enough to create a defect report from the scanner results, move on to the next finding.
4. As the team begins working on fixes together, invite them to think about how to avoid introducing similar vulnerabilities in the future. Record on a wiki page whatever defenses you agree on. This becomes the *Secure Coding Guidelines*.
5. Ask the team how often they want to run the scanner and what kinds of problems they will commit to fixing. Capture those decisions in a working agreement.
6. When new people join the team, be sure they know at least as much as you do about vulnerabilities. If they don't, train them.
7. Periodically, perhaps quarterly, review the scanner results and defect reports to identify progress and problems.
8. If your business is regulated (by HIPAA or PCI, for example), or if you have customers who sometimes want to audit your security practices, be sure the working agreement includes creating records of ongoing vulnerability management efforts—scanner results, bug reports, and notes from periodic reviews.

Talk to management and engage their support for automating parts of the security work and integrating it with the build pipeline. As you gain experience with multiple types of vulnerabilities, bring that knowledge into design discussions. One new testing tool can be the first step in creating a culture of quality and security.

Resources

Criteria for Evaluating Vulnerability Scanners

Black, Paul E.; Elizabeth Fong; Vadim Okun; and Romain Gaucher. 2007. *Software Assurance Tools: Web Application Scanner Functional Specification Version 1.0.* NIST Special Publication 500-269. National Institute of Standards and Technology (NIST).

Chen, Shay. 2012. "A Step-by-Step Guide for Choosing the Best Scanner." InfoSec Island. http://www.infosecisland.com/blogview/21926-A-Step-by-Step-Guide-for-Choosing-the-Best-Scanner.html (accessed August 14, 2019.)

Filkins, Barbara. 2017. *Asking the Right Questions: A Buyer's Guide to Dynamic Scanning to Secure Web Applications.* A SANS Whitepaper.

Web Application Security Consortium. 2009. "Web Application Security Scanner Evaluation Criteria." http://projects.webappsec.org/w/page/13246986/Web%20Application%20Security%20Scanner%20Evaluation%20Criteria (accessed August 14, 2019.)

Comparisons of Vulnerability Scanners

Chen, Shay. 2017. "Evaluation of Web Application Vulnerability Scanners in Modern PenTest/SSDLC Usage Scenarios." http://sectooladdict.blogspot.com/ (accessed August 14, 2019.)

InfoSec Institute. 2019. *14 Best Open Source Web Application Vulnerability Scanners.* https://resources.infosecinstitute.com/14-popular-web-application-vulnerability-scanners/ (accessed August 14, 2019.)

Upguard. 2019. "Arachni vs OWASP ZAP." https://www.upguard.com/articles/arachni-vs-owasp-zap (accessed August 14, 2019.)

Vulnerability Scanners Discussed in This Paper

Arachni Web Application Security Scanner Framework
https://www.arachni-scanner.com/

OWASP Zed Attack Proxy Project (ZAP)
https://www.owasp.org/index.php/OWASP_Zed_Attack_Proxy_Project

Scan My Server
https://scanmyserver.com

w3af Web Application Attack and Audit Framework
http://w3af.org/

Wapiti
http://wapiti.sourceforge.net

Vulnerable Websites Mentioned in This Paper

Mutillidae
http://www.irongeek.com/i.php?page=mutillidae/mutillidae-deliberately-vulnerable-php-owasp-top-10

OWASP Juice Shop Project
https://www.owasp.org/index.php/OWASP_Juice_Shop_Project

Help Understanding Vulnerabilities

DevCentral, a technology community sponsored by F5, has posted talks on YouTube describing common web application vulnerabilities.

https://www.youtube.com/user/devcentral

https://devcentral.f5.com/s/

Hacksplaining is a training project sponsored by Netsparker. The Hacksplaining site has free visually appealing animated online explanations of common vulnerability types. https://www.hacksplaining.com/lessons

OWASP local chapters. The Portland chapter meets monthly for networking and presentations. Anyone is welcome to attend. Here you can find people to talk to about application security issues. Look for meeting announcements on Meetup.

https://www.owasp.org/index.php/Portland

https://www.meetup.com/OWASP-Portland-Chapter/

OWASP Top Ten – 2017: The Ten Most Critical Web Application Security Risks. 2017. This PDF from The Open Web Application Security Project has a page for each of the top ten vulnerability types. Each page has a short explanation of the vulnerability along with information about the risk it represents, how it can be exploited, and sources of further information.

https://www.owasp.org/images/7/72/OWASP_Top_10-2017_%28en%29.pdf.pdf

https://www.owasp.org/index.php/Category:OWASP_Top_Ten_Project

Udemy has several inexpensive courses on web application security.

https://www.udemy.com/course/web-application-security/

https://www.udemy.com/course/web-application-security-for-absolute-beginners-no-coding/

---

[1] For example, the Hacksplaining site (sponsored by NetSparker) has good visual explanations for a number of common vulnerability types including SQL injection: https://www.hacksplaining.com/lessons.

Testing AI and Bias

Jason Arbon
test.ai

Abstract

Testing the functionality of AI-based features and systems is a whole new world. Bias in AI systems is an even newer and more important aspect of testing modern AI products. The world is awash with AI-based features, the question is how can we test these features and ensure they are high quality? Perhaps more importantly, how can we ensure these products don't have an undesirable bias.

Jason Arbon shares learnings from testing the relevance and bias in some of the most popular and important AI-based software services today such as Microsoft Bing and Google search. Jason shares tips on testing AI-based systems in the stages of gathering training data, training processes and productization. Make sure you are on the leading edge of testing techniques in a world of AI and ensure your product doesn't suffer avoidable gaffes. This is a nerdy, but important, topic as the scope of testing increases dramatically with the introduction of AI.

Biography

Jason Arbon is the CEO at test.ai where the mission is to test all the world's apps. Google's AI investment arm lead test.ai's latest funding round. Jason previously worked on several large-scale products: web search at Google and Bing, the web browsers Chrome and Internet Explorer, operating systems such as Windows and ChromeOS, and crowd-sourced testing at uTest.com. Jason has also co-authored books such as *How Google Tests Software* and *App Quality: Secrets for Agile App Teams*.

Arbon Published by:

Test.ai

Bias: "prejudice in favor of or against one thing, person, or group compared with another, usually in a way considered to be unfair."
- Google

As our world increasingly depends on AI-based software, our engineering focus needs to broaden from avoiding bugs to understanding bias. These AI systems are already controlling our cars, diagnosing diseases, influencing the legal system, and influencing the information we are exposed to. Biases in these critical systems can not only produce incorrect results but can also make unethical decisions. We can't blame the AI because it is *us* who are training and enabling these biases. In this new world of software engineering, we have engineers who don't truly understand bias on one side, and on another we have testers who don't truly understand machine learning. In short, we need to understand these issues and add new tools and techniques to ensure a safe and ethical world.

In this discussion, we will investigate bias in the software, specifically AI systems. We'll walk through where biases can appear and how to minimize unwanted bias across the following major stages of building these AI-powered apps:

- **Stage 1:** Training Data
- **Stage 2:** Training Processes
- **Stage 3:** Productization

We'll use real world examples from web search engines to illustrate bias. We picked these examples because most people are familiar with what search engines do and most people agree that they shouldn't be biased. I also happen to have intimate experience testing the world's most well-known search engines and will share some of those stories.

Spoiler Alert: It's Not Possible to Eliminate Bias

If you remember just one thing, remember that it's not possible to eliminate bias**.** There will *always* be bias in an AI system. This is because there is always bias in the training data that AI learns from. Most people want to eliminate all bias. However, that is not possible and is also unnecessary because not all bias is bad. The term *bias* is typically used to suggest some AI system is negatively biased against a particular group of people. As we'll see, AI can also be biased in constructive ways toward different groups of people or situations.

You may wonder if there is truly such a thing as an unbiased training set. An unbiased training set would be random noise where AI would learn nothing. In other words, you can't train an AI system with random noise. The moment a human or machine selects data to train with, bias has entered the picture. Even if the human is ethical, intends well, and is super smart, there are still many sources of bias that are introduced at every point along the way.

AI-based software systems reflect the biases of their makers and their environment. Although it's impossible to eliminate all bias, our job is to understand the biases that exist and then minimize the unwanted ones.

Not Familiar with AI?

If you're not familiar with AI, think of AI as a student at school. Much like a teacher selects the books and tests used to teach students, AI engineers select the training data and models to teach AI systems. But unlike actual students, AI will learn and take a test hundreds (or even millions) of times until it gets it 'right'. With enough data, the AI will almost always get it right on average.

So, if our training data is correct and ethical, will AI be correct and ethical too? Nope. If our training data is 'bad', will AI also be 'bad'? Yes. Even the most well-intentioned teachers and engineers have their own biases, and it leaves an impression on the student's and AI's brains.

In practice, there are three major types of AI:

1. *Supervised learning* - Supervised learning closely matches the teacher/student model, as the teacher is supervising the training material and testing process. The vast majority of commercial deployments are supervised learning.

2. *Reinforcement learning* - Reinforcement learning is more like the reward and punishment used to train a new puppy. You can easily extend the lessons here to the rewards of reinforcement learning. By definition, the bias in training data (or rewards) will result in bias in the AI system.

3. *Unsupervised learning* - Unsupervised learning is a branch of AI where the machine organizes, or clusters, information based on its similarity without using training data. This may sound like a less biased way to build AI, but the selection of the data to train on, and even the interpretation of the data still invite many opportunities for bias to creep in.

All three major branches of AI and machine learning suffer from many of the biases that we will discuss in this document.

Stage 1: Training Data

The first stage in building your AI-powered app is acquiring the right training data. This is actually a group of steps that involve:

1. Sourcing data
2. Sampling data
3. Labeling data
4. Defining training sets

Sourcing data refers to acquiring the data set to train your app on. Sampling data means picking which specific examples from the data set to train on. Labeling is the process of applying tags to sample data for use in machine learning models. Defining training sets refers to identifying which labeled data samples will be used for training, testing and validation. Even at these early stages, bias is already introduced in each of these steps.

Bias in Sourcing

One of the biggest challenges in training an AI system is sourcing data. Imagine that you are tasked with building an AI-powered search engine. There are two types of data needed to train an AI-based search engine: search queries and websites. Our AI needs to learn how to match search queries to the best websites. A logical way to get website data is to build a web crawler that indexes as many pages as it can find on the web. It's here that we see our first bias challenge. Web crawlers find websites by starting at one site and then following all the links on the page, and then every link on those linked pages, and so on. We might be able to get millions of web pages indexed, but ask yourself:

Where did the web crawler start?

The web crawlers probably started on popular, top websites. Given that the web crawlers only find millions of the possible billions of websites, there is now a bias in the data set towards top web sites. Many of those unpopular, unlinked websites that weren't found are left out of the data set, which means the AI can't learn from them. The resulting AI-based search engine will only be learning from the most well-formed and well-written websites. The search engine will not be learning how to deal with less popular and possibly poorly written, misspelled pages with broken or malformed HTML code in them.

But what if we had *all* the web pages?

Can we address this bias by applying more data? Many engineers are tempted to build a better web crawler to find all those tiny websites. That *could* relieve some bias, but there are a few problems with this approach. By definition, you can't actually know if you have crawled the entire web, because you don't know what you don't know. If you did, you'd know about it. There are also technical reasons why you can't actually crawl all websites. For example, many web pages are behind a login, or a paywall, or on private corporate or government web servers, not linked at all, or will even tell the web crawler not to view them. Therefore, our data set is only going to be comprised of publicly available, accessible web sites.

Even with a truly complete data set, you cannot eliminate all bias. There are socio-economic and demographic factors that are inherently part of all data. If we magically did have all of the world's web pages, you'll still find that most websites are written in English. That the richest countries produce more web pages per-capita. That democratic countries produce more web pages. Even if every demographic bias was somehow adjusted for, the AI learns from the average of all the data. As most humans aren't average, bias creeps in again because the outliers don't get much of a vote in how the search engine AI will be trained.

While it may seem that we're attempting to solve an impossible problem, our job is to acknowledge the bias and understand it. We need to ask ourselves: *Is this an OK form of bias?* and *Do we understand how bias will manifest itself in our app?*

You might say that this bias is OK because the best results will probably come from top web pages. Or you might think this is concerning because the search engine will have a bias for commercial sites and a bias against sites from underfunded, non-technologists. Do we deliberately seek out these less-connected web sites? How do we know when we have enough of them? Determining if these biases are acceptable, or even preferable, is actually up to you.

Did You Know? MSN in the 90s

In my previous life, I had the opportunity and privilege to contribute to Microsoft's MSN search engine. This was one of the early search engines born in the 1990's. At MSN, we had a dominant position as the default search engine in most of machines around the world. With this market position, you would think we'd have a lot of great training data. But since you have read this far, I'm sure you already know that is likely a wrong assumption and you are already starting to see problems.

Where are all those search queries coming from? If we think about it, we might think the bias is OK because our operating system is the dominant desktop operating system so our query samples are coming from all sorts of different demographics and locations. Wrong. The people who were using MSN Search back then were people that either weren't aware of Google, didn't know how to change their search engine default, or as we found out later, thought MSN search results were actually Google search results. (At that time, almost every engineer at Microsoft was using Google as their default search engine.) Given that our queries are coming from these people, there was a new bias we are feeding to the AI. The bias was toward lower-income, lower-education, located in the Midwest of the country. We were training AI to be great at search queries for this demographic, but not other demographics such as engineers, doctors, lawyers, etc.

We might look at this and say one of two things. One, this bias will deliver subpar results to knowledge workers and this is a bad bias. Or two, this bias is OK because we are making a search engine positively biased toward the very people that are using our search engine, and therefore are more likely to be able to monetize queries. There is a bias, but determining if it is good or bad is sometimes also a business decision.

Myth: I Should Source Production Data

Machine learning engineers often want to train on the data gathered in production, but this can introduce additional unintended bias and should only be done with great care. In the world of search engines, an example of this is click-through data. Most search engineers and average search engine users believe that you can simply rate search results higher if they are clicked more often by the search engine users. There are a few problems with this. One, this data is biased by your user demographics. More importantly though, humans semi-trust the search result ordering, so they are far more likely to click an irrelevant search result at the top versus the best result if it occurs at position six. There are ways to try and get around this positional bias problem, but they are fraught with bias themselves and can be very expensive to run. A naive way to do this is to have many different flights so that your users get the results in a

randomized order to remove the positional bias. This means we have deliberately added random bias to the results for many of our production users. Many queries (some 15%) are unique and many more have only been executed a few times. Training with this clickthrough data biases the engine for doing better on frequent queries and likely worse on infrequent queries. It is tempting for engineers to use their production data, but it needs to be done carefully to avoid inadvertent bias loops in the training and productization process.

Bias in Sampling

Sampling is the process of picking examples in your data set to train on. There are many different ways to sample data, and of course, many different ways bias can creep in.

Say we needed 50,000 queries to train the AI (any more doesn't improve the system, takes more time to train, and reaches a point of diminishing returns). As a search engine, you have millions of searches happening each day. What if we picked a single point in time and took the last 50,000 search queries? What bias have we introduced? If 50,000 search queries happen every hour, and we took our sample of queries between 4pm and 5pm Pacific Time from a random machine in production, we have now introduced a bias based on time of day. People generally search differently (e.g. technical searches) when they are at work versus on the way home from work (e.g. restaurant searches). Since we also picked a single machine, albeit at random, individual machines are often serving different regions of the country, so we also just introduced bias based on location.

To avoid building a search engine that is biased toward time of day, or location, we could take a random sample of queries from a random set of machines in production. From our earlier discussion, we know that this will still be biased based on search frequencies and higher population density regions, but maybe that is OK because our user base also follows these biases. But, we still have a day-of-week bias. If we take the sample on Monday, a weekday, the Monday-based trained-AI probably won't fare as well on the weekend. So we sample from a whole week of data. But was that week a holiday? Was that week in the winter or summer? Was there a major world news event, such as an election?

Sample Randomly

One solution to this problem is to sample randomly. Utilize data from the most recent hour, and mixing in fewer samples from previous times such as last week, even fewer from last month and even last year. That way our sample is at least sprinkled with time-varying bias, with a recency bias, and will probably work well in general, on the average, and not be what is called over-fit to a particular time. That said, the resulting search engine won't be the best weekday search engine, but on average it will be as good as it can be.

Sample Sizes

How do you know if you have enough data? How do you know how much more you need? This question is often very domain-specific. The amount of data required varies widely between different machine learning algorithms. Some are data hungry like deep neural networks while others like reinforcement learning may only need a few examples. Some problem domains have very noisy data, or even data that contradicts itself (aka 'disagreement', 'confusion' or 'entropy') in the training data. Generally, the more variety in possible training values and the more confusion there is in the data set, the more data is needed to train a great AI, and avoid a poorly biased system. For example, if you were teaching a student to identify pictures of cats vs. dogs, you might need a lot of examples as there are a wide variety of dogs and cats. But if you were training an AI to discriminate between a picture of a night sky (mostly black with white stars) and a sky during the day (mostly blue/white), you may not need as many training examples.

For a very simple example of bias due to sample sizing, consider a political poll that only asked 50 people for their opinion. It is very likely several people from large demographics will be included in the poll. But what about the opinion of people that represent 1% of the population? The odds of their opinion being represented in the summary poll can be less than 50%. And, what if we did manage to catch that 1% in the poll? They would be overrepresented in the polling data, being 1/50th of the people polled, which is 2%. Their voice would have twice the weight it should have. To understand the right sample size, the data engineer needs to understand the texture of the data, the underlying differences and frequency of those differences in the data and ensure the sample size is large enough to avoid bias in the sampling.

Remember, the AI algorithms have both the training and test data and can learn and take the test thousands of times during training. The AI training process is continually testing the AI's output against the expected output (test or validation data set), so most AI training processes can tell you precisely how accurate the model is given the training/test and validation data. In addition to giving a % correct, these training systems often also provide a confidence interval and other measures of quality such as a confusion score, records of false-positives and false-negatives, and precision and recall. Often, teams will add more data (or change hyperparameters) to the training process until they see diminishing returns on these scores. For your given application, you need to balance the time it takes to train, the amount of data, and these training results to fit your engineering goals.

Bias in Labelling

Labeling is the process of getting humans, or raters, to look at some output and describe what they see. After applying labels to your data set, you can apply labeled data to machine learning models for training your AI system. It may sound pretty simple in principle, but it is actually far from it in practice.

In labeling, there are two major areas where bias is found:

1. In the labeling process
2. In the raters

Bias in the Labeling Process

In our search engine example, when labeling, the data you would show raters are search queries and possible search results. We'd then ask the raters to rate how good that result is on a scale of 1-10. Let's look at the guidelines Google gives to these people today:

https://static.googleusercontent.com/media/www.google.%20com/de//insidesearch/howsearchworks/assets/searchqualityevaluatorguidelines.pdf.

The guidelines themselves introduce some intentional and possibly unintentional bias. Here are just three biases introduced by the rating instructions:

- **Ads-based Bias:** The guidelines encourage raters to discount web pages that have distracting ads. This biases raters to favor websites by entities like governments or large corporations who don't need to advertise to pay for their costs. The person who has the best content or answer may not be rated highly because they have to have a giant banner ad to pay for their web hosting.
- **Business-based Bias:** You could also even read some accidental business bias into these guidelines. Google, which is a web advertising business, wouldn't serve annoying ads based on their definition, so sites that have Google-powered ads will likely receive a few more page views and ad clicks and that means more money for Google. Whether intentional or not, this type of bias can lead to business and perception issues.
- **Authority-based Bias:** The guidelines instruct raters to prefer websites that are authoritative and from experts. If there are two web pages written about a political topic, one written by a professor, and the other by someone who has first hand knowledge on the topic who is not a professor, Google is essentially asking raters to favor the professor. The rater may interpret

anything as expertise. Perceived expertise might be the fact that the name of the author of the page is well-known, or in their community, or agrees with their position on a topic. Is this bias a good thing in all cases? What about in some cases?

Companies rarely have the money and time to even think about how to test for bias in the labeling process, but it can be done. A great tester and bias investigator will want to see search ratings from people that have or have not received different versions of these instructions and measure how the results of the AI-based search engine performs. The search quality engineer should inspect which search results are affected by different clauses in the instructions, document the variation, and judge if this is a good or bad bias. You can define what a good or bad bias is in terms of the impact on the business, customers, users, and even social impact.

Applied more broadly, exceptional testers will understand the biases inherent in their process and make a judgement on the bias.

Entropy

As you enlist the help of multiple raters, you'll quickly realize that people rarely agree. If you ask the same labeling question to multiple people, you will get multiple answers. One person's best search result may be another's worst. This is called *entropy* in the training data set. The AI wants to learn the best answer, but how can it do that if the training data set conflicts with itself?

This is akin to a teacher giving textbooks that have conflicting versions of history and facts. Rather than risk getting just one person's opinion, data scientists will often generate overlap, which is simply asking more than one person the same question to see how much they agree or disagree.

"Bush"

Let's look at an example I investigated in the past: the search term "bush". If a rater enjoys gardening in the mornings, the rater may justifiably think it obvious that a website describing shrubbery is the best result. If you are over a certain age, have a political bent, or have heard of recent news about one of the two former U.S. presidents, then you might think their Wikipedia pages, or a news article, is the best search result. If you are a fan of alternative music, the website or a music video of a band called "Bush" is the best search result. With this single and simple query, we could get wildly different answers if we asked a few random people what the best website results should be. This happens to be a very common problem when labeling data for training AI systems. Knowing that our training data isn't consistent, there are several bias and correctness issues we need to tackle.

To mitigate bias in the labeling process, we need to:

1. Quantify Entropy
    a. Identify Areas with the Most Variance
    b. Identify Areas with the Least Variance
2. Increase Overlap Where Needed

The first step is to quantify the amount of entropy in the system. We want to understand the areas with the most variance, the least variance, and the distribution. If we don't take this step and decide to pass this data to the AI training system, the AI will be unlikely to get 100% of the tests correct because it will generally average the results. With this step, let's take a look at:

- **Areas with the Most Variance:** In our search engine example, we want to test the queries with the most variance in ratings. If these differences are understandable, have we captured a representative sample of these ratings? On an ambiguous query like "bush", with an overlap of 3, and all three have given us different answers, we need to increase the overlap. Increasing overlap is simply asking more people to rate the results. Maybe there are other interpretations of the best results for "bush" and we haven't found them yet, and that bias is missing in our training set. Maybe there are really only three major opinions on the best results for "bush" and we were lucky to catch all three of them by asking three people at random. But, if we train now, the AI will learn the average of these opinions and equally weight the three opinions. That may sound like a reasonable bias, but with only three ratings, we don't know the relative ratio of biases. If seven out of ten raters think the best results are websites with plants on them, our training data doesn't represent that. We need to get far more overlap in ratings to capture the entropy for this query. You can add more and more overlap until the relative ratios converge to a value. The best mathematical result from this is training data that is biased to popularly held beliefs and suppresses the outliers. But, is this the correct bias?
- **Areas with the Least Variance:** Counterintuitively, you also need to test the queries with the least variance in ratings. On simple, navigational queries such as "CNN", almost every human rater believes https://www.cnn.com is the best answer. You would think we don't need a whole lot of overlap, but it's quite the opposite. Our search engine is going to show at least ten web results for this query. Figuring out what the second and third best results for a query like this requires *more* overlap to discover alternative and minority results such as those for 'Convolutional Neural Networks', a search result only nerds reading this would appreciate. This is another form of bias and whether we address these issues or not is our decision.

Our task is to apply the necessary overlap needed to mitigate entropy. Using benchmarks such as relative ratios are good indicators of how close or far you are from an ideal data set. But because this is often very costly, knowing when enough overlap is enough becomes a balancing act of risk in the bias and the cost of the human labeling data program which can run into the many tens of millions of dollars each year. Since we live in a world with scarce resources, we need to balance the amount of overlap needed versus its financial cost.

Myth: I should clean training data

All too often, well-intentioned data scientists try to clean up the training data thinking *good data in, good data out.* Cleaning up training data is not only another point where bias is introduced, but it is almost always it is a bad idea. Here are some examples:

- ***Misspellings:*** If you look through search queries and find some that are obviously misspelled such as 'buush', or 'CNNN'. Most engineers' instinct is to remove these from the training set or fix the spelling because it might confuse the AI--much like a teacher is likely to hide errata from a textbook so as not to confuse the students. But, in the real world, search queries are often misspelled, and more interestingly, certain types of misspellings are shared across different query strings. Leaving these queries out of the training set introduces a bias toward searchers who spell correctly, making it more difficult for people with lazy typing, learning disabilities, or poor educational backgrounds to find information on the web.

- ***Weird / Rare Data:*** With any form of sampling, strange samples will inevitably show up in the training data. A real-world example is the search for a GUID. It doesn't much matter what that is, but the point is that it can look like garbage data and be tempting to remove from the training set. For example, the query "{72631e54-78a4-11d0-bcf7-00aa00b7b32a}" is a deliberately unique string. If we throw out this example query, we don't provide the AI the data it needs to learn how to rank similar long strings of similar letters and numbers. To some folks, this particular GUID string may be super valuable (computer engineers working on battery systems in this case). If the data looks odd, there is probably a good reason for it; leave it in the training set.

- ***Scientist's Bias:*** It is always tempting for a Data Scientist/Engineer to fix up a bad result. If the training data is 'obviously' wrong, they want to fix it. But, their idea of 'obviously wrong' now introduces more bias, i.e. the bias of this individual scientist who probably has a different view of the world than most humans that will use the AI in production.

- ***Excluding Raters:*** Tendencies to clean or scrub the training data are most dangerous when they are automated or systematized and invisible to the data science team. The task of gathering labels/ratings is often passed to an external vendor and not performed by the data scientist. Vendors will often try to clean up the data to make it look 'good'. This data cleansing can take many forms, from removal of outlier data to the systematic firing of raters who constantly disagree with their peers. Think about your training sets, even publicly available sets--do you know what data was excluded? Perhaps a strange looking cat was excluded from the data set, or the label of what is obviously a dog (but is really a cat) had its label fixed by someone who knew better. Or perhaps, semi-nefariously, someone wanted an improved AI by the metrics and got rid of some confusion from their training or test set. These hidden sources of bias are dangerous in that they are often never noticed. The mitigation here is obvious: control as much of your data sourcing as possible.

- ***Social Pressure:*** Imagine a traditional, functional software engineering company pivoting to data science and building search engines. You can imagine that the small, fragile, search engine team would get pressure from other parts of the organization to 'fix' bugs in the search results. For example, what if you searched for "best search engine" and your competitor showed up at the top of the search results? The AI might have learned that your competitor is a better search engine, but what does a fledgling data science team do when a senior VP complains? Of course, they hard code the correct answer and bypass the AI subsystem. This rarely works out because it reduces user trust in your system for other search queries. It is best not to introduce hard coded bias. The mitigation here is twofold. First, analyze the system code looking for places where hardcoded results might lie (especially in the rendering/UI system). Second, employ psychology. For example, make it easy for people to give feedback and thank them kindly for it. But, since this is just another form of bias, ignore this anecdotal data and stick to statistics and sampling.

Bias in the Raters (Demographics)

Perhaps the most dominant and overwhelming bias introduced into supervised learning systems is the bias inherent in the people doing all that labeling work. The judgements of the people creating all that labeled training data directly influences the resulting AI. The AI-based search engine is effectively trying to mimic the collective wisdom and reasoning of these human raters.

Raters are far from demographically diverse or representative of the users of the search engine. These raters are unsurprisingly all paid the same amount of money for their time. They are paid between $4 and $15 dollars an hour for their work. This means the labeled data is unlikely to match the thinking of a physician, engineer, retired or young person. Moreover, what demographics desire this type of work? Often, they are single parents of multiple children working from home, living in the Midwest. It is a great job because they can tend to their children and work their own hours while making a decent income. But, this means that a very specific demographic bias is training our AI-search engine.

It is often cost-prohibitive and sometimes impossible to get labeled data from the right mix of demographics. It is difficult to imagine even Microsoft or Google being able to afford and find people from highly paid professions such as lawyers, engineers, or scientists willing to do such mundane work. Further, consider that people who cannot see cannot perform these tasks. The practicalities of labeling has significant bias of its own and needs to be understood.

Ironically, this labeler demographic bias may not always be a bad bias. If your search engine was primarily used by and designed to serve this demographic, it might be OK. In practice though, the business wants to attract and monetize more affluent demographics and the engineers want the search engine they work on to be the one they use on a daily basis.

It is also worth noting that this demographic bias in the human labeling may not be as concerning for different applications. In the training of an AI to discriminate cats versus dogs for example, a data scientist could argue that there would be little difference in the bias from the demographics not represented. Some applications might also not be interesting or very-low risk in practice, and not warrant concern.

There are several ways to mitigate the bias stemming from this demographic homogeneity. The most direct way is to systematically ensure that you include the demographic variety that is appropriate by hiring at great expense those underrepresented demographics to perform some labeling. If the labeling activity is infrequent, this might be feasible. At minimum, this data set can be used to test the bias in the system. With data from different demographics, it is possible to check for the amount of disagreement within the larger training set. This can guide directed labeling efforts on the types of queries where there is significant demographic differences. This data can also be used to identify which demographics and queries the search engine does poorly on to understand the basic characteristics of the labeling bias.

Bias in Defining Training Sets

The concept of the test set is taking all the samples that you have to train the AI and splitting them into two different parts: the training set and the testing set. Often a third part called the validation set will be used outside of the training process for additional verification. What happens during AI-training is that the training data is used much like a teacher's book and other materials to teach concepts. The test data is just what it sounds like, which is data that may have been shared in the teaching process but also tests how well the student does with new data or new concepts given their learnings from the training materials. If you have a lousy exam built from poor test data, you'll give A's to the wrong students. The integrity and bias of the test dataset is critical to the training of the AI system.

Apply Random Sampling

Typically, the split between test and training sets is done by random sampling from the data. As with a teacher's tests, this means some test data may be shared with the training set. The importance of this testing is that the student (AI) has learned the concepts and not just memorized the answers. Random selection is interesting because it seems to minimize this bias, or at least is an attempt to do so. Generally speaking, it is best to make sure the test set is as equally a random sample as the training set--it is OK for some test questions to also be in the training data. If queries for "Obama" are very popular, you do want them to also appear in the testing set, not just the training set. But it is important to test that the training and test data are not equivalent to ensure that the test data has a degree of independence from the training set that reflects the variation of queries expected in your production system.

Step 2: Training Process

Now that you've acquired the right data, training is the second stage in building an AI-powered app. AI training systems are composed of many parts, including: feature detection, initial weights, hyperparameters, model updates and quantified precision and recall of the trained system. For our discussion, we'll focus on bias from features.

Generally speaking, machines can't actually see pictures of dogs and cats, let alone webpages. The AI training system can only see numbers in the range of 0 to 1. Training data must be converted into lists of these numbers that we call *features*. Features are the characteristics of a machine learning model that significantly influence its output. In the case of a web page, we might create features such as:

- # Queries in Document: Number of times the query string appears in the document
- % Queries in Document: Percent of words in the document that match the query string
- # Queries in Title: Number of times the query string appears in the Page Title
- % Queries in Title: Percent of words in the title that match the query.
- % Spammy: Percent of raters that think the result might be spam.

Engineers will write features that take the text of a web page and compute the corresponding training values for every training sample. The training process is then simply a loop:

1. Presenting these feature values to a randomly configured model
2. The AI guesses at the correct output value (score between 0-1)
3. That guess is compared to the raters assessment of how good that web result is given the query
4. If the AI guesses incorrectly, it will reconfigure itself for the next try
5. If the AI gets guesses correctly, the AI configuration is reinforced as it is guessing well

After many loops the AI gets smarter and smarter at guessing through small, semi-random changes in the model.

These features were used because they are intuitively good indicators of the quality of the search result, but there are an almost infinite number of features we could have written. The very process of a human (or system in the case of AutoML) deciding which features to use introduces bias in that it decided what aspects of the data the AI can and cannot see.

An often overlooked form of bias can happen when the code that computes the feature values is numerically incorrect. Perhaps the algorithm misses the first word or last word on the page.

Perhaps the math is off and the feature never produces a value greater than 0.00001--this would effectively turn off that feature. The functional code used to generate features for training needs to be extensively tested, much like traditional code. If the AI can't see correctly, it can bias the training of the AI in unexpected ways.

A machine learning engineer's job is to evaluate the quality of the resulting AI and iterate by creating or removing features to help the AI perform better. A well-intentioned machine learning engineer may notice that the AI is performing poorly on pages with pictures of flowers, as the pages have very similar page layouts and very similar looking images of flowers. So she creates a new feature called AveragePageColor(), which looks at all the pixels on the page and determines the average color, and normalizes this to 0-1 values for the training system. She then retrains the AI and gets a better score because the AI can now realize the difference between two flower web pages that differ almost only on the color of the image of the flower.

She has made a better search engine according to the mathematical analysis, but on deeper inspection she should measure which other queries were also affected by this change. It is easy to imagine the AI might have rated other pages better or worse because the AI is now also considering the color of the page, and those need to be inspected for unintentional bias. It is easy to imagine that giving the search engine the ability to see color could lead to additional unwanted, unethical or offensive bias as the AI-engine might now also be able to detect correlations in skin color, or hair color, or clothes on non-flower search queries.

Remember that we have demographic bias in the training data from raters. If those raters have their own bias, and the machine learning engineer writes features that expose the features the raters used for demographic bias, she is enabling the AI to easily reflect those same biases.
Interestingly, the inverse is also true. If the machine learning engineer considered adding a feature for color, but realized that feature might add the possibility of demographic bias, she might choose not to add the feature. The search engine might not be as good at discriminating flowers, but might also be less likely to have unwelcome bias elsewhere!

We can mitigate for this type of feature selection bias by:

- Considering the types of discriminations the feature may enable in the resulting AI
- Proactively analyzing the queries heavily influenced by specific features
- Proactively considering test queries that might reflect even the perception of unwanted bias
- Generating synthetic training data based on variations of existing examples for training to balance the data. This can be very dangerous and add its own bias, so be careful!

The training process also enables engineers to literally add their own initial bias, or *weights*, to the different input features. The machine learning engineers are continually trying to coax the AI to get better by messing around with all these little training bias hints. The hints reflect the intuition, judgement and bias of the engineer resulting in the AI having a heavy bias for color, or spamminess, or any other feature. Care should be taken when adding initial weights to feature inputs in training as the AI might get stuck in a local maximum that directly reflects unwanted bias from the engineer.

A Note on Drift

It is important to note that every new AI training session can result in a search engine with the same overall score but have very different characteristics and biases. This is often called *drift*. Due to inherent randomization in the training process, changes in the training data, training configuration, hyperparameters, etc, each new search engine with the same score might behave very differently on any given query. On average, the two AI's are equally good, but may be better or worse on different types of queries. Today's trained AI engine may be better at acronyms but worse at proper names versus yesterday, but on average it is the same relevance. Today's AI engine may also be better at getting the top result in the top spot, is far worse with results in position 4 and 5, but still have the same net score. For some AI-based applications, consistency may be incredibly important (e.g. medical, legal, financial) and might need a great deal of time spent on identifying drift in the sub-topical behavior of the system.

Stage 3: Productization

The last stage in building an AI-powered app is productization. Ultimately, we build most AI systems for people like us. Whether it's a search engine, medical analytics tool, or autonomous driving system, these AI systems all try to produce the right data. But what really matters is how that data or those predictions are translated into real world user interfaces and actions. We need to understand the bias that exists in the end-to-end user experience.

In search engines, the user experience manifests in a list of search results in a ranked order. People see a list of ten blue links and read these results from top to bottom. We rarely look at results past the fourth one on the web page. On the other hand, machines (and often data scientists) can see all of the results. They can even see when the first result is 10x better than the second. They can see if the first and second results are virtually indiscernible. Some of that context and texture is lost when translating the underlying numbers output by the AI-based search ranker into a simple, clean user interface.

The underlying AI system is only optimized to score each individual website for a given query. The AI isn't smart enough to measure itself from the user's perspective. Rather than rely on the AI's own assessment of its correctness, we need a way to score how well the AI's output is perceived by the user.

Quantifying end-to-end user experience

One simple approach to measure the end-to-end user experience of AI systems that rank (i.e. search engines) is called Normalized Discounted Cumulative Gain (NDCG). It sounds complicated, but for our search engine example, it is simply a mathematical way to quantify the perceived search engine quality to humans using the search engine's user interface. NDCG gives the search engine a score for a search query and set of search results that favors getting the best results at the top of the page. This measurement penalizes the search engine more for getting the top results in the second row than it would penalize the engine for getting the fourth best results in position ten. This encapsulates the understanding that if a *good* but not *best* result is in the top position, many users will never see the best link. It also encapsulates the notion that users rarely get to the results below position four or five. For AI systems, it is important to measure the relevance of the system as it is productized, deployed and factored into the human perception of relevance.

However, be wary that these productized measurements of bias can also add their own bias to the AI system. NDCG doesn't account well for the fact that some queries are informational.

Medical queries are often of this type where the user really wants to read all of the top results, and they are almost all equally relevant. NDCG is optimizing on the assumption that there are right answers and the result positions are exponentially more valuable at the top. Using NDCG as a test for the relevance of the end to end search product, and for deciding which AI-based rankers to deploy into production means there is a bias against informational types of queries.

Bias from performance

Another aspect of end-to-end relevance of the AI-based search engine is reliability. The way search engines often work is a machine receives the user's query, and that machine talks to over a hundred other machines and asks them for the best results they have. These machines are given as little as 100ms to reply back to the querying server and return the merged results to the end user. If the network is slow, or a machine that happens to have the best URL has a functional bug and crashes, the search results might be missing the best URL, dramatically impacting NDCG. It is often important for large scale AI systems to be functionally reliable and performant, or the net relevance of the AI based system can be compromised.

AI Bias and Testing

By now it should be clear that testing AI systems is really the process of identifying, understanding and making a judgement on the bias of these systems. Training AI systems and testing those systems are really one and the same. They are both systematically trying to understand the bias inherent in the system. The testing of AI based systems is just glorified testing and quality work. At Google Search, the AI and machine learning engineers aren't called Software Engineers, or even AI Engineers, they are called Search Quality Engineers. These engineers are constantly running experiments and testing their hypotheses. Most of their time is spent testing and building testing infrastructure and analytic tools.

If you are a functional software tester today and are asked to test an AI system, your primary job will be to identify bias and judge whether it is good or bad. If you are a classic, functional software engineer transitioning to an AI role, much of your new work should be focused on quantifying and managing the bias in the system. Transitioning into an AI role means becoming more of a tester than a standard engineer. Testing in this new world of AI is looking for bias.

Looking for bias in AI systems means testing

While we primarily used a search engine as an example of an AI-powered app, the examples of bias above are generally applicable to most AI software projects. Search is a complex and large-scale project and is vulnerable to most of the biases that smaller systems will also encounter. I ask that engineers working on AI-based projects to consider which of these biases and testing issues should be considered for their own projects.

References

Production experimentation at Bing:
https://blogs.bing.com/search-quality-insights/2013/08/08/large-scale-experimentation-at-bing

Testing at Bing:
https://brendan-regan.com/3-testing-optimization-tenets/

Testing Mobile Software with Machine Learning: An Introduction

Aaron Briel
PinkLion
aaron@pinklion.ai

Chris Navrides
Test.ai
chris@test.ai

Jennifer Bonine
PinkLion
jennifer@pinklion.ai

Abstract

User Interface testing has changed very little since its inception. It is still completely reliant upon knowing the state and actions available on the screen. However, this way of testing is incompatible with current development methodologies such as A/B flighting and dynamic data, as well as variations by test platform. These new methodologies present a significant challenge to the current paradigm in that the current state of the application may not be known. Platform variations contribute to automation framework bloat and test cycle time. This paper demonstrates how Machine Learning can assist in closing the gap by removing reliance on the state of the application and its underlying DOM.

Biography [DS1]

Aaron Briel is a seasoned engineer with over 15 years of experience in development, QA automation, DevOps, cybersecurity, AI and Machine Learning. Applications he built for a Fortune 100 company produced data presented in Congressional hearings to demonstrate post-breach compliance progress. His work in AI started at the University of Minnesota in the early 2000's, where he developed a genetic algorithm capable of generating hip-hop drum sequences. Aaron is currently Chief AI Architect for PinkLion and a graduate student in ML/AI at Georgia Tech.

Jennifer Bonine has been a strategic C-suite advisor for some of the most respected Fortune 100 companies in the areas of technology strategic roadmap, Quality Assurance, organizational development, and change management. She is a well-known speaker, teacher and trainer, keynoting at both national and international technology conferences. Jennifer has held executive level positions at leading development and quality engineering teams for Fortune 100 companies in several Industries. She is currently the CEO of PinkLion.

Chris Navrides has worked in the software automation and testing industries for 10 years at large tech companies such as Google, Microsoft and Dropbox. He holds patents for temporal content selection and entity-based summarization from his work at Google. Chris is currently a Software Engineer at test.ai.

1. Introduction

User Interface (UI) testing was originally developed when applications were far more static and development cycles were on the order of quarters to years. Tests that made assumptions regarding the state of the UI and underlying application were logical at the time. Webpages and applications today, however, are dynamically changing based upon Machine Learning (ML) models determining the optimal items to place on them. An example of this is content customized for users on Amazon. New versions of native applications are released every few weeks filled with A/B experiments.

Test authors and framework designers are having an increasingly hard time writing reliable tests while using technology and techniques developed 15 to 20 years ago. While the introduction of automated testing into the development lifecycle promised to more closely accommodate increasingly agile methodologies, the holy grail of Continuous Delivery has rarely been realized much less sustained.

A traditional automated testing solution relying on the DOM is likely to break when faced with modified content or elements, whereas an AI/ML driven testing solution can demonstrate flexibility. For example, an image-based element classification approach has no dependency on the DOM. Renamed elements with the same images would have no effect on this class of tests, and even visually modified elements might only require a few training iterations.

What if minor details in the flow of a specific validation change? A traditional automated test would likely fail, even with bloated and fragile conditionals. However, an ML-based approach to navigation would intelligently find the correct path to the pertinent location required for the test.

Automated testing must adapt and become smarter in order to meet the business and quality challenges of the modern software development lifecycle. Development of traditional automation solutions is often so time consuming that the final product, once completed, is no longer compatible with the application it was initially meant to test. Maintenance of these frameworks consistently exceeds the release cycle timeline itself, rendering the approach infeasible in the current fast-paced reality of software development. Hard coding all of the possible scenarios to make "intelligent tests" is one approach but is inflexible and doesn't scale. Machine Learning is designed specifically for challenges such as these by offering solutions more compatible with rapid release cycles.

2. What is Machine Learning?

Machine Learning (ML) is a software development technique that allows a program, often called an agent, to generalize about data it has not yet seen. Instead of programming a set of predefined commands, a model or computer brain is trained by presenting the agent with sets of examples or input to learn from. The model essentially provides the agent with confidence percentages for behaviors or actions to take given specific states it is presented with. Using this model allows it to handle both previously seen, and unseen challenges in the future.

2.1 Supervised Learning

The approach of training by providing feedback based on existing examples is known as supervised learning, or function approximation. A simple example might include an image classifier. The supervised aspect of learning consists of the fact that a human provides feedback as to the correctness of the agent's predictions. This feedback could consist of well-labeled training data. The image classification example is relevant to test automation not only for validations but also for element identification. [DS2] An example of image classification is an agent that can classify number images. In training, it is presented with thousands of examples of hand written- numbers with correct labels. Depending on the number of samples, training sessions, and other factors, this can produce an agent that is able to correctly classify well written test samples. (Briel, 2018).

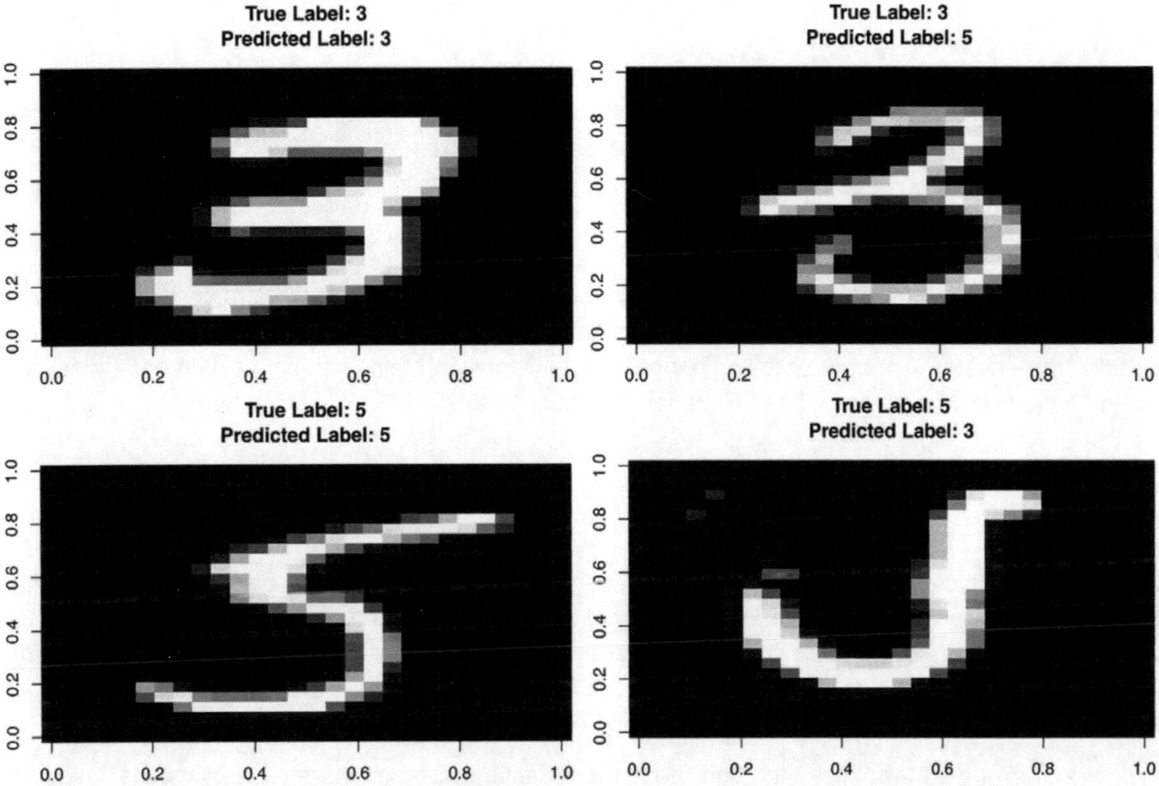

Figure 1: Test samples and predictions given by a number classification agent

2.2 Unsupervised Learning [DS3]

In unsupervised learning the agent only has whatever data is presented to it without any behavioral directives. One popular unsupervised learning technique is called Clustering. Clustering is an exploratory approach to data analysis that allows for the discovery of previously unknown relationships in data. The EM Algorithm is often used as the basis for clustering algorithms, where parameters are estimated to describe an underlying probability distribution when only part of the data produced by the said distribution is observable. Dissimilarity in data objects becomes apparent in Clustering, making it an optimal technique for anomaly detection. This is highly relevant in the testing context, as anomaly detection could be used to discover defects in applications.

Deep Learning has provided many opportunities to explore unsupervised learning. DeepMind, for example, introduced its AlphaZero system that was able to teach itself how to play chess, shogi, and Go, defeating previous world-champion AI applications in the process (Silver, 2018).

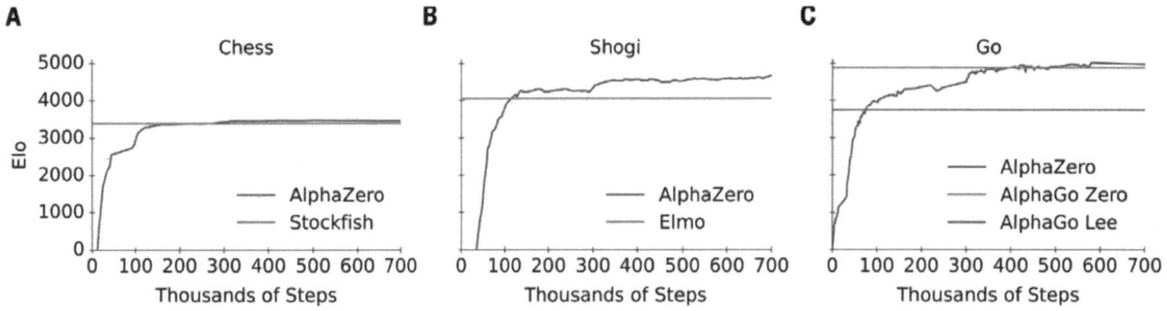

Figure 2: DeepMind's AlphaZero system training for 700,000 steps, showing exponential performance increases after learning occurs

2.3 Reinforcement Learning

Reinforcement Learning (RL) is a hybrid ML approach that can leverage aspects of supervised and unsupervised learning. Constructing a model and optimal behavioral in RL becomes a balancing process of exploring the environment and exploiting rewards. The Q-table contains values for different states, and is updated based on the classic Bellman Equation (Littman, 1996):

$$Q_i(s,\vec{a}) = (1 - \alpha)Q_i(s,\vec{a}) + \alpha[R_i + \gamma V_i(s')] \quad (1)$$

The maximum Q-values for actions and states represent the optimal policy of the agent, or the best action to take given a specific state. A fundamental property of the Q-update function is that the values are updated recursively as the agent progresses through its tasks. A discount factor (*y*) is applied to future rewards, allowing flexibility with respect to how much an agent values immediate versus delayed actions. Introduction of the learning rate (*a*) ensures eventual convergence of the Q-updates.

An example of an agent that uses RL might be a robot vacuum cleaner. As the robot moves a specific distance without hitting an obstacle it might be presented with a positive reward, while hitting an obstacle or staying in place might present it with a negative reward. A reward system in this context might be set up to emulate walking on a hot beach. The agent wants to keep moving around in order to prevent its feet from burning, and stepping on broken glass would teach it to avoid such obstacles in the future.

3. Element Classification

The easiest way to leverage ML models in testing is through element classification. Similar to how a human can look at an app they have never seen before and determine what is a menu button or search button, the same can be achieved by a well-trained ML model. This is something that traditional test automation is simply incapable of achieving because there is no standard naming or app design convention for commonly occurring elements such as search icons and menus. For example, search icons aren't always going to have an ID of "search_icon". In the ML scenario, an image of the page might be broken up into sub-images which constitute element contenders. The human tester may go in and provide feedback on the labels provided to the elements by the agent. Rewards are allocated based on these adjustments and the model is updated appropriately. Over time, the model is able to correctly predict the label to assign to elements it has never seen.

3.1 Shopping cart classifier

To illustrate element classification, we will present an example of the steps that would be taken in building a shopping cart classifier. One would first obtain a significant number of shopping cart images. These will be used to train a model on how to classify the element icon.

A large number of samples is necessary in the data selection process in order to cover the wide range of what constitutes the shopping cart element. An example of the variance encountered includes an empty cart compared to one with items in it, possibly denoted with a number over the top. Other examples needed to increase the diversity of items presented include carts enclosed in a circle and ones with varying background colors. The reason such a wide range of examples is needed is so that the agent is able to generalize and classify cart examples that have not yet been seen. [DS4] Fig. 1 illustrates the extent of diverse cart items that might be considered (Frost, 2019).

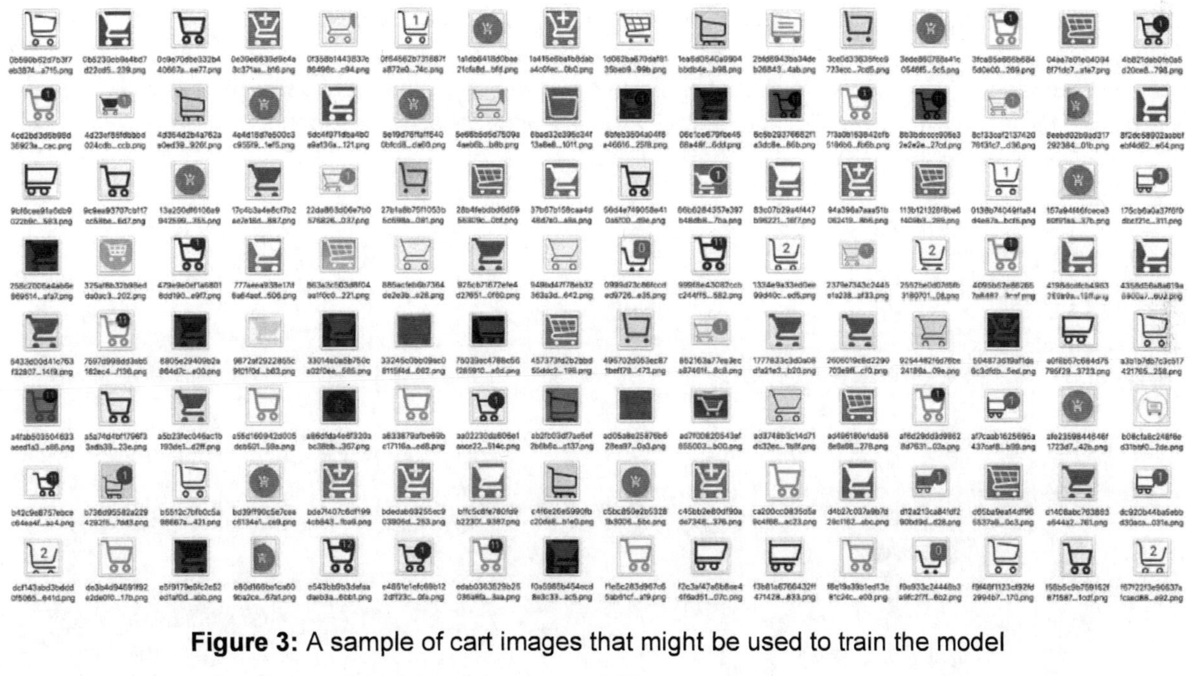

Figure 3: A sample of cart images that might be used to train the model

4. Reinforcement Learning for Exploratory Testing [DS5]

Another area where Machine Learning can augment the testing effort is with exploratory testing. RL [DS6] would be an appropriate contender for this, as it involves a process discussed previously of exploration of the environment. When an RL agent using Q-learning crawls a webpage, it will initially execute random actions leading to exploratory application behaviors. It's Q-table in this case could be populated with page element and action combinations, Actions like 'click' executed on certain elements such as buttons may have a higher reward than a 'swipe' action on a text field, and its Q-table will be updated accordingly.

With respect to element labelling, when an agent crawls an app it may apply some correct and some incorrect labels. When the human tester provides feedback to the agent as to the correctness of its labeling, a strong positive reward is assigned in the cases of elements labeled correctly, while a negative reward is allocated to incorrect labels. Over a few iterations of this training the agent improves its labeling process for subsequent crawls.

This approach can also apply to paths taken by the agent within the application. A strong practical benefit of such an RL approach in test development is that the exploratory phase may lead to testing paths that may have never been considered. Positive rewards can be distributed in the case where the agent discovers novel screens within the application, while negative rewards might be given in situations where progress in discovery has stalled or the agent has browsed to an external application. Situations such as these are analogous to the beach walking example earlier, where the stalling corresponds to standing on hot sand, which browsing away from the app is similar to stepping on broken glass. The fact that the approach provides value in automating a previously expensive human task is a strong ancillary benefit.

5. ML for Testcase Creation

We saw that it is indeed possible for RL-driven exploratory testing to produce novel test flows. It would thus by no means be unrealistic to postulate the feasibility of an agent capable of generating test cases. Along with element classification, another model could contain more abstract information related to common flows of application behavior. Such a system that combines these areas of functionality has indeed been proposed (Santiago, 2018). In this proposal, test flows are modeled as “sequences”, where specific phrases or words can be processed as application behaviors and others constitute elements.

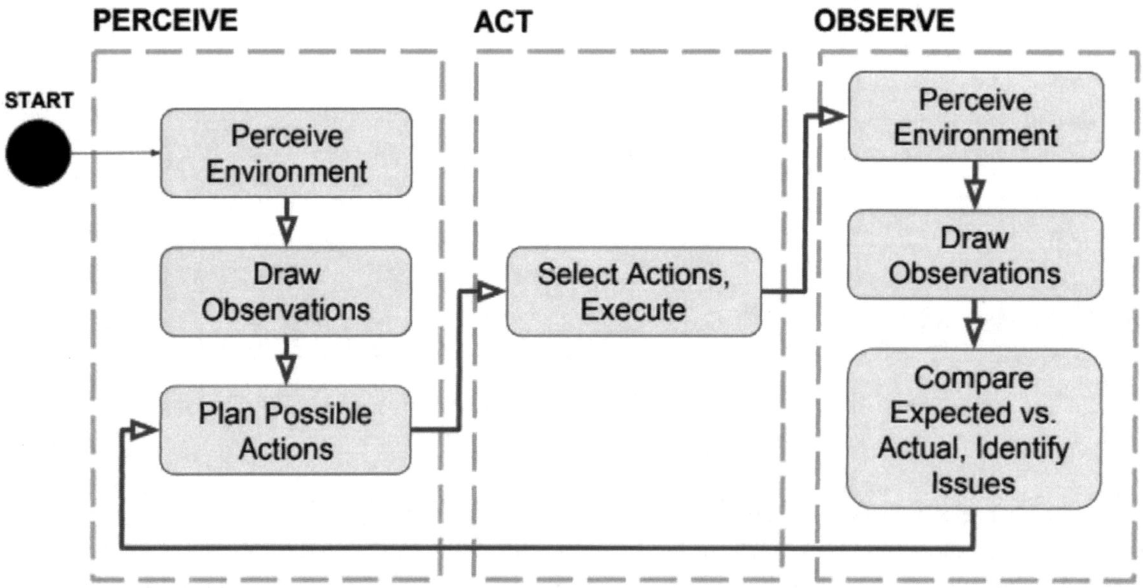

Figure 4: Modeling testing as a sequence or test flow

The elements training discussed previously could occur within a "web classifier" sub-system, with additional human feedback provided to a test flow generator. A grammar module could then convert said flows to a "test generator" that produces executable tests.

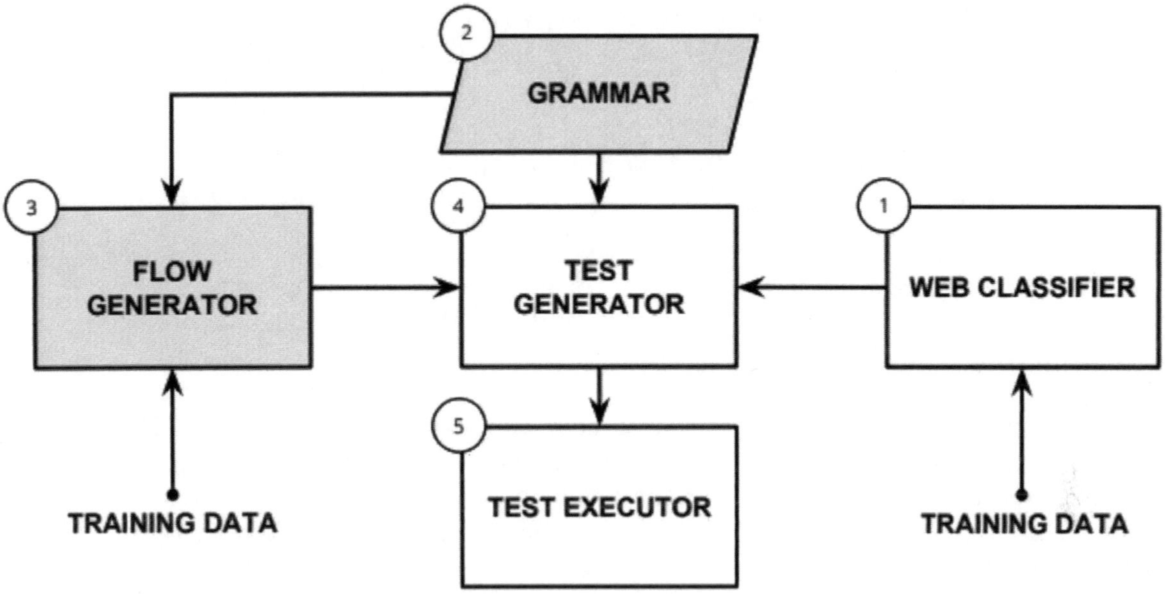

Figure 5: AI driven test generation system

Test cases [DS7] themselves could be simplified to only include validations instead of sequences of prior steps. When a human engineer is asked to test that a guest login page loads, we are not concerned with how she got there. ML presents us with the ability to replicate this human-like behavior, where navigation to a specific page for validation is possible without having to explicitly code all steps it may take to get there – steps which are likely to change and break a traditional automation test. This is illustrated in Fig. 2 and Fig. 3. A traditional automation approach would require conditional logic to deal with the environment loading page and the android-specific popup, while an ML approach would not.

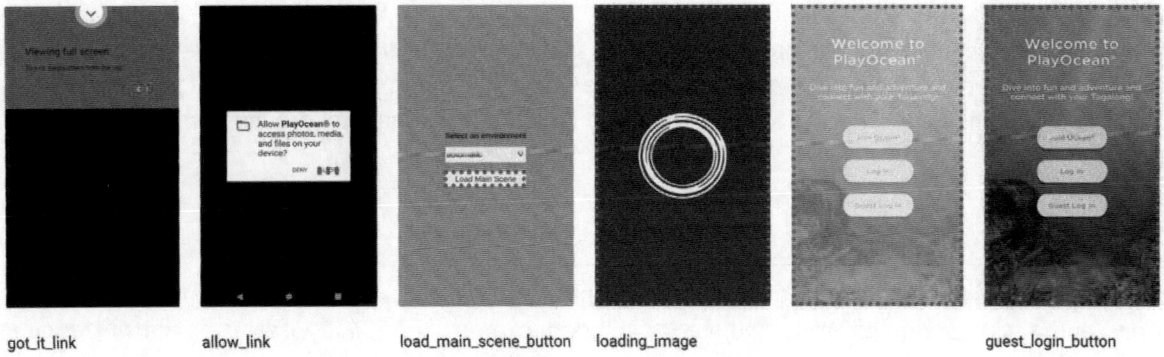

Figure 6: Running a test to validate that the welcome page loads on a certain android device

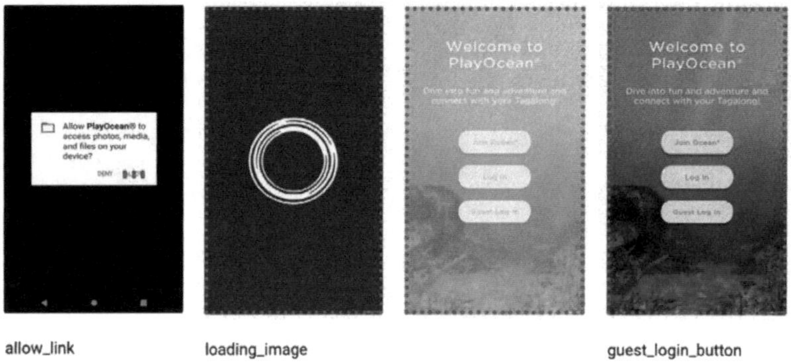

Figure 7: The same test run on a different device and environment

6. ML Solutions in Practice

PinkLion and test.ai have applied the techniques above to thousands of applications. Reinforcement Learning in particular is a technique frequently leveraged, wherein a process called "crawling" is executed, consisting of exploratory testing and element extraction. This is analogous to the initial phase of exploration in RL, where the Q-table is populated with values for actions and corresponding states. Many defects are often discovered in this initial phase, and release dates have frequently been pushed forward as a result of this process, even before any customized test flows have been developed.

7. Challenges and Limitations [DS8] [AB9]

As with any technology there are limitations, problems and challenges. One limitation is that complex use cases still require customized automation flow development. Although test case creation was briefly touched, it is nowhere near the point of being able to capture complete business requirements. A paradigm shift in application testing focused on more granular validations combined with more simplified test case creation may result in a convergent satisfaction of this limitation.

Maintenance and bias can also introduce challenges. If elements change to a point where the model no longer recognizes them, additional training may be necessary. Although this may initially take longer than a minor code modification in a traditional automation script, it could provide an added benefit of making the model more generalizable and adaptable to future element changes.

Finally, it is possible that a human may introduce bias into a model. This bias could be the result of an error in classification. In this case repeated training may be necessary in order for the model to balance itself to the correct classification. This is a small price to pay for the benefits provided by novel element classification.

8. The Future

Industries are disrupted by technological advancements, forcing a change in the way humans are needed. QA and automation are no different, and the rapid introduction of AI and ML into this space will require a paradigm shift in the approaches taken. As applications are ultimately consumed by humans, human input will be needed in their development and testing. ML will first replace the need for automation of menial and repetitive tasks but will eventually evolve to higher level test creation. Human feedback will be needed to guide these systems, although even this might eventually be provided through beta or crowd-sourced behavior analysis.

References

Briel, Aaron. 2018. "Image Classification using Logistic Regression with Stochastic Gradient Descent." https://github.com/aaronbriel/logistic-regression/blob/master/logistic_regression.pdf (accessed July 31, 2019).

Frost, Nick. 2019. "Training Data for Our Open-Sourced AI Classifier for Appium." https://www.test.ai/blog/training-data-for-app-classifier/ (accessed August 1, 2019).

Littman, Michael. 1994. "Markov games as a framework for multi- agent reinforcement learning." In Proceedings of the Eleventh International Conference on Machine Learning (July 1994), pages 157–163.

Santiago, Dionny. 2018. "AI Driven Test Generation. Machines Learning from Human Testers." In 36th Annual Pacific NW Software Quality Conference. http://uploads.pnsqc.org/2018/papers/119-Santiago-AI%20Driven%20Test%20Generation.pdf (accessed August 1, 2019).

Silver, David. 2018. "A general reinforcement learning algorithm that masters chess, shogi, and Go through self-play." Science: Vol. 362, Issue 6419 (Dec 2018), pages 1140-1144

[DS1]Try to expand upon the bios just a bit so the first page is a bit more "full".
[DS2]Consider expanding upon this. These reasons are obvious to some.
[DS3]Clustering is a popular unsupervised approach that is not mentioned here. It has been used for anomaly detection which is relevant to testing.
[DS4]This doesn't seem quite right.
[DS5]Great improvement to this section! Like the discussion on concrete reward function examples.

You might want to consider explaining the Q-update function in more detail.
[DS6]Consider moving some of this to background section, under a section dedicated to Reinforcement Learning. You might want to move the content currently under unsupervised learning to the new RL section and focus more on clustering under the unsupervised learning section.
[DS7]Test cases
[DS8]Would it be possible to share some numbers from test.ai or PinkLion.ai on how many apps these various different techniques have been applied to, and how many bugs have been found with these techniques? This wouldn't be under this section, but perhaps under a new section right before this one that discusses applications in practice, and current results.
[AB9]Although I am unable to provide exact figures at this time, I've added a MLSolutions in Practice section that discusses some current observations and achievements.

This page intentionally left blank.

Semi-Autonomous, Site-Wide A11Y Testing Using an Intelligent Agent

Briggs, K.A., Santiago, D., Adamo, D., Daye, P., King, T.M.
keith_briggs@ultimatesoftware.com

Abstract

Most countries across the globe have now ratified and/or signed the United Nations Convention on the Rights of Persons with Disabilities, the culmination of an effort started in the 1980's to protect the rights and dignity of people with disabilities. W3C's Web Content and Accessibility Guidelines documents, WCAG 2.0 (2008), ISO/IEC 40500 (2012), and WCAG 2.1 (2018), establish conformance requirements, which most nations have adopted as their de jure standard for determining website compliance with the UN convention. Although several tools support static WCAG web page analysis, present tools lack the automation required to automatically evaluate an entire website. In addition, current techniques are capable of discovering less than 30% of WCAG Level A and Level AA conformance issues. This paper presents an intelligent testing agent, Agent A11Y, capable of semi-autonomously exploring a website and more thoroughly evaluating its compliance with WCAG guidelines. To expand the system's automated WCAG guideline coverage, Agent A11Y employs novel dynamic testing strategies in combination with existing static web page analysis solutions. Additional tooling focuses manual testing activities on WCAG requirements that are difficult to fully automate. Supporting the generation of effective and actionable reports, Agent A11Y utilizes site exploration information to improve the aggregation and categorization of site-wide testing results. In conjunction with a discussion of the aforementioned Agent A11Y exploration, testing, and reporting methods, the paper presents experimental results and analysis to illustrate the comparative usefulness of the described techniques for conducting site-wide accessibility assessments.

Biography

Keith Briggs is a Software Architect at Ultimate Software, a leading cloud provider of human capital management solutions. With over 35 years of experience across diverse electrical, bio-electrical, software and systems engineering applications, Keith brings a unique perspective to his current AI for software testing research.

Dionny Santiago is a Quality Architect at Ultimate Software. Dionny is focused on research and development efforts to apply artificial intelligence and machine learning to software testing.

David Adamo Jr. holds a PhD in Computer Science from the University of North Texas and multiple years of experience conducting research and developing tools for automated software testing.

Philip Daye is a Software Test Lead for Ultimate Software. In his current role, Philip contributes to the development of patterns and practices with a special emphasis on accessibility.

Dr. Tariq M. King is the Senior Director and Engineering Fellow for Quality and Performance at Ultimate Software. Tariq heads Ultimate Software's quality program and is a frequent presenter at conferences and workshops. He has published more than thirty research articles in IEEE and ACM sponsored journals, and he has developed and taught software testing courses in both industry and academia.

1. Introduction

Approximately 1.125 billion people, or 15% of the worldwide population, experience significant difficulties in their everyday lives due to disability (World Bank 2018; World Health Organization 2011). Recognizing that people with disabilities face many barriers to full and effective participation in society, the United Nations adopted the Convention on the Rights of Persons with Disabilities, see Figure 1. Its primary aim is "to promote, protect and ensure the full and equal enjoyment of all human rights and fundamental freedoms by all persons with disabilities, and to promote respect for their inherent dignity."

Focused on promoting universal access to web technologies, the World Wide Web Consortium (W3C) developed Web Content Accessibility Guidelines (WCAG). In 2008, WCAG 2.0 (2008) was formally adopted; in 2012, WCAG 2.0 became an international standard, ISO/IEC 40500, as approved by the International Organization for Standardization and the International Electrotechnical Commission; finally, in 2018, WCAG 2.1 added 17 new criteria to address issues with mobile accessibility, people with low vision, and people with cognitive and learning disabilities. Not only do website owners have a moral obligation to construct universal access websites and web applications, in most countries they have a legal obligation. In 2018, at least 2258 lawsuits alleging websites were not adequately accessible were filed in the United States, an increase of 177% over 2017. Starting on January 1, 2021, publicly accessible websites operating in Ontario, Canada must comply with WCAG 2.0 AA, except for WCAG success criteria 1.2.4 and 1.2.5. Failure to do so may result in fines of up to $100,000 per day for the organization and up to $50,000 per day for its officers and directors.

Despite the moral and legal imperative to adopt the WCAG standards, few web applications fully comply. A study, conducted in 2019 by Yan and Ramachandran, found that 94.8% of evaluated websites violated WCAG 2.0 guidelines.

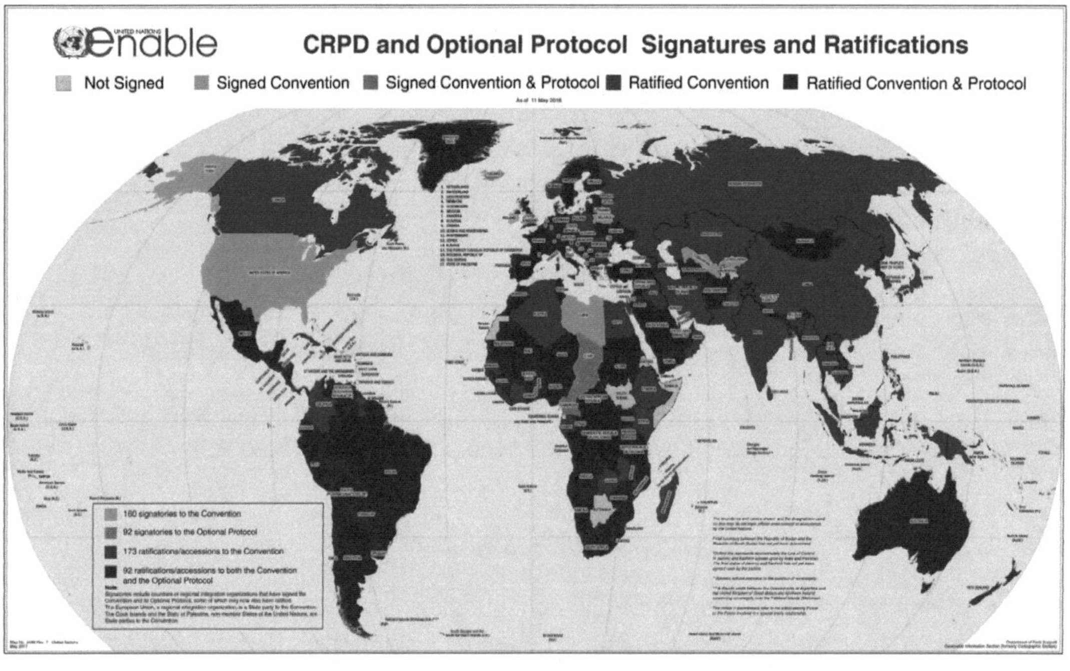

Figure 1: Most of the world has adopted, or is generally following, as in the case of the United States, the UN Convention on the Rights of Persons with Disabilities (CRPD).

To help companies address accessibility compliance, several automated evaluation tools have been developed. In 2019, Vigo, Brown and Conway assessed six of the most popular tools in use today, and they found that 50% or less of the WCAG success criteria were evaluated. And, for the criteria which were assessed, the tools discovered less than 40% of the known problems. These tools determine if a web page complies with a set of best practices, or rules, derived from the WCAG guidelines. In general, the evaluations are conducted statically against the DOM in much the same way as LINT tools statically evaluate source code. Unfortunately, as is evident in the above study, the current static analysis tools cannot identify a majority of WCAG compliance failures.

Some existing tools can perform their analysis on a set of URLs, or they employ a crawler to develop additional web page targets from a single URL. However, the current techniques employed by the most popular accessibility conformance testers are not particularly effective at navigating websites with significant dynamic content, required forms, or difficult to reach pages.

This paper presents a new approach for dynamically evaluating WCAG conformance using an intelligent testing agent, Agent A11Y. The agent is capable of semi-autonomously exploring a website, developing a limited understanding of page context, and activating dynamic content to more completely evaluate compliance with the accessibility guidelines.

To expand the system's automated WCAG guideline coverage, Agent A11Y employs novel dynamic testing strategies in combination with existing static web page analysis solutions. Additional tooling focuses manual testing activities on WCAG requirements that are difficult to fully automate. Supporting the generation of effective and actionable reports, Agent A11Y utilizes site exploration information to improve the aggregation and categorization of site-wide testing results.

In conjunction with a discussion of the aforementioned Agent A11Y exploration, testing, and reporting methods, the paper presents experimental results and analysis to illustrate the comparative usefulness of the described techniques for conducting site-wide accessibility assessments.

2. Web Content Accessibility Guidelines

While the WCAG are imperfect, they represent a critical resource for companies as they attempt to ensure their websites and web applications are legally compliant with local laws such as the American with Disabilities Act (ADA) and the Accessibility for Ontarians with Disabilities Act (AODA), amongst others. Over the last decade, the WCAG have become either the de facto or de jure standard for assessing website compliance throughout much of the world.

WCAG 2.0 consists of four overarching principles, twelve guidelines, and 61 success criteria. WCAG's success criteria are testable statements which may be applied to websites independent of any specific technology. The following sections provide a brief overview of the WCAG principles and a few selected guidelines relevant to the paper. For a more complete understanding, please visit the Web Accessibility Initiative's (WAI) home page, https://www.w3.org/WAI/. This page includes links to a number of resources for content writers, designers, developers, and testers including the full WCAG 2.0 and 2.1 documents.

2.1 Perceivable

In order for a website to be usable, the information presented must be provided in a manner that can be perceived by the user. Several guidelines follow from this principle:

1. Text alternatives should be provided for non-text content,
2. Time-based media should provide captions or textual descriptions,
3. The content should be adaptable to different presentations without loss of information, and
4. Data should be distinguishable.

For data to be distinguishable, mechanisms must allow individuals with limited hearing or sight to adequately perceive the data. For example, one success criterion specifies that color should not be the sole method of communicating information, as colorblind individuals may not be able to properly perceive differences in the data as presented.

2.2 Operable

It is not enough to specify that a user is able to perceive a website component, they must also be able to use its features. Several guidelines follow from this principle.

1. Some disabled users lack the motor control to be able to effectively utilize a pointing device; consequently, all functionality should be accessible using a keyboard alone.

2. Many disabled users require more time to complete standard functions; therefore, websites should provide enough time for users to read and use the content.

3. Flashing images or animations may cause difficulties for some users; thus, these features of a website, if employed, should be able to be turned off.

4. To operate a website, users must be able to navigate through the website. And,

5. WCAG 2.1 adds a fifth guideline addressing input modalities associated with mobile applications.

The fourth guideline concerning website navigation is divided into ten success criteria. The third criterion states, "If a Web page can be navigated sequentially and the navigation sequences affect meaning or operation, focusable components receive focus in an order that preserves meaning and operability.

On its surface, this success criterion is straightforward. If a user tabs through a website, the focus shouldn't shift from the first item in a list to the last item in a list and then to a middle item. However, in practice, this criterion can be met through a wide range of web programming constructs. To simplify the problem, many accessibility validation tools define "best practices," which build on WAI's definition of sufficient techniques, see Figure 2.

Another sufficient technique specifies that the content order matches the visual order. If the DOM follows this approach, everyone may read and interact with the content in the same order. Assuming this technique is used, developers should not use positive HTML tabindex numbers, as the use of positive tabindex values may cause the focus order to follow something other than the order in the DOM. However, it is possible to independently implement a logical focus order using tabindex values greater than one to programmatically define the order in explicit terms. Current validation tools, such as aXe generate an error in such cases, even if the focus order is logical and satisfies the WCAG criteria.

2.3 Understandable

The third principle states, "Information and the operation of user interface must be understandable." The success criteria derived from this principle are difficult for current static accessibility tools to evaluate. They generally require active, rather than passive, assessments, i.e. clicking on a button, which current tooling does not support.

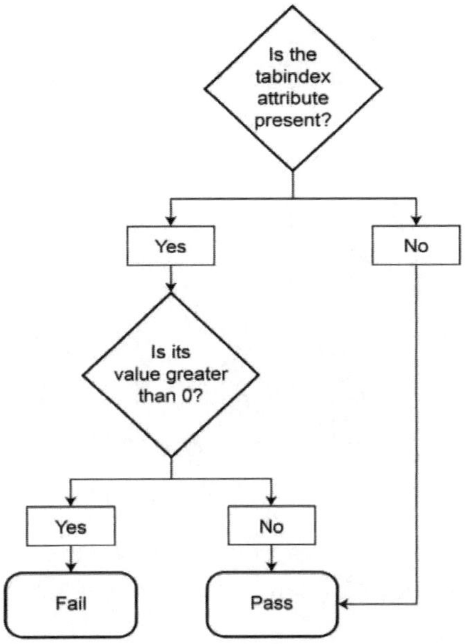

Figure 2: While some validation tools will indicate a webpage violates WCAG 2.4.3 if it uses a positive tabindex value, webpages can use positive tabindex values in a compliant manner. This should not infer that positive tabindex values are recommended. Rather, this example serves to expose the opinionated checking performed by compliance tools.

As shown in Figure 3, six of the most popular tools offered only minimal coverage of this principle. (Vigo 2019).

WCAG's Understandable principle is divided into three guidelines:

1. Content must be readable and understandable. This guideline primarily focuses on language definitions and word use (unusual words, abbreviations, etc.)

2. Web pages should appear and operate in consistent ways. That is, similar pages and components operate similarly across a website. And,

3. A website should help users avoid and correct mistakes.

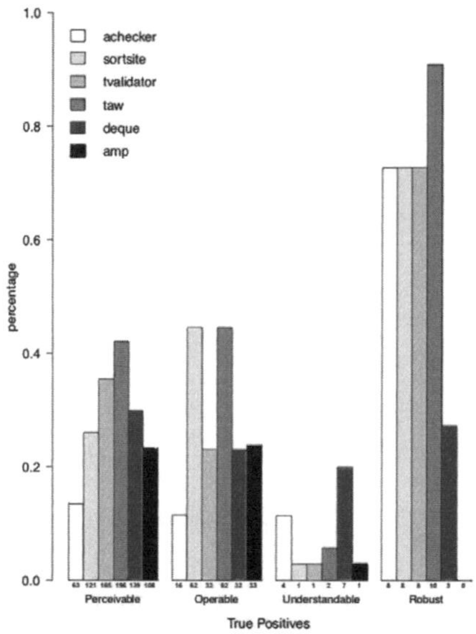

Figure 3: Completeness per tool and principle, where completeness is the number of true violations found by tools with respect to the actual number of violations reported by experts.

The evaluated tools do not compare pages across a site; thus, many success criteria associated with the second guideline, Predictable, cannot be validated.

None of the tools studied support the testing of the third guideline, Input Assistance, which aims to ensure that users with disabilities have the tools to avoid and correct mistakes. The automated testing of this guideline requires that the testing system support: 1) the natural language processing of input recommendations and error correction suggestions, and 2) an ability to actively follow happy and sad testing paths based on a functional understanding of page inputs.

3. Current A11Y Testing Strategies

Comprehensively and efficiently evaluating the accessibility conformance of a website requires the use of multiple techniques. Effective strategies to reduce a11y issues within a website application should employ multiple testing techniques. Static assessments may detect issues such as an insufficient contrast level; whereas, dynamic, workflow testing is necessary to evaluate many other usability issues, such as a cognitive issues which may prevent a user from completing a task.

Ultimately, to keep costs down, companies should try to employ accessibility training and testing such that issues can be addressed as early in the design and development process as possible. Training content writers and developers on the specific issues associated with a set of persona profiles is helpful, as content authors and developers will be more apt to address accessibility design issues before they reach the testing process (Henke 2019).

Once in testing, verification tasks can be broken down into technical accessibility evaluations, and usable accessibility evaluations, see Table I (Bai 2017).

TABLE I. ACCESSIBILITY TESTING GROUPS.

#	*Group*	*Technical accessibility*	*Usable accessibility*
1	Automated checkers	x	
2	Checklist and guidelines	x	x
3	Simulation kits		x
4	Assistive technology	x	
5	Walkthrough		x

Because of the nature of A11y validation and testing, no one strategy can catch all possible accessibility defects. In 2017, Bai measured the percentage of defects discovered by various testing methodologies. Interestingly, the automated tools in use failed to discover any critical or cognitive failures, see Table 2.

While Table 2 indicates that manual techniques can be effective in discovering accessibility defects, it also illustrates the significant limitations of current automated tools. The automated tools studied by Bai only performed static analysis. The automated tools only caught 7.3% of all discovered issues. Further, they were not able to identify any of the errors that were classified as critical or cognitive. At the same time, even though manual techniques are capable of discovering such defects, manual accessibility testing is expensive. Further, as Bai has shown, multiple manual techniques are required to catch the errors. No single technique is sufficient.

	Total	Critical	Cognitive
Automated tools	7,3 %	0,0 %	0,0 %
Checklists	24,6 %	29,4 %	15,5 %
Assistive Technology	20,3 %	31,0 %	14,1 %
Simulation kit	31,4 %	17,5 %	36,6 %
Expert walkthrough	16,5 %	22,2 %	33,8 %

Table 2: Percentage of errors discovered by method.

Given the high lifecycle costs of manual testing, if companies are to reduce the costs of accessibility testing substantially, it will be necessary to improve upon available automated techniques.

3.1 Surveying Available Accessibility Testing Tools

Prior to embarking on the development of Agent A11y, Ultimate Software, a leading provider of Human Capital Management (HCM) software, conducted a broad survey of commercially available accessibility tools. The list of tools reviewed was derived from the Web Accessibility Evaluation Tools List published by the W3C (W3C 2016).

In general, five categories of tools were considered.

1. **Content creation tools:** These products aid users in the development of accessible content, primarily Word and PDF documents;

2. **Color, contrast, and visual acuity evaluators:** These tools aid a user in determining if a given combination of background and foreground content satisfies the WCAG guidelines for color, contrast and text readability;
3. **Page scanners:** These tools support the semi-automated evaluation of a web page using various static analysis techniques primarily focusing on DOM structure, proper page source formatting, and color, contrast, and visual acuity evaluations;
4. **Accessibility testing libraries:** These libraries allow the web-based functionality of plug-ins or stand-alone tools to be controlled via an Application Program Interface (API), thus allowing the tools to be integrated with other automated testing platforms; and,
5. **Out-sourced evaluation services:** Due to the contract nature of their work, the quality and capabilities of out-sourced evaluation services were not considered beyond what was available from their published marketing materials.

Ultimate Software's assessment primarily focused on the page scanners and associated accessibility testing code libraries. Web based page scanners often encounter difficulties when working with sites that require a login, and they may have limited or no ability to navigate a complex site with forms, required fields, etc. Since many of the scanners run in the vendor's own datacenter, there is the additional risk of exposing confidential data during the testing process. However, some of these tools are built on code libraries, which can be executed locally and via programmatic control. While the accessibility testing libraries can be used to scan pages, they do not generally support site exploration, form entry, or scripting. As a consequence, they must be used in conjunction with other GUI test automation tools.

As part of the study, Ultimate Software evaluated numerous tools. The conclusions drawn from the assessment were in general agreement with those reported by Bai, Henke, and Vigo as reported in the sections above. The study identified several approaches for conducting web page analysis, assuming the desired System Under Test (SUT) page was discoverable. These solutions were capable of identifying a wide range of static formatting and page display issues to include missing alternative text, insufficient contrast, improperly structured data, and missing guides such as skipped heading levels or landmarks.

It was found that all of the tools evaluated lacked seven key capabilities, which were critical to determining the accessibility compliance of enterprise scale, web applications in a cost-effective and repeatable manner. The tools did not support:

1. An automated, or semi-automated (i.e. scripted), ability to navigate to all application states, or at least a representative set of application states, within a web-based, enterprise application;
2. A capability to assess site-wide accessibility criteria, such as WCAG success criteria 3.2.3, Consistent Navigation;
3. The ability to dynamically interact with a webpage to actively assess compliance with certain WCAG guidelines, such as Guideline 2.1, Keyboard [Accessibility];
4. Company specific accessibility design verification, which may look to the enforcement of site-specific guidelines for a website or company;
5. Natural language or machine learning capabilities capable of evaluating page layout, form labeling, help content, and error text;
6. An ability to effectively deduplicate and present aggregated, actionable results across multiple states of an application feature or page; and,
7. A workflow assessment capability capable of determining the accessibility of a series of pages and actions necessary to complete a task within an application.

Agent A11y targeted items 1, 3, and 6 for further evaluation. The approach and findings are presented in the following sections.

3.2 Automated Testing

Static page analyzers, such as Deque's aXe and Level Access' Continuum (AMP), are capable of discovering a number of important WCAG violations, but they cannot detect critical or cognitive accessibility defects, see Table 2. As reported by Bai (2017), these tools failed to detect issues associated with more than 50% of the WCAG success criteria, see Figure 4. Further, even where success criteria defects are detected, the tools cannot determine full compliance.

Tool	P	O	U	R	overall
AChecker	3 (38%)	3 (25%)	1 (25%)	1 (50%)	8 (31%)
SortSite	3 (38%)	5 (42%)	1 (25%)	1 (50%)	10 (38%)
TV	3 (38%)	3 (25%)	1 (25%)	1 (0.5)	9 (35%)
TAW	3 (38%)	5 (42%)	2 (50%)	2 (100%)	13 (50%)
Deque	3 (38%)	3 (25%)	4 (100%)	1 (50%)	11 (42%)
AMP	2 (25%)	3 (25%)	1 (25%)	0 (0%)	6 (23%)

Figure 4: The evaluated tools were unable to detect any failures associated with 50% of the WCAG success criteria.

Fundamentally, these tools are limited in what they can evaluate, as they presently only perform static evaluations of a webpage's DOM and limited rendering tests. As most enterprise applications utilize dynamic web pages to support complex workflows, statically focused, single page, static evaluation systems cannot evaluate most critical application features. The researched, commercially available validation tools share these common limitations:

1. The evaluated systems are not able to evaluate multi-state or multi-page defects. As these systems operate on pages independently, even if they are utilized in conjunction with a web crawler, they cannot effectively assess cross-page conformance requirements. For example, WCAG success criterion 3.2.3 specifies that a website use consistent navigation such that, "Navigational mechanisms that are repeated on multiple Web pages within a set of Web pages occur in the same relative order each time they are repeated, unless a change is initiated by the user."
2. The evaluated systems cannot assess dynamically changing content. As the systems are statically employed, and as they determine compliance through an analysis of a single DOM instance, they are unable to evaluate the results of a button push, form submission, or other action. This limits the ability of the systems to detect violations of success criteria such as WCAG 3.2.2, On Input. This criterion specifies, "Changing the setting of any user interface component does not automatically cause a change of context unless the user has been advised of the behavior before using the component."
3. The evaluated systems do not attempt to understand the functional operation of the website in performing their evaluation. As such, they are not able to develop the models and contextual information needed to evaluate whether or not an error described to the user is adequate as required by WCAG 3.3.1.

Further, when evaluating multi-page websites and websites with dynamic content, it is critical that automated testing solutions provide actionable, consolidated information to guide developers in correcting the failure. While many of the tools mentioned provide impressive reporting mechanisms and guidance when applied to individual pages, none offer the ability to consolidate accessibility errors generated across different states of the same page, and neither can they evaluate information that may be presented across multiple similar pages, such as error messages. Lacking these capabilities, if current automated solutions are directly applied to multiple instances of the same page in different states, or similar pages with duplicative issues, the user may be inundated with massive quantities of largely duplicative data. This can make finding and acting on web application design issues particularly difficult.

3.3 Evaluating Design Quality Versus Simple Conformance

None of the solutions evaluated were capable of evaluating the sufficiency, rather than the existence, of a particular solution. Consider the case of a button label; the evaluated tools only test that a label is provided. They cannot determine if the information can effectively support the operation of the web application by a person who uses a screen reader or other assistive device. For example, a webpage may contain several buttons whose context within the page establishes its functionality. While a shopping page might have several buttons labeled "add" on a page, in many cases, each instance of the button may add a different item to a user's shopping cart. For a sighted user, the function of each "add" button may be easily determined from the location of the button in relation to the surrounding context. However, unless additional information is provided in the accessible version of the label provided to a screen reader, a person who is blind may be unable to determine which item will be placed in their cart when any of the multiple "add" buttons are selected. Consequently, merely testing for the existence of a label is often insufficient to determine if a given label provides adequate accessibility.

While neither the evaluated tools nor Agent A11y can currently address this deficiency using automated testing techniques, Agent A11y's approach allows for the introduction of dynamic tests, techniques and oracles which could be capable of addressing this issue in the future. Agent A11y could click on all commonly labeled buttons (using the accessible label) on a page and flag an error if the resulting action is not identical. Such a solution would build on the existing technology and capabilities of the Agent framework already incorporated in functional testing versions of the system and its predecessors. Not only is the framework capable of clicking on buttons and modeling the results, Agent and its predecessors can extract semantic information from labels, error messages, links and workflows. However, applying these techniques to support evaluating the effectiveness of accessibility designs and labels remains a work-in-progress. While a machine learning enabled solution which completely eliminates the need for manual verification of such content may be decades away, considerable opportunities to reduce the amount of manual verification required may be attainable within much shorter timescales, see Section 5, Future Work.

4. Agent A11Y

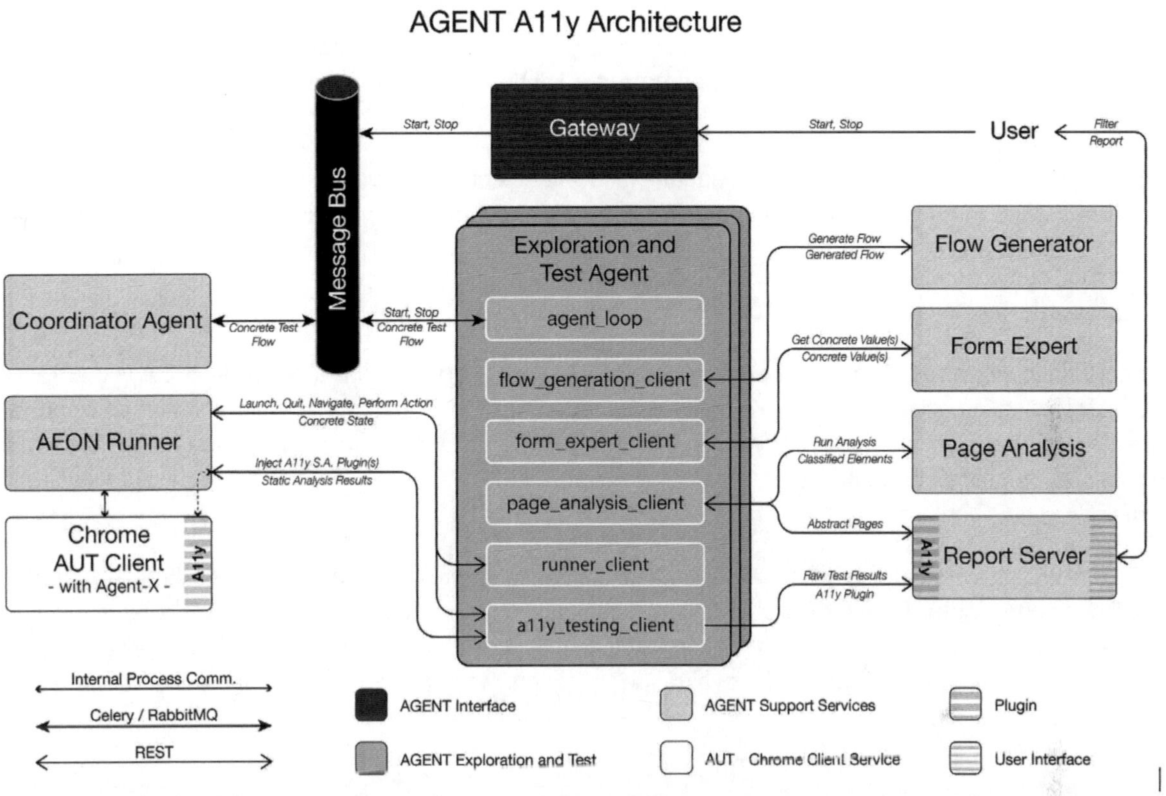

Figure 5: Agent A11y automatically explores a web application, conducts both static and dynamic accessibility testing, and reports consolidated test results.

Based on Ultimate Software's survey of available accessibility testing tools, a review of current research, and an evaluation of ongoing internal automated testing research projects, the team began efforts to integrate available commercial technologies with associated AI driven testing research. The project sought to combine both static and dynamic accessibility testing solutions with an agent based, autonomous testing system. The resulting research, Ultimate Software's Agent A11y project, is the focus of this paper. Other efforts have pursued the integration of the non-agent-based testing features into the company's Aeon open source project. Aeon is available under an Apache 2.0 license on GitHub.

To enable context sensitive and site-wide accessibility testing features, it is necessary to evaluate the capabilities of the SUT over multiple states, preferably a collection which abstractly represents the full functionality of the product. Without the benefit of the contextual information gathered across multiple product pages and states, an autonomous testing solution cannot reasonably determine if adequate accessible information is available in a form suitable for people with a variety of disabilities. With this in mind, the Agent A11y system, based on the open sourced AGENT (AGENT 2019), is constructed around an Exploration and Test Agent capable of exploring a web application without significant direction or human intervention. Agent A11y is capable of identifying, navigating, evaluating, and acting on the actions, fields, and forms constituting an application's pages and workflows. Agent A11y deploys one or more exploration and testing agents to navigate a system, and it applies appropriate test flows as testable patterns are recognized.

A coordinator dispatches testing assignments through a message queue. The queued tasks are distributed to multiple distributed, concurrent execution and testing agents. Each agent is capable of independently interacting with the SUT via an instrumented Chrome client and AEON runner. This AI for Software Testing solution, designed for research and development applications, illuminates a new path for advancing the state-of-the-art in testing automation.

As the agents explore the site, they conduct static accessibility evaluations for every, sufficiently new, discovered state. In addition, the agents execute supported dynamic accessibility tests as relevant testable patterns are recognized.

4.1 Automatic Exploration

The automatic exploration process begins with a start request from an end-user of Agent A11y. The start request includes information about how many exploration agents to instantiate, a completion criterion (e.g. a specific number of exploration actions per agent or a fixed amount of time) and a seed URL from which the exploration process should begin. Each agent's goal is to visit as many distinct pages of the SUT as possible.

Traditional web crawlers use a breadth-first or depth-first strategy to collect and visit links (typically identified by HTML anchor tags). Agent A11y interacts directly with buttons, text fields, checkboxes, scrollbars and other web page elements in ways similar to actual users. Automated exploration in Agent A11y is a precursor to automated accessibility evaluation of each web page / state that constitutes a SUT.

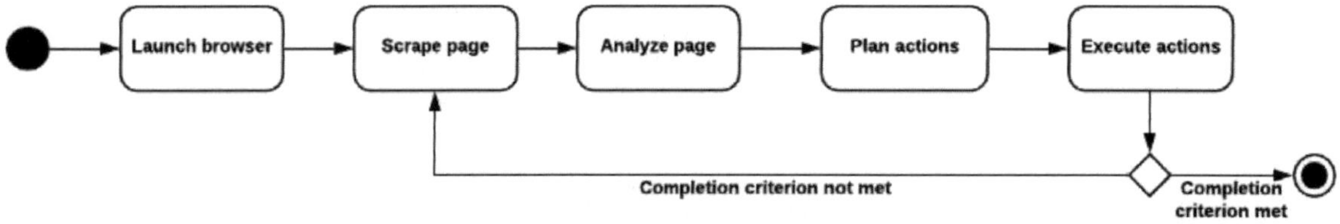

Figure 6: The automatic exploration process with a single browser.

The start request from an end user initiates an exploration session, which can be uniquely identified and later retrieved with all associated data. As shown in Figure 6, automatic exploration involves a sequence of steps (browser launch, page scraping, page analysis, action planning and execution) that occur in a loop until a specified completion criterion is met.

Browser launch: At the start of the exploration process, Agent A11y spawns one or more exploration agents, launches web browsers, and navigates to a specified seed URL.

Page Scraping: Agent A11y extracts a Computed Render Tree (CRT) representation and stores a screenshot of each web page it visits. The CRT is generated by injecting JavaScript into each web page during exploration. The CRT contains data about the structure, content and visual characteristics of each web page. This is in contrast to HTML source which focuses on structure and content but has limited information about visual characteristics of a web page. Web page screenshots are useful for further analysis and reporting at different stages of the exploration process.

Page Analysis: Agent A11y uses information derived from CRTs to generate unique identifiers for similar pages, to classify web page elements (e.g. page titles, labels, commit buttons, error messages, etc.), to identify groups of elements (e.g. forms, navigation bars, label-form field mappings), and to identify actionable elements and construct selectors for actionable elements.

Action Planning and Execution: The information derived from page analysis serves as input for action planning. During exploration, Agent A11y uses page analysis information to determine a sequence of actions that have a high likelihood of leading to previously unseen web pages. Once such a sequence of actions has been chosen, Agent A11y uses Selenium and JavaScript injection to execute the chosen sequence of actions. Executing one or more actions typically results in navigation to a different web page. It is important to note that this stage also includes actions used to assess the accessibility of each web page (e.g. execution of an accessibility analysis tool).

The exploration agent loop tracks exploration state and determines whether the completion criterion has been met. Agent A11y, as implemented, is a highly scalable, distributed system capable of running multiple exploration and accessibility evaluation processes in parallel across multiple agent/browser instances. The goal of automatic exploration is to visit as many distinct pages as possible in as little time as possible. The comprehensiveness of accessibility evaluations across an application, in large part, depends on how deeply Agent A11y is able to explore the SUT.

4.2 Form Recognition

During the exploration process, it is important for the system to be able to recognize forms and fill out valid values for form elements. This is especially true for enterprise applications that contain many forms with complex form validation requirements. The inability to complete a form may prevent the Agent from reaching subsequent portions of the SUT. Once the system learns to successfully complete a form, Agent A11y may recognize applicable test flows, which may then be executed to validate the accessibility of the form. A comprehensive accessibility evaluation requires testing the form under both positive (i.e. with valid values for all form fields) and negative (i.e. at least one field with an invalid or missing value) conditions. Negative tests are required to determine the SUT's compliance with WCAG Guideline 3.3, Input Assistance. Agent A11y is capable of learning and applying both positive and negative tests on recognized forms.

To understand a form, it is necessary to first extract the actionable widgets that comprise the form. The page analysis client employs ML techniques to recognize different types of form elements (e.g., labels, error messages, form and page titles). The problem of understanding web page components is framed as a supervised learning classification problem (Santiago 2018). A standard web-based render tree includes information such as: (1) hierarchy; (2) element types; (3) element attributes; and (4) style sheet information. We extend this basic structure by collecting the render tree only once the web browser has finalized rendering, and by calculating additional information such as: (1) element positions; and (2) element sizes. The result is a Computed Render Tree (CRT) representation of the webpage.

Using the CRT representation, a feature synthesis step is then performed. An element-wise pass is done through all of the elements in the CRT, synthesizing several features for each element. Although the synthesis is done at the local level for each element, the full global context (information on the entire set of elements) is used to compute several features. The feature synthesis results in the generation of training data that can be annotated for the purpose of training ML models. A set of example synthesized features is described in Table 3.

Table 3: An example set of features that can be collected or synthesized from the CRT.

Feature	Description
HTML Tag	The tag for the given element.
Parent HTML Tag	The tag for the given element's parent.
"For" Attribute	The existence of a value for the HTML "For" attribute.
Num. Children	The number of HTML nodes that are children of the given element's node.
Num. Siblings	The number of HTML nodes that are siblings of the given element's node.
Depth	The depth of the given element's node within the CRT.
Horizontal Percent	The relative horizontal position (in percentage) of the given element.
Vertical Percent	The relative vertical position (in percentage) of the given element.
Font Size	The relative (normalized against the full set of elements) font size of the given element.
Font Weight	The relative (normalized against the full set of elements) font weight of the given element.
Is Text	Describes whether a given element is a text node.
Nearest Color	The closest color computed using CIEDE2000 algorithm.
Nearest Background Color	The closest background color computed using CIEDE2000 algorithm.
Distance from Input	The relative (normalized against the full set of elements) distance to the closest input widget from the given element.
Text	The actual text associated with the given element.

Using the synthesized feature values, the Agent A11y ML-based classification system is capable of recognizing key web elements (Page Title, Widget Labels, and Error Messages) critical to navigation within the SUT and the recognition of form elements, see Figure 7. As mentioned, the ability to properly fill-in forms is necessary to the navigation of the SUT, as invalid values can block further progress into the SUT. Form recognition is an important first step in the process of completing a form.

As the system must first navigate to a SUT state to evaluate the accessibility of the page in a given state, Agent A11y must be capable of successfully completing encountered forms. Additionally, the recognition of form components and their associated error messages is required to evaluate a web application's compliance with WCAG's Input Assistance Guideline (WCAG 3.3). To comply with this guideline, a web application must provide suitable labels, instructions and help so that a user who is disabled may properly understand how to fill-out the form. Further, when an error is generated, WCAG 3.3 requires that the error suggestions correctly identify the user error so that it can be corrected. While the parsing and evaluation of error messages for the purpose of evaluating WCAG 3.3 compliance has not yet been implemented in Agent A11y, related work associated with understanding form semantics and interpreting error messages provides encouragement that future implementations may be capable of validating the accessibility of common error messages.

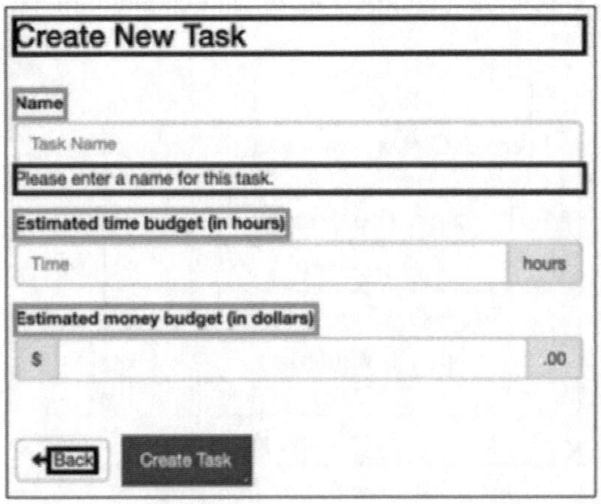

Figure 7: The Agent A11y ML-based classification system is capable of automatically identifying page title, widget label associations, and error messages (not shown) on an untrained web page.

In addition to identifying a page title or form label, the ML classifiers also construct bounding boxes for each of these elements. While the system is currently able to recognize individual web page elements; oftentimes, it is useful to recognize a group of elements as a single semantic entity, see Section 5, Future Work.

4.3 Understanding Form Semantics, Form Filling

The information collected from the previous step (Form Recognition) enables additional reasoning concerning the functional and semantic context of the form under exploration. To help define the domain of valid input values associated with an element, Agent A11y attempts to first determine which data types may be associated with the element, and subsequently, any relationships that may exist between associated form elements. This process involves creating an abstraction of the page under exploration.

Abstraction

A full CRT contains information about every DOM element for a given web page. To effectively support further reasoning about key elements, Agent A11y creates a simplified representation, or abstraction, of the page. This abstraction mechanism also supports Agent A11y's SUT navigation task by reducing the number of duplicative paths which must be explored, and by improving the effectiveness of Agent A11y's reinforcement learning algorithms. Theoretically, multiple approaches to state abstraction are not only possible, but appropriate, as the state abstraction methodology directly impacts the mechanics of exploration and the type of test flows which the system can detect. For this implementation, the Exploration and Testing Agent constructs a hierarchical semantic model leveraging the information collected during the form recognition stage.

Each node within the semantic model contains information that identifies a specific form control. Nodes are hierarchically organized based on element positioning relative to form headers and page titles. Generally, web forms are composed of inputs and labels. As such, we employ a label extraction process that associates each control with the nearest label that may be used to describe the control (Becce 2012, Lin 2017). The labels may range from singular words to phrases or sentences. Continuing with the form from Figure 7, the semantic model identifies the key components and one or more suggested data types for completing the form, see Figure 8. While not shown in this example, Agent A11y is also capable of identifying other important form characteristics such as required fields, hints, and error messages.

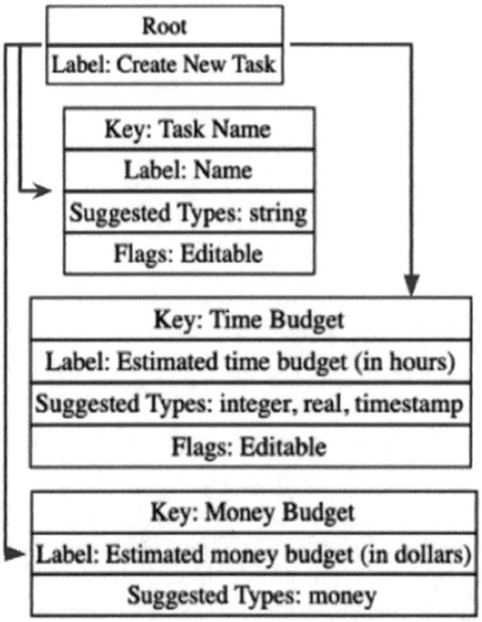

Figure 8: The Agent A11y ML-based classification system supports the generation of a semantic model representation, which identifies the key form components and likely input types.

Actionable State

Agent A11y constructs a class representing a page state of the SUT as a collection of widgets, the actionable state, from the semantic model. A hashing function that only depends on the actionable widgets for a given page is applied to the semantic model. The output of the hashing function is a hash that is used to determine uniqueness among all explored abstract states. Concretely, any variant of the form explored in Section 4.2 (e.g., one of the fields is filled out, or the field is empty, or multiple fields are filled out) will be represented by the same abstract state (that is, all form variants are represented by the "same" semantic model). As mentioned above, multiple abstraction techniques may be applied to the CRT, and its associated semantic models. This particular abstraction technique, which focuses on the actionable components of the

CRT, has proven useful for identifying states important to the completion of forms and the successful navigation of a SUT.

Data Type Detection

Agent A11y's Form Expert Client consumes discovered semantic models and determines potential valid values for completing the form. The form expert includes a natural language processing (NLP) engine built on top of the Stanford CoreNLP Toolkit (Manning 2014). The NLP engine recursively processes each node of the model. For each node and parameter therein, the engine has one primary goal: to suggest likely types of each parameter. The NLP engine processes the text label of each parameter using an internal knowledge base which maps likely types to names. The output is an array of suggested types from most to least probable. For example, a text label "First Name" containing the substring "Name" is most likely a string data type. Conversely, a label such as "Starting Date" containing "Date" may refer to either a date control, a timestamp control, or a string, in order of likelihood.

If an exact match is not found in the knowledge base, a text similarity search is conducted with the label against the members of the knowledge base to see if it is similar in concept to any member of the knowledge base. If so, the search result is used as a proxy, with an adjusted confidence based on how strong the similarity score is. As part of the NLP process, the semantic model is augmented with the new, derived information representing the likely data types.

Form Filling

The augmented semantic model is then passed into the form filling subsystem of the form expert client. The form filling subsystem faces two distinct challenges: (1) providing correct values given labels on a form; and (2) contextually generating values for a given form. Typically, form controls are provided with labels, and natural language descriptions of the value types. Some of these controls maintain contextual relationships. For instance, a form's structure may change when selecting a country that may or may not have states or provinces. Many forms, such as registration or payment forms, contain similar controls, differing by only a small number of controls. Given the augmented semantic model, the form filling subsystem leverages ML (specifically, the K-Nearest Neighbor algorithm) to find the semantic model within a training dataset that is closest to the provided model. Levenshtein distance is used to measure label distances across label sequences (Levenshtein 1966). To support form filling given a limited training set of data, an analogy-based reasoning approach is employed (Aamodt 1994, Veloso 1992).

The form filling subsystem may not find a semantic model that matches one-to-one for all form fields. It is entirely possible that the training data includes enough information to fill out a subset of the target form under exploration, but not enough data to fill out the entire form. To compensate, the form filling algorithm employs a recursive subset filling approach. That is, the algorithm explores a search space of all possible form field subset combinations until it converges to a combination for which as much of the form is filled as possible.

4.4 Static Tool Execution

Given the ability to automatically explore the SUT, the AGENT system serves as a platform that supports the integration of additional testing tools. For accessibility testing purposes, aXe Core and Continuum static analysis tools are used. Both of these tools provide a JavaScript library for simple injection and execution against any web page. Since the AGENT web execution system is based on Selenium, the system is able to leverage the existing JavaScript execution capabilities available in the Selenium toolchain.

In order to seamlessly leverage multiple tools such as aXe Core and Continuum, it is necessary to create a common A11y domain model to capture accessibility issues. The system maps the specialized aXe Core and Continuum results into this common A11y domain model. This allows the system to generate an aggregated report that leverages the results of multiple A11y static analysis tools to improve rule coverage while limiting report complexity.

As mentioned in Section 4.3, the AGENT platform is able to create abstractions for all of the pages found during exploration. ML classifiers are used to recognize the page title for each page. Common pages are then clustered together. This approach allows the system to aggregate A11Y issues across all known variants of a given page abstraction, see Figure 9. If the system did not aggregate results based on an abstract understanding of a SUT, and rather reported the accessibility test results associated with each concrete page instance discovered, the report would be tens or hundreds of times longer, as each abstract page is visited many times in a typical session.

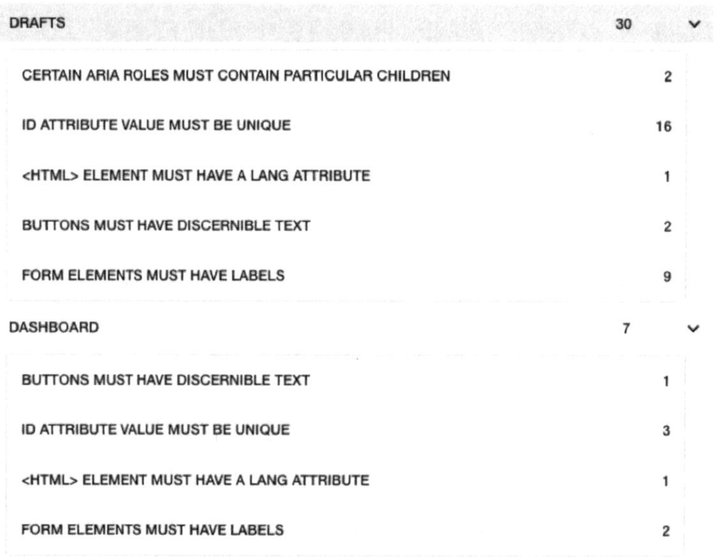

Figure 9: This screenshot from the Agent A11Y accessibility reporting page illustrates the identification of multiple a11y issues as discovered on multiple SUT abstract pages.

4.5 Dynamic Accessibility Testing

As described in Section 4.4, Agent A11Y is able to utilize a range of static analysis tools including the popular aXe Core and Level Access Continuum plug-ins. Further, the system is capable of aggregating the results into a single report, which organizes discovered issues according to the abstract SUT page on which they were discovered. The system aggregates duplicative information discovered on multiple concrete pages, or by multiple testing tools to reduce information overload. While such a capability is powerful and useful in it of itself, static analysis tools are currently only able to cover a small percentage of all a11y compliance concerns. As such, there is a need for dynamic a11y testing. Our system extends the static a11y testing tooling by introducing dynamic tests which are executed on every abstract page encountered during exploration.

An example of a dynamic a11y test involves the testing web element focus order. While it is difficult to build an automated oracle for what the correct focus order should be on any arbitrary web page, it is possible to develop oracles for simpler problems such as ensuring there are no keyboard traps on the page. A keyboard trap occurs when a person using a keyboard is unable to shift focus away from a certain element or control. Agent A11Y is able to test for keyboard traps by employing the following algorithm:

1. Scrape the contents of the page under test
2. Identify the actionable elements on the page
3. Based on the number of actionable elements, determine an upper bound for the number of times the Tab key should be hit
4. Identify the currently focused element and add it to a running list of focused elements. At the end of the algorithm, this running list will represent the element focus order on the page
5. Hit the tab key
6. Scrape the contents of the page under test
7. Jump to Step 4 as long as we have not exceeded the upper bound on the number of times to hit the Tab key. Else, continue to Step 8
8. Check the element focus order list for cyclicity, and for the presence of a keyboard trap (duplicate controls, especially when contiguous)

In addition to testing for keyboard traps, Agent A11y supports other oracles capable of verifying if all actionable controls can be reached (i.e. focused on) by tabbing. The system employs a similar algorithm that identifies the "actionable" elements which are reachable from a given concrete state and then the system checks to ensure each element is accounted for within the focus order list.

There are many promising avenues for future work to expand the range of dynamically testable, accessibility compliance concerns, see Section 5, Future Work.

4.6 Web Page Clustering and Accessibility Reports

Agent A11y generates and stores large amounts of data as a result of its automated exploration and accessibility evaluation processes. Reporting this data to end users requires techniques that enable derivation and presentation of useful information that end users can understand and act upon.

Agent A11y organizes and presents accessibility reports in a page-centric manner. The goal is to help users identify, in as specific a manner as possible, web pages in the SUT that have accessibility issues. During automatic exploration, Agent A11y may visit many slightly different instances of the same page, and it is potentially undesirable to present the results of accessibility evaluation for every instance of each visited page as part of an application-wide report. A key objective of Agent A11y's reporting scheme is to organize accessibility evaluation data into representative groups based on characteristics shared between multiple instances of each web page. Other key aspects of Agent A11y reports include web page screenshots and descriptions of identified accessibility issues.

Agent A11y utilizes an unsupervised machine learning algorithm, k-medoids (Shubert), to identify clusters (i.e. representative groups) of visited web pages and associated accessibility evaluation data. Each member of a cluster has more characteristics, or features, in common with other members of the same cluster than with members of other clusters. The centroid of each cluster is the most representative instance of a single web page that potentially has several instances. Rather than present accessibility information about all members of each cluster, Agent A11y focuses on the centroid of each cluster to provide tractable reports.

Clustering algorithms generally require a vectorized representation of each entity that is to be analyzed. In the context of accessibility evaluation, the entities are web pages. Table 4 shows the list of features that are used to represent each web page as part of the clustering process.

Table 4: Web page features for clustering.

Feature	**Description**
Tag frequency	The number of times each HTML tag appears in a web page.
Word frequency	The number of times each word appears in a web page.
URL	Levenshtein distance between a web page's URL and the URL of all other explored web pages.
Document Object Model (DOM)	Tree edit distance [1] between the DOM tree of a web page and the DOM tree of all other explored web pages.

One of the inputs to the k-medoids clustering algorithm is the number of clusters into which data points should be grouped. In the context of accessibility reporting for web pages, it is unlikely that the appropriate number of clusters is known prior to accessibility evaluation for a given application. Algorithm 1 illustrates how Agent A11y determines an appropriate number of clusters to use for reporting.

```
function identifyRepresentativeWebPages(vectorizedWebPages, maxClusters)

      bestNumberOfClusters = 2

      bestSilhouetteScore = -1

      bestClustering = vectorizedWebPages

      currentNumberOfClusters = 2

      while currentNumberOfClusters <= maxClusters:

      clusters = kMedoids(vectorizedWebPages, currentNumberOfClusters)

      silhouetteScore = calculateSilhouetteScore(clusters)
```

```
if silhouetteScore > bestSilhouetteScore:
        bestSilhouetteScore = silhouetteScore
        bestNumberOfClusters = currentNumberOfClusters
        bestClustering = clusters
currentNumberOfClusters = currentNumberOfClusters + 1
representativeWebPages = getCentroids(bestClustering)
return                                        representativeWebPages
```

Algorithm 1: Web page clustering with silhouette coefficients

Algorithm 1 takes the set of featurized web pages and a user-defined maximum number of clusters as input. The algorithm produces a subset of representative web pages from the superset of all explored web pages. For a given SUT, Agent A11y repeatedly clusters the set of visited and evaluated web pages until it identifies a number of clusters within a specified bound (e.g. 2 to 50) that yield the best silhouette coefficient for clustering (Selecting 2019). The silhouette coefficient is a measure of how close each entity in a cluster is to points in neighboring clusters. The silhouette coefficient provides a way to assess the quality of a set of web page clusters. Once an appropriate number of clusters has been identified, Agent A11y uses the resulting subset of representative web pages to produce a report that is assumed to be more tractable than one based on the superset of all visited pages.

5. Future Work

While Agent A11y has demonstrated the capability to autonomously evaluate a broad set of WCAG success criteria, the system is still in its infancy and many opportunities to expand upon its supported test strategies remain.

5.1 Evaluating Information Content Versus Existence

In most cases, current solutions, including those currently supported by Agent A11y, evaluate the existence of a label and not the sufficiency of its content. While the construction of a system capable of interpreting the meaning of all labels, help messages, captioning content, and errors is well beyond the present state-of-the-art, cross-site comparison algorithms, NLP techniques, and machine learning classification systems may be applied to assess the sufficiency of certain information content. Consider these examples:

- A site uses many common form elements across a site, such as name, address and phone number. Using several examples, a testing module is trained to determine if adequate instructions and help are provided. Later, when evaluating the SUT, Agent A11y encounters a field labeled, "emergency contact phone number." While this particular variation on a phone number field label may not have been seen by Agent A11y before, the trained system recognizes that the field represents a phone number, which it has previously learned should be paired with accessible input guidance consistent with that provided within its training set.

- Input guidance for the entry of a password specifies the length, types and number of characters that constitute a valid password. Using NLP and/or REGEX techniques, Agent A11y programmatically interprets the input guidance and actively validates that a password constructed according to the input guidance is accepted by the SUT.

- An image alt-text label is compared to the classification returned by an image classification module. If the alt-text label conflicts with the returned image classification, the alt-text label – image pair is flagged for further evaluation by a manual tester.

- A link to a common web page is provided in several places throughout the SUT. The accessible labels for the links are compared and inconsistencies flagged, see WCAG 3.2.4, Consistent Identification.

5.2 Form Recognition

While the system is currently able to recognize individual web page elements such as First Name and Last Name; oftentimes, it is useful to recognize a group of elements as a single semantic entity. For example, groupings of fields such as Contact Information, Shopping Cart, or Midterm Grades can provide important semantic information concerning the function, types, and value ranges of the group's contained fields.

5.3 Dynamic Accessibility Testing

There are many promising avenues where new dynamic testing algorithms might successfully expand the range of WCAG success criteria which could be addressed through automated testing. WCAG's Input Assistance Guidance category represents one area where substantial gains may be achieved as current static methods are insufficient. In particular, the Error Identification, Suggestion, and Prevention success criteria under WCAG 3.3 could all benefit from appropriate dynamic testing algorithms. While full verification of these success criteria is beyond the state-of-the-art of current machine learning and NLP capabilities, it is likely that many aspects of these success criteria may be evaluated using available techniques, at least for some significant percentage of situations.

6. Conclusions

At its core, AGENT A11y's ability to automatically explore a SUT, with all of its page and form variants, broadly supports autonomous, site-wide, accessibility testing. With Agent A11y, it is possible to simultaneously support multiple accessibility testing modules, strategies, oracles, and report aggregation capabilities to achieve more comprehensive WCAG coverage. Perhaps most critically, Agent A11y's modular architecture and site-wide exploration capabilities establish a framework for the application of new multi-page and dynamic testing algorithms suitable for evaluating additional WCAG Guidelines which presently require expensive manual testing. Certainly, much work remains to be done to develop testing techniques and oracles capable of evaluating many of the more complex WCAG criteria. However, Agent A11y has already demonstrated that an autonomous, self-exploring agent-based solution can expand the capabilities of current single-page, static accessibility assessment tools.

References

Chillarege, Ram, I.S.Bhandari, Jarir Chaar, M.J.Halliday, D.S.Moebus, Bonnie Ray, M.-Y.Wong. 1992. "Orthogonal Defect Classification - A Concept for In-Process Measurements." IEEE Transactions on Software Engineering 18: 943 - 956.

Aamodt, A., Plaza, E. 1994. "Case-based reasoning: Foundational issues, methodological variations, and system approaches." AI Communications 7(1): 39–59.

AGENT. 2019. "AI Generation and Exploration in Test." https://github.com/ultimatesoftware/AGENT (accessed August 16, 2019).

Bai, A., Camilla, H., Viktoria, S. 2017. "A Cost-Benefit Analysis of Accessibility Testing in Agile Software Development Results from a Multiple Case Study." International Journal on Advances in Software 10(1,2). http://www.iariajournals.org/software/, (accessed August 27, 2019).

Becce, G., Mariani, L., Riganelli, O., Santoro, M. 2012. "Extracting widget descriptions from GUIs." International Conference on Fundamental Approaches to Software Engineering: 347–361.

Levenshtein, V. I. 1966. "Binary codes capable of correcting deletions, insertions, and reversals." Soviet Physics 10(8): 708–710.

Lin, J.-W., Wang, F., Chu, P. 2017. "Using semantic similarity in crawling-based web application testing." 2017 IEEE International Conference on Software Testing, Verification and Validation (ICST): 138–148.

Manning, C., Surdeanu, M., Bauer, J., Finkel, J., Bethard, S., McClosky, D. 2014. "The Stanford CoreNLP Natural Language Processing Toolkit." Proceedings of the 52nd Annual Meeting of the Association for Computational Linguistics: System Demonstrations: 55–60.

Pawlik, M., Augsten, N. 2015. "Efficient Computation of Edit Tree Distance." ACM Transactions on Database Systems, vol. 40 (1), No. 3. https://dl.acm.org/citation.cfm?id=2699485, (accessed August 27, 2019).

Santiago, D. 2018. "A Model-Based AI-Driven Test Generation System." FIU Electronic Theses and Dissertations: 3878. https://digitalcommons.fiu.edu/etd/3878, (accessed August 27, 2019).

"Selecting the number of clusters with silhouette analysis on k-means clustering." https://scikit-learn.org/stable/auto_examples/cluster/plot_kmeans_silhouette_analysis.html (accessed August 27, 2019).

Shubert, E., Rousseeuw, P.J., "Faster k-medoids clustering: improving the PAM, CLARA, and CLARANS algorithms." https://arxiv.org/abs/1810.05691 (accessed August 27, 2019).

Veloso, M. 1992. 'Learning by analogical reasoning in general problem solving." Carnegie Mellon University, 40. https://apps.dtic.mil/dtic/tr/fulltext/u2/a256573.pdf (accessed August 27, 2019).

Vigo, J., Brown, J., Vivienne, C. 2013. "Benchmarking Web Accessibility Evaluation Tools: Measuring the Harm of Sole Reliance on Automated Tests." Proceedings of the 10th International Cross-Disciplinary Conference on Web Accessibility.

Acknowledgements

We thank Brian Muras and Justin Phillips for their contributions to Agent A11y and this paper.

This page intentionally left blank.

Understanding and Testing Blockchain

John Cvetko
John.Cvetko@Tekasc.com

Abstract

Cryptocurrency, especially Bitcoin has received a lot of attention in the past couple of years. No matter what you think of cryptocurrency, the underlying technology known as blockchain, is finding its way into mainstream enterprise systems. When there is a business need to have distributed, secure and immutable transaction records between various organizations, blockchain is a natural fit. Understandably, the first to see the potential value of this technology has been the financial industry.

Blockchain was originally designed to enable untrusted parties to transact business using cryptocurrency. Instead of using a trusted middleman (like a bank) to complete the transaction, this role was shifted to technology. This, however, came at a cost; it can take several hours or even days to validate a single transaction, in addition to a significant amount of compute power and electricity to operate each node on the network.

But, what if blockchain technology was modified to accommodate different levels of trust and expanded to do more than just transfer cryptocurrency? Blockchain is now being tailored to achieve shorter transaction times, require less power, and provide integrated multi-use flexibility. As the technology is enhanced and shaped to specific markets, more organizations are seeing potential value for their operations.

Blockchain is a paradigm shift in the way we think of traditional networking, application development and deployment. Like all new disruptive technologies, it will require extensive testing, conducted by skilled and agile resources throughout its lifecycle. This paper looks at blockchain from many perspectives and discusses what the testing needs will be over time.

Biography

As a Principal of TEK Associates, Mr. Cvetko works with companies and government agencies to improve their organizations by helping them manage the IT challenges they face. He applies state of the art solutions to evolve business processes, creating more efficiency and productivity, all while maintaining and/or improving quality. In the span of 25 years he has held positions in systems engineering, product and program management and management consulting. The last 12 years have been primarily focused on assessing and implementing large enterprise software systems. He has worked with the state governments of Washington, Oregon, North Carolina, North Dakota, Mississippi, Utah, Kentucky, and Oklahoma. Earlier in his career he worked as a technical consultant for firms such as NIKE and Boeing, and in product development and program management for Tektronix, PGE/Enron and ASCOM.

1. Introduction

Many transaction workflows span a series of different companies, often with each company entering the same data into their systems. It is also not uncommon to have several intermediaries in the workflow that impose delays and charge fees for marginal services. Aside from being inefficient, it makes the transaction and all the companies in the workflow vulnerable to compromise by the least secure system in the network. If a centralized system (for example, a bank) is compromised due to fraud, cyberattack, or even a simple mistake, the entire business network can be affected.

Blockchain, also known as distributed ledger technology (DLT), is emerging as more than just a cryptocurrency platform. Its unique characteristics are fostering new ideas in the minds of technologist and business executives alike. The expectations are that it will be a platform consisting of peer-to-peer, consensus and data ledger layers that will usher in a new breed of Distributed Applications (DApps), see figure 1. This combination of technologies will change how commerce is conducted, assets are tracked, products and services are delivered. Moving beyond recording transactions, DLT can track and manage assets. These assets may be tangible (cars, packages, lettuce), or intangible (trade settlements, intellectual property, identity, software).

Because this technology will be evolving for many years, it will have challenges that IT professionals will need to work through to make it a reality. By relying on standard business and engineering practices, these systems will be deployed in a reliable and secure manner. Developing, deploying and testing these systems will require a shift in thinking about traditional networks and applications. This shift in thinking will require new testing strategies, methods, skills and technologies, some of which have yet to be conceived. This paper will discuss the characteristics of DLT, the technology lifecycle, and the potential challenges faced by IT testing professionals throughout this lifecycle.

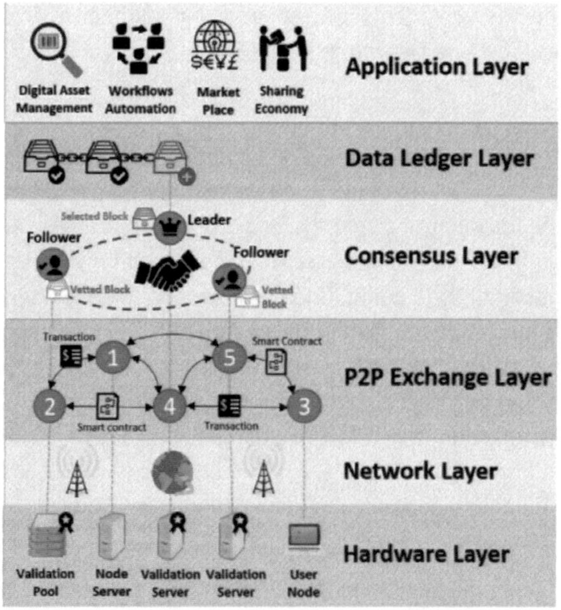

Figure 1. Blockchain Transactions

Source: Consortium Blockchains: Overview, Applications and Challenges [DIB 2018]

2. Blockchain Fundamentals

The blockchain architecture gives participants the ability to share a ledger, i.e., a permanent transaction record that's updated through peer-to-peer replication and validation. Peer-to-peer replication means that each node in the network acts as both a publisher and a subscriber. A node can receive or send transactions to other nodes, and the data is synchronized across the network as it's transferred. This information is available to all pertinent parties simultaneously, eliminating duplication of effort and reducing the need for intermediaries. It's also less vulnerable because it uses consensus algorithms to validate the information, prior to it being recorded on the blockchain.

A blockchain platform has the following key characteristics:

- **Consensus:** For a block to be appended to the chain, all participants must agree on its validity.
- **Provenance:** Participants know where the asset came from and how its ownership has changed over time.
- **Immutability:** No participant can tamper with a transaction after it has been recorded to the ledger. If a transaction is in error, a new transaction must be used to reverse the error, and both transactions are then visible.
- **Finality:** A single, shared ledger provides one place to go to determine the ownership of an asset or the completion of a transaction.

The Block and Chain

Blockchain owes its name to the way it stores data - in blocks that are linked together to form a chain. As the number of blocks grow, so does the blockchain. Blocks record and confirm the time and sequence of transactions, which are then are appended to the blockchain network, that is governed by rules agreed on by the network participants (consensus). A *transaction* represents an interaction between parties. With cryptocurrencies for example, a transaction represents a transfer of the cryptocurrency between network users. For business-to-business scenarios, a transaction is a way of recording activities occurring on digital or physical assets.

Each block contains a hash (a digital fingerprint), timestamped batches of recent valid transactions, and the hash of the previous block. The previous block hash links the blocks together and prevents any block from being altered or inserted between two existing blocks (see figure 2 below). In this way, each subsequent block strengthens the verification of the previous block, and therefore, the entire blockchain. This method renders the blockchain tamper-evident, lending to the key attribute of immutability. To be clear, while the blockchain contains data, it's not a replacement for databases, messaging technology, transaction processing, or business processes. Instead, the blockchain contains verified proof and security of the data; these benefits extend far beyond those of a traditional database. For example, it removes the possibility of tampering by a malicious actor, e.g., a disgruntled database administrator.

Figure 2. Blockchain

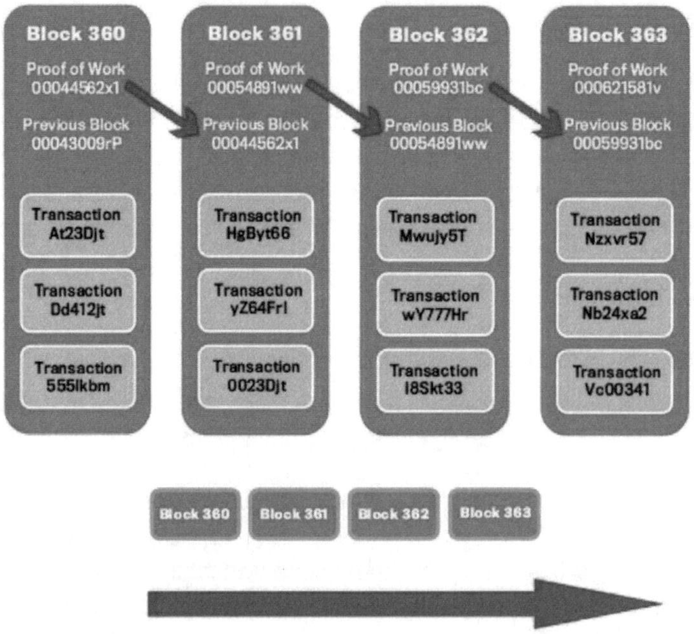

In a blockchain, network participants submit candidate transactions to the blockchain network via software (desktop applications, smartphone applications, digital wallets, web services, etc.). The software sends these transactions to a node or nodes within the blockchain network to create a candidate block.

Each network node will take any number of transactions, validate that they are "legitimate" – and put them into a candidate block. The candidate blocks generated by the participant nodes will vary arbitrarily, due to network latency, or intentionally because of network rules or incentives. So essentially, each node is building their own unique candidate block for presentation to all other nodes on the network. A candidate block is then selected by the network nodes to be appended to the chain based on the consensus method used. [Yaga 2018]

Chaincode

Chaincode, also known as a Smart Contract, is essentially code or business logic that can reside in a block transaction that has been appended to the blockchain. There are two classes of chaincode in blockchain, system and application.

System chaincode

System chaincode is distinguished as software that defines operating parameters and rules for some or all nodes within the network. For example, a Configuration System Chaincode (CSC) can be utilized to enforce network identity policies, ensuring that all participants meet specific security conditions before their digital signatures are considered valid, thus allowing them to operate on the network.

Application chaincode

Application chaincode is also known as user chaincode and is used to execute business logic when a specific condition is valid. Application chaincode incorporates business logic with metadata about its function, including the name, version, and counterparty signatures required to ensure the integrity of the code. Additionally, application chaincode can't be invoked directly by other chaincode on the blockchain; however, it can be queried.

Application chaincode can be as simple as a data update, or as complex as executing a business contract with conditions attached. For example, a contract can be written between two parties on the network that stipulates the terms and cost of shipping an item based on the desired delivery date and mode of transport. When this information is agreed on by both parties, it is permanently written to the blockchain, and when the item is received by the purchaser, the appropriate funds can then be automatically sent to the supplier. [Hyperledger VII 2018]

3. Consensus Models

Consensus is a central component of the blockchain technology. Without a trusted, central intermediary, the network of participating users that implement the decentralized system need to agree on the validity of what's being added to the chain. Consensus algorithms are used to validate that the block of transactions meets the requirements set forth by the network participants to append blocks to the chain.

There are a variety of consensus protocols that can be deployed and are dependent on the requirements of the participants. International standards' organizations are working towards defining standards for consensus protocols; this will allow product vendors the ability to implement whichever consensus mechanism is deemed best for the system in which it is deployed, and, in a more modular fashion. [Hyperledger VI 2017] [Morris 2019]

A consensus protocol has three main characteristics that determine its use in the network design.

Security
A consensus protocol is defined to be safe if enough nodes offer the same valid outputs as the algorithm dictates. This is also known as "consistency of the shared state".

Real-time
A consensus protocol requires a sufficient number of nodes participating in real-time to provide consensus that a candidate block is valid.

Participants
A consensus protocol operates best in environments where there is a large number of diverse participants...the more, the better. This ensures network "fault tolerance".

Balancing all the elements above is challenging, and each consensus protocol has characteristics that emphasize specific elements for the environments in which they are deployed. For example, public cryptocurrencies may focus more on security than on the time it takes to validate a block.

There are many different consensus mechanisms and only a few are discussed here.

Proof of Work

Proof of work (PoW) is a network consensus protocol utilized most notably by Bitcoin. This protocol is not desirable for general business use due to its significant operational costs. The proof of work comes in the form of an answer to a mathematical problem, one that requires considerable work to arrive at, but is easily verified to be correct once the answer has been found.

The problem to be solved is that the node must generate a block hash number that is below the "target hash" set in the network, in order to be selected to append their candidate block to the chain.

A target hash is generated as part of the PoW algorithm. Each node calculates this based on the level of desired difficulty. The target hash is continually adjusted and updated by the network nodes to keep the work needed to a specific range. For the Bitcoin blockchain this target was originally set so that it would take 10 minutes to solve the problem.

The only way to solve this problem is by the nodes on the network running a long and random process of generating block hashes, for the candidate block, on a trial and error basis. The result of the original hash function on the block is completely unpredictable, so there is no control over what the initial block hash value will be. To change the initial block hash value, the node will vary one specific value in the block header known as a nonce. The nonce will be changed, and the block contents will be rehashed until a block hash is found that is below the network target hash. The node that manages to solve the problem the quickest wins the right to append their candidate block to the chain. [De Angelis 2018]

Proof of Elapsed Time (PoET)

This concept was first introduced by Intel through the HyperLedger consortium and is considered a "lottery" protocol. The PoET consensus mechanism was developed specifically for Internet of Things (IoT) applications. This protocol is highly efficient and capable of scaling to thousands of nodes. The key element enabling the PoET model relies on Intel's Software Guard Extension (SGX) technology, currently available in some Intel CPUs. SGX is considered a Trusted Execution Environment (TEE) within the CPU that ensures that the code executing within the TEE cannot be tampered with by external software.

The PoET model relies on randomly distributing the "leader" (block publisher) election among all available participating nodes. This randomness is a secure way for other nodes to verify that a given leader was correctly selected, i.e., without any manipulation.

In each round of the lottery, network nodes receive a signed, randomized timer object from the TEE code within their CPU's. Each node subsequently waits for their randomized timer to expire. The node's timer that is the first to expire propagates a signed certificate to the network indicating that they are the block leader for that round. The message is authenticated by other nodes in the network, and the block is appended to the chain. Once the block is appended to the chain the next network lottery round begins.

When a node wins the lottery and is determined the leader, other nodes can easily verify the nodes authenticity because the leader will produce a signed attestation from their TEE that provides proof that the code has been correctly initialized in a trusted environment. [Cachin 2017]

While PoET is highly efficient and not nearly as resource intensive as Proof of Work systems, the technology is not without its critics. The main concerns are that a single vendor would control the underlying technology (the CPU), and if a security vulnerability was detected, it would be very difficult to correct it at scale.

Proof of Authority

This protocol does not depend on nodes solving arbitrarily difficult mathematical problems or a lottery, but instead uses a specific set of "authority" or "validator" nodes in the network. These are nodes that are explicitly allowed to approve candidate blocks produced by non-authority nodes. The proposed block must be validated and approved by a majority of authorities to be appended to the chain. This approach can be utilized by a private chain (internal network) to keep the block issuers accountable.

With PoA, security is maintained by earning the right to become and remain a validating node, so there is an incentive to retain the position that has been achieved. By attaching a "reputation" to the node's identity, validator nodes are incentivized to uphold the transaction process by gaining and maintaining trust over time. If a node produces the wrong validation of a block, or does not act as expected, its reputation suffers, and the node is no longer trusted with the authority role.

Practical Byzantine Fault Tolerance

The Practical Byzantine Fault Tolerance (pBFT) model primarily focuses on providing a practical Byzantine state machine that tolerates faults or malicious nodes. The algorithm is designed from the perspective that there are node failures and/or compromised nodes in the network acting maliciously.

Essentially, all the nodes in the pBFT model are ordered in a sequence with one node being the primary node (leader) and the others referred to as the backup nodes. In this method, all the nodes participate in the voting process and consensus is reached when more than two-thirds of all nodes agree that the candidate block is valid. pBFT can tolerate malicious behavior from up to one-third of all nodes to perform normally. For instance, in a system with 1 malicious node, there should be at least 4 nodes to reach a correct consensus. Once a majority of the nodes agree, the leader appends the block to the chain. In this method, consensus is reached quicker and more economically compared to a number of other consensus models.

PBFT has high throughput, low latency, and low computational requirements – all of which are desirable for IoT networks. However, its high network overhead limits scalability, thus, it would likely be applied to only small IoT networks.

4. Blockchain System Classifications

A public blockchain's most native environment is where there is no central authority and no point of trust between participants on a network…this is the most challenging environment for any system. To accomplish this task, the system uses raw compute power and complex algorithms to establish a high degree of trust among network participants. Trust through technology, while an impressive feat of engineering, increases the cost of deployments to a point that it is not feasible for the average private or hybrid (public/private) environment.

In general, all blockchain systems are constrained by three main properties: (a) decentralization, (b) scalability and (c) security. This is referred to as the "trilemma" of elements that need to be balanced to ensure an optimum design is employed for its intended purpose. [Qin 2018] Each class of blockchain discussed below will struggle to find the needed balance for its intended purpose. For example, a small ecosystem of 100 private companies may need a global decentralized and secure system that doesn't need to scale beyond this size for many years. On the other end of the spectrum, you may have a single company that tracks many IoT devices and may value scalability and decentralization over security. These lopsided trilemma deployments will drive new methods and technologies to satisfy consumer needs, e.g., Intel's PoET consensus model.

At a high level, there are two main classes of blockchains - permissionless and permissioned. The needs of these classes vary greatly and will undoubtedly expand the current limits of the trilemma.

Permissionless

Permissionless blockchains are considered public, which means that anyone can join and use it for the intended purpose. Permissionless blockchains are designed and operate with the perspective that their environment is hostile. These systems require the use of crypto-techniques, and robust consensus models to protect against malicious actor's intent on exploiting or breaching the system.

Companies that provide services to the public will have monetary transactions and or sensitive information as part of their exchange with (B2C), and between, their consumers (C2C). These systems will require scalable, cost-efficient consensus methods to make their business models viable. [Qin 2018]

Permissioned

In permissioned blockchains, participants are more trusted, and the use of on-chain and off-chain authentication mechanisms are tolerated. These systems operate in a limited decentralized environment and have rules and policies that participants will adhere to for the right to use the network. To ensure compliance to these rules and policies, independent auditors are employed to review, validate and attest to the transactions on the blockchain. There are two sub-classes of permissioned blockchain, consortium and private networks.

Consortium

Consortium networks have different companies operate in a specific context on a network, e.g., a manufacturer, transport company and a raw material supplier. Participant nodes are incentivized to behave honestly, because, if misbehavior is detected they may have their network privileges curtailed or even revoked.

An example of two independent companies formed by a consortium are Vakt and Komgo SA. These organizations will work in tandem to build a commodity exchange and settlement platform for oil companies, trading firms, banks and goods inspection companies. The companies associated with Vakt will handle the contract and terms processing and the companies associated with Komogo will act as the financial settlement arm of the exchange. This platform will be essential for the member companies to efficiently transact business in the future. [Rathod 2019]

Private

Private blockchains are where participants are known, and access is extremely limited, to either internal operations or among a select few companies. In this scenario, there are a predetermined set of nodes that participate in the network and they operate in a very limited decentralized environment. This use of blockchain would likely be for large organizations that have the need to permanently record information between divisions or trusted partner companies. For example, BNP is an international banking firm that conducted a private blockchain trial to determine if it could be utilized by their Asset Liability and Management (ALM) Treasury department. The trial was used to determine blockchain's feasibility for improving existing internal processes and providing immutable records between different business units on an international level. [Sundararajan 2017]

5. Centralized and Decentralized Applications

Blockchain, in-and-of-itself, isn't very useful if applications can't leverage the technology. When organizations design blockchain networks they will have two application options. They can continue to use legacy applications, or they can deploy new Decentralized Applications (DApps).

Legacy Applications

Existing application vendors will look to adapt their legacy, (centralized products) to work with blockchain. Integration to legacy applications is done through connectors called "oracles". Oracles provide a method for legacy applications to quickly adapt to decentralization by enabling them to leverage whichever blockchain architectures emerge as the dominate approach within their target vertical market. Another approach that can be taken by an application vendor, is to integrate blockchain into their existing products to provide a packaged solution, e.g., SAP's Leonardo technologies.

Decentralized Applications

In addition to the legacy application vendors, there will be many new companies that will develop enterprise decentralized applications (DApps), exclusively from a decentralized perspective. DApps not only communicate with the underlying blockchain, but can also manage the state of network actors.

A good example of a DApp for supply chain management, is being developed by four Chinese entities, Xiamen, Innov, Corelink, and VeChain. Their intent is to integrate a DApp, blockchain, IoT (RFID), artificial intelligence and cloud technologies to track physical assets and inventories as they are being shipped and stored. [Nugent 2018] Supply chain management involves multiple stakeholders operating in a coordinated effort, often resulting in a complex workflow. There are multiple levels of suppliers, manufacturers, service providers, distributors, and retailers that make recordkeeping and communications inefficient. The integration of DApps, IoT and chaincode can simplify the process by coordinating sensory data, documentation, and transparency to regulations.

For example, a participating manufacturing company would utilize a DApp to order, pay and monitor a shipment of raw material to a factory. If the shipment was delayed, it would be detected by the RFID component of the system, which would relay the information to the chaincode and ultimately the DApp. Using Artificial Intelligence, the DApp may determine the delay is out of acceptable limits for the factory and initiate an order on a commodity exchange for new material from another vendor. The new supplier agrees to fulfill the order and the contract would be recorded in the blockchain. Once the new material is received and verified by the factory, the DApp then communicates this information to the chaincode, which releases payment to the supplier via the same blockchain network. In this case, numerous emails, telephone communications and intermediaries are replaced by a highly integrated network.

6. When Does Blockchain Make Sense?

Because there are countless news articles and videos describing the "magic" of blockchain, it is important to understand the limitations of the technology to balance expectations. The current hype around the use of blockchain is much greater than the understanding of it, and as with all new technology, there is a tendency to want to apply it to every sector in every way imaginable. [Wüst 2017]

If cost and return on investment are satisfactory for the business case, then from a functional perspective, considering blockchain as a solution today makes sense when:

- No single participant requires sole authority to write data to the blockchain.
- Immutability of the data is necessary.
- A high degree of data security and redundancy is needed.
- All participants have the same incentives to participate.
- All participants require data transparency.
- The transaction speed is not a paramount concern for the participants.

But the list above is only relative to a point-in-time in the Technology Adoption Lifecycle (TAL) (see figure 3 below). This lifecycle represents the adoption of the technology by consumers over time, and as the technology matures, the deployment guidance will change with it.

The adoption lifecycle is a descriptive framework that classifies the adoption of technologies into five consumer phases: innovators, early adopters, early majority, late majority and laggards. These phases overlap and are subject to market forces, technology innovations and business advances that can affect the speed of adoption. [Moore 1991] The first three stages of the Technology Adaption Lifecycle will be the most dynamic and challenging for consumers and are further discussed below.

- Innovators seek out novel technology. They experiment, demonstrate, conduct pilot deployments, develop business cases, cost analysis, etc., to investigate the feasibility of use. These companies are keenly aware that failure to identify technical issues and real costs before investing are the main causes for significant schedule delays and (potentially) project failure. As these consumers review the feasibility of the technology, they also assess high risk areas that will need to mature in order to reach their desired business goals. They develop a close relationship with their vendors and often will shape the vendor's short-term product roadmap.

  Non-technical challenges are addressed during this phase as well, e.g., how decentralized governance models, business relationships and legal liabilities need to be handled between participating entities. [Hogan Lovells 2016] [Zetzsche 2018] Even in this high-risk environment companies forge ahead, often because they are in hyper competitive markets or have needs that are not satisfied by existing technologies.

- Early adopters stand on the shoulders of the innovators. The failures and successes of the innovators are found through published case studies, total cost of ownership models and more viable products available in the market.

- The innovators have reduced the risk of failure for the early adopters by paving the way through fundamental technology and business barriers. For early adopters, the viability risk has been diminished and their concern turns to selecting the system that will become the "dominate design" over time...the BETA vs. VHS risk. [Kwong 2019] This risk is difficult to mitigate because many factors are out of the control of the consumer. The main risk mitigation technique is to limit the size and scope of deployments to non-core areas of the business.

- If the technology enters the Early Majority phase, it has "crossed the chasm," and the stage is now set for rapid deployment growth (see figure 3). [Moore 1991] Dominate designs and standards coalesce and begin to drive interoperability among product vendors, further reducing risk and driving down prices. Early Majority consumers are practical, and if a product provides obvious value with tolerable risk, they will use it.

DApps will also follow the same adoption lifecycle but will have a "chicken and egg" relationship with independent blockchain vendors. As DApp vendors create and deliver more features that can be utilized by the business, the underlying blockchain deployment may not be efficient or powerful enough to deliver the desired services. DApp vendors may vertically integrate by incorporating a desired blockchain as part of their solution, or partner with blockchain vendors to present a coordinated solution to their clients.

As the technology matures and finds its way towards industry vertical dominant designs, the "when does blockchain make sense" list (mentioned above), will also evolve and be tailored to specific industry applications.

Figure 3. Technology Adoption Lifecycle

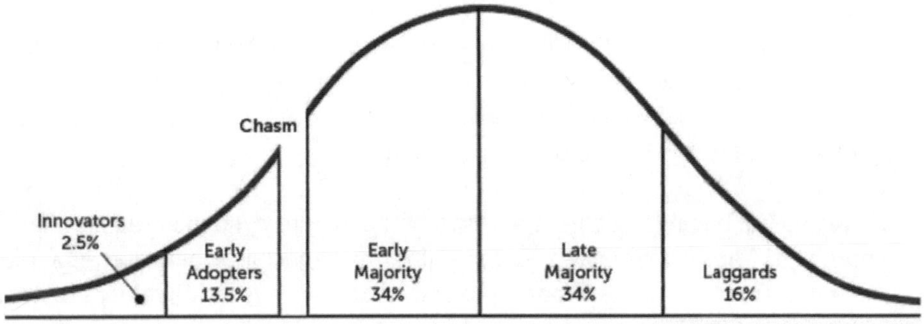

Source: Crossing the Chasm [Moore 1991]

7. Technology Adoption Lifecycle and Testing Lifecycle

The technology adoption lifecycle has a direct relationship to the quality assurance skillsets, testing strategies and tools needed to ensure that stable and secure systems are put into production. In general, when testing tools and strategies are immature then the testing staff knowledge, judgement and skillsets will be highly leveraged. As the testing tools and strategies mature the reliance on tester skillsets are greatly reduced. As mentioned above, the first three stages of the adoption lifecycle will be the most dynamic and challenging and will require QA teams to be agile.

- **Innovator Phase:** The innovator phase is primarily used by consumers to learn and evaluate new technology. It is marked by consumer demonstrations and trials that are often intense and run for short periods of time. System requirements at this stage will be fluid as consumers struggle to understand the technology and its application in their environment, i.e., they don't know what they don't know on a variety of fronts. As consumers refine their requirements and developers adjust and readjust their design approaches, testing is heavily focused on basic operation and stability.

This stage of the lifecycle will require highly skilled testers that can move across many domains and at a deep level. These individuals will be adept at programming, have a sound understanding of system engineering and will be working side by side with the system developers, designers, and client technical staff. This is sometimes referred to as "shifting left," but shifting left in this context is not done to increase productivity, quality, etc., but rather out of basic necessity.

Testing tools at this stage are usually "home-grown", minimal and not deployed for simulating large system loads or precision regression testing, but rather, they'll be used as coarse monitors and simulators for working through specific development problems.

- **Early Adopter Phase:** In this phase, product vendors will seek out "friendly" consumers that believe their products and long-term vision will be the dominate design or product in their specific industry. The systems will be deployed into limited production environments and will have constant system refinements. The pre-deployment testing periods will be much longer and will be conducted in close collaboration with other participants using the system. System testing will focus on the elements of the trilemma most applicable to the network deployment objectives.

  The network products will come with more internal monitoring capabilities allowing testers to validate and monitor many system elements during testing. Product vendors will support these consumers with a high degree of attention due to the immaturity of their products and the semi-custom nature of each deployment.

  QA teams will begin to segment and specialize in core system areas, i.e., the DApp or the blockchain. These segmented teams will further specialize between new feature testers and regression testers. New feature or core system changes will require testers with a high degree of system knowledge to develop increasingly nuanced tests that may be heavily instrumented.

  In decentralized deployments, there may be many companies, sometimes competitive, simultaneously testing a release for deployment. [ACT-IAC 2017] This will require a high degree of coordination and be conducted by cross company teams or independent firms, i.e., consortiums.

  Permissioned system deployments will have an inherent need for independent, continuous security and accounting audits. These audits will focus on processes, products, software releases and system operations. [Smith 2018] [Jefferson 2019] Consortium participants will require testing teams to leverage these tools for assurance that the appropriate battery of standardized audit tests will be conducted for all releases.

- **Early Majority Phase:** In this phase there will be tremendous growth in system deployments by consumers that need to keep pace with their competitors. These consumers will look to deploy products that conform to technology standards when they can, even at a premium. These premiums can be justified by ensuring that when these systems are built, participants can deploy any vendor product they prefer to use on the chain. This modularity will be further driven by consumers needing products that can be easily configured by technicians and that best suit the multiple needs of business and enterprise roadmaps.

Consumers will expect to find sufficient IT resources to execute their business strategies. This will create more demand for skilled, specialized resources to work in the decentralized networking field. Quality assurance strategies and processes will be mature at this point and the focus will be on finding greater efficiencies through the utilization of independent testing tools that are geared more towards non-developers.

8. Conclusion

As decentralized systems are introduced, companies will need quality assurance teams comprised of highly skilled testers to ensure these systems meet the desired quality expectations. This paper provided an overview of the technology and its lifecycle as it relates to quality assurance.

The pace of decentralized system adoption will be slow at first, and there will many setbacks and retrenching. Any estimate as to the time required for significant adoption by consumers is foolhardy, at best. However, understanding some of the high-level challenges will help to stimulate awareness and discussion among QA professionals early in the process. Hopefully, QA teams will document their decentralized testing experiences for public consumption and inclusion into the QA body of knowledge.

There are many additional aspects of blockchain and DApps that are not addressed in this introductory paper, e.g., specific industry case studies, Blockchain as a Service (BaaS), side chains, etc. These topics will be addressed by the author in future work.

Acknowledgement

The author would like to thank Dima Itkis, David E. Burgess and Tom Kapusta for their insight and constructive comments.

References

[DIB 2018] Dib, O., et. al., "Consortium Blockchains: Overview, Applications and Challenges" International Journal on Advances in Telecommunications, vol 11 no 1 & 2, year 2018, http://www.iariajournals.org/telecommunications/

[Yaga 2018] Yaga, D., Mell, P., Roby, N., Scarfone, K., "Blockchain Technology Overview," National Institute of Standards and Technology Internal Report 8202, October 2018

[Hyperledger VII 2018] Hyperledger Architecture Workgroup Volume II, Smart Contracts, Linux Foundation, 2018. Available: Hyperledger Architecture VII

[Hyperledger V1 2017] Hyperledger Architecture Workgroup Volume II, "Introduction to Hyperledger Business Blockchain Design Philosophy and Consensus," Linux Foundation 2017 Available: https://www.hyperledger.org/wp-content/uploads/2017/08/Hyperledger_Arch_WG_Paper_1_Consensus.pdf

[Morris 2019] Morris, N., 2019, "ISO Blockchain Standards Planned for 2021," Ledger Insights, June 2019 Available: https://www.ledgerinsights.com/iso-blockchain-standards/

[De Angelis 2018] De Angelis, D., 2018, "Assessing Security and Performances of Consensus Algorithms for Permissioned Blockchains," Rome, Sapienza University.

[Cachin 2017] Cachin, C., Vukoli´c, M., Whitepaper "Blockchain Consensus Protocols in the Wild," 2017, Zurich, IBM Research

[Qin 2018] Qin, K., Gervis, A., 2018, "An overview of blockchain scalability, interoperability and sustainability," Imperial College London

[Rathod 2019] Rathod, A., 2019, "Oil Giants BP and Shell Launch Oil-Trading Blockchain Platform," Toshi Times, January. Available: https://toshitimes.com/oil-giants-launch-oil-trading-blockchain-platform/

[Sundararajan 2017] Sundararajan, S., "BNP, EY Complete Blockchain Trial for Internal Treasury Operations" CoinDesk, October 17th. Available: https://www.coindesk.com/bnp-ey-complete-blockchain-trial-for-internal-treasury-operations

[Nugent 2018] Nugent, D., 2018, "Smart Corelink Joins VeChain's Strategic Partnership with Xiamen Innov" Cointrust, April 14th. https://www.cointrust.com/news/smart-corelink-joins-vechains-strategic-partnership-with-xiamen-innov

[Wüst 2017] Wüst, K., Gervais, A.,2017," Do you need a Blockchain?" 1st Crypto Valley Conference on Blockchain Technology. Available: https://eprint.iacr.org/2017/375

[Moore 1991] Moore, G.A. Crossing the Chasm, Harper Business, New York, 1991.

[Hogan Lovells 2016] Hogan Lovells 2016, "Blockchain Bites... twenty key legal issues to navigate," Hogan Lovells Blockchain Blog, June 7th
https://www.hoganlovells.com/en/blogs/blockchain-blog/blockchain-bites-twenty-key-legal-issues-to-navigate

[Zetzsche 2018] Zetzsche, D., Buckley, R., Arner, D., The Distributed Liability of Distributed Ledgers: Legal Risks of Blockchain," University of Illinois Law Review Vol. 2018 p. 1362 – 1407 Available: https://illinoislawreview.org/wp-content/uploads/2018/10/BuckleyEtAl.pdf

[Kwong 2019] Kwong, Y., Lew, P., McDowell, J., 2019 "Software Based Disruptive Change Initiatives Require a Culture of Quality," Excerpt from PNSQC 2019 Proceedings.

[ACT-IAC 2017] 2017 "Enabling Blockchain Innovation in the Federal Government," American Council for Technology – Industry Advisory Council October 16, 2017

[Smith 2018] Smith, M., 2018 "The blockchain challenge nobody is talking about." Price Waterhouse Coopers blog, March 15th. http://usblogs.pwc.com/emerging-technology/the-blockchain-challenge/

[Jefferson 2019] Jefferson, D., et. al., 2019, "What We Don't Know About the Voatz "Blockchain" Internet Voting System," https://cse.sc.edu/~buell/blockchain-papers/documents/WhatWeDontKnowAbouttheVoatz_Blockchain_.pdf

This page intentionally left blank.

Testing Benefits of SOLID Principles

Easa El Sirgany
easaemad14@gmail.com

Abstract

SOLID design principles are well known for their impact on flexibility and maintainability of software development, but it is rare (if ever) that these principles are touted for their benefits with respect to testing.

In my quest to find a testing library to suit my needs for testing C++ libraries, I found that most frameworks were merely extensions of older C testing libraries, allowing for classes and member methods. The problem with this was that it failed to address some of the more important aspects of Object Oriented Programming (OOP) languages, specifically inheritance. Due to this shortcoming, any tests built for a library would only work for the library, and all derivations would need to implement their own test; this goes against everything software stands for.

After understanding the problem with building a framework that could do this for any library or base class, the following two-step solution was developed: build testing assertions into the source (something that should be done regardless of testing) and abstract test functions to work for any derivation of a base class.

This paper details the general approach taken in creating actionable steps for existing software to allow for proper software testing ideologies and strategies. The first was identifying SOLID design principle violations in the source and educating the developers why these violations are important (and how fixing them simplifies their lives), and the second was educating developers and SQA engineers alike on how to build templated testing functions in order to build proper unit tests.

Biography

Easa El Sirgany studied computer engineering with an emphasis in security (primarily encryption) and mathematics. With his love of breaking things in order to understand how to better them, the transition to a Software Quality Assurance Engineer was seamless.

More recently, he has spent his time building automated testing frameworks and tools for industrial-grade 3D printers.

1. Introduction

One day my boss tasked me with writing unit tests for a suite of C++ libraries under development at the time. I had limited knowledge in existing testing tools, most of which came from testing C and Hardware Description Languages (HDLs), due to my background in Embedded Systems. After some research, I concluded that a framework to handle my needs did not exist. The problem stemmed from the fact that the few frameworks that I looked into could not address one of the strongest benefits of OOP languages: inheritance.

The idea of testing libraries piqued my interest because building a test suite that was complete and verifiable seems impossible without having knowledge of the implementation. Firstly, it is possible for objects of a library to be abstract, i.e. have at least one pure virtual method. In such cases, it is not possible to instantiate the class for testing, since we will need to create a derivation in order to override the pure virtual methods.

Another problem with this approach was the fact that writing a unit test for a library would only apply to the methods of the base classes. For example, if I were to write a suite of tests for a base class with expected output of a virtual method, this test is no longer valid as soon as someone overrides the virtual method.

From the understanding of the two problems noted above, I implemented two different solutions. The first solution was the more obvious approach: write a program that generates all possible combinations of derivations, and test these against a framework of templates. This idea was very ambitious and required me to use C++ in ways I did not know were possible, but still failed even though it compiled and ran just as I expected.

The underlying problem of all of this was the code that I was testing was not built with testing in mind. Those crazy people that spend their days on the sidewalk preaching about Test Driven Development (TDD) were right all along. Even though I was able to automate the process of building derivations of the base class, I had no way to assert the success of the test run. This new understanding of the problem led to the second solution: documenting the problems of the source (libraries) using SOLID design principles.

SOLID design principles are composed of five design principles used by Object Oriented Programming (OOP) languages in order to increase flexibility and maintainability of software, but it also comes with some lesser-known testing benefits. The five paradigms are as follows: Single Responsibility Principle (SRP), Open/closed principle, Liskov's Substitution Principle (LSP), Interface-Segregation Principle (ISP), and Dependency Inversion Principle (DIP).

This paper will showcase the testing benefits a couple of the SOLID design principles provide, as well as a practical application to using these paradigms for testing; namely SRP and LSP. The example code used in this paper is written (not compiled nor tested) in modern C++, and is just that: example code. There are several guidelines and rules ignored in order to optimize for space and/or complexity.

2. Single Responsibility Principle

SRP is the easiest to implement and understand how this makes unit testing and TDD much easier to utilize. Robert C. Martin (Uncle Bob) states, "A class should only have one reason to change" (Martin 2003, 95). The idea was an expansion of a paper written by D.L. Parnas on the strengths of simplifying large solutions into smaller components, starting with components "which are likely to change" (Parnas, 1972). This has been a common idea well before OOD, and those familiar with the Unix Philosophy will know this to be very similar to the first rule: "Make each program do one thing well...." (McIlroy, Pinson, Tague 1978).

2.1 Implementing Single Responsibility Principle

The core idea behind SRP is that each change should require only one modification to a single piece of the system. For example, the following logger class is responsible for logging messages to a log file maintained by the class:

```
void Logger::log(const std::string& message, const std::string& level)
{
    if(lFile.is_open()) {
        std::lock_guard<mutex> lock(logMutex);
        lFile << "[" << level << "]" << message << std::endl;
        lFile.flush();
    }
}
```

The third line of this method checks to ensure that our log file is open, if not the logger does nothing. After this, the std::mutex is locked to save any threaded implementation of the logger. Line 5 is the area of interest covered in depth below, and the sixth line synchronizes the file with the underlying device in order to prevent any data loss in the event of an unexpected shutdown.

The first issue with line five is that any derivation of our logger will have to override the whole ::log() method in order to modify the formatting of the logged message; this breaks the open/closed principle. Every logger should log the same way, i.e. write to a file and flush to sync with the underlying device with mutual exclusion. Furthermore, there are at least two reasons to change the ::log() method above: *how* the logger class logs messages and *what* the logger logs to the log file. Separating the "how" and the "what" could look something like the following:

```
1.  void Logger::log(const std::string& message, const std::string& level)
2.  {
3.      if(lFile.is_open()) {
4.          std::lock_guard<mutex> lock(logMutex);
5.          lFile << formatMessage(message, level) << std::endl;
6.          lFile.flush();
7.      }
8.  }
```

Going back to the fifth line of the above example, the ::formatMessage() method makes use of our two parameters passed to the ::log() method in order to generate a formatted log message. This allows the logger to format the message as needed, as well as any derivation of this class to override the formatting of a message (assuming ::formatMessage() is a virtual method).

Before moving on to analyzing testing benefits of SRP, I should note that this is a very simple example and differentiating between reasons for change is a common problem. Uncle Bob wrote a blog articulating this in more depth, stating the "reason is about people" (Martin 2014).

2.2 Testing Single Responsibility Principle

More importantly (for the purpose of this document) than the flexibility that SRP provides, breaking the formatting of messages into different methods simplifies testing strategies. It may be difficult to understand the full impact that SRP has on testing from the example above due to the simplicity of the ::log() method since there are only two operations that are performed, neither of which addressing points of failure. The following example initializes the logger class:

```
bool Logger::init(bool verbose)
{
    auto retVal{false};
    if(preInit()) {
        lFile.open(fileName);
        retVal = lFile.is_open();
    }

    postInit(retVal);
    return retVal;
}
```

This example initialized our logger class, using a ::preInit() and ::postInit() method on lines 4 and 9, respectively. This is a common open/closed practice to allow derivations to extend upon the logger initialization, without modifying the inherent initialization process. Consequently, these two methods ensure the ::init() method conforms to SRP, assuming they are both virtual, since they allow changes to be contained to one method. If our pre-initialization succeeds, we attempt to open the (member variable) log file and set our return value before returning.

Testing the initialization of the logger, there are two conditions that are required to be true in order to assert success: ::preInit() returns "true" and we are able to open the file lFile. The beauty of conforming to SRP is that if we fail, we can differentiate between the operation that failed by checking ::preInit() directly. Assuming that Logger is a base class, ::preInit() should always return true if it is a virtual function to allow the least amount of restrictions if a derived class chooses to not override this method. Therefore, if the initialization fails, there is a direct correlation with opening the file.

Furthermore, if we override ::preInit() to always return false, we can double-check this against the result of testing the ::init() method. If ::preInit() returns false but ::init() succeeds, it can be stated with confidence that there is a bug in the initialization of the logger. This ties nicely into LSP since this test will work for any derivation of the logger.

3. Liskov Substitution Principle

The formal definition of LSP states the following subtype requirement: "Let $\phi(x)$ be a property provable about objects x of type T. Then $\phi(y)$ should be true for objects of type S where S is a subtype of T." (Liskov and Wing 1994, 1812). I find this terminology confuses many (not completely from the usage of mathematical notation) due to the "$\phi(y)$ should be true" portion of the quote. This statement does not mean that every subsystem that returns true for type S should return true for type T, but rather *how* the subtype is determined should be true for all derivations. The following example demonstrates the use of LSP by calculating the area of rectangles:

```
1.  class Rectangle {
2.  protected:
3.      int width, height;
4.  public:
5.      Rectangle(int w, int h) { width = w; height = h; }
6.      virtual ~Rectangle() = default;
7.      int getWidth() { return width; }
8.      int getHeight() { return height; }
9.      long int calculateArea() { return width * height; }
10. protected:
11.     virtual void setWidth(int w) { width = w; }
12.     virtual void setHeight(int h) { height = h; }
13. };
```

The Rectangle class contains width and height private member integers, along with their public getters and protected setters. The setters on lines 9 and 10 are virtual because the Square class below will override the functionality of these methods. The ::calculateArea() method is important for testing and conforms to LSP; further explanation below. Since (mathematically) a square is a rectangle, the following example should be correct:

```
class Square : public Rectangle {
public:
   Square(int w, int h) : Rectangle(w, h)
   {
      if(w not_eq h) {
         throw invalid_argument("Sides not same size!");
      }
   }
   virtual ~Square() = default;

protected:
   void setWidth(int w) override { width = w; height = w; }
   void setHeight(int h) override { height = h; width = h; }
};
```

Since a square is a rectangle with all four sides being the same length, the Square class requires both width and height to match, and a call to ::setWidth() and ::setHeight() set both values to ensure our square is always valid. The inherited ::calculateArea() method works for both the Square and Rectangle classes, so it conforms to LSP. The following test function tests this functionality for any type of rectangle.

```
1.  bool testArea(Rectangle& r)
2.  {
3.     r.setWidth(3);
4.     r.setHeight(4);
5.     return (r.getWidth() * r.getHeight() == r.calculateArea());
6.  }
```

If a base class Rectangle is passed to the testArea() function, it can be verified that the area is equal to the product of the width and the height (12 in this case). This validation is the same for a Square class, with the difference being that the width and the height always being equivalent. After line 3 in the test function, all sides of a square will have a value of three until the call on line 4 changes all sides to four. Regardless of order of setting width or height of a Square class (or the values used in the setters), it will always have correct implementation when tested with line 5.

The use of the rectangle and square classes is a popular example for LSP, and Uncle Bob wrote an article on LSP using a very similar example (Martin 1996, 3-7). Before moving onto testing strategies using LSP, it is important to understand why Uncle Bob and I disagree as to whether a square is a rectangle or not.

The following is the test function used by Uncle Bob:

```
1.  void g(Rectangle& r)
2.  {
3.     r.setWidth(5);
4.     r.setHeight(4);
5.     assert(r.GetWidth() * r.GetHeight() == 20);
6.  }
```

The only difference between the testArea() and the g() test functions is the assertion (or Boolean return value of success) on line 5 for both functions. The problem with Uncle Bob's test function is due to the Rectangle class being incomplete or the implementation of the test is just wrong.

If the Rectangle class has requirements (depending on expectations of the class itself and how it will be used) to calculate the area of a rectangle, this **must** be built into the class and tested in the same manner as the testArea() function. If no such requirement exists, however, testing this functionality is not a valid test of any type of rectangle. Rewriting the test in order to ignore the calculation of area better demonstrates the requirements of the Rectangle class:

```
1. void gPrime(Rectangle& r)
2. {
3.     r.setWidth(5);
4.     r.setHeight(4);
5.     assert(r.GetWidth() == 5); // Square classes will fail here
6.     assert(r.GetHeight() == 4);
7. }
```

gPrime() has the same error as the g() test function without the noise of area calculation, i.e. this test makes the assumption that the width will not be changed for any rectangle when setting the height. **If** this were a requirement of a Rectangle, **then** it would not be possible for a Square to be a Rectangle. Without this requirement, however, this test is invalid and should be two different tests: testing validity of setting the width and testing the validity of setting the height of a Rectangle. This could be also be done by switching lines 4 and 5 in the gPrime() test, which will work for any type of Rectangle.

3.1 Testing Benefits of Liskov Substitution Principle

One of the biggest benefits of LSP are the testing benefits provided by merely conforming to LSP. Since "ϕ(y) should be true for objects of type S where S is a subtype of T", any test written for an interface or base class can be used for all derived classes. Before moving onto testing our Rectangle class, it would be helpful to have a class that does some error checking:

```
class Rectangle {
protected:
    int width, height;

public:
    Rectangle(int w, int h)
    {
        if(not setWidth(w) or not setHeight(h) {
            throw invalid_argument("Invalid dimensions");
        }
    }

    //...
protected:
    // ...

    virtual bool setHeight(int h)
    {
        auto retVal{false};
        if(h > 0) {
            height = h;
            retVal = true;
```

```
    }
    return retVal;
}
```

Now that we have a Rectangle class that asserts valid dimensions, the following tests are valid for any type of rectangle:

```
template<class R>
bool testGetWidth(int w, int h)
{
    auto retVal{false};
    try {
        R rect(w, h);
        retVal = (w == rect.getWidth());
    } catch(...) {} // This demonstration does nothing with caught exceptions

    return retVal;
}

//...

template<class R>
bool testCalculateArea(int w, int h)
{
    auto retVal{false};
    try {
        R rect(w, h);
        retVal = (rect.getWidth() * rect.getHeight() == rect.calculateArea());
    } catch(...) {}

    return retVal;
}
```

Each of these tests attempt to instantiate a Rectangle object and determine success of the method tested. The benefit of this approach, as compared to the assertion method used in the last section, is that the test allows for failures when expected. For example, if I run testGetWidth<Square>(-1, 3), this test will fail (for multiple reasons), but this is still a valid test that should be run to ensure that it fails gracefully.

The importance of the above test functions is that the testing implementation for any type of rectangle can utilize these for their testing strategies, since success or failure is not inherent within these functions. This is an abstraction layer between the implementation and the expectation of a Rectangle class object. The following example test will implement a discrete test for evaluating the area of a Square specifically, using the knowledge of the expected behavior of a Square:

```
void validAreaSquareTest() {
    for(auto side{1}; side > 0; side++) { // Overflow will terminate
        if(not testCalculateArea<Square>(side, side)) {
            cerr << "Area test failed for square with side: " << to_string(side) << endl;
        }
```

```
6.      }
7.  }
```

Since the expectation of any Square object is that this should pass for all positive width/height values, this test should pass for all values without having to modify the template test function. For example, in the event that requirements change and operating in two dimensions is no longer sufficient, these tests are still valid for testing anything that derives from a Square object (much like it did when testing a Square object derived from a rectangle base class).

4. Conclusion

In conclusion, implementing SOLID design principles not only benefits the flexibility and maintainability of the software itself, but also simplifies testing strategies by reducing redundancy of testing functions and allowing for inherent assertions of expected behavior.

Software contains more functions that are easier to understand when it conforms to SRP and, therefore, simplifies maintainability when deriving from base classes and interfaces. This allows tests to more thoroughly test the software and provide better feedback when the system does not perform as expected, while allowing specific tests to cater to expected behaviors of different types of objects.

Likewise, test functions built for interfaces and base classes are valid for all derivations when the software complies with LSP. Even though there will be a greater number of smaller test functions written (the side effect of SRP), these functions hold true for all children when abstracted from the implementation of the test, meaning fewer tests are written in total and redundancy is removed.

Since everyone loves a happy ending, I will share the outcome of the implementation of this work when applied to the project I was asked to work on. I wrote many stories and bugs relating to violations of SOLID design principles for a handful of existing libraries so that I could begin working on templated test functions. During the refactor of the libraries, developers found bugs that had existed for years, before I even started implementing test.

References

Martin, Robert C. 2003. Agile Software Development, Principles, Patterns, and Practices. Prentice Hall

Parnas, D.L. "On the Criteria To Be Used in Decomposing Systems into Modules." Communications of the ACM 15, no.12 (December 1972): 1058

McIlroy, Doug, Pinson, E.N., Tague, B.A. "Unix Time-Sharing System: Foreword" (PDF). The Bell System Technical Journal. Bell Laboratories. (8 July 1978): 1902–1903

Martin, Robert C. 2014 "The Single Responsibility Principle." The Clean Code Blog. https://blog.cleancoder.com/uncle-bob/2014/05/08/SingleReponsibilityPrinciple.html (accessed June 20, 2019)

Liskov, Barbara H. and Wing, Jeannette M. "A Behavioral Notion of Subtyping". ACM Transactions on Programming Languages and Systems 16, no. 6 (November 1994): 1811-1841

Martin, Robert C. 1996 "The Liskov Substitution Principle." C++ Report. https://web.archive.org/web/20151128004108/http://www.objectmentor.com/resources/articles/lsp.pdf (accessed June 20, 2019)

Achieving a Culture of Software Quality for Android Robots

Vivek Kumar[1], Shreyes Joshi[2], Catherine Lee[3], Anya Bohra[4], Krish Aditya[5], Sneha Jeyasingh[6], and Bo Li[7]
totalchaosftc@gmail.com, bo.a.li@intel.com

Abstract

Robotics software quality is very crucial to control robot hardware while interacting with the physical world to accomplish a set of tasks. The software needs to tackle sensor errors, software exceptions, robot hardware failures and uncertainties from the external environment. This paper describes the challenges of achieving a culture of software quality for an Android platform robot based on the experiences of the First Tech Challenge (FTC) robotics team, Total Chaos.

To maximize the quality of FTC work, Charles Handy Athena culture model was employed to provide a small-team culture, working with flexibility, adaptability, and empowerment. The optimum level of power distributions and cooperation was established to maximize team efficiency. The use of the machine learning, embedded with modular software and hardware, further increased the effectiveness of the design process. The case study of an FTC Android robot demonstrates how the culture of teamwork and collaboration improved the development process, how modular design and documentation drastically improved the efficiency and quality of Android robot design and implementation, and how Deep Learning TensorFlow based Neural Network enabled accurate autonomous object detections.

Biography

The authors are high school students from the Total Chaos robotics team. The team is a four-year veteran FIRST Tech Challenge (FTC) team from Portland, Oregon. They have participated at the state and world level competitions. In 2016, they advanced to the world championships getting recognitions for their competitive robot, programming and contribution to the communities. The team developed a streamlined design and building process while ensuring software quality. The team also focuses on outreach activities in educating young students in communities about Science, Technology, Engineering and Mathematics (STEM) through Tech Talks, community open houses, and mentoring younger robotics teams.

Bo Li works in software developments and managements for Logic Technology Development in Technology and Manufacturing Group (TMG) at Intel. He joined Intel in 1999 after receiving Ph.D. from Georgia Institute of Technology. Since then, he has been focusing on software development, quality, performance, and testing for variety of software applications. Outside of work, he volunteers to mentor robotics teams in the community for students to foster passion and knowledge in STEM.

1. Introduction

It has long been recognized that experiential and hands-on education provides superior motivation for students to start at a young age. Robotics has been shown to be a superb tool for hands-on learning, not only of robotics itself, but of general topics in Science, Technology, Engineering, and Mathematics (STEM). Learning with robotics gives students an opportunity to engage with real life problems that require STEM knowledge. Mataric et al [1] describes the approach of enabling hands-on experiential robotics for all ages through the introduction of a robot programming workbook and robot test-bed. The workbook and test-bed provide readily accessible materials to K-12 students for direct immersion in hands-on robotics. Additionally, the success of learning science through robotics is explored by Chow et al [2] through their experiences.

For Inspiration and Recognition of Science and Technology (FIRST) is a team-based robotics program created for students aged 6-18. Within the FIRST program, there are four different sub-programs: Jr. FIRST Lego League (Jr. FLL) for students aged 6-9, FIRST Lego League (FLL) for students aged 9-13, FIRST Tech Challenge (FTC) for students aged 12-18, and FIRST Robotics Challenge (FRC) for students aged 14-18 [3]. As the programs progress, the tasks become more difficult and require deeper STEM knowledge to accomplish. Jr. FLL and FLL are Lego based programs, while FTC and FRC require teams to use Java programming and build with metal parts. Teams are required to develop strategy and build robots based on sound engineering principles. The ultimate goal of FIRST is to reach more young people with a lower-cost and more accessible opportunity to discover the excitement and rewards of STEM.

1.1 Background for FIRST Tech Challenge Robot Programming

In the FTC program, teams of 5-15 members build, program, and operate robots that compete in a head-to-head challenge. The field the robots compete on are 12ft by 12ft in size, and the robots have a size limit of 18in by 18in by 18in.

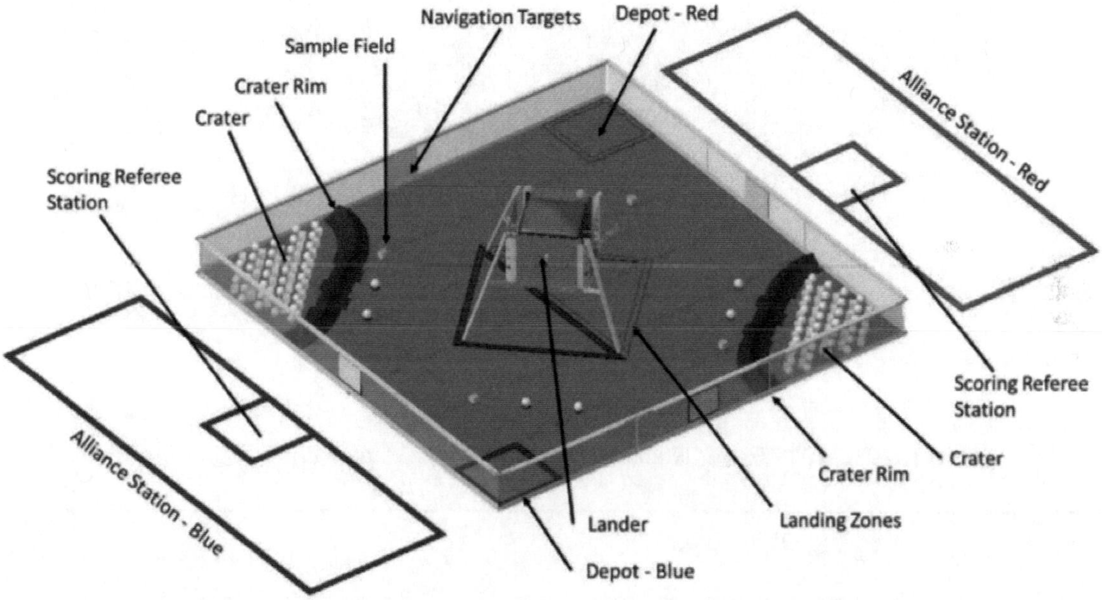

Figure 1. FTC field setup for 2018-19 season [4]

Figure 1 showcases a digital drawing of the field for the 2018-2019 Rover Ruckus FTC challenge. Although the challenges change every year, there are time-based rules that stay the same. All of the matches are 2 minutes and 30 seconds long. The first 30 seconds is the autonomous period where the robot is required to accomplish tasks autonomously. For the Rover Ruckus challenge, every robot starts in the parking zone or hung on the lander via the lander support bracket (See *Figure 2*). Driver control period begins 5 seconds after the autonomous period ends. For the driver control period, each team designates two team members to be in charge of controlling the robot, and one coach who helps the drivers keep track of time and looks for ideal positions. End game period is the last 30 seconds of driver control time. During end game, a new set of challenges are open for the teams to complete. For the most part, the challenges during end game are the hardest and highest scoring. The more challenges the robots complete, the more points the team scores. The play style is 2 teams vs. 2 teams. Each team is paired up with another team to form an alliance. Two alliances compete against each other during every match. Alliances are chosen randomly and change from match to match. The alliance that accumulates the most points wins the match.

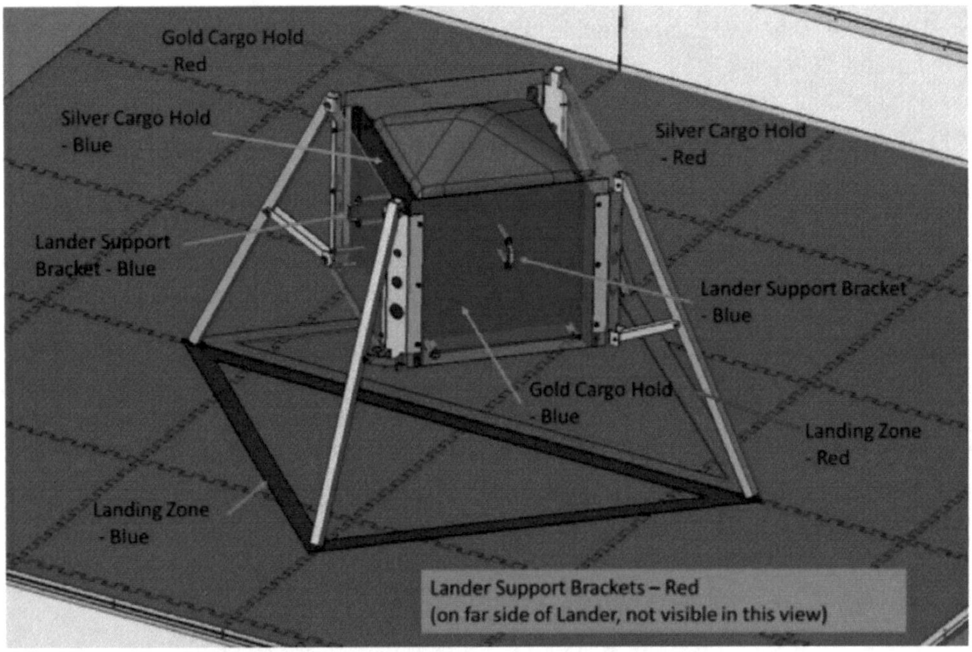

Figure 2. FTC Rover Ruckus Lander Details [4]

Table 1 shows the Rover Ruckus FTC challenge Game Period and Scores:

Table 1: 2018-2019 Rover Ruckus FTC Challenge Game Period and Scores

Game Period	Scoring Objectives
A — Autonomous Period	• Drop down and unlatch from the lander (30 points) • Knock off only the gold mineral from the tape mark (25 points) • Drop a small team marker in their corresponding depot (15 points) • Park in a parking zone (10 points)

B — Driver Control Period Scoring	• Collect minerals from the crater and deposit them in the lander (5 points each). The minerals have to be deposited in the corresponding cargo hold to be counted for points. The robot can only hold 2 minerals at a time. • Collect minerals and deposit them in the depot (2 points each)
C — End Game Scoring	• Continue scoring minerals (5 points each) • Latch and hang on the lander (50 points). • Partially park in crater (15 points) • Fully park in crater (25 points).

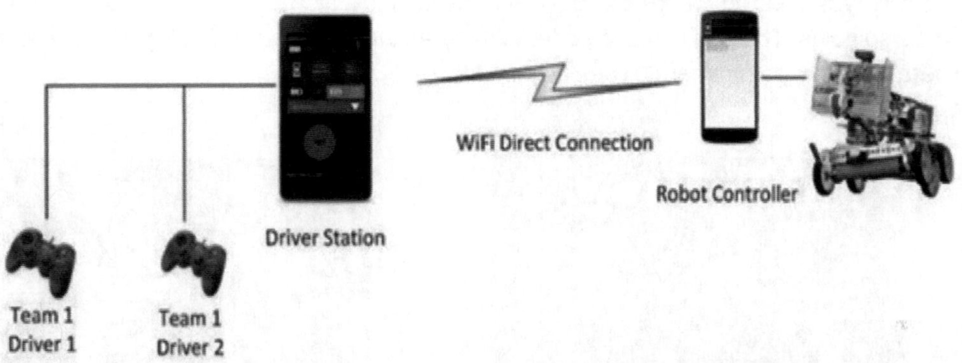

Figure 3. The control system of an FTC robot and its subsystems consisting of joysticks (used by drivers), Android smartphones with pre-loaded software programs, and core components (e.g., external sensors, motors, power, etc.) to detect and control FTC robot [5]

FTC utilizes Java through the Android Studio platform to program the robot to move and compete (See Figure 3). The Android programs are downloaded and run on a phone which is called the robot controller. The robot controller is wired to the Rev Expansion hub, which is connected to the motors and servos. Through this, the robot controller can tell the module when to give servos power. The robot controller also uses Wifi direct to communicate with the Driver Station, which is a phone that is kept near the user. The Driver Station acts almost like a remote control, where certain programs can be selected and be told to run. Gamepads are connected to the driver station through a USB hub. When a driver clicks a button on the gamepad, it registers with the driver station, which sends a signal to the robot controller through Wifi direct. Using the downloaded program, the Robot Controller tells the Expansion hub what motors or servos to give power to, making the robot move.

1.2 Introduction to FTC Robot for Rover Ruckus Challenge

The robot design is the foundation to solve the challenge for the FTC season. For 2018-2019 Rover Ruckus challenge, the robot drivetrain from Total Chaos team is a four wheel drive with mecanum wheels for added maneuvering ability, including sideways and diagonal movement. The wheels are powered by NeveRest 40 motors mounted vertically, attached by bevel gears in each of the corners of the robot. This is advantageous as it empties out the center of the robot, which not only provides more space for other robot modules, but also enables easier access when making repairs and troubleshooting issues. The lower central space of the robot features the REV electronic interface modules while the upper side holds the Moto G4 Play robot controller to aid with Vuforia. The entirety of the robot was built to produce an efficient scoring system that had the ability to stand its ground.

A major part of the robot is the mineral scoring module, which was used to retrieve and score gold and silver minerals during the tele-op period. The mineral scorer takes up a large portion of the robot, due to its overwhelming value in this year's game as a major differentiator amongst top teams. The scoring mechanism utilizes two sets of linear slides that can extend 35 inches, which allows to collect minerals by extending over the crater walls. The whole mechanism is attached to two motors which allows it to pivot up and down to score minerals into the lander.

The box can hold two minerals and has the ability to sort the minerals. It is observed that gold minerals have a height of 2 inches while silver minerals have a height of 2.75 inches. Using the measurements of the minerals, a box was created where the gold and silver minerals go in opposite directions, into their corresponding cargo holds. The addition of a sorter eliminates the need to sort through the crater and collect only silver minerals or only gold minerals (See Figure 4).

(a)

(b)

Figure 4. Total Chaos FTC Robot a) Box b) Depositing Mechanisms

Three sensors were utilized to maximize the efficiency during both the tele-op and autonomous (Figure 5).

1. The motor encoders, which are sensors built into each NeverRest motor that use counts to track the rotations of each motor. By using the diameter of the wheel and a counts per rotation constant specific to the motor, the robot is able to convert inches into counts. This meant that the software can tell the robot to move x inches and it would. However, these encoders aren't entirely accurate. While this doesn't cause too many problems with straight movements, the issues really appear with turns, which are more dependent on accuracy. Because of the inconsistency, it was decided to use the REV IMU gyro sensor for turns. This sensor was built into the Rev power distribution module, which gave power to all of our motors.
2. The gyro tracked the angle of the robot, and allowed the robot to make turns to specific angles, instead of depending on encoder counts.

3. The final sensor that was used is the phone camera, which allowed the robot to locate the gold and silver minerals, and knock the correct one.

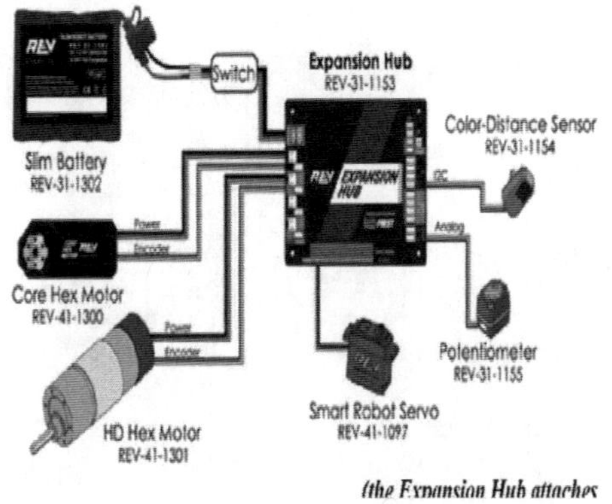

Figure 5. Total Chaos FTC Robot Sensors

1.3 Introduction to a Culture of Software Quality

FTC software quality is very crucial due to the high expectations of consistent performance during FTC competitions. If the software fails, it can significantly impact FTC competition results. A quality-focused culture leads to high quality products, which allow for high scoring capabilities during competitions.

This paper presents two main challenges in accomplishing a culture of software quality for FTC robotics competitions. The first challenge is ensuring that the software can be adapted rapidly while ensuring high software quality. Rover Ruckus was released on September 8th, 2018, and the first competition was on January 27th, 2019. This means we had a short four months to design, build, test, program and refine a competition-ready robot. The second challenge is ensuring that the robot can utilize machine learning software to minimize the effects of the constantly changing physical world and make the right decisions in different situations. The machine learning algorithms have to be tested thoroughly to ensure high quality robot performance.

2. Achieving a Culture of Software Quality in Android Robots

With a small team of six members, efficiency was crucial to produce a functional and competitive robot within the 4 month build season. As our team gained experience, we refined our work ethic to complete all of our tasks in a timely manner. We found it necessary to develop a structure that would utilize the strengths and interests of every team member. We've found that the Athena Culture of Charles Handy's management theory has helped us accomplish those goals best. Along with the Athena Culture, we also utilized modular design, effective documentation and Tensor Flow machine learning to further increase the quality of our robot.

Charles Handy is an author and philosopher known for his work in organizational behavior and mechanics. He is also known for developing the Charles Handy Theory, in which he describes four different management structures - based on power, role, task, and person (See Figure 6 [5]). Each of these structures is commonly connected to four Greek Gods: Zeus (power), Apollo (role), Athena (task), and Dionysus (person). The Athena culture is a task-based culture that centers around flexibility and adaptability. The core of this structure involves subteams that are formed to complete different tasks. By having subteams, individuals are enabled to work on a myriad of projects based on their own skills and interests. It also saves time because tasks can be done in parallel [6].

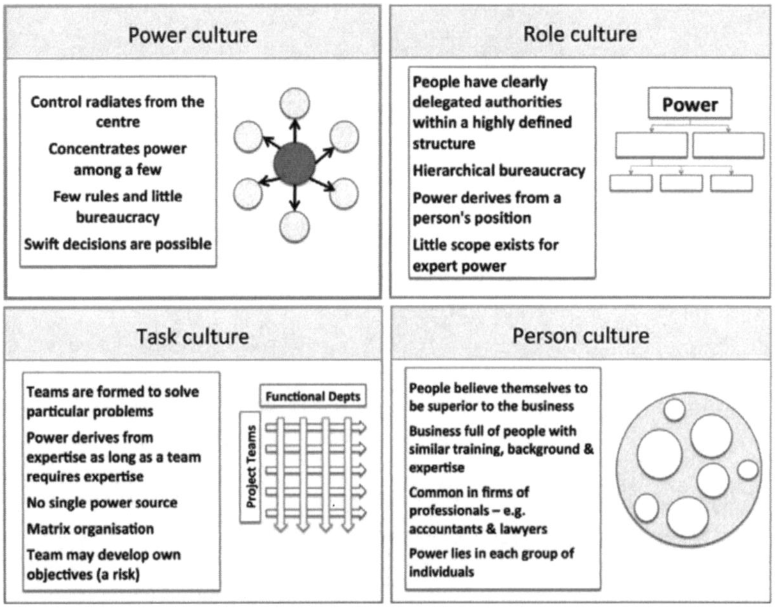

Figure 6. Charles Handy Model of Team Management

We also utilized modular design to allow changes to certain elements of the robot to be fast and efficient. The independent nature of each mechanism allowed us to isolate different parts of the robot to easily pinpoint a problem. After pinpointing a problem, we could easily remove the mechanism and make changes without altering the rest of the robot.

Performance expectations for the robot increase after every elimination tournament, meaning that constant improvements need to be made. The use of effective documentation allowed us to note past robot performance, previous iterations, stress tests, and test runs to more easily brainstorm and create the next design.

Lastly, we employed TensorFlow machine learning technology for software quality improvements. TensorFlow is a deep learning library recently open-sourced by Google [7]. TensorFlow provides primitives for defining functions on tensors and automatically computing their derivatives. Formally, tensors are multilinear maps from vector spaces to the real numbers and fundamental mathematical constructs in fields such as physics and engineering. Historically however, tensors have made fewer inroads in computer science, which has traditionally been more associated with discrete mathematics and logic. The state of affairs has started to change significantly with the advent of machine learning and its foundation on continuous, vectorial mathematics. Modern machine learning is founded upon the manipulation of tensors and the calculus of tensors. The TensorFlow Machine Learning process utilizes image recognition (Vuforia) to record the location of the minerals for later use. When hanging, the robot phone camera activates Vuforia, allowing the TensorFlow image recognition to initialize and scan the field for objects. The TensorFlow Machine Learning system is trained to recognize the gold/silver mineral by being shown numerous images of the objects from multiple angles, allowing for a complete perspective to be produced for the high quality of object detection software.

3. Case Study: FTC Android Robot Culture of Software Quality

3.1 Charles Handy's Athena Culture (Task Based Work Culture)

The Athena culture is a team-based culture that centers around flexibility and adaptability. The core of this structure involves subteams that are formed to complete specific tasks. Additionally, the Athena culture is flexible; individuals are enabled to work with several subteams based on their own skills and interests to accomplish different tasks and missions.

As described in sections 1.1, 1.2 and 1.3, the Rover Ruckus challenge requires robots to accomplish a multitude of varying tasks. One robot must have several subassemblies to accomplish them all. We created several subteams for each subassembly, in addition to programming and outreach (See Figure 7). Following the Athena Culture team management enabled our team to design, build, and program every subassembly in parallel and accomplish the robot control tasks to meet the critical need dates.

By utilizing the Athena culture, we were able to drastically decrease our overall build, programming and testing time. Without the sub-teams system, it would've taken an estimated 12 months to complete our robot (See Figure 8). Being able to work on many tasks in parallel allowed us to completely design, build, program, and test our robot in 4 months. Furthermore, software development was accelerated as we were able to create and validate code for each assembly without it being on the completed robot. When all subassemblies were implemented onto the robot, we already had reliable code that was developed alongside the hardware design and implementations.

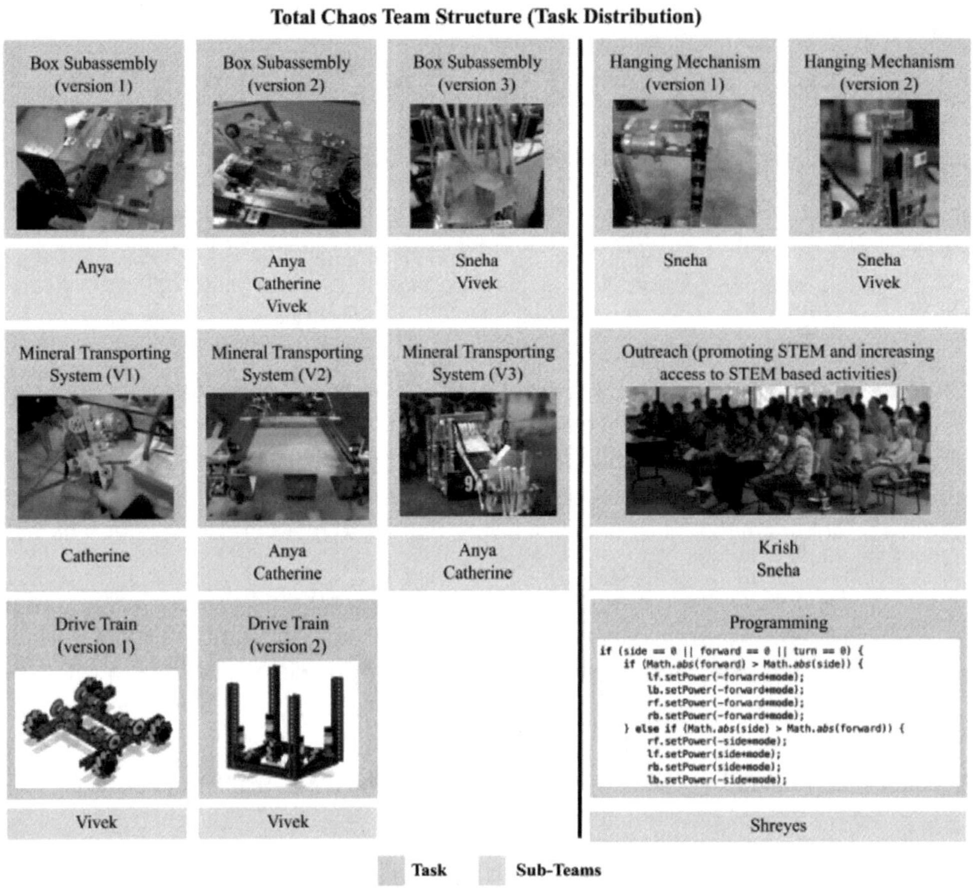

Figure 7. FTC Robot Subteams for Each Subassembly

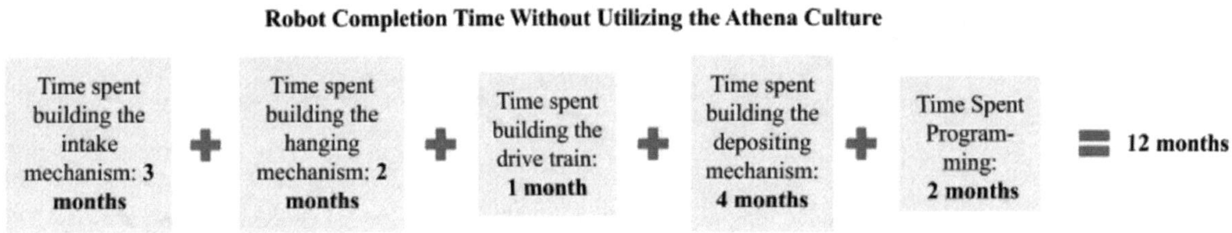

Figure 8. FTC Robot Completion Time without Utilizing the Athena Culture

3.1.1 Modular Designs for Charles Handy's Athena Culture

We split our robot into four separate modules: 1) box subassembly 2) mineral transporting system, 3) hanging mechanism and 4) drive train.

Figure 9. Total Chaos FTC Robot (a) Drive Train (b) Mineral Intake Mechanism (c) Hanging Mechanism

After employing the Athena culture within our team, we decided to split our robot into separate modules for each subteam to focus on (See Figure 9). The independent nature of the modules proved to be beneficial at many points during the season. After our first competition in January 2019, we began preparing for the state competition in March 2019. We wanted to increase our scoring capability by fixing the drive train -- at our first competition, the robot began swerving left instead of driving straight-- and rebuilding our pivoting platform to decrease the weight. When rebuilding the platform, we were able to easily remove the mechanism from our robot and rebuild it without implicating the rest of the robot. When we finished building and testing the new mechanism, the installation process took a mere 20 minutes. The ease of this process was only made possible because of the separate modules that we utilized.

Before reducing the weight of the platform by 1.25 lbs, it required more torque to rotate the platform from intake to scoring position. As a result, the motors on the platform would periodically stall because they could not provide the necessary torque to rotate the mechanism. When the motors stalled, the gears would slip due to the weight of the platform forcing the gear in motion without any motor power. As a result, the slippage created low rotational accuracy, so we were unable to use the motor's encoder counts to track the position of the motor. After decreasing the weight of the platform, the encoder counts became reliable, so we were able to utilize them for driver control enhancements during tele-op. For example, we were able to prevent the box on the platform from slamming against the ground when rotating to collecting position. If the encoder counts were between 125 and 0, we knew the platform was between around 30 degrees of its starting position, so we stopped giving power to the motors and allowed gravity to slowly bring the mechanism down (See Figure 10).

```
if (gamepad2.right_trigger > 0 && rotateLeft.getCurrentPosition() > 300) {
    rotateLeft.setPower(0);
    rotateRight.setPower(0);
}else if (gamepad2.right_trigger > 0) {
    rotateLeft.setPower(gamepad2.right_trigger);
    rotateRight.setPower(gamepad2.right_trigger);
} else if (gamepad2.left_trigger > 0 && rotateLeft.getCurrentPosition() < 125) {
    rotateLeft.setPower(0);
    rotateRight.setPower(0);
} else if (gamepad2.left_trigger > 0) {
    rotateLeft.setPower(-gamepad2.left_trigger);
    rotateRight.setPower(-gamepad2.left_trigger);
} else {
    rotateLeft.setPower(0);
    rotateRight.setPower(0);
}
```

If the position of the left motor that powers the platform is less than 125 encoder counts, then set the power of the left and right motors to zero

Figure 10. Software Sample to Control the Platform When Rotating to Collecting Position

At our first competition, the autonomous encountered a drivetrain swerving issue. The modular nature of our robot allowed us to test the drivetrain motors while rebuilding the pivoting platform because the two mechanisms were completely independent (See Figure 11). After discovering the motors attached to the wheels were still functional, we realized the swerving issue stemmed from the wheels; many of the rollers on the mecanum wheels were too tight and could no longer rotate freely. After loosening the rollers, we conducted 10 tests and the autonomous program worked perfectly.

(a) | (b)

Figure 11. Total Chaos FTC Robot Drivetrain Swerving (a) Drivetrain (b) wheel

3.1.2 Effective Documentations for Charles Handy's Athena Model

A practical and easy method to maintaining quality and consistency over the course of the season lies within the engineering notebook [8]. Our notebook contained thorough technical descriptions of the robot design, in addition to meeting notes that described our journey in designing the robot. Throughout the season, we made sure that we thoroughly documented every single meeting. Any changes made to the robot, code, or outreach activity planning is described in detail, alongside reasoning behind the change. Testing procedures and results were also documented in full detail, giving us a reliable source of data from which we could evaluate the strengths and weaknesses of our subassemblies or program. In the latest Rover Ruckus season, documenting every program iteration proved helpful during many stages of the programming process. At the beginning of the season, we planned and documented the ideal path the robot should take during autonomous. Having a reference as to where the robot needed to be made programming far easier; whenever we finished programming a section of the path, we knew exactly what to program next.

Documenting the steps to solve a problem was another effective practice (See Figure 12.a). When coding the robot, issues sometimes resurfaced even after we had attempted to solve it. When our continuous servo motors would not function as we wanted them to, we were able to refer to meeting notes that detailed a similar issue. By referencing how we solved the problem last time, we were able to build upon the previous solution and solve the issue quickly.

One of the most important documentation practices was recording our goals and criteria (See Figure 12.b). Whenever we began a new subassembly or a new program, we made sure to thoroughly document our goals, our timeline, and our criteria for the finished product. When we set these goals on paper, we are able to orient ourselves to these high-level goals throughout the season, always being able to refer to an agreed-upon list of requirements and ideas.

Session # 14	2/15/2019

Objectives	Reflections
Fixing issues with continuous servos	• We were having issues with setting the power of the continuous servo • It would only set power when we took readings from the joystick • If we tried to set the power to one the servo wouldn't move at all • When the joystick controlled the power it would move inaccurately, sometimes very slowly • To solve the problem we simply tried giving it an double number slowly lowered the power • Once the power reached 0.8 the servo started moving at full speed • The power was constant, and did not slow down like I did before

(a)

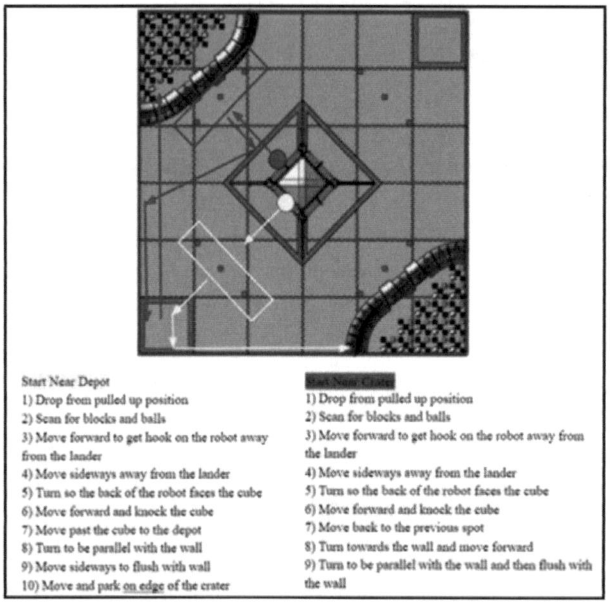

(b)

Figure 12. Total Chaos FTC Robot Documentation Examples: (a) Steps to Solve Servo Problems (b) Autonomous Period Goals and Criteria

3.2 TensorFlow Machine Learning for Autonomous Phases

We have two different autonomous combinations to complement our alliance partners. The diagram below shows both paths we take (See Figure 13), which consistently scores all 80 points.

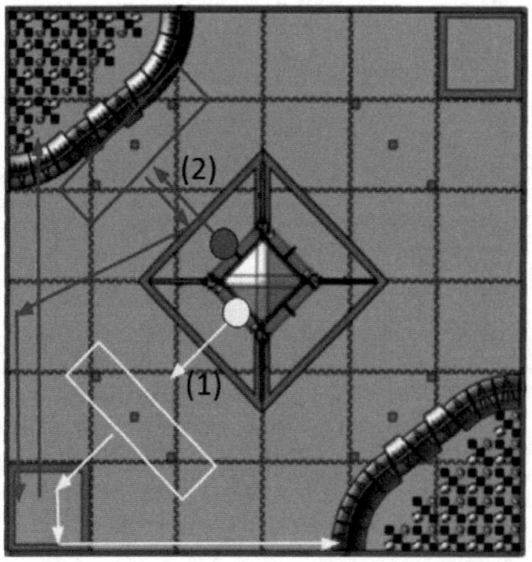

Figure 13. Illustration of Total Chaos Autonomous Robot Movements

Table 2: Rover Ruckus FTC Challenge Autonomous Robot Action Sequence Example

Path (1): Near the Lander	**Path (2): Near the Crater**
1) Drop from pulled up position 2) Scan for blocks and balls 3) Move forward to get hook on the robot away from the lander 4) Move sideways away from the lander 5) Turn so the back of the robot faces the cube 6) Move forward and knock the cube 7) Move past the cube to the depot 8) Turn to be parallel with the wall 9) Move sideways to flush with wall 10) Move and park on the edge of the crater	1) Drop from pulled up position 2) Scan for blocks and balls 3) Move forward to get hook on the robot away from the lander 4) Move sideways away from the lander 5) Turn so the back of the robot faces the cube 6) Move forward and knock the cube 7) Move back to the previous spot 8) Turn towards the wall and move forward 9) Turn to be parallel with the wall and then flush with the wall 10) Move to the depot and drop the marker 11) Move and park on the edge of the crater

One important part of the autonomous objectives is to identify the location of the gold mineral accurately. We utilized Vuforia software and Google's TensorFlow to locate the position of the two silver balls and the gold cube. Our initial idea for finding the location of the gold mineral was to use a long metal piece with a color sensor on it and attach the piece to a servo. The mechanism would sense the color of the gold cube and knock it by rotating the servo. We decided to use the TensorFlow software instead because it is more reliable. Additionally we saved a lot of time by doing a quick scan using the camera instead of moving close to every mineral to scan for the color.

The TensorFlow Machine Learning [9] process utilized image recognition (Vuforia) to record the location of the minerals for later use. When hanging, the robot phone camera activated Vuforia, allowing the TensorFlow image recognition to initialize and scan the field for objects. The Machine Learning system has been trained to recognize the gold/silver mineral by being shown numerous images of this object from multiple angles, allowing for a complete perspective to be produced. Once the objects are visually scanned, it compares previously learned images to the real life situation. Additionally, every iteration of the scanned objects are added to a cloud recognition database to enhance future accuracy of scanning. In some scenarios, some images are related with the object tucked behind another object, so the TensorFlow can recognize the gold/silver mineral with only a partial image. After recognizing the location of the gold/silver mineral, the camera utilizes the xy plot of a Cartesian plane to generate an exact location for gold/silver mineral. Based on previous testing, we were able to narrow down the expected ranges of the gold/silver mineral, then allowing us to locate the xy location. With the paths for each mineral programmed, we are ready to begin detecting the mineral arrangement. We wanted to use it so we could recognize which position the gold mineral was in, and tell the robot to push that mineral away accordingly.

Furthermore, when we mounted the phone and started the test program, we found that when the phone was in an upright, portrait position, the phone camera was not wide enough to see all three minerals. Switching to landscape allowed the phone to see the whole arrangement. After adjusting the setup, the camera was positioned appropriately in order to compare the images in the right directions. For example, when the robot is hanging, the phone camera will have to be angled down to see the arrangement. It is very important to have the right inputs to the machine learning algorithm (e.g., the positioning and angle of the phone mount.). With the advanced troubleshooting practice and methodology, we can detect the right mineral 100% of the time (See Figure 14)

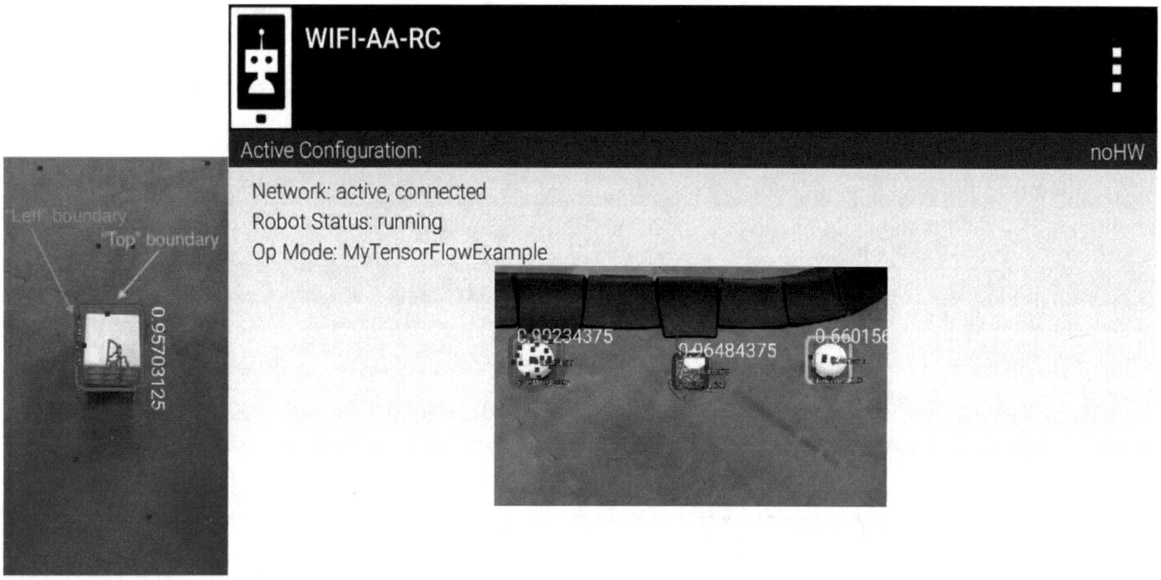

Figure 14. Illustration of Golden Mineral Detections Using TensorFlow Machine Learning [10]

4. Summary

This paper presented our approaches to achieve a culture of software quality in Android robots that integrates robot software and physical worlds together. Case studies were shared to utilize Charles Handy's Athena Culture model to improve software quality in Android robots for the robot performance improvements in FTC robot competitions. The detail-oriented team structure, effective document, and modular designs were presented to take into considerations of multiple factors including robot design, build, programming and team coordination. With the evolvement of robot performances and capabilities, the software quality was improved. It was proved that the software quality Charles Handy's model is a very powerful tool to guide the team to close software quality gaps in critical areas for consistent robot performances. Furthermore, the paper also presented TensorFlow Machine Learning to improve the software quality in autonomous phase to minimize dependencies on the external physical sensor readings.

All of these methods can be utilized in industries to improve software quality when handling the physical world uncertainties and complicities.

Acknowledgements

The authors wish to thank the reviewer Joseph Ruskiewicz for his invaluable assistance and discussions on the culture of software quality. In addition, the authors also wish to thank the Oregon Robotics Tournament & Outreach Program (ORTOP) whose assistance is very crucial for the success of FTC events in Oregon.

References

[1] Mataric, Maja J., Koenig, Nathan and Feil-Seifer, David. 2007. "Materials for Enabling Hands-On Robotics and STEM Education", *AAAI Spring Symposium on Robots and Robot Venues: Resources for AI Education, Stanford, CA.*

[2] Chow, Kingsum, Chow, Ida, Niu, Vicki, Takla, Ethan and Brillhart, Danny. 2010. "Software Quality Assurance in the Physical World", *Proceedings of the Pacific Northwest Software Quality Conference. Portland, Oregon. USA.*

[3] FIRST Homepage: http://www.usfirst.org/ (accessed July 18, 2019).

[4] FIRST, 2018-2019 Game Manual: https://firstinspiresst01.blob.core.windows.net/ftc/2019/gemf2.pdf (accessed July 18, 2019).

[5] Tutor2u. Handy's Model of Organisational Culture. https://www.tutor2u.net/business/reference/models-of-organisational-culture-handy (accessed July 18, 2019).

[6] Dininni, Jeanne. 2011. "Management Theory of Charles Handy". https://www.business.com/articles/management-theory-of-charles-handy/ (3.1 Athena Culture) (accessed July 18, 2019).

[7] Qualcomm. 2019. "2019-2020 FTC Android Studio Tutorial". https://www.firstinspires.org/sites/default/files/uploads/resource_library/ftc/android-studio-tutorial.pdf (accessed July 18, 2019).

[8] Qualcomm. 2019. "2019-2020 FTC Wiring Guide". https://www.firstinspires.org/sites/default/files/uploads/resource_library/ftc/robot-wiring-guide.pdf (accessed July 18, 2019).

[9] "TensorFlow for Deep Learning". https://www.matroid.com/dlwithtf/chap1-2.pdf (accessed July 18, 2019).

[10] FTC Engineering. "Java Sample TensorFlow Object Detection Op Mode". https://github.com/ftctechnh/ftc_app/wiki/Java-Sample-TensorFlow-Object-Detection-Op-Mode (accessed July 18, 2019).

---

[1] Sunset High School, Portland, Oregon
[2] Sunset High School, Portland, Oregon
[3] Sunset High School, Portland, Oregon
[4] Westview High School, Portland, Oregon
[5] Jesuit High School, Portland, Oregon
[6] Westview High School, Portland, Oregon
[7] Logic Technology Development, Technology and Manufacturing Group, Intel Corporation

Testing for Cognitive Bias in AI Applications

Peter Varhol, Gerie Owen
peter@petervarhol.com, gerie.owen@gerieowen.com

Abstract

We would like to think that AI-based machine learning systems always produce the right answer within their problem domain. However, in reality their performance is a direct result of the data used to train them. The answers in production are only as good as that training data.

But data collected by human means, such as surveys, observations, or estimates can have built-in human biases, such as the confirmation bias or the representative bias. Even seemingly objective measurements can be measuring the wrong things, or can be missing essential information about the problem domain.

The effects of biased data can be even more insidious. AI systems often function as black boxes, which means technologists are unaware of how an AI came to its conclusion. This can make it particularly hard to identify any inequality, bias, or discrimination feeding into a particular decision.

This paper explains how AI systems can suffer from the same biases as human experts, and how that could lead to biased results. It examines how testers, data scientists, and other stakeholders can develop test cases to recognize biases, both in data and the resulting system, and how to address those biases.

Biography

Peter Varhol is a software strategist and evangelist who closely observes the testing industry and uses his knowledge and experience to identify new technologies to identify trends and help companies respond to those trends. He speaks frequently at conferences, local meetups, and on webinars on software development, testing, machine learning, and DevOps topics. He also writes for popular technology publications such as Information Week and InfoWorld.

Peter has been a tenure-track professor in computer science and mathematics, technology journalist and editor, software developer and tester, and software product manager. He has MS degrees in computer science, applied mathematics, and psychology, along with doctoral work in data science.

Gerie Owen is a Testing Strategist and Evangelist. She is a Certified Scrum Master, Conference Presenter and Author on technology and testing topics. She enjoys mentoring new QA Leads and brings a cohesive team approach to testing. Gerie is the author of many articles on technology including Agile and DevOps topics. Gerie chooses her presentation topics based on her experiences in technology, what she has learned from them and what she would like to do to improve them.

1. Introduction

The uses for artificial intelligence (AI) and machine learning systems have exploded into the mainstream over the last couple of years. These types of systems are unique in that they "learn" based on data that is available about the problem domain. For example, by taking thousands or even hundreds of thousands of readings of the price of a stock in the stock market, we might be able to predict future movements of that stock with some accuracy.

These AI, or machine learning, systems are dependent upon data to enable them to learn. Machine learning systems consist of layered sets of mathematical algorithms that attempt to model a particular problem domain. It's not really learning as we understand it; it is simply using data to model a problem domain, and using that model to make decisions within that domain.

The most common type of machine learning architecture is the neural network. At a high level, neural networks model the neurons of the human brain. They include an input layer of neurons, an output layer, and one or more hidden layers of neurons. Each neuron, or node, contains a mathematical algorithm that transforms the data sent to it in some way. The network produces one or more outputs that are then compared to the known "correct" answer.

These systems are trained by applying data representing the problem and its solution. The algorithms manipulate that data at each stage of the process, until an output is obtained. After each training run, the software goes back and adjusts the algorithms and tries again. At first, the answers produced likely bear little resemblance to the correct ones, but after a number of training runs, the algorithm solutions should converge to the known correct solutions.

If an acceptable solution is not forthcoming from a particular neural network after a number of training runs, then it is time to go back and redesign the network. Perhaps more hidden layers can provide better accuracy, or different data are needed. But it is common for teams to go back and rethink their original assumptions regarding the data or the design.

That is the primary reason why issues are difficult to uncover and address. You won't get the exact right answer; instead, the goal is to get answers that are "good enough". What does good enough mean? It really all depends on the goals of the application. For an e-commerce recommendation engine, an advantage is usually worthwhile. For self-driving cars, it has to be pretty exact.

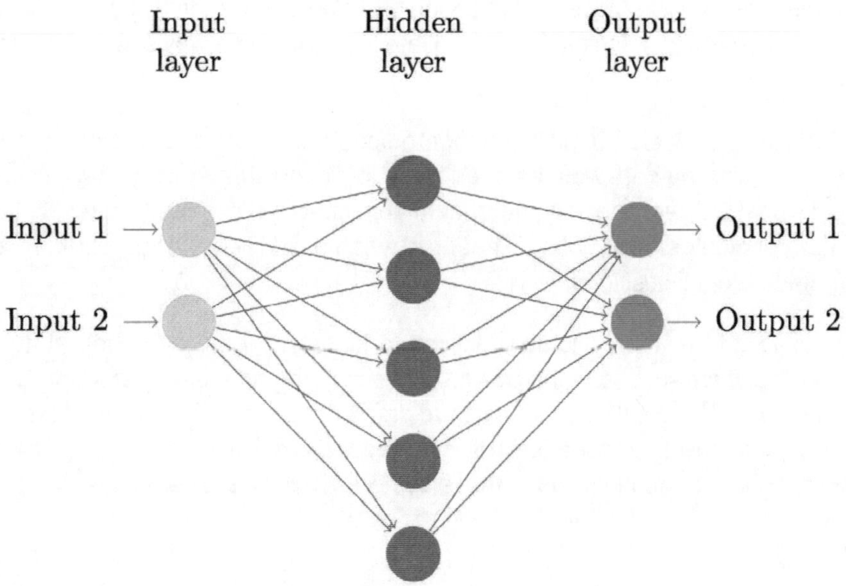

Figure 1. The basic neural network architecture, with an input layer for data, one or more hidden layers, and an output layer with the results.

1.1. About That Learning

AI and machine learning systems don't learn in the way that we normally think about learning. In humans, learning is a cognitive process that incorporates physiological changes to the brain and a change in behavior. Often as we learn new things, we integrate those into our existing knowledge, and are able to synthesize new concepts and applications.

While researchers are attempting to create machines with more general intelligence (which will introduce an entirely new and more complex series of problems), today's AI systems are almost entirely domain-specific, using algorithms and training techniques designed to operate in a particular problem domain.

Simply, what is occurring here in many cases is relatively straightforward curve-fitting, according to longtime researcher Judea Pearl. We can introduce advanced mathematical techniques that take into account things like prior probabilities or N-dimensional discriminant analysis, but the fundamental idea is that we are doing an advanced and largely black-box form of regression analysis. It's a black box in that we can't see inside these groups of algorithms to determine why a particular result has occurred.

2. What Causes Bias?

How can an intelligent system like this be biased? How can it produce results that don't appropriately reflect the problem domain? If it's trained with data that doesn't accurately represent the problem domain, it could produce results that aren't the best or most accurate responses. That can be difficult to determine, especially if the relationship between the training data and the domain isn't well-defined.

Further, it's very difficult to identify biases because many different types of tests are needed to determine whether or not bias exists in the first place. Even if we are looking for possible bias, we may not be looking at the domain and solution in the right way (Wachter-Boettcher, 2017).

So the training data is the key to a successful machine learning application. Data that accurately reflects the problem domain in all aspects will minimize bias. Data that is in some way skewed against the problem domain will likely cause biased results.

For example, in 2016 Amazon wrote an intelligent bot to search the Web and find potential candidates for jobs (Quartz, 2018). The training data was resumes from applicants that Amazon had received for the last ten years. For IT positions, the overwhelming number of applicants were men. As a result, the bot "learned" that men were better candidates for IT jobs. That bias was so pervasive in the algorithms that Amazon decided not to use the bot for IT positions.

This kind of bias is difficult to test for, and very difficult to identify, because the neural network itself is a black box, making it difficult for anyone in the design, development, and testing process to peer under the hood in order to understand where individual results are derived from. Yet as machine learning applications move more and more into the mainstream, unbiased results are critical to making the right business decisions. So identifying and correcting bias in these systems becomes a very high priority.

3. Bias Isn't a Bug

It's important to note that bias is not a bug, even though it may sound like one. A bug is an identifiable and measurable error in process or result of the software execution, and can usually be fixed with a code change. A bias, instead, is a bending of most or all results in a particular direction. In other words, it is incorrect, usually in a particular way. More importantly, bias cannot be fixed by a code change. The problem is deeper than that.

How does bias manifest itself? Because the AI system learns from data, how we choose our data affects the results that we obtain. If we choose data that doesn't represent the entire problem domain objectively, then we have a strong potential for bias. So testers need to be able to identify if the data is biased, how it is biased, and how it might be corrected.

A lot of data used to train AI systems today is at least partially subjective. For example, opinions on physical attractiveness are used to train these systems that judge beauty contests. Those opinions may differ among reasonable people, but those whose opinions are included in the training data are those that matter. Also, parole officers' opinions are used as data to predict criminal recidivism. Both data sets are not generally used in isolation, but in combination with other data. Still, it is likely that any bias in those opinions will influence the results.

But even seemingly objective data can be biased. The data may simply not reflect actual use of the system once it reaches production, even if it is objectively measured.

For example, an electronic wind sensor, which uses the cooling of filaments to determine wind speed and direction, uses training data collected in a wind tunnel. The data are scientifically accurate, but were collected under the same humidity and temperature conditions. That could well produce biased results when deployed into the wild, which has often substantially different values in both factors. These authors created just such a design (Figure 2), in the 1990s, and found bias when the system was deployed into the wild (Varhol, 1993).

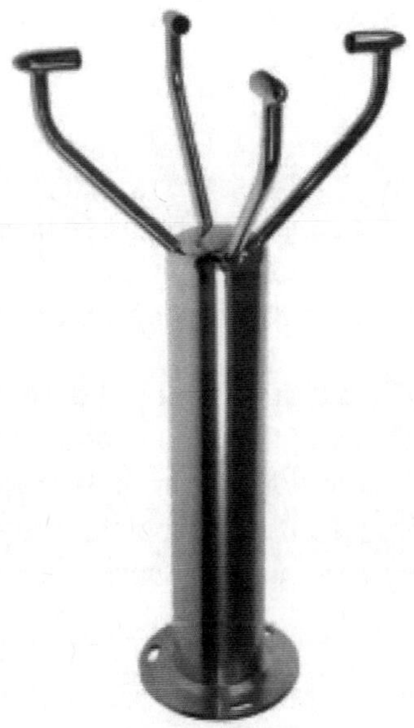

Figure 2. An electronic wind sensor that used wind tunnel data to train algorithms to estimate wind speed and direction (courtesy Armtek Industries).

4. Sources of Bias

There are three primary different sources of bias in AI systems. First is **data selection**; we have simply selected training data that represents only a part of the problem domain, or over represents part of the problem domain. This was Amazon's problem with its applicant application; it simply overrepresented male job candidates.

Data selection is probably the most common source of bias in AI systems, but it can be difficult to identify because the AI results seem to reflect real human decisions rather than an accurate view of the problem space.

A second source of bias is known as **latent bias**. This is where concepts become incorrectly correlated. Correlations are relationships between variables that can be used in prediction. To at least some extent, correlation is at the heart of many machine learning technologies, because we are using algorithms to relate known data to the results we want to use.

However, correlation doesn't mean causation. There may be a correlation between human intelligence and monetary income level, for example, but that doesn't mean that higher intelligence causes higher income. Instead, higher intelligence may result in people being more educated, which may in fact be the root cause of higher income. Without a good deal of further analysis, causation is difficult or sometimes even impossible to achieve.

The third source of bias is through **interactions**. If it is an AI that people interact with, those interactions can be misunderstood by the AI because it is being used in a way that was not intended. Microsoft Tay is a case in point. Tay was a Twitter bot that Microsoft launched to interact with others and dynamically learn from those interactions. Twitterdom quickly came to the realization that Tay could be trained for any behavior, without any conventional boundaries. As a result, nefarious tweets within the space of hours rapidly turned Tay into a racist and bigoted creation. As this was learned behavior, Microsoft had to withdraw it from use until it could start over again.

5. Testing for Bias

Testing for bias in AI systems is a significant challenge, because bias is difficult to identify in a limited period of testing time. Bias is, after all, a tendency, not a clear-cut right or wrong. It's not like a particular test case succeeds or fails. Therefore, it requires a different approach than traditional applications.

The sources of bias listed above also provide a guidepost on how to identify and test for that particular bias. Testers need to carefully examine the data used for training, and ideally have similar data for use in testing. Saying that data does not reflect the problem domain, or underrepresents or overrepresents the problem domain, has to be demonstrated. Testers also need to look for unintended correlations, and ways that the AI can be incorrectly trained by interaction with people. Data that is seemingly innocuous may well have a significant influence on the results.

Testing for bias is substantially different than testing for defects in a traditional application. It starts with requirements. Rather than stating requirements in terms of feature capability or user interface controls, AI requirements have to be very specific in terms of both results and required margin of error. Depending on the problem domain, the quantitative requirements will be very different.

The electronic wind sensor developed by these authors is a case in point. Like any wind sensor, even a mechanical one, it was not going to precisely determine the exact wind speed and direction. In the wild, there is always an uncertainty factor. The question then became how much uncertainty was acceptable. In this case, we determined that for 95 percent of the readings, within 2 degrees of direction and within 2.5

knots of wind speed was acceptable, following a normal curve. With our testing data, we were able to achieve this goal, although subsequent tests in the wild were mixed because of confounding factors, such as dust.

Actual test planning and testing for bias can be accomplished through an analysis similar to that used for testing safety critical systems such as medical devices or aviation systems. With these systems, we look at potential risks, and attempt to determine the likelihood of those risks. For example, a cardiac monitoring device may have exposed leads, with the potential for electric shock from those leads. Safety critical testing involves determining the risk, the hazard inherent from that risk, and the likelihood that the risk will happen in reality. From that analysis you derive your test plan and test cases.

Likewise, testing for bias involves looking at any potential for a systemic incorrect response, the hazard inherent in that incorrect response, the likelihood that the hazard will manifest itself, and the harm it may do as a result.

For example, machine learning systems are being actively developed and used for health care applications, especially diagnosis and treatment regimens. Diagnosis is both difficult and uncertain; one of the authors in the recent past had been diagnosed with a terminal condition by multiple doctors that turned out not to be the case (obviously). The information was incomplete, and these doctors relied on their experience to fill in the blanks (Quartz, 2017).

Now imagine an AI system coming to such a conclusion. Was the AI making a truly objective diagnosis based on data, or did that data introduce bias based on a lack of causation or an overreliance on certain diagnostic outcomes? The only way to know is to go back and attempt to find flaws in the data methodology.

Testing for bias requires many more test cases than traditional functional testing. Testing individual requirements in traditional testing for correct or incorrect results usually only requires a handful of test cases; with AI system, each requirement may have hundreds or even thousands. That's because bias will be very difficult to uncover with just a few tests. The entire range of responses has to have representative test cases, including both mainstream and edge cases.

Further, testers must exercise discipline in running these cases. A methodology that runs test cases in a logical sequence will usually make it easier to identify trends. Exploratory testing, while valuable in many circumstances, doesn't exercise the discipline needed to identify bias.

6. Beginning the Testing Process

The best place to start such test cases is with the causes of bias mentioned above – data selection, latent bias, and interaction bias. Starting with data selection, testers quantify the problem domain, then map out how the planned data fully encompasses that domain. In the Amazon applicant case, the company could have looked at the number of resumes for each gender they had in the applicant pool and determined a method for equalizing them.

With latent bias, testers have to ask the question of why a particular data collection accurately reflects the causation behind a particular outcome. We want causation in order to ensure validity rather than a simple random relationship. Past performance does not always predict future results, as investment companies keep telling us.

Last, interaction bias determines if the data and architecture used can withstand use in the wild, especially in interactions with actual users. That will be the most difficult to determine, and requires looking into future use of the application. Will interactions with users influence future results? For static systems, those that don't learn after deployment, this is not a problem, but for those that do continue to learn, which are often referred to as adaptive or dynamic systems, it could be an issue. Adaptive systems require ongoing testing after deployment to ensure that the original intent of the application isn't subverted by ongoing use and changes.

How would this type of testing occur? The best approach is to maintain a set of test cases that you use initially to determine bias and correctness of results, then execute those same test cases at regular intervals throughout the life of the application. Ideally, those results should be approximately the same, with some accuracy improvements due to adaptive training.

However, if results start to diverge from correctness, testers have to consider the possibility of an interaction bias or other data-based bias. That could come from unexpected interactions, an over-reliance on a particular data set in adaptive training, or even that the problem domain has gradually changed over time. While a problem can be identified in a fairly straightforward fashion, the cause of that problem is much more difficult to determine. Ultimately, testers looking for a source of bias in adaptive systems may have to make educated guesses based on their domain knowledge and deep understanding of the underlying data.

If there is bias in an AI system, addressing it is a difficult problem. As mentioned above, in most cases a code change won't fix the problem. In general, it will require starting over again with an untrained neural network, and retraining it with different data or an entirely different network. Although it won't require starting the development process all over again, it can be a time-consuming process. As mentioned earlier, unlike a bug, a bias encompasses virtually all of the code base, rather than a small section that can be easily changed (Barkan, 2018).

Teams and users that are concerned about bias will have to take into account the possibility that multiple trainings, and even algorithm changes, will be needed to get it right. It is best that the potential for bias is determined prior to the final selection of training data sets, so that any issues can be addressed before serious development begins.

7. Beyond AI Systems

It's important to note that all software is biased in some way, because it is designed and written by humans, who are biased in general. The biases may be trivial and unimportant, or they may have serious consequences. It doesn't necessarily have to be an AI application.

For example, a woman wasn't able to access the women's locker room of her gym, as her programmed RFID card wouldn't work. While the gym acknowledged that there was an error, it had no idea what was wrong or how to address it.

The software development team knew what was wrong. Among the registration information for the gym was the salutation. For expediency, the team had hard-coded the salutation "Doctor" as male, allowing access only to the men's locker room. This and similar biases can conceivably be fixed with a code change, although identifying the cause of the bias can be challenging (The Atlantic, 2017).

Biases such as this occur in many applications. Many of these types of biases are just as difficult to find, although they are usually easier to fix. Developers can code solutions that address the example above, as long as the problem can be found. Because developers can also introduce bias, design and development are the most appropriate places to observe and address it (King, 2010).

In the above example, such a decision may not have been designed or even documented; it may have just been an unconscious decision that an individual developer did under pressure to finish code. But it was bias, and it had implications to users.

8. Bias is Not Clear-Cut

There is some controversy in testing and fixing bias. If we want any bias to be uncovered and removed, then testing is an important aspect of the development process. But there may be circumstances where we want to reflect human bias in our AI systems. Bias isn't always bad, although we need to be aware that it is present. There may be problem domains where we believe the human expert is the best decision-maker, such as in medical diagnosis. Doctors may jump to a correct conclusion based on their experience and the bias that comes from that experience, and we may want the AI system to react in a similar way.

In problem domains such as this, we may want the AI system to reflect the expert biases. But are we getting the best diagnosis, or simply the same human diagnosis? And more importantly, which of these outcomes do we want in practice?

There is also ongoing research on "explainable AI", which is an attempt to offer an explanation of why a particular result occurred (Dosilovic, Brcic, and Hlupic, 2018). This research typically uses alternative AI techniques, such as decision trees, that may not provide the power of neural networks or genetic algorithms in solving domain-specific problems.

One approach that may be possible is to incorporate code that looks at what each algorithm does at each layer, and explains how a particular piece of data was interpreted by that algorithm. While this approach may not provide a human rationale for a decision, it could provide insight into what occurred at each step of the process (Müller and Bostrom, 2016).

These types of questions will continue to haunt bias in AI systems, and there is no easy answer. But until we can identify, quantify, and potentially remove bias, we won't understand what alternatives are available.

References

Müller, Vincent C. and Bostrom, Nick (2016), 'Future progress in artificial intelligence: A survey of expert opinion', in Vincent C. Müller (ed.), Fundamental Issues of Artificial Intelligence (Synthese Library; Berlin: Springer), 553-571.

Dosilovic, Filip; Brcic, Mario; Hlupic, Nikica (2018-05-25). "Explainable Artificial Intelligence: A Survey" (PDF). *MIPRO 2018 - 41st International Convention Proceedings*. MIPRO 2018. Opatija, Croatia. pp. 210–215.

M King, Tariq. (2010). A self-testing approach for autonomic software. ProQuest ETD Collection for FIU.

[Bar 18] Personal correspondence with Joseph Barkan, director of IBM Research Labs, 2018.

Wachter-Boettcher, Sara, 2017. Technically Wrong: Sexist Apps, Biased Algorithms, and Other Threats of Toxic Tech. New York: W.W. Norton.

Quartz, 2017. "When a Robot AI Doctor Misdiagnoses You, Who's to Blame?" Posted May 23, 2017, https://qz.com/989137/when-a-robot-ai-doctor-misdiagnoses-you-whos-to-blame/ (accessed July 12, 2019).

Quartz, 2017. "AI hacks are trying to turn code into intelligence like alchemists tried turning lead into gold." Posted September 28, 2017. https://qz.com/1089555/artificial-intelligence-programmers-are-trying-to-turn-code-into-intelligence-like-alchemists-tried-turning-lead-into-gold/ (accessed July 12, 2019).

The Atlantic, 2017. “The Coming Software Apocalypse.” Posted September 28, 2017. https://www.theatlantic.com/technology/archive/2017/09/saving-the-world-from-code/540393/ (accessed July 12, 2019).

Quartz, 2018. “Amazon’s sexist hiring algorithm could still be better than a human.” Posted November 7, 2018. https://qz.com/work/1454396/amazons-sexist-hiring-algorithm-could-still-be-better-than-a-human/ (accessed July 12, 2019).

Varhol, Peter D. “Neural Networks for Predicting Behavior.” Dr. Dobbs Journal, February 1993. http://collaboration.cmc.ec.gc.ca/science/rpn/biblio/ddj/Website/articles/DDJ/1993/9302/9302h/9302h.htm